THE
ECONOMIST
ATLAS

THE ECONOMIST ATLAS

A Henry Holt Reference Book
HENRY HOLT AND COMPANY
NEW YORK

Editor Ian Castello-Cortes
Art Editor Keith Savage
Editorial Team Sue Turner, Penny Butler,
Isla MacLean, Jennifer Mussett,
Tina Norris, Jane Devane
Assistant Designer Stephen Moore
Production Controller Christine Campbell
DTP Production Jeremy Haworth
Indexer Fiona Barr

Editorial Director Stephen Brough
Art Director Douglas Wilson
Managing Editor Fay Franklin
Production Manager Charles James

Contributors John Ardagh, George Blazyca, Carl Bridge, Ian Campbell,
Duncan Campbell-Smith, Mike Chapman, Rory Clarke, Chris Cramer,
Andrew Draper, Alison Flint, Jeremy Gaunt, Martin Giles, Anthony
Goldstone, Edmund Gritt, Phil Gunson, Charles Gurdon, Martin
Macauley, John McEniff, John McLachlan, David Perman, Philippa
Potts, Charles Powell, Rod Prince, Martin Rhodes, Graham Richardson,
Matt Ridley, Ed Roby, Jack Spence, Keith Sword, Richard Synge

A Henry Holt Reference Book
First published in the
United States in 1992 by Henry Holt and Company, Inc. ,
115 West 18th Street, New York, New York 10011

Originally published in Great Britain in 1991 by Business Books Ltd,
an imprint of Random Century Limited, in association with
The Economist Books Ltd

Library of Congress Catalog Card number: 91-58152
ISBN 0-8050-1987-1

Henry Holt Reference Books are available at special discounts for bulk
purchases for sales promotions, premiums, fund-raising, or educational
use. Special editions or book excerpts can also be created to specification.

For details contact:
Special Sales Director
Henry Holt and Company, Inc.
115 West 18th Street
New York, New York 10011

First American Edition – 1992

World Comparisons and World Encyclopedia maps
and graphics by Lovell Johns, Oxford, England

Printed in Italy

1 3 5 7 9 10 8 6 4 2

The greatest care has been taken in compiling this book. However, no
responsibility can be accepted by the publishers or contributors for the
accuracy of the information presented. Where opinion is expressed it is
that of the author and does not necessarily coincide with the editorial
views of *The Economist* newspaper.

CONTENTS

WORLD MAPS

MAP CONTENTS

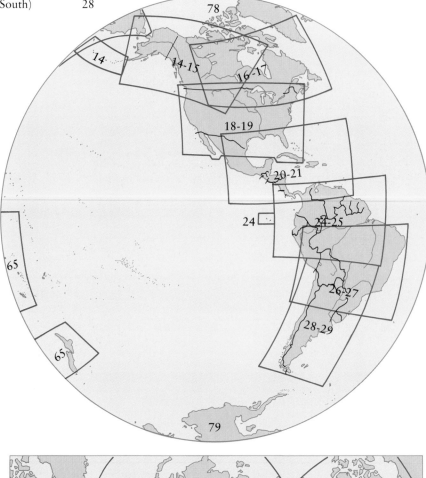

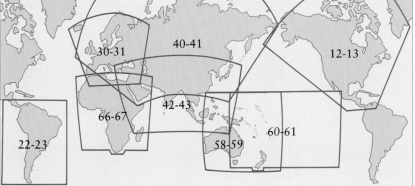

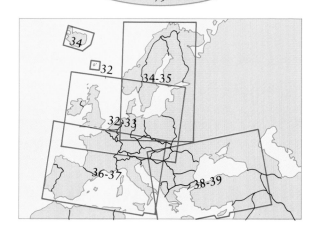

MILITARY POLITICS

AMERICAN ASPECT
centre Chicago

EUROPEAN ASPECT
centre London

EAST ASIATIC ASPECT
centre Peking

N.A.T.O. A.N.Z.U.S. (under reorganization 1991)

Warsaw Pact

Other communist states

Arab League

Other states

W. William-Ols projection

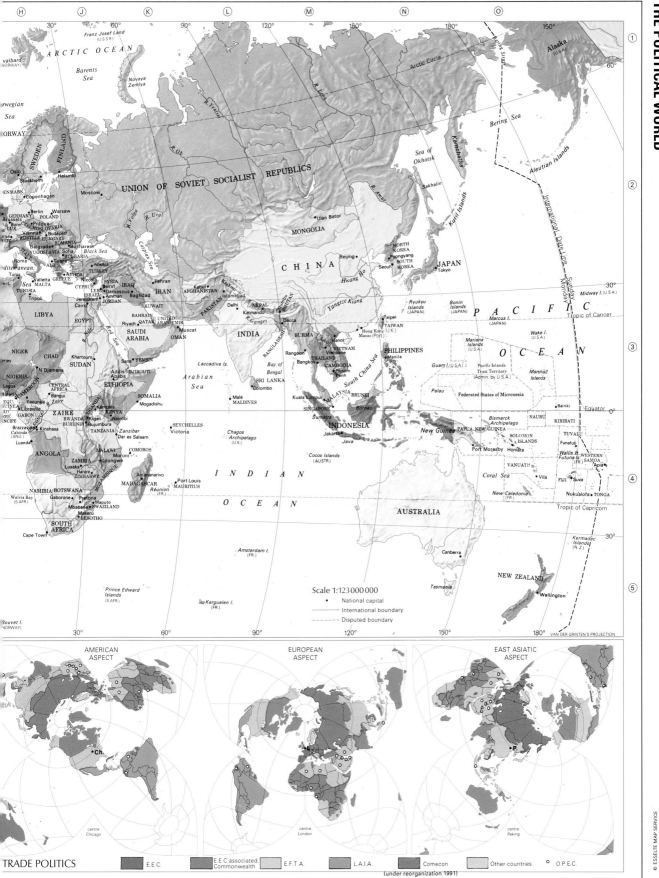

H   J   K   L   M   N   O

ARCTIC OCEAN

Franz Josef Land (U.S.S.R.)

Svalbard (NORWAY)

Barents Sea

Arctic Circle

Alaska (U.S.A.)

Bering Strait

Bering Sea

Aleutian Islands

International Date Line

Novaya Zemlya

Norwegian Sea

NORWAY

SWEDEN

FINLAND

Oslo

Stockholm

Helsinki

Moscow

UNION OF SOVIET SOCIALIST REPUBLICS

Kamchatka

Sea of Okhotsk

Sakhalin

Kuril Islands

Sunday / Monday

DENMARK

Copenhagen

GERMANY

Berlin

Warsaw

POLAND

Brussels

Bonn

Prague

CZECHOSLOVAKIA

Vienna

Budapest

AUSTRIA

HUNGARY

ROMANIA

Belgrade

Bucharest

YUGOSLAVIA

Sofia

BULGARIA

Rome

Tirana

ITALY

Mediterranean Sea

MALTA

GREECE

TURKEY

Ankara

Athens

Nicosia

CYPRUS

LEB.

Beirut

Damascus

SYRIA

ISRAEL

Amman

Jerusalem

JORDAN

Baghdad

IRAQ

Tehran

IRAN

AFGHANISTAN

Kabul

Islamabad

PAKISTAN

Delhi

NEPAL

Katmandu

BHUTAN

Dacca

BANGLADESH

BURMA

INDIA

Hanoi

VIETNAM

Vientiane

LAOS

Bangkok

THAILAND

CAMBODIA

Phnom Penh

MONGOLIA

Ulan Bator

CHINA

Beijing

Hwang Ho

Yangtze Kiang

NORTH KOREA

Pyongyang

SOUTH KOREA

Seoul

JAPAN

Tokyo

Sea of Japan

Ryukyu Islands (JAPAN)

Taipei

TAIWAN

Hong Kong (U.K.)

Macao (Port.)

Bonin Islands (JAPAN)

Marcus I. (JAPAN)

Midway I. (U.S.A.)

Tropic of Cancer

Wake I. (U.S.A.)

PACIFIC OCEAN

LIBYA

EGYPT

Cairo

Tripoli

Tunis

TUNISIA

Valletta

R. Nile

Red Sea

Riyadh

SAUDI ARABIA

KUWAIT

BAHRAIN

QATAR

UNITED ARAB EMIR.

OMAN

Muscat

Sana

YEMEN

DJIBOUTI

Addis Ababa

ETHIOPIA

SOMALIA

Mogadishu

Laccadive Is.

Arabian Sea

SRI LANKA

Colombo

MALAYSIA

Kuala Lumpur

SINGAPORE

Sumatra

Borneo

BRUNEI

INDONESIA

Jakarta

Java

PHILIPPINES

Manila

South China Sea

Mariana Islands (U.S.A.)

Guam I. (U.S.A.)

Palau

Pacific Islands Trust Territory (Admin. by U.S.A.)

Marshall Islands

Federated States of Micronesia

Bairiki

Equator

NAURU

KIRIBATI

NIGER

CHAD

SUDAN

Khartoum

N'Djamena

NIGERIA

Lagos

CAMEROON

CENTRAL AFRICA

Bangui

Yaounde

GABON

Libreville

EQU. GUINEA

SÃO TOMÉ & PRÍNCIPE

ZAIRE

Kinshasa

Brazzaville

Cabinda (ANG.)

Luanda

ANGOLA

RWANDA

Kigali

BURUNDI

Bujumbura

UGANDA

Kampala

KENYA

Nairobi

TANZANIA

Zanzibar

Dar es Salaam

SEYCHELLES

Victoria

Chagos Archipelago (U.K.)

Malé

MALDIVES

Cocos Islands (AUSTR.)

New Guinea

PAPUA NEW GUINEA

Port Moresby

Bismarck Archipelago

SOLOMON ISLANDS

Honiara

TUVALU

Funafuti

WESTERN SAMOA

Apia

Wallis & Futuna Is. (FR.)

INDIAN OCEAN

MALAWI

ZAMBIA

Lusaka

ZIMBABWE

Harare

MOZAMBIQUE

COMOROS

Moroni

Lilongwe

MADAGASCAR

Antananarivo

Réunion (FR.)

Port Louis

MAURITIUS

VANUATU

Vila

FIJI

Suva

New Caledonia (FR.)

Coral Sea

NAMIBIA

BOTSWANA

Gaborone

Pretoria

SOUTH AFRICA

Walvis Bay (S.AFR.)

Maputo

SWAZILAND

Mbabane

Maseru

LESOTHO

Cape Town

Amsterdam I. (FR.)

AUSTRALIA

Canberra

Tropic of Capricorn

Nukualofa

TONGA

Kermadec Islands (N.Z.)

Prince Edward Islands (S.AFR.)

Kerguelen I. (FR.)

NEW ZEALAND

Tasmania

Wellington

Bouvet I. (NORWAY)

Scale 1:123 000 000

- • National capital
- —— International boundary
- - - - Disputed boundary

VAN DER GRINTEN'S PROJECTION

TRADE POLITICS

AMERICAN ASPECT

Ch.

centre Chicago

EUROPEAN ASPECT

centre London

EAST ASIATIC ASPECT

P.

centre Peking

| E.E.C. | E.E.C. associated, Commonwealth | E.F.T.A. | L.A.I.A. | Comecon | Other countries | ○ O.P.E.C. |

(under reorganization 1991)

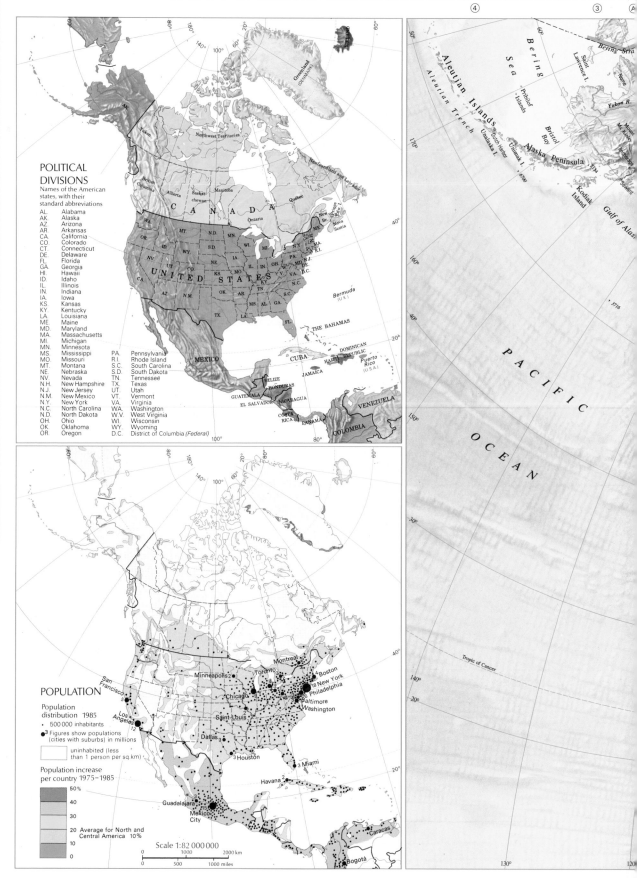

POLITICAL DIVISIONS

Names of the American states, with their standard abbreviations

AL.	Alabama	PA.	Pennsylvania
AK.	Alaska	R.I.	Rhode Island
AZ.	Arizona	S.C.	South Carolina
AR.	Arkansas	S.D.	South Dakota
CA.	California	TN.	Tennessee
CO.	Colorado	TX.	Texas
CT.	Connecticut	UT.	Utah
DE.	Delaware	VT.	Vermont
FL.	Florida	VA.	Virginia
GA.	Georgia	WA.	Washington
HI.	Hawaii	W.V.	West Virginia
ID.	Idaho	WI.	Wisconsin
IL.	Illinois	WY.	Wyoming
IN.	Indiana	D.C.	District of Columbia (Federal)
IA.	Iowa		
KS.	Kansas		
KY.	Kentucky		
LA.	Louisiana		
ME.	Maine		
MD.	Maryland		
MA.	Massachusetts		
MI.	Michigan		
MN.	Minnesota		
MS.	Mississippi		
MO.	Missouri		
MT.	Montana		
NE.	Nebraska		
NV.	Nevada		
N.H.	New Hampshire		
N.J.	New Jersey		
N.M.	New Mexico		
N.Y.	New York		
N.C.	North Carolina		
N.D.	North Dakota		
OH.	Ohio		
OK.	Oklahoma		
OR.	Oregon		

POPULATION

Population distribution 1985

· 500 000 inhabitants

●³ Figures show populations (cities with suburbs) in millions

☐ uninhabited (less than 1 person per sq.km)

Population increase per country 1975–1985

50%
40
30
20 Average for North and
10 Central America 10%
0

Scale 1:82 000 000

0   1000   2000 km
0   500   1000 miles

Scale 1:34 000 000

0   500   1000 km
0   200   400   600 miles

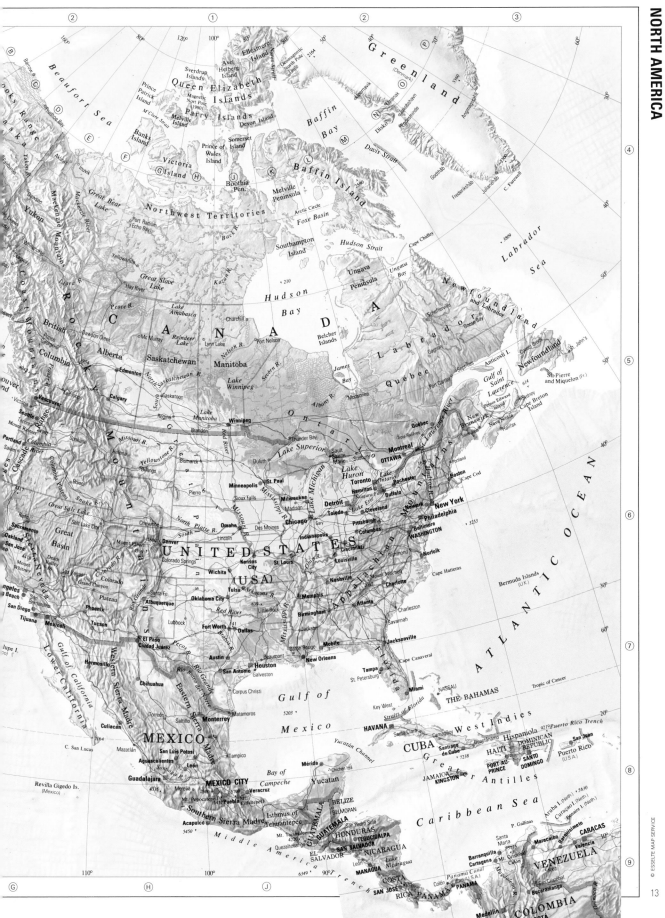

Scale 1:14 000 000

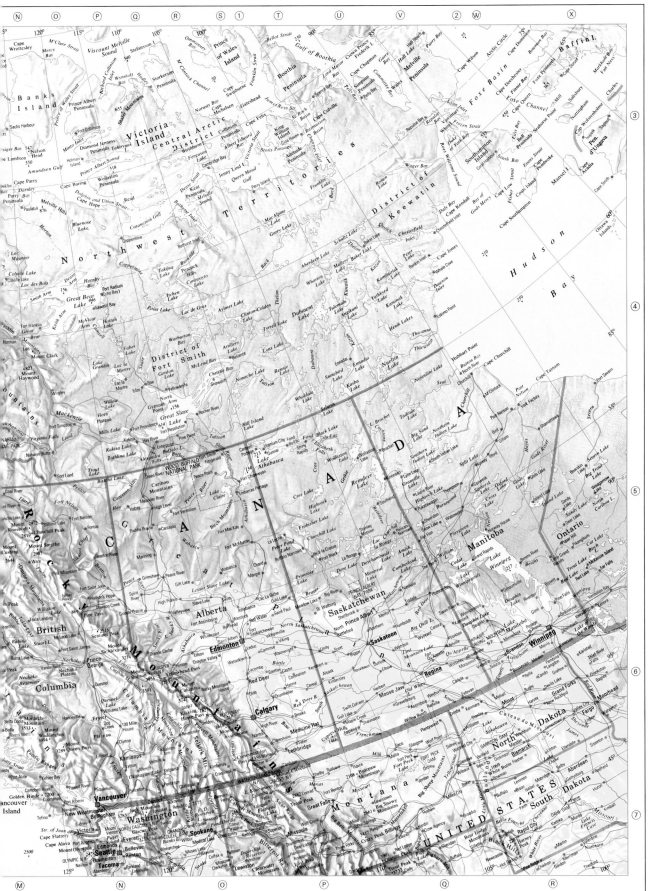

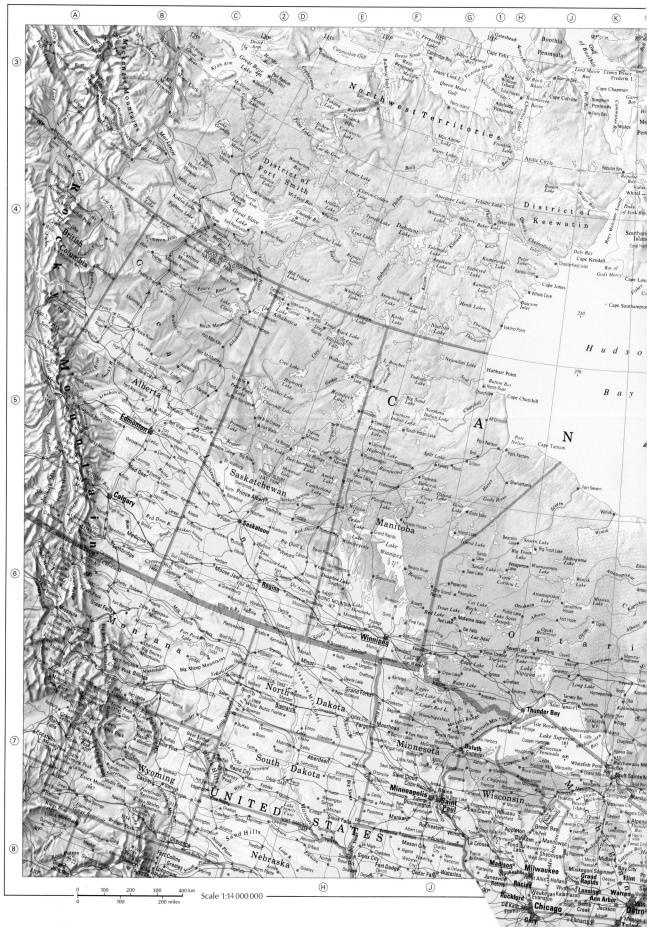

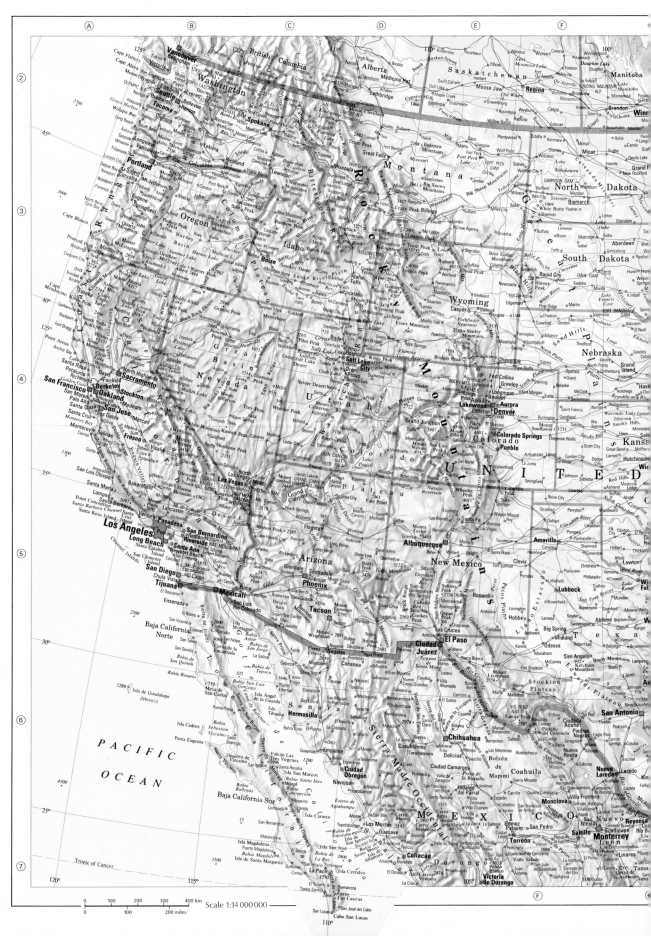

Scale 1:14 000 000

0   100   200   300   400 km
0   100   200 miles

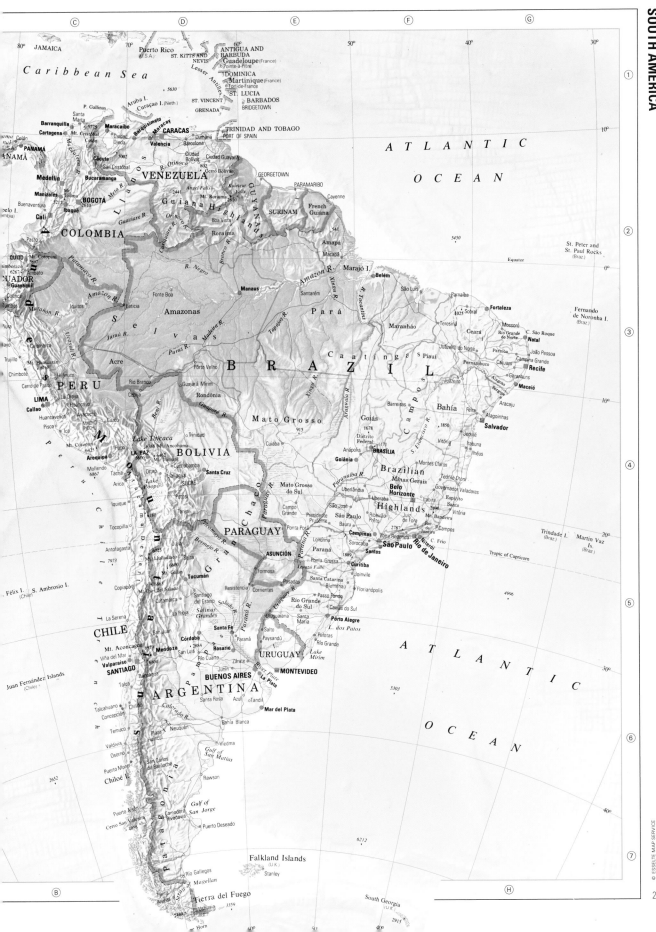

Caribbean Sea

JAMAICA
80°
70°
Puerto Rico
(USA)
ST. KITTS AND
NEVIS
ANTIGUA AND
BARBUDA
Guadeloupe (France)
Pointe-à-Pitre
DOMINICA
Martinique (France)
Fort-de-France
ST. LUCIA
ST. VINCENT
BARBADOS
GRENADA
BRIDGETOWN
60°
Lesser Antilles
5630

ATLANTIC

OCEAN

P. Gallinas
Aruba I.
Curaçao I. (Neth.)
Santa
Marta
Barranquilla
Cartagena
Maracaibo
Barquisimeto
Maracay
CARACAS
Cumaná
Ojeda
TRINIDAD AND TOBAGO
PORT OF SPAIN
Mt. Cristóbal
Colón
PANAMÁ
Medellín
Bucaramanga
Valencia
Barcelona
Ciudad
Bolívar
Ciudad Guayana
R. Orinoco
Cerro Bolívar
802
VENEZUELA
GEORGETOWN
PARAMARIBO
Manizales
Mt. Tolima
BOGOTÁ
Ibagué
Angel Falls
Kaieteur Falls
GUYANA
SURINAM
French
Guiana
Cayenne
Cali
COLOMBIA
Guaviare R.
Mt. Roraima
Boa Vista
Guiana Highlands
R. Negro
Roraima
51°
Amapá
Macapá
QUITO
Mt. Cotopaxi
R. Putumayo
Marajó I.
Belém
ECUADOR
Guayaquil
Cuenca
Amazon R.
Iquitos
Leticia
Fonte Boa
Manaus
Santarém
Amazon R.
Xingu R.
R. Tocantins
São Luís
Parnaíba
Fortaleza
Equator
PERU
Amazonas
Pará
Maranhão
Teresina
Ceará
Sobral
Mossoró
C. São Roque
Natal

ATLANTIC

OCEAN

Acre
Porto Velho
B R A Z I L
Barreiras
Bahia
Feira
Salvador
BOLIVIA
LA PAZ
Santa Cruz
Mato Grosso
Cuiabá
Goiás
Distrito
Federal
Goiânia
BRASÍLIA
Brazilian
Minas Gerais
Belo
Horizonte
Highlands
SUCRE
PARAGUAY
ASUNCIÓN
Mato Grosso
do Sul
Campo
Grande
São José
São Paulo
Bauru
Campinas
Paraná
Londrina
Santos
São Paulo
Rio de Janeiro
CHILE
PARAGUAY
Formosa
Resistencia
Corrientes
Posadas
Santa Catarina
Blumenau
Florianópolis
Rio Grande
do Sul
Caxias do Sul
Pôrto Alegre
Santa Fe
Rosario
URUGUAY
MONTEVIDEO
BUENOS AIRES
La Plata
ARGENTINA
Mar del Plata

ATLANTIC

OCEAN

Bahía Blanca
Falkland Islands
(U.K.)
Stanley
Tierra del Fuego
Horn

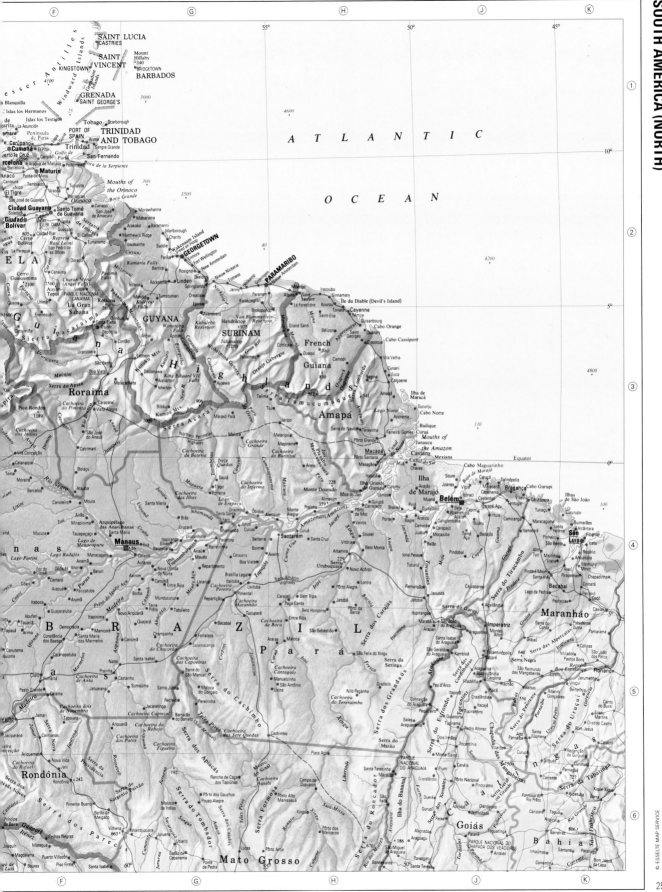

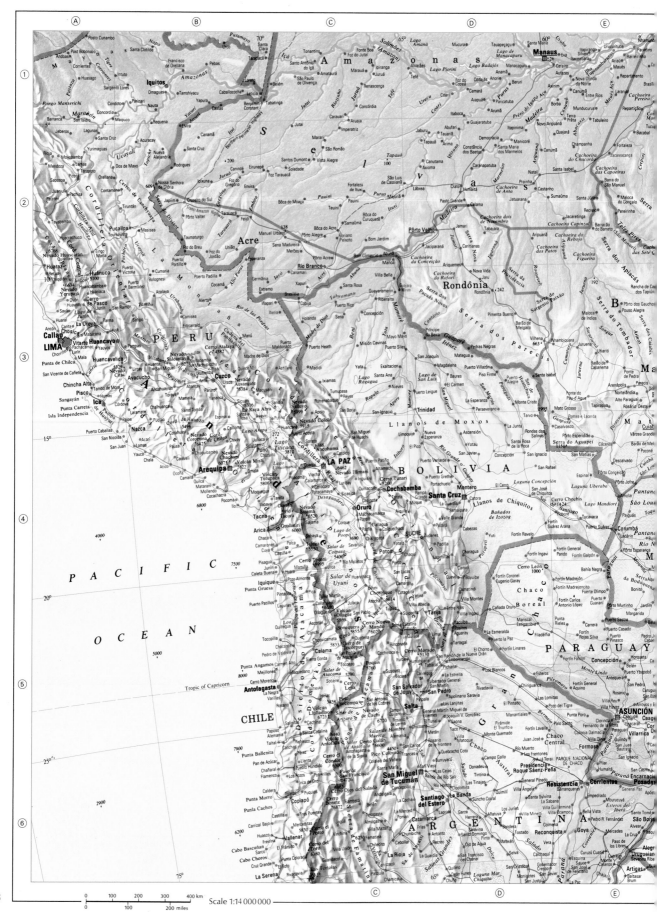

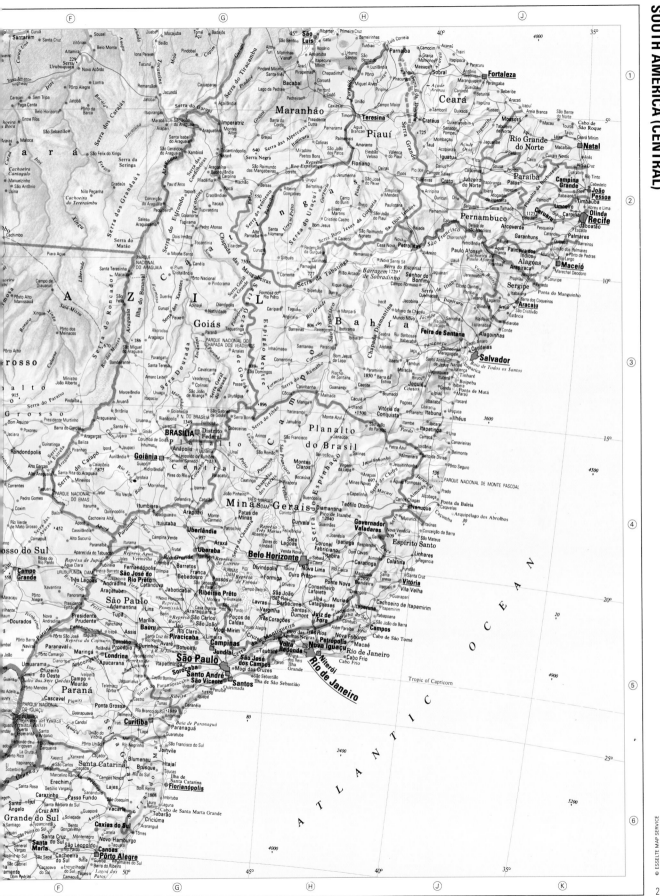

Scale 1:14 000 000

0   100   200   300   400 km

0   100   200 miles

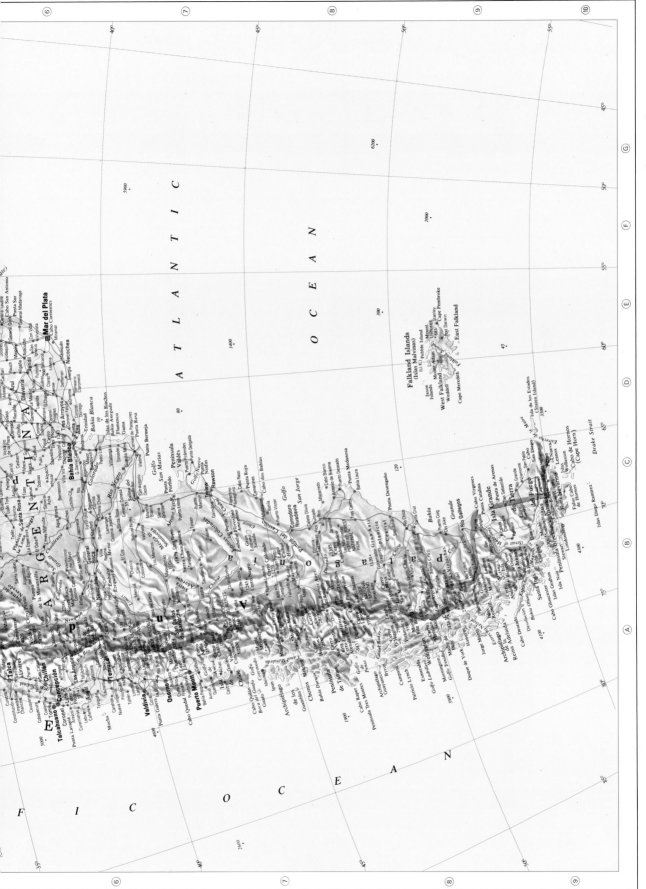

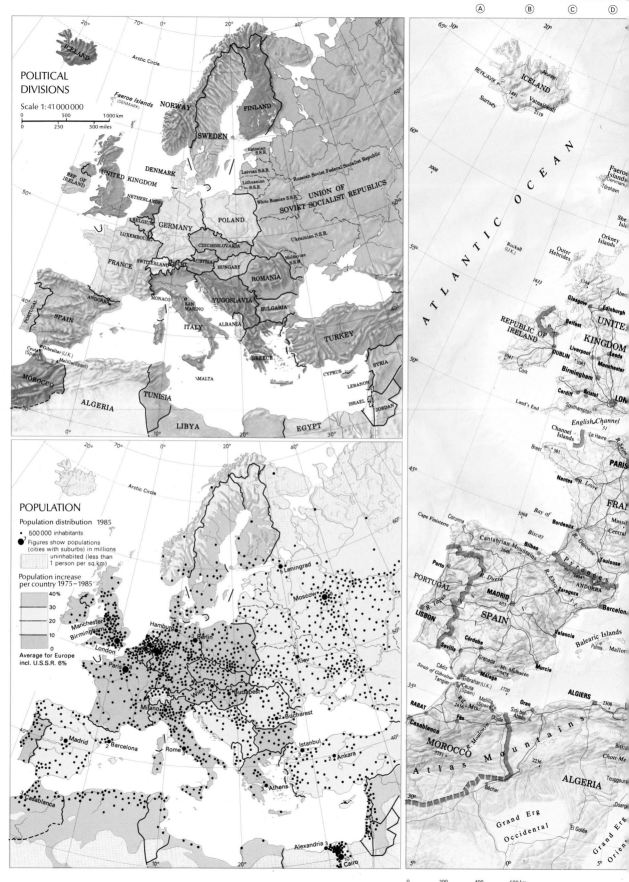

3

Barents

Sea

260

Kanin
Peninsula

Murmansk

Kola
Peninsula

R. Pechora

Mt. Narodnaya
1894

R. Ob

Sergut

Khanty-Mansiysk

North Cape

Tromsø

Vesterålen Is.

1191

Narvik

2111
Kebnekaise

Kiruna

Bodø

Arctic Circle

Lofoten Is.

Arctic Circle

245

White Sea

Arkhangel

R. Pechora

Ukhta

U
r
a
l

M
o
u
n
t
a
i
n
s

1569

Serov

Nizhniy Tagil

65°

Trondheim

Oulu

117

Umeå

Severodvinsk

North Dvina R.

R. Vychegda

Syktyvkar

Kotlas

NORWAY

Östersund

FINLAND

Lake Onega

Petrozavodsk

R. Sukhona

Berezniki

Perm

Sverdlovsk

Zlatoust

55°

Galdhöpiggen
2469

R. Glåma

Sundsvall

SWEDEN

Lake
Ladoga

R. Vyatka

Kirov

Izhevsk

R. Kama

Ufa

1640

Bergen

Åland Is.

Gulf of Finland

HELSINKI

Leningrad

Novgorod

Rybinsk
Reservoir

Yaroslavl

Ivanovo

Nizhniy
Novgorod

Yoshkar
Ola

Kazan

Sterlitamak

Magnitogorsk

Stavanger

690

Norrköping

459

STOCKHOLM

Turku

Tallinn

Estonian S.S.R.

347

R. Volga

Tver

Vladimir

MOSCOW

Ulyanovsk

Tolyatti

Kuybyshev

Orenburg

Skagerrak

Jutland

Kattegat

DENMARK

North Sea

COPENHAGEN

Gothenburg

Vänern

Göteborg

Malmö

Bornholm

Gotland

Öland

Latvian S.S.R.

Riga

Valdai Hills

Russian Soviet Federal Socialist Republic

Ryazan

Tula

Penza

Saratov

R. Ural

50°

Kiel

Lithuanian S.S.R.

Kaliningrad

Kaunas

Vilnius

West Dvina R.

Smolensk

Bryansk

Orel

Lipetsk

Tambov

R. Volga

Astrakhan

45°

Kazakh S.S.R.

Guryev

Hamburg

Bremen

Hanover

BERLIN

Szczecin

Gdańsk

Poznań

Łódź

R. Vistula

WARSAW

Minsk

White Russian S.S.R.

Gomel

R. Neman

Kursk

R. Don

Voronezh

UNION OF SOVIET SOCIALIST REPUBLICS

Kharkov

119

Volgograd

R. Volga

Caspian

Sea

HERLANDS

TERDAM

terdam

SELS

TUM

Essen

Ruhr

Dortmund

Cologne

BONN

GERMANY

1142

Leipzig

Dresden

Sudeten Mts.

Wrocław

Katowice

POLAND

Cracow

Lvov

Pripet Marshes

Kiyev

Ukrainian S.S.R.

Donets Basin

Gorlovka

Makeyevka

Voroshilovgrad

567

Rostov-
na-Donu

.28

Grozny

40°

Frankfurt

Nuremberg

PRAGUE

Brno

CZECHOSLOVAKIA

Bratislava

2663

Vinnitsa

Dnepropetrovsk

Krivoy Rog

Donetsk

Mariupol

LUXEMBOURG

Strasbourg

Stuttgart

518

Munich

R. Danube

VIENNA

AUSTRIA

BUDAPEST

HUNGARY

Moldavian S.S.R.

Kishinev

Nikolayev

Zaporozhye

R. Don

R. Dnieper

Sea of Azov

Stavropol

Caucasus Mts.

5632

Mt. Elbrus

Georgian S.S.R.

Sochi

Tbilisi

BOURG

BERNE

SWITZERLAND

Zürich

LIECHTEN-
STEIN

1247

Graz

R. Drava

Graz

R. Tisza

ROMANIA

Cluj-
Napoca

346

Brasov

2543

R. Danube

Crimea

Simferopol

1545

Krasnodar

Armenian S.S.R.

Yerevan

5165

Azerbaijan S.S.R.

Blanc
4810

THE

ALPS

Milan

R. Po

Venice

Zagreb

BELGRADE

YUGOSLAVIA

Sarajevo

Transylvanian
Alps

Iron Gate

BUCHAREST

R. Danube

Constanta

Sevastopol

Black Sea

2244

Mt. Ararat
5165

Turin

Bologna

Florence

SAN
MARINO

Adriatic Sea

307

Split

2522

Balkan Mountains

SOFIA

Varna

Pontic

Mountains

2600

Samsun

3340

Tabriz

Nice

MONACO

Genoa

Ligurian Sea

Apennines

BULGARIA

Mt. Musala
2925

Plovdiv

Skopje

Istanbul

ANKARA

870

Kayseri

4168

Corsica

2710

ROME

ITALY

Naples

Mt. Vesuvius
1277

Bari

Taranto

TIRANA

ALBANIA

Mt. Olympus
2911

Thessaloniki

Sea of
Marmara

Bursa

Eskişehir

TURKEY

Anatolia

Konya

3916

Nineveh

Mosul

Kirkuk

35°

Sardinia

Cagliari

Tyrrhenian

3550

Sea

Palermo

Mt. Etna
3340

Messina

Catania

Sicily

Ionian

Sea

Patras

ATHENS

GREECE

Aegean Sea

Izmir

3086

Antalya

Taurus Mts.

Adana

Latakia

Aleppo

SYRIA

R. Euphrates

BAGHDAD

IRAQ

Bizerta

TUNIS

VALLETTA

MALTA

M
e
d
i
t
e
r
r
a
n
e
a
n

S
e
a

Peloponnese

Rhodes

3864

Crete

2456

Iráklion

Sa

NICOSIA
1952

1463

CYPRUS

LEBANON

BEIRUT

Homs

DAMASCUS

30°

TUNISIA

Sfax

Gabès

ott

erid

TRIPOLI

Misrātah

Tripolitania

Gulf of Sirt

Cyrenaica

Beida

As Sallūm

Benghazi

Alexandria

Tanta

Suez Canal

Port Said

Dead Sea
ISRAEL

Tel Aviv-Yafo

JERUSALEM

JORDAN

AMMAN

Nafud

SAUDI

ARABIA

Qattara
Depression
-134

Giza

CAIRO

Suez

Sinai
2637

Gulf of Suez

10°

15°

LIBYA

20°

25°

EGYPT

R. Nile

30°

35°

40°

Scale 1:7 000 000

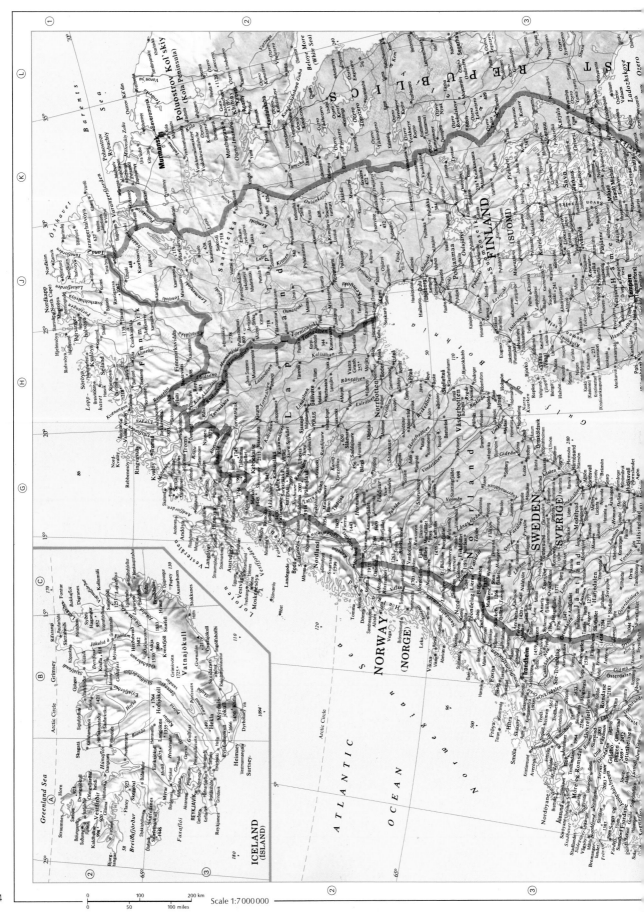

Scale 1:7 000 000

0   100   200 km
0   50   100 miles

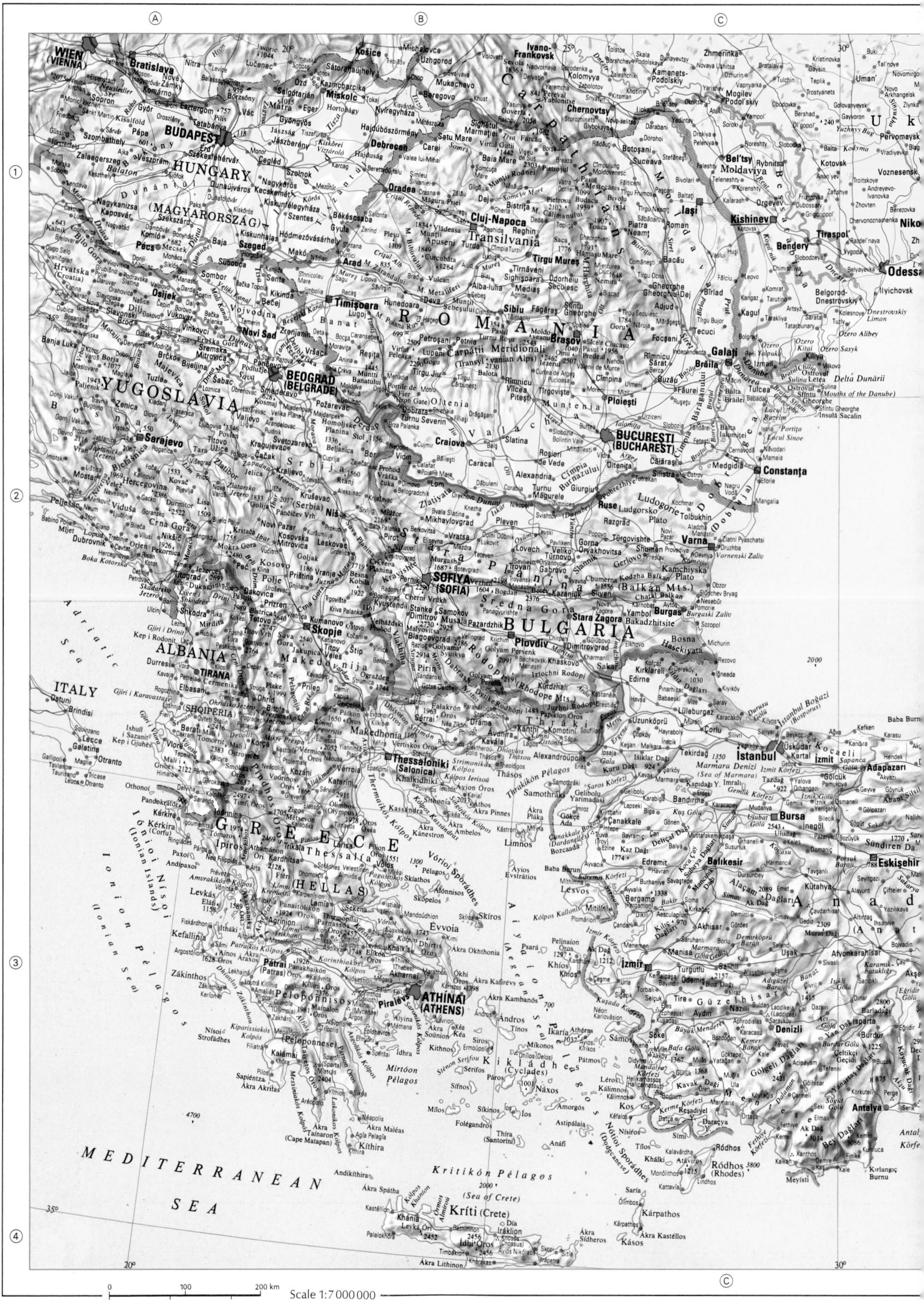

WIEN (VIENNA)
Bratislava
BUDAPEST
HUNGARY
(MAGYARORSZÁG)
Debrecen
Miskolc
Košice
Ivano-Frankovsk
Chernovtsy
Kishinev
Iaşi
Bel'tsy
Moldaviya
Cluj-Napoca
Transilvania
Tîrgu Mureş
ROMANIA
Arad
Timişoara
Oradea
Novi Sad
Subotica
YUGOSLAVIA
BEOGRAD (BELGRADE)
Sarajevo
Hrvatska (Croatia)
Osijek
Bendery
Tiraspol
Odessa
Galaţi
Brăila
Ploieşti
BUCUREŞTI (BUCHAREST)
Constanţa
Craiova
Srbija (Serbia)
Niš
Ruse
Varna
SOFIYA (SOFIA)
Plovdiv
BULGARIA
Stara Zagora
Burgas
Skopje
Makedonija
ALBANIA
TIRANA
SHQIPERIA
Thessaloníki (Salonica)
Edirne
İstanbul
İzmit
Bursa
Eskişehir
Balıkesir
Manisa
İzmir
Denizli
Antalya
ITALY
Brindisi
Adriatic Sea
GREECE
HELLAS
Ípiros
Thessalía
Pátrai (Patras)
Pelopónnisos (Peloponnese)
ATHÍNAI (ATHENS)
Piraiévs
Kérkira (Corfu)
Ionian Sea
Iónioi Nísoi (Ionian Islands)
Kikládhes (Cyclades)
Náxos
Ródhos (Rhodes)
Kárpathos
Kríti (Crete)
Iráklion
Khaniá

MEDITERRANEAN SEA

Kritikón Pélagos (Sea of Crete)

Aegean Sea

Sea of Marmara (Marmara Denizi)

Black Sea

0   100   200 km
0   50   100 miles
Scale 1:7 000 000

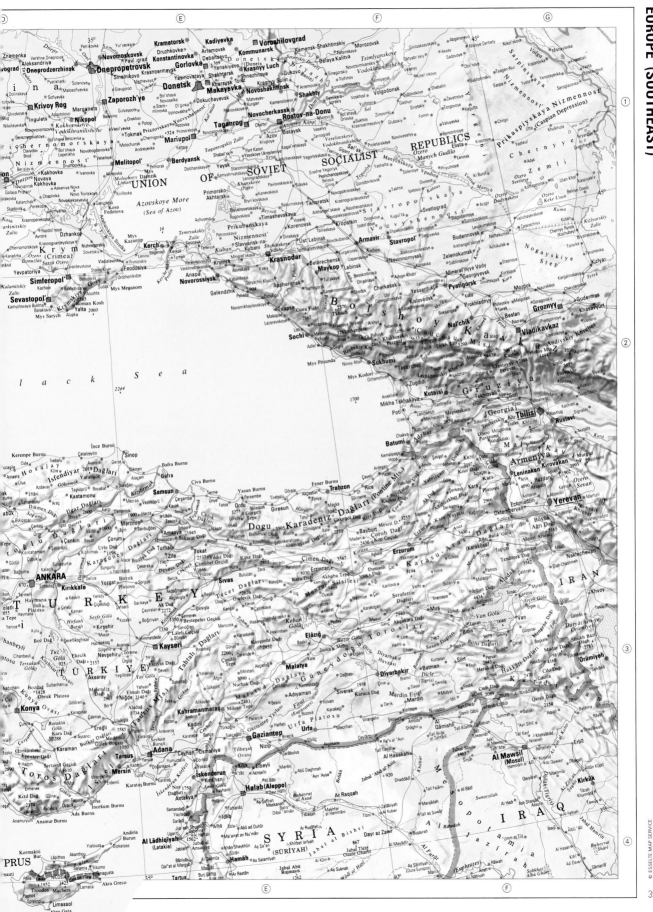

OCEAN

East Siberian
Sea

Bering
Strait

Chukotsk
Peninsula

Saint Lawrence I.

Providenya

Bering

Sea

Aleutian Islands
(USA)

Aleutian Trench

Wrangel I.

New Siberian
Islands

C. Chelyuskin

Laptev Sea

Anadyr

Pevek

Ambarchik

Indigirka R.

Kolyma R.

Koryak Range

Komandorsk Islands
(Komandorskie Ostrova)

O. Bering
O. Mednyy

Central Siberian
Plateau

Chersky Range

Verkhoyansk Range

Kamchatka

Petropavlovsk
Kamchatskiy

PACIFIC

Tiksi

Yana R.

Verkhoyansk

Oymyakon

Okhotsk

Sea of
Okhotsk

Severo Kurilsk

OCEAN

R. Lena

Dzhugdzhur Range

Kuril Trench

R. Olenek

Yakutsk

Aldan R.

Nizhnekolymsk

Sakhalin

Kuril Islands

Japan Trench

R. Lena

Magadan

Okha

Lensk

Stanovoy Range

Aleksandrovsk
na Amure

Yuzhno Sakhalinsk

Nikolayevsk na Amure

Soya Strait

Wakkanai

Mirnyy

Skovorodino

Svobodnyy

Amur R.

Komsomolsk
na Amure

Asahikawa

Hokkaido

SOCIALIST REPUBLICS

Ust Kut

Kirensk

Heilong Jiang

Sovetskaya Gavan

Sapporo

Hakodate

R. Angara

Bratsk

Chita

Shilka R.

Nenjiang

Sikhote Alin Range

Aomori

Honshu

Japan

ALIST REPUBLICS

Cheremkhovo

L. Baykal

Ulan Ude

Blagoveshchensk

Belogorsk

Hegang

Akita

Sendai

Niigata

Irkutsk

Angara R.

Kyakhta

Borzya

Hailar

Qiqihar

Jiamusi

Sungari R.

Utsunomiya

Great Khingan Mts.

Harbin

Manchuria

Jilin

Vladivostok

Chongjin

TOKYO

Yokohama

Kyzyl

Ulaan Baatar

R. Kerulen

Changchun

Shenyang

Fushun

NORTH KOREA

Kyoto

Nagoya

Osaka

MONGOLIA

Gobi

Nei Monggol (Inner Mongolia)

Jinzhou

Anshan

Dandong

PYONGYANG

SEOUL

SOUTH KOREA

Kobe

Matsuyama

Shikoku

Sea of Japan

Kita Kyushu

Hiroshima

Pusan

Saynshand

Benxi

Sea of Japan

Dalandzadgad

BEIJING (PEKING)

Tangshan

Lüda

Taejon

Taegu

Fukuoka

Kyushu

Hohhot

Baotou

Datong

Zhangjiakou

Tianjin

Yellow
Sea

Kwangju

Nagasaki

Kagoshima

Ordos Plateau

Yinchuan

Shijiazhuang

Jinan

Qingdao

Yumen

Nan Shan

Zhangye

Taiyuan

Handan

Lianyungang

Koko Nor

Ningxia Huizu

Yanan

Xinxiang

Kaifeng

Huang Ho

Grand Canal

Tsaidam

Xining

Lanzhou

Xianyang

Luoyang

Zhengzhou

Xuzhou

Zhenjiang

Bayan Har

Huang Ho

Baoji

Xian

CHINA

Huainan

Nanjing

Wuxi

Shanghai

East China
Sea

Ryukyu Islands

Chengdu

Red
Basin

Nanchong

Wuhan

Yangtze Kiang

Hangzhou

Ningbo

Zigong

Chongqing

Dongting Hu

Changsha

Nanchang

Wenzhou

Naha

Tropic of Cancer

Luzhou

Zunyi

Guiyang

Hengyang

Fuzhou

TAIPEI

Kunming

Nan Ling

Guilin

Liuzhou

Guangzhou

Shantou

Xiamen

Tainan

Kaohsiung

TAIWAN

Guangxi Zhuangzu

Nanning

Hong Kong (U.K.)

Macao (Port.)

Luzon Strait

BURMA

Mandalay

VIETNAM

HANOI

LAOS

Haiphong

Zhanjiang

PHILIPPINES

Kazan Is. (Japan)

Iwo Jima

Bonin Is. (Japan)

Ramapo Deep

Mariana Trench
(Adm. by USA)

Mariana Islands
(Adm. by USA)

Guam I. (USA)

Challenger Deep

UNION OF SOVIET

Mediterranean Sea

Black Sea

GREECE
ATHENS
Benghazi
LIBYA
Cyrenaica

TURKEY
ANKARA
Anatolia
CYPRUS
Alexandria
BEIRUT
LEBANON
DAMASCUS
SYRIA
ISRAEL
JERUSALEM
AMMAN
JORDAN
IRAQ
BAGHDAD
EGYPT
CAIRO
Giza

Kazakh S.S.R.
Kirghiz Steppe
Kyzyl-Kum
Uzbekistan S.S.R.
Kara-Kum
Turkmenistan S.S.R.

Caspian Sea
TEHRÁN
IRAN
Zagros Mountains

SAUDI ARABAIA
RIYADH
Nejd
Hejaz
Nafud
Red Sea

Rub al Khali

OMAN

UNITED ARAB EMIRATES
QATAR
BAHRAIN
Persian Gulf
KUWAIT

AFGHANISTAN
KABUL
Hindu Kush
Pamir
PESHAWAR

PAKISTAN

Tien Shan
East Turkistan
Tarim Basin
Sink
Uig

Kunlu
Plateau of Ti
Tibe

Himalaya
DELHI
NEPAL
KATHMANDU

INDIA

SUDAN
KHARTOUM
Nubian Desert

ETHIOPIA
ADDIS ABABA
Ethiopian Plateau

YEMEN
SAN'Á
Hadramawt
Gulf of Aden
Aden
Socotra

SOMALIA
MOGADISHU
Ogaden

KENYA

Arabian
Sea

Bombay
Poona
Hyderabad

Western Ghats
Eastern Ghats
Deccan

Madras
Bangalore
Coimbatore

Laccadive Is.
(India)

Cochin
Trivandrum
C. Comorin

SRI LANKA
COLOMBO

Mombasa
Pemba I.
Zanzibar
DAR ES SALAAM

Equator

MALDIVES
MALÉ

VICTORIA
SEYCHELLES
Amirante Is.
(Sey.)
Aldabra Is.
(Sey.)

COMOROS
MORONI
Mayotte
(Fr.)

Mozambique Channel

Chagos
Archipelago
(U.K.)

INDIAN OC

MADAGASCAR
ANTANANARIVO

0   500   1000 km
0   200   400   600 miles
Scale 1:34 000 000

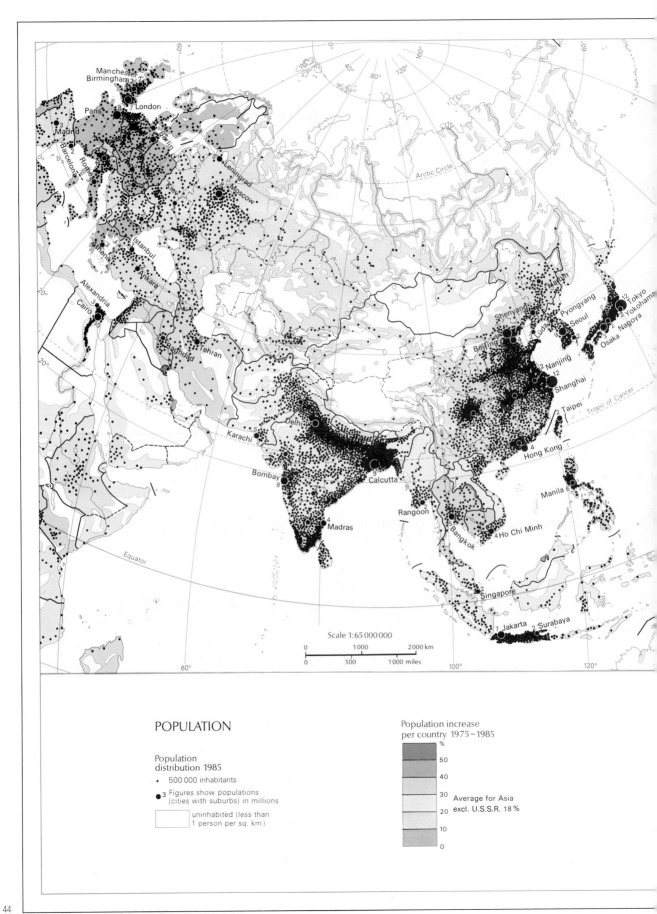

POPULATION

Population distribution 1985

- · 500 000 inhabitants
- ●3 Figures show populations (cities with suburbs) in millions

☐ uninhabited (less than 1 person per sq. km)

Population increase per country 1975–1985

%
50
40
30
Average for Asia excl. U.S.S.R. 18 %
20
10
0

Scale 1:65 000 000

0 — 1000 — 2000 km
0 — 500 — 1000 miles

Manchester
Birmingham 2
8 Paris 7 London
Madrid 3
Barcelona 2
Rome 3
Berlin
Kiev
5 Leningrad
Moscow
Athens
Istanbul
Ankara 2
Alexandria
Cairo 3
Baghdad 3
Tehran
Karachi
Delhi 5
Bombay 8
Madras 4
Calcutta 9
Rangoon
Bangkok 5
Ho Chi Minh 4
Singapore
Jakarta 7
Surabaya 2
Harbin
Shenyang
Beijing
Luda 2
Pyongyang
Seoul 9
Tokyo 12
Yokohama 2
Osaka 3 Nagoya 2
Nanjing 2
Shanghai 12
Taipei 2
Hong Kong 4
Manila 6

Arctic Circle
Tropic of Cancer
Equator

60°   60°
20°
20°
40°   80°   120°   160°
100°   120°

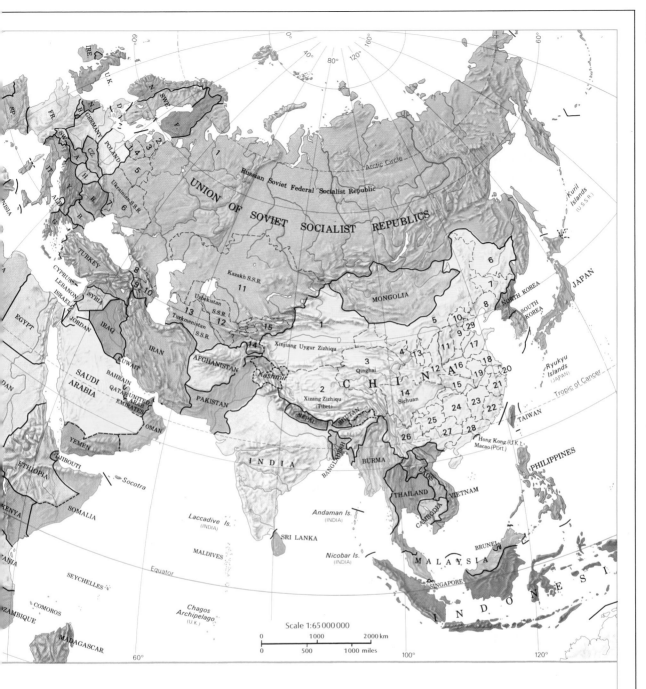

POLITICAL DIVISIONS

Republics of the U.S.S.R.

1 Russian S.F.S.R.
2 Estonian S.S.R.
3 Latvian S.S.R.
4 Lithuanian S.S.R.
5 Belorussian S.S.R.
6 Ukrainian S.S.R.
7 Moldavian S.S.R.
8 Georgian S.S.R.
9 Armenian S.S.R.
10 Azerbaijan S.S.R.
11 Kazakh S.S.R.

12 Uzbek S.S.R.
13 Turkmen S.S.R.
14 Tadzhik S.S.R.
15 Kirgiz S.S.R.

Administrative regions in China
(Zizhiqu = Autonomous region)

1 Xinjiang Uygur Zizhiqu
2 Xizang Zizhiqu (Tibet)
3 Qinghai

4 Gansu
5 Nei Monggol Zizhiqu
6 Heilongjiang
7 Jilin
8 Liaoning
9 Hebei
10 Beijing Shi
11 Shanxi
12 Shaanxi
13 Ningxia Huizu-Zizhiqu
14 Sichuan
15 Hubei
16 Henan

17 Shandong
18 Jiangsu
19 Anhui
20 Shanghai Shi
21 Zhejiang
22 Fujian
23 Jiangxi
24 Hunan
25 Guizhou
26 Yunnan
27 Guangxi Zhuangzu Zizhiqu
28 Guangdong
29 Tianjin Shi

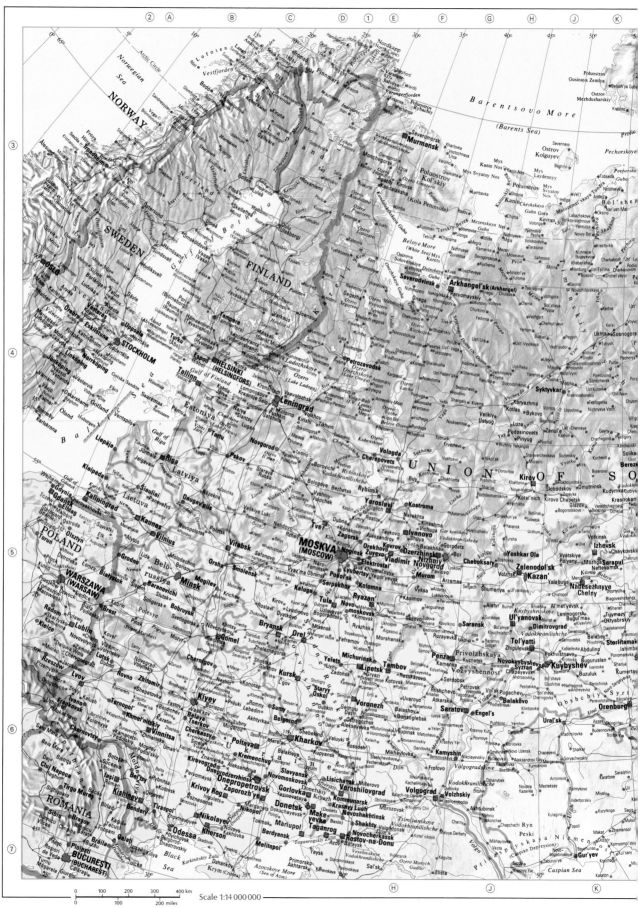

Scale 1:14 000 000

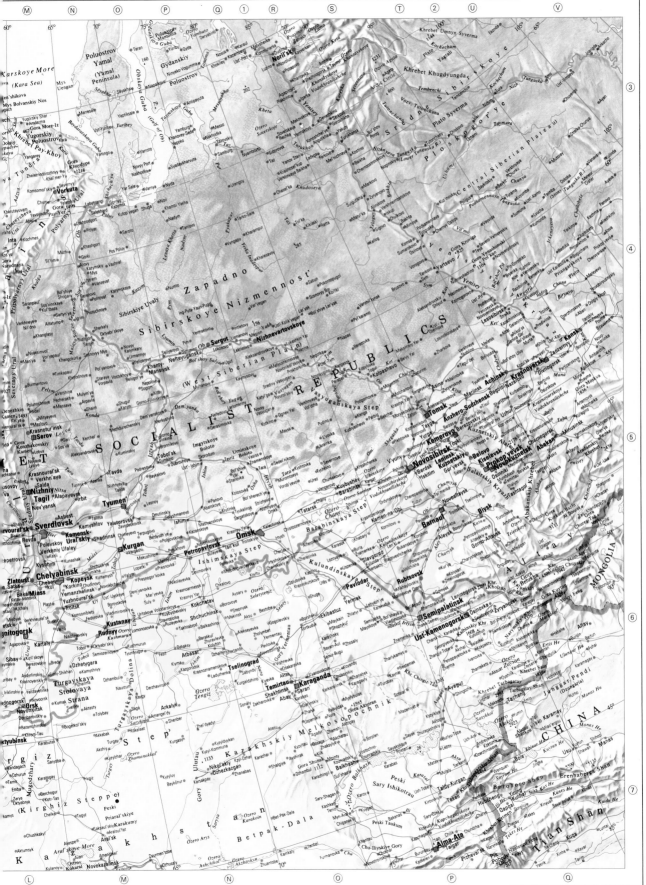

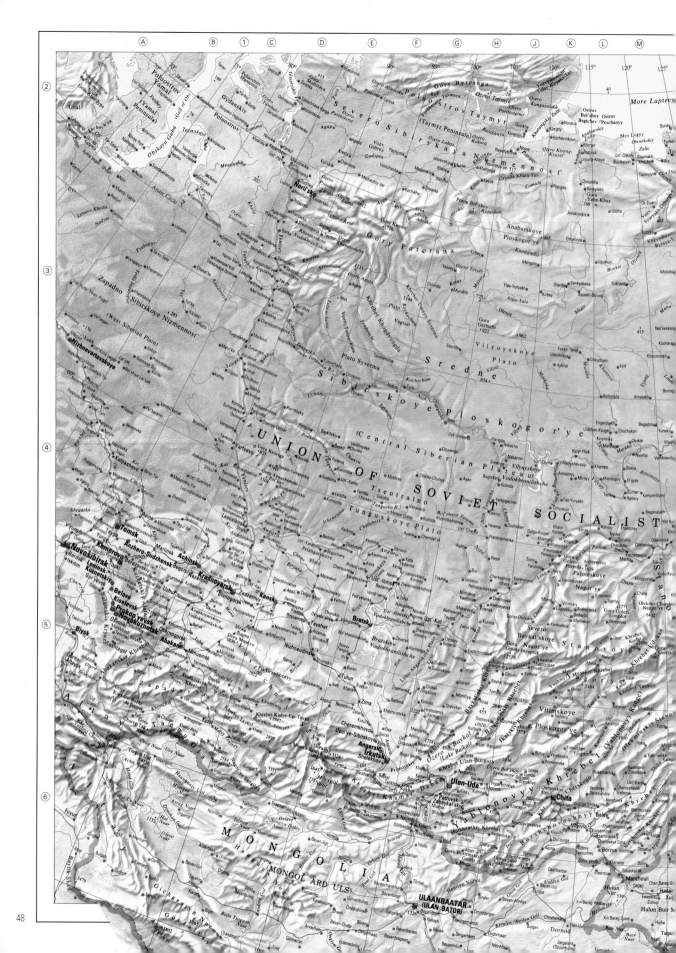

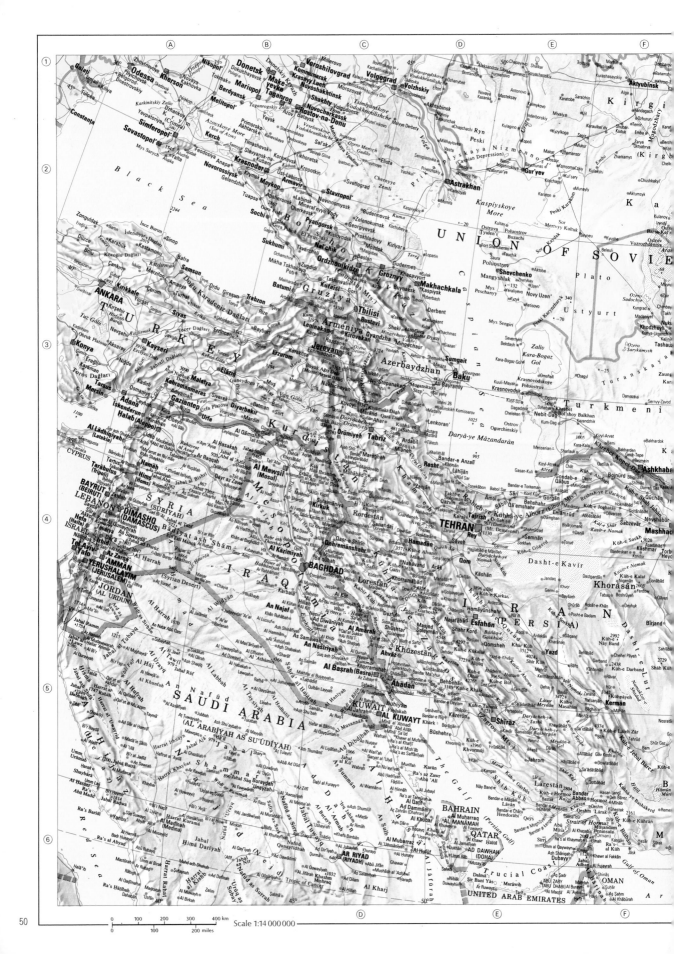

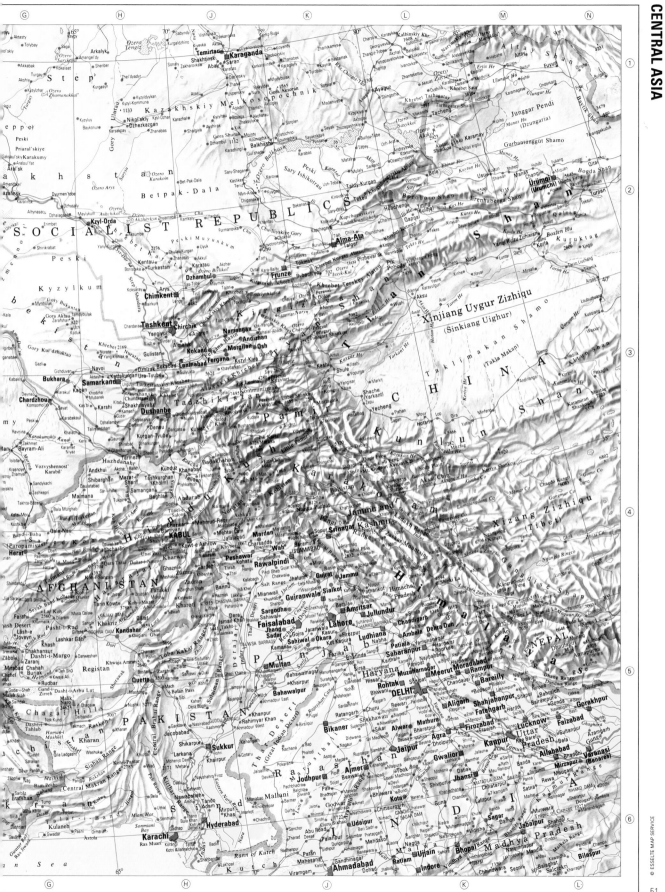

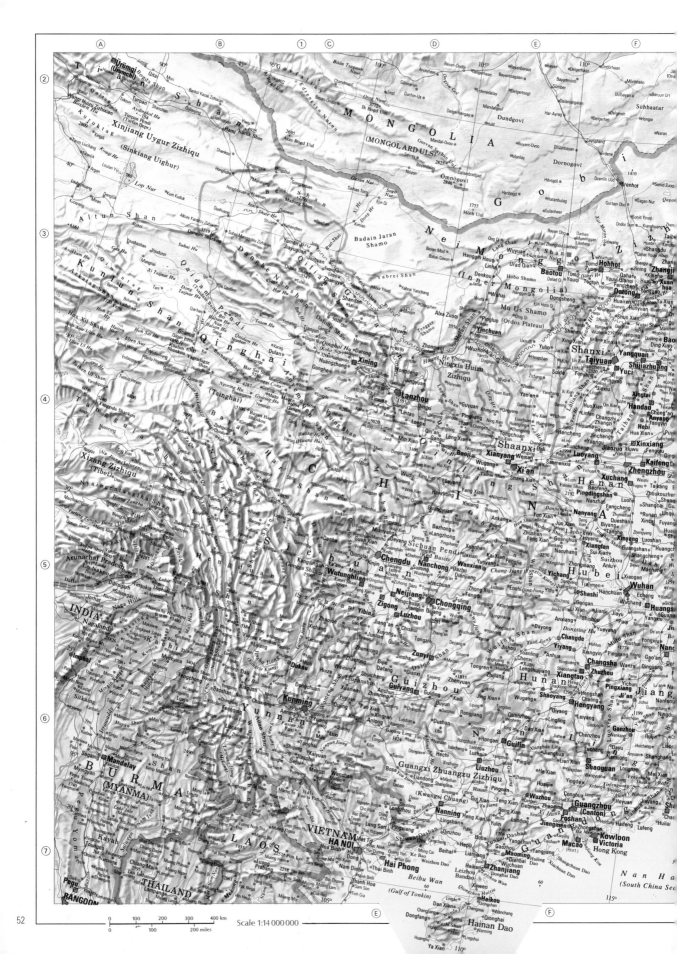

G   H   J   K   L   1   M

②

③

④

⑤

⑥

Busr
Nuur
120° 1712
Moguge Nanzishan   Qiqihar   Hailun   Nancha   Huachuan   Maksimovka
Longjiang An'ang   Qingang   Tieli   Tangwang   Baoqing   Sichote-Alin
125°   Jiamusi   Shuangyashan
Heilongjiang   Huanan   Hulin   Lesozavodsk
135°

Harbin   U.S.S.R.   Hokkaidō

P'YONGYANG

NORTH
KOREA   Sea of Japan   JAPAN

Honshū   TOKYO   Yokohama

SOUTH
KOREA

Huang Hai
(Yellow Sea)

Shanghai

Dong Hai
(East China Sea)

PACIFIC

TAIWAN
(FORMOSA)

OCEAN

TAIPEI

Kaohsiung

Tropic of Cancer

Luzon Strait

120°   125°   130°   135°   140°

H   J   K   L

53

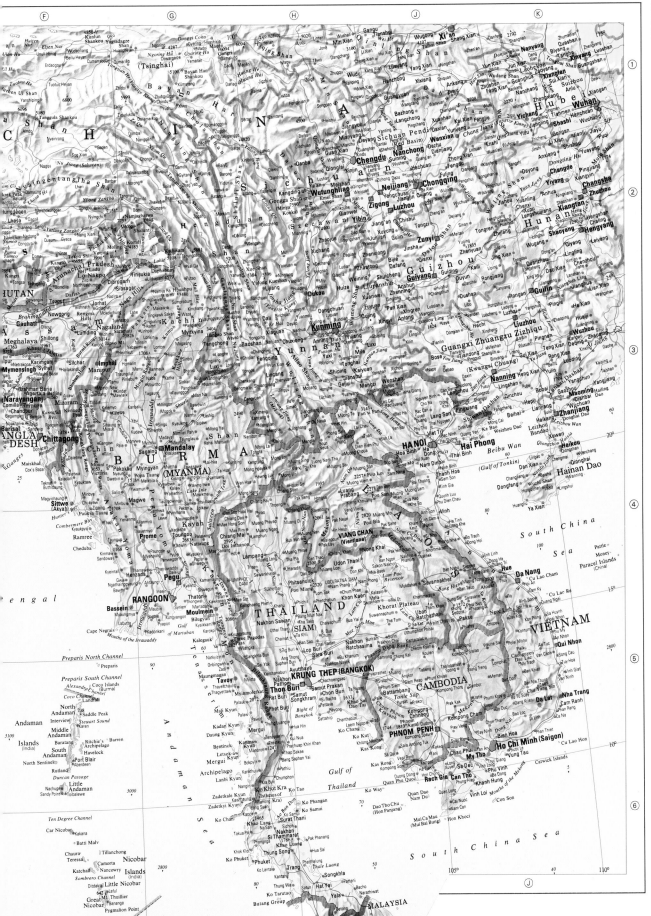

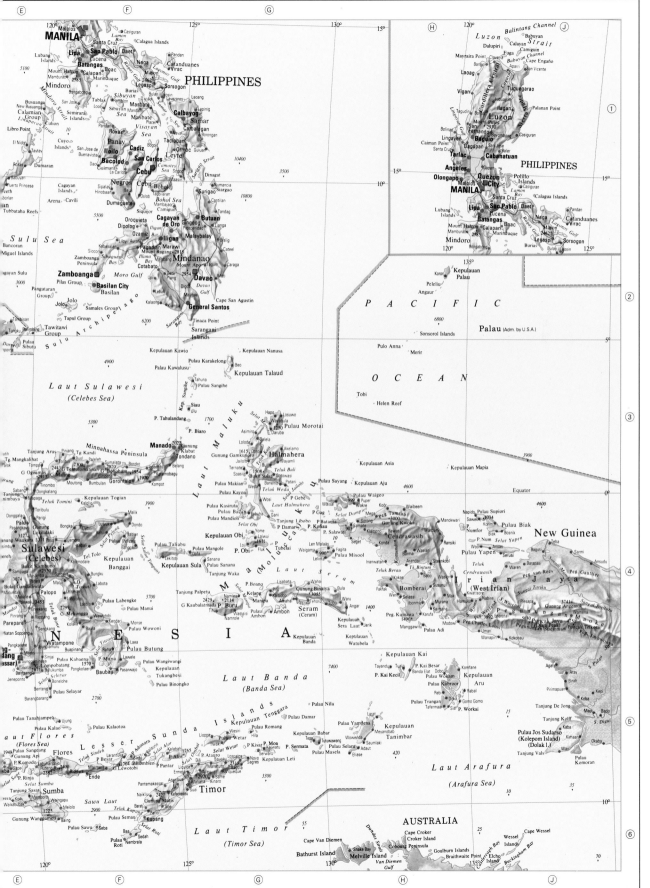

POLITICAL DIVISIONS

Scale 1:82 000 000

POPULATION

Population distribution 1985

- 500 000 inhabitants

•³ Figures show populations (cities with suburbs) in millions

uninhabited (less than 1 person per sq. km)

Population increase per country 1975–1985

0 10 20 30 40 50 % Average for Oceania 17%

Scale 1:34 000 000

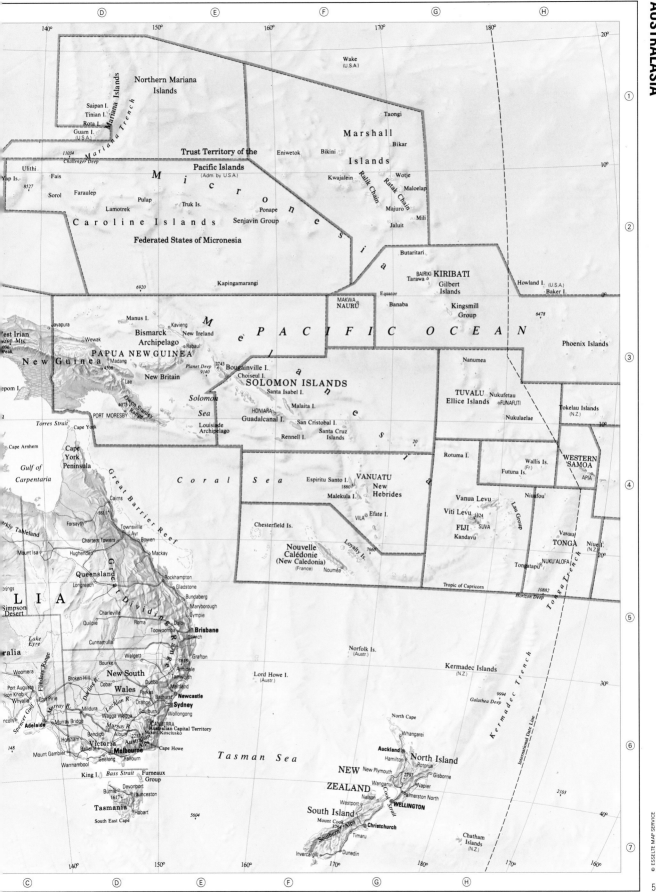

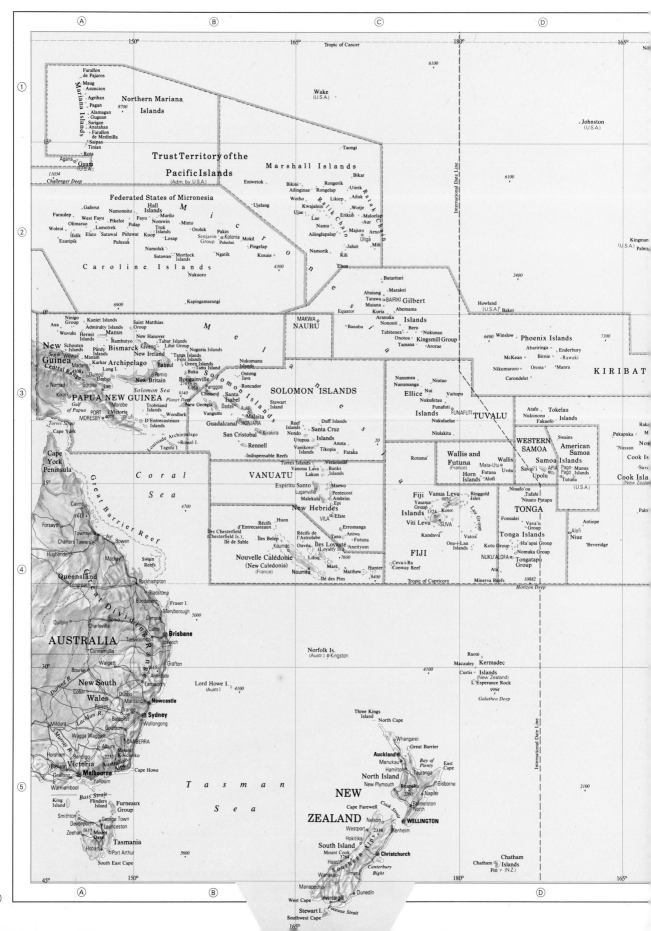

A   B   C   D

150°   165°   Tropic of Cancer   180°   165°

① Farallon de Pajaros
Maug
Asuncion
6100
Agrihan
Pagan
8700
Alamagan   Northern Mariana
Guguan   Islands   Wake
Sarigan   (U.S.A.)   Johnston
Anatahan   (U.S.A.)
15°   Farallon
de Medinilla
Saipan
Tinian   Taongi

Agana Rota
(U.S.A.) Guam
11034   Trust Territory of the
Challenger Deep   Pacific Islands   Marshall Islands
(Adm. by U.S.A.)

Bikar
Bikini Rongerik Utirik
Eniwetok Ailinginae Rongelap Ailuk   6100
Wotho   Likiep Wotje
Ujelang Kwajalein Erikub
Ujae Lae Maloelap
Federated States of Micronesia   Namu Aur
Gaferut   Hall   Murilo   Majuro
Faraulep   Namonuito   Islands   Ailinglapalap Uliga
② West Fayu   Fayu Nomwin   Minto   Mili
Woleai Pikelot   Lamotrek   Pulap Truk   Oroluk   Jaluit
Olimarao   Elato Satawal Puluwat   Islands   Pakin   Namorik
Ifalik   Kuop   Senjavin   Kolonia   Kili
Eauripik   Pulusuk   Group Pohnhei   Kingman
Namoluk   Mokil   Ebon   (U.S.A.)
Satawan Mortlock   Ngatik   Pingelap   Palmy
Islands Kusaie

Caroline Islands   4300   Butaritari   2400
Nukuoro   Abaiang Marakei
Tarawa Bairiki Gilbert
Kapingamarangi   Maiana Howland
Equator   Kuria   Abemama (U.S.A.) Baker
Makwa   Aranuka   Islands
Nauru   Banaba Nonouti   Beru Nukunau
6900   Tabiteuea   Kingsmill Group   6400 Winslow   Phoenix Islands   7300
0°   Ninigo   Saint Matthias   Onotoa Tamana   Abariringa   Enderbury
Aua Group   Kaniet Islands Group   Arorae   McKean Birnie Rawaki
Wuvulu Admiralty Islands   Nikumaroro Orona Manra
Hermit Manus   New Hanover   Carondelet   KIRIBAT
New Islands Rambutyo   Tabar Islands   KIRIBAT
Guinea Schouten Purdy Kavieng Lihir Group
Islands   Bismarck Nuguria Islands Nanumea Niutao
Sepik R. Manam Long I.   Archipelago Tanga Islands   Nukumanu   Nanumanga   Nui
Madang Karkar   Feni Islands Islands   Ellice   Vaitupu
Central Range Dampier   New Ireland Green Islands   Nukufetau   Atafu Tokelau
4508 Umboi   Babau Ontong   Islands   Funafuti Nukunonu Islands
Nomad Goroka Tami New Britain Java   FUNAFUTI Fakaofo
③ Kikori   Goroka Buka   Nukulaelae
PAPUA NEW GUINEA Bougainville   SOLOMON ISLANDS   TUVALU
Gulf Solomon Sea Kieta   Niulakita   Atafu Tokelau
of Papua Morobe Panggoe   Swains
PORT 9140 New Georgia Choiseul Santa   American
MORESBY 4073 Lae Planet Deep   Isabel   WESTERN Samoa
Trobriand Dadali   SAMOA Islands
Torres Strait D'Entrecasteaux Vangunu Aulu   Samoa Is.
Cape York Islands Malaita   Rotuma   Savai'i APIA   Pago Manua
Guadalcanal HONIARA   Reef   Duff Islands   Upolu   Pago Islands
San Cristobal Kirakira   Nendo Santa Cruz   Wallis   Tutuila
Rennell   Utupua   Islands   Wallis and   Wallis   (U.S.A.)
Cape   Vanikoro Anuta   Futuna Mata-Utu
York   Indispensable Reefs   Tikopia   (France) Uvéa
Peninsula   Fataka Futuna   Cook Is.
Torres Islands Vetaoundé   Horn Alofi
Vanua Lava Banks   Islands   Cook Isla
Coral VANUATU Lakon Islands   Niuafo'ou   (New Zeala
15° Sea Espíritu Santo Maewo   Tafahi
Luganville Pentecost   Fiji Vanua Levu Ringgold   Niuatoputapu
4700 Malekula Ambrim   Islands Yasawa 1031 Isles
Epi Group   TONGA
Huon New Hebrides   Koro   Lau Group
Récifs VILA Efate   Viti Levu 1324   Fonualei   Vava'u Group
Îles Chesterfield d'Entrecasteaux   Erromanga   SUVA   Tonga Islands
(Chesterfield Is.) Aniwa   Kandavu   Ono-i-Lau   Kotu Group   Antiope
Île de Sable Récifs de Tana Futuna   Vatoa   Ha'apai Group   Alofi Niue
Îles Belep l'Astrolabe Aneityum   FIJI   Islands   Nomuka Group   Beveridge
Koumac Ouvéa   Iles Loyauté   Ceva-i-Ra   NUKU'ALOFA Tongatapu
Nouvelle Calédonie Lifou (Loyalty Is.) 7600   Conway Reef   Group
(New Caledonia) Maré   Hunter   Ata   10882
④ (France) Nouméa Matthew   Minerva Reefs   Horizon Deep
Île des Pins 6400   Tropic of Capricorn
Queensland Rockhampton
Longreach Gladstone   Norfolk Is.   Raoui
Bundaberg Fraser I.   (Austr.) Kingston   Macauley Kermadec
Quilpie Roma Maryborough   4100 Curtis   Islands
Charleville Gympie   L'Esperance Rock
Dalby 5000   9994
AUSTRALIA Toowoomba Brisbane   Galathea Deep
Cunnamulla Ipswich
Bourke   1615 Grafton
30°   Walgett   Tenterfield   Lord Howe I.   Three Kings
Cobar New South Armidale   (Austr.) 4100   Island North Cape
Wales Tamworth   Whangarei
Dubbo   Great Barrier
Maitland Newcastle   Auckland   Bay of East
Mildura Parkes Orange   Manukau Plenty Cape
Bathurst Sydney   Hamilton Tauranga
Wagga Wagga Goulburn Wollongong   North Island
Albury CANBERRA   New Plymouth Gisborne
Horsham Mount   Wanganui Napier
2237 Kosciusko Australian   NEW 3764
Bendigo 1922 Alps   2797 Palmerston
Ballarat Victoria Cape Howe   ZEALAND   North
Geelong Melbourne   WELLINGTON
⑤ Warrnambool Yallourn Tasman   Nelson
Bass Strait   Sea   Cape Farewell Blenheim
King Flinders   Westport 2338
Island Island Furneaux   Hokitika   2100
Smithton Group   South Island
Devonport George Town   Mount Cook Christchurch
1617 Launceston   3764   Chatham
Zeehan Mount Ossa   Timaru   Canterbury Islands
Tasmania   Southern Bight   Chatham (N.Z.)
Hobart Port Arthur   5600   Alps Wanaka   Pitt
South East Cape   Haast   South Island
Manapouri Dunedin
West Cape   Invercargill
Stewart I. Foveaux Strait
Southwest Cape

45°   150°   180°   165°

A   B   D

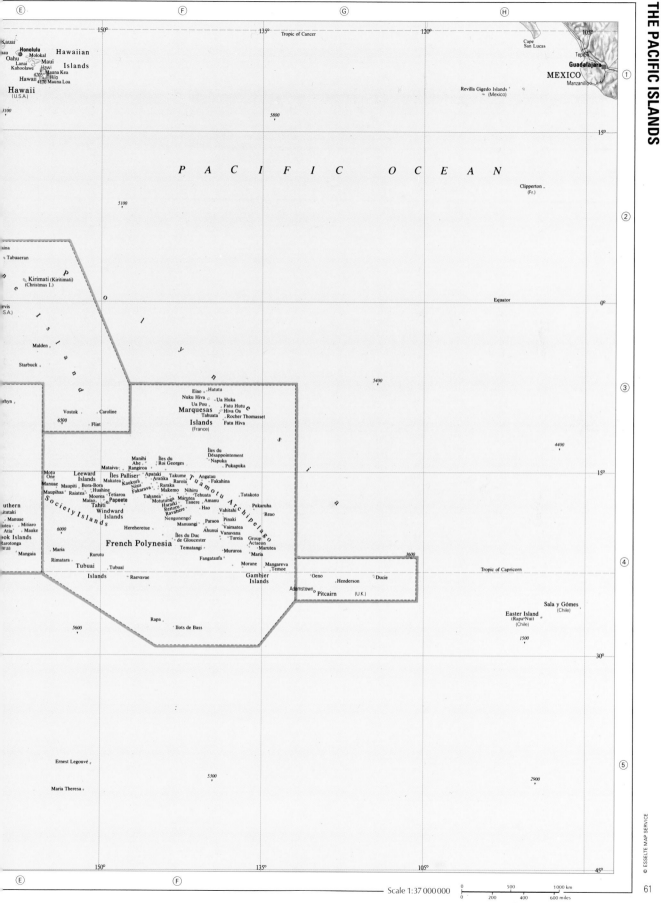

115°   120°   125°   130°   135°

6600

2200

Pulau Sawu   Seba   Baä   Sedah   Timor

INDONESIA

Pulau Roti   Nembrala

①

Ashmore Reef   Hibernia Reef   Cartier Island

T i m o r   S e a

140

55

Cape Van Diemen   Cape Croker   Croker Island
Bathurst Island   Melville Island   Snake Bay   Cobourg Peninsula   Goulburn Islands   Braithwaite Point
Beagle Gulf   Van Diemen Gulf   Oenpelli   Maningrida
Seringapatam Reef   Port Darwin   Darwin   Point Stuart   East Alligator River
Scott Reef   Browse Island   Rum Jungle   Batchelor   Oenpelli   Mainoru   Nurl

I N D I A N

Bonaparte Archipelago   Admiralty Gulf   Pago Mission   310   Joseph Bonaparte Gulf   El Sharana
Mount Connor   Kalumburu   259   Mount Casuarina   Port Keats   Brock's Creek   Daly River   Pine Creek   Katherine R.   Beswick
Adele Island   Cambridge Gulf   Queens Channel   Adelaide River   KATHERINE GORGE   Roper R.
Buccaneer Archipelago   York Sound   DRYSDALE RIVER NATIONAL PARK   Adolphus I.   Legune   Katherine   *Arnhem Land*   ARNHEM LAND N.P.
Collier Bay   Wyndham   Carlton Hill   Bradshaw   Willeroo   Larrimah   Blyth R.

15°

O C E A N

5500   Sunday Strait   King Leopold Ranges   Kimberley   Mount Elizabeth   853   Karunjie   Durack Range   ORD RIVER DAM   Victoria River Downs   Montejinnie   Dunmarra
Cape Lévêque   King Sound   Mount Ord   936   Kimberley Plateau   Mount John   536   Stirling Creek   Pigeon Hole   Sturt   Newcastle River   Beetaloo
Lacepede Islands   Pender   Derby   Mount Broome   Mount Leake   697   Mount Maiyu   479   Inverway   Plain   Newcastle Waters   Elliott
Dampier Land   Beagle Bay   Lennard River   Yeeda River   Margaret River   Halls Creek   Hooker Creek   Lake Woods   Powell Creek   Anthony

②

5500   Broome   Fitzroy River   Liveringa   Fitzroy Crossing   Old Cherrabun   Gordon Downs
Rowley Shoals   230   Roebuck Bay   Thangoo   Noonkanbah   Bohemia Downs   Birrindudu
Cape Latouche Treville   Cape Bossut   Lagrange   Edgar Range   *N o r t h e r n*
Anna Plains   Billiluna   Lake Buck   Tanami   *T a n a m i   D e s e r t*   Mount Samuel   436
Larrey Point   Poissonnier Point   Eighty Mile Beach   Wallal Downs   *Canning Basin*   TANAMI DESERT   Tennant Cre

100   Dampier Archipelago   Dampier   Port Hedland   Goldsworthy   *Great Sandy Desert*   Lake Gregory   436   The Granites   Wauchope
Monte Bello Islands   Nickol Bay   Wickham   Yarrie   Warrawagine   Lake Lucas   WILDLIFE SANCTUARY   Murray Downs   Barrow
Barrow Island   Roebourne   De Grey R.   Lake   Percival Lakes   Lake Wills   *T e r r i t o r y*   Tea Tree   Uto

20°

Muiron Islands   Yarraloola   Marble Bar   Waukarlycarly   Lake Tobin   Lake Hatlett   Lake White   *A U S T R A L I A*
North West Cape   CHICHESTER RANGE NATIONAL PARK   Nullagine   Lake Mackay   Napperby   Harts Range
Exmouth Gulf   Onslow   Minderoo   *Hamersley*   Wittenoom   RUDALL RIVER NATIONAL PARK   Lake Dora   Lake Auld   Lake Eaton   1524   1510   Narwietooma   Mount
Point Cloates   Giralia   Mount Brockman   1141   Mount Bruce   1235   Lake Blanche   Lake George   Lake Mackay   Mount Liebig   901   1058   Alice Springs
Boolaloo   Tom Price   Marillana   Roy Hill   HAMERSLEY RANGE   Lake Macdonald   Mount Leisler   *Macdonnell Ranges*

③

Point Cloates   Ningaloo   Koolina   Ethel Creek   NATIONAL PARK   Newman   *Tropic of Capricorn*   Lake Hopkins   Lake Neale   Henbury   Deep Well
Cape Farquhar   Winning   *Ashburton R.*   Paraburdoo   *Lake Disappointment*   Lake Amadeus   FINKE GORGE NATIONAL PARK   Bundo
Lyndon River   Mount Vernon   *W e s t e r n*   Lake Macdonald   Mount Olga   Petermanns Ranges   Erldunda
Cape Cuvier   Minilya   Barlee Range   Mount Deering   1069   AYERS ROCK - MOUNT OLGA   Lake R.
Minilya R.   Williambury   Salt Lakes   *Gibson Desert*   Giles   1219   Mount Davies   NATIONAL PARK   Kulgera
Geographe Channel   Lake McLeod   Mount Augustus   COLLIER RANGES   Mount Essendon   BROWNE RANGE   705   Barrow R.   Mulga Park   Victory Downs   Wall Creek

25°

Bernier I.   Gascoyne R.   370   Mount Sandiman   NATIONAL PARK   Carnarvon Range   NATURE RESERVE   Warburton Mission   Barrow Range   1058   *Musgrave Ranges*   1440
Dorré I.   994   Mount Egerton   910   Mount Woodroffe
Naturaliste Channel   Gascoyne Junction   Lake Buchanan   Warburton Range   555   Tomkinson Ranges   Everard
Cape Inscription   Shark Bay   Macadam Plains   Robinson Ranges   802   Lake Gregory   Carnegie   Mount Squires   Simpson Hill   Birksgate Range   773   *S o*   Range
Dirk Hartog Island   Denham   Callytharra Springs   Mount Gould   Lake   Mount Fraser   705   Lake Gillen   Baker   Mount Sir Thomas   Everard   Welbo
Hamelin Pool   Byro   732   Nabberu   Lake   Lake   Lake   Wintinna   Mount
Edel Land   Tamala   Milly Milly   Mount Hale   Meekatharra   Wiluna   Lake Carnegie   Breaden   *Great Victoria Desert*   *A u s t*   Willoughby

④

Mount Murchison   Nannine   Lake Way   Lake Throssell   Serpentine Lakes   Coober Pedy
520   Meadow   Murgoo   Sanford R.   Annean   Lake Maitland   Lake Yeo   Lake Dey Dey   Lake Maurice   1186
Meeberrie   Big Bell   Lake Austin   Lake Mason   Mount Shenton   594   Lake Rason   Jubilee Lake   Mount Willoughby   Mount
Billabong R.   Cue   Agnew   Lake Darlot   Lake Ell   Maralinga   Oldea
KALBARRI NATIONAL PARK   Geraldine   Boogardie   Painswick   Sandstone   Laverton   Lake Carey   Lake Gidgi   Shell Lakes   GREAT VICTORIA DESERT   Maralinga   Wynbring
Kalbarri   Northampton   Yalgoo   Mount Magnet   Mount Redcliffe   576   Leonora   Malcolm   Lake Minigwal   Plumridge Lake   Lake Nyanga   NATURE RESERVE   Cook
Bluff Point   Greenough River   Mullewa   Thundelarra   Kookynie   Lake Shepperd   Christie   1186
Houtman Abrolhos   Geraldton   Mingenew   Menzies   Lake Rebecca   Mundabilla   Hughes   Cook   Mount

30°

100   Dongara   Moora   698   Lake Barlee   Goongarrie   *Nullarbor Plain*   Forrest   Kingoonya   Nullarbor   Colona   Penong
5000   Three Springs   Carnamah   Mount Singleton   Lake Moore   686   Loongana   Rawlinna   Naretha   Rawlinna   Head of Bight   Fowlers Bay
Yarra Yarra Lakes   Mount Lesueur   313   Dalwallinu   Beacon   Mount Jackson   Lake Lapage   Karonie   Kalgoorlie   Cocklebiddy   Eucla   Wilson Bluff   65   Streaky Ba
Jurien Bay   Watheroo   Pithara   Bonnie Rock   Coolgardie   Boulder   Zanthus   Eyre   Fowlers Bay
Lancelin   Moora   Koorda   Mukinbudin   Southern Cross   Kambalda   Lake Cowan   Fraser Range   Nanambinia   *G r e a t*
Wannaroo   Gingin   Toodyay   Northam   Merredin   Widgiemooltha   Higginsville   Lake Lefroy   Balladonia   Anx
New Norcia   Kellerberrin   Coolgardie   Norseman   Lake Dundas   Cap

⑤

Perth   Fremantle   York   Quairading   Corrigin   Hyden   658   Lake King   Charles Peak   Point Culver   *A u s t r a l i a n   B i g h t*
Rockingham   Beverley   Brookton   Stretton   Kondinin   Daniell   Lake Magenta   Ravensthorpe   CAPE ARID NATIONAL PARK
Mandurah   Pingelly   Wickepin   Lake Grace   Nyabing   Hopetoun   Esperance   Cape Arid   Pollock Reef
Waroona   Boddington   Wagin   Lake Grace   Archipelago of the Recherche
Harvey   Narrogin   Katanning   FITZGERALD RIVER   Gnowangerup   NATIONAL PARK
Bunbury   Collie   Darkan   Nyabing   Esperance Road   Hood Point
Cape Naturaliste   Geographe Bay   Bonnybrook   Kojonup   STIRLING RANGE N.P.   1109   Bremer Bay
Busselton   Bridgetown   Cranbrook   Bluff Knoll   Cheyne Bay

35°

2600   Margaret River   Witchcliff   Manjimup   Mount Barker
Augusta   Pemberton   Northcliff   Denmark   Albany
Cape Leeuwin   Flinders Bay   Point D'Entrecasteaux   West Cape Howe   King George Sound   Bald Head

⑥

2500   5700   4000

110°   115°   120°   125°   130°

0   100   200   300   400 km
0   100   200 miles

Scale 1:14 000 000

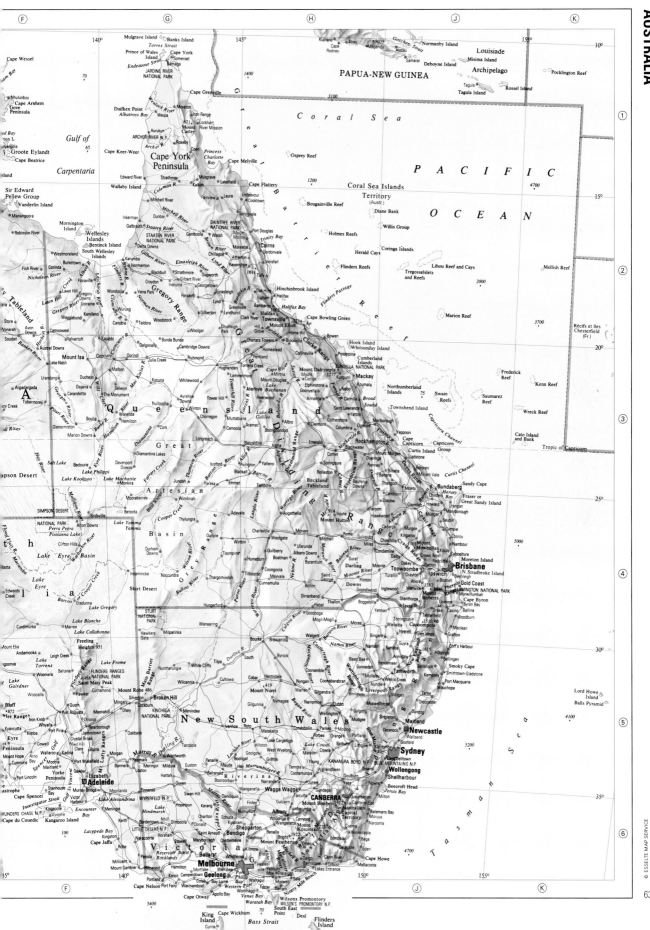

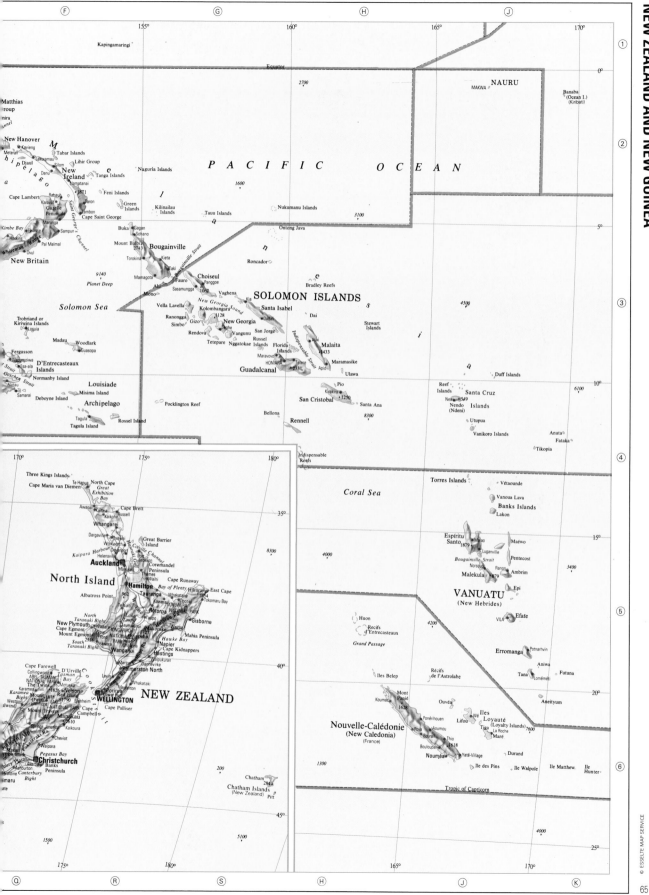

Kapingamaringi

Equator

2700

NAURU

MAKWA

Banaba
(Ocean I.)
(Kiribati)

Matthias
Group

mira
Channel

New Hanover
Kavieng
Metefan
Tabar Islands
Djaul
Lakonamau
Lihir Group
Danu
New
Ireland
Namatanai
Tanga Islands

P A C I F I C   O C E A N

Nuguria Islands

Cape Lambert
Rabaul
1871
Baron
Feni Islands
1600
Kilinailau
Islands
Tauu Islands
Nukumanu Islands
3100

Karavai
Gazelle
Peninsula
Cape Saint George
Green
Islands

Kimbe Bay
Kwasse
Hoskins
Sampun
Pal Malmal
Buka
Gagan
Sohano
Ontong Java
5°

Whiteman Range
Dvul
Mount Balbia
Bougainville
n

New Britain
Torokina
Kieta
Roncador

9140
Planet Deep
Mamagota
Taki
Choiseul
Panggoe
Bradley Reefs
e

Solomon Sea
Mono
Fauro
Sasamungga
1067
Vaghena
Gia
SOLOMON ISLANDS
s
4500

Trobriand or
Kiriwina Islands
Loiuia
Vella Lavella
New Georgia Sound
Kolombangara
Santa Isabel
Dai
Stewart
Islands
i

Madau
Guasopa
Ranongga
Simbo
Gizo
1128
New Georgia
Vanghe
Dadali

Fergusson
Watmugiwa
Esa-ala
Rendova
Tetepare
Russel
Nggatokae
Islands
San Jorge
Florida
Islands
Auki
Malaita
1433
a

D'Entrecasteaux
Islands
Normanby Island
Maravovo
Tetere
Maramasike
Apid
Duff Islands

Gosclei Strait
Samarai
Louisiade
Misima Island
HONIARA
2331
Guadalcanal
Ulawa
6100

Deboyne Island
Archipelago
Pocklington Reef
Pio
Kirakira
1250
San Cristobal
Santa Ana
Reef
Islands
Nea
Santa Cruz
549
Nendo
(Ndeni)
Islands
10°

Tagula
Tagula Island
Rossel Island
Bellona
Rennell
8300
Utupua
Vanikoro Islands
Anuta
Fataka

Tikopia

Indispensable
Reefs

Three Kings Islands
North Cape
Te Hapua
Torres Islands
Vétaounde

Cape Maria van Diemen
Great
Exhibition
Bay
Coral Sea
Vanoua Lava
Banks Islands
15°

Awanui
Kaitaia
Cape Brett
Russell
Kaikohe
Lakon

Whangarei
35°
Espíritu
Santo
Malao
1879
Maéwo

Dargaville
Great Barrier
Luganville
Pentecost

Kaipara Harbour
Helensville
8300
4000
Bougainville Strait
Norsup
Rangon
Ambrim
3400

Auckland
Manukau
Coromandel
Peninsula
Thames
Waihi
Malekula
1879
Epi

North Island
Hamilton
Tauranga
Cape Runaway
East Cape
VANUATU
(New Hebrides)

Albatross Point
Kawerau
1254
Tokomaru Bay

New Plymouth
Rotorua
UREWERA
NATIONAL PARK
Gisborne
Huon
Recifs
d'Entrecasteaux
4200
VILA
Efate
5°... VILA
Efate

Cape Egmont
Mount Egmont
Napier
Mahia Peninsula
Grand Passage
Erromanga
Potnarhvin

South
Taranaki Bight
Hastings
Cape Kidnappers
Aniwa
Futuna

Wanganui
Dannevirke
Tana
Lomémét

Cape Farewell
D'Urville
Palmerston North
Iles Belep
Récifs
de l'Astrolabe
20°

Collingwood
ABEL TASMAN
NATIONAL PARK
Tasman Bay
Levin
Whatakai
Mont
Panié
1628
Ouvéa
Iles
Loyauté
(Loyalty Islands)

Karamea
1826 Nelson
Red Hill
Masterton
WELLINGTON
NEW ZEALAND
Nouvelle-Calédonie
(New Caledonia)
(France)
Ponérihouen
Lifou
Tiga
La Roche
7600
Maré

Westport
Cape Campbell
Cape Palliser
Koumac
Pova
Aoumou
Thio
Wé

Manukau
2610
Kaikoura
Bouloupari
1618
Nouméa
Ile des Pins
Durand

Christchurch
Banks
Peninsula
1300
Yaté-Village
Ile Matthew
Ile Hunter
Ile Walpole

Pegasus Bay
Cheviot

Canterbury
Bight
Chatham
284
Chatham Islands
(New Zealand)
Pitt
Tropic of Capricorn

1500
5100
4000

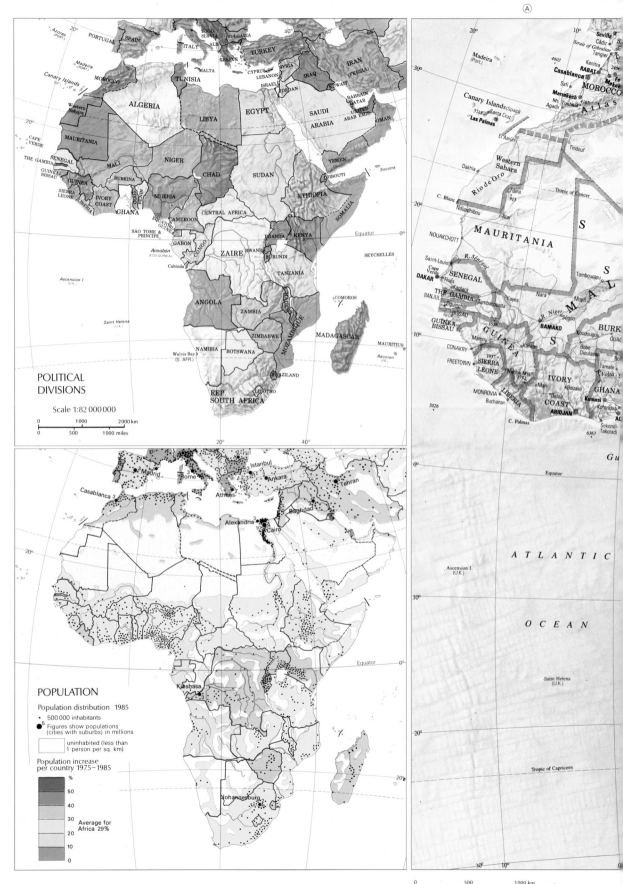

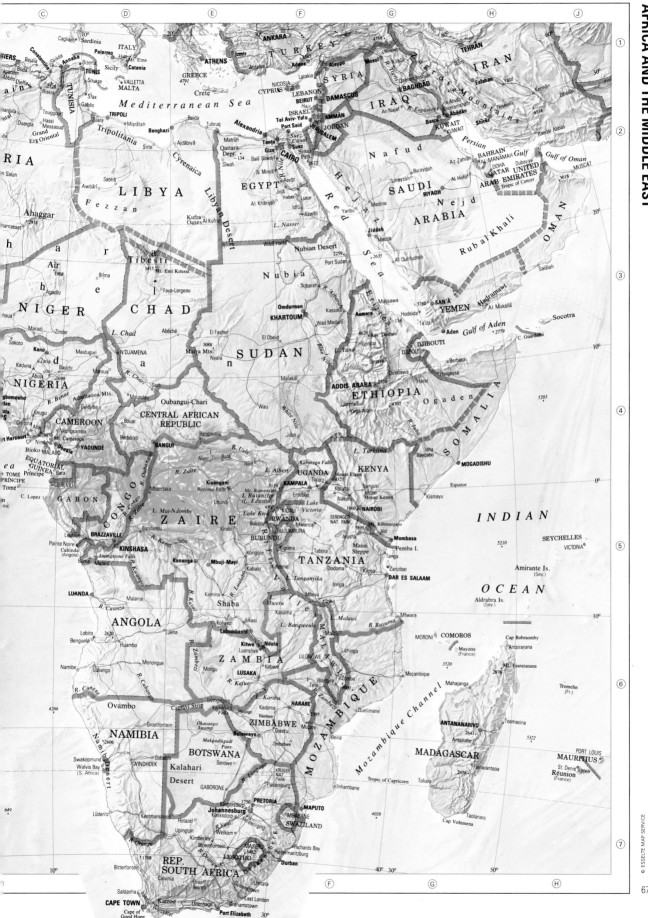

© ESSELTE MAP SERVICE

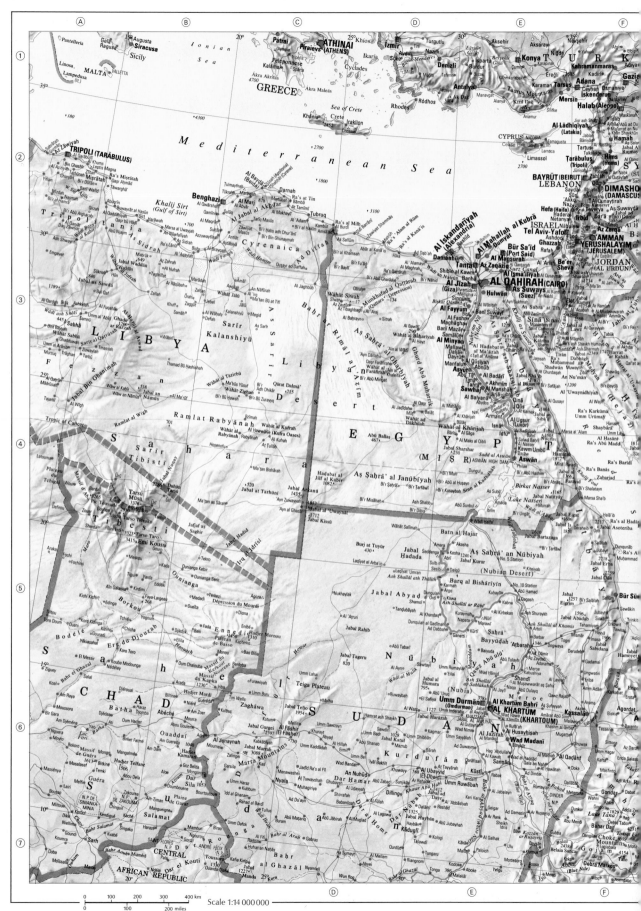

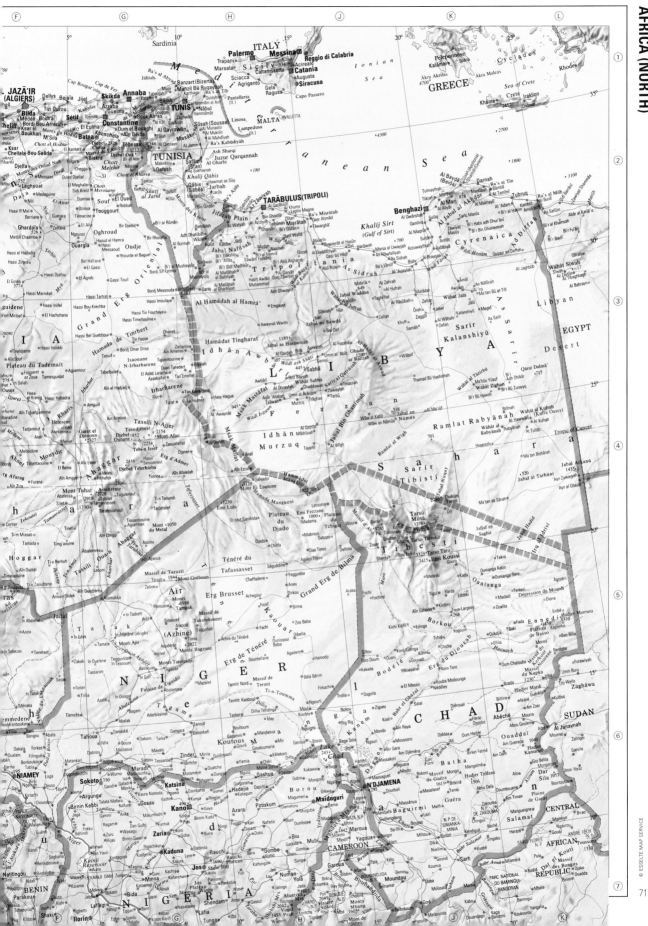

© ESSELTE MAP SERVICE

Scale 1:14 000 000

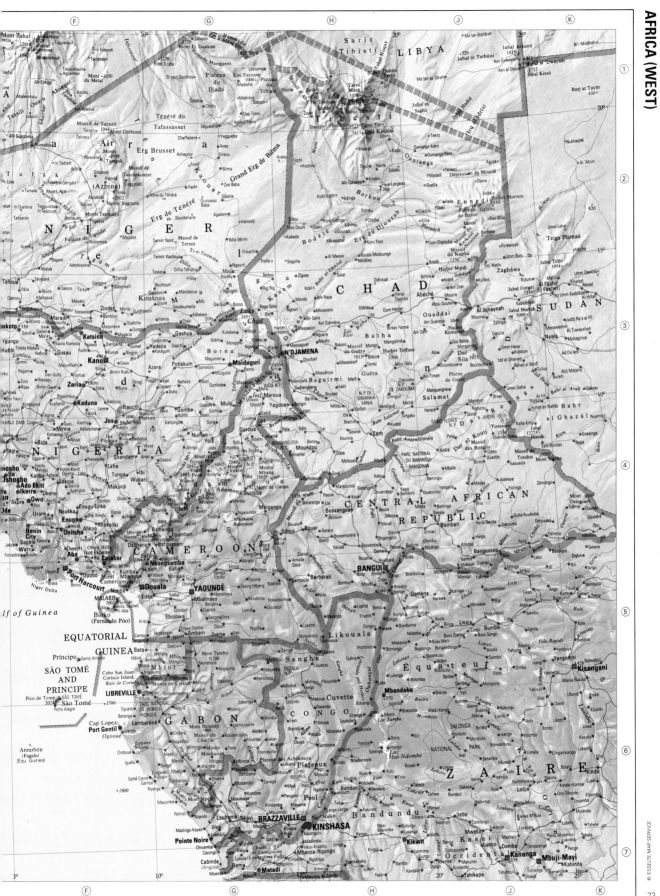

© ESSELTE MAP SERVICE

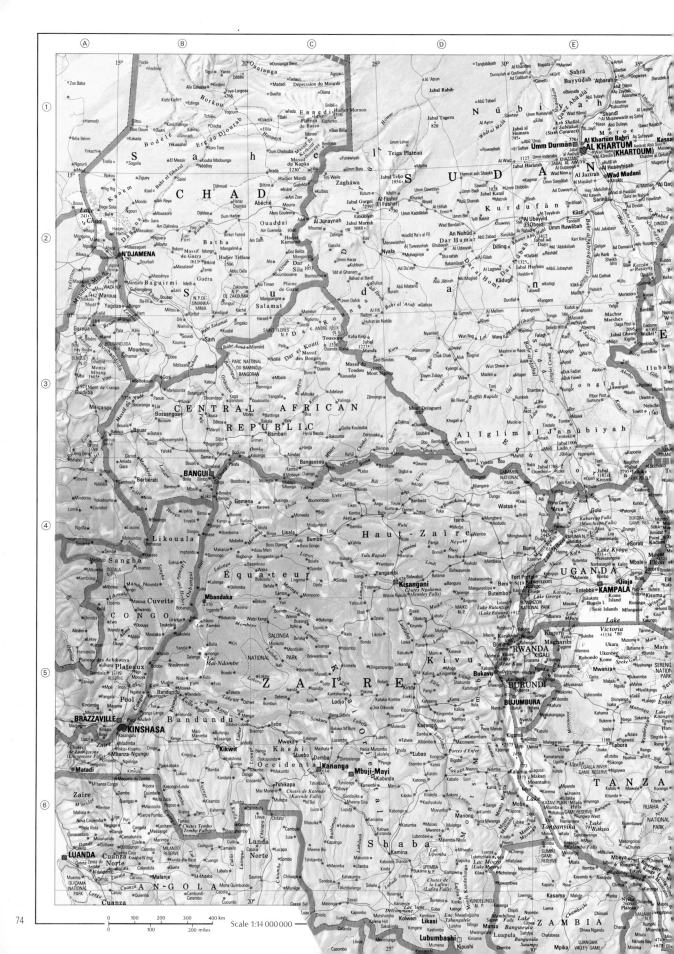

© ESSELTE MAP SERVICE

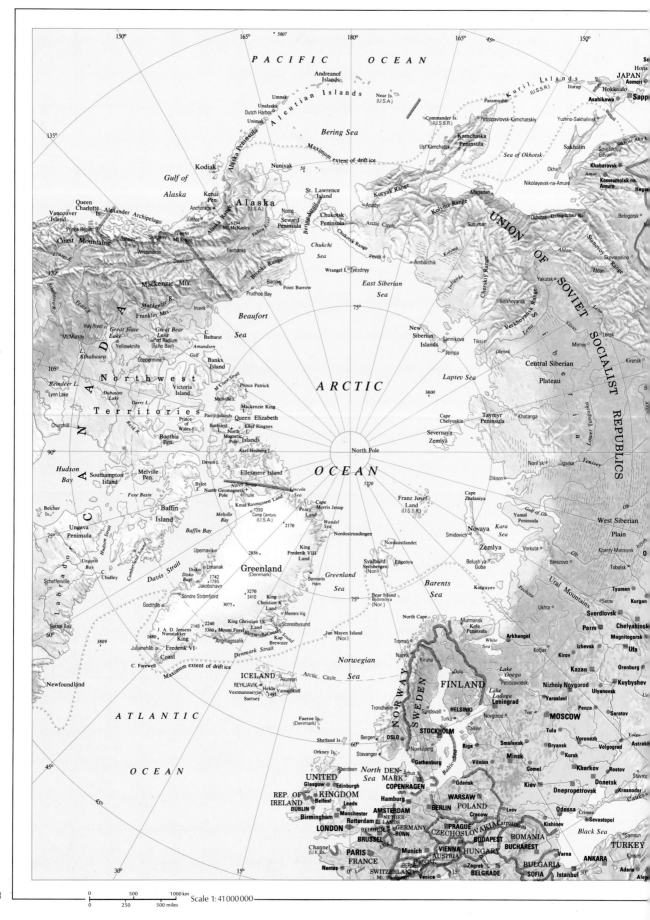

PACIFIC OCEAN

JAPAN

Honshu
Aomori

150°
165°
180°
165°
45°
150°

5807

Andreanof
Islands

Hokkaido

Umnak

Near Is.
(U.S.A.)

Kuril Islands
(U.S.S.R.)

Iturup

Asahikawa

Sapp

Aleutian Islands

Unalaska
Dutch Harbor

Paramushir

Commander Is.
(U.S.S.R.)

Petropavlovsk-Kamchatskiy

Yuzhno-Sakhalinsk

Unimak

Bering Sea

Ust'-Kamchatsk

Sakhalin

Sovetskaya
Gavan

Maximum extent of drift ice

Kamchatka
Peninsula

Sea of Okhotsk

Khabarovsk

135°

Kodiak

Alaska Peninsula

Nunivak

50

Koryak Range

Magadan

Okha

Komsomolsk-na-
Amure

Nikolayevsk-na-Amure

Amur

Hega

Gulf of
Alaska

Kenai
Pen.

Anchorage

Alaska
(U.S.A.)

Nome

St. Lawrence
Island

Anadyr

Susuman

Okhotsk Dzhugdzhur Ra.

Belogorsk

Valdez

6194
Mt. McKinley

Seward
Peninsula

Chukotsk
Peninsula

Arctic Circle

Kolyma Range

UNION

Stanovoy
Range

Skovorodino

Queen
Charlotte
Islands

Alexander Archipelago

Alaska Range

Bering Strait

Chukchi
Sea

Chukotsk Range

Pevek

Kolyma

Kolyma

Aldan

OF

Aldan

Vancouver
Island

Juneau

Skagway

5950
Mt. Logan

Fairbanks

Barrow

Point Barrow

Wrangel I. Zvezdnyy

Ambarchik

Indigirka

Cherskiy Range

Lena

Yakutsk

Lensk

SOVIET

Coast Mountains

Whitehorse

Dawson

Brooks Range

Prudhoe Bay

East Siberian
Sea

Verkhoyansk

Verkhoyansk Range

Mirnyy

Fraser R.

120°

Mackenzie Mts.

Inuvik

Beaufort
Sea

75°

New
Siberian
Islands

Sannikova

Tiksi

Olenek

Lena

i

SOCIALIST

Kirensk

Hay River

Mackenzie R.

Franklin Mts.

C.
Bathurst

Tempa

b

REPUBLICS

McMurray

Great Bear
Lake
Port Radium
(Echo Bay)

Amundsen
Gulf

Banks
Island

Laptev Sea

Central Siberian

e

Great Slave
Lake

Coppermine

Plateau

r

Yellowknife

Athabasca

105°

Reindeer L.

Northwest

M'Clure Strait

Victoria
Island

Prince Patrick

Melville I.

Mackenzie King

ARCTIC

3800

Cape
Chelyuskin

Taymyr
Peninsula

Khatanga

i

Lower Tunguska

B

Lynn Lake

Dubawnt
Lake

Garry L.

Back R.

Territories

Parry Islands

Bathurst

Queen Elizabeth

Ellef Ringnes

Severnaya
Zemlya

a

Yenisey

Churchill

Prince
of
Wales I.

North
Magnetic
Pole

Islands

Axel Heiberg I.

Noril'sk

Igarka

Dikson

90°

Boothia
Pen.

Devon I.

North Pole

OCEAN

5220

Franz Josef
Land
(U.S.S.R.)

Cape
Zhelaniya

West Siberian

Hudson
Bay

Southampton
Island

Melville
Pen.

Ellesmere Island

Yamal
Peninsula

Gulf of Ob

Plain

Belcher
Is.

Foxe Basin

Bylot
I.

Nares Strait

North Geomagnetic
Pole

Thule
1390

Lincoln
Sea

Cape
Morris Jesup

Peary
Land

Novaya

Smidovich

Kara
Sea

Vorkuta

Berezovo

Ob

Khanty-Mansiysk

Irtysh

O

Ungava
Peninsula

Hudson Strait

Baffin
Island

Knud Rasmussen Land

Melville
Bay

Camp Century
(U.S.A.)

2170

Wandel
Sea

Nordstrundingen

Zemlya

Belush'ya
Guba

Kolguyev

Pechora

Ukhta

Ural Mountains

Tyumen

75°

Schefferville

Chidley

Ungava
Bay

Davis Strait

Cumberland Sound

Baffin Bay

Upernavik

Umanak

Disko
Bugt

2836

King
Frederik VIII
Land

Svalbård
Spitsbergen
(Nor.)

Edgeøya

Nordaustlandet

Barents
Sea

Serov

Tobolsk

Tyumen

Izhevsk

Kurgan

Sverdlovsk

Chelyabinsk

60°

Goose Bay

3809

Labrador

Disko

1742
1795

Jakobshavn

Greenland
(Denmark)

3270
3410

Christian X
Land

Danmarks
Havn

Greenland
Sea

75°

Bear Island
Björnöya
(Nor.)

Perm

Magnitogorsk

Ufa

Søndre Strømfjord

3075

Mesters Vig

Ura

Godthåb

2140
3360

2240

King Christian IX
Land

Scoresbysund

North Cape

Murmansk
Kola
Peninsula

Arkhangel

White
Sea

Kotlas

Kirov

Izhevsk

Kazan

Orenburg

Kuybyshev

Julianehåb

J. A. D. Jensens
Nunatakker

1680

Mount Forel
Blosseville Coast

King
Frederik VI·
Coast

Angmagssalik

Kap
Brewster

Scoresby Sound

Jan Mayen Island
(Nor.)

Tromsø

Narvik

Kiruna

Murmansk

Kotlas

Nizhniy Novgorod

Ulyanovsk

Perm

Saratov

Newfoundland

C. Farewell

Maximum extent of drift ice

Denmark Strait

ICELAND

Akureyri

Arctic Circle

Norwegian
Sea

NORWAY

SWEDEN

Oulu

Petrozavodsk

Lake
Onega

FINLAND

Lake
Ladoga

Leningrad

Tver

MOSCOW

Penza

Tula

Yaroslavl

Saratov

Astrakh

Volga

REYKJAVIK

Hekla

Vatnajökull

1491

HELSINKI

45°

ATLANTIC

Vestmannaeyjar

Surtsey

STOCKHOLM

Turku

Tallinn

Novgorod

Smolensk

Bryansk

Voronezh

Volgograd

Kursk

OCEAN

Trondheim

Sundsvall

Norrköping

Riga

Vilnius

Minsk

Gomel

Kharkov

Rostov

Krasnodar

Caucasus

Stavro

Shetland Is.

60°

Bergen

OSLO

Gothenburg

Baltic Sea

Kiev

Dnepropetrovsk

Odessa

Crimea

Sevastopol

Black Sea

Samsun

Orkney Is.

Stavanger

Aberdeen

North
Sea

DEN-
MARK

COPENHAGEN

Gdańsk

Vilnius

Lvov

Kishinev

Varna

ANKARA

Kayseri

REP. OF
IRELAND

UNITED
KINGDOM

Glasgow

Edinburgh

Belfast

Hamburg

WARSAW

BERLIN

POLAND

Cracow

TURKEY

Adana

DUBLIN

Birmingham

Manchester
Rotterdam

Leeds

AMSTERDAM

NETHER-
LANDS

GERMANY

BONN

PRAGUE

CZECHOSLOVAKIA

Carpathians

BUDAPEST

ROMANIA

BUCHAREST

BULGARIA

SOFIA

Istanbul

30°

LONDON

BRUSSEL

BELGIUM

Munich

VIENNA

AUSTRIA

HUNGARY

Varna

Channel
(U.K. Is.)

PARIS

FRANCE

BERNE

Zagreb

BELGRADE

Nantes

Loire

SWITZERLAND

Mt. Blanc

Venice

30°

15°

0°

15°

78

0   500   1000 km

0   250   500 miles

Scale 1: 41 000 000

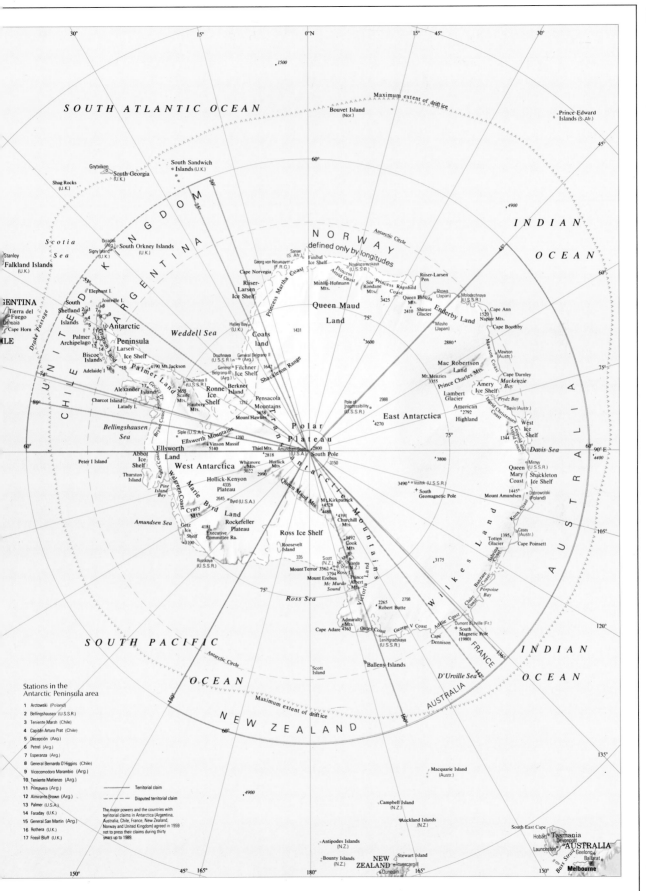

SOUTH ATLANTIC OCEAN

1500

Maximum extent of drift ice

Bouvet Island
(Nor.)

Prince Edward
Islands (S. Afr.)

South Sandwich
Islands (U.K.)

Grytviken

South Georgia
(U.K.)

Shag Rocks
(U.K.)

4900

60°

Antarctic Circle

INDIAN

OCEAN

45°

NORWAY

defined only by longitudes

Sanae
(S. Afr.)

Georg von Neumayer
(F.R.G.)

Fimbul
Ice Shelf

Novolazarevskaya
(U.S.S.R.)

Rüiser-Larsen
Pen.

Scotia
Sea

Orcadas
(Arg.)

South Orkney Islands
(U.K.)

Signy Island
(U.K.)

Cape Norvegia

Rüiser-
Larsen
Ice Shelf

Princess Martha Coast

Princess
Astrid Coast

Sör
Rondane
Mts.

Princess Ragnhild
Coast

Showa
(Japan)

Molodezhnaya
(U.S.S.R.)

Stanley

Falkland Islands
(U.K.)

Mühlig-Hofmann
Mts.

Queen Maud

Land

Queen
Maud
Mts.

3425

Shirase
Glacier

Enderby Land

1520
Cape Ann

Napier Mts.

GENTINA

Tierra del
Fuego

Ushuaia

Cape Horn

ILE

Elephant I.

South
Shetland
Islands

Joinville I.

Antarctic

Peninsula

Weddell Sea

Halley Bay
(U.K.)

Coats
land

1431

75°

3600

2410

Mizuho
(Japan)

2880

Cape Boothby

Palmer
Archipelago

Larsen
Ice Shelf

Mawson
(Austr.)

Mac Robertson
Land

Cape Darnley

Biscoe
Islands

Palmer Land

Druzhnaya
(U.S.S.R.)

General Belgrano II
(Arg.)

General
Belgrano III
(Arg.)

General Filchner
Ice Shelf

1642

Shackleton Range

Mt. Menzies
3355

Prince Charles Mts.

Amery
Ice Shelf

Mackenzie
Bay

Prydz Bay

Davis (Austr.)

Adelaide I.

Druzhnaya II
(U.S.S.R.)

3655
Scaife
Mts.

Ronne
Ice
Shelf

Berkner
Island

1312

Pensacola
Mountains

Lambert
Glacier

American
*2792
Highland

Inград Christensen
Coast

75°

West
Ice
Shelf

Charcot Island

Latady I.

Hauberg
Mts.

3658

Mount Hawkes

Pole of
Inaccessibility
(U.S.S.R.)

2988

East Antarctica

1344

Kemp Land Coast

Davis Sea

Bellingshausen
Sea

Siple (U.S.A.)

Ellsworth Mountains

1780

Polar
Plateau

South Pole

4270

3800

Mirny
(U.S.S.R.)

60° 90° E

4400

Peter I Island

Abbot
Ice
Shelf

Ellsworth

Land

4190 Mt. Jackson

Alexander
Island

5140
Vinson Massif

Thiel Mts.

Amundsen-Scott
(U.S.A.)

2800

2818

3150

3490

3490

Vostok (U.S.S.R.)

South
Geomagnetic Pole

Queen
Mary
Coast

Shackleton
Ice Shelf

Thurston
Island

Whitmore
Mts.
3022

Horlick
Mts.
2990

1445

Mount Amundsen

Dobrowolski
(Poland)

Knox
Coast

Casey
(Austr.)

West Antarctica

Hollick-Kenyon
Plateau
4335

Queen Maud Mts.

Mt. Kirkpatrick
4528

4480

1395

Totten
Glacier

Cape Poinsett

Eights Coast

Marie Byrd

Crary
Mts.

2645

Byrd (U.S.A.)

Rockefeller
Plateau

4391

Churchill
Mts.

Sabrina
Coast

Amundsen Sea

Getz
Ice
Shelf

4181

Executive
Committee Ra.

Land

Ross Ice Shelf

3492

Cook
Mts.

3175

Knox
Coast

Budd
Coast

Banzare
Coast

Walgreen Coast

3100

Russkaya
(U.S.S.R.)

Roosevelt
Island

335

Scott
(N.Z.)

Vanda
(N.Z.)

Prince
Albert
Mts.

Clarie
Coast

Porpoise
Bay

Mount Terror
Mount Erebus

3794 Ross I.

Mc Murdo
Sound

3362 *4163*

2265
Robert Butte

2798

Wilkes Land

AUSTRALIA

Ross Sea

Victoria Land

Admiralty
Mts.

Cape Adare *4163*

Oates Coast

George V Coast

Adélie Coast

Dumont d'Urville (Fr.)

South
Magnetic Pole
(1980)

SOUTH PACIFIC

Antarctic Circle

OCEAN

Scott
Island

Leningradskaya
(U.S.S.R.)

Cape
Dennison

FRANCE

105°

120°

INDIAN

OCEAN

D'Urville Sea

Balleny Islands

4900

Maximum extent of drift ice

60°

NEW ZEALAND

135°

150°

Macquarie Island
(Austr.)

**Stations in the
Antarctic Peninsula area**

1 Arctowski (Poland)

2 Bellingshausen (U.S.S.R.)

3 Teniente Marsh (Chile)

4 Capitán Arturo Prat (Chile)

5 Decepción (Arg.)

6 Petrel (Arg.)

7 Esperanza (Arg.)

8 General Bernardo O'Higgins (Chile)

9 Vicecomodoro Marambio (Arg.)

10 Teniente Matienzo (Arg.)

11 Primavera (Arg.)

12 Almirante Brown (Arg.)

13 Palmer (U.S.A.)

14 Faraday (U.K.)

15 General San Martín (Arg.)

16 Rothera (U.K.)

17 Fossil Bluff (U.K.)

Territorial claim

Disputed territorial claim

The major powers and the countries with
territorial claims in Antarctica (Argentina,
Australia, Chile, France, New Zealand,
Norway and United Kingdom) agreed in 1959
not to press their claims during thirty
years up to 1989.

Campbell Island
(N.Z.)

Auckland Islands
(N.Z.)

South East Cape

Hobart

Tasmania

Devonport

AUSTRALIA

Launceston

Geelong

Ballarat

Bass Strait

Melbourne

Antipodes Islands
(N.Z.)

Bounty Islands
(N.Z.)

NEW
ZEALAND

Stewart Island

Invercargill

Dunedin

150°

165°

180°

165°

150°

MAP LEGEND

Symbols
Scale 1:7 000 000, 1:14 000 000

Bombay More than 5 000 000 inhabitants

Milano 1 000 000 – 5 000 000 inhabitants

Zürich 250 000 – 1 000 000 inhabitants

Dijon 100 000 – 250 000 inhabitants

Dover 25 000 – 100 000 inhabitants

Torquay Less than 25 000 inhabitants

Tachiumet Small sites

WIEN National capital

Atlanta State capital

—————— Major road

—————— Other road

– – – – – Road under construction

—————— Railway

– – – – – Railway under construction

- - - - - - - Train ferry

National boundary

Disputed national boundary

State boundary

Disputed state boundary

Undefined boundary in the sea

4807 Height above sea-level in metres

3068 Depth in metres

National park

Nineveh Ruin

Pass

KAINJI DAM Dam

Wadi

Canal

Waterfall

Reef

Symbols
Scale 1: 21 000 000, 1:34 000 000, 1:37 000 000, 1:41 000 000

Shanghai More than 5 000 000 inhabitants

Barcelona 1 000 000 – 5 000 000 inhabitants

Venice 250 000 – 1 000 000 inhabitants

Aberdeen 50 000 – 250 000 inhabitants

Beida Less than 50 000 inhabitants

Mawson Scientific station

CAIRO National capital

—————— Major road

—————— Railway

– – – – – Railway under construction

National boundary

Disputed national boundary

State boundary

Disputed state boundary

Undefined boundary in the sea

8848 Height above sea-level in metres

11034 Depth in metres

2645 Thickness of ice cap

Dam

Thebes Ruin

Wadi

Canal

Waterfall

Reef

Colour Key

Tundra

Glacier

Coniferous forest

Mixed forest

Deciduous forest

Tropical rain forest

Chacos

Arable land

Grassland, pasture

Savanna

Steppe, semi-desert

Sand desert

Other desert

Mountain

Marshland

Salt lake

Intermittent lake

Salt desert, salt pan, dry lake

Lava field

WORLD
COMPARISONS

ECONOMIC STRENGTH

The map plots gross domestic product (GDP) per head of population for every country where data are available or can be estimated. GDP is generally regarded as the yardstick for the economic activity of a country; it measures the total value of the goods and services produced annually. GDP can be measured in a number of different ways; the most common, used here, is GDP at market prices, which includes indirect taxes and subsidies.

Many socialist countries use net material product (NMP) to measure economic performance. This differs from GDP in that it excludes the value of services and discounts for depreciation. To enable comparison, standard adjustments have been made to NMP figures.

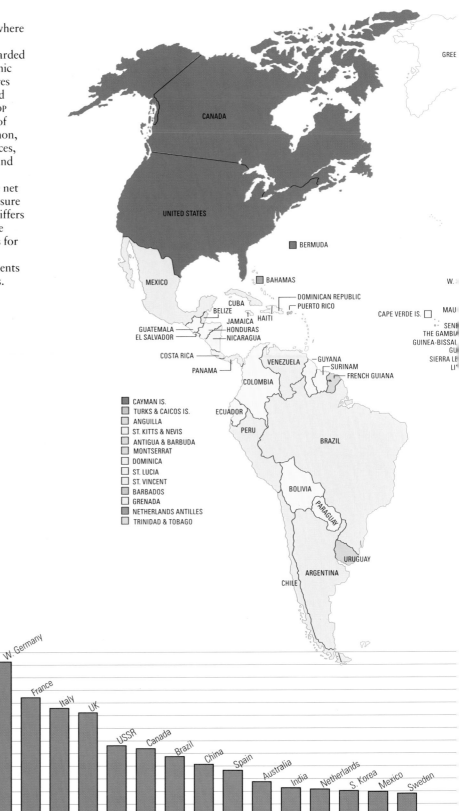

GDP per head
$
17,500
15,000
12,000
10,000
7,500
5,000
2,500
1,250
500

no reliable data

CAYMAN IS.
TURKS & CAICOS IS.
ANGUILLA
ST. KITTS & NEVIS
ANTIGUA & BARBUDA
MONTSERRAT
DOMINICA
ST. LUCIA
ST. VINCENT
BARBADOS
GRENADA
NETHERLANDS ANTILLES
TRINIDAD & TOBAGO

GREE
W.
CAPE VERDE IS.
MAU
SEN
THE GAMBIA
GUINEA-BISSA
GU
SIERRA LE
LI

CANADA
UNITED STATES
BERMUDA
BAHAMAS
MEXICO
CUBA
BELIZE
DOMINICAN REPUBLIC
PUERTO RICO
JAMAICA HAITI
GUATEMALA
EL SALVADOR
HONDURAS
NICARAGUA
COSTA RICA
PANAMA
VENEZUELA
GUYANA
SURINAM
FRENCH GUIANA
COLOMBIA
ECUADOR
PERU
BRAZIL
BOLIVIA
PARAGUAY
URUGUAY
ARGENTINA
CHILE

GDP $bn

USA 5,167
Japan 2,818
W. Germany
France
Italy
UK
USSR
Canada
Brazil
China
Spain
Australia
India
Netherlands
S. Korea
Mexico
Sweden

1200
1100
1000
900
800
700
600
500
400
300
200
100
0

Sources: EIU *Country Profiles;* Business International *Country Risk Service;* IMF *International Financial Statistics* (1989 figures or latest available).

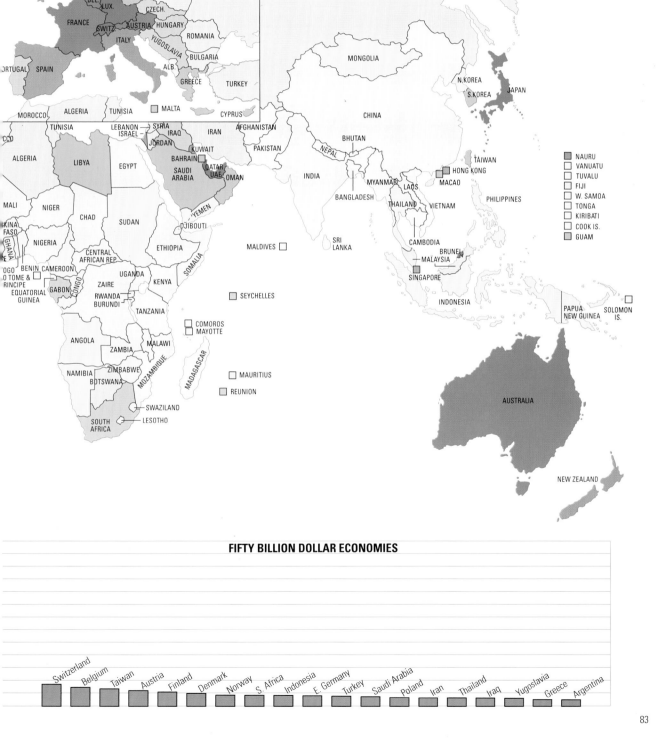

ICELAND
NORWAY
SWEDEN
FINLAND
DENMARK
UNITED KINGDOM
IRELAND
NETH.
GERMANY
BEL.
LUX.
POLAND
FRANCE
SWITZ.
CZECH.
AUSTRIA
HUNGARY
ITALY
YUGOSLAVIA
ROMANIA
BULGARIA
ALB.
GREECE
TURKEY
SPAIN
RTUGAL
MALTA
CYPRUS
UNION OF SOVIET SOCIALIST REPUBLICS
UNION OF SOVIET SOCIALIST REPUBLICS

MOROCCO
ALGERIA
TUNISIA
TUNISIA
CCO
ALGERIA
LIBYA
EGYPT
LEBANON
ISRAEL
SYRIA
IRAQ
JORDAN
KUWAIT
BAHRAIN
SAUDI ARABIA
QATAR
UAE
OMAN
IRAN
AFGHANISTAN
PAKISTAN
INDIA
NEPAL
BHUTAN
MYANMAR
BANGLADESH
MONGOLIA
CHINA
N.KOREA
S.KOREA
JAPAN
TAIWAN
HONG KONG
MACAO
MALI
NIGER
CHAD
SUDAN
YEMEN
DJIBOUTI
KINA FASO
KE
GHANA
NIGERIA
CENTRAL AFRICAN REP.
ETHIOPIA
SOMALIA
MALDIVES
SRI LANKA
THAILAND
LAOS
VIETNAM
CAMBODIA
PHILIPPINES
OGO
O TOME & RINCIPE
BENIN
CAMEROON
EQUATORIAL GUINEA
GABON
CONGO
ZAIRE
UGANDA
RWANDA
BURUNDI
KENYA
TANZANIA
SEYCHELLES
BRUNEI
MALAYSIA
SINGAPORE
ANGOLA
ZAMBIA
MALAWI
MOZAMBIQUE
MADAGASCAR
COMOROS
MAYOTTE
INDONESIA
PAPUA NEW GUINEA
SOLOMON IS.
NAMIBIA
ZIMBABWE
BOTSWANA
MAURITIUS
REUNION
SWAZILAND
SOUTH AFRICA
LESOTHO
AUSTRALIA
NEW ZEALAND

NAURU
VANUATU
TUVALU
FIJI
W. SAMOA
TONGA
KIRIBATI
COOK IS.
GUAM

FIFTY BILLION DOLLAR ECONOMIES

Switzerland · Belgium · Taiwan · Austria · Finland · Denmark · Norway · S. Africa · Indonesia · E. Germany · Turkey · Saudi Arabia · Poland · Iran · Thailand · Iraq · Yugoslavia · Greece · Argentina

FOREIGN DEBT

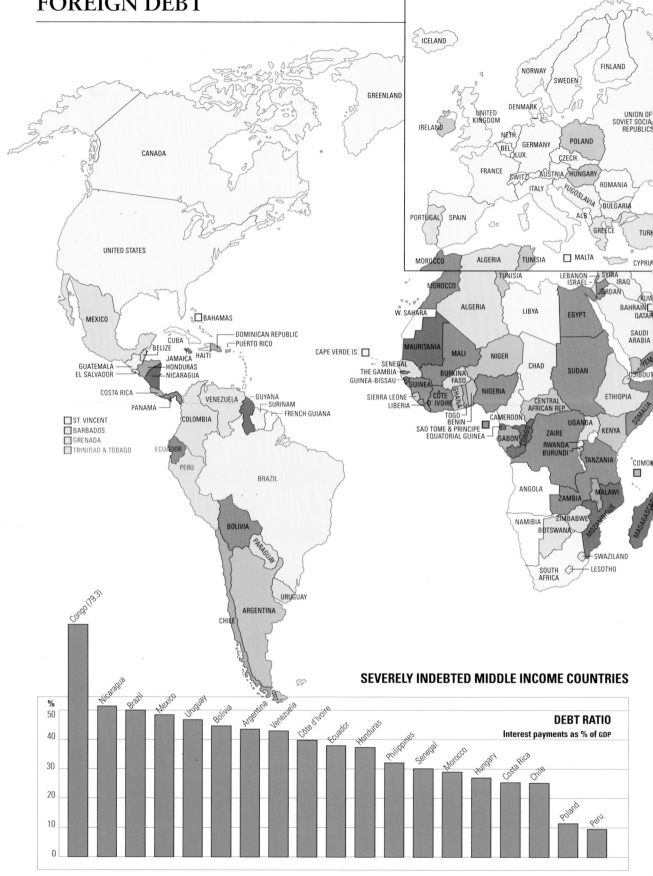

SEVERELY INDEBTED MIDDLE INCOME COUNTRIES

DEBT RATIO
Interest payments as % of GDP

Source: World Bank *World Debt Tables* (1988-89 figures); EIU *Country Profiles* (1988 figures).

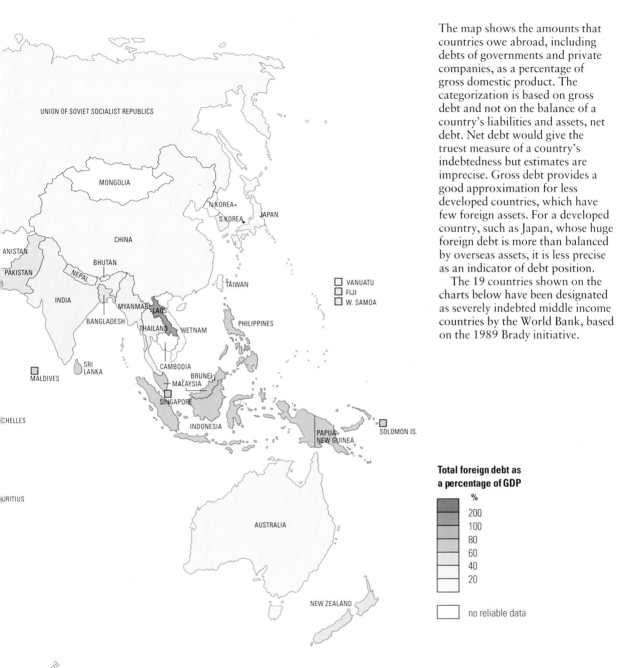

The map shows the amounts that countries owe abroad, including debts of governments and private companies, as a percentage of gross domestic product. The categorization is based on gross debt and not on the balance of a country's liabilities and assets, net debt. Net debt would give the truest measure of a country's indebtedness but estimates are imprecise. Gross debt provides a good approximation for less developed countries, which have few foreign assets. For a developed country, such as Japan, whose huge foreign debt is more than balanced by overseas assets, it is less precise as an indicator of debt position.

The 19 countries shown on the charts below have been designated as severely indebted middle income countries by the World Bank, based on the 1989 Brady initiative.

Total foreign debt as a percentage of GDP

%
200
100
80
60
40
20

no reliable data

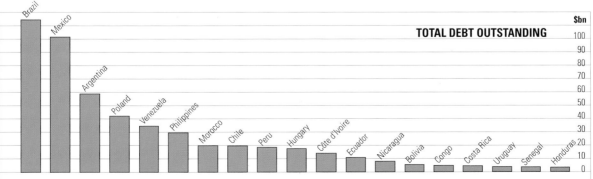

TOTAL DEBT OUTSTANDING

$bn
100
90
80
70
60
50
40
30
20
10
0

Brazil, Mexico, Argentina, Poland, Venezuela, Philippines, Morocco, Chile, Peru, Hungary, Côte d'Ivoire, Ecuador, Nicaragua, Bolivia, Congo, Costa Rica, Uruguay, Senegal, Honduras

THE BALANCE OF TRADE

A country which runs a deficit on the current account of the balance of payments is usually consuming more than it produces. Deficits have to be financed by a capital inflow and imbalances must be remedied sooner or later by measures such as devaluing the currency, raising taxes and cutting government spending.

The current account includes visible imports and exports (raw materials and manufactures) as well as invisibles (payments relating to services rather than goods, and investment income). The map shows the balance of visible trade. The chart showing the top trading nations is based on the sum of visible imports and exports, including imports for re-export. Eastern European countries include only hard currency trade. Figures can also be distorted by illegal trade or government "massaging"

The map also indicates which countries are signatories to the General Agreement on Tariffs and Trade (Gatt), which came into force in 1948.

BERMUDA
ST. KITTS & NEVIS
ANTIGUA & BARBUDA
MONTSERRAT
DOMINICA
ST. LUCIA
BARBADOS
GRENADA
NETHERLANDS ANTILLES
TRINIDAD & TOBAGO

Sources: EIU *Country Profiles*;
Business International *Country Risk Service*;
IMF *International Financial Statistics*
(1989 figures or latest available).

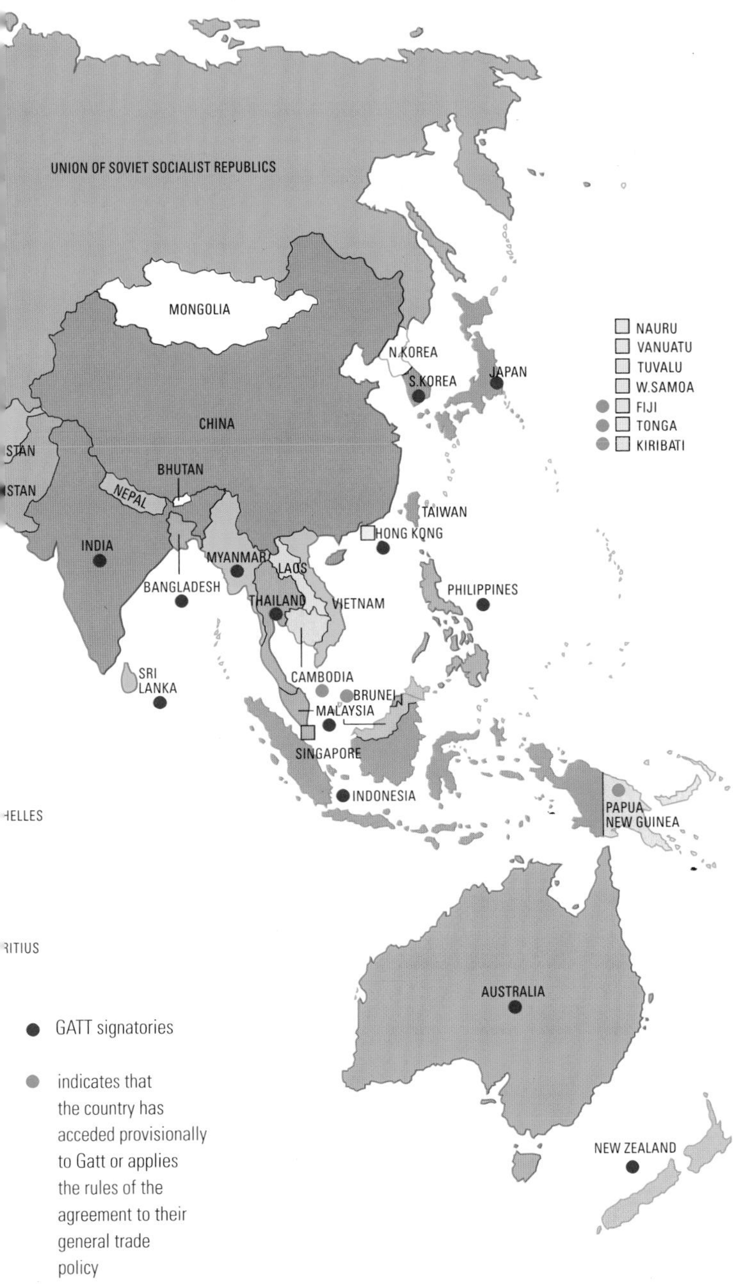

TOP 50 TRADERS $bn

Trade Balance $m

5,000	
1,000	
250 surplus	
0	
250 deficit	
1,000	
5,000	

☐ no reliable data

USA 781.2
W. Germany 620.4
Japan 462.6
France 371.0
UK 363.0
Canada 321.0
Italy 289.3
Netherlands 217.9
Belgium 196.2
Hong Kong 152.9
Taiwan 125.4
S. Korea 125.3
Spain 116.0
Switzerland 114.4
China 113.1
Sweden 101.0
Singapore 83.2
Austria 78.4
Australia 73.4
Denmark 63.0
USSR 55.0
Norway 54.2
Brazil 51.2
Finland 50.0
Saudi Arabia 47.3
Malaysia 46.2
Thailand 45.3
Mexico 43.9
Ireland 41.6
S. Africa 40.0
India 38.0
Indonesia 36.9
Portugal 29.0
Iran 28.0
Turkey 27.6
Iraq 26.7
UAE 24.0
Israel 22.8
Yugoslavia 22.0
Venezuela 19.4
Algeria 18.1
Philippines 18.1
New Zealand 15.9
Greece 15.4
E. Germany 15.1
Poland 15.0
Argentina 14.8
Chile 14.5
Nigeria 14.2
Kuwait 13.6

UNION OF SOVIET SOCIALIST REPUBLICS

MONGOLIA

N.KOREA

S.KOREA

JAPAN

CHINA

BHUTAN

NEPAL

☐ NAURU
☐ VANUATU
☐ TUVALU
☐ W.SAMOA
● FIJI
● TONGA
● KIRIBATI

STAN

STAN

TAIWAN

INDIA

MYANMAR

LAOS

BANGLADESH

THAILAND

VIETNAM

PHILIPPINES

HONG KONG

SRI LANKA

CAMBODIA

BRUNEI

MALAYSIA

SINGAPORE

INDONESIA

PAPUA NEW GUINEA

HELLES

RITIUS

AUSTRALIA

● GATT signatories

● indicates that the country has acceded provisionally to Gatt or applies the rules of the agreement to their general trade policy

NEW ZEALAND

TRADE IN MANUFACTURES

The bar chart ranks the principal categories of manufactured goods by the total dollar value of imports and exports, free on board (excluding transport and insurance costs). The pie charts identify the biggest exporters and importers in each category. Only market economies are included; members of Comecon traded with barter and non-convertible currencies, making an evaluation of trade in dollar terms difficult.

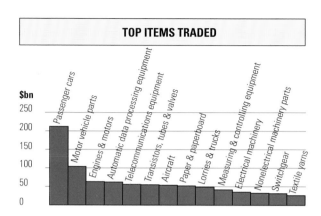

PASSENGER CARS

IMPORTS

EXPORTS

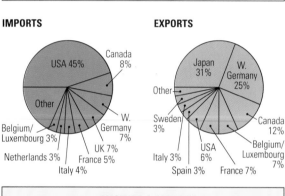

ENGINES & MOTORS

IMPORTS

EXPORTS

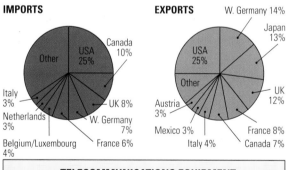

TELECOMMUNICATIONS EQUIPMENT

IMPORTS

EXPORTS

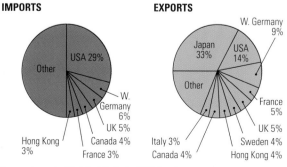

MOTOR VEHICLE PARTS

IMPORTS

EXPORTS

AUTOMATIC DATA PROCESSING EQUIPMENT

IMPORTS

EXPORTS

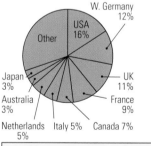

TRANSISTORS, TUBES & VALVES

IMPORTS

EXPORTS

Source: UN *International Trade Statistics Yearbook* (1986 figures).

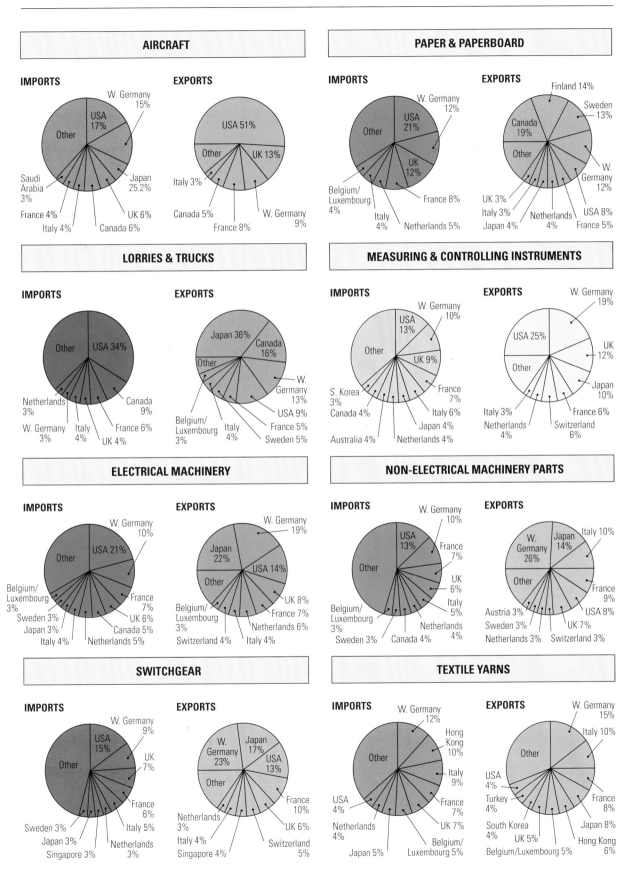

AIRCRAFT

IMPORTS

USA 17%
W. Germany 15%
Japan 25.2%
Other
Saudi Arabia 3%
France 4%
Italy 4%
Canada 6%
UK 6%

EXPORTS

USA 51%
UK 13%
Other
Italy 3%
Canada 5%
France 8%
W. Germany 9%

LORRIES & TRUCKS

IMPORTS

Other
USA 34%
Canada 9%
Netherlands 3%
W. Germany 3%
Italy 4%
UK 4%
France 6%

EXPORTS

Japan 36%
Canada 16%
Other
W. Germany 13%
USA 9%
France 5%
Sweden 5%
Italy 4%
Belgium/ Luxembourg 3%

ELECTRICAL MACHINERY

IMPORTS

USA 21%
W. Germany 10%
Other
France 7%
UK 6%
Canada 5%
Netherlands 5%
Italy 4%
Japan 3%
Sweden 3%
Belgium/ Luxembourg 3%

EXPORTS

W. Germany 19%
Japan 22%
USA 14%
Other
UK 8%
France 7%
Netherlands 6%
Italy 4%
Switzerland 4%
Belgium/ Luxembourg 3%

SWITCHGEAR

IMPORTS

USA 15%
W. Germany 9%
UK 7%
Other
France 6%
Italy 5%
Netherlands 3%
Singapore 3%
Japan 3%
Sweden 3%

EXPORTS

W. Germany 23%
Japan 17%
USA 13%
Other
France 10%
UK 6%
Switzerland 5%
Netherlands 3%
Italy 4%
Singapore 4%

PAPER & PAPERBOARD

IMPORTS

W. Germany 12%
USA 21%
UK 12%
Other
France 8%
Netherlands 5%
Italy 4%
Belgium/ Luxembourg 4%

EXPORTS

Finland 14%
Sweden 13%
Canada 19%
Other
W. Germany 12%
USA 8%
France 5%
Netherlands 4%
Japan 4%
Italy 3%
UK 3%

MEASURING & CONTROLLING INSTRUMENTS

IMPORTS

USA 13%
W. Germany 10%
UK 9%
Other
France 7%
Italy 6%
Japan 4%
Netherlands 4%
Canada 4%
Australia 4%
S. Korea 3%

EXPORTS

W. Germany 19%
USA 25%
UK 12%
Japan 10%
Other
France 6%
Switzerland 6%
Netherlands 4%
Italy 3%

NON-ELECTRICAL MACHINERY PARTS

IMPORTS

USA 13%
W. Germany 10%
France 7%
UK 6%
Italy 5%
Other
Netherlands 4%
Canada 4%
Sweden 3%
Belgium/ Luxembourg 3%

EXPORTS

W. Germany 26%
Japan 14%
Italy 10%
France 9%
Other
USA 8%
UK 7%
Switzerland 3%
Netherlands 3%
Sweden 3%
Austria 3%

TEXTILE YARNS

IMPORTS

W. Germany 12%
Hong Kong 10%
Italy 9%
Other
Italy 9%
France 7%
UK 7%
Belgium/ Luxembourg 5%
Japan 5%
Netherlands 4%
USA 4%

EXPORTS

W. Germany 15%
Italy 10%
Other
USA 4%
Turkey 4%
South Korea 4%
UK 5%
Belgium/Luxembourg 5%
Hong Kong 6%
Japan 8%
France 8%

BANKING AND FINANCE

$bn at the end of December

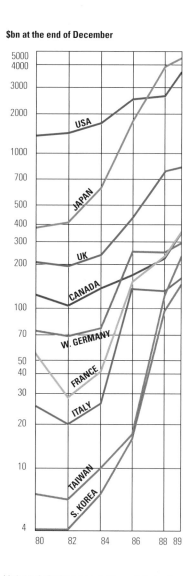

Market capitalization is the sum of the market value of stocks. The figures use an index, based on liquidity, market capitalization and industrial classification, representing approximately 60% of the total market capitalization in each country. Crashes and peaks, such as Black Monday in October 1987, are not depicted as the figures show annual averages, spreading the effects of any temporary market situations. The growth of the Japanese market was spectacular, although the future outlook has not been as optimistic since the crash in 1990.

TOP INTERNATIONAL BANKS

Rank 1989	Rank 1984		Capital ($m) 1989–90
1	6	Sumitomo Bank (Osaka)	13,357
2	2	Dai-Ichi Kangyo Bank (Tokyo)	12,322
3	3	Fuji Bank (Tokyo)	11,855
4	9	Crédit Agricole (Paris)	11,802
5	8	Sanwa Bank (Osaka)	11,186
6	5	Mitsubishi Bank (Tokyo)	10,900
7	12	Barclays Bank (London)	10,715
8	14	National Westminster Bank (London)	9,761
9	18	Deutsche Bank (Frankfurt)	8,462
10	15	Industrial Bank of Japan (Tokyo)	8,184
11	36	Union Bank of Switzerland (Zürich)	8,150
12	1	Citicorp (New York)	7,319
13	31	Compagnie Financière de Paribas (Paris)	6,968
14	17	Tokai Bank (Nagoya)	6,821
15	–	Hong Kong Bank (Hong Kong)	6,746
16	–	Bank of China (Beijing)	6,611
17	23	Long-Term Credit Bank of Japan (Tokyo)	6,463
18	7	Banque Nationale de Paris (Paris)	6,177
19	41	Swiss Bank Corp (Basel)	6,153
20	22	Bank of Tokyo (Tokyo)	5,928
21	21	Mitsui Bank (Tokyo)	5,675
22	10	Crédit Lyonnais (Paris)	5,617
23	–	Japan Development Bank (Tokyo)	5,532
24	11	Société Générale (Paris)	5,528
25	39	Banco de Brasil (Rio de Janeiro)	5,503
26	32	Dresdner Bank (Frankfurt)	5,405
27	57	Rabobank Nederland (Utrecht)	5,336
28	30	Sumitomo Trust & Banking (Osaka)	4,970
29	68	Westpac Banking Corporation (Sydney)	4,931
30	65	Crédit Suisse (Zürich)	4,898
31	25	Mitsubishi Trust & Banking Corp. (Tokyo)	4,770
32	4	Bank America Corp (San Francisco)	4,764
33	–	Banco Bilbao Vizcaya (Madrid)	4,691
34	27	Taiyo Kobe Bank (Tokyo)	4,556
35	66	Cariplo (Milan)	4,513
36	104	National Australia Bank (Melbourne)	4,404
37	20	Midland Bank (London)	4,372
38	24	Royal Bank of Canada Montreal)	4,291
39	42	Banca Nazionale del Lavoro (Rome)	4,153
40	38	Canadian Imperial Bank of Commerce (Toronto)	4,080
41	26	JP Morgan & Co. (New York)	3,997
42	–	Abbey National (London)	3,940
43	101	Banco Central (Madrid)	3,899
44	–	Groupe des Caisses d'Epargne Ecureuil (Paris)	3,853
45	29	Mitsui Trust & Banking (Tokyo)	3,835
46	16	Chase Manhattan Corp (New York)	3,813
47	54	Commerzbank (Frankfurt)	3,803
48	100	Skandinaviska Enskilda Banken (Stockholm)	3,708
49	62	Toronto-Dominion Bank (Toronto)	3,703
50	59	Istituto Bancario San Paolo di Torino (Turin)	3,697

The table shows the top 50 banks, ranked by capital. The second column shows how each bank was ranked in 1984. The rise of Japan's banks has been dramatic, although there has been a slow-down in growth throughout the last few years.

Source: International Financial Corporation *Emerging Stock Markets Factbook 1990*.

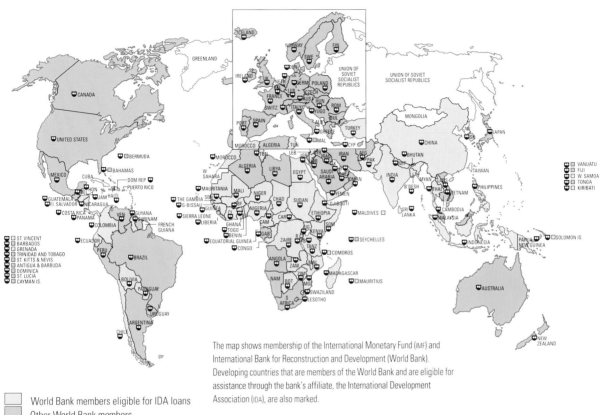

The map shows membership of the International Monetary Fund (IMF) and International Bank for Reconstruction and Development (World Bank). Developing countries that are members of the World Bank and are eligible for assistance through the bank's affiliate, the International Development Association (IDA), are also marked.

World Bank members eligible for IDA loans
Other World Bank members
IMF members

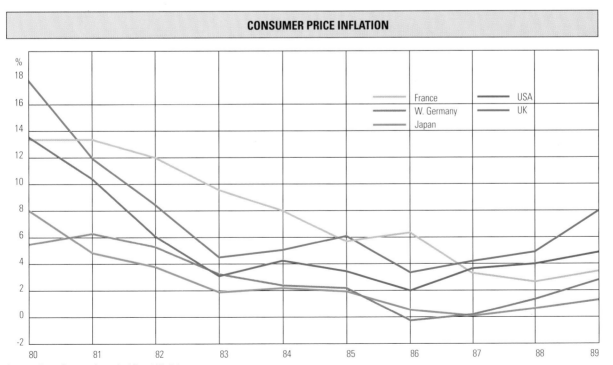

CONSUMER PRICE INFLATION

France   USA
W. Germany   UK
Japan

Source: EIU *Country Reports*; IMF *International Financial Statistics*.

INDUSTRIAL PRODUCTION

The map plots industrial growth rates in 1989, or the latest available year. Growth has been rapid in parts of East Asia throughout the last decade, whilst output is falling in states vulnerable to commodity price falls or political upheaval.

The pie charts show the top producers of a selection of manufactured goods.

Average industrial growth rate

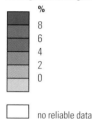

%
8
6
4
2
0

no reliable data

TOP PRODUCERS
1 tonne = 1.10 US (short) tons

Passenger cars Total 32.7m units

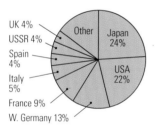

UK 4%
USSR 4%
Spain 4%
Italy 5%
France 9%
W. Germany 13%
Other
Japan 24%
USA 22%

Crude steel Total 681.1m tonnes

Other
USSR 24%
Japan 14%
France 3%
Italy 3%
W. Germany 5%
China 8%
USA 12%

Cigarettes Total 5,033.0bn units

Other
China 29%
USA 14%
USSR 8%
Japan 6%
W. Germany 3%
Brazil 3%

Ships (launched) Total 9.8m gross registered tons

Other
Japan 41%
S. Korea 23%

TV sets Total 102.0bn units

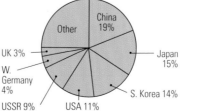

China 19%
Other
Japan 15%
S. Korea 14%
USA 11%
USSR 9%
W. Germany 4%
UK 3%

Nitrogenous fertilizers Total 87.9m tonnes

USSR 18%
Other
China 15%
USA 11%
India 6%
Indonesia 5%
Egypt 5%
Canada 3%

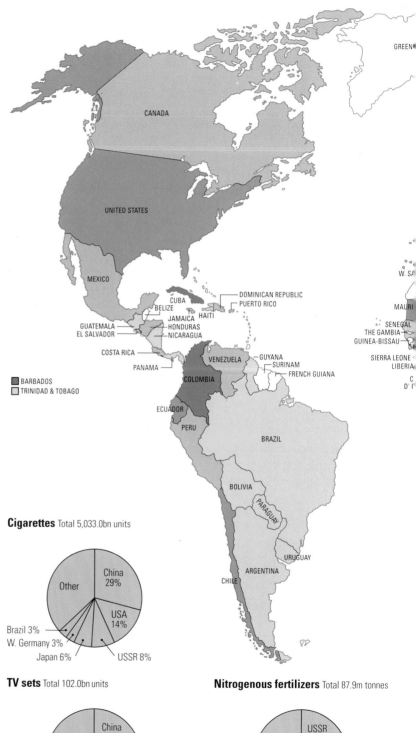

GREEN

CANADA

UNITED STATES

MEXICO

CUBA
BELIZE
GUATEMALA
EL SALVADOR
HONDURAS
NICARAGUA
COSTA RICA
PANAMA
JAMAICA
HAITI
DOMINICAN REPUBLIC
PUERTO RICO

BARBADOS
TRINIDAD & TOBAGO

VENEZUELA
GUYANA
SURINAM
FRENCH GUIANA
COLOMBIA
ECUADOR
PERU
BRAZIL
BOLIVIA
PARAGUAY
URUGUAY
ARGENTINA
CHILE

W. SA
MAURI
SENEGAL
THE GAMBIA
GUINEA-BISSAU
SIERRA LEONE
LIBERIA
C
D'I

Source: Industrial growth rate EIU *Country Profiles*; UN *Industrial Statistics Yearbook* (1989 figures or latest available); Top producers UN *Industrial Statistics Yearbook* (1987 figures).

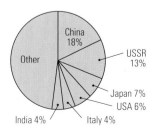

Cement Total 1,045.0m tonnes

China 18%
Other
USSR 13%
Japan 7%
USA 6%
India 4%
Italy 4%

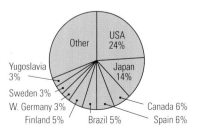

Paper & paperboard Total 249.4m tonnes

USA 24%
Other
Japan 14%
Yugoslavia 3%
Sweden 3%
W. Germany 3%
Finland 5%
Brazil 5%
Canada 6%
Spain 6%

Synthetic rubber Total 9.4m tonnes

Other
USSR 25%
Brazil 3%
UK 3%
USA 24%
W. Germany 5%
France 6%
Japan 13%

ENERGY

The map plots energy consumption per head for fuels
that are commercially exploited, and the charts show
the biggest producers and consumers of energy, fuel by
fuel as well as overall. Consumption figures are shown
for nuclear energy and hydroelectricity; these are
generally equal to production figures. Commercial
utilization of other energy resources satisfies an
insignificant proportion of the world's energy needs,
though wood is the principal fuel source for an
estimated 80% of the population of the developing
world.

COAL
Production 3.19 billion tonnes coal equivalent

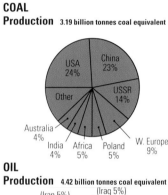

China 23%
USA 24%
USSR 14%
Other
Australia 4%
India 4%
Africa 5%
Poland 5%
W. Europe 9%

Consumption
3.19 billion tonnes coal equivalent

(China) 23%
Asia 35%
USA 21%
Other
Africa 3%
USSR 13%
E. Europe 12%
W. Europe 12%

OIL
Production 4.42 billion tonnes coal equivalent

(Iran 5%) (Iraq 5%)
(Saudi Arabia 8%)
Middle East 26%
USSR 20%
USA 14%
Other
Venezuela 3%
UK 3%
China 5%
Mexico 5%
Africa 9%

Consumption 4.43 billion tonnes coal equivalent

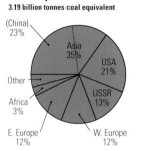

(Japan) 8%
Asia & Australia 20%
USA 26%
(China) 4%
W. Europe 19%
Other
Africa 3%
USSR 14%
Middle East 5%
Latin America 8%

NATURAL GAS
Production 2.46 billion tonnes coal equivalent

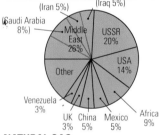

USSR 37%
USA 25%
Other
Africa 3%
Canada 5%
W. Europe 9%
Middle East 5%
Latin America 5%
Asia & Australia 8%

Consumption 2.44 billion tonnes coal equivalent

USSR 33%
USA 29%
Other
Canada 3%
Middle East 5%
W. Europe 12%
Latin America 5%
Asia & Australasia 7%

NUCLEAR POWER
Consumption 0.64 billion tonnes coal equivalent

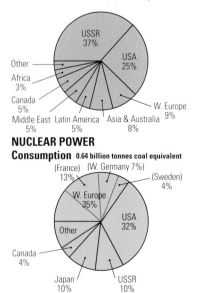

(France) 13%
(W. Germany 7%)
(Sweden) 4%
W. Europe 35%
USA 32%
Other
Canada 4%
Japan 10%
USSR 10%

HYDROELECTRICITY
Consumption 0.75 billion tonnes coal equivalent

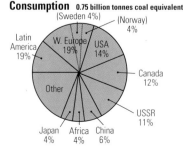

(Sweden 4%)
(Norway) 4%
Latin America 19%
W. Europe 19%
USA 14%
Canada 12%
Other
USSR 11%
Japan 4%
Africa 4%
China 6%

Map labels: CANADA, UNITED STATES, ST PIERRE & MIQ., BERMUDA, MEXICO, BAHAMAS, CUBA, DOMINICAN REPUBLIC, PUERTO RICO, BELIZE, JAMAICA, HAITI, CAPE VERD, GUATEMALA, HONDURAS, EL SALVADOR, NICARAGUA, COSTA RICA, PANAMA, VENEZUELA, COLOMBIA, GUYANA, SURINAM, FRENCH GUIANA, ECUADOR, PERU, BRAZIL, BOLIVIA, PARAGUAY, URUGUAY, ARGENTINA, CHILE

CAYMAN IS.
US VIRGIN IS.
BRITISH VIRGIN ISLANDS
ST. KITTS & NEVIS
ANTIGUA & BARBUDA
MONTSERRAT
GUADELOUPE
DOMINICA
MARTINIQUE
ST. LUCIA
ST. VINCENT
BARBADOS
GRENADA
NETHERLANDS ANTILLES
TRINIDAD & TOBAGO
ARUBA

Energy consumption per head
tonnes of coal equivalent per year

5.0
2.5
1.0
0.5
0.25

no reliable data

Sources: UN *Energy Statistics Yearbook* (1988 figures); BP *Statistical Review of World Energy* (1989 figures).

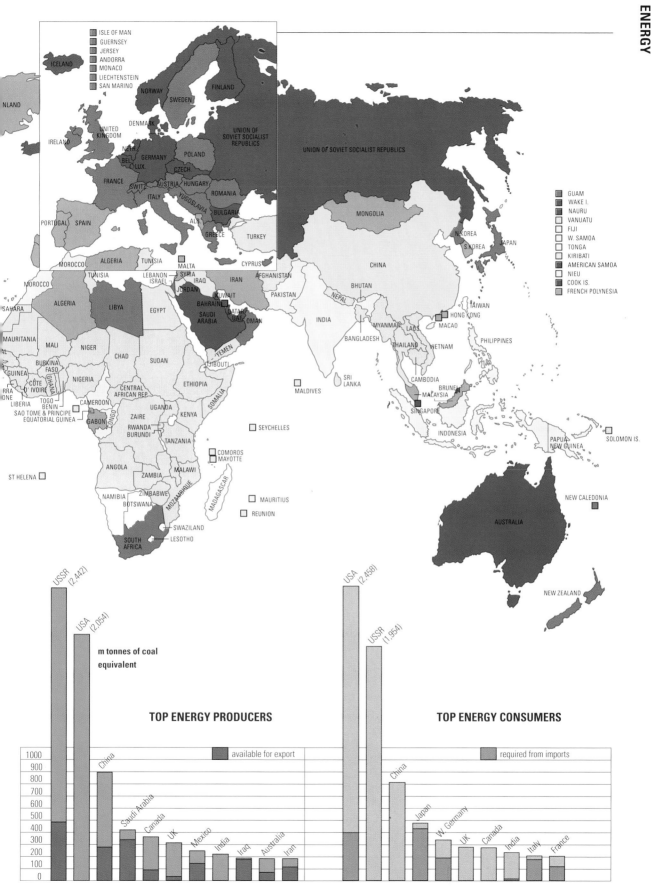

ISLE OF MAN
GUERNSEY
JERSEY
ANDORRA
MONACO
LIECHTENSTEIN
SAN MARINO

GUAM
WAKE I.
NAURU
VANUATU
FIJI
W. SAMOA
TONGA
KIRIBATI
AMERICAN SAMOA
NIEU
COOK IS.
FRENCH POLYNESIA

ICELAND
NORWAY
SWEDEN
FINLAND
DENMARK
UNITED KINGDOM
IRELAND
NETH.
BEL.
LUX.
GERMANY
POLAND
CZECH
UNION OF SOVIET SOCIALIST REPUBLICS
UNION OF SOVIET SOCIALIST REPUBLICS
FRANCE
SWITZ.
AUSTRIA
HUNGARY
ITALY
YUGOSLAVIA
ROMANIA
BULGARIA
ALB.
GREECE
TURKEY
PORTUGAL
SPAIN
CYPRUS
MALTA
MOROCCO
ALGERIA
TUNISIA
MONGOLIA

NLAND

MOROCCO
TUNISIA
LEBANON
ISRAEL
SYRIA
JORDAN
IRAQ
IRAN
AFGHANISTAN
PAKISTAN
CHINA
N.KOREA
S.KOREA
JAPAN
SAHARA
ALGERIA
LIBYA
EGYPT
KUWAIT
BAHRAIN
QATAR
SAUDI ARABIA
UAE
OMAN
YEMEN
NEPAL
BHUTAN
INDIA
TAIWAN
HONG KONG
MACAO
PHILIPPINES
MAURITANIA
MALI
NIGER
CHAD
SUDAN
DJIBOUTI
BANGLADESH
MYANMAR
LAOS
GUINEA
BURKINA FASO
NIGERIA
CÔTE D'IVOIRE
GHANA
TOGO
BENIN
CENTRAL AFRICAN REP.
ETHIOPIA
SOMALIA
THAILAND
VIETNAM
CAMBODIA
BRUNEI
MALAYSIA
SRI LANKA
MALDIVES
RRA ONE
LIBERIA
SAO TOME & PRINCIPE
EQUATORIAL GUINEA
GABON
CAMEROON
CONGO
ZAIRE
UGANDA
KENYA
RWANDA
BURUNDI
TANZANIA
SINGAPORE
SEYCHELLES
INDONESIA
PAPUA NEW GUINEA
SOLOMON IS.
ANGOLA
ZAMBIA
MALAWI
COMOROS
MAYOTTE
ST HELENA
NAMIBIA
ZIMBABWE
BOTSWANA
MOZAMBIQUE
MADAGASCAR
MAURITIUS
REUNION
NEW CALEDONIA
SWAZILAND
SOUTH AFRICA
LESOTHO
AUSTRALIA
NEW ZEALAND

m tonnes of coal
equivalent

USSR (2,442)
USA (2,054)

USA (2,458)
USSR (1,954)

TOP ENERGY PRODUCERS

China
Saudi Arabia
Canada
UK
Mexico
India
Iraq
Australia
Iran

	available for export

TOP ENERGY CONSUMERS

China
Japan
W. Germany
UK
Canada
India
Italy
France

	required from imports

1000
900
800
700
600
500
400
300
200
100
0

MINERAL WEALTH

The map symbols identify major producers, those with more than a 3% share of world production. The charts indicate total world mine output and the percentage mined by each of the largest producers. Production volumes for most minerals are for metal content, but output of iron, chromium and bauxite is instead measured as ore weight.

Figures for uranium production in Eastern Europe are not available; even informed sources are reluctant to estimate output.

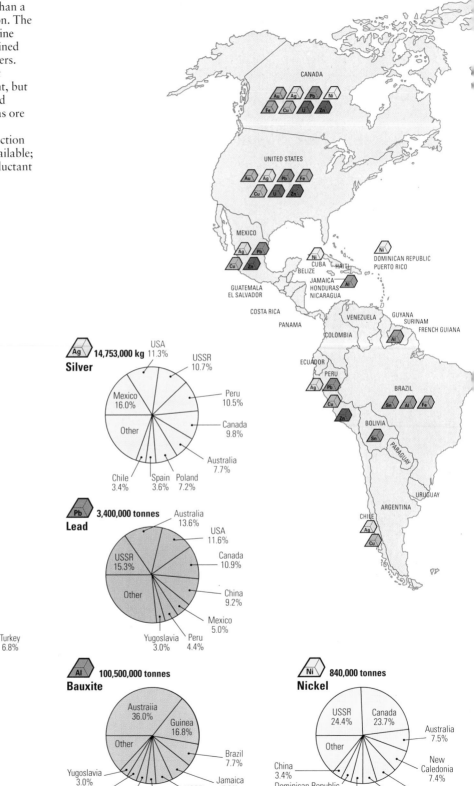

1 tonne = 1.1025 US tons

Au 1,797,000 kg
Gold

- Other
- South Africa 34.5%
- China 4.3%
- Canada 7.5%
- USSR 15.6%
- Australia 8.7%
- USA 11.2%

Ag 14,753,000 kg
Silver

- USA 11.3%
- USSR 10.7%
- Mexico 16.0%
- Peru 10.5%
- Other
- Canada 9.8%
- Australia 7.7%
- Chile 3.4%
- Spain 3.6%
- Poland 7.2%

Cr 11,700,000 tonnes
Chromium

- South Africa 36.3%
- USSR 27.7%
- Other
- Finland 4.6%
- Zimbabwe 4.8%
- Albania 6.4%
- India 6.5%
- Turkey 6.8%

Pb 3,400,000 tonnes
Lead

- Australia 13.6%
- USA 11.6%
- USSR 15.3%
- Canada 10.9%
- Other
- China 9.2%
- Mexico 5.0%
- Yugoslavia 3.0%
- Peru 4.4%

Sn 204,000 tonnes
Tin

- Australia 3.4%
- Other
- Brazil 21.6%
- Bolivia 5.1%
- Thailand 7.0%
- China 14.7%
- USSR 7.4%
- Malaysia 14.2%
- Indonesia 14.5%

Al 100,500,000 tonnes
Bauxite

- Australia 36.0%
- Guinea 16.8%
- Other
- Brazil 7.7%
- Yugoslavia 3.0%
- Jamaica 7.3%
- India 3.4%
- Surinam 3.4%
- China 3.5%
- USSR 5.9%

Ni 840,000 tonnes
Nickel

- USSR 24.4%
- Canada 23.7%
- Australia 7.5%
- Other
- New Caledonia 7.4%
- China 3.4%
- Dominican Republic 3.5%
- South Africa 4.1%
- Cuba 5.0%
- Indonesia 7.1%

Source: British Geological Survey *World Mineral Statistics* (1988 figures or latest available).

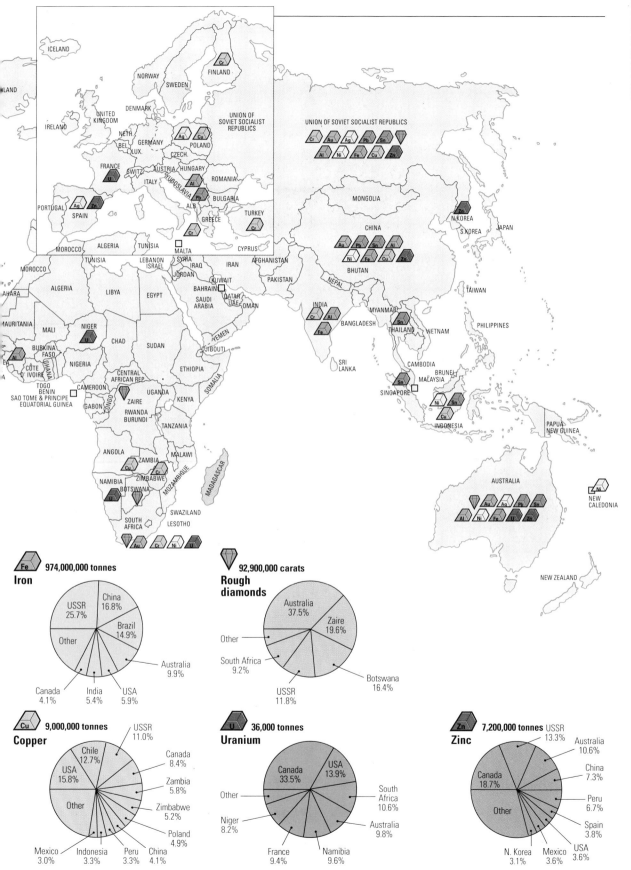

Iron ⬡ Fe 974,000,000 tonnes

Pie chart:
- China 16.8%
- Brazil 14.9%
- Australia 9.9%
- USA 5.9%
- India 5.4%
- Canada 4.1%
- Other
- USSR 25.7%

Rough diamonds ◆ 92,900,000 carats

Pie chart:
- Australia 37.5%
- Zaire 19.6%
- Botswana 16.4%
- USSR 11.8%
- South Africa 9.2%
- Other

Copper ⬡ Cu 9,000,000 tonnes

Pie chart:
- USSR 11.0%
- Canada 8.4%
- Zambia 5.8%
- Zimbabwe 5.2%
- Poland 4.9%
- China 4.1%
- Peru 3.3%
- Indonesia 3.3%
- Mexico 3.0%
- Other
- USA 15.8%
- Chile 12.7%

Uranium ⬡ U 36,000 tonnes

Pie chart:
- Canada 33.5%
- USA 13.9%
- South Africa 10.6%
- Australia 9.8%
- Namibia 9.6%
- France 9.4%
- Niger 8.2%
- Other

Zinc ⬡ Zn 7,200,000 tonnes

Pie chart:
- USSR 13.3%
- Australia 10.6%
- China 7.3%
- Peru 6.7%
- Spain 3.8%
- USA 3.6%
- Mexico 3.6%
- N. Korea 3.1%
- Canada 18.7%
- Other

97

POLITICAL SYSTEMS

RELATED TERRITORIES

AUSTRALIA
Christmas I.
Cocos Is.
Norfolk Is.
CHILE
Easter I.
DENMARK
Faeroe Is.
Greenland
FRANCE
French Guiana
French Polynesia
Guadeloupe
Mayotte
Martinique
Monaco
New Caledonia
Reunion
St. Pierre & Miquelon
Wallis & Futuna
ITALY
San Marino
NETHERLANDS
Aruba
Netherlands Antilles
NEW ZEALAND
Cook Is.
Niue
Tokelau
PORTUGAL
Azores
Macao
Madeira
SPAIN
Canary Is.
SWITZERLAND
Liechtenstein
UNITED KINGDOM
Anguilla
Bermuda
Virgin Is.
Cayman Is.
Channel Is.
Falkland Is.
Gibraltar
Hong Kong
Isle of Man
Montserrat
Pitcairn Is.
St. Helena
Turks & Caicos Is.
UNITED STATES
Samoa
Palau
Guam
Marshall Is.
Federated States of Micronesia
Northern Mariana Is.
Puerto Rico
Virgin Is.
FRANCE/SPAIN
Andorra

The map charts political rights, on a scale from 1 for the highest degree of political freedom to 7 for the lowest. Among the criteria for a high rating are: recent free and fair elections, a parliament with effective power, a significant opposition and recent shifts in power through election. Factors contributing to a lower rating include military or foreign control, the denial of self-determination to major population groups and lack of decentralized political power.

Human rights generally go hand-in-hand with political rights. A country that denies its citizens the right to participate in a free electoral process will often also deny them free assembly, demonstration and organization, and freedom from political terror and unjustified imprisonment.

Countries which have become independent since 1945 are indicated by their date of independence. Aruba, formerly one

Source: Freedom House, NY, *Survey of Freedom 1991.*

of the Netherland Antilles, was granted separate status in 1986 with a view to full independence by 1996.

Related territories of each country are listed separately, but their status and degree of autonomy varies widely; some are under military occupation; some, such as the overseas departments of France, are considered to be integral parts of the sovereign state; others have a large degree of self-determination.

Political freedom

1 Most free
2
3
4
5
6
7 Least free

ISLE OF MAN
GUERNSEY
JERSEY
ANDORRA
MONACO
LIECHTENSTEIN
SAN MARINO
FAEROE IS.

NAURU '68
VANUATU '80
TUVALU '78
WALLIS & FUTUNA
FIJI '70
W. SAMOA '62
TONGA '70
KIRIBATI
TOKELAU
AMERICAN SAMOA
NIUE
COOK IS.
FRENCH POLYNESIA
MARSHALL IS.
PALAU
N. MARIANA IS.
GUAM
NORFOLK IS.
EASTER IS.
FEDERATED STATES OF MICRONESIA

INTERNATIONAL GROUPINGS

WORLD

UN *non*-members of the United Nations

OECD Organization for Economic Co-operation and Development

Opec Organization of the Petroleum Exporting Countries

Commonwealth

Countries that have only partial membership, such as observer status, are not marked; neither are dependencies and other non-sovereign states.

For a fuller explanation of these terms, and of the aims of the organizations shown, *see the Glossary* and the relevant sections of the *World Encyclopedia.*

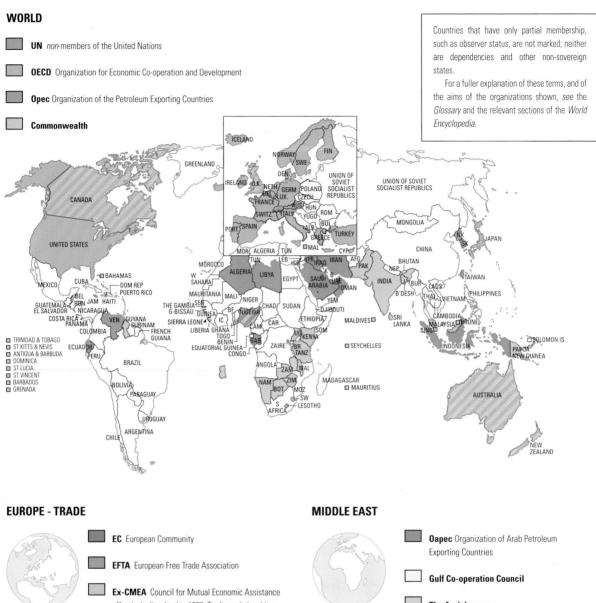

EUROPE - TRADE

EC European Community

EFTA European Free Trade Association

Ex-CMEA Council for Mutual Economic Assistance effectively dissolved in 1990. Trading relationships remain important, though many members are now seeking entry to other trading groups such as the EC. Cuba, Mongolia and Vietnam were also members.

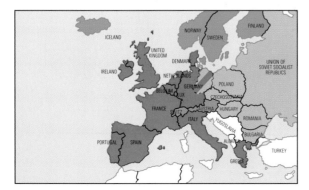

MIDDLE EAST

Oapec Organization of Arab Petroleum Exporting Countries

Gulf Co-operation Council

The Arab League

Arab Co-operation Council

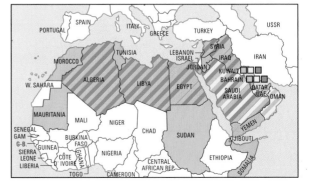

THE NORTHERN HEMISPHERE - DEFENCE

Nato North Atlantic Treaty Organization

Ex-Warsaw Pact Treaty of "friendship, co-operation and mutual assistance" formed May 1955 under Moscow's control, effectively dissolved 1990.

AFRICA

OAU *non-*members of the Organization for African Unity

Franc Zone

SADCC Southern Africa Development Co-ordination Conference

PTA Preferential Trade Area for Eastern and Southern Africa

Ecowas Economic Community of West African States

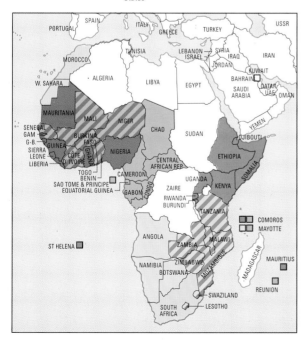

PACIFIC BASIN

Apec Asia and Pacific Economic Community

Asean Association of South East Asian Nations

LATIN AMERICA AND CARIBBEAN

Aladi Asociación Latinoamericana de Integratión

Andean Pact

Caricom Caribbean Community and Common Market

Organization of River Plate Basin Countries

TRINIDAD & TOBAGO
BRITISH VIRGIN IS.
ANGUILLA
ST. KITTS & NEVIS
ANTIGUA & BARBUDA
MONTSERRAT
DOMINICA
ST. LUCIA
ST. VINCENT
BARBADOS
GRENADA

DEFENCE SPENDING

The map shows the proportion of national government expenditure allocated to defence. It gives an indication of the state's budgetary priorities, rather than absolute military strength. Where actual figures are unavailable, budgeted figures or, as a last resort, informed estimates have been used. Accurate figures are not available for ex-Warsaw Pact members and therefore these should be seen as estimates. For the USSR, these vary by as much as $100 billion, because much Soviet procurement, research and development expenditure is not included in published defence budgets.

BILLION DOLLAR SPENDERS

$bn

USA 292.2
USSR 119.4
UK 33.4
France 28.6
Japan 28.1
W. Germany 27.6
Italy
Saudi Arabia
Iraq
E. Germany
S. Korea
Vietnam
Canada
India
Iran
Taiwan
Spain
Netherlands
Egypt
Australia
Israel
China
Sweden
N. Korea

Source: International Institute for Strategic Studies *The Military Balance* (1990 figures or latest available).

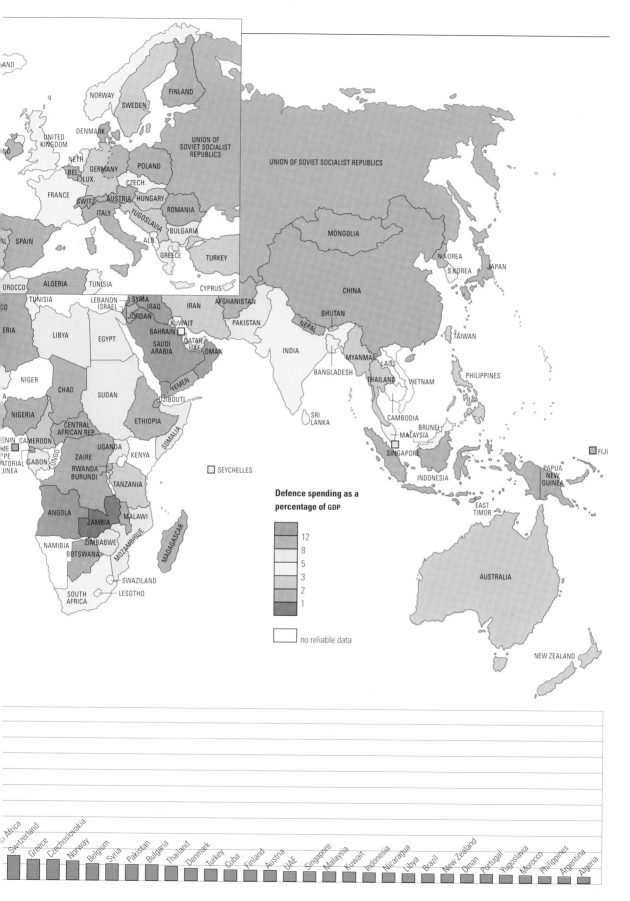

FOREIGN AID

The map shows the amount of official aid received by each country per head of population by members of the OECD Development Assistance Committee (DAC), Opec and Comecon. The figures, in US dollars, cover grants, loans and technical assistance and show actual disbursements, rather than commitments. Both bilateral – government to government – and multilateral aid through agencies such as the World Bank are included. Military aid is excluded.

The pie chart shows the share of aid contributed by major donors, including the individual shares of EC members and the proportion of French aid that goes to its overseas departments and territories.

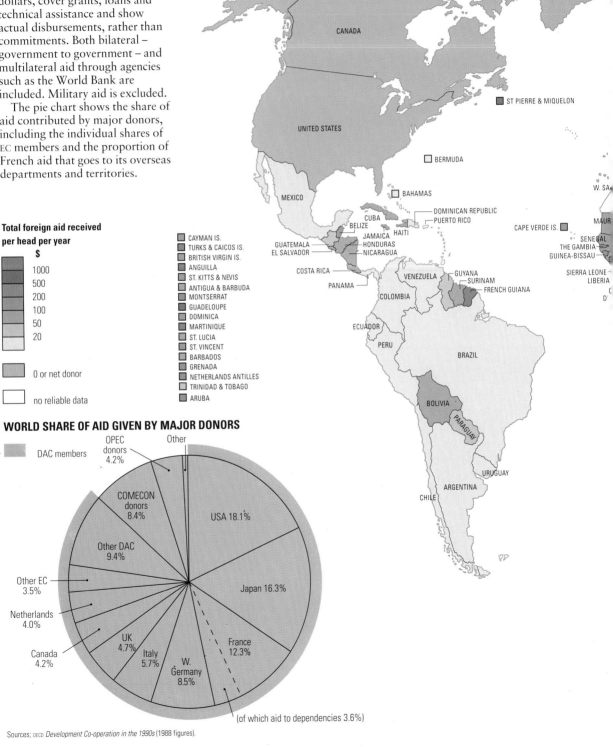

Total foreign aid received per head per year

$

1000
500
200
100
50
20

0 or net donor

no reliable data

CAYMAN IS.
TURKS & CAICOS IS.
BRITISH VIRGIN IS.
ANGUILLA
ST. KITTS & NEVIS
ANTIGUA & BARBUDA
MONTSERRAT
GUADELOUPE
DOMINICA
MARTINIQUE
ST. LUCIA
ST. VINCENT
BARBADOS
GRENADA
NETHERLANDS ANTILLES
TRINIDAD & TOBAGO
ARUBA

WORLD SHARE OF AID GIVEN BY MAJOR DONORS

DAC members

OPEC donors 4.2%
Other
COMECON donors 8.4%
USA 18.1%
Other DAC 9.4%
Other EC 3.5%
Netherlands 4.0%
Canada 4.2%
UK 4.7%
Italy 5.7%
W. Germany 8.5%
France 12.3%
Japan 16.3%
(of which aid to dependencies 3.6%)

Sources; OECD *Development Co-operation in the 1990s* (1988 figures).

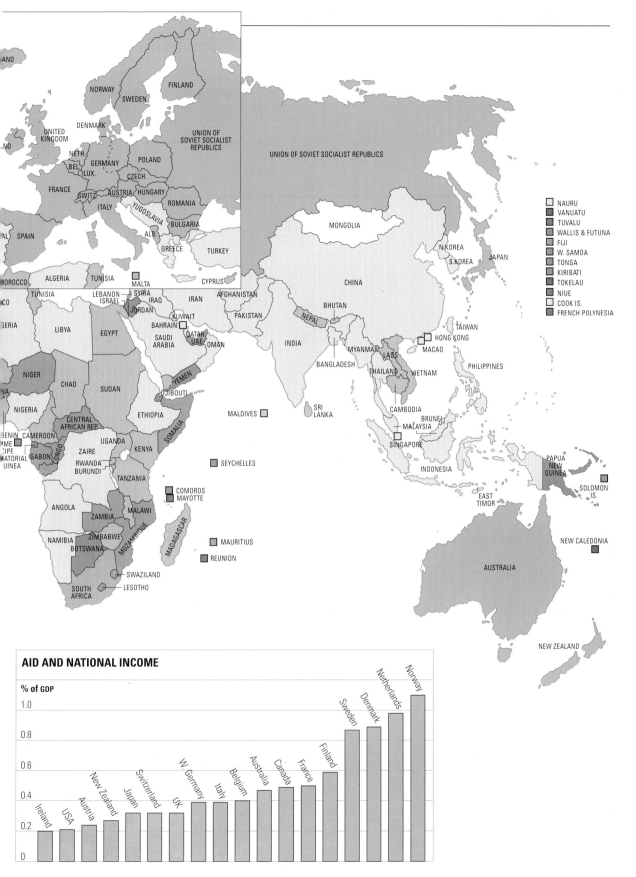

NAURU
VANUATU
TUVALU
WALLIS & FUTUNA
FIJI
W. SAMOA
TONGA
KIRIBATI
TOKELAU
NIUE
COOK IS.
FRENCH POLYNESIA

AID AND NATIONAL INCOME

% of GDP

1.0

0.8

0.6

0.4

0.2

0

Ireland
USA
Austria
New Zealand
Japan
Switzerland
UK
W. Germany
Italy
Belgium
Australia
Canada
France
Finland
Sweden
Denmark
Netherlands
Norway

FOOD AND HUNGER

The map shows the calorie consumption per head of population, and countries where on average protein requirements are not met. A moderately active man needs to consume about 3,000 calories per day, a sedentary one 2,500. Their female counterparts require respectively 2,200 and 2,000 calories per day.

This century, the use of fertilizers, pesticides and new hybrids has meant that the world now produces enough to feed everyone. The production of food is unevenly distributed, however, and as a commodity its transport costs are usually high in relation to its market price. Most foodstuffs are subject to price fluctuations related to weather. Few government attempts to stabilize prices by subsidies, controls or international stockpiling have met with much long-term success.

Calories per head per day

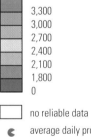

- 3,300
- 3,000
- 2,700
- 2,400
- 2,100
- 1,800
- 0

no reliable data

ᗧ average daily protein consumption per head per day less than 45gm

ST. KITTS & NEVIS
ANTIGUA & BARBUDA
DOMINICA
MARTINIQUE
ST. LUCIA
ST. VINCENT
BARBADOS
GRENADA
NETHERLANDS ANTILLES
TRINIDAD & TOBAGO

STAPLE FOOD PRODUCTION

The charts show world production of staple foods. Figures indicate the yield in kilograms per hectare.
1,000kg ha = 8.92 US cwt acre

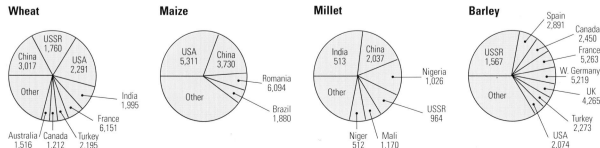

Wheat
- USSR 1,760
- China 3,017
- USA 2,291
- Other
- India 1,995
- France 6,151
- Australia 1,516
- Canada 1,212
- Turkey 2,195

Maize
- USA 5,311
- China 3,730
- Other
- Romania 6,094
- Brazil 1,880

Millet
- India 513
- China 2,037
- Nigeria 1,026
- Other
- USSR 964
- Niger 512
- Mali 1,170

Barley
- Spain 2,891
- Canada 2,450
- France 5,263
- W. Germany 5,219
- UK 4,265
- USSR 1,567
- Other
- Turkey 2,273
- USA 2,074

Source: Food and Agriculture Organization *Production Yearbook* (1987 figures).

VANUATU
FIJI
TONGA
KIRIBATI
FRENCH POLYNESIA

Sorghum

Argentina 3,347
Sudan 789
Nigeria 1,098
Mexico 3,056
China 3,215
India 688
USA 4,005
Other

Oats

Sweden 3,310
Australia 1,261
W. Germany 4,297
Poland 2,614
Canada 2,111
USA 1,404
USSR 1,375
Other

Rice

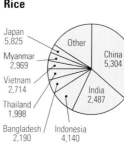

Japan 5,825
Myanmar 2,969
Vietnam 2,714
Thailand 1,998
Bangladesh 2,190
Indonesia 4,140
India 2,487
China 5,304
Other

Rye

China 1,538
W. Germany 4,177
E. Germany 2,941
Poland 2,366
USSR 1,778
Other

POPULATION DENSITY AND GROWTH

Populations are hard to measure and change constantly, therefore all the figures presented here are estimates. Even the more reliable ones may be based on a census carried out up to ten years ago.

The map shows population density, obtained by dividing population by land area. However, the larger and more geographically varied the country, the cruder this measure becomes. In the USSR, the vast majority of the population lives west of the Urals. Even in a smaller country the density figure can be deceptive; if the uninhabitable area of Japan is excluded, the population density rises from 324 people per sq km to 1,500.

Also indicated on the map are the world's largest cities, their populations based on central areas; the population of the conurbation is shown beneath in brackets.

People per sq km

500
250
100
50
25
10

no reliable data

Largest cities population in millions: Metropolitan Area (conurbation)

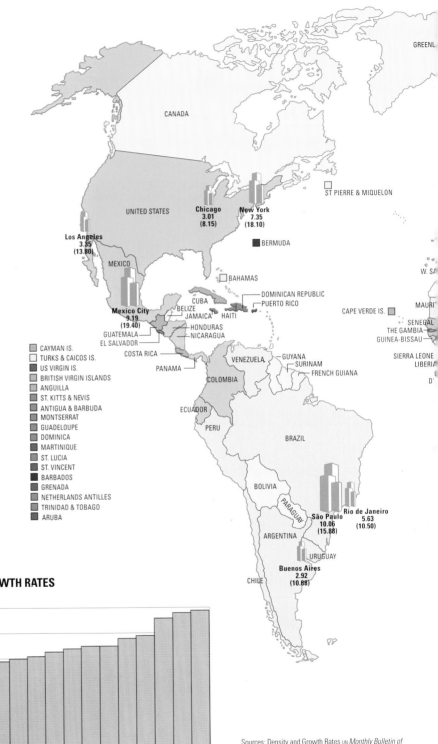

CANADA

GREENL

ST PIERRE & MIQUELON

UNITED STATES

Chicago
3.01
(8.15)

New York
7.35
(18.10)

BERMUDA

Los Angeles
3.35
(13.80)

MEXICO

W. SA

BAHAMAS

DOMINICAN REPUBLIC
PUERTO RICO

CUBA
BELIZE
JAMAICA HAITI

CAPE VERDE IS.

MAURI

Mexico City
9.19
(19.40)

HONDURAS
GUATEMALA NICARAGUA
EL SALVADOR

SENEGAL
THE GAMBIA
GUINEA-BISSAU

CAYMAN IS.
TURKS & CAICOS IS.
US VIRGIN IS.
BRITISH VIRGIN ISLANDS
ANGUILLA
ST. KITTS & NEVIS
ANTIGUA & BARBUDA
MONTSERRAT
GUADELOUPE
DOMINICA
MARTINIQUE
ST. LUCIA
ST. VINCENT
BARBADOS
GRENADA
NETHERLANDS ANTILLES
TRINIDAD & TOBAGO
ARUBA

COSTA RICA

PANAMA

VENEZUELA

GUYANA
SURINAM
FRENCH GUIANA

SIERRA LEONE
LIBERIA

D'

COLOMBIA

ECUADOR

PERU

BRAZIL

BOLIVIA

PARAGUAY

São Paulo
10.06
(15.88)

Rio de Janeiro
5.63
(10.50)

ARGENTINA

URUGUAY

Buenos Aires
2.92
(10.88)

CHILE

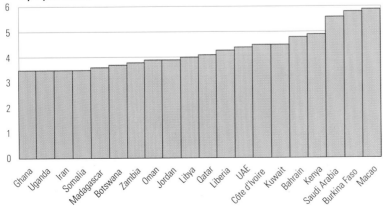

POPULATION: TOP TWENTY GROWTH RATES
% per year 1980-88

Ghana, Uganda, Iran, Somalia, Madagascar, Botswana, Zambia, Oman, Jordan, Libya, Qatar, Liberia, UAE, Côte d'Ivoire, Kuwait, Bahrain, Kenya, Saudi Arabia, Burkina Faso, Macao

Sources: Density and Growth Rates UN *Monthly Bulletin of Statistics*; UN *World Population Prospects*; EIU *Country Reports*; Europa *Yearbook* (1989 figures or latest available); Population increase and City populations UN *Demographic Yearbook* (1987 figures or latest available).

108

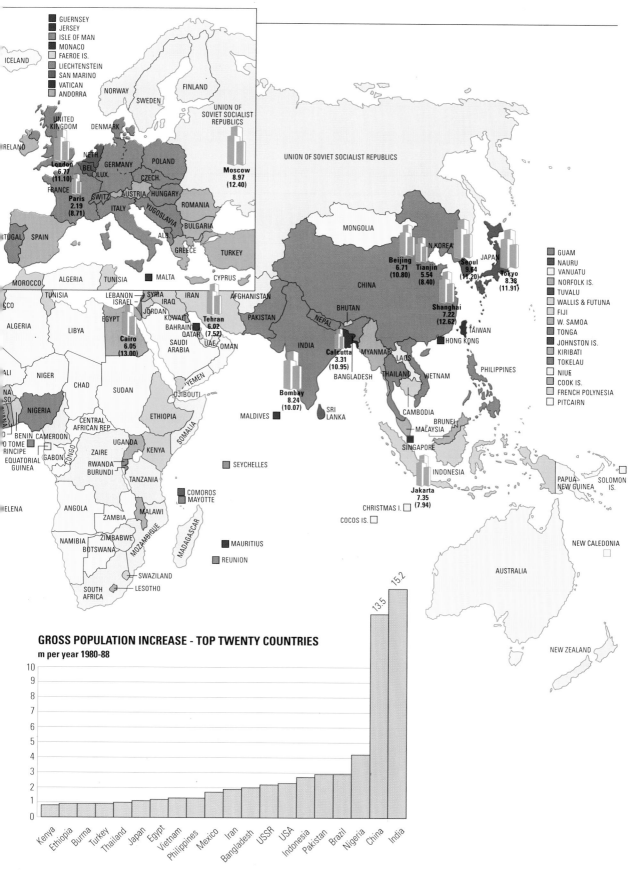

GUERNSEY
JERSEY
ISLE OF MAN
MONACO
FAEROE IS.
LIECHTENSTEIN
SAN MARINO
VATICAN
ANDORRA

ICELAND

NORWAY
SWEDEN
FINLAND

UNION OF
SOVIET SOCIALIST
REPUBLICS

UNION OF SOVIET SOCIALIST REPUBLICS

IRELAND

UNITED
KINGDOM
DENMARK

London
6.77
(11.10)

NETH.
BEL.
LUX.
GERMANY
POLAND
CZECH.
AUSTRIA HUNGARY

Moscow
8.97
(12.40)

FRANCE

Paris
2.19
(8.71)

SWITZ.
ITALY
YUGOSLAVIA
ROMANIA
BULGARIA
ALB.
GREECE
TURKEY

TUGAL
SPAIN

MONGOLIA

N.KOREA
JAPAN

Beijing
6.71
(10.80)
Tianjin
5.54
(8.40)
Seoul
9.64
(11.20)
Tokyo
8.38
(11.91)

MOROCCO
ALGERIA
TUNISIA
MALTA
CYPRUS

CCO
TUNISIA
LEBANON
ISRAEL
SYRIA
IRAQ
IRAN
AFGHANISTAN

Shanghai
7.22
(12.62)

CHINA

EGYPT
JORDAN
KUWAIT
Tehran
6.02
(7.52)
PAKISTAN
BHUTAN
NEPAL
TAIWAN
HONG KONG

LIBYA
Cairo
6.05
(13.00)
BAHRAIN
QATAR
SAUDI
ARABIA
UAE
OMAN
INDIA
Calcutta
3.31
(10.95)
MYANMAR
LAOS

GUAM
NAURU
VANUATU
NORFOLK IS.
TUVALU
WALLIS & FUTUNA
FIJI
W. SAMOA
TONGA
JOHNSTON IS.
KIRIBATI
TOKELAU
NIUE
COOK IS.
FRENCH POLYNESIA
PITCAIRN

ALGERIA
MALI
NIGER
CHAD
SUDAN
YEMEN
DJIBOUTI
BANGLADESH
THAILAND
VIETNAM

NA
SO
NIGERIA
Bombay
8.24
(10.07)
MALDIVES
SRI
LANKA
CAMBODIA

PHILIPPINES

BENIN
CAMEROON
CENTRAL
AFRICAN REP
ETHIOPIA
SOMALIA
BRUNEI
MALAYSIA

O TOME
RINCIPE
EQUATORIAL
GUINEA
GABON
CONGO
ZAIRE
UGANDA
KENYA
RWANDA
BURUNDI
SINGAPORE

SEYCHELLES

ELENA
ANGOLA
TANZANIA
INDONESIA
Jakarta
7.35
(7.94)

COMOROS
MAYOTTE

CHRISTMAS I.
COCOS IS.

PAPUA
NEW GUINEA
SOLOMON
IS.

ZAMBIA
MALAWI
ZIMBABWE
MOZAMBIQUE
MADAGASCAR
MAURITIUS
REUNION

NAMIBIA
BOTSWANA

NEW CALEDONIA

SWAZILAND
SOUTH
AFRICA
LESOTHO

AUSTRALIA

NEW ZEALAND

GROSS POPULATION INCREASE - TOP TWENTY COUNTRIES
m per year 1980-88

13.5
15.2

10
9
8
7
6
5
4
3
2
1
0

Kenya
Ethiopia
Burma
Turkey
Thailand
Japan
Egypt
Vietnam
Philippines
Mexico
Iran
Bangladesh
USSR
USA
Indonesia
Pakistan
Brazil
Nigeria
China
India

LIFE EXPECTANCY AND HEALTH

LIFE EXPECTANCY

The map shows average life expectancy in years. Men generally have a lower life expectancy than women, but the gap between the sexes varies widely. In a few countries, notably those of the Indian subcontinent, men have a slightly higher life expectancy than women.

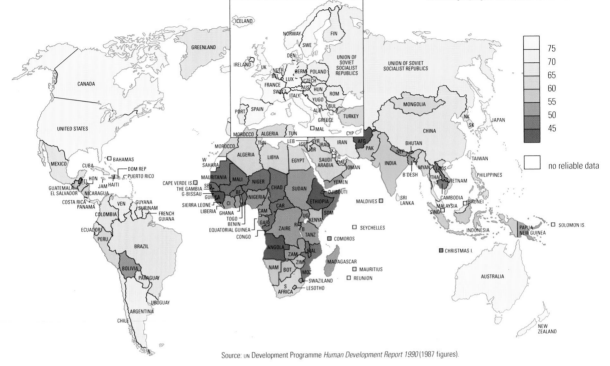

Source: UN Development Programme *Human Development Report 1990* (1987 figures).

INFANT MORTALITY

The map shows the number of children per 1,000 who die before reaching their first birthday. Many of the deaths in countries with high infant mortality rates are caused by poor water and sanitation, disease and a lack of health education.

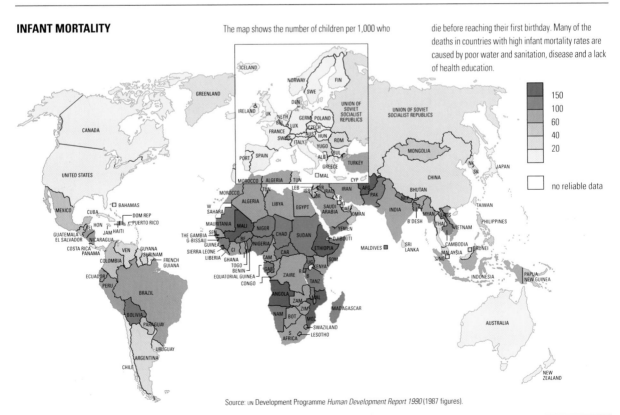

Source: UN Development Programme *Human Development Report 1990* (1987 figures).

PEOPLE PER PHYSICIAN

Comparing this map with those showing infant mortality and life expectancy reveals that the number of physicians is not a straightforward indicator of a state's standards of health. The available figures are for all qualified physicians, not only those in medical practice, and exclude paramedics.

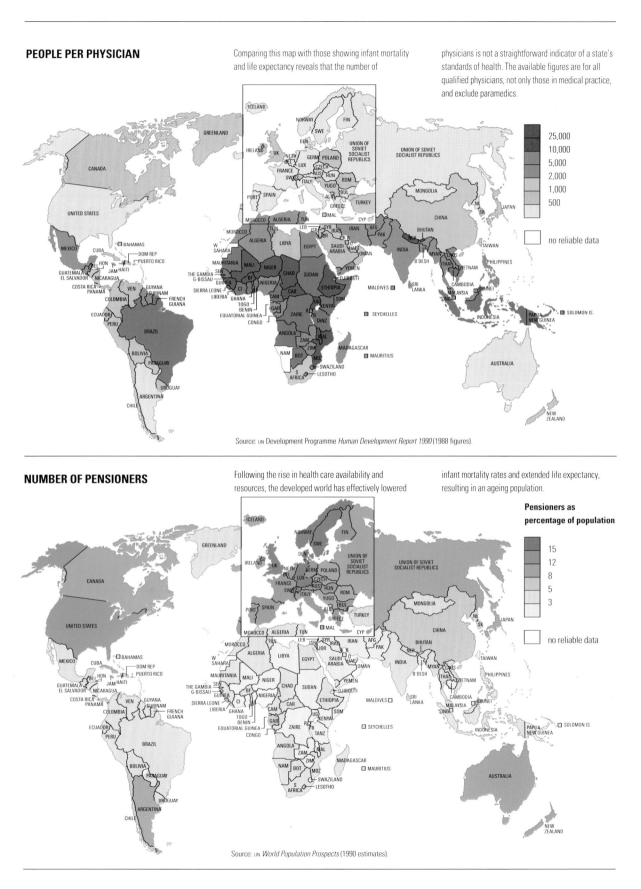

25,000
10,000
5,000
2,000
1,000
500

no reliable data

Source: UN Development Programme *Human Development Report 1990* (1988 figures).

NUMBER OF PENSIONERS

Following the rise in health care availability and resources, the developed world has effectively lowered infant mortality rates and extended life expectancy, resulting in an ageing population.

Pensioners as percentage of population

15
12
8
5
3

no reliable data

Source: UN *World Population Prospects* (1990 estimates).

ENVIRONMENT

Burning fossil fuel releases large quantities of carbon dioxide which, with other gases, traps heat in the atmosphere and is causing a slow increase in global temperatures. This "greenhouse effect" could have disastrous consequences: widespread crop failures and flooding of vulnerable lowland areas. The first chart identifies the countries that generate the most carbon dioxide from fossil fuels. The second chart shows global temperature rise, with future predictions based on three models.

Burning of tropical rainforests releases yet more carbon dioxide; this is just one of the many problems of deforestation. The third chart shows the scale of forest loss and the map identifies where the destruction is taking place.

The meagre environment on the fringe of the world's deserts is being destroyed by over-grazing and deforestation. The map indicates where the threat of desertification is most serious.

Acid rain, the product of industrial emissions of sulphur dioxide and nitrogen oxides, is a major contributor to forest destruction and water pollution in the northern hemisphere. The map shows the regions of great acidity. Some countries, the members of the "30% club" (Austria, Canada, Denmark, Finland, France, the Netherlands, Norway, Sweden, Switzerland and Germany), have begun to tackle the problem with an agreement to cut sulphur emissions to 70% of present levels by 1993.

DESERTIFICATION

Very high degree of desertification hazard
High degree of desertification hazard

Source: UN *Map of desertification.*

RAINFOREST DESTRUCTION

Present distribution of forest area
Area originally forested

Source: Smithsonian Institute *Tropical Rainforests: A Disappearing Treasure.*

ACID DEPOSITION

Estimated acidity of precipitation in the northern hemisphere

5.0 least acid
4.5
4.0 most acid

Source: World Meteorological Organisation *Long-Range Transport of Sulphur in the Atmosphere and Acid Rain.*

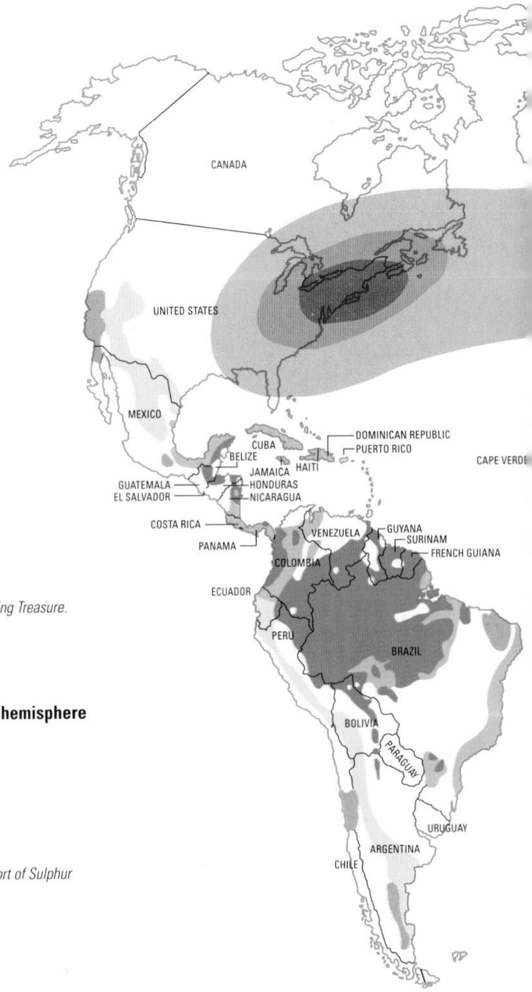

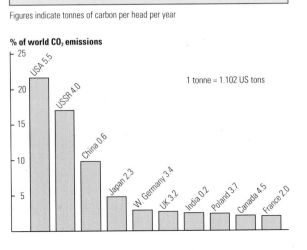

CARBON DIOXIDE EMISSIONS

Figures indicate tonnes of carbon per head per year

1 tonne = 1.102 US tons

% of world CO_2 emissions

USA 5.5
USSR 4.0
China 0.6
Japan 2.3
W. Germany 3.4
UK 3.2
India 0.2
Poland 3.7
Canada 4.5
France 2.0

Source: Carbon Dioxide Information Analysis Centre (1986 figures).

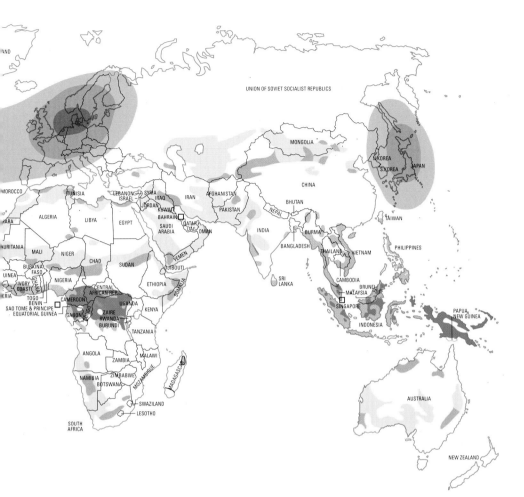

GLOBAL WARMING

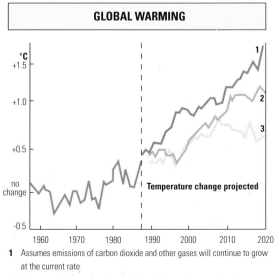

°C
+1.5
+1.0
+0.5
no change
-0.5

1960   1970   1980   1990   2000   2010   2020

Temperature change projected

1

2

3

1 Assumes emissions of carbon dioxide and other gases will continue to grow at the current rate

2 Assumes emissions of carbon dioxide continue at the current level

3 Assumes drastic cuts in emissions in the 1990s

Source: Nasa Goddard Institute for Space Studies.

DEFORESTATION IN TROPICAL COUNTRIES

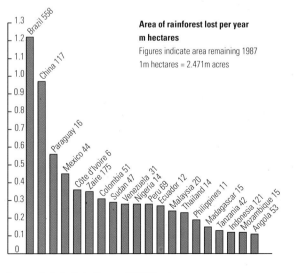

**Area of rainforest lost per year
m hectares**
Figures indicate area remaining 1987
1m hectares = 2.471m acres

1.3
1.2
1.1
1.0
0.9
0.8
0.7
0.6
0.5
0.4
0.3
0.2
0.1
0

Brazil 558
China 117
Paraguay 16
Mexico 44
Côte d'Ivoire 6
Zaire 175
Colombia 51
Sudan 47
Venezuela 31
Nigeria 14
Peru 69
Ecuador 12
Malaysia 20
Thailand 14
Philippines 11
Madagascar 15
Tanzania 42
Indonesia 121
Mozambique 15
Angola 53

Source: FAO *Production Yearbook* (average 1982–87 figures).

EDUCATION

The map shows government spending on education as a percentage of GDP, while the chart ranks those independent countries which spend most per head on education, rounding figures to the nearest $50. In countries where many are educated privately the actual spending on education is, of course, significantly higher.

Average education spending as a percentage of GNP

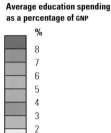

%
8
7
6
5
4
3
2
1

☐ no reliable data

CAYMAN IS.
TURKS & CAICOS IS.
US VIRGIN IS.
BRITISH VIRGIN ISLANDS
ST. KITTS & NEVIS
ANTIGUA & BARBUDA
GUADELOUPE .
MARTINIQUE
ST. LUCIA
ST. VINCENT
BARBADOS
GRENADA
TRINIDAD & TOBAGO

GOVERNMENT SPENDING PER HEAD

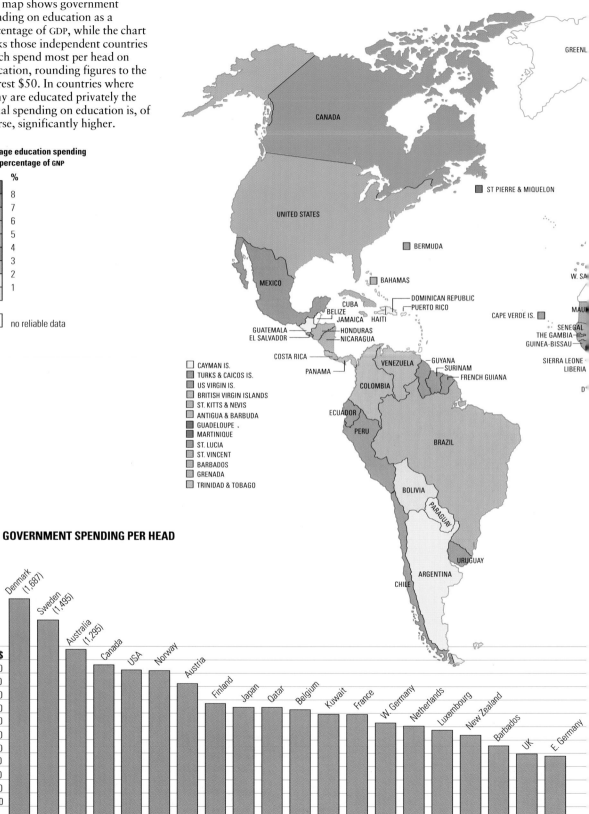

Denmark (1,687)
Sweden (1,495)
Australia (1,295)
Canada
USA
Norway
Austria
Finland
Japan
Qatar
Belgium
Kuwait
France
W. Germany
Netherlands
Luxembourg
New Zealand
Barbados
UK
E. Germany

$
1100
1000
900
800
700
600
500
400
300
200
100

Source: UNESCO *Statistical Yearbook* (1987 figures or latest available).

GUAM
NORFOLK IS.
FIJI
W. SAMOA
TONGA
KIRIBATI
NIUE
COOK IS.
FRENCH POLYNESIA

LANGUAGE

Countries are coloured according to the official language or languages; the accompanying graphic gives a breakdown of world population by mother tongue. The contrast between the two is striking, reflecting the tension between the official and the colloquial. The map could be one of the great empires, with six international languages, English, French, Spanish, Portuguese, Arabic and Russian, covering most of the globe. Yet, as the chart shows, a majority have as their native tongue one spoken by fewer than 1% of the world's population. These minor languages are included in "Others".

It is in Africa that the dichotomy between *lingua franca* and mother tongue is strongest. Nations divided along tribal lines have tended to adopt the language of their colonizers, a common denominator, as their official language; inhabitants thus fall into one category and the country into another. Similarly, in the USSR, India, Peru and Paraguay there are large linguistic minorities which often find it expedient to understand the dominant language, but do not adopt it as a mother tongue.

☐ CAYMAN IS.
☐ TURKS & CAICOS IS.
☐ US VIRGIN IS.
☐ BRITISH VIRGIN ISLANDS
☐ ANGUILLA
☐ ST. KITTS & NEVIS
☐ ANTIGUA & BARBUDA
☐ MONTSERRAT
☐ GUADELOUPE
☐ DOMINICA
☐ MARTINIQUE
☐ ST. LUCIA
☐ ST. VINCENT
☐ BARBADOS
☐ GRENADA
☐ NETHERLANDS ANTILLES
☐ TRINIDAD & TOBAGO

MOTHER TONGUES

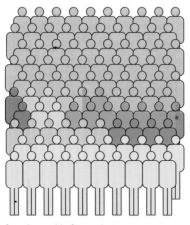

Source: Larrouse *Atlas Geostrategique*.

LIVING STANDARDS

CAR OWNERSHIP

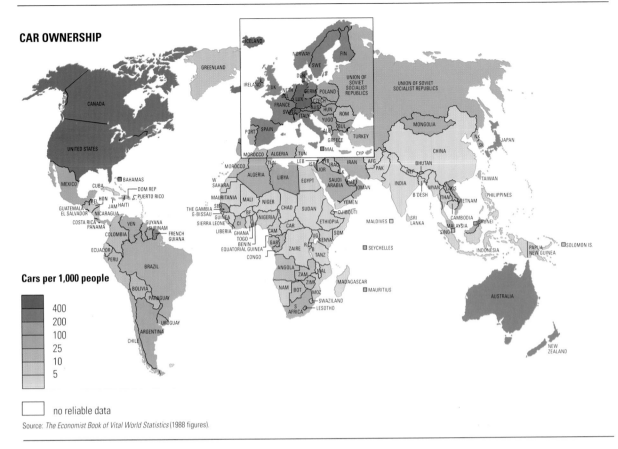

Cars per 1,000 people

400
200
100
25
10
5

no reliable data

Source: *The Economist Book of Vital World Statistics* (1988 figures).

TELEPHONE OWNERSHIP

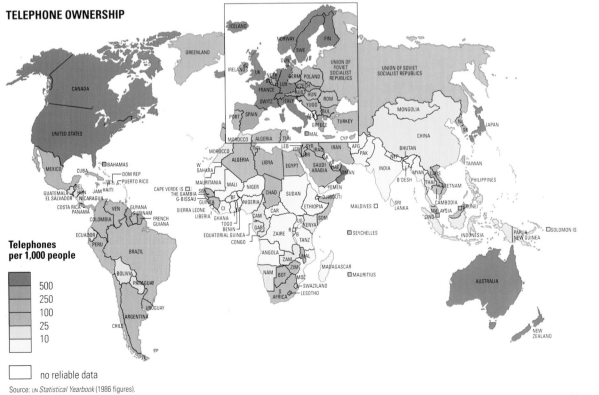

Telephones per 1,000 people

500
250
100
25
10

no reliable data

Source: UN *Statistical Yearbook* (1986 figures).

WORLD ENCYCLOPEDIA

NORTH AMERICA

Climate

North American climatic conditions range from tropical desert to Arctic. The central plains have a continental climate with cold winters and hot summers; temperatures range from below -15°C (5°F) in winter to above 30°C (86°F) in summer. Temperature ranges are less extreme on the west coast; the Gulf coast has a subtropical climate, subject to hurricanes and tornadoes moving north-east from the Caribbean. Most of the northern coast of Canada is ice-bound throughout the year.

Canadian-US trade

With nearly three-quarters of Canadian exports going to the USA and two-thirds of imports arriving from there, Canada and the USA have the largest trade flow between two countries in the world. Canadian manufacturers have become increasingly dependent on US demand since the first world war, to the extent that the Canadian economy generally mirrors recession and boom in its neighbour. The high degree of integration of the North American economy also dampens relative currency movements. The free-trade agreement between Canada and the USA, ratified in 1989, aims to eliminate all remaining tariffs by the year 2000.

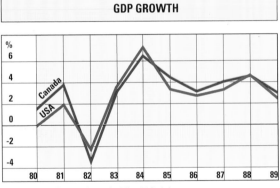

GDP GROWTH

Source: EIU *Country Report;* IMF *International Financial Statistics.*

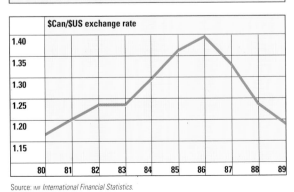

CURRENCY TRENDS

Source: IMF *International Financial Statistics.*

Alaska

The territory was purchased by the USA from Russia for $7.2m in 1867. This was regarded by many Americans as a waste of money until gold was discovered at Nome in 1889.

Alaska received territorial status in 1912 and became the 49th state of the union in 1959. Large oil reserves were discovered in 1968; production peaked in 1990.

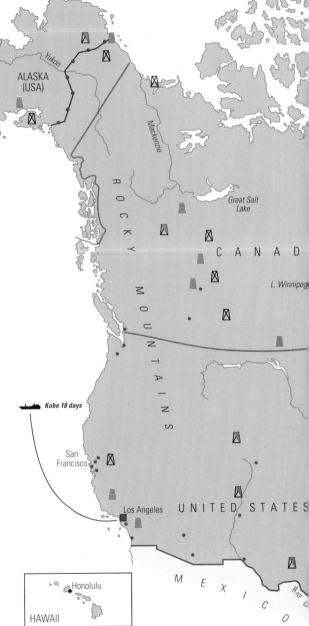

Hawaii

Hawaii became the 50th US state in 1959, some 60 years after it was formally annexed. Food processing, fishing and tourism are the main industries. Pearl Harbor remains an important naval base. Hopes for future growth rest on financial services and scientific research.

The Arctic

Since the discovery of oil and USS Nautilus's crossing under the ice in 1958, the Arctic has gained considerable economic and political significance. The world's smallest ocean has become both an arena and a possible cause of conflict, patrolled by Soviet and US ballistic missile submarines. Territorial claims by Canada to what the USA insists is an international waterway have led to disputes over the transit of US vessels. US economic interest in the region focuses on the large oil reserves, which would help to reduce dependence on foreign energy supplies; but there are logistical difficulties in production and mounting international concern for a fragile ecology.

The St Lawrence Seaway and the Great Lakes

The St Lawrence Seaway, a 3,500km (2,200-mile) system of canals, locks and dams, was built in the late 1950s to open up navigation between the Atlantic and the Great Lakes for ocean-going vessels. The seaway is closed by ice for about four months of the year; but from May to December it carries huge volumes of bulk commodities from the Great Lakes. The seaway was built jointly by the USA and Canada but US cargo is the main beneficiary of its subsidized tolls.

The Great Lakes – Superior, Michigan, Huron, Erie and Ontario – are the largest group of freshwater lakes in the world. They have a total surface area of 245,000 sq km (94,710 sq miles), of which about one-third is in Canada; only Lake Michigan is entirely within the USA.

St Pierre and Miquelon

These eight islands, 25km (16 miles) from the coast of Newfoundland, are a territorial collectivity of France. The population of 6,200 is dependent on fishing. Economic problems caused by disputes over territorial waters with Canada should be reduced following a compromise reached in 1990.

- ■ More than 5 million
- • 250,000 - 1 million

- ⊠ Major oil fields
- ▲ Major gas fields
- ⊠ Oil & gas fields
- ✈ Alaska oil pipeline

Oil and gas

US oil production is concentrated in four states, Texas, Louisiana, California and Alaska; the first two, along with Oklahoma, are also the leading natural gas producers. Dependence on imports is increasing. Low prices have made many small wells unprofitable and there have been few substantial new discoveries. Alaskan production, which came to the rescue in the late 1970s, is expected to go into a rapid decline in the 1990s.

In Canada, Alberta is the main oil-producing province and there are substantial reserves as yet unexploited in the Arctic. Canada is producing more energy than it needs and exports grew during the 1980s; a new gas pipeline from Canada to New York and New England opened in 1991.

THE AMERICAS

 # UNITED STATES OF AMERICA

Since the second world war, the United States has been the world's pre-eminent political and economic power. Abroad it used this pre-eminence not so much to project its own influence – that was left to private enterprise – as to contain communism's. After 45 years of cold war its rival is largely discredited. Economically the USA has increasingly seen its habits emulated across the world: free trade, free markets, technical inventiveness, low taxation and the use of debt. During this time America's self-confidence has been repeatedly shaken: by an unsuccessful war in Vietnam, by the turmoil of the struggle for black civil rights, by the near-impeachment of President Nixon, by the success of foreign imports and by the stagnation of productivity and the growth of debt. Despite these difficulties, it entered the 1990s having won a war, resumed economic growth after a brief recession and with its most popular president since polling began.

The US economy has always been firmly hitched to the star of free enterprise and a great deal of its vitality springs from the entrepreneurial spirit of the American people. Americans invented the transistor, the laser, the communications satellite, the personal computer and genetic engineering. For two decades after 1950, economic growth was steady and real incomes climbed. In the 1970s, however, productivity ceased to grow, inflation took off (reaching 18% as Ronald Reagan took office in 1981) and imports undermined many manufacturing sectors. A steep recession in 1981–82 left much of the manufacturing mid-west a ruined "Rust Belt". But inflation was tamed by firm control of the money supply and investment was stimulated by cuts in income tax and increases in defence spending. A swift boom resulted, with growth hitting 7% in 1983. But with federal taxes taking 18% of GNP and federal spending amounting to 22%, the government had to borrow ever more money to fund its annual deficits. This meant keeping interest rates high, which overvalued the dollar, encouraging imports and discouraging exports. By 1985 the USA was a net debtor; by 1986 its trade deficit was $145 billion.

George Bush came into office in 1989 refusing to raise taxes to balance the federal budget. By the second year of his administration, however, the economy had slowed and the budget deficit was climbing fast. In addition, taxpayers faced a huge bill for having insured a spree of property speculation by the lightly-regulated savings and loan industry during the 1980s. President Bush rethought his position. A divided and acrimonious budget debate in 1990 ended with a new five-year agreement to cut the deficit by spending cuts and taxes in equal measure. But despite a weakening dollar and easing of interest rates by the Federal Reserve, there was a brief recession in 1990–91.

WAGES AND PRICES

1983=100

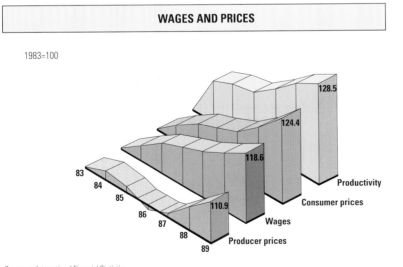

Source: IMF *International Financial Statistics*.

OFFICIAL NAME United States of America.
CAPITAL CITY Washington DC.
GEOGRAPHY The great plains that are the USA's agricultural – and in the north, industrial – heartland sweep down from the Canadian Shield to the Gulf of Mexico. To the east they are bordered by the old rocks of the Appalachians, to the west by the younger Rockies. South and east of the Appalachians is a coastal plain, often swampy, and with generally poor soils except around the Mississippi. West of the Rockies a series of intermontane plateaus and basins rises up into the coastal ranges of the Sierras and the Cascades. The USA also includes the mountainous Arctic region of Alaska and the volcanic Pacific islands of Hawaii. *Highest point* Mt McKinley 6,190 metres (20,300 feet). *Area* 9,372,570 sq km (3,618,700 sq miles).
PEOPLE *Population* 249m. *Density* 26.4 per sq km. *Ethnic groups* White 76.8%, Afro-Caribbean 11.7%, Hispanic 6.4%, Asian/Pacific 1.5%, Amerindian/Inuit/Aleut 0.6%.
RELIGION Protestant 33%, RC 22%, Jewish 2%.
LANGUAGE English. Also Spanish and other languages.
EDUCATION Free to age 18, generally compulsory for ages 7–16. Mostly organized at state and local level, with some federal funding. Enrolment in private schools is around 13% at primary level, 9.5% at secondary level.
CLIMATE Enormous variety, from sub-tropical in Florida – annual average temperature 29°C (84°F) to arctic in Alaska – annual average temperature -13°C (9°F). Most of the country is temperate, though the centre gets continental extremes. Average annual rainfall 735mm (29ins); large deserts in south-west and south.
CURRENCY US dollar.
PUBLIC HOLIDAYS (*some states only) Jan 1, 21, Feb 12*, 18, Mar 29*, Apr 1*, May 27, Jul 4, Sep 2, 9*, Oct 14, Nov 11, 28, Dec 25. Also many regional, state and city holidays.
GOVERNMENT Federal republic. There are 50 states and 1 federal district (Columbia), all internally self-governing; the federal government is responsible for defence, foreign affairs, internal security, the posts and the coinage. The chief executive is the president, elected for a 4-year term by a college elected by direct vote in each state. He appoints the rest of the executive, subject to Senate approval. The legislative Congress has 2 elected houses: the Senate has 2 members for each state elected for a 6-year term, with elections for a third of the seats held every 2 years; the 435 members of the House of Representatives are elected for 2-year terms. The judiciary is headed by the Supreme Court, which can veto legislation and overturn executive decisions on constitutional grounds. The written constitution, drawn up in 1787, is the oldest in existence. Subsequent amendents include 10 made in 1791 and known as the Bill of Rights.

IMPORTS AND EXPORTS

☐ Canada
☐ Japan

☐ Mexico
☐ W. Germany

☐ UK
☐ Taiwan

☐ Other

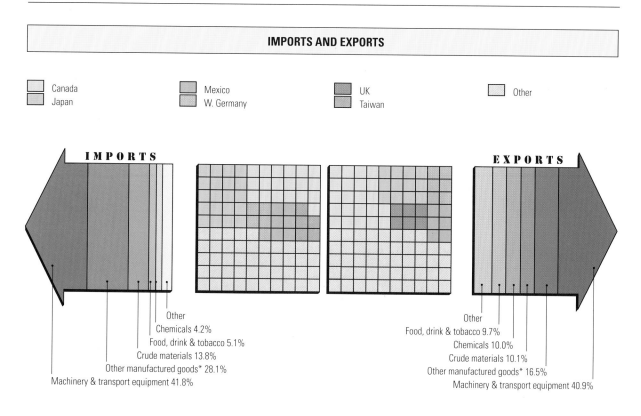

IMPORTS

EXPORTS

Other
Chemicals 4.2%
Food, drink & tobacco 5.1%
Crude materials 13.8%
Other manufactured goods* 28.1%
Machinery & transport equipment 41.8%

Other
Food, drink & tobacco 9.7%
Chemicals 10.0%
Crude materials 10.1%
Other manufactured goods* 16.5%
Machinery & transport equipment 40.9%

* Excluding machinery, transport equipment & chemicals

Source: EIU *Country Report* (1989 figures).

WORK FORCE

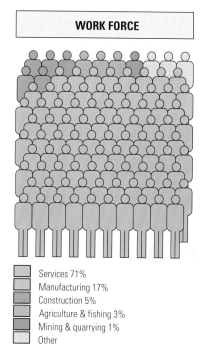

☐ Services 71%
☐ Manufacturing 17%
☐ Construction 5%
☐ Agriculture & fishing 3%
☐ Mining & quarrying 1%
☐ Other

Source: EIU *Country Profile* (1989 figures).

BALANCE OF PAYMENTS

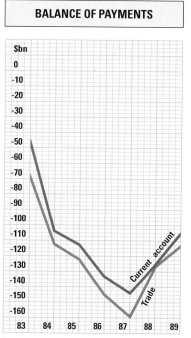

$bn

Current account

Trade

Source: IMF *International Financial Statistics.*

FEDERAL BUDGET DEFICIT

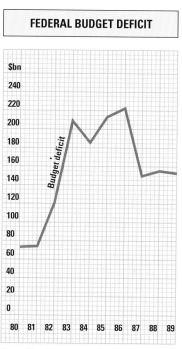

$bn

Budget deficit

Source: Office of Management and Budget
Budget of the United States Government.

THE AMERICAS

POPULATION - THE BIG SEVEN

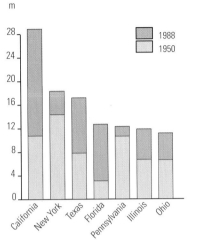

m

Legend: 1988, 1950

Source: *Statistical Abstract of the United States* (1986 figures).

Seven states in the USA have a population of more than 10m. They dominate the winner-takes-all presidential election: a candidate who takes the Big Seven would be more than two-thirds of the way to victory. In evenly-balanced presidential elections the seven are usually split; the Sun Belt leaning towards the Republicans and the Rust Belt towards the Democrats. The population growth of the Sun Belt has increased its electoral importance; during the 1980s, the population of Florida overtook Ohio, Illinois and Pennsylvania, and Texas will soon surpass New York. The Department of Commerce projects that Los Angeles will have become the largest city in the USA by the year 2000.

THE MELTING POT

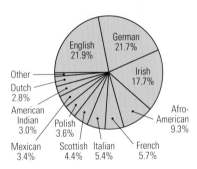

Source: *Statistical Abstract of the United States* (1980 figures).

Statistically, the inhabitants of the USA are demonstrably heterogeneous: no ethnic group accounts for much more than a fifth of the total. As the identities of the various European communities become blurred, continuing immigration of Central Americans and Asians sustains ethnic variety. The official breakdown under-represents these groups because of the large numbers of illegal immigrants; there are an estimated 5m Mexicans living illegally in the USA.

The centre of gravity of America, economic and demographic, continues to move west and south. The 1990 census found that Florida, Arizona and Nevada were the fastest-growing states, while California's population had jumped by more than a quarter in a decade to nearly 30m and Texas's had almost equalled New York's. In the 1980s more immigrants (especially Hispanics and Asians) came to the USA than in any decade since the second world war. By the year 2000, whites will be in a minority in California.

The degeneration of many inner cities is America's most serious social problem. The arrival of plentiful cheap "crack" cocaine triggered drug wars that took murder rates to record levels in many cities. In inner cities education standards have deteriorated, racial tension increased and job opportunities moved away to the suburbs. The gap between rich and poor has grown.

Even so, US society and politics continue to display considerable stability. At the root of the national consciousness is a civic orthodoxy that places personal liberty above the claims of authority, awards the right of privacy to individuals but denies it to bureaucracy, and encourages suspicion of all who exercise power. Americans have made astute use of the governmental checks and balances laid down by the constitution by habitually electing a president from one party while giving control of Congress to the other.

In both world wars it was the entry of the USA that assured victory for the

Rust Belt to Sun Belt

The shift in the US economy from manufacturing to services over the past 30 years has been accompanied by a movement of output and workers from the old industrial heartland, the northern "Rust Belt" states, to the booming south and west, the "Sun Belt".

The proportion of America's population living in the Rust Belt has fallen from 47% to 39% since 1970. Arizona, Nevada and Florida have had the fastest-growing populations over the past 20 years; the populations of West Virginia, Iowa and Michigan have declined.

Immigration

The USA practised an open-door policy on immigration from independence until the 1960s. During the 1970s immigration, estimated at 500,000 a year, accounted for around 20% of the population growth, declining to 10% throughout the 1980s. The official figures give no indication of illegal immigration, mostly across the Mexican border.

Drugs

American politicians regard the war against drugs as one of the most important problems they face. About 30m Americans are thought to take an illegal drug regularly. About 2m are thought to be addicts: about a quarter to heroin, the rest to cocaine. Drug-related deaths are on the increase, but, at about 10,000 a year, still fall short of deaths linked to the use of tobacco (390,000) or alcohol (100,000). The cost of America's drug habit is estimated at anywhere from $50 billion to $100 billion a year. Concern is focused on the growing availability and low price of cocaine – despite all efforts at control – and the crime and violence associated with it. Recently the USA has subsidized campaigns, especially in South America, to control production.

Agriculture

The US agricultural sector is a victim of its own success. It is immensely productive; of the world's exports, it provides a third of the wheat and three-quarters of the maize and soybeans, at prices with which most other producers cannot fairly compete. Widespread international agricultural protectionism, the USA's greatest trade grievance, constrains the country's capacity to export more. The government, at substantial cost and against its *laissez-faire* instincts, has mitigated the consequences through price support and subsidies, sustained by production quotas. But its efforts to expand the overseas market for US produce have not had significant effect, and so improvements in productivity have manifested themselves in a shrinking workforce and a declining share of GDP – just over 2% in the late 1980s – rather than in increased output.

Smaller farmers have taken the brunt of the contraction, but larger businesses have also suffered. Many borrowed heavily in the late 1970s and early 1980s on the security of property which fell in value throughout the 1980s; the value of an average acre of farmland dropped by 33.4% between 1982–87. Land prices recovered slightly in the late 1980s, however, and debt is showing a decline.

Rust Belt
Sun Belt

■ More than 1 million
• 250,000 - 1 million

The Mississippi

The Mississippi and its major tributaries, the Missouri and Ohio, form the largest river system in the USA. The Missouri is the country's longest river; 3,725km (2,330 miles) from its source in Montana to its confluence with the Mississippi north of St Louis. The Mississippi itself is the second longest, flowing for 1,884km (1,178 miles) from Lake Itasca in Minnesota to the Gulf of Mexico. The rivers form a major transport artery: the Mississippi is navigable as far as Minneapolis, the Ohio for its entire length from Pittsburgh to Cairo, Illinois, and the Missouri as far as Fort Benton, Montana.

THE AMERICAS

allies, and since 1945 the country has assumed the role of defender of the free world. After the experience of Vietnam, US presidents were reluctant to intervene directly in foreign wars, and in the 1980s the "Reagan doctrine" instead emphasized the arming and support of anti-communist guerrillas, especially in Nicaragua and Afghanistan. Meanwhile, following the Iranian revolution, the holding of hostages in Tehran and Beirut and an upsurge in anti-American Islamic terrorism, the United States grew gradually more embroiled in confronting militant regimes. In 1991 this culminated in the quick and overwhelming destruction of Iraq's forces after their invasion of Kuwait, an event which marked both the return of US forces to direct foreign intervention on a large scale and the return of American support for the United Nations and alliance-building, rather than unilateralist leadership.

The USA entered the 1990s having to adjust to a new world order. The Soviet Union had ceased to be an ideological rival. Japan, though, had become an increasingly effective technological competitor and America's main creditor. The European Community, meanwhile, found itself more and more at odds with America over trade policy. But Americans have never been a people with a tendency to live in the past. They are less concerned with their reduced pre-eminence than with the new challenges and opportunities that lie ahead.

GNP BY ORIGIN

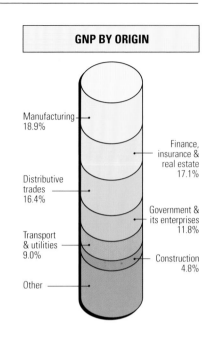

Manufacturing 18.9%

Finance, insurance & real estate 17.1%

Distributive trades 16.4%

Government & its enterprises 11.8%

Transport & utilities 9.0%

Construction 4.8%

Other

INCOME DISTRIBUTION

Average income of families with children
% change in real terms, 1979 - 1987

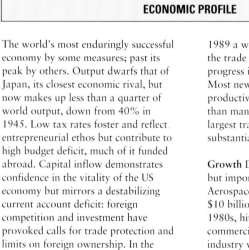

Richest fifth

Next richest fifth

Middle fifth

Second poorest fifth

Poorest fifth

Source: *The Economist*.

COMPONENTS OF GNP

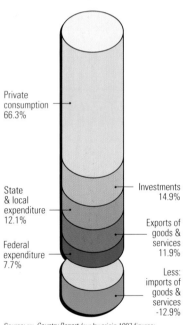

Private consumption 66.3%

State & local expenditure 12.1%

Investments 14.9%

Federal expenditure 7.7%

Exports of goods & services 11.9%

Less: imports of goods & services -12.9%

Source: EIU *Country Report* (GNP by origin 1987 figures; Components of GNP 1989 figures).

ECONOMIC PROFILE

The world's most enduringly successful economy by some measures; past its peak by others. Output dwarfs that of Japan, its closest economic rival, but now makes up less than a quarter of world output, down from 40% in 1945. Low tax rates foster and reflect entrepreneurial ethos but contribute to high budget deficit, much of it funded abroad. Capital inflow demonstrates confidence in the vitality of the US economy but mirrors a destabilizing current account deficit: foreign competition and investment have provoked calls for trade protection and limits on foreign ownership. In the 1980s tax reductions, tight monetary policy, high interest rates and an overvalued dollar caused inflation to fall and the economy to boom, and pushed budget, trade and current account deficits to record levels. After

1989 a weakening dollar led to a fall in the trade gap but there has been little progress in reducing the budget deficit. Most new jobs in low-wage, low-productivity service industries rather than manufacturing, which is the largest tradable sector but in substantial deficit and relative decline.

Growth Dynamic computer industry, but imports rising faster than exports. Aerospace sector, which produced a $10 billion-plus trade surplus in the 1980s, hit by a slump in demand for commercial aircraft. Pharmaceutical industry very profitable.

Problems Agricultural production hit by falling world demand. Import dependence on oil has been rising. Automobile industry constrained by saturated market.

CANADA

The world's second largest country, Canada has a lower population density than virtually any other nation. Almost 90% of the country is uninhabited and 85% of the population lives within 100 miles of the US border. Proximity to the vast US market and a wealth of natural resources have contributed greatly to Canada's prosperity. Yet despite its close links with the USA, Canada has assiduously maintained a separate political and cultural identity, retaining strong ties with other Commonwealth countries and the francophone world.

Canada's vastness divides the country into a string of economic islands linked by excellent transport services and centralized media. The province of Ontario has the largest manufacturing base and agricultural sector and contributes about 40% of GNP. Toronto, its capital, is the country's business and financial centre. By the late 1980s the economy appeared to have recovered well from a sharp downturn at the start of the decade. However, by 1990 tight monetary policies had helped push the economy back into recession, with little sign of a quick or strong recovery.

Concern about the implications of the free-trade agreement with the USA, which was highly controversial and formed the centrepiece of the 1988 election debate, has recently been overshadowed by worries over the future of the federal system. The 1980s saw considerable wrangling over constitutional reform. Canada's ten provinces have considerable autonomy and it was difficult for the federal government to persuade them to relinquish some of their independence and agree to the 1982 Constitution Act. Francophone Québec never did accept the act and it was hoped that the Meech Lake accord would finally lure Québec back into the constitutional fold by acknowledging it as a "distinct society".

OFFICIAL NAME Canada.

CAPITAL CITY Ottawa.

GEOGRAPHY The second largest country in the world. Half its area is the central Canadian Shield, a glaciated platform of ancient rock centred on Hudson Bay which is largely covered by lakes and forests. Only 8% of Canada is suitable for cultivation. There are three lowland zones: the sparsely populated western plains, the ice-covered Arctic plains, and the area around the Great Lakes and the St Lawrence where most of the population live. In the far west are the Cordillera, parallel mountain ranges whose westernmost outriders make up Vancouver, and the Queen Charlotte Islands. The Appalachians run from Quebec through the Gaspé peninsula to Newfoundland. *Highest point* Mt Logan 6,050 metres (19,850 feet). *Area* 9,976,139 sq km (3,851,810 sq miles).

PEOPLE *Population* 27m. *Ethnic groups* UK/Irish 44%, French 27%, German 5%, Italian 3%, Ukrainian 2%, Amerindian/Inuit 2%, Dutch 2%, Chinese 1%, Scandinavian 1%, Jewish 1%, Polish 1%.

RELIGION Christian 90% (RC 47%, Protestant 41%, other 2%), Jewish 1%.

LANGUAGE English and French.

EDUCATION Free and compulsory; ages vary by province, though 85% of ages 12–17 attend secondary school.

CLIMATE Continental: fairly dry inland, monthly average temperature range -17–19°C (1–66°F) in the prairies; very cold in north. Pacific coast mild and wet.

CURRENCY Canadian dollar.

PUBLIC HOLIDAYS Jan 1, 20, Mar 8, Good Fri, Easter Mon, Jun 1, Jul 5, Sep 12, Dec 25.

GOVERNMENT Parliamentary and federal monarchy. There are 10 provinces, each with its own legislature, and 2 territories. The British monarch, represented by the governor-general, is head of state. The legislature has a 112-member Senate nominated by the provinces and the prime minister and a 295-seat House of Commons elected from single-member constituencies for a term of up to 5 years. Executive power is held by a prime minister and cabinet drawn from the majority party in the Commons.

Québec

Separatism in French-speaking Québec first peaked in the 1970s and the Meech Lake accord of 1987 recognized Québec as a "distinct society". But the failure of some other provinces to ratify it led to renewed demands for autonomy.

The Inuit

About 14,500 Inuit, or Eskimos, live in the Canadian Arctic. In 1974 they demanded the creation of an autonomous state, Nunavut, consisting of part of the mainland of the Northwest Territories and several Arctic islands, including Baffin Island, which was expected to be completed in 1991.

The Canadian provinces

Canada's ten provinces have responsibility for most social services, labour matters and the civil law. However, the failure of some states to ratify the 1987 Meech Lake accord, and the resurgence of Québecois demands for separation has led to a distinct possibility the federal structure could collapse before the end of the century.

More than 1 million
250,000 - 1 million
100,000 - 250,000

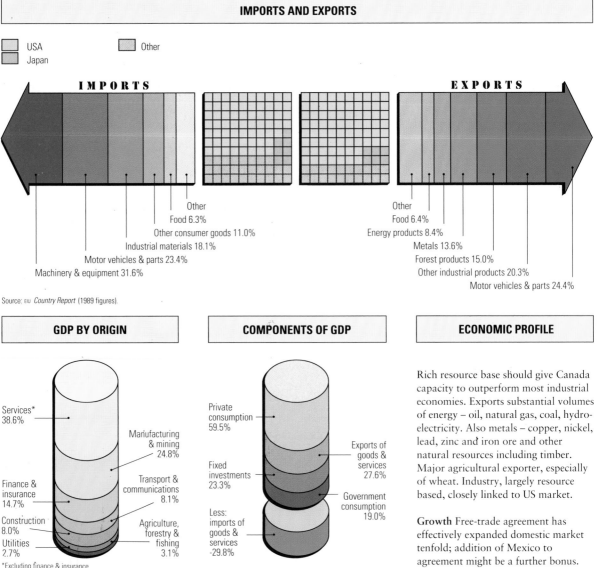

IMPORTS AND EXPORTS

USA
Japan
Other

IMPORTS

EXPORTS

Other
Food 6.3%
Other consumer goods 11.0%
Industrial materials 18.1%
Motor vehicles & parts 23.4%
Machinery & equipment 31.6%

Other
Food 6.4%
Energy products 8.4%
Metals 13.6%
Forest products 15.0%
Other industrial products 20.3%
Motor vehicles & parts 24.4%

Source: EIU *Country Report* (1989 figures).

GDP BY ORIGIN

Services*
38.6%

Manufacturing
& mining
24.8%

Finance &
insurance
14.7%

Transport &
communications
8.1%

Construction
8.0%

Agriculture,
forestry &
fishing
3.1%

Utilities
2.7%

*Excluding finance & insurance

Source: EIU *Country Report* (1989 figures).

COMPONENTS OF GDP

Private
consumption
59.5%

Exports of
goods &
services
27.6%

Fixed
investments
23.3%

Government
consumption
19.0%

Less:
imports of
goods &
services
-29.8%

ECONOMIC PROFILE

Rich resource base should give Canada capacity to outperform most industrial economies. Exports substantial volumes of energy – oil, natural gas, coal, hydro-electricity. Also metals – copper, nickel, lead, zinc and iron ore and other natural resources including timber. Major agricultural exporter, especially of wheat. Industry, largely resource based, closely linked to US market.

Growth Free-trade agreement has effectively expanded domestic market tenfold; addition of Mexico to agreement might be a further bonus. Sales of all forms of energy to USA are expanding rapidly. Sales of metal products also strong.

Problems Worldwide surpluses have hit agriculture. Industry faces problems competing in high-technology sectors, particularly electronics. Persistent deficit in invisible trade, including investment income, travel and financial services. Spending cutbacks to reduce a still-large budget deficit have hurt some sectors. A tight monetary policy, initially to control inflation, helped push the economy into recession and, through bolstering the value of the Canadian dollar, caused some problems for exporters.

The collapse of the accord in mid-1989 after the refusal of several other provinces to ratify it provoked a resurgence of Québecois separatism. Many Canadians became more concerned about the survival of Canada as a nation state, than about preserving its particular cultural identity.

Canadian politics has traditionally been dominated by the left-of-centre Liberals and the right-leaning Progressive Conservatives (PCP). After two decades in power the Liberals were ousted in 1984 by the PCP under Brian Mulroney. His first term was affected by ministerial scandals and the government was accused of being indecisive. His second started in 1988 on a more confident note but despite (or perhaps because of) radical tax reforms and substantial deregulation of the economy Mr Mulroney's popularity had fallen to a record low by the end of the decade, as the traditional Canadian political scene began to fragment . Labour-PCP dominance was under challenge in many areas, notably by the left-of-centre New Democrats who were the surprise victors of the 1990 Ontario provincial elections. Elsewhere Québec separatism has been mirrored by the rise of the strongly anglophone Reform Party.

MEXICO

"So far from God and so close to the United States": Mexico, the world's largest Spanish-speaking country, sits uneasily in the shadow of its powerful neighbour. The first century after independence in 1810 was one of political instability culminating in the bitter revolution of 1910–20, in which 500,000 people died. 1929 ushered in over 60 years of stability under the Partido Revolucionario Institucional (PRI). The nationalizations and social reforms of the 1930s (especially land reform) and the four decades of economic growth which followed helped ensure the PRI's dominance of power.

That stability is now showing signs of stress. Carlos Salinas de Gortari won the 1988 presidential elections only narrowly, amid allegations of fraud and after a bitter contest. As a result he was not able to rely on the almost unquestioning support of Congress afforded to his predecessors. Opposition has been spearheaded by Cuauhtémoc Cárdenas, son of the reforming president of the 1930s, who broke with the PRI to contest the elections with his Frente Democrático Nacional (FDN).

The government has dominated the economy since oil was nationalized in 1938. Efforts to reduce economic inequality by using the revenues from vast new oil discoveries in the early 1970s failed. Growth slowed and inflationary and balance of payments strains became intolerable. In 1982, Mexico gave the world the term "debt crisis" when it admitted that it could no longer service its debt of more than $100 billion.

OFFICIAL NAME United Mexican States.
CAPITAL CITY Mexico City.
GEOGRAPHY Most of Mexico is highland, a complex of mountains, some volcanic, and plateaus criss-crossed by valleys and canyons. The only extensive lowlands are the long, narrow, desert peninsula of Baja California and the limestone Yucatán Peninsula. *Highest point* Orizaba 5,700 metres (18,700 feet). *Area* 1,972,547 sq km (761,610 sq miles).
PEOPLE *Population* 80.5m. *Density* 41 per sq km. *Ethnic groups* Mestizo 55%, Amerindian 30%, European 15%.
RELIGION RC 93%, Protestant 3%.
LANGUAGE Spanish. Also some Amerindian dialects.
EDUCATION Free to age 18; compulsory for ages 6–12. There are 82 universities. The government has invested heavily in drives to improve adult literacy.
CLIMATE Temperate in the north and central highlands, with an average temperature of 15°C (59°F), although winters can be severe; tropical in the south and the coastal lowlands, with an annual average temperature of 18°C (64°F). Extensive deserts in the north and west.
CURRENCY Mexican peso.
PUBLIC HOLIDAYS Jan 1, Feb 5, Mar 21, Good Fri–Easter Mon, May 1, 5, Sep 1, 16, Oct 12, Nov 2, 20, Dec 12, 24–25.
GOVERNMENT Federal republic. There are 31 states, each with its own governor and legislature, and a federal district. Both houses of the National Congress are directly elected: the 64 members of the Senate – 2 from each confederation member – for 6 years, and the 500-member Chamber of Deputies for 3 years. 300 deputies come from single-member constituencies, the remainder from PR lists.

Unemployment

The unemployment rate in 1990 was estimated at around 13.5% compared with 18.5% in 1988; but only workers covered by the state-affiliated trade unions enjoy full benefit and under-employment generally is estimated at 38%.

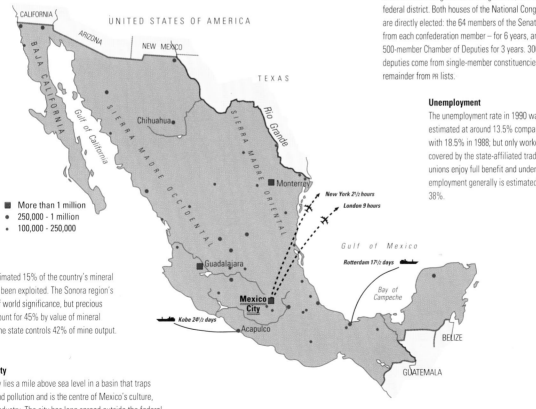

More than 1 million
250,000 - 1 million
100,000 - 250,000

Minerals

Only an estimated 15% of the country's mineral wealth has been exploited. The Sonora region's copper is of world significance, but precious metals account for 45% by value of mineral reserves. The state controls 42% of mine output.

Mexico City

Mexico City lies a mile above sea level in a basin that traps rising air and pollution and is the centre of Mexico's culture, trade and industry. The city has long spread outside the federal district and 19.4m people live in the metropolitan area, creating horrendous problems of overcrowding, failing water supply, and inadequate drainage and sewage disposal.

Oil

The largest oil-producing region is the Gulf of Campeche; 65% of Mexico's oil output comes from here.

THE AMERICAS

For five years the government pursued a conventional course of successive austerity programmes, but with little initial sign of success; growth averaged no more than 0.1%. Recovery was not helped by the mixed response to some of the government's efforts to deal with the country's debt problems, notably the debt equity swap and debt-for-bond auction schemes of 1987 and 1988. More successful rescheduling arrangements were hammered out in 1989, with both sides under pressure from the USA which had earlier unveiled the Brady plan for debt relief with Mexico specifically in mind. For geopolitical reasons the USA has a greater commitment to resolving Mexico's debt crisis than any other.

The Salinas government committed itself to liberalizing the economy, and began pressing ahead with privatization. The economic solidarity pact with business and unions introduced in December 1987 and the pact for stability and growth, combined with measures to cut the public sector deficit, were successful in reducing inflation from 159% in 1987 to 29% by late 1990. There has also been a recovery in GDP growth, which rose from 1.4% in 1988 to an estimated 3.3% in 1990. Internationally the Salinas government's most daring initiative was the pursuit of a free-trade area with the USA and Canada. However, while economic liberalization suggested good prospects for sustained growth and low inflation, doubts remained over President Salinas's commitment to tackling electoral fraud and easing the PRI's stranglehold over Mexican politics in the run-up to the 1994 elections.

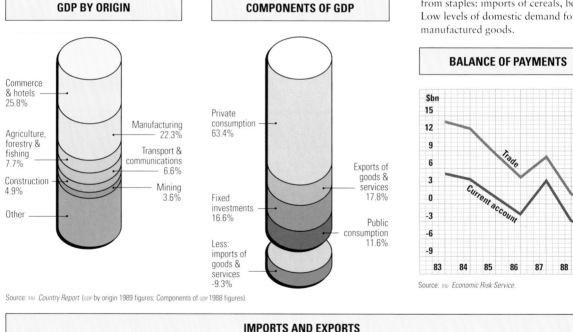

GDP BY ORIGIN

Commerce & hotels 25.8%
Manufacturing 22.3%
Agriculture, forestry & fishing 7.7%
Transport & communications 6.6%
Construction 4.9%
Mining 3.6%
Other

COMPONENTS OF GDP

Private consumption 63.4%
Exports of goods & services 17.8%
Fixed investments 16.6%
Public consumption 11.6%
Less: imports of goods & services -9.3%

Source: EIU *Country Report* (GDP by origin 1989 figures; Components of GDP 1988 figures).

BALANCE OF PAYMENTS

$bn — Trade, Current account — 83 84 85 86 87 88 89

Source: EIU *Economic Risk Service*.

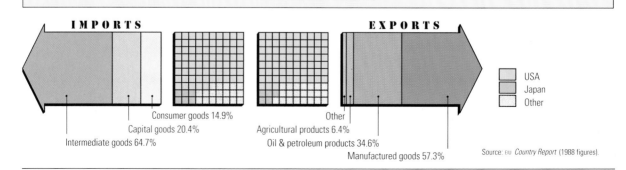

IMPORTS AND EXPORTS

IMPORTS

Consumer goods 14.9%
Capital goods 20.4%
Intermediate goods 64.7%

EXPORTS

Other
Agricultural products 6.4%
Oil & petroleum products 34.6%
Manufactured goods 57.3%

USA
Japan
Other

Source: EIU *Country Report* (1988 figures).

CENTRAL AMERICA

Independent from Spain since 1821, Central America split into five separate states more than a century ago. Many Central Americans, however, see economic and political arguments for reunification. The last serious attempt to bring the states together was the Central American Common Market (CACM) set up in 1961. This increased intra-regional trade threefold in seven years, but fell apart in 1969. Attempts are now being made to revive it with outside assistance, notably from the EC. The major obstacle to unification as a single market is that the region's economies tend to be competitive rather than complementary. All remain backward, linked too closely for comfort to the fortunes of a single export crop such as coffee, bananas or sugar. Growth has been achieved through new export crops, notably cotton, but development remains threatened by political instability and periodic outbursts of violence in an area also notoriously prone to natural disasters.

Guatemala

Guerrilla warfare has been endemic in parts of the country since the 1960s. From late 1970s the army pillaged traditional Indian settlements in the north-west, touching off a virtual race war and driving thousands of refugees into southern Mexico. The rate of killing increased again in 1987: in 1990 the USA cut off military aid because of human rights violations.

Honduras/Nicaragua

"Contras" – 12,000-strong US-backed Nicaraguan Democratic Force – operated covertly across the Honduran border into Nicaragua in the 1980s. With the electoral defeat of the Sandinist government in February 1990, they signed a peace agreement with the pro-US government of Violeta Chamorro.

El Salvador

The Farabundo Marti National Liberation Front (FMLN), has fought successive governments since 1980. Nicaraguan aid largely dried up after 1981 and US-backed government troops forced a stalemate using so-called "low-intensity" strategy. Talks, opened in 1983, were repeatedly postponed but later resumed with UN mediation; death squads remain active.

New York 8 hours

London 18 hours

Rotterdam 17 days

Panama Canal

Kobe 26 days

MEXICO

Belmopan

BELIZE

GUATEMALA

Guatemala

HONDURAS

Tegucigalpa

San Salvador

EL SALVADOR

NICARAGUA

Managua

COSTA RICA

San José

■ More than 1 million
● 250,000 - 1 million
• 100,000 - 250,000

PANAMA

Panama

COLOMBIA

Panama

Because of its canal and US military bases, Panama is at the centre of US strategic interests in the Caribbean basin, as was clear from the 1989 US invasion which overthrew General Manuel Noriega. Although the USA's power in the region would seem unchallenged, Central America dominated the concerns of its policy-makers during the 1980s because of growing fears that Cuba, as the Soviet Union's representative, was exploiting latent unrest to gain a strategic advantage. The collapse of the Soviet bloc and the defeat of Nicaragua's Sandinists have rendered such an analysis largely superfluous. The Panamanian flag flies from the masts of over 11% of the world's merchant fleet – only Liberia has more shipping tonnage registered.

THE AMERICAS

GDP GROWTH

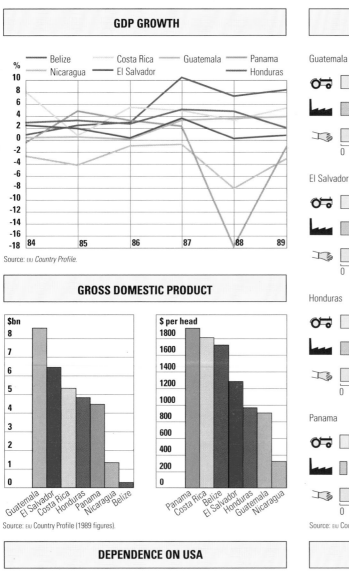

Belize — Costa Rica — Guatemala — Panama
Nicaragua — El Salvador — Honduras

Source: EIU *Country Profile*.

GROSS DOMESTIC PRODUCT

$bn

Guatemala, El Salvador, Costa Rica, Honduras, Panama, Nicaragua, Belize

$ per head

Panama, Costa Rica, Belize, El Salvador, Honduras, Guatemala, Nicaragua

Source: EIU Country Profile (1989 figures).

GDP BY ORIGIN

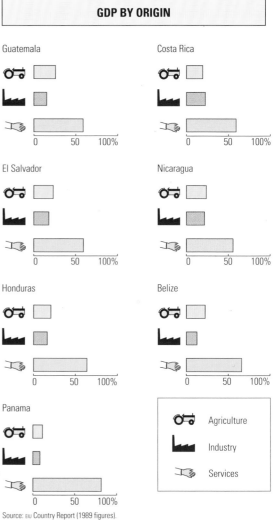

Guatemala

Costa Rica

El Salvador

Nicaragua

Honduras

Belize

Panama

Agriculture
Industry
Services

Source: EIU Country Report (1989 figures).

DEPENDENCE ON USA

imports from USA as % of total   exports to USA as % of total

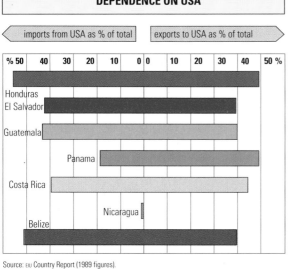

% 50 40 30 20 10 0 0 10 20 30 40 50 %

Honduras
El Salvador
Guatemala
Panama
Costa Rica
Nicaragua
Belize

Source: EIU Country Report (1989 figures).

TOTAL EXTERNAL DEBT

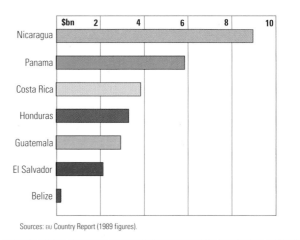

$bn 2 4 6 8 10

Nicaragua
Panama
Costa Rica
Honduras
Guatemala
El Salvador
Belize

Sources: EIU Country Report (1989 figures).

GUATEMALA

Guatemala, the largest economy in Central America, is torn by bitter and seemingly irreconcilable tensions. Once the centre of a major civilization, it remains primarily an Indian society, with languages such as Quiché, Man and Cakchiquel widely spoken. However, economic wealth is concentrated in the hands of large landowners who dominate export crop production in the fertile lowlands. The Indians have been steadily forced back into the less productive uplands and land reform, frustrated in the 1950s by a US-inspired coup, remains a bitter issue. The start of oil production in 1979 only exacerbated the struggle over land rights in the north-west.

Indians were also the main victims of the military's savage counter-insurgency campaign against left-wing guerrillas in the early 1980s. Deliberate, indiscriminate killings left thousands dead and only temporarily repressed the guerrillas. The election in 1985 of a moderate Christian Democrat president, Vinicio Cerezo Arévalo, ostensibly brought a return of democracy after 30 years of military rule. However, the armed forces remained the most powerful force in Guatemala, blocking vital reforms in such areas as taxation and land rights, and in 1991 electors shifted back to the right with the victory of conservative Jorge Serrano in the presidential poll.

Guatemala still depends to an unhealthy degree on exports of primary agricultural products; coffee accounts for over a third of foreign exchange earnings. Economic diversification was given a boost in the late 1970s when the country became an oil exporter. However, the oil is of poor quality and has not fulfilled its initial potential. Among newer crops, cotton has been the most successful.

Guatemala's ability to export these surpluses would benefit from a settlement of the territorial dispute with Belize, which has hampered access to the Caribbean. After the Serrano government took office there were clear signs that this was in prospect.

OFFICIAL NAME Republic of Guatemala.
CAPITAL CITY Guatemala City.
GEOGRAPHY Most of the population lives in the central highlands. To the north is the sparsely populated limestone tableland of the Petén and in the south there is a fertile region of alluvial and volcanic soils. *Highest point* Tajumulco 4,220 metres (13,850 feet). *Area* 108,889 sq km (42,040 sq miles).
PEOPLE *Population* 8.6m. *Density* 80 per sq km. *Ethnic groups* Amerindian 50%, Mestizo 42%, European 4%.
RELIGION Christian 100% (RC 80%).
LANGUAGE Spanish. Also Amerindian languages.
EDUCATION Free for ages 7–14, compulsory in urban areas only. There are 5 universities.
CURRENCY Quetzal.
CLIMATE Sub-tropical in the lowlands, with an average annual temperature of 28°C (82°F); milder – 20°C (68°F) – in the highlands. The rainy season is May–Nov, except on Caribbean coast where it falls year-round.
PUBLIC HOLIDAYS Jan 1, 6, Good Fri–Easter Mon, May 1, Jun 30, Aug 15, Sep 15, Oct 12, 20, Nov 1, Dec 24–25, 31.
GOVERNMENT The head of state is a president, elected for 5 years, who shares executive power with a cabinet appointed from the 100 members of the legislative Congress. Congress members are also elected for a 5-year term, 75 of them from single constituencies, the rest by PR.

BELIZE

A former British colony, independent since 1981, Belize is a parliamentary democracy which has been dominated for most of the past three decades by its prime minister, George Price. The UK has maintained a small military presence since independence but this is due to be replaced by a US-trained national defence force. Settlement of a long-standing dispute with neighbouring Guatemala, which has laid claim to the entire Belizean territory, is also in prospect.

The country suffered badly in the early 1980s from heavy dependence on sugar, which replaced timber and bananas as the economic mainstay. Efforts at diversification have encouraged a small but expanding industrial base, founded primarily on agri-processing – especially of citrus fruits – but with a growing emphasis on other light industries such as shoes and textiles. Plans by Coca-Cola to develop large areas of land to supply the US market with fruit concentrates caused a national debate about foreign domination and the environment, and in 1987 the company withdrew from the project.

Notwithstanding this the citrus industry has continued to expand. There has also been growing investment in tourism, much of it by overseas interests, adding to continuing fears about foreign influence over the economy. By 1990, however, there were signs that the investment boom, which helped push GDP growth to over 8% a year in the late 1980s, was waning. And with the future of preferential markets in the EC and United States for vital agricultural exports looking increasingly uncertain, the outlook for the economy was problematic.

OFFICIAL NAME Belize.
CAPITAL CITY Belmopan.
GEOGRAPHY Mostly jungle; the south is dominated by the Maya Mountains, an ancient plateau with deep-cut valleys; the north is lowland, much of it swamp. *Highest point* Victoria Peak 1,222 metres (3,680 feet). *Area* 22,963 sq km (8,870 sq miles).
PEOPLE *Population* 180,000. *Density* 8 per sq km. *Ethnic groups* Creole 40%, Mestizo 33%, Garifuna 8%, Maya 7%, European 4%, Ketchi 3%, East Indian 2%.
RELIGION RC 62%, Protestant 18%.
LANGUAGE English 56%, Spanish 28%, Carib 6%, Maya 5%.
EDUCATION Free for ages 6–19, compulsory to age 14.
CLIMATE Sub-tropical. Dry season Feb–May, wet season Jun–Nov. Annual rainfall in the south is 1,290mm (51ins), three times as much as in the north.
CURRENCY Belizean dollar.
PUBLIC HOLIDAYS Jan 1, 1st Mon in Mar, Good Fri–Easter Mon, May 1, Mon after Jun 7, Sep 10, 21, Oct 12, Nov 19, Dec 25–26.
GOVERNMENT Parliamentary democracy. The head of state is the British monarch, represented by a governor-general. Executive power is held by the prime minister and cabinet drawn from the majority party in the 28-member House of Representatives.

HONDURAS

Independent since 1838, Honduras is a poor, sparsely populated country which gained strategic significance during the 1980s by playing host to the US-backed "contra" rebels in their war against Nicaragua's revolutionary Sandanist government. The Honduran army also collaborated, albeit more reluctantly, with US efforts to defeat left-wing rebels in El Salvador. Many of the rebel strongholds were in border areas disputed by the two countries. The territorial dispute led to a ten-day war in 1969 and has yet to be fully resolved.

The army remains extremely influential even though formal electoral democracy was restored in 1981. The economy is one of the least developed in Latin America and is characterized by sharp income inequalities and entrenched business and union interests. During the 1980s Honduras became increasingly dependent on US aid: a more or less direct payment for hosting the contras. Little attempt was made at reform until the 1989 election of President Rafael Leonardo Callejas who began an IMF-backed programme aimed at overcoming severe balance of payments and budgetary crises and reorienting the economy to export-led growth. A priority is to reduce dependence on bananas and coffee, which account for 60% of export earnings. Banana production is concentrated on the north coast and dominated by two US food conglomerates. Coffee production began in the 1950s and expanded rapidly to become the second largest export, although Honduras remains a small producer compared with its central American neighbours.

OFFICIAL NAME Republic of Honduras.
CAPITAL CITY Tegucigalpa.
GEOGRAPHY 70% of the population lives in the central highlands where there are sheltered valleys with fertile soils. The east of the country is thickly forested. There are extensive alluvial plains to the north, and good harbours on the long Caribbean coast. *Area* 112,088 sq km (43,280 sq miles).
PEOPLE *Population* 4.9m. *Density* 44 per sq km. *Ethnic groups* Mestizo 90%, others (Amerindians, Europeans, Africans) 10% .
RELIGION RC 96%, Protestant 3%.
LANGUAGE Spanish. Also Indian dialects.
EDUCATION Free to age 18, compulsory for ages 7–13. There are 3 universities.
CLIMATE Tropical on the coast but more moderate inland. Rainy season May–Nov.
CURRENCY Lempira.
PUBLIC HOLIDAYS Jan 1, Maundy Thu–Easter Sun, Mar 14, May 1, Sep 15, Oct 3, 12, 21, Dec 25.
GOVERNMENT The 134-member legislature is elected every 4 years. Executive power is in the hands of the president; he is elected, also for a 4-year term, but in practice is the leader of the majority party.

NICARAGUA

A beautiful land of lakes and volcanoes, Nicaragua could have been the richest of the Central American republics. But it lost out to Panama as the site for the isthmian canal and for more than four decades was looted by the Somoza dynasty, which came to control more than 40% of the economy. The 1979 revolution ousted the Somozas at a cost of 50,000 lives. The new left-wing Sandinist government, under Daniel Ortega, was confirmed in power by elections in 1984.

The Sandinists' ambitious policies combined literacy, health and land reform programmes with economic reconstruction. But by 1988 the economy was in crisis: inflation was running at 33,000%; earnings from the key exports, coffee, cotton and sugar, had collapsed. The crisis was partly due to government incompetence. But equally important was US policy. Since 1981 the USA had waged undeclared war on Nicaragua, imposing trade and financial embargoes, and arming and training the "contra" rebels. Backed by its Central American neighbours the Sandinist government agreed to peace talks. It also initiated drastic austerity measures which controlled inflation but exacerbated the economic recession.

In February 1990, weary of war and deprivation Nicaraguans voted for the pro-US Unión Nacional Opositora (UNO) coalition, headed by Violeta Chamorro. The demobilization of the "contra" rebels was one of the few successes of UNO's first year in power. Its efforts to tackle the economic crisis were not helped by the slow arrival of promised US aid or by its inept handling of the introduction of a new currency. Hyperinflation returned and the country faced food shortages. The army, still under Sandinist control, was forced to support the government when a general strike threatened to escalate into civil war. Its decision helped pave the way for national unity talks between UNO and the Sandinists, but the prospect of splits by the extremes of the two parties and of renewed contra violence meant that a return to political chaos was an ever-present threat.

OFFICIAL NAME Republic of Nicaragua.
CAPITAL CITY Managua.
GEOGRAPHY The eastern plains are largely jungle, and the Caribbean coast is marked by sandbanks, lagoons and reefs. Most settlement is in the west, in a triangular mountainous area with fertile valleys and basins. In the south a large basin contains lakes Managua and Nicaragua, the largest in Central America. A range of volcanoes separates the lakes from the Pacific. *Highest point* Pico Mogoton 2,107 metres (6,910 feet). *Area* 130,000 sq km (50,000 sq miles).
PEOPLE *Population* 3.7m. *Density* 28 per sq km. *Ethnic groups* Mestizo 69%, European 14%, African 8%, Zambo 5%, Amerindian 4%.
RELIGION RC 90%, Protestant 5%.
LANGUAGE Spanish. Some English is spoken.
EDUCATION Free to age 18, compulsory for ages 7–13.
CLIMATE Tropical, with an average temperature of 26°C (79°F), milder in the highlands and the east. Annual rainfall 3,800mm (150ins) in the east, half as much in the west.
CURRENCY Córdoba.
PUBLIC HOLIDAYS Jan 1, Maundy Thu, Good Fri, May 1, Jul 19, Aug 10, Sep 14–15, Nov 2, Dec 25.
GOVERNMENT Democratic republic. The head of state is a president elected for a 6-year term, who appoints a cabinet. The 92-member unicameral legislative National Assembly is elected for a 6-year term by PR.

EL SALVADOR

The smallest and most densely populated of the Central American states, El Salvador has a long history of military rule and political violence. Historically a coffee planters' oligarchy, it also has a strong artisan tradition and industrial potential, notably in food processing, textiles and clothing. The country has been torn by civil war since 1980, when a frustrated political left joined forces with the guerrillas of what became the FMLN (Frente Farabundo Martí de Liberación Nacional). US backing for the armed forces brought about a stalemate. The FMLN has been prepared to negotiate, but neither the Christian Democrats under José Duarte nor Alfredo Christiani of the Arena party, which came to power in 1989, has been able or willing to force the necessary concessions on an army with close ties to the extreme right. US pressure on the government has stopped short of cutting-off military and economic aid, and violence and human rights abuses have continued unabated.

OFFICIAL NAME Republic of El Salvador.
CAPITAL CITY San Salvador.
GEOGRAPHY Most people live in the lake-strewn central plain, bounded by mountains and volcanoes. *Area* 21,041 sq km (8,120 sq miles).
PEOPLE *Population* 5.1m. *Density* 239 per sq km. *Ethnic groups* Mestizo 94%, Amerindian 5%, European 1%.
RELIGION RC 96%, Protestant 3%.
LANGUAGE Spanish.
EDUCATION Free and compulsory for ages 7–16.
CURRENCY El Salvador colón.
PUBLIC HOLIDAYS Jan 1, Good Fri–Easter Mon, May 1, Corpus Christi, Aug 5–6, Sep 15, Oct 12, Nov 2, 5, Dec 24–25.
GOVERNMENT Republic. Head of state and chief executive is a president, elected for a 5-year term, who appoints a cabinet drawn from the 60-member National Assembly. The assembly is elected every 3 years.

COSTA RICA

For 100 years Costa Rica has been an oasis of democracy in Central America. The abolition of the army in 1948 by José (Pepe) Figueres saved the country from militarism and its formal neutrality has enabled it to play a key role in resolving regional disputes. Power regularly changes hands in keenly contested elections between the socialist Partido de Liberación (PLN) and the conservative Partido Unidad Social Cristiano (PUSC). Their policies have started to converge as both have accepted IMF-style programmes to restructure an economy badly affected by high levels of indebtedness.

A more even distribution of land and wealth has contributed to a stable society but opposition to austerity measures led to the defeat of the PLN in the 1990 elections and has caused problems for its PUSC successor. The economy is still dominated by agriculture; coffee and bananas are the main exports. Diversification programmes have recently led to the growth of new exports.

OFFICIAL NAME Republic of Costa Rica.
CAPITAL CITY San José.
GEOGRAPHY There are three mountain chains and swampy lowlands on the Caribbean shore. *Area* 50,700 sq km (19,600 sq miles).
PEOPLE *Population* 2.9m. *Density* 57 per sq km. *Ethnic groups* European 85%, Mestizo 10%.
RELIGION RC 92%, Protestant 7%.
LANGUAGE Spanish.
CURRENCY Costa Rican colón.
PUBLIC HOLIDAYS Jan 1, Mar 19, Maundy Thu, Good Fri, Apr 11, May 1, Corpus Christi, Jun 29, Jul 25, Aug 2, 15, Sep 15, Oct 12, Dec 1, 8, 25.
GOVERNMENT The head of state is a president elected every 4 years, at the same time as the 57 members of the legislative assembly.

PANAMA

Panama was part of Columbia until it seceded with US assistance in 1903, and is still often regarded as part of South America. It is set apart by the canal which has made the country a world crossroads and enabled it to develop the free-trade zone, "open-registry fleet" and offshore banking sector on which much of its revenue has depended. Like the country, the canal was the creation of the USA, which retains a controlling interest until 1999. The future of the canal is problematic because of competition from other routes and its inability to accommodate supertankers. As a result, a policy priority has been to develop the extra-canal zone economy.

However, the political crisis of 1987–89, which culminated in the US invasion and ousting of General Manuel Noriega, head of the armed forces and de facto leader since 1983, severely damaged confidence in Panama's stability and provoked massive capital flight. The Adoc coalition under Guillermo Endara, which won the May 1989 elections annulled by General Noriega, was sworn in at a US military base just hours before the December invasion. It found government increasingly difficult, suffering from waning popularity and internal splits over President Endara's plans to liberalize trade and contain public spending.

OFFICIAL NAME Republic of Panama.
CAPITAL CITY Panama City.
GEOGRAPHY Apart from volcanic mountains in the south, most of the land is below 700 metres (2,300 feet). The majority of people live on the Pacific side. *Area* 77,082 sq km (29,760 sq miles).
PEOPLE *Population* 2.4m. *Density* 31 per sq km. *Ethnic groups* Mulatto/Mestizo 70%, African 12%, European 12%.
RELIGION RC 89%, Protestant 5%, Muslim 4%.
LANGUAGE Spanish.
EDUCATION Free to university level, compulsory for ages 6–15.
CURRENCY Balboa.
PUBLIC HOLIDAYS Jan 1, 9, Shrove Tue, Good Fri, May 1, Aug 15, Oct 11, Nov 1–5, 10, 28, Dec 8, 12, 25.
GOVERNMENT The head of state and chief executive is a president elected for a 5-year term. Two elected vice-presidents assist the president, who appoints the cabinet. The unicameral legislative assembly has 67 members elected every 5 years.

THE CARIBBEAN

The Caribbean is one of the world's most diverse regions, containing two dozen countries, ranging in population from a few thousand to more than 10m. Five main languages (Spanish, English, French, Dutch and Creole) are spoken by people from a great variety of ethnic and religious backgrounds.

Just over half the countries are politically independent. The rest are colonial dependencies of European powers or the USA. There are three constitutional oddities: Puerto Rico has associated status with the USA, and Guadeloupe and Martinique are overseas departments of France. Apart from Cuba the region is firmly – although sometimes reluctantly – in the US sphere of influence.

Most of the smaller island states are classified as "less developed", with externally dependent economies, but the region also includes countries with a strong financial base and incomes per head approaching those of the industrialized world.

Island groupings

The islands of the West Indies separate the Caribbean and the Gulf of Mexico from the Atlantic, though the region as a whole is commonly referred to as the Caribbean. Three island groups make up the chain: the Bahamas; the Greater Antilles, comprising Cuba, Jamaica, Haiti, the Dominican Republic and Puerto Rico; and the smaller islands of the Lesser Antilles in the east. The last group is often further divided into the Leeward Islands, stretching from the Virgin Islands to Dominica; the Windward Islands from Martinique to Grenada; Trinidad & Tobago; and the southern group of the Netherlands Antilles and Aruba.

Climate

The climate of most of the region is tropical or sub-tropical; temperatures, which vary throughout the year, are generally in the range of 22–32°C (62–72°F). Trade winds temper the climate of the north-east Caribbean making this area cooler and drier than the western parts. The rainy season generally lasts from June–July to November–December.

Time

Time is 5 hours behind GMT in the western Caribbean, and 4 hours behind in the east.

Trade and industry

The USA is the main trading partner of almost all countries in the region. A large proportion of tourists are American, and US companies are increasing their investment in tourism, manufacturing, mining, energy and agri-business. The USA has promoted duty-free access to its market through the Caribbean Basin Initiative, launched in 1984, but benefits have been fewer than expected; the region's trade balance with the USA went from surplus to deficit during the 1980s, principally because of reduced oil exports.

Tourism and the supply of raw materials and agricultural produce to the developed world remain the main economic activities. Only the larger countries have significant industrial sectors, often based on one predominant commodity, such as bauxite in Jamaica. During the 1980s, though, new export industries developed, notably electronic components assembly and garment manufacturing.

Almost every country runs a trade deficit, and the earnings from tourism and financial sector services are badly needed to correct the overall payments balance. A shortage of low-cost development finance has meant frequent resort to commercial borrowing, resulting in a heavy repayment burden. Structural adjustment programmes overseen by the IMF have been adopted by the Dominican Republic, Haiti, Jamaica, Dominica, Trinidad & Tobago and Guyana.

Caricom

Founded in 1973 to replace the Caribbean Free Trade Association, the Caribbean Community and Common Market aims to promote unity and economic integration in the region. However, the economic difficulties of the member states have hindered this attempt at regional cooperation, and moves towards free trade have made slow progress. Wider integration involving the non-English-speaking countries that are not members of Caricom is an even more distant prospect.

The Organization of Eastern Caribbean States

The seven members of this associate institution of Caricom formerly comprised the West Indies Associated States. The organization was formed in 1981 to foster closer economic and political ties between the member states in the Windward and Leeward Islands.

The Lomé Convention

Twelve Caribbean states are parties to the Lomé Convention, which provides privileged access to the European Community for (mainly agricultural) exports from former French and British possessions in Africa, the Caribbean and the Pacific (ACP states). Lomé conventions signed in 1976, 1981, 1984 and 1989 also provide aid for these territories.

Eastern Caribbean geography

The Windward and Leeward Islands are so-called because they are swept by the prevailing NE trade winds. The islands vary in size from over 60 km (37 miles) across, down to tiny low-lying islands without lakes or rivers. Many are formed from coral, but some are volcanic in origin.

GROSS DOMESTIC PRODUCT

	$m
Cuba	34,070
Puerto Rico	20,030
Dominican Republic	6,691
Trinidad and Tobago	4,047
Jamaica	3,881
Haiti	2,068
Martinique	1,998
Bahamas	1,801
Barbados	1,707
Guadeloupe	1,525
Netherland Antilles	1,452
US Virgin Is	1,030
Bermuda	980
Aruba	724
Cayman Is	463
Antigua and Barbuda	286
St Lucia	220
Dominica	126
Grenada	139
St Vincent and the Grenadines	130
St Kitts and Nevis	112
British Virgin Is	102
Turks and Caicos Is	63
Montserrat	54
Anguilla	28

GDP PER HEAD

	$
Cayman Is	18,269
Bermuda	16,897
Aruba	11,602
Bahamas	10,280
British Virgin Is	8,322
US Virgin Is	7,780
Barbados	6,828
Puerto Rico	6,144
Martinique	6,003
Netherland Antilles	5,378
Turks and Caicos Is	4,854
Guadeloupe	4,560
Montserrat	4,168
Antigua and Barbuda	3,671
Anguilla	3,495
Trinidad and Tobago	3,373
Cuba	3,245
St Kitts and Nevis	2,239
Jamaica	1,637
Dominica	1,572
St Lucia	1,540
Grenada	1,394
St Vincent and the Grenadines	1,100
Dominican Republic	956
Haiti	369

Source: EIU Country Reports; *Europa Yearbook* (1989 figures or latest available).

ork 5 days

Rotterdam 13 days

VIRGIN IS. (USA)
VIRGIN IS. (UK)

Road Town

ANGUILLA
The Valley

San Juan

Charlotte Amalie

PUERTO RICO

NETHERLANDS ANTILLES

ANTIGUA & BARBUDA

Basseterre

ST KITTS & NEVIS
1, 2, 3

St. John's

Plymouth
MONTSERRAT
1, 2

Basse-Terre

GUADELOUPE

Leeward Islands

Antilles

DOMINICA 1, 2, 3

Roseau

Fort-de-France

MARTINIQUE

Lesser

Castries

ST LUCIA 1, 2, 3

ST VINCENT & THE GRENADINES
1,2,3

BARBADOS 1,3

Kingstown

Bridgetown

Windward Islands

St. George's

GRENADA
1,2,3

■ More than 1 million
● 250,000 - 1 million
• 100,000 - 250,000

TRINIDAD & TOBAGO
1,3

Port of Spain

1 Caricom
2 Organization of Eastern Caribbean States
3 EEC ACP states

 CUBA

Since 1959 Cuba has been the Caribbean's only one-party socialist state, with a highly centralized economy. Significant achievements of Fidel Castro's regime have included a creditable health and education system, determined efforts to eliminate racial inequality, and a strong national identity.

However, the economic growth enjoyed in the 1960s and 1970s was financed by vast amounts of Soviet aid. In the 1980s Cuba's fortunes steadily declined and the country is now in a desperate position, forced to ration even basic goods. Since Mikhail Gorbachev came to power, the Soviet Union has sought to reduce the level of aid and, in particular of oil it supplies to Cuba on highly concessional terms. The Soviet Union's own crisis and the thaw in relations with the USA have made Cuba still less of a Soviet priority. A further blow to Cuba was the collapse of socialist regimes in Eastern Europe and the consequent winding down of Comecon, within which most of Cuba's trade had been conducted. The government's response to this crisis has been to try to adjust to its reduced circumstances. Since 1990 many urban workers have been redeployed to the countryside because fuel and spare parts are not available for machines.

Cuba has restored relations with almost all Latin American countries. Its influence in the Caribbean, however, remains small, a legacy of its Comecon trading days. Relations with the USA, which since 1959 have ranged from the dangerous to the lukewarm, are unlikely to be normalized in the foreseeable future. Castro continues to run the country on his own terms, and despite some changes to the internal political structure in recent years, with debate becoming a little more open, he still has no obvious successor.

OFFICIAL NAME Republic of Cuba.
CAPITAL CITY Havana.
GEOGRAPHY A long narrow island with a complex of eroded mountain ranges interspersed with small plains, Cuba is the summit of a marine tableland. The highest mountains are the Sierra Maestra on the south-east coast. There is a well-developed underground river system and a long coastline of bays, beaches, swamps and cliffs. *Highest point* Turquino 2,005 metres (6,580 feet). *Area* 110,861 sq km (42,800 sq miles).
PEOPLE *Population* 10.4m. *Density* 94 per sq km. *Ethnic groups* European 72%, Mulatto 15%, African 12%.
RELIGION RC 40%.
LANGUAGE Spanish.
EDUCATION Free and compulsory for ages 6–12. Schooling combines study and manual work.
CURRENCY Cuban peso.
PUBLIC HOLIDAYS Jan 1, May 1, Jul 25–27, Oct 10.
GOVERNMENT Communist republic. The only authorized party is the Partido Comunista de Cuba. The 1976 constitution provides for a 481-member National Assembly of People's Power, elected for 5 years by municipal assemblies. The national assembly appoints 31 members as the council of state, whose president is head of state and head of government.

 JAMAICA

Jamaica's externally dependent economy has undergone sharp changes of fortune in recent years. In the later years of Michael Manley's democratic socialist experiment in the 1970s, the economy underwent a deep recession, brought on by factors including the 1973 oil price rise, a prolonged conflict with the major bauxite companies and a high level of political tension, culminating in the pre-election violence of 1980. A modest return to economic growth took place in the first years of the Edward Seaga government, which started a programme of deregulation, reduction of government expenditure and encouragement of tourism and export-oriented, free-zone manufacturing, in association with the United States and the IMF.

The programme, which imposed considerable hardship on the poorer sections of the population, led to increasing government unpopularity and periodic outbreaks of violence. A sharp decline in real GDP in 1985 was followed by a recovery in 1987, but the upturn was checked by the severe damage caused by Hurricane Gilbert in September 1988.

The Manley government, returned in February 1989, continued many of Mr Seaga's policies, and in September 1990 announced plans for further economic deregulation including floating the Jamaican dollar. While tourism, bauxite and export manufacturing were all performing well, the economy remained plagued by an external debt of more than $4 billion and a persistent trade deficit vulnerable to oil price increases.

OFFICIAL NAME Jamaica.
CAPITAL CITY Kingston.
GEOGRAPHY The island has a spine of limestone mountains and plateaus, much of it covered in rain forest. Most settlement is on the coastal plains. *Area* 10,991 sq km (4,240 sq miles).
PEOPLE *Population* 2.4m. *Density* 215 per sq km. *Ethnic groups* African 76%, mixed 15%, European 3%, Asian Indian 2%.
RELIGION Church of God 18%, Baptist 10%, Anglican 7%, Seventh Day Adventist 7%, Pentecostal 5%, RC 5%, Presbyterian 5%, Methodist 3%. There are also many Rastafarians.
LANGUAGE English. Also English/African patois.
CURRENCY Jamaican dollar.
PUBLIC HOLIDAYS Jan 1, Ash Wed, Good Fri–Easter Mon, May 23, 1st Mon in Aug, 3rd Mon in Oct, Dec 25–26.
GOVERNMENT Parliamentary democracy. A governor-general, representing the British monarch, appointed on the recommendation of the prime minister. The prime minister is the head of the majority party in the 60-member House of Representatives, elected every 5 years. The upper house, the Senate, has 21 members.

HAITI

Political turmoil has gripped Haiti for much of its history since Toussaint L'Ouverture led the slaves to freedom from France in 1804, and made the country the Caribbean's first independent state. Sporadic conflict between the mulatto and black populations led the USA to intervene in 1915 and take control of the country for nearly 20 years. The 29-year dictatorship of the Duvalier family, which ended with the flight of Jean-Claude Duvalier in 1986, kept the majority of Haitians in wretched poverty, with the worst housing, health and education record in the Caribbean, while millions of dollars were embezzled by the presidential elite.

Attempts to establish a constitutional, elected government have been frustrated by partisans of the old regime, using every means including open terror. The November 1987 general election was cancelled after voters were shot down at the polling stations. The army, itself by no means united, has resumed the habit, formed before the Duvalier regime, of intervening in politics. The second of 1988's two military coups departed from the norm: it was led by sergeants, although they installed a former Duvalier confidant, Lt-Gen Prosper Avril, as president. Popular opposition forced Avril's resignation, and in December 1990, Father Jean-Bertrand Aristide won a landslide victory to become Haiti's first freely-elected president.

The country's political upheaval has increased economic difficulties. Agriculture and fishing provide a bare level of subsistence for 65% of the population. A number of US-owned manufacturers provide employment in the Port-au-Prince area, but several moved to other countries in the region, increasing the ranks of the capital's unemployed. The USA is Haiti's main aid donor, and the suspension of disbursements between 1987 and 1989 further exacerbated the country's problems.

OFFICIAL NAME Republic of Haiti.
CAPITAL CITY Port-au-Prince.
GEOGRAPHY Haiti is the western part of Hispaniola, with two long, rocky, calcareous peninsulas joined by an alluvial plain and a central plateau. Earthquakes are common. *Highest point* Pic de la Selle 2,674 metres (8,770 feet). *Area* 27,750 sq km (10,710 sq miles).
PEOPLE *Population* 5.5m. *Density* 199 per sq km. *Ethnic groups* African 95%, Mulatto 5%.
RELIGION RC 80%, Protestant 14%; Voodoo is recognized by the state.
LANGUAGE French. Also Creole.
EDUCATION Compulsory for ages 7–13. State system supplemented by many fee-paying RC schools.
CURRENCY Goude.
PUBLIC HOLIDAYS Jan 1, 2, Shrove Mon–Tue, Good Fri, May 1, 18, 22, Nov 1, 18, Dec 5, 25.
GOVERNMENT Republic since 1804. The March 1987 constitution provides for a president, elected every 5 years, to form the executive with a prime minister and cabinet drawn from the majority party in the legislature. There is a 27-member Senate and a 77-member Chamber of Deputies.

DOMINICAN REPUBLIC

A booming tourist industry, rapid expansion of duty-free industrial zones and a grandiose programme of public works have produced high economic growth and new employment opportunities for the Dominican Republic. Forcing the pace, though, has brought problems. A headlong fall of the national currency set off a sharp rise in food and fuel prices which led to widespread rioting in early 1988. The government subsequently reasserted control over the exchange rate by closing the privately run exchange offices, but mounting inflation brought two currency devaluations in 1990.

The shortage of hard currency has compounded the problem of maintaining production in the face of a grossly inadequate electric power supply system, which in 1989–90 produced frequent and prolonged power cuts. A persistent fuel shortage was worsened by oil price rises caused by the Gulf crisis. With an external debt of over $4 billion and growing payment arrears, a return to the IMF appeared inevitable.

The government's dilemma has been that an earlier IMF-led austerity drive in 1984 brought an explosion of angry demonstrations, violently repressed at the cost of 100 lives. The octogenarian President Joaquin Balaguer, narrowly re-elected in May 1990 amid charges of electoral fraud, announced steep price increases aimed at curtailing the fiscal deficit in preparation for an IMF pact. A general strike followed in which 12 people were killed. His sixth term promised to be a difficult one, the more so as the election deprived him of overall control of Congress.

OFFICIAL NAME Dominica.
CAPITAL CITY Santo Domingo.
GEOGRAPHY The country is dominated by a series of hills and mountain ranges running north-west to south-east. There is an abundance of fertile soils, especially in the south-eastern lowlands. *Highest point* Pico Duarte 3,175 metres (10,420 feet). *Area* 48,374 sq km (18,820 sq miles).
PEOPLE *Population* 6.9m. *Density* 142 per sq km. *Ethnic groups* Mulatto 75%, European 15%, African 10%.
RELIGION RC 98%, Protestant 1%.
LANGUAGE Spanish.
EDUCATION Free to university level; compulsory for ages 7–14.
CURRENCY Dominican Republic peso.
PUBLIC HOLIDAYS Jan 1, 6, 21, 26, Feb 27, Good Fri, Apr 4, May 1, Ascension, St Peter and St Paul's, Corpus Christi, Jul 16, Aug 16, Sep 24, Oct 12, 24, Nov 1, Dec 25.
GOVERNMENT Republic since 1821. The chief executive, the president, is directly elected for a 4-year term and is assisted by a vice-president and a cabinet. The national Congress has a 30-member Senate and 120-member Chamber of Deputies.

THE BAHAMAS

Tourism contributes more than 50% of GNP and provides jobs for almost half the working population of the Bahamas; 90% of the tourists come from the USA. Offshore banking, insurance and one of the largest "open-registry" shipping fleets in the world help to offset a substantial trade deficit: 80% of food is imported. Attempts are being made to develop fishing and agriculture, particularly citrus fruit for export.

The country's exposed position close to the US coast, with its 700 widely dispersed islands, made it a haven in the 1980s for international drug traffickers, with officials up to ministerial level implicated in drug-related corruption. Anti-smuggling efforts appeared to have diverted much of the traffic to other routes by 1990.

OFFICIAL NAME The Bahamas.
CAPITAL CITY Nassau.
GEOGRAPHY An archipelago, with more than 700 low-lying islands, 29 of them inhabited. *Area* 13,935 sq km (5,380 sq miles).
PEOPLE *Population* 244,000. *Density* 18 per sq km. *Ethnic groups* African 70%, mixed 14%, European 13%.
RELIGION Christian 95% (Protestant 47%, RC 25%, Anglican 21%, other 2%).
LANGUAGE English.
CURRENCY Bahama dollar.
PUBLIC HOLIDAYS Jan 1, Good Fri, Easter Mon, May 20, Jun 7, Jul 10, Aug 5, Oct 12, Dec 25–26.
GOVERNMENT Parliamentary monarchy. A governor-general represents the British monarch and acts on the advice of the prime minister and cabinet.

PUERTO RICO

Puerto Rico is subject to US law, with the US administration responsible for defence, taxation and immigration procedures. It has a measure of internal self-government, electing its own Congress and governor, but Puerto Ricans cannot vote in US presidential elections.

The island is largely industrialized, and about a third of the population lives in the San Juan urban area. Agriculture plays only a small part in the economy; the two major growth areas are tourism and manufacturing.

The US internal revenue code grants tax exemption to US companies based in Puerto Rico, provided that they pay 10% of their profits into the government development bank. These funds amount to more than $7 billion, and the Puerto Rican administration has offered to use $840m to assist industrial development in countries benefiting from the Caribbean Basin Initiative, by setting up twin plants for the finishing of semi-manufactured goods.

Past controversy over the island's status appears to have waned, with the retention of the current position gaining support over the alternative extremes of US statehood or independence.

OFFICIAL NAME Commonwealth of Puerto Rico.
CAPITAL CITY San Juan.
GEOGRAPHY A rugged, hilly island. Mountains slope steeply to the sea in the south, but give way in the north to a plateau and rain forest cut by deep valleys. *Area* 9,104 sq km (3,520 sq miles).
PEOPLE *Population* 3.3m. *Density* 365 per sq km. *Ethnic groups* European (mostly Spanish) 75%, African 15%, Mulatto 10%.
RELIGION RC 85%, Protestant 5%.
LANGUAGE Spanish and English.
CURRENCY US dollar.
PUBLIC HOLIDAYS Jan 1, 6, 12, 3rd Mon in Feb, 4th Wed in Mar, Apr 16, Good Fri, last Mon in May, Jul 4, 17, 25, 27, 1st Mon in Sep, Oct 12, Nov 11, 19, last Thu in Nov, Dec 25.
GOVERNMENT "Free associated state" of the USA. The chief executive is the governor. There is a cabinet of 15 secretaries. The legislature is a 27-member Senate and 51-member House of Representatives.

TRINIDAD & TOBAGO

The fall in international oil prices during the 1980s wrought havoc on Trinidad & Tobago's economy. Petroleum products account for about 70% of exports, and falling production brought a steady decline in GDP, coupled with adverse trade and payments figures. At the same time, rising interest payments on loans contracted for extravagant and badly managed development projects helped almost exhaust once-ample reserves.

An abrupt change in political direction came in December 1986, when the electorate turned its back on the People's National Movement after 30 years in power. The incoming government, headed by Prime Minister Arthur Robinson, was an uneasy coalition under the banner of the National Alliance for Reconstruction (NAR); by 1988, a prolonged internal wrangle had led to the expulsion of its pro-labour representatives. The NAR faced the run-up to the elections, due by mid-1992, with seven fewer seats in the House of Representatives than when it took office, but the economic recovery which began in 1990 was expected to boost its chances at the polls.

OFFICIAL NAME Republic of Trinidad & Tobago.
CAPITAL CITY Port of Spain.
GEOGRAPHY Trinidad has mountains on the north, a central plain and volcanic hills to the south. Tobago is surrounded by coral reefs. *Area* 5,128 sq km (1,980 sq miles).
PEOPLE *Population* 1.2m. *Density* 241 per sq km. *Ethnic groups* African 41%, Asian Indian 40%, mixed 17%.
RELIGION Christian 62%, Hindu 25%, Muslim 6%.
LANGUAGE English.
CURRENCY Trinidad & Tobago dollar.
PUBLIC HOLIDAYS Jan 1, Shrove Mon–Tue, Good Fri–Easter Mon, Id al-Fitr, Whit Mon, Corpus Christi, Jun 19, Aug 1, 31, Sep 24, Divali, Dec 25, 26.
GOVERNMENT Republic since 1962. The president is elected by a college of the legislature which comprises an elected 36-member House of Representatives and a 31-member Senate.

CAYMAN ISLANDS

OFFICIAL NAME Colony of the Cayman Islands.
CAPITAL CITY Georgetown.
GEOGRAPHY An archipelago of low-lying rocky islands surrounded by coral reefs. There are no rivers.
PEOPLE *Population* 24,900. *Density* 96 per sq km. *Ethnic groups* Mixed 50%, African 25%, European 25%.
RELIGION Protestant 85%, RC 5%.
LANGUAGE English.
CURRENCY Cayman Islands dollar.
PUBLIC HOLIDAYS Jan 1, Ash Wed, Good Fri–Easter Mon, 3rd Mon in May, Mon after Jun 8, 1st Mon in Jul, 2nd Mon in Nov, Dec 25–26.
GOVERNMENT UK colony. A governor represents the British monarch. Small executive council and legislative assembly.

The Cayman Islands has become the world's largest offshore financial centre, offering secrecy and freedom from taxes to more than 18,000 companies. Since 1986, however, US law enforcement agencies have been allowed access to banking records, as part of a crackdown on drug-trafficking. The islands' thriving tourist industry, based overwhelmingly on the US market, accounts for 70% of GDP and 75% of foreign exchange earnings. A property boom shows no signs of slackening, and a labour shortage is met by the employment of foreigners, who make up a third of the population.

TURKS & CAICOS Is

OFFICIAL NAME Colony of Turks & Caicos Islands.
CAPITAL CITY Cockburn Town.
GEOGRAPHY More than 30 islands, 8 inhabited, in two groups.
PEOPLE *Population* 13,000. *Density* 30 per sq km. *Ethnic groups* Mixed 63%, African 33%.
RELIGION Protestant 78%.
LANGUAGE English.
CURRENCY US dollar.
PUBLIC HOLIDAYS Jan 1, Easter (4 days), May 30, Jun 13, Aug 1, Oct 10, Dec 25–26.
GOVERNMENT UK colony. A governor represents the British monarch. Executive and legislative councils.

The Turks & Caicos Islands regained an elected government in 1988; a period of direct rule by a council headed by the British governor had followed the conviction in 1986 of three ministers on drugs charges in the USA. The new government, headed by Chief Minister Oswald Skippings, negotiated a £15m aid package from the UK, aiming to eliminate the need for budgetary support over three years. Tourism and offshore financial services are being developed to supplement the main foreign exchange earner, lobster.

BERMUDA

OFFICIAL NAME Bermuda.
CAPITAL CITY Hamilton.
GEOGRAPHY An archipelago of 120 coral islands, 20 of them inhabited.
PEOPLE *Population* 58,050. *Density* 1.095 per sq km. *Ethnic groups* African 61%, European 37%.
RELIGION Christian 88%, Muslim 1%.
LANGUAGE English.
CURRENCY Bermuda dollar.
PUBLIC HOLIDAYS Jan 1, Good Fri, 2nd Mon in Jun, last Thu and Fri in Jul, 1st Mon in Sep, Nov 11, Dec 25–26.
GOVERNMENT UK colony. A governor represents the British monarch. House of Assembly and Senate.

A British colony since 1620, Bermuda lies in the Atlantic Ocean, 1,450km (900 miles) north-east of Nassau. Like several of the Caribbean islands, it makes handsome earnings from tourism and offshore financial services; GNP per head is among the highest in the world. Income from services offsets a severe trade deficit; the island imports 80% of its food – much of it eaten by the tourists – and manufactured goods. Almost all tourist and commercial business originates in the USA and the economy has followed that of the USA in and out of recession in recent years.

The government is discussing constitutional issues with the UK, USA and Canada, but a referendum is promised before any moves are made towards independence, which public opinion has traditionally opposed.

US VIRGIN ISLANDS

OFFICIAL NAME US Virgin Islands.
CAPITAL CITY Charlotte Amalie.
GEOGRAPHY A group of more than 50 islands.
PEOPLE *Population* 103,200. *Ethnic groups* African 80%, European 15%.
RELIGION Christian 98%.
LANGUAGE English. Also Spanish, French, Creole.
CURRENCY US dollar.
GOVERNMENT Unincorporated US territory with a measure of self-government.

Tourism is the dominant industry in the 68-island group, of which St Thomas, St John and St Croix are the main islands. Condominium and hotel construction is continuing rapidly, and industry is also expanding, helped by the extension of US tax concessions.

BRITISH VIRGIN Is

OFFICIAL NAME British Virgin Islands.
CAPITAL CITY Road Town.
GEOGRAPHY Four large islands and about 36 islets and cays.
PEOPLE *Population* 12,200. *Density* 80 per sq km. *Ethnic groups* African 88%, European 7%.
RELIGION Protestant 73%, RC 6%.
LANGUAGE English.
CURRENCY US dollar.
GOVERNMENT UK colony. A governor represents the British monarch. Two councils.

A successful drive to promote luxury tourism has brought substantial foreign earnings to this British dependency. A recent growth sector has been offshore business, with nearly 6,000 companies registered by early 1988.

ANGUILLA

OFFICIAL NAME Anguilla.
CAPITAL CITY The Valley.
GEOGRAPHY Low-lying coral island covered in scrub.
PEOPLE *Population* 8,000. *Density* 83 per sq km. *Ethnic groups* Mainly African or mixed.

THE AMERICAS

RELIGION Mainly Christian.
LANGUAGE English.
CURRENCY East Caribbean dollar.
GOVERNMENT UK colony. A governor represents the British monarch. Council and assembly.

Anguilla has achieved a balanced budget virtually without taxation. Most revenue comes from customs duties, and income from the still-expanding tourist industry and other services offsets a big trade deficit. Unemployment is now a negligible 2%.

ST KITTS-NEVIS

OFFICIAL NAME Federation of Saint Christopher and Nevis.
CAPITAL CITY Basseterre.
GEOGRAPHY Three mountainous islands: St Kitts, Nevis and Sombrero.
PEOPLE *Population* 47,000. *Ethnic groups* African 94%, Mulatto 3%, European 1%.
RELIGION Protestant 85%, RC 7%.
LANGUAGE English.
CURRENCY East Caribbean dollar.
GOVERNMENT Parliamentary monarchy. A governor-general represents the British monarch. Elected parliament and prime minister.

Tourism is replacing the declining sugar industry; manufacturing and service sectors are also growing fast. The construction of a new road in the late 1980s opened up the south-east peninsula of St Kitts for housing, industry and tourism.

ANTIGUA & BARBUDA

OFFICIAL NAME Antigua & Barbuda.
CAPITAL CITY St John's.
GEOGRAPHY The main islands of the group are Antigua and Barbuda. Redonda is uninhabited.
PEOPLE *Population* 79,000. *Ethnic groups* African 94%, European 1%.
RELIGION Christian 96%, mainly Anglican.
LANGUAGE English.
CURRENCY East Caribbean dollar.
GOVERNMENT Parliamentary monarchy. A governor-

general represents the British monarch. Senate and House of Representatives.

Governed almost without interruption since 1956 by the Antigua Labour Party, the islands have relied for growth on tourism. Attempts to diversify the economy have encountered difficulties. There is some manufacturing, but farming is in decline; food imports add to the serious trade deficit. Borrowing to finance development projects has built up a large external debt and debt service takes almost a fifth of government revenue.

MONTSERRAT

OFFICIAL NAME Montserrat.
CAPITAL CITY Plymouth.
GEOGRAPHY A mountainous island with active volcanoes.
PEOPLE *Population* 12,300. *Ethnic groups* African 96%, European 3%, mixed 1%.
RELIGION Christian 97%.
LANGUAGE English.
CURRENCY East Caribbean dollar.
GOVERNMENT British dependent territory. A governor represents the British monarch. Legislative council includes 7 elected members.

Tourism is the island's mainstay, but is not allowed to dominate the economy. Electronic components account for over half of exports; agricultural produce is also exported and the island aims to be self-sufficient in food.

GUADELOUPE

OFFICIAL NAME Guadeloupe.
CAPITAL CITY Basse-Terre.
GEOGRAPHY The main islands in the seven-island group are Grande-Terre and Basse-Terre.
PEOPLE *Population* 336,000. *Ethnic groups* Mulatto 77%, African 10%, Mestizo 10%, European 2%.
RELIGION Christian, mainly RC.
LANGUAGE French. Also patois.
CURRENCY French franc.
GOVERNMENT French overseas department.

Guadeloupe has a strong independence movement which has mounted sporadic bombings. French aid has ensured a high living standard, but unemployment is almost 40%. Main exports are bananas, sugar and rum, mostly to France. Tourism is thriving.

DOMINICA

OFFICIAL NAME Commonwealth of Dominica.
CAPITAL CITY Roseau.
GEOGRAPHY A ridged volcanic island. Two-thirds of the land is forested.
PEOPLE *Population* 81,200. *Ethnic groups* African 90%, Mulatto 7%, Amerindian 2%, Carib 0.5%.
RELIGION RC 90%, Protestant 8%.
LANGUAGE English. Also French patois.
CURRENCY East Caribbean dollar.
GOVERNMENT Republic since 1978. 30-member House of Assembly.

An IMF loan has aided development of public utilities; plans for an international airport have been mooted. Agriculture is the mainstay, and bananas the leading export crop. Luxury tourism is being encouraged.

MARTINIQUE

OFFICIAL NAME Martinique.
CAPITAL CITY Fort-de-France.
GEOGRAPHY The island rises steeply from the sea to the northern volcanic massif of Mount Pelée.
PEOPLE *Population* 337,000. *Ethnic groups* Mulatto 95%, European 2%, Asian Indian 2%.
RELIGION RC 91%, Protestant 5%.
LANGUAGE French. Also patois.
CURRENCY French franc.
GOVERNMENT French overseas department.

French government expenditure on the island accounts for 70% of GNP, providing jobs and social services to cushion high unemployment. Bananas, rum and pineapples are the chief exports, but tourism is important. The industrial sector includes an oil refinery, cement works and agro-processing plants.

ST LUCIA

OFFICIAL NAME Saint Lucia.
CAPITAL CITY Castries.
GEOGRAPHY A mountainous volcanic island.
PEOPLE *Population* 142,000. *Density* 231 per sq km. *Ethnic groups* African 90%, Mulatto 6%, Asian Indian 3%, European 1%.
RELIGION RC 86%, Protestant 11%.
LANGUAGE English. Also French patois.
CURRENCY East Caribbean dollar.
GOVERNMENT Parliamentary monarchy. A governor-general represents the British monarch. Senate and House of Representatives.

Vigorous infrastructure development is taking place as St Lucia strives to overcome a persistent trade deficit and chronic unemployment. Tourism, bananas and manufacturing are the main sources of foreign exchange.

ST VINCENT & THE GRENADINES

OFFICIAL NAME Saint Vincent and the Grenadines.
CAPITAL CITY Kingstown.
GEOGRAPHY The group comprises St Vincent, Bequia, Mustique, Canouan, Mayreau and Union.
PEOPLE *Population* 113,000. *Ethnic groups* African 65%, Mulatto 19%, Asian Indian 5%, European 3%.
RELIGION Protestant 77%, RC 19%.
LANGUAGE English.
CURRENCY East Caribbean dollar.
GOVERNMENT Parliamentary monarchy. A governor-general represents the British monarch. House of Assembly.

Conservative budgeting and infrastructure development – notably the construction of an international airport – are the main planks of the government's programme. Foreign aid supports land reform and other projects, but unemployment remains a problem. The trade gap is narrowing, thanks to increased agricultural exports. Luxury tourism is developing on the smaller islands.

BARBADOS

OFFICIAL NAME Barbados.
CAPITAL CITY Bridgetown.
GEOGRAPHY A rugged island ringed by a reef.
PEOPLE *Population* 255,200. *Ethnic groups* African 92%, European 3%, mixed 3%.
RELIGION Protestant 88%, RC 6%.
LANGUAGE English.
CURRENCY Barbados dollar.
GOVERNMENT Parliamentary monarchy. A governor-general represents the British monarch. Senate and House of Assembly.

Tourism has taken over as Barbados's leading industry but sugar remains an important source of foreign exchange. Oil and natural gas extraction satisfies about a quarter of domestic demand. Manufacturing has suffered from depressed markets, and hopes of economic growth are pinned on service industries. Barbados is an important communications centre for the eastern Caribbean, and is the base for several regional institutions. Foreign debt, unemployment and a widening trade gap are serious problems, but the country enjoys political stability and good welfare services.

GRENADA

OFFICIAL NAME Grenada.
CAPITAL CITY St George's.
GEOGRAPHY Main island and arc of smaller islands running north to St Vincent.
PEOPLE *Population* 112,000. *Ethnic groups* African 84%, Mulatto 11%, Indian 3%.
RELIGION Christian 99% (RC 64%).
LANGUAGE English. Also patois.
CURRENCY East Caribbean dollar.
GOVERNMENT Parliamentary monarchy. A governor-general represents the British monarch. Senate and House of Representatives.

The traumatic events of 1983, when the violent overthrow of Prime Minister Maurice Bishop's government led to armed intervention by the USA, are still keenly felt in Grenada. Despite US financial support, the government has found it hard to balance the budget.

Price fluctuations for nutmegs have caused a planned trade pact with Indonesia to fall through, and other traditional export crops, cocoa and bananas, also face problems. Efforts to diversify the economy have been impeded by considerable debt and the need to rebuild manufacturing infrastructure after the upheaval of 1983. The revival of tourism should help to offset the trade deficit.

NETHERLANDS ANTILLES

OFFICIAL NAME Netherlands Antilles.
CAPITAL CITY Willemstad.
GEOGRAPHY Comprises the Leeward and Windward groups some 800km (500 miles) apart.
PEOPLE *Population* 189,000. *Ethnic groups* Mulatto 84%, European 6%.
RELIGION RC 87%, Protestant 10%.
LANGUAGE Dutch. Also Spanish, English, patois.
CURRENCY Netherlands Antilles guilder.
GOVERNMENT Netherlands dependency. A governor represents the Dutch monarch. Council and parliament.

The federation of six islands became five in 1986 when Aruba seceded; Curaçao seeks to follow. The federation is dependent on Dutch aid; tourism, finance and, to a decreasing extent, oil refining are the main economic activities.

ARUBA

OFFICIAL NAME Aruba.
CAPITAL CITY Oranjestad.
GEOGRAPHY The dry and flat limestone island lies 25km (16 miles) north of Venezuela.
PEOPLE *Population* 62,400. *Ethnic groups* Dutch, mixed, American Indian, Portuguese.
RELIGION RC 80%.
LANGUAGE Dutch. Also a patois, Papiamento.
CURRENCY Aruba guilder.
GOVERNMENT Netherlands dependency.

Aruba gained seperate status in 1986. Since then the island's economy has grown rapidly, assisted by the reopening of its oil refinery in 1990. Independence from The Netherlands is scheduled for 1996.

SOUTH AMERICA

Cocaine

US government agencies estimated that in 1987 retail sales of South American cocaine totalled $22 billion, although only about $2 billion is earned by the producer states. Bolivia and Peru are the main producers and Colombia the centre for refining and export. The USA has backed crackdowns in the area with varied reactions. A campaign of terror, in response to the Colombian government's all-out war on drug cartels, eventually gave way to negotiations. The Bolivian government, with $18m in US aid and military assistance, has had more success in using incentives and reimbursements to cocaine-producing peasants. Having turned down US aid, probably to avoid the problems evident in Colombia, Peru has decided to work on its own to encourage crop substitution.

The Galapagos islands

The Galapagos islands, on the Equator 970km (610 miles) west of the South American mainland, have been administered by Ecuador since 1832. Four of the islands are inhabited. The Galapagos' unique wildlife, particularly iguanas and giant tortoises, has made the islands a focus of scientific study since Charles Darwin visited in 1835. Isabela, the largest island, was a prison colony until 1958.

Trade

Prospects of South American states uniting to repudiate their debt are much reduced by the fact that they depend on the outside world much more than they do on each other. Trade between the 11 member countries of the Asociación Latinoamericana de Integración (Aladi) runs at only about 10% of their total exports and imports.

This may be starting to change. Brazil and Argentina, which once competed for dominance of the subcontinent, are edging towards a customs union following a trade agreement in 1986, which Uruguay will also join. Both are looking at bilateral agreements with other countries that could greatly reduce their dependence on traditional US and European markets.

Aladi, whose members are the 10 Portuguese and Spanish-speaking South American states, plus Mexico, was set up in 1980 to promote freer trade and economic integration.

The Falkland Islands/Malvinas

The question of whose flag should fly over the Falklands/Malvinas Islands dates from long before Argentina and the UK went to war in 1982. Costly in lives and physical damage, the war did not end the dispute. Although Anglo-Argentine diplomatic relations were restored in 1990, the UK refuses to enter negotiations on the question of sovereignty.

The economy, previously sheep-based, now centres on the presence of British troops. Commercial quantities of oil and natural gas may exist offshore and, under British protection, a fishing industry is beginning to flourish.

Tierra del Fuego

At the southern tip of the continent, Tierra del Fuego is split between Argentina and Chile. The two countries' territorial dispute over the Beagle Channel, south of the island, was settled in 1984, after Vatican mediation.

The Amazon basin

The Amazon, the world's largest river by volume and the second longest, rises in the Peruvian Andes only 150km (95 miles) from the Pacific and flows into the Atlantic through a huge delta; its total length is 6,750km (4,218 miles). It has more than 1,100 tributaries, draining a basin of 7m sq km/2.7m sq miles; together they carry one-fifth of the world's running water.

Burning of the Amazon forest, the world's largest, for new settlements and agriculture is estimated to reduce its area by 4% a year. The global environmental implications of this destruction are causing mounting concern.

Indigenous peoples

Latin America's indigenous peoples are becoming the victims of the race for development. The Indians of the Amazon basin, once insulated from the outside world by impenetrable forest, are increasingly exposed as new roads open up their homelands to development and settlement. Hundreds of thousands of landless migrants have settled in Rondônia and Acre provinces, on Brazil's western border, invading Indian land, destroying the forest and polluting the rivers. Farther east, the state of Para has been opened up by huge mining projects, hydroelectric dams and cattle ranches. Amazonia is thought to have supported an Indian population of 2m in 230 tribal groups 500 years ago. Today the number has dwindled to less than 50,000; many tribes have vanished altogether.

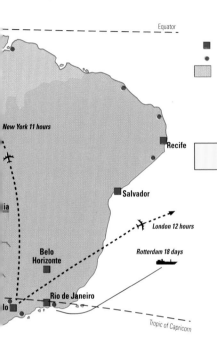

NCH
ANA

- ■ More than 1 million
- • 250,000 - 1 million
- ▨ Natural extent of tropical rainforest

New York 11 hours

Recife

Salvador

London 12 hours

Rotterdam 18 days

Belo Horizonte

Rio de Janeiro

Io

Equator

Tropic of Capricorn

EXTERNAL DEBT

The debt crisis

The focus of concern about Latin American debt has shifted. In the early 1980s, the future of the world financial system seemed to be at stake, as debtors could no longer repay the huge loans banks had been eager to make in the heyday of Opec surpluses. By the end of the decade the problem was the stability of Latin America. Banks have written down the value of their debt, traded some of it on the secondary market, often at huge discounts, and sometimes put up new loans to help debtors pay off old ones. The banks have survived, but South American countries have had their prospects for growth squeezed by the struggle to service debt.

Various schemes have been tried to reduce indebtedness. With debt trading at a deep discount, debtors can buy back their debt for a quarter or half its face value. Debt can be swapped for equity: a company will buy debt in foreign currency in exchange for an agreed amount of local currency to invest in businesses in the debtor country. Some countries have tried debt-for-nature swaps: an environmentalist group buys debt at a discount, then sells it back to the debtor at a premium, using the proceeds for local conservation projects. In 1989 external debts were reduced by about 5% using schemes such as these.

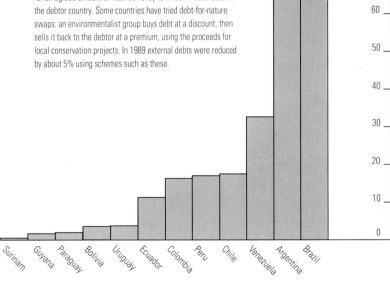

$bn

110 —
100 —
90 —
80 —
70 —
60 —
50 —
40 —
30 —
20 —
10 —
0 —

Surinam · Guyana · Paraguay · Bolivia · Uruguay · Ecuador · Colombia · Peru · Chile · Venezuela · Argentina · Brazil

Sources: EIU *Country Reports* (1989 figures).

ECUADOR

Although Ecuador's history has been characterized by coups, elected civilians have ruled since 1979. Rodrigo Borja Cevallos was inaugurated in August 1988. Unlike his two predecessors he became president without winning Guayaquil, Ecuador's commercial centre. Also unlike his predecessors, he enjoyed a working majority in Congress – at least until 1990, when his Izquierda Democrática became a victim of the notoriously fickle allegiances of Ecuador's numerous political parties. The loss of the government's majority threatened to increase both political instability and the problems of implementing a coherent economic reform programme.

Dr Borja inherited an economy in the grips of "stagflation". Tight fiscal and monetary policies were aimed at reducing inflation, but did little for his government's popularity. There were also efforts to ease balance of payments pressures, especially those of servicing the $11 billion external debt. Structural changes to restore growth included trade liberalization, tax reform and upgrading state enterprises. Unlike many of his Latin American peers, Dr Borja eschewed privatization, preferring to increase state control over key sectors such as oil. Another target was export diversification; Ecuador depends on oil, shrimps, coffee, cocoa and bananas for 90% of export earnings. One area of diversification the government has been keen to suppress, however, is the production of chemicals for the Colombian cocaine industry.

ECONOMIC PROFILE

Traditionally a producer of cocoa, coffee, pyrethrum and Panama hats; world's leading banana exporter. Oil produced since 1917 but exports began only after new discoveries in early 1970s; natural gas and hydroelectric resources ensure plentiful energy supplies. Intermediate and capital goods imported.

Growth Fruit, vegetables and cut flowers increasingly important exports. Fishing industry, particularly shrimps, growing rapidly. Gold production also rising.

Problems Sugar, once exported, now has to be imported. Manufacturing suffering due to small domestic market, inadequate investment and shortage of skilled labour.

OFFICIAL NAME Republic of Ecuador.
CAPITAL CITY Quito.
GEOGRAPHY The Andes run north-south through the country in three parallel ranges separated by wide basins; one of the peaks is Cotopaxi, the highest active volcano in the world. On the Pacific coast is a lowland area, part cultivated, part rain forest. Almost all the population live on the coast or in the mountain valleys; the east of the country, an impenetrable forest lowland at the edge of the Amazon basin, is almost uninhabited. *Highest point* Chimborazo 6,267 metres (20,560 feet). *Area* 270,670 sq km (104,506 sq miles).
PEOPLE *Population* 10.2m. *Density* 37 per sq km. *Ethnic groups* Amerindian (mainly Quechua) 50%, Mestizo 40%, European 8%.
RELIGION RC 96%, Protestant 2%.
LANGUAGE Spanish. Also Amerindian languages, especially Quechua.
EDUCATION Compulsory for six years for ages 6–14. Free in state schools, but there is a large private sector. There are 16 universities. State-run literacy centres and adult schools boost government educational spending to 28% of total budget.
CLIMATE Tropical, but moderated by altitude and the Humboldt current. Coastal temperature 23–25°C (73–77°F), wet season Jan–May. Beyond the mountains, temperature 23–27°C (73–81°F), humidity 90% and annual rainfall 6,000mm (240ins).
CURRENCY Sucre.
PUBLIC HOLIDAYS Jan 1, Jan 6, Feb 11–12, Easter, May 1, 24, Jul 24, Aug 10, Oct 9, 12, Nov 1–3, Dec 6, 25.
GOVERNMENT Republic since 1830. The head of state and chief executive is a president elected for a single 4-year term. The legislative Congress has 72 members: 12 elected nationally for 4 years, the remainder elected on a provincial basis for a single 2-year term.

IMPORTS AND EXPORTS

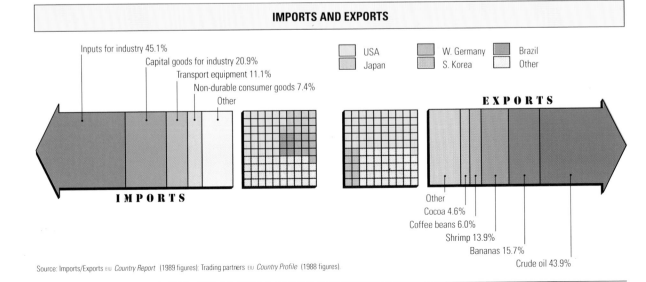

Inputs for industry 45.1%
Capital goods for industry 20.9%
Transport equipment 11.1%
Non-durable consumer goods 7.4%
Other

USA
Japan
W. Germany
S. Korea
Brazil
Other

EXPORTS

IMPORTS

Other
Cocoa 4.6%
Coffee beans 6.0%
Shrimp 13.9%
Bananas 15.7%
Crude oil 43.9%

Source: Imports/Exports EIU *Country Report* (1989 figures); Trading partners EIU *Country Profile* (1988 figures).

COLOMBIA

Colombia's unhappy record of political strife and violence dates back to its emergence as a republic in 1830. Bitter civil wars between the federalist Liberal and centralist Conservative parties punctuated much of the 19th century. Blood was spilled on an epic scale in the final outburst of conflict between the two, "La Violencia" of 1948–57. About 300,000 died before a coalition government was agreed. This arrangement remained intact, in one form or another, until Virgilio Barco became president in 1986. But by then violence had plenty of new perpetrators: guerrillas, death squads and the drug trafficking cartels.

President Barco continued the task of trying to encourage guerrillas to stop fighting and bring change to Colombia by participating in the political mainstream. In this he had a certain amount of success. Mr Barco also took on the drug cartels whose influence over many areas of political and economic life – not to mention the judiciary – had reached dangerous levels. In his last year of office he launched an all-out attack on the drug barons which propelled Colombia into a new phase of violence.

When César Gaviria Trujillo, a Liberal like Mr Barco, became president in August 1990 he attempted to restore power-sharing, using a broad-based cabinet to ensure support for constitutional change and continuing the war against the drug barons, both considered key factors in bringing an end to the violence. The constitutional reforms, initiated by Mr Barco, should widen access to the political system and make the government more accountable.

Economic policy in the 1990s is expected to maintain the priorities of the previous decade: fiscal restraint, a flexible exchange rate and prompt servicing of the $17 billion external debt. Colombia's refusal to reschedule its debts brought costs in the late 1980s in the form of slower GDP growth. Economic liberalization based on export promotion is the strategy for restoring growth favoured by the government. It should be helped by the continuing broadening of the country's economic base. Development of the Guajira and other coal deposits, an increase in oil production and plans to mine gold offer a much brighter future than coffee and cocaine alone could have done.

OFFICIAL NAME Republic of Colombia.
CAPITAL CITY Bogotá.
GEOGRAPHY 80% of Colombians live in the high valleys and intermontane plateaus of the Andes. Most of the coastal plains and the interior lowlands, stretching from the Andes to the Orinoco, are covered in tropical rain forest. *Highest point* Colón 5,775 metres (18,950 feet). *Area* 1,141,748 sq km (440,831 sq miles).
PEOPLE *Population* 30.2m. *Density* 26 per sq km. *Ethnic groups* Mestizo 50%, Mulatto 23%, European 20%, African 5%.
RELIGION RC 97%, Protestant 1%.
LANGUAGE Spanish.
EDUCATION Free and compulsory for five years to be taken between ages 6–12. Education takes up nearly 20% of the country's budget.
CLIMATE Tropical, with a range of 23–27°C (73–81°F) on the coast, colder at higher altitudes; temperatures seldom exceed 18°C (64°F) in Bogotá. Annual rainfall 2,500mm (100ins) in the Amazon basin and on the coast, less in other regions.
CURRENCY Colombian peso.
PUBLIC HOLIDAYS Jan 1, 6, Mar 19, Maundy Thu, Good Fri, May 1, Ascension, Corpus Christi, Jun 9, 29, Jul 20, Aug 7, 15, Oct 12, Nov 1, 11, Dec 8, 25.
GOVERNMENT Republic since 1830. The chief executive is a president elected for a 4-year term. He governs with the help of a cabinet drawn from the bicameral Congress which consists of a 112-member Senate and a 199-member House of Representatives.

ECONOMIC PROFILE

Economy based on growing coffee and, to a much lesser extent, cotton and bananas. Well endowed with mineral resources: gold, oil, emeralds, coal, nickel, platinum and silver. Some manufactures exported to Andean neighbours. Major supplier of cocaine to USA and other markets.

Growth Resurgence of oil production; exports resumed in 1986. Development of Cerrejón Norte coalfields could mean coal overtakes coffee as leading export.

Problems Agriculture has suffered from violence in rural areas; food imported although Colombia has capacity to feed itself. Financial sector still recovering from crisis in early 1980s. Disorder deters investors.

IMPORTS AND EXPORTS

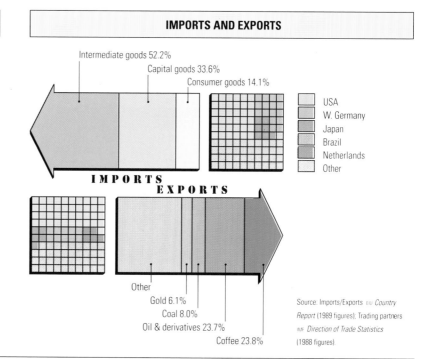

Intermediate goods 52.2%
Capital goods 33.6%
Consumer goods 14.1%

USA
W. Germany
Japan
Brazil
Netherlands
Other

IMPORTS
EXPORTS

Other
Gold 6.1%
Coal 8.0%
Oil & derivatives 23.7%
Coffee 23.8%

Source: Imports/Exports EIU *Country Report* (1989 figures); Trading partners IMF *Direction of Trade Statistics* (1988 figures).

VENEZUELA

Venezuela became a republic in 1830 and for the next century its history was largely one of dictatorships. However, since 1958 it has enjoyed stable democracy, with power normally alternating between the slightly left-of-centre Acción Democrática (AD) and the Christian Democrat party, Copei. The military has concentrated on border disputes with Guyana and Colombia and, more recently, the unwelcome presence of Colombian guerrillas. Venezuela's own guerrillas have been persuaded to swap the gun for the ballot box.

The picture has less attractive aspects. Occasional outbursts of unrest have been dealt with harshly and there are periodic allegations of corruption in high places. The use of the country's oil wealth to erect a vast state machinery has presented ample opportunities for venality.

Until oil was discovered in commercial quantities in 1914, Venezuela's economy was based on coffee and, to a lesser extent, cocoa and cattle. By 1930 the country had become the world's first major oil exporter and the largest producer after the USA. Oil gave Venezuela the chance to develop into a modern country; in the 1950s and 1960s it had the highest GDP per head in Latin America. The state took an increasing share of oil profits, finally nationalizing the industry in 1976. Its role grew throughout the 1970s, as oil prices rose to unprecedented heights. But the effects of excessive dependence on a single commodity started to be felt. This dependence remains a problem, despite recent attempts to diversify the economy; oil still accounts for 80% of export earnings.

The governments of the 1980s had to contend with lower oil prices, which made balancing the budget and external accounts difficult. The AD administration of Jaime Lusinchi (1984–89) failed to address these problems effectively. It was Carlos Andrés Peréz, also of the AD, who instituted swingeing austerity measures immediately after he took office in January 1989. Violent riots followed, in which around 300 people died.

Mr Peréz's liberal economic programme was in complete contrast to the nationalistic and populist tenor of his first term in office in the 1970s and went as far as to envisage greater private sector involvement in the oil industry, which he had nationalized. However, implementation of some key aspects, notably restructuring public sector enterprises, was expected to provoke widespread opposition, not least from conservative elements within the AD.

OFFICIAL NAME Republic of Venezuela.

CAPITAL CITY Caracas.

GEOGRAPHY The west two arms of the Andes enclose the shallow, freshwater coastal Lake Maracaibo, whose basin is a large oil field. East of the lake is a range of coastal mountains containing most of the population and the capital. From here a wide plain stretches to the swampy delta of the Orinoco. Inland is the heavily forested and sparsely populated granite mass of the Guiana highlands. *Highest point* Pico Bolívar 5,007 metres (16,430 feet). *Area* 912,050 sq km (352,144 sq miles).

PEOPLE *Population* 19.2m. *Density* 21 per sq km. *Ethnic groups* Mestizo 69%, European 20%, African 9%, Amerindian 2%.

RELIGION RC 92%.

LANGUAGE Spanish.

EDUCATION Free and compulsory for 6 years to be undertaken between ages 7–14. There are 11 universities.

CLIMATE Tropical, with a rainy season Apr–Oct. On the coast, average temperature 28°C (82°F) and appreciably lower rainfall. Cooler in the highlands, with an average of 21°C (70°F) in Caracas.

CURRENCY Bolívar.

PUBLIC HOLIDAYS (* = half day) Jan 1, Feb, Carnival, Easter, Apr 19, May 1, Jun 24, Jul 5, 24, Oct 12, Dec 24*–25, 31.

GOVERNMENT Federal republic. The head of state and chief executive is a president, elected for a single 5-year term, as is the legislative National Congress, made up of a 196-member Chamber of Deputies and a Senate of 47 elected members and all past presidents.

ECONOMIC PROFILE

Oil provides 80% of export earnings, although Venezuela is no longer world's largest exporter due to Opec constraints. Overseas refining and distribution facilities have been bought. Iron, steel and aluminium are also exported.

Growth Bauxite reserves and abundant hydroelectricity could encourage expansion of aluminium production. Iron ore, coal, natural gas and gold being developed. Agriculture beginning to revive with investment.

Problems Manufacturing for domestic market hurt in 1980s by price controls and import curbs.

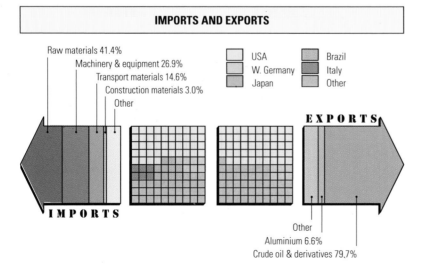

IMPORTS AND EXPORTS

Raw materials 41.4%
Machinery & equipment 26.9%
Transport materials 14.6%
Construction materials 3.0%
Other

USA
W. Germany
Japan
Brazil
Italy
Other

EXPORTS

IMPORTS

Other
Aluminium 6.6%
Crude oil & derivatives 79.7%

Source: EIU *Country Profile* (1988 figures).

GUYANA

A former British territory, Guyana became independent in 1966. It was ruled by Forbes Burnham, a member of the Afro-Guyanese minority in a racially divided country, from 1964 until his death in 1985. Steadily increasing his own and the state's influence, he became intolerant of opposition and attracted condemnation from human rights activists.

The economy has preoccupied his successor, Desmond Hoyte. Foreign companies, whose operations had been nationalized, were encouraged to return to help manage the key sugar and bauxite industries. The IMF and other multilateral agencies initially supported the policy changes, and foreign debts were rescheduled. But economic growth remained elusive; real GNP declined by an average 4.9% a year between 1984–88. By 1989 the government had fallen into disfavour with the IMF over payments arrears, and with human rights activists over allegations of renewed repression following strikes over food shortages and austerity measures. Notwithstanding this, lack of cohesion in the opposition was expected to enable Mr Hoyte to remain at the helm.

Bauxite, rice and sugar are Guyana's economic foundations. Considerable potential also lies in huge timber reserves, livestock, gold and diamonds. Dependence on imported oil could be reduced by exploiting hydroelectricity.

OFFICIAL NAME Co-operative Republic of Guyana.
CAPITAL CITY Georgetown.
GEOGRAPHY Much is rain forest. A fertile coastal strip with a central plateau supports most of the population. *Area* 215,000 sq km (83,000 sq miles).
PEOPLE *Population* 811,000. *Density* 4 per sq km. *Ethnic groups* Asian Indian 51%, African 31%, Mixed 12%, Amerindian 4%.
RELIGION Protestant 34%, Hindu 34%, RC 18%, Muslim 9%.
LANGUAGE English. Also Urdu, Hindi, Amerindian and Creole.
EDUCATION Free and compulsory for ages 6–14.
CLIMATE Tropical, with a rainy season Apr–Aug.
CURRENCY Guyana dollar.
PUBLIC HOLIDAYS Jan 1, Feb 23, Good Fri, Easter Mon, May 1, Id al-Fitr, May 1, Jul 1, Id al-Adha, 1st Mon in Aug, Mouloud, Dec 25–26.
GOVERNMENT Republic within the UK Commonwealth. Head of state and chief executive is the president. The 65-member legislative assembly sits for a 5-year term.

SURINAM

The former Dutch Guiana gained independence in 1975, and was under military domination for most of the 1980s. Colonel Desi Bouterse, leader of a 1980 coup, so outraged world opinion by murdering 15 opponents two years later that Dutch, American and EC aid was cut off. The economic consequences were disastrous and forced Colonel Bouterse gradually to return to a more democratic posture. After elections in November 1987, Ramsewak Shankar became president, but Colonel Bouterse remained on the scene.

The elections brought the resumption of Dutch aid, made all the more vital because of rebel disruption of the crucial bauxite/aluminium industry. However, Dutch aid was again frozen after a military coup in December 1990 which ousted President Shankar. It was followed by the reinstatement as military commander of Colonel Bouterse, viewed as the driving force behind the military intervention and Mr Shankar's replacement by a more compliant civilian administration.

OFFICIAL NAME Republic of Surinam.
CAPITAL CITY Paramaribo.
GEOGRAPHY Much is jungle. Most people live in a narrow coastal zone. *Area* 163,265 sq km (63,040 sq miles).
PEOPLE *Population* 395,000. *Ethnic groups* Asian Indian 35%, Creole 32%, Indonesian 15%, Bush Negro 10%, Amerindian 3%, Chinese 3%.
RELIGION Hindu 27%, RC 23%, Muslim 20%, Protestant 19%.
LANGUAGE Dutch. Also Hindi, Javanese and Creole.
EDUCATION Free to age 18 and compulsory 6–14.
CLIMATE Sub-tropical; high rainfall on coast.
CURRENCY Surinam guilder.
PUBLIC HOLIDAYS Jan 1, Feb 25, Phagwa, Easter, May 1, Id al-Fitr, May 1, Jul 1, Nov 25, Dec 25–26.
GOVERNMENT Military-dominated republic. A 54-member National Assembly elects the executive president who is advised by a civilian-military Council of State.

FRENCH GUIANA

The only remaining European colony on the South American mainland, French Guiana is sparsely inhabited, with most people confined to the coastal strip; the interior is heavily forested. A French overseas department, it houses the Kourou base of the European Ariane satellite-launching rocket, together with a French military base.

Except for rice, agriculture is little developed. The interior has valuable reserves of tropical hardwoods and large deposits of bauxite and kaolin but transport difficulties have limited their exploitation. The territory is overwhelmingly dependent on French aid and on imports from France and the USA. The government is by far the largest employer, but unemployment is high.

OFFICIAL NAME Department of French Guiana.
CAPITAL CITY Cayenne.
GEOGRAPHY Mostly tropical rain forest. *Area* 91,000 sq km (35,000 sq miles).
PEOPLE *Population* 93,600. *Ethnic groups* Creole 43%, Chinese 14%, French 11%.
RELIGION RC 87%, Protestant 4%, Animist 4%.
LANGUAGE French. Also a Creole patois.
EDUCATION Compulsory for ages 6–16.
CURRENCY French franc.
PUBLIC HOLIDAYS Jan 1, Shrove Tue, Good Fri, Easter Mon, May 1, Ascension, Whit Mon, Jul 14, Nov 11, Dec 25.
GOVERNMENT French overseas department. 2 deputies are sent to the French National Assembly.

BRAZIL

Brazil has boundless potential and has experienced spectacular growth, but it has still not crossed the divide between the developing and developed worlds. With about half South America's population, Brazil has the eighth largest economy in the world and is a prime producer of coffee and sugar. The country has barely begun to exploit its vast mineral and energy resources, but its manufacturing sector has grown dramatically in recent years. During the economic miracle years of 1968–73 GDP growth averaged over 10% a year.

One reason why Brazil remains part of the third world is its failure to find the right political structure. After two decades of military rule, the country took a step towards democracy in 1985 when an electoral college picked a civilian president. In 1989 another landmark was achieved with the first free, direct presidential elections since 1960. However, the new president, Fernando Collor de Mello, lacked a secure base in Congress. This encouraged him to govern by decree and added fuel to the debate over whether Brazil should have a parliamentary rather than presidential style of government. A referendum in 1993 is expected to resolve the issue.

Another obstacle to Brazil's membership of the developed world is the extreme poverty of most of the population. Income inequality is probably greater than in any other newly industrializing country, and has been exacerbated since 1980. About 60% of the population is estimated to be living outside the modern economy, a third is malnourished and the pressures of poverty have resulted in at least 16m children being abandoned.

OFFICIAL NAME Federative Republic of Brazil.

CAPITAL CITY Brasilia.

GEOGRAPHY Two-thirds of Brazil is covered by forest. The great majority consists of plateaus, low mountain ranges and tablelands. The only large lowland area is the upper Amazon basin. There is no coastal plain, but sheltered bays provide several excellent deep-water harbours, especially in the south-east. *Highest point* Pico da Neblina 3,014 metres (9,890 feet). *Area* 8,511,965 sq km (3,286,490 sq miles).

PEOPLE *Population* 144.4m. *Density* 17 per sq km. *Ethnic groups* Mulatto 22%, Portuguese 15%, Italian 11%, Spanish 10%, other European 17%, Mestizo 12%, African 11%, Japanese 1%.

RELIGION RC 89%, Protestant 7%.

LANGUAGE Portuguese.

EDUCATION Free to age 19, and compulsory for ages 7–14. There is a parallel private system. There are 47 state and 21 private universities.

CLIMATE Tropical, wet and unchanging in the Amazon basin, average temperature around 25°C (77°F). Cooler in the highlands and on the coast, with more definite seasons and rainfall of 1,000–1,500mm (40–60ins), most falling in Dec–Apr.

CURRENCY Cruzeiro.

PUBLIC HOLIDAYS Jan 1, Good Fri, Easter Mon, Apr 21, May 1, Ascension, Corpus Christi, Sep 7, Oct 12, Nov 2, 15, Dec 25.

GOVERNMENT Federal republic of 25 states, plus the federal district of Brasilia and 3 territories. The legislative National Congress has a 75-member Senate representing the regions and a 90-member Chamber of Deputies elected for 4 years by compulsory popular vote. The executive president is elected by direct ballot.

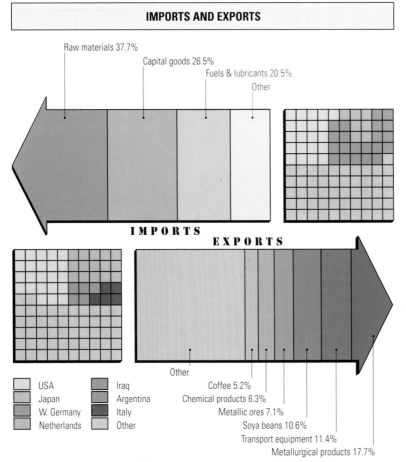

IMPORTS AND EXPORTS

Raw materials 37.7%
Capital goods 26.5%
Fuels & lubricants 20.5%
Other

IMPORTS

EXPORTS

USA
Japan
W. Germany
Netherlands
Iraq
Argentina
Italy
Other

Other
Coffee 5.2%
Chemical products 6.3%
Metallic ores 7.1%
Soya beans 10.6%
Transport equipment 11.4%
Metallurgical products 17.7%

Source: Imports/Exports EIU *Country Profile* (1989 figures); Trading partners IMF *Direction of Trade Statistics* (1988 figures).

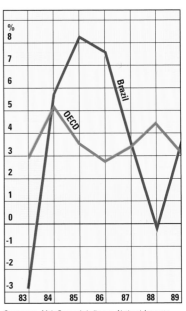

GDP GROWTH

Brazil

OECD

83 84 85 86 87 88 89

Source: OECD *Main Economic Indicators, National Accounts*; EIU *Economic Risk Service*.

Poverty is compounded by a relatively high population growth rate and deteriorating educational standards. In 1985 over a fifth of the adult population was estimated to be illiterate, with a much higher proportion in the north-east than in the wealthiest states of the south-east: Rio de Janeiro, São Paulo and Minas Gerais. The north-east is prone to drought and its poverty is exacerbated by the structure of land holding. Holdings of less than 10 hectares represent 68% of all titles. The nine states of the region, home to 40m people, have the highest rates of infant mortality and malnutrition. Not surprisingly they have become a hotbed of political unrest.

In the past governments tried to defuse such tensions by encouraging landless peasants and the urban unemployed to move into the vast virgin territories of the Amazon region. The tax incentives and government funds designed for this purpose were misused and no greater equity has resulted. Constitutional changes to land ownership have been strongly resisted by those who stood to lose by the reforms. The government has, however, decided to inhibit the expansion of agriculture in the Amazon because of the ecological consequences of slash-and-burn farming.

Brazil's foreign debt, at over $114 billion, is higher than that of any other South American country and on a par with Mexico's. Servicing this debt has been beyond Brazil's means. Instead, it has muddled through with a mixture of new loans, reschedulings and rollovers, not to mention the accumulation of interest arrears. In mid-1990 these amounted to $9 billion but Mr Collor's government gave priority to other problems, notably the country's deep-rooted hyperinflation. His radical "New Brazil Plan" unveiled in March 1990 subjected the economy to a brutal liquidity squeeze and aimed at transforming a public sector deficit of 8% of GDP into a surplus. Structural reforms to raise revenues and reduce expenditure included a wide-ranging privatization programme, dismissals of federal employees, the removal of import barriers and the de-indexation of wages. Progress was slower than hoped for, impeded by a difficult political situation and labour resistance. But provided that the arrears problem is resolved and new debt relief negotiated, Brazil appears to have a chance of removing another obstacle to membership of the developed world.

ECONOMIC PROFILE

Largest coffee producer for over 100 years, growing about one-third of world total. Sugar and cocoa are other important traditional crops; soya and oranges are being developed as part of export drive. Manufacturing has grown rapidly since the 1960s, with heavy government involvement, first to meet domestic requirements and then for export.

Growth New agricultural exports have captured strong market share; Brazil supplies 85% of the world's orange juice concentrates. Need for large trade surpluses has stimulated exploitation of mining and energy resources, particularly oil, hydroelectricity and nuclear power. Use of new technology is increasing industrial productivity.

Problems Agriculture neglected as investment went to industry; coffee harvest perennially vulnerable to drought and frost. Food, oil and many raw materials imported. Capital to sustain development is in short supply. Falling oil prices have made alcohol fuel programme uneconomic.

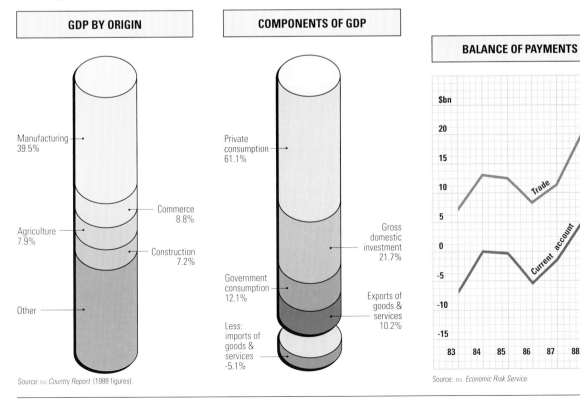

GDP BY ORIGIN

Manufacturing 39.5%
Commerce 8.8%
Agriculture 7.9%
Construction 7.2%
Other

Source: EIU *Country Report* (1988 figures).

COMPONENTS OF GDP

Private consumption 61.1%
Gross domestic investment 21.7%
Government consumption 12.1%
Exports of goods & services 10.2%
Less: imports of goods & services -5.1%

BALANCE OF PAYMENTS

$bn

Trade
Current account

83 84 85 86 87 88 89

Source: EIU *Economic Risk Service.*

PERU

Peru has had an extremely difficult time for more than a decade. Successive governments have failed to find a remedy for economic imbalances with the result that inflation has soared and living standards have plummeted. At the same time enormous arrears have accrued on the external debt, preventing new foreign loans and deterring overseas investors.

The deterioration in the economy has been matched by a decline in the security situation. Since 1980 the Maoist Sendero Luminoso (Shining Path) terrorists have widened their theatre of operations from the department of Ayacucho to the capital, Lima. Thousands have died as a result of the guerrilla war, but the security forces have come nowhere near defeating the insurgents. With the economy stagnating, Sendero Luminoso has been able to find many new recruits.

Immediately after being elected in June 1990, President Alberto Fujimori embarked on a tough reform programme aimed at stabilizing the economy and restoring Peru's reputation with international creditors and lenders. However, his "Fujishock" proposals offered the poor only greater hardship. They were also unlikely to improve the chances of a positive response by the Sendero Luminoso to Mr Fujimori's initial peaceful overtures. The president and his Cambio-90 party, which lacked a congressional majority, could also expect close scrutiny by the military, which in the late 1980s had become a law unto itself.

ECONOMIC PROFILE

Silver, gold, copper, lead and zinc are the main foreign exchange earners, followed by coffee, cotton, fishmeal, textiles; also coca and cocaine. Agriculture has declined as manufacturing has expanded. Food and capital goods imported.

Growth Considerable growth potential exists in the mining and energy sectors.

Problems Once important fishing industry in decline, because of overfishing and appearance of warm Niño current. Oil production dwindling due to inadequate investment in exploration. Manufacturing suffering from foreign exchange constraints and weak domestic demand.

OFFICIAL NAME Republic of Peru.
CAPITAL CITY Lima.
GEOGRAPHY A narrow strip of desert lowland along the coast has less rainfall than the Sahara, but still maintains the bulk of the population. Most of the country is the high Andes, with some cultivation and pastureland up to 4,000 metres (13,000 feet). To the east are the lower forested slopes of the Montaña, giving way to marshy jungle lowlands at the edge of the Amazon basin. *Highest point* Nevado Huascarán 6,768 metres (22,200 feet). *Area* 1,285,216 sq km (496,230 sq miles).
PEOPLE *Population* 21.2m. *Density* 16 per sq km. *Ethnic groups* Amerindian 54% (mainly Quechua), Mestizo 32%, European 12%.
RELIGION RC 92%, other Christian 2%.
LANGUAGE Spanish and Quechua. Also Aymará and Autoctonos.
EDUCATION Free and compulsory for ages 6–15. There are 25 state and 10 private universities.
CLIMATE Tropical, but moderated by altitude. Cool Humboldt current makes coast temperate; rainfall is negligible. Monthly average temperatures in Lima in the range 16–23°C (61–73°F).
CURRENCY Inti.
PUBLIC HOLIDAYS (* = half day) Jan 1, Maundy Thu, Good Fri, May 1, 2nd Sun of May, Jun 24*, 3rd Sun of Jun, Jul 28–29, Aug 30, Oct 8, Nov 1, Dec 8, 25.
GOVERNMENT Republic since 1824. The head of state and chief executive is a president elected every 5 years. The legislative national Congress has a 60-member Senate elected on a district basis and a 180-member Chamber of Deputies elected from the constituencies.

IMPORTS AND EXPORTS

Intermediate goods 50.4%
Capital goods 35.3%
Consumer goods 13.1%
Other

IMPORTS **EXPORTS**

USA
W. Germany
Japan
Argentina
Brazil
Other

Other
Oil & oil products 6.0%
Zinc 11.2%
Fishmeal 12.0%
Copper 23.2%
Non-traditional products 28.1%

Source: EIU *Country Report* (Imports/Exports 1989 figures; Trading partners 1988 figures).

BALANCE OF PAYMENTS

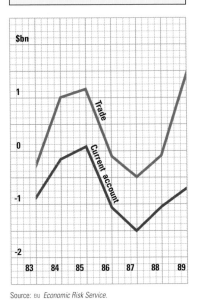

$bn

Trade

Current account

83 84 85 86 87 88 89

Source: EIU *Economic Risk Service*.

BOLIVIA

After no fewer than 189 coups in 154 years, Bolivian politics have been fairly stable since the early 1980s. Civilian presidents have held power since 1982. Víctor Paz Estenssoro, president from 1985 to 1989, inherited a dizzying rate of inflation driven by enormous budget and balance of payments deficits. To make matters worse, the price of tin, the most important export after gas, collapsed. Dr Paz, who in the 1950s had nationalized tin mines and made sweeping agrarian reforms, decided on drastic cuts in government spending and lifted restrictions on foreign trade.

The policy paid dividends in as much as the rot of five years' economic decline was stopped, inflation fell from its 1985 rate of nearly 12,000% and foreign loans began to flow in again. But it was only the start of a long and painful restructuring process which has been continued by Dr Paz's successor, Jaime Paz Samora, who took office in August 1989.

Agriculture is the main sector of the economy, employing half of the working population. It is largely labour-intensive and in the central highlands subsistence farming predominates, so productivity levels are low. A succession of droughts and floods has also dogged the sector in recent years. Mining is beginning to show a comeback but large reserves of petroleum and natural gas remain unexploited because of lack of investment. Official figures make Bolivia the poorest country in South America. There is, however, another side to the story: a vast black economy run on dollars earned by the cocaine trade and, to a lesser extent, contraband. Bolivia not only grows coca but also produces paste and unrefined cocaine. More than half a million people make a living from the drugs trade, but with US support the government is trying to stifle the industry.

OFFICIAL NAME Republic of Bolivia.
CAPITAL CITY La Paz (administrative); Sucre (legal).
GEOGRAPHY Most Bolivians live in the high Altiplano, with Lake Titicaca at its northern end. The Oriente, east of the Andes, is a sparsely populated lowland area. *Highest point* Nevado Sajama 6,520 metres (21,390 feet). *Area* 1,098,581 sq km (424,160 sq miles).
PEOPLE *Population* 6.9m. *Density* 6 per sq km. *Ethnic groups* Amerindian 45% (Quechua 25%, Aymará 17%), Mestizo 31%, European 15%.
RELIGION RC 94%.
LANGUAGE Spanish. Also Quechua and Aymará.
EDUCATION Free and compulsory for ages 6–14.
CLIMATE Annual mean temperature of 10°C (50°F) in the Altiplano, with dry winters and wet summers; southern Altiplano is desert. Hot, 25°C (77°F), and wet year-round in the Oriente.
CURRENCY Boliviano.
PUBLIC HOLIDAYS Jan 1, Good Fri, May 1, Corpus Christi, Aug 6, Nov 1, Dec 25.
GOVERNMENT Republic since 1825. The constitution provides for a 27-member Senate and 130-member Chamber of Deputies, both elected for 4 years, and an executive president also elected for 4 years by popular vote.

PARAGUAY

After 34 years in power General Alfredo Stroessner was sent into exile in Brazil in February 1989 after a coup engineered by his erstwhile supporters. The general had remained in power only partly because of his control of the ruling Colorado party; more important had been the prizes for those loyal to him and the at-times brutal repression of opposition. The system he created finally dislodged him: as two factions within the ruling party jostled for the succession, one led by General Andrés Rodríguez seized the initiative by ousting the man at the top. The convincing victory of General Rodríguez in the May 1989 presidential election legitimized the takeover. The general has permitted some political liberalization. Just how far such reforms should go is a bone of contention within the still-divided Colorado party. But while the opposition remains fragmented, its monopoly of power and patronage seems secure.

Rapid economic growth in the 1970s and early 1980s had undoubtedly helped to keep General Stroessner in power. It came about mainly as a result of the $20 billion Itaipú hydroelectric project, a joint venture with Brazil that brought thousands of jobs to Paraguay. As work on Itaipú tailed off, another hydroelectric scheme, Yacyretá, was planned to take up the slack but this has been delayed by financial difficulties. As a result, slower – and occasionally negative – growth, fiscal deficits, high inflation and balance of payments difficulties have become as familiar in Paraguay as elsewhere in the subcontinent.

The country's fortunes now once again rest on agriculture and to an unknown extent on the contraband trade with Brazil and Argentina. The unpalatable choice facing Paraguay's government is whether to tackle the country's economic problems with swift but painful austerity measures or to stick to the policies of the past in the interests of preserving the political status quo.

OFFICIAL NAME Republic of Paraguay.
CAPITAL CITY Asunción.
GEOGRAPHY The country is landlocked, but has access by river to the Atlantic. The eastern third is a forested plateau, bounded by low mountains to the north and by the Paraná river to the south and east. Most people live in the centre. The Paraguay basin is swampy. *Highest point* 700 metres (2,300 feet). *Area* 406,752 sq km (157,050 sq miles).
PEOPLE *Population* 4m. *Density* 10 per sq km. *Ethnic groups* Mestizo 90%, Amerindian 3%.
RELIGION RC 96%, Protestant 2%.
LANGUAGE Spanish. Also Guaraní.
EDUCATION Free and compulsory for six years. 2 universities.
CLIMATE Sub-tropical, with monthly average temperatures in the range 17–29°C (63–84°F). Annual rainfall 1,250mm (50ins) in the west and 800mm (30ins) in the east.
CURRENCY Guaraní.
PUBLIC HOLIDAYS Jan 1, Mar 1, Maundy Thu, Good Fri, May1, 15, Jun 12, Aug 15, Immaculate Conception, Dec 25.
GOVERNMENT Republic. The president holds extensive executive powers. The bicameral legislature consists of a lower house of 72 seats and a Senate of 36 seats. Two-thirds of the seats are allocated to the majority party, the remainder are divided among the minority parties in proportion to the votes cast.

URUGUAY

Once a model of democracy, Uruguay had a traumatic period of military domination from 1973 to 1985. With the return to civilian rule came demands that those in the military accused of horrendous human rights abuses should be called to account. But a referendum decided that such an inquisition could do more harm than good. This decision undoubtedly helped to guarantee a smooth transfer of power in March 1990 from one elected president to another.

President Luis Alberto Lacalle faced a number of economic challenges, the most immediate of which was to strike a decisive blow against obstinately high inflation. This involved tackling the fiscal deficit – and at times falling foul of organized labour. To achieve this aim, in a country which has in the past enjoyed social security and other benefits unparalleled in Latin America, the president has attempted to govern by consensus, seeking backing within the ranks of the Colorado opposition party as well as from his own Blanco party.

Like his predecessor, Mr Lacalle has pursued diversification of an economy largely dependent on two export commodities: beef and wool. Capital investment in agriculture is needed to introduce new technology and – since the domestic market is so small – new export industries must be encouraged. Another, perhaps more formidable, task is to reduce the country's vulnerability to events in Argentina and Brazil, which can cause violent fluctuations in export earnings, tourism receipts and capital flows.

OFFICIAL NAME Oriental Republic of Uruguay.
CAPITAL CITY Montevideo.
GEOGRAPHY The smallest country in South America, it has a plateau to the north and west and a region of low, granitic hills to the east and south. There is lowland around the coast, where there are tidal lakes and dunes, and along the valleys of the Uruguay and the Negro. Almost half of the population live in the capital. *Highest point* Cerro de las Animas 501 metres (1,640 feet). *Area* 176,215 sq km (68,040 sq miles).
PEOPLE *Population* 3.1m. *Density* 17 per sq km. *Ethnic groups* European 92%, Mestizo 3%, Mulatto 2%.
RELIGION RC 60%, Protestant 2%, Jewish 2%.
LANGUAGE Spanish.
EDUCATION Free and compulsory for ages 6–15. 1 university.
CLIMATE Temperate, with a monthly average temperature range of 10–22°C (50–72°F). Annual rainfall of around 900mm (35ins), evenly distributed through the year.
CURRENCY Uruguayan new peso.
PUBLIC HOLIDAYS Jan 1, 6, Feb/May Carnival Week, Easter, April Tourist Week, Apr 19, May 1, 18, Jun 19, Jul 18, Aug 25, Oct 12, Nov 2, Dec 8, 25.
GOVERNMENT Republic since 1825. The government has undertaken to overhaul the constitution, which currently provides for an executive president elected for 5 years and a bicameral legislative Congress, which consists of a 30-member Senate and a 99-member Chamber of Representatives elected for 5 years by PR.

ECONOMIC PROFILE

Abundant good grassland fostered livestock industry. Beef and wool brought prosperity until 1950s and are still the leading exports. Rice, citrus and dairy products also exported. No oil or gas, but hydroelectric power provides 90% of energy; electricity exported to Argentina. Few mineral resources. Principal industries process agricultural produce.

Growth Developing non-traditional exports including textiles, leather, plastics and chemicals. Fishing and free trade zones offer potential.

Problems Badly hit by loss of European and US markets for beef, although new buyers have been found in Middle East and Asia. Small domestic market restricts growth.

IMPORTS AND EXPORTS

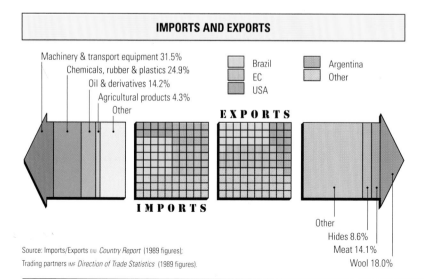

Machinery & transport equipment 31.5%
Chemicals, rubber & plastics 24.9%
Oil & derivatives 14.2%
Agricultural products 4.3%
Other

Brazil
EC
USA
Argentina
Other

EXPORTS
IMPORTS

Other
Hides 8.6%
Meat 14.1%
Wool 18.0%

Source: Imports/Exports EIU *Country Report* (1989 figures);
Trading partners IMF *Direction of Trade Statistics* (1989 figures).

BALANCE OF PAYMENTS

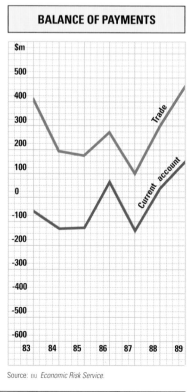

$m
500
400
300
200
100
0
-100
-200
-300
-400
-500
-600

Trade
Current account

83 84 85 86 87 88 89

Source: EIU *Economic Risk Service*.

CHILE

After 16 years of authoritarian military rule the Chilean presidency passed to a civilian in March 1990. Patricio Aylwin, leader of the centre-left Concertación coalition had been elected president in December 1989, a year after a plebiscite had put an end to General Augusto Pinochet's bid for a further eight-year term.

Mr Aylwin inherited the government of a country which, atypically in Latin America, had enjoyed rapid growth in the previous five years, with inflation at manageable levels and exports booming, thanks to General Pinochet's bold free-market policies. From these the new president is unlikely to depart significantly, although the Christian Democrat bent of his government will mean more state spending in social areas and a revision of labour laws to give workers somewhat more security.

Economic prospects for the country are good. Private (domestic and foreign) investment in Chile's extensive natural resources continue to give the economy momentum, and repayments of the foreign debt (reduced by debt equity swaps and buybacks under General Pinochet) are unlikely to present the government with undue problems. Mr Aylwin does, however, have to deal with the thorny issue of human rights violations during the long spell of military rule, a task which will be more difficult as long as General Pinochet remains commander-in-chief of the armed forces. Aylwin may also find that left-wing terrorism, far from dying out now that a civilian government is in power, proves to be another difficult problem.

OFFICIAL NAME Republic of Chile.
CAPITAL CITY Santiago.
GEOGRAPHY The Atacama desert in the north is one of the driest places on earth, while the southern region of islands, lakes and mountains is one of the bleakest and wettest. The population is concentrated in the centre, mostly in the mineral-rich sedimentary plains that lie between the high Andes and the coastal mountains that block access to the sea. Chile is seismically active, with frequent earth tremors and several active volcanoes. *Highest point* Ojos del Salado 6,880 metres (22,570 feet). *Area* 756,945 sq km (292,260 sq miles).
PEOPLE *Population* 12.9m. *Density* 17 per sq km. *Ethnic groups* Mestizo 90%, Amerindian 6%, European 4%.
RELIGION RC 80%, Protestant 6%.
LANGUAGE Spanish.
EDUCATION Free and compulsory for ages 6–14.
CLIMATE Generally temperate, moderated by the cool Humboldt current. Desert-dry in the north. Over 4,000mm (160ins) of rain a year in extreme south, mostly in winter. Mean annual temperature in Santiago is 15°C (59°F).
CURRENCY Chilean peso.
PUBLIC HOLIDAYS Jan 1, Good Fri, Holy Sat, May 1, 21, Jun 29, Aug 15, Sep 18–19, Oct 12, Nov 1, Dec 8, 25.
GOVERNMENT Republic. Executive power is vested in the president who is directly elected for a 4-year term. The legislative bicameral National Congress comprises the 47-member Senate and 120-member Chamber of Deputies.

IMPORTS AND EXPORTS

USA
Japan
W. Germany
Brazil
France
UK
Argentina
Italy
Other

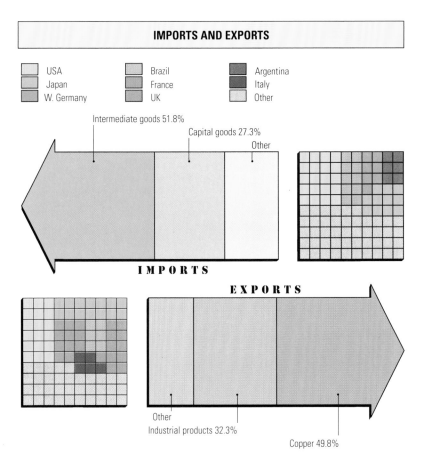

Intermediate goods 51.8%
Capital goods 27.3%
Other

IMPORTS

EXPORTS

Other
Industrial products 32.3%
Copper 49.8%

Source: EIU *Country Report* (1989 figures).

BALANCE OF PAYMENTS

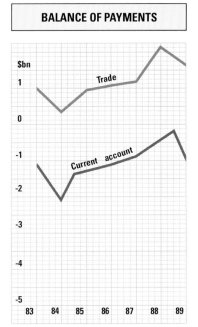

$bn

Trade

Current account

83 84 85 86 87 88 89

Source: EIU *Economic Risk Service*.

THE AMERICAS

ECONOMIC PROFILE

Agriculture and mining most important sectors. Exports of copper, also fruit, timber products, fishmeal. Nearly self-sufficient in many basic foods. Diverse manufacturing sector.

Growth Output of gold, silver, molybdenum and cobalt; La Escondida copper reserves, world's largest, started production in 1991. Coal, natural gas and hydroelectricity resources are being exploited.

Problems Economy still vulnerable to drop in copper prices and increases in the price of oil, domestic production of which is declining. Industry shaken by impact of trade liberalization and increased foreign competition.

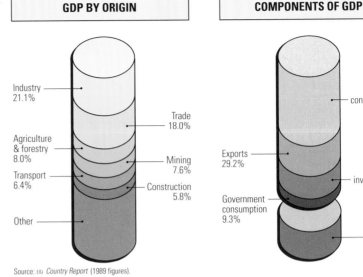

GDP BY ORIGIN

Industry 21.1%
Trade 18.0%
Agriculture & forestry 8.0%
Mining 7.6%
Transport 6.4%
Construction 5.8%
Other

Source: EIU *Country Report* (1989 figures).

COMPONENTS OF GDP

Private consumption 67.4%
Exports 29.2%
Fixed investments 21.8%
Government consumption 9.3%
Less: imports -27.7%

ARGENTINA

A military coup in 1930, some 80 years after the foundation of the federal republic of Argentina, marked the start of a long period of military intervention. Although the country enjoyed two periods of civilian rule under Presidents Frondizi and Illia (1958–62 and 1963–66) and a brief spell of democracy under military presidents in the early 1970s, it returned to direct military control in 1976. However, badly demoralized by defeat in the Falklands/Malvinas war in 1982, as well as by the negative political climate created by the brutal campaign (the "dirty war") waged against alleged subversives and terrorists in the late 1970s, during which 10,000–15,000 people "disappeared", the regime called elections in October 1983.

The new Radical Party president, Dr Raúl Alfonsín sought to prevent future military interventions and political instability by building a stable democracy. He failed, however, to come up with effective prescriptions for the serious inflationary and balance of payments problems besetting the country, partly because he was hamstrung by opposition from the Peronists – the party founded in the 1940s by General Juan Domingo Perón – and partly because he was afraid that

ECONOMIC PROFILE

Economy's wealth based on rich agricultural produce of the pampas – beef, grains and wool. Industry developed to cut imports of consumer goods but still heavily based on agricultural processing. Some capital goods and manufactures imported. Abundant energy resources.

Growth Natural gas being developed to supply growing petrochemicals industry. Burgeoning computer industry. Great potential, as yet

unexploited, in fishing, forestry and copper and uranium mining.

Problems Manufacturing suffering from domestic recession and likely to feel the pinch of import competition. Oil production has declined due to lack of incentives for exploration and competition from other energy sources. Troubled financial sector cannot mobilize sufficient development funds; capital flight a serious problem and foreign investment disappointing.

OFFICIAL NAME Argentine Republic.
CAPITAL CITY Buenos Aires.
GEOGRAPHY Mostly an alluvial plain between the Andes and the Atlantic, covered in the north by forest and savannah and in the south by the rolling, fertile grasslands and marshes of the pampas. In the west are the Andes, high and wild in the north, but lower in Patagonia, a glaciated region of forests, lakes and meadows. Much of the coast is swampy, especially around the mouth of the Plata. *Highest point* Aconcagua 6,960 metres (22,830 feet). *Area* 2,766,889 sq km (1,068,300 sq miles).
PEOPLE *Population* 31.9m. *Density* 11.5 per sq km. *Ethnic groups* European 98%, Mestizo 2%.
RELIGION RC 92%, Protestant 3%, Jewish 2%.
LANGUAGE Spanish.
EDUCATION Free to university level and compulsory for ages 6–14. There are 29 state and 23 private universities.
CLIMATE Mostly temperate, though sub-tropical in the north-east and sub-Arctic in the extreme south. Temperatures in Buenos Aires around 23°C (73°F) in summer, 9°C (48°F) in winter. Widespread winter frosts. Most rain falls in the east.
CURRENCY Austral.
PUBLIC HOLIDAYS Jan 1, Good Fri, May 1, 25, Jun 10, Jul 9, Aug 17, Dec 8, 25.
GOVERNMENT Federal republic with 22 provinces and 1 national territory. The legislative Congress has a Senate whose 46 members are appointed for 9 years by the provinces and a Chamber of Deputies whose 254 members are elected every 4 years. The chief executive and head of state, the president, is chosen by an electoral college every 6 years.

any signs of social unrest resulting from austerity measures could give the armed forces a pretext to return to the political stage. When he left office in July 1989 inflation was running at nearly 4,000% and the country was unable to meet all the payments due on its $62 billion foreign debt.

Dr Alfonsín's successor was Carlos Saúl Menem, a Peronist who had won the presidential elections held in May 1989 because of his populist rhetoric. This evaporated as soon as he took office, when the new president instantly embarked on economic reforms which promised liberalization, free-market principles and, most importantly, a reduction in the state's pervasive involvement in many areas of the economy.

This course has brought Mr Menem into direct conflict with labour, traditionally one of the pillars of the Peronist movement, as well as costing him the support of some sections of his own party. Because his austerity programme has been somewhat erratically followed it has also been slow to yield results, but Mr Menem's "capitalist revolution" should eventually help Argentina to grow out of its unhealthy dependence on a handful of agricultural products.

The beef, grains and wool that made Argentina the richest country in Latin America and one of the richest in the world in the early part of the 20th century still account for nearly half of export earnings. The manufacturing sector, built up behind high tariff barriers in the 1960s, is in no fit state to compete with imports. However, as long as progress is made on the economic front, the threat of renewed military intervention must fade.

GDP BY ORIGIN

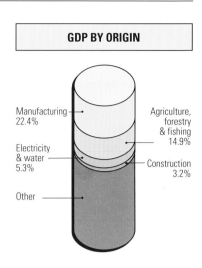

Manufacturing 22.4%
Agriculture, forestry & fishing 14.9%
Electricity & water 5.3%
Construction 3.2%
Other

COMPONENTS OF GDP

Public & private consumption 79.8%
Exports 17.9%
Investment 12.0%
Less: imports -9.7%

Source: EIU *Country Report* (1988 figures).

IMPORTS AND EXPORTS

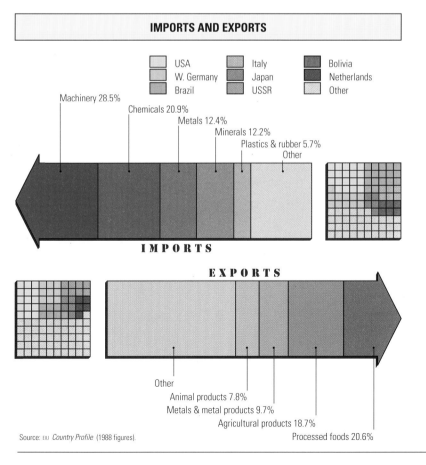

USA
W. Germany
Brazil
Italy
Japan
USSR
Bolivia
Netherlands
Other

Machinery 28.5%
Chemicals 20.9%
Metals 12.4%
Minerals 12.2%
Plastics & rubber 5.7%
Other

IMPORTS

EXPORTS

Other
Animal products 7.8%
Metals & metal products 9.7%
Agricultural products 18.7%
Processed foods 20.6%

Source: EIU *Country Profile* (1988 figures).

BALANCE OF PAYMENTS

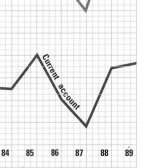

Trade
Current account

$bn

Source: EIU *Economic Risk Service.*

EUROPEAN COMMUNITY

EC institutions

The **Commission** initiates, implements and supervises community action. Its 17 members are appointed by member governments, but their loyalty is pledged to the community as a whole.

The **Council of Ministers** directly represents governments and takes final decisions on proposals presented by the Commission. Its composition depends on the subject under discussion. Each state is represented by one minister but states are allocated voting rights in proportion to their size.

The 518-member **European Parliament** was directly elected for the first time in 1979. Elections are held every 5 years. The parliament has joint responsibility with the Council of Ministers for finalizing the EC's annual budget; its role in legislation is mainly advisory. In theory it also has the power to dismiss the Commission. Parliamentary sessions are held in Strasbourg, its secretariat is based in Luxembourg, most committees sit in Brussels. In January 1989 a parliamentary vote made a move to Brussels probable, but the final decision rests with the member governments.

The **Economic and Social Committee** is an advisory body consulted by the Commission and the Council of Ministers on a variety of issues. Its members come from interest groups including employers, trade unions, consumers and farmers.

The **European Council**, consisting of the heads of government of member states, meets twice a year.

Economic and Monetary Union

Jacques Delors, president of the European Commission, has proposed a three-stage plan for union. Stage One aims to bring each member country into the European Monetary System. Stage Two, projected for 1994, would set up a system of central banks, with the European Central Bank at its head, and continue the monetary convergence of members. Stage Three centres on the creation of a European currency with permanently-fixed exchange rates.

1992 and the internal market

A white paper prepared by the Commission lists some 300 actions to be taken to achieve a single market by the end of 1992. They fall into three categories:

Removal of physical barriers: the abolition of frontier controls.

Removal of technical barriers: the programme to harmonize national manufacturing standards to be replaced by mutual recognition of national standards, pending the adoption of European standards.

Removal of fiscal barriers: levels of VAT and excise duty to be adjusted to fall within 2.5% of a target level.

1951 Treaty of Paris establishes European Coal & Steel Community (members: Belgium, France, West Germany, Italy, Luxembourg, Netherlands).

1955 Six ECSC members form committee to investigate the feasibility of a common market.

1957 Treaty of Rome establishes European Economic Community (EEC). European Atomic Energy Community (Euratom) set up.

1961 UK, Ireland, Denmark, Norway apply for EEC membership.

1962 Common market in agriculture established.

1963 France vetoes UK membership of EEC; Ireland, Norway and Denmark withdraw applications.

1966 UK again applies for membership; France again vetoes.

1967 EEC, ECSC and Euratom amalgamate as European Community (EC).

1972 Renewed applications for membership from UK, Ireland, Denmark and Norway accepted; Norway rejects membership in referendum, other three become members on January 1, 1973.

1979 European Monetary System established. First direct elections to European Parliament.

1981 Greece becomes a member of the EC.

1985 Greenland (no longer under full Danish rule) withdraws.

1986 Spain and Portugal join. Single European Act signed.

1987 Turkey and Morocco apply to join. Morocco's application rejected, further negotiations on Turkey's membership may begin in 1993.

1988 Committee established to discuss European monetary union.

1990 East Germany joins EC with German unification. Formal talks between EC and Efta on creation of European Economic Area (EEA).

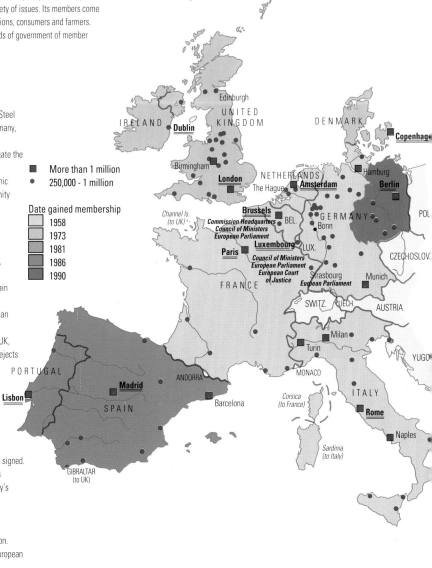

More than 1 million
250,000 - 1 million

Date gained membership
1958
1973
1981
1986
1990

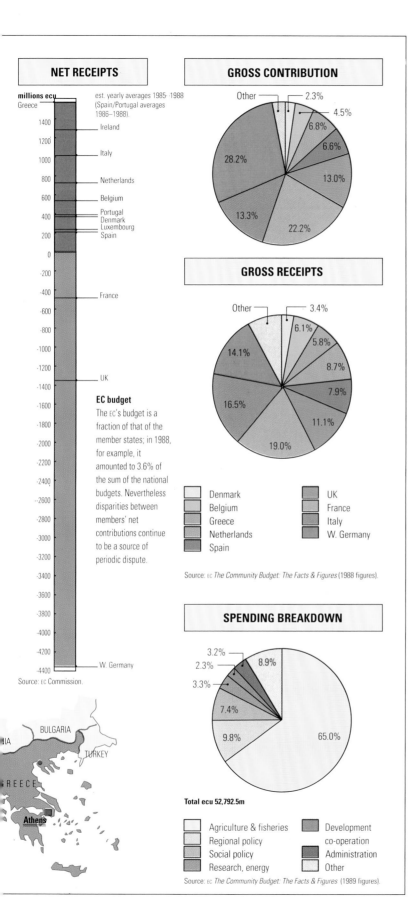

NET RECEIPTS

millions ecu

est. yearly averages 1985–1988 (Spain/Portugal averages 1986–1988).

Greece

- 1400 — Ireland
- 1200
- 1000 — Italy
- 800 — Netherlands
- 600 — Belgium
- 400 — Portugal / Denmark / Luxembourg
- 200 — Spain
- 0
- -200
- -400 — France
- -600
- -800
- -1000
- -1200
- -1400 — UK
- -1600
- -1800
- -2000
- -2200
- -2400
- -2600
- -2800
- -3000
- -3200
- -3400
- -3600
- -3800
- -4000
- -4200
- -4400 — W. Germany

Source: EC Commission.

EC budget

The EC's budget is a fraction of that of the member states; in 1988, for example, it amounted to 3.6% of the sum of the national budgets. Nevertheless disparities between members' net contributions continue to be a source of periodic dispute.

GROSS CONTRIBUTION

Other — 2.3%
4.5%
6.8%
6.6%
13.0%
28.2%
13.3%
22.2%

GROSS RECEIPTS

Other — 3.4%
6.1%
5.8%
8.7%
7.9%
14.1%
11.1%
16.5%
19.0%

- Denmark
- Belgium
- Greece
- Netherlands
- Spain
- UK
- France
- Italy
- W. Germany

Source: EC *The Community Budget: The Facts & Figures* (1988 figures).

SPENDING BREAKDOWN

3.2% — 8.9%
2.3%
3.3%
7.4%
9.8%
65.0%

Total ecu 52,792.5m

- Agriculture & fisheries
- Regional policy
- Social policy
- Research, energy
- Development co-operation
- Administration
- Other

Source: EC *The Community Budget: The Facts & Figures* (1989 figures).

BULGARIA

TURKEY

GREECE

Athens

UNITED KINGDOM

Britain in the 1990s is a country gradually coming to terms with a profound reorientation. As one immediate legacy of Margaret Thatcher's 11-year premiership that ended in late 1990, what happened to Britain between the second world war and 1979 already appears to belong to a different age. Those were decades of a seemingly inexorable decline in Britain's relative wealth and standing in the world. Neither Labour nor Conservative administrations had much success applying a corporatist philosophy to the management of the economy: sluggish growth, by international standards, was accompanied by a succession of sterling crises, problems over the balance of payments and ever more acute confrontations between government and organized labour. The 1980s brought sweeping changes in almost every area of national life, with consequences that are still playing themselves out.

A string of government initiatives were devoted to unleashing a supply-side revolution in the economy and a reversal of many deeply embedded cultural attitudes towards industry, private enterprise and the role of the state. It is still unclear whether, as a result, Britain is now capable of combining steady growth with low inflation through most of a normal economic cycle – or whether many of the achievements of the 1980s have made little difference to the underlying weaknesses of Britain as a modern industrial competitor.

The equivocal nature of the inheritance left by Mrs Thatcher to her successors is exemplified by the record on privatization. The sale of billions of pounds worth of state assets into the private sector has left the state with a dramatically reduced role. It is also clear that many of the companies involved – most notably, perhaps, British Airways and British Steel – are now performing significantly better than at any time in their state-owned past. But many remain, like British Gas or British Telecom, powerfully dominant within their domestic sectors. How far their privatization will lead to an influx of new competitors and a better deal for consumers must still depend on future regulatory action.

Similarly, deregulation changed the face of the City of London in the 1980s; but a successful restructuring of the securities industry is not yet assured. The City still shares with New York and Tokyo the status of a leading financial centre; the accelerating integration of Europe's national capital markets offers it the opportunity to consolidate that position. But it will also draw other European capitals, notably Paris and Frankfurt, to challenge London's pre-eminence. The original rationale behind the "Big Bang" revolution of 1986 was that, by blowing apart the cartelized structure of the old City, it would lay the basis for a more

OFFICIAL NAME United Kingdom of Great Britain and Northern Ireland.

CAPITAL CITY London.

GEOGRAPHY The UK's varied landscape ranges from the relatively undeveloped uplands of north Wales and Scotland to the intensively farmed lowlands of south-east England. Over 75% of land is used for agriculture. The UK's largest lake, Lough Neagh, is in Northern Ireland, most of which is lowland. Major ports are dotted around the long, indented coastline. A tunnel under the English Channel, due for completion in June 1993, will provide the first rail link between Great Britain and the rest of Europe. The highly urbanized population is densest in the south-east – around 20% live in Greater London. The other main cities are in the more heavily industrialized areas of the centre and north. *Highest point* Ben Nevis 1,343 metres (4,410 feet). *Area* 244,100 sq km (94,250 sq miles).

PEOPLE *Population* 57.1m. *Density* 234 per sq km. *Ethnic groups* White 94%, Indian 1%, West Indian/Guyanese 1%, Pakistani 1%, mixed 0.4%, Chinese 0.2%, African 0.2%, Bangladeshi 0.2%.

RELIGION Christian 85% (Church of England 50%, RC 13%, Church of Scotland 4%, Methodist 2%, Baptist 1%), Muslim 2%, Jewish 1%, Hindu 1%, Sikh 1%.

LANGUAGE English. Also Welsh and Gaelic.

EDUCATION Compulsory for ages 5–16 and free at all levels. Some 6% of pupils attend private schools. There are 45 universities. Scotland and Northern Ireland have separate educational systems.

CLIMATE Temperate and variable. Monthly average temperatures 15°C (60°F) in summer, 5°C (40°F) in winter. Annual rainfall 900–1,000mm (35–40ins), less in London, heaviest Oct–Feb.

CURRENCY Pound sterling.

PUBLIC HOLIDAYS Jan 1, Good Fri, Easter Mon, first and last Mon in May, last Mon in Aug, Dec 25–26.

GOVERNMENT Parliamentary monarchy. There is no written constitution. The legislature has 2 chambers: the House of Commons has 650 members elected for a term of up to 5 years from single-member constituencies; the less important House of Lords consists of hereditary and appointed life peers. Executive power is in the hands of the prime minister, usually leader of the majority party in the Commons, and a cabinet drawn mainly from the House of Commons.

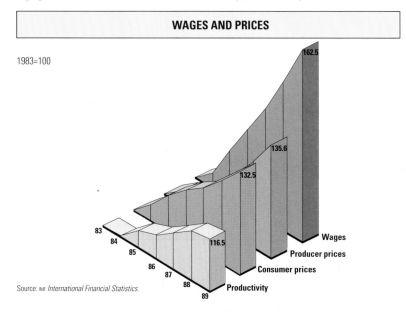

WAGES AND PRICES

1983=100

162.5
135.6
132.5
116.5

83
84
85
86
87
88
89

Wages
Producer prices
Consumer prices
Productivity

Source: IMF *International Financial Statistics.*

Northern Ireland

The six north-eastern counties of Ireland remained part of the UK when the rest of Ireland won its independence in 1921. About 60% of the population is Protestant. Anti-Catholic discrimination led to increasingly violent opposition. In an attempt to quell the violence, the British government sent troops to the province in 1969. By the end of the first quarter of 1991, 898 members of the security forces and 1,963 civilians had lost their lives as a result of the "troubles".

The devolved parliament at Stormont was prorogued and direct rule imposed from Westminster in 1972. Subsequent attempts to impose a new administrative structure fell foul of growing religious and political polarization.

The Anglo-Irish agreement, signed in November 1985, allows the Irish government the right of consultation on Northern Ireland's affairs. It is vigorously opposed by Northern Ireland's Unionists.

Isle of Man

A dependency of the crown, and not part of the United Kingdom, the Isle of Man has its own legislative assembly and legal system. The Manx government controls direct taxation and the island has developed as a tax shelter and financial centre.

North Sea oil

North Sea oil transformed Britain from an oil importer to the world's fifth largest oil exporter within a decade. Benefits to the economy included savings on imports of around $10 billion a year and export earnings of $8 billion a year by the mid-1980s and an oil industry employing 100,000 people. Oil also fuelled the growth of Britain's foreign assets, income from which will assume greater importance as the oil runs out. On the negative side, oil gave a boost to the exchange rate at a time when manufactures were struggling to compete in export markets. Between 1979 and 1984, the UK changed from being a net exporter of manufactures to a net importer.

Oil production passed its peak in 1985 and fields coming online in the 1990s are smaller than those discovered in the 1970s. Although oil production has fallen, that of natural gas has increased, a trend which is expected to continue.

Shetland Is.

Orkney Is.

Outer Hebrides

Inner Hebrides

Loch Ness

SCOTLAND

■ More than 1 million
● 250,000 - 1 million

Edinburgh

NEW YORK 7 hours
(3¾ hours by Concorde)

NORTHERN IRELAND

Belfast

NORTH

Isle of Man

YORKSHIRE AND HUMBERSIDE

E I R E

NORTH WEST

EAST MIDLANDS

WEST MIDLANDS

EAST ANGLIA

E N G L A N D

Birmingham

WALES

Severn

Cardiff

London

Thames

SOUTH EAST

SOUTH WEST

Tokyo 15 hours

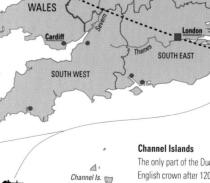

New York 11½ days

Channel Is.

Kobe 38 days (via Suez Canal)

Regional tensions

Despite the UK's small size and relatively long history as a unified state, national and regional differences persist in many areas of social, political, economic and cultural life. Some differences are enshrined in the law; Scotland, for example, has separate legal and educational systems. Nationalist sentiment in Wales and Scotland and support for devolution are fuelled by an increasingly marked political divide; in the 1987 general election, the Conservatives won a majority in parliament but took only 10 of the 72 Scottish seats and 8 of the 38 Welsh seats.

The gap in living standards between north and south is more perceived than actual; regional income variations are less marked in the UK than in most other Western European countries. Also the early 1990s recession particularly affected the south-east, bringing incomes more in line with other regions.

Channel Islands

The only part of the Duchy of Normandy retained by the English crown after 1204, the Channel Islands do not form part of the United Kingdom and have their own legislative assemblies and legal systems. Low income tax has encouraged the development of Jersey and Guernsey, the largest islands, as financial centres, supplementing tourism and agriculture as the islands' main source of income.

efficient and homogenous securities industry – in which several British firms might eventually emerge as world players. This could still be achieved. But as yet the industry remains crippled by surplus capacity; new technologies have been only half-digested and structural changes in many of the City's individual markets are still far from complete.

Popular attitudes have undergone a sea-change in many respects. Most Britons no longer expect their trade unionists to play an important role in the day-to-day politics of their country. The notion that government should actively intervene in the economy, to redress any shortcomings in the working of the free market, is now widely regarded as part of a defunct ideology – though opinions still vary widely over the extent to which government policies might influence the effectiveness of British industry at the margin. Unemployment is tolerated at levels which, though unexceptional by European standards, would have seemed shocking in earlier decades. On the other hand, sharply lower levels of state taxation are probably entrenched for good. And home ownership remains a peculiar obsession of the British.

In its relations with the rest of the world, Britain continues to see itself in two contexts at once: on the one hand enjoying a special relationship with America – undoubtedly strengthened by events during the Gulf war of early 1991 – while, on the other, fulfilling its role as a leading member of the EC. A widespread antipathy towards closer links with the continent, which even lingered on for some years after Britain's entry into the EC in 1973, seems now to have gone for good. The result in the 1990s may be that Britain can prosper from its unique Janus-like status, facing East and West. But a good many politicians from both main parties, fearing a federalist future, remain deeply ambivalent about the steady encroachment of the EC on the UK parliament's affairs. This largely explains why foreign policy has assumed an unusual importance in British politics over recent years – and Mrs Thatcher's failure to handle the central issues with sufficient sensitivity led directly to her fall from power.

Three fundamental problems are as evident in the 1990s as in every other post-war decade – with ever-more damaging consequences. The structure of both central and local government looks barely adequate to the administrative tasks of government in a modern state. Reforms of the time-honoured working practices of the House of Commons and the degree of public access to official information are not yet high on the political agenda; the need to reform local government has been highlighted by the failure of the poll tax, introduced in 1990–91 with disastrous political results. The British educational system provides a hopelessly inadequate background for far too many young people, forcing them to enter the labour market with few if any qualifications and no practical skills. Last, and as intractable as ever, the problem of a divided society in Northern Ireland goes on generating terrorist violence that afflicts mainland Britain as well as the province itself.

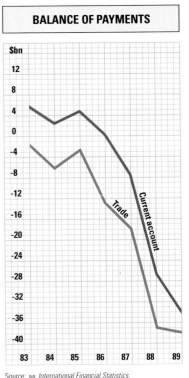

BALANCE OF PAYMENTS

Source: IMF *International Financial Statistics.*

ECONOMIC PROFILE

Manufacturing has declined in importance since 1960s, while service sector has grown to become the mainstay of the economy. Severe contraction of traditional industries – textiles, coal, steel, engineering, transport equipment. Recovery in 1980s of some manufacturing industries due in part to greater productivity, also evident in shrinking agricultural sector which provides efficiently for two-thirds of food needs. Level of state ownership in industry greatly reduced.

Growth Chemicals, expanding into high-technology, high value-added products. Financial services, particularly through strengthening of London's global position. UK is favourite location for Japanese and American investment in EC.

Problems Oil production declining. Further rationalization still needed in capital goods, shipbuilding, truck and coal industries. High unemployment persists despite skilled labour shortages.

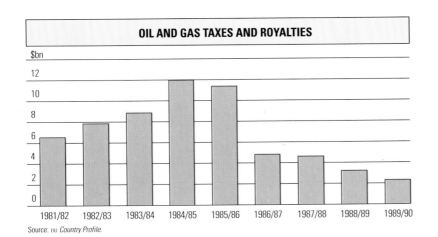

OIL AND GAS TAXES AND ROYALTIES

Source: EIU *Country Profile.*

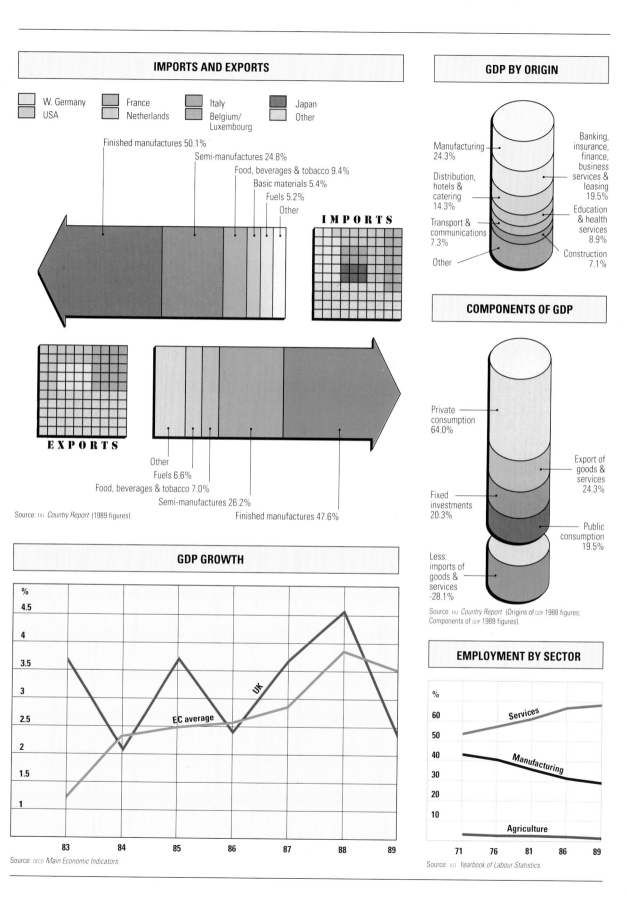

IMPORTS AND EXPORTS

W. Germany
USA
France
Netherlands
Italy
Belgium/
Luxembourg
Japan
Other

Finished manufactures 50.1%
Semi-manufactures 24.8%
Food, beverages & tobacco 9.4%
Basic materials 5.4%
Fuels 5.2%
Other

IMPORTS

EXPORTS

Other
Fuels 6.6%
Food, beverages & tobacco 7.0%
Semi-manufactures 26.2%
Finished manufactures 47.6%

Source: EIU *Country Report* (1989 figures).

GDP GROWTH

%
4.5
4
3.5
3
2.5
2
1.5
1

UK
EC average

83   84   85   86   87   88   89

Source: OECD *Main Economic Indicators*.

GDP BY ORIGIN

Manufacturing
24.3%

Distribution,
hotels &
catering
14.3%

Transport &
communications
7.3%

Other

Banking,
insurance,
finance,
business
services &
leasing
19.5%

Education
& health
services
8.9%

Construction
7.1%

COMPONENTS OF GDP

Private
consumption
64.0%

Fixed
investments
20.3%

Less:
imports of
goods &
services
-28.1%

Export of
goods &
services
24.3%

Public
consumption
19.5%

Source: EIU *Country Report* (Origins of GDP 1988 figures;
Components of GDP 1989 figures).

EMPLOYMENT BY SECTOR

%
60
50
40
30
20
10

Services
Manufacturing
Agriculture

71   76   81   86   89

Source: ILO *Yearbook of Labour Statistics*.

IRELAND

In 1921, after a war of independence, the Anglo-Irish treaty was signed conceding dominion status within the British Commonwealth to the 26 counties of the Irish Free State; the six northern counties had been given their own parliament within the UK the year before. Opposition to partition continued and two years of civil war ensued. In 1949 the last remaining constitutional ties with Britain were cut and the Free State became a republic.

Ireland's economy has always lagged behind that of the industrialized countries of Western Europe. The 1960s was a period of growth, then in 1973 Ireland joined the EC; but after the oil price rises of the same year, it soon ran into the problems of recession, rising inflation and a mounting balance of payments deficit. In the late 1970s the Fianna Fail government borrowed heavily to finance an ambitious programme of public spending. The habit continued in the early 1980s when governments came and went in quick succession. Ireland has been paying for this profligacy ever since: cutting public spending and borrowing are now the government's main priorities. A new consensus between government, unions, employers and agricultural interests on how to tackle economic problems, and the underpinning of investment by EC structural funds until 1993, should help offset the effects of higher oil prices in the wake of the Gulf crisis, and the slowdown in the US and UK economies.

The country has a tradition of mass emigration dating back to the great famine of 1847–50 when a million people left for Britain and the USA. Its demographic structure is similar to that of many developing nations; half the population is under 25. Industrial growth, encouraged by government incentives, has been greatest in high-technology rather than more labour-intensive sectors, and emigration is once again rising.

Irish unity remains high on the political agenda. The Anglo-Irish agreement signed in 1985 has been the vehicle for progress in this direction, and 1991 saw the start of new initiatives to resolve the problem of Northern Ireland. Recent governments have taken stronger measures against terrorism and can claim some success in stopping the Irish Republican Army (IRA) from using bases in the south for incursions into the north. Meanwhile, thousands of southerners cross the border every week to shop where prices are considerably lower.

OFFICIAL NAME Republic of Ireland.

CAPITAL CITY Dublin.

GEOGRAPHY Most of Ireland's high ground is around the coast; the centre is a lush, sometimes boggy, limestone plain dotted with lakes and low hills and drained by slow, winding rivers. The west coast is wild and rocky, with wide bays, while the east is much more sheltered. *Highest point* Carantuohill 1,041 metres (3,420 feet). *Area* 70,283 sq km (27,140 sq miles).

PEOPLE *Population* 3.5m. *Density* 51 per sq km. *Ethnic groups* Irish 96%, English and Welsh 2%, Northern Irish 1%.

RELIGION RC 94%, Church of Ireland 3%, Presbyterian 1%.

LANGUAGE Irish and English. Irish is the official first language but is not widely spoken.

EDUCATION Compulsory for ages 6–15 and free to university level, in either state or subsidized private schools. There are 7 universities.

CLIMATE An equable maritime climate greatly influenced by the Gulf Stream. Average temperatures around 5°C (40°F) in winter, rising to not more than 16°C (60°F) in summer. Annual rainfall around 1,500mm (60ins) in the west, half that in the east.

CURRENCY Punt.

PUBLIC HOLIDAYS Jan 1, Mar 17, Good Fri, Easter Mon, 1st Mon in Jun, 1st Mon in Aug, last Mon in Oct, Dec 25–26.

GOVERNMENT Republic since 1949. The head of state is a president elected by direct vote every 7 years. The legislature has two chambers. The upper house, the Senate, which has no power of veto, has 60 members, 11 nominated by the prime minister, the others indirectly elected. The lower house, the Dail, has 166 members elected by PR every 5 years. The chief executive, the Taoiseach (prime minister), is leader of the majority in power; the Taoiseach appoints the cabinet.

IMPORTS AND EXPORTS

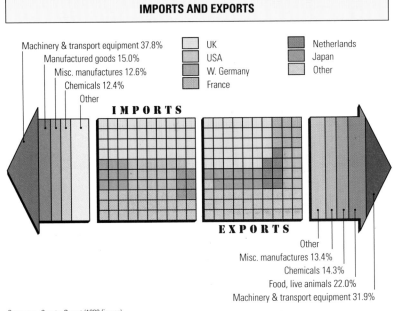

Machinery & transport equipment 37.8%
Manufactured goods 15.0%
Misc. manufactures 12.6%
Chemicals 12.4%
Other

UK
USA
W. Germany
France

Netherlands
Japan
Other

IMPORTS

EXPORTS

Other
Misc. manufactures 13.4%
Chemicals 14.3%
Food, live animals 22.0%
Machinery & transport equipment 31.9%

Source: EIU *Country Report* (1989 figures).

ECONOMIC PROFILE

Agriculture, traditionally dominant, now less important. Industrial expansion, largely financed by foreign capital, based on producing high-value goods for export.

Growth High-tech industries such as electronics, pharmaceuticals. Service industries, particularly tourism.

Problems Older industries such as textiles and footwear hit by foreign competition. Job creation not keeping pace with growth of labour force.

FRANCE

France has been described as an "idea necessary to civilization". It is also a nation essential to Europe. With both Atlantic and Mediterranean coastlines, it is the only country that belongs to northern and southern Europe, and its national culture embraces both mercurial Latin flair and the methodical industriousness more usually associated with northern societies. For centuries, France has played a focal role in European affairs, and not only politically: Paris has long paraded as the cultural champion of the West, the arbiter of artistic fashion and the melting-pot of new ideas. Economically, France has been slower to develop. Despite a notable record of scientific invention in the 19th century, it has only recently become a major industrial power in the forefront of technology. This remarkable post-war modernization has also helped it to secure the de facto political leadership of the EC, along with Germany.

Since the 1950s, France has become a dynamic, prosperous and confident country, with a well-balanced and open society. But the earlier part of the century was not a happy period. The 1914–18 war drained French strength. The interwar years were a time of decline, unrest and economic stagnation, leading to the defeat of 1940 and the German occupation. This humiliation spurred post-war renewal, though the recovery was obscured by political instability and divisive colonial wars (notably in Algeria) until General de Gaulle returned to power in 1958.

Modernization has shifted the economic focus from farming to industry, as more than 6m people have moved off the land and the cities have swelled. Agriculture still plays an important role, in this fertile and relatively spacious country, but the peasant has been replaced by the business-minded farmer. With many ups and downs, and despite recurrent problems with inflation and trade balances, the economy has moved steadily forward, especially in high-tech fields.

In foreign affairs and defence, General de Gaulle has left France with a strong legacy of independent-mindedness, coupled with dislike of American dominance of the Western alliance. He took France out of the military structure of Nato in 1966, though it remains part of the political wing. But the French have skilfully managed to identify EC interests with their own; they are among the most dedicated and enthusiastic of "Europeans". Not only has French agricul-

OFFICIAL NAME French Republic.
CAPITAL CITY Paris.
GEOGRAPHY The geography and economy of France are centred on five great river systems, those of the Rhine, the Rhône, the Seine, the Loire – whose fertile valley is known as the Garden of France – and the Garonne. In the centre are the old, eroded, largely forested ranges of the Massif Central and the Massif Armoricain. In the east are newer mountains, the Alps and the Jura; and the Pyrénées form the border with Spain in the south-west. To the north are the fertile, rolling hills and plateaus of the Paris basin. The Aquitaine basin forms a lowland area in the south-west and south-eastern lowlands surround the valley and delta of the Rhône. *Highest point* Mont Blanc 4,810 metres (15,780 feet). *Area* 547,062 sq km (211,210 sq miles).

PEOPLE *Population* 55.2m. *Density* 101 per sq km. *Ethnic groups* French 93%, Algerian 1.5%.
RELIGION RC 80%, Muslim 2%, Protestant 2%, Jewish 1%.
LANGUAGE French. Also Breton and Basque.
EDUCATION Compulsory for ages 6–16 and free in state schools; private schools, mainly RC, highly subsidized.
CLIMATE Temperate and wet on north coast; long hot summers and dry winters in the south; wet springs and autumns in the west; a continental climate in the centre and east. Temperatures in Paris are generally between 0°C (32°F) and 24°C (75°F).
CURRENCY French franc.
PUBLIC HOLIDAYS Jan 1, Easter Mon, May 1, 8, Ascension, Whit Mon, Jul 14, Aug 15, Nov 1, 11, Dec 25.
GOVERNMENT Republic. The head of state and chief executive is the president, elected by a simple majority in a 2-round election every 7 years. The president appoints the prime minister and the rest of the council of ministers. The 577-member National Assembly is elected for 5 years; PR has been used, but the current system is based on single-member constituencies. The second chamber, the Senate, is elected by a college of local councillors and members of the National Assembly.

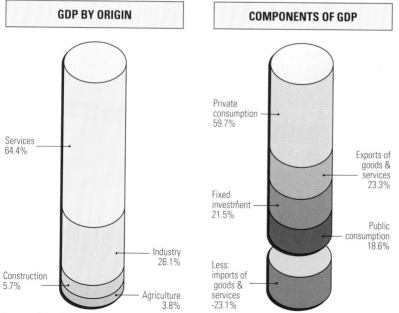

GDP BY ORIGIN

Services 64.4%
Industry 26.1%
Construction 5.7%
Agriculture 3.8%

COMPONENTS OF GDP

Private consumption 59.7%
Exports of goods & services 23.3%
Fixed investment 21.5%
Public consumption 18.6%
Less: imports of goods & services -23.1%

Source: EIU *Country Report* (1989 figures).

ture benefited greatly from the EC, but French vision and single-mindedness have enabled France to dominate many high-tech projects, such as Eureka, Airbus and the Ariane space programme. By retaining close economic ties with its former African possessions, France has also kept a good deal of influence in the third world.

In a highly centralized country with a tradition of state intervention, France has certainly benefited from intelligent state planning and the dynamic leadership of state technocrats, especially in regional development. France has been centralized since medieval times, when the Capetian monarchs forged its diverse elements into one nation. Napoléon Bonaparte continued the process, setting up the system of government by local state-appointed prefects. But Paris tended to suck the life-blood from the provinces, leaving them lethargic and resentful. The post-war revival brought new life to the regions and with it a new regional awareness and demands for more autonomy. In the 1980s, these demands finally began to be met by the Socialists' devolutionary reforms.

Today, many argue that the *étatiste* tradition, once valuable, is a liability in an age of open frontiers. Recent governments, of both the right and left, have begun to reduce state power in local affairs and the economy. This trend seems likely to continue, even though in 1988 the Socialist government halted the extensive privatization programme begun by its right-of-centre predecessor. But state influence remains strong, both structurally and informally: much real power is still in the hands of graduates of a handful of *grandes écoles*, who hold many key posts in the upper civil service and in both public and private agencies and corporations.

Class divisions remain strong. Wealth is still very unevenly shared and trade unions are weak. Yet in many other ways society has changed enormously since the war. Social formality has given way to a new free-and-easiness. Moral attitudes have relaxed, abortion has been legalized, the influence of the Catholic church has waned. Parental authority too has declined and parent-child relations have become more equal, while rigid classroom discipline has been replaced by informality, sometimes at the cost of high academic standards. In

BALANCE OF PAYMENTS

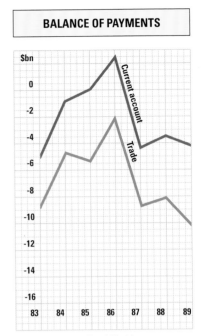

Source: IMF *International Financial Statistics.*

ECONOMIC PROFILE

Industry traditionally strong in heavy engineering, including railways and power stations; also vehicles, aircraft and weapons. Agriculture now modernized and very diverse; a big net exporter of food. Luxury goods like perfumes still play a role.

Growth Economy slowing due to high real interest rates. After expanding aggressively – particularly in America – companies are cutting costs. Public work contractors and telecommunications businesses well placed to benefit from the single European market. Growth in service and leisure industries also slowing.

Problems State companies – about one-third of GNP – lack capital. Car, steel and shipbuilding industries threatened by competition and saturated markets. Some high-tech businesses like computers and semi-conductors in serious trouble. Financial markets slow to expand and vulnerable to foreign competition post-1992.

IMPORTS AND EXPORTS

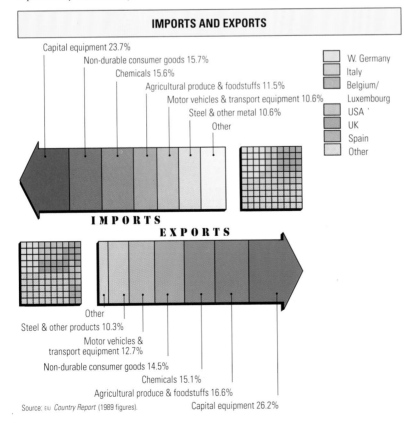

Capital equipment 23.7%
Non-durable consumer goods 15.7%
Chemicals 15.6%
Agricultural produce & foodstuffs 11.5%
Motor vehicles & transport equipment 10.6%
Steel & other metal 10.6%
Other

W. Germany
Italy
Belgium/
Luxembourg
USA
UK
Spain
Other

IMPORTS

EXPORTS

Other
Steel & other products 10.3%
Motor vehicles & transport equipment 12.7%
Non-durable consumer goods 14.5%
Chemicals 15.1%
Agricultural produce & foodstuffs 16.6%
Capital equipment 26.2%

Source: EIU *Country Report* (1989 figures).

Population

As a population centre, Paris still dominates the country: about 10m of France's 55m people live within the boundaries of Greater Paris. Only three other conurbations – Lyons, Marseilles and Lille – have populations over the 1m mark.

The past few years have seen a drift in population away from the capital for the first time. The new growth areas are where high-tech industries are expanding, in cities like Toulouse, Grenoble and Montpellier, coinciding with a southward shift in the centre of economic gravity as heavy industry in the Nord-Pas-de-Calais region has declined.

Railways

The high-speed TGV, transporting 90m travellers in its first seven years of operation, has enjoyed continued domestic success. In mid-1990 plans to develop a 350km/hour "Super-TGV" passenger train were announced. Proposed investment in 3,560km of new and updated TGV lines is expected to further cut travelling times on a network already offering strong competition to domestic air services.

The Community of European Railways' plans for 30,000 km of high-speed lines is being promoted as the harbinger of European economic integration, with Paris potentially just over two hours from London and three hours from Frankfurt.

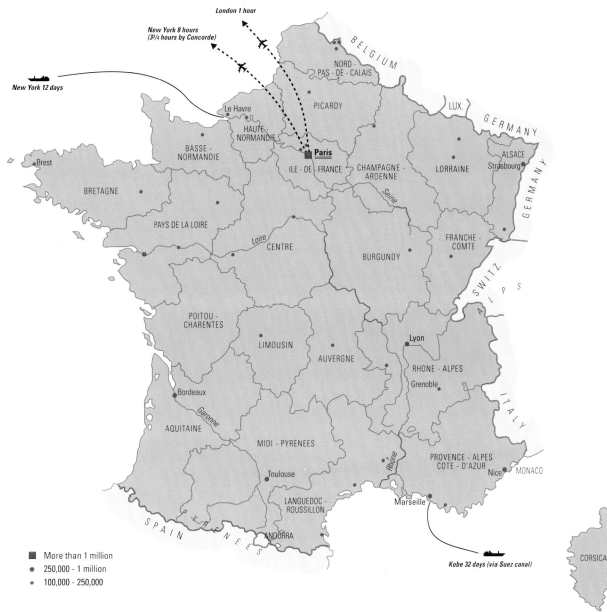

Monaco

An outpost of Genoa in the 12th century, Monaco has since been more or less independent and ruled by members of the Grimaldi family. It occupies about 1.5 sq km (0.6 sq miles) on France's Mediterranean coast; the economy depends on service industries, notably tourism and banking and finance.

Corsica

The fourth largest island in the Mediterranean was in turn under Arab, Pisan and Genoan rule until France annexed it in 1768, a few months before the birth of Napoléon Bonaparte, the island's most famous son.

Corsica gained the status of *collectivité territoriale* in 1982, with increased autonomy and its own directly elected assembly. This did not satisfy separatist movements, which have continued to mount sporadic terrorist attacks.

the cultural field, this seems to be the age of the dazzling performing arts, full of visual fireworks, rather than solid creativity: literature, philosophy and painting are all somewhat in the doldrums.

Despite class divisions, society has become more cohesive and less polarized, and this is reflected in recent political changes. General de Gaulle, during his decade as president from 1958 to 1969, did much to give the French new self-confidence and political stability, but the old French tendency to split into warring camps of right and left survived. In the 1980s, however, the trend was towards consensus. Not only has the once-powerful Communist Party declined, now representing a mere 10% of the electorate; but the Socialist Party, largely as a result of its experience of power from 1981 to 1986, has shifted from doctrinaire crypto-Marxism towards a moderate social-democratic stance that accepts the market economy. This change has loosened the old left-right divide and made possible hitherto unimaginable forms of partnership, such as "cohabitation" between a Socialist president and a right-wing government. The constitution devised for the Fifth Republic by General de Gaulle gives substantial powers to a directly elected president and seems well suited to the age-old French love of strong leaders. But the problem of relations between president and parliament has yet to be resolved.

France's economic problems are causing growing concern. Many state industries need capital to restructure their operations, but the government is cutting aid to industry. Large privatizations, the obvious solution, are unlikely until after legislative elections in 1993. Despite significant technological successes, France is still weak in crucial high-tech industries like computing. French companies have expanded aggressively abroad recently – notably in the United States – and are having trouble digesting large acquisitions. Capital investment is still relatively low and structural unemployment remains high. Added to this is the traditional weakness of the financial markets which risk losing out to London and Frankfurt, after 1992.

But the French enjoy such challenges. There is no lack of enthusiasm for new projects, and old chauvinistic attitudes have been abandoned in favour of a new international outlook, exemplified by France's leading role in the drive towards monetary and political union within the EC. Modernism is welcomed and enjoyed, and the latest gadgets find a ready market. But traditional values have not been forsaken. Good food and wine are still important, as are style and elegance, albeit in a new, more informal interpretation.

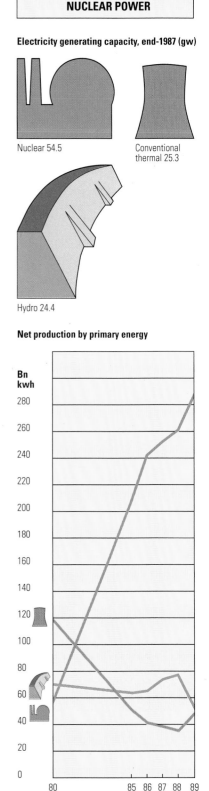

NUCLEAR POWER

Electricity generating capacity, end-1987 (gw)

Nuclear 54.5

Conventional thermal 25.3

Hydro 24.4

Net production by primary energy

Bn kwh

Source: EIU *Country Profile.*

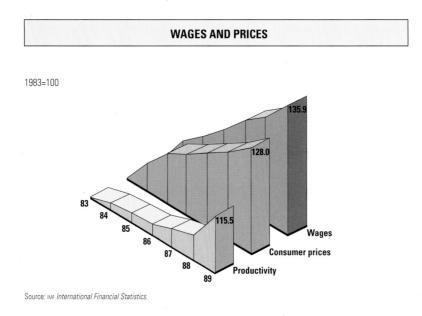

WAGES AND PRICES

1983=100

135.9

128.0

115.5

83
84
85
86
87
88
89

Wages

Consumer prices

Productivity

Source: IMF *International Financial Statistics.*

BELGIUM

The Dutch-speaking Flemings and the French-speaking Walloons have shown every sign of regretting at leisure a union created in haste in 1830. And yet, despite some superficial indications to the contrary, the Belgian state is unlikely to fall apart. Rather, new coherence and new emphasis on what the two linguistic communities have in common can be expected now that agreement has largely been reached on a federal solution to the country's internal divisions.

With an undeveloped sense of national identity by general European standards, Belgium has rarely attempted to limit movement of goods or people across its boundaries. Instead, Belgium has capitalized on its position as a crossroads of continental Europe. Typically, exports and imports are each equivalent to around 90% of GDP. Not unexpectedly, Belgium plays a leading role in European economic integration, both physically by virtue of the presence in Brussels of the EC's headquarters, and in terms of strong popular and government commitment.

Governments, whose composition reflects not only the electorate's verdict but also a delicate balance between the two main communities, find themselves with relatively few policy choices. The enormous public deficit, will determine the direction of economic policy well into the 1990s, as governments focus their energies on curbing public spending and improving the balance of payments. Though there are government plans for the reform of financial markets, Belgium should remain one of the most *laissez-faire* economies in Europe.

This means that much of Belgian business is moving towards the European single market with considerable trepidation. In the absence of clear government policy-guidance, there is still too much emphasis on relatively low-added-value industries. Increased competition in a market wide open to countries with much lower labour costs could prove deeply problematic.

This vulnerability betokens a certain inflexibility in Belgium's industrial structure. Company ownership is concentrated among a few large groups. Seen as under-utilizing their assets, these big corporations are increasingly likely to become targets for foreign takeover attempts, which could effect changes that government policies have so far failed to make.

OFFICIAL NAME Kingdom of Belgium.

CAPITAL CITY Brussels.

GEOGRAPHY Except for the forested plateau and foothills of the Ardennes in the south-east, most of the country is low-lying, an extension of the Paris Basin, with sandy and clay soils; much of the coastal region has been reclaimed from the sea. *Highest point* Botrange 694 metres (2,270 feet). *Area* 30,513 sq km (11,780 sq miles).

PEOPLE *Population* 9.8m. *Density* 323 per sq km. *Ethnic groups* Belgian 91%, Italian 3%, Moroccan 1%, French 1%, Dutch 1%, Turkish 1%.

RELIGION RC 96%.

LANGUAGE Dutch (Flemish) 57%, French (Walloon) 42%, German 1%.

EDUCATION Free and compulsory for ages 6–18. 15% of the government's budget goes on education, through either the state secular system or subsidies to the parallel private denominational system. There are 19 universities.

CLIMATE Temperate, with mild, foggy winters and cool summers. Monthly temperature range is 0–23°C (32–73°F). Annual rainfall from 750mm (30ins) on the coast to 1,000mm (40ins) inland.

CURRENCY Belgian franc.

PUBLIC HOLIDAYS Jan 1, Easter Mon, May 1, Ascension, Whit Mon, Jul 21, Aug 15, Nov 1, 11, Dec 25.

GOVERNMENT Parliamentary monarchy. The 212-member Chamber of Representatives is elected for 4 years, while the Senate has 106 directly elected members plus 50 from the provincial councils, 25 co-optees and the heir to the throne. Voting, through PR, is compulsory. The chief executive is the prime minister.

IMPORTS AND EXPORTS

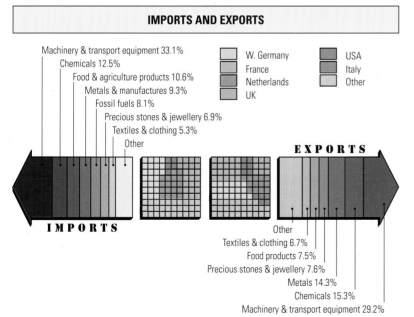

Machinery & transport equipment 33.1%
Chemicals 12.5%
Food & agriculture products 10.6%
Metals & manufactures 9.3%
Fossil fuels 8.1%
Precious stones & jewellery 6.9%
Textiles & clothing 5.3%
Other

W. Germany
France
Netherlands
UK
USA
Italy
Other

EXPORTS

IMPORTS

Other
Textiles & clothing 6.7%
Food products 7.5%
Precious stones & jewellery 7.6%
Metals 14.3%
Chemicals 15.3%
Machinery & transport equipment 29.2%

Source: EIU *Country Report* (1989 figures).

ECONOMIC PROFILE

Decline in older industries – coal, steel, textiles, heavy engineering, chemicals and food – and rapid expansion of service industries. Agriculture, small in scale, provides meat, fruit, vegetables and dairy products for domestic consumption. Few mineral or energy resources; nuclear power has replaced coal and oil as main energy source, though further development suspended.

Growth Light industry expanding, backed by government incentives. Brussels continues to grow as centre for European and international institutions.

Problems Large industrial combines lack flexibility in competitive environment.

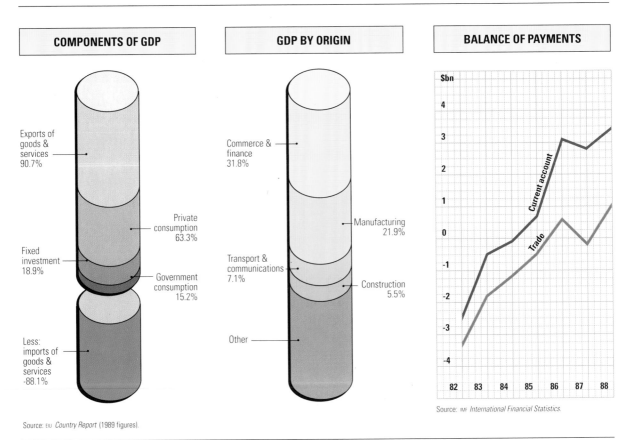

COMPONENTS OF GDP

Exports of goods & services 90.7%

Private consumption 63.3%

Fixed investment 18.9%

Government consumption 15.2%

Less: imports of goods & services -88.1%

Source: EIU *Country Report* (1989 figures).

GDP BY ORIGIN

Commerce & finance 31.8%

Manufacturing 21.9%

Transport & communications 7.1%

Construction 5.5%

Other

BALANCE OF PAYMENTS

$bn

Current account

Trade

82 83 84 85 86 87 88

Source: IMF *International Financial Statistics*.

LUXEMBOURG

Unabashed by its anachronistic status as a grand duchy, Luxembourg has seen itself as a spectator, rather than participant, in the relationships between nations.

Emphasis, however, is now being placed on playing a full role in an integrated Europe, notably as a home for European institutions, and neutrality is being abandoned in favour of commitment to Nato; but such moves represent Luxembourg's public face. Official and private attitudes are still often inward-looking and almost reclusive, possibly as a means of preserving a national identity otherwise defended by only 630 regular soldiers.

Continuity is provided by a succession of coalition governments whose policies differ as marginally as their composition. Inflation is low, unemployment negligible, public finances and the balance of payments healthy. The perpetually troubled iron and steel industry, however, will preoccupy government well into the 1990s until the growth of financial services, manufacturing and chemicals deprive it of its central role in the economy.

Banking and financial services have become increasingly important, as Luxembourg has established a leading role in the Eurocurrency markets and in offshore Deutschmark deposits. A high number of holding companies – over 5,000 – are registered in the duchy, attracted by a law exempting them from tax on dividends or interest and capital gains tax. Portfolio management services have been doing well, boosted by legislation to guarantee Swiss-style banking secrecy and the absence of stamp duty on security transactions.

OFFICIAL NAME Grand Duchy of Luxembourg.

CAPITAL CITY Luxembourg-Ville.

GEOGRAPHY Luxembourg is a landlocked upland. The northern section, the Oesling, is part of the plateau of the Ardennes, a windswept area cut by rocky valleys. The southern section, the Gutland, is heavily wooded and contains most of the important towns and industries. Almost all the rivers drain into the Moselle on the south-eastern boundary. *Highest point* 559 metres (1,830 feet). *Area* 2,586 sq km (1,000 sq miles).

PEOPLE *Population* 374,900. *Density* 145 per sq km. *Ethnic groups* Luxembourger 74%, Portuguese 8%, Italian 6%, French 3%, German 2%.

RELIGION RC 93%, Protestant 1%.

LANGUAGE French, German and Letzeburgish.

EDUCATION Compulsory and free for ages 6–15. There is 1 university.

CLIMATE Temperate. Annual rainfall is 750–1000mm (30–40ins).

CURRENCY Luxembourg franc.

PUBLIC HOLIDAYS Jan 1, Easter Mon, May 1, Ascension, Whit Mon, Jun 23, Aug 15, Nov 1, Dec 25–26.

GOVERNMENT Parliamentary monarchy. The grand duke appoints a council of ministers responsible to a 60-member Chamber of Deputies elected by PR for 5 years.

BENELUX COUNTRIES

Benelux and Bleu

The Benelux treaty, signed in 1958 by Belgium, Luxembourg and the Netherlands, created the first free international labour market and established free movement of services and capital; most border formalities were abolished in 1971. Benelux has served as a model for the EC's internal market.

Belgium and Luxembourg also form a tighter union, Bleu. Their foreign trade and payments accounts are amalgamated and they operate a joint central bank.

Rotterdam

A natural harbour in the centre of the west European coastline, Rotterdam is now the largest port in the world, handling the majority of continental Europe's sea-trade. It is one of the Netherlands' biggest generators of foreign exchange and the Dutch have concentrated on encouraging its development as an entrepôt. New proposals to modernize and enlarge the Rotterdam docks will enhance its trading position, along with the new and expanding markets of eastern Europe and the EC's single market.

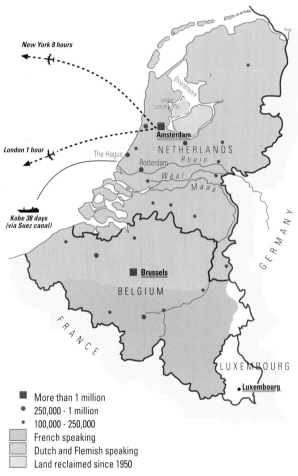

Shipping

In 1990 a new shipping register enabled Luxembourg to register foreign vessels under its own flag. The advantages of lower corporate tax, lower tax for crews and lower social security payments were expected to encourage shipowners from Belgium to be among the first to fly Luxembourg's flag. The development of ship finance and ship broking is a natural extension of the Grand Duchy's expanding financial services sector.

Devolution

Differences between the Flemish-speaking community in the north of Belgium and the French-speaking Walloons in the south led to the creation in 1982 of two regional assemblies: one for Flanders and one for Wallonia. In 1988 further reform created a third assembly for largely French-speaking Brussels. Responsibility for education now rests with local communes, in an attempt to defuse tension in French-speaking areas of Flanders and Flemish-speaking areas of Brussels and Wallonia.

Energy

Nuclear power supplies only 1% of the Netherlands' energy and 6% of its electricity. This compares with an average nuclear share in Westen European electricity supply of 30%-35%. A 1989 poll showed that almost 85% of the Dutch population opposed the building of new nuclear reactors. However, global warming, renewed uncertainty about oil supplies created by the 1990-1991 Gulf crisis, and worries about the Netherlands' dependence on its abundant but finite supplies of natural gas, have forced the nuclear issue back onto the political agenda.

NETHERLANDS

The Dutch obsession with consensus could only be found in a country fearful of the internal diversity that has threatened to pull it apart. Differences of political and religious orientation, singly and in every conceivable combination, have been resolved by allowing the major groups to become pillars of society. Nowhere is this seen more clearly than in the television networks: Protestants, Catholics, Socialists and Liberals each have their own station. Reflecting this ambivalence the political scene has, since 1958, been characterized by shifting coalitions, usually without coherence or a clear sense of direction.

At the political level, the search for consensus tends to mean that differences rarely become polarized. Compromise always has to prevail in the end, not least because no single party ever gets enough votes to rule alone. Personalities are important, and above party politics; there was little surprise when Ruud Lubbers, the high-profile Christian Democrat prime minister who for seven years led a coalition with the conservative Liberal party, switched to lead a centre-left coalition with Labour in 1989.

Economic policies tend as a result to be equivocal in both conception and implementation. The economy's fundamental strength may have prevented any real disasters, but indecision has recently carried the penalty of slow growth, below the EC average in the 1980s. The need to improve economic performance receives lip-service but forceful policies for growth have tended to founder among objections from small, but key, members of governmental coalitions. Thus the political agenda is headed by subjects such as education, the environment and, above all, welfare .

How to pay for the most extensive welfare system in Europe is the principal dilemma of Dutch politics. A product of the post-war consensus that all should share in increasing wealth, it now swallows up around 7% of GNP. The dilemma was exacerbated by the 1990 downturn in the economy, as the centre-left coalition struggled to fulfill its election pledges to link increases in welfare payments to wage rises in the private sector. To many Europeans, aspects of the Dutch welfare system seem incredulous. In the Netherlands, however, suggestions that its size and cost could damage future Dutch competitiveness have yet to enter the political mainstream.

The industrial base, which benefited from the restructuring forced by the

OFFICIAL NAME Kingdom of the Netherlands.
CAPITAL CITY Amsterdam.
GEOGRAPHY With the exception of a small area on the southern border, the Netherlands is totally flat and criss-crossed with canals. Much of it, especially in the west, is below sea level and protected by dykes and dunes. 7,700 sq km (3,000 sq miles) of land have been reclaimed from the sea. *Highest point* Vaalserberg 321 metres (1,050 feet). *Area* 41,785 sq km (16,130 sq miles).
PEOPLE *Population* 14.8m. *Density* 437 per sq km. *Ethnic groups* Dutch 96%, Turkish 1%, Moroccan 1%.
RELIGION RC 36%, Dutch Reformed Church 19%, other Reformed Church 8%.
LANGUAGE Dutch.
EDUCATION Free and compulsory for ages 5–16. There are 21 universities.
CLIMATE Generally temperate, though winter temperatures can fall to -17°C (1.5°F). Summers warm but unsettled and windy. Driest in spring; annual rainfall is around 800mm (32ins).
CURRENCY Guilder
PUBLIC HOLIDAYS Jan 1, Good Fri–Easter Mon, Apr 30, May 5, Ascension, Whit Mon, Dec 25.
GOVERNMENT Parliamentary monarchy. The 2 chamber legislature, the States-General, has a 75-member upper chamber elected for 6 years by 12 provincial councils and a 150-member lower chamber directly elected by PR for 4 years. Executive power lies with a council of ministers headed by the prime minister.

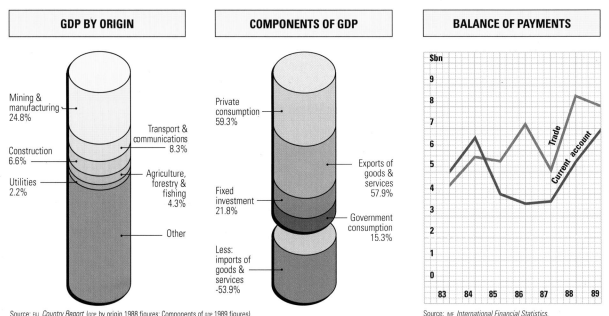

GDP BY ORIGIN

Mining & manufacturing 24.8%
Construction 6.6%
Utilities 2.2%
Transport & communications 8.3%
Agriculture, forestry & fishing 4.3%
Other

COMPONENTS OF GDP

Private consumption 59.3%
Fixed investment 21.8%
Exports of goods & services 57.9%
Government consumption 15.3%
Less: imports of goods & services -53.9%

Source: EIU *Country Report* (GDP by origin 1988 figures; Components of GDP 1989 figures).

BALANCE OF PAYMENTS

$bn

Trade
Current account

83 84 85 86 87 88 89

Source: IMF *International Financial Statistics*.

recession of the early 1980s, remains, however, among the most efficient in Europe, and places it in a key position to take advantage of new business opportunities created by German unification (West Germany was by far the Netherlands' biggest export partner.), and by the change to more market-oriented policies in Eastern Europe. The farming sector has retained substantial importance, making the Netherlands not only self-sufficient in most foods, but also the world's second biggest exporter of agricultural products.

The Netherlands has always been more environmentally aware than most countries, the result of a long tradition established by the need to reclaim and protect land from the sea. Pollution of the Rhine, which provides nearly three-quarters of the country's fresh water, is a major concern.

The conflicting demands of meeting the Netherlands' rising energy requirements and complying with the targets for reducing carbon dioxide emissions under the national environment policy plan (Nepp) have also led to a re-opening of the nuclear energy debate. Under the Nepp the aim is to stabilize carbon monoxide emissions by 1994–5 and achieve a steady reduction thereafter. With dependence on natural gas already high (it provides 52% of energy consumed) and further expansion of coal-fired stations considered incompatible with the Nepp, the government argues that a significant increase in nuclear power capacity is necessary if target levels are to be reached. However, memories of the 1986 Chernobyl nuclear plant melt-down and fire in the USSR are still vivid and public opinion remains strongly opposed to nuclear power.

Traditions of consensus politics make the Dutch natural Europeans and they have justifiably acquired a reputation as the EC's pragmatic conciliators. It was a Dutch plan that was accepted, by all except Britain, as the model for achieving stage two of the Delors plan for political and monetary union by 1994. The Dutch have long realized that their economy, more than most, depends on an international outlook. Because of that the Netherlands is likely to play an important role in EC affairs.

ECONOMIC PROFILE

Historically a major trading nation, importing raw materials for processing and manufacture and exporting the products; today, exports and imports are each equivalent to about 60% of GDP. Efficient, high-yielding agriculture, specializing in horticulture and dairy products. Europe's leading producer and exporter of natural gas.

Growth Chemicals, rubber, paper, food and drink have led economic growth. Service industries growing strongly. Good marketing and advanced technology have boosted worldwide flower and bulb exports.

Problems Fluctuating gas prices. Textiles and heavy engineering contracting in face of competition from low-cost overseas producers. Export-led economy susceptible to recession in overseas markets.

IMPORTS AND EXPORTS

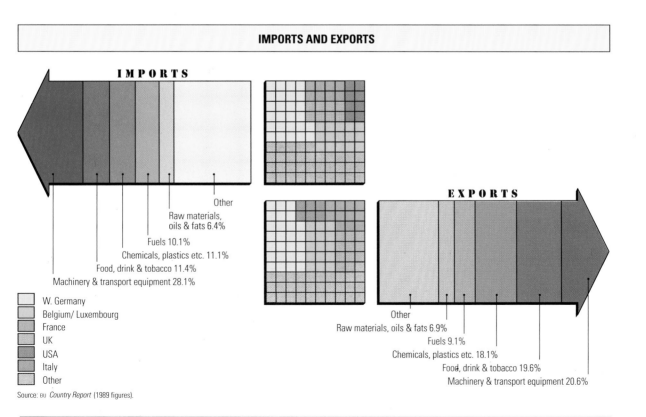

IMPORTS

Other

Raw materials, oils & fats 6.4%

Fuels 10.1%

Chemicals, plastics etc. 11.1%

Food, drink & tobacco 11.4%

Machinery & transport equipment 28.1%

W. Germany
Belgium/ Luxembourg
France
UK
USA
Italy
Other

EXPORTS

Other

Raw materials, oils & fats 6.9%

Fuels 9.1%

Chemicals, plastics etc. 18.1%

Food, drink & tobacco 19.6%

Machinery & transport equipment 20.6%

Source: EIU *Country Report* (1989 figures).

DENMARK

Denmark has for many years been ranked at the top of European surveys of personal satisfaction with life. This result owes much to the excellence of the country's welfare state system. However, national concern with achieving the good life has tended to reinforce criticisms that the country lives way beyond its means.

Traditionally the current account deficit has posed major problems, but in 1990 the account recorded its first annual surplus since 1963. The government has had some recent success in bringing down the rate of inflation which, at just over 2.5% in 1990, was among the lowest in the OECD. But rising unemployment, high interest rates and shortfalls in tax and duty revenues have added to the problems of controlling the public debt.

Political fragmentation has undoubtedly made it harder to implement the tighter economic policies necessary to restore financial discipline. The 21 general elections since the second world war have left no party with an absolute majority in parliament. Minority and coalition governments have had to rely on support from other parties which have frequently proved reluctant to share responsibility for painful measures. The most contentious issues remain labour reform in the public sector, the cost of welfare payments and tax levels, which are the highest in the EC.

Denmark nevertheless is still one of the most prosperous members of the EC, which it joined in 1973. The single European market programme, with its objective of fiscal harmonization, may cause problems, however, because of Denmark's high direct and indirect tax rates. In 1986 a programme of EC trade reforms only just scraped a majority in a national referendum called after parliament threw out the proposals. Danish opponents of EC membership base their arguments on the desirability of Nordic unity. They feel Denmark belongs to Scandinavia and object to it being drawn into the European cultural sphere. The other Scandinavian countries, by contrast, view Denmark as their gateway to the European market.

Ambivalence about membership of Nato is even greater. Denmark has not met military spending targets and is firmly opposed to the presence of nuclear

OFFICIAL NAME Kingdom of Denmark.

CAPITAL CITY Copenhagen.

GEOGRAPHY Denmark is the Jutland Peninsula and a total of 483 low-lying islands, 97 inhabited. The number of islands and the fjords of Jutland give Denmark a disproportionately long coastline. Average elevation is less than 30 metres (100 feet); much of the land is sandy or moraine gravels, though the peninsula has much fertile loam. *Highest point* Yding Skovhöj 179 metres (590 feet). *Area* 43,069 sq km (16,630 sq miles).

PEOPLE *Population* 5.1m. *Density* 119 per sq km. *Ethnic groups* Danish 99%.

RELIGION Evangelical Lutheran 96%, RC 1% .

LANGUAGE Danish.

EDUCATION Free and compulsory for ages 7–16. 90% of children are educated at municipal schools.

CLIMATE Temperate and changeable, moderated by the Gulf Stream. Average temperatures 16°C (61°F) in Jul, 0°C (32°F) in Feb. Rainfall all year round, with most in summer and autumn; annual totals around 800mm (31ins) in the west, half that in the eastern islands.

CURRENCY Danish krone.

PUBLIC HOLIDAYS Jan 1, Maundy Thu, Good Fri, Easter Mon, 4th Fri after Good Fri, Ascension, Jun 5, Whit Mon, Dec 25–26.

GOVERNMENT Constitutional monarchy. The unicameral legislature, the Folketing, has 179 members elected for 4 years by PR. The cabinet is headed by a prime minister responsible to the Folketing.

IMPORTS AND EXPORTS

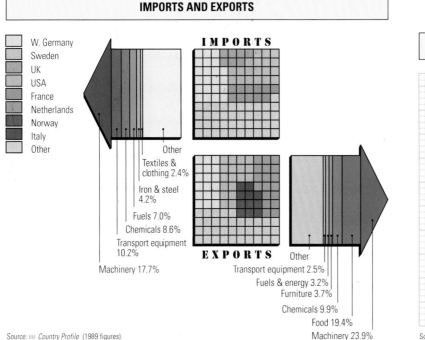

W. Germany
Sweden
UK
USA
France
Netherlands
Norway
Italy
Other

IMPORTS

Other
Textiles & clothing 2.4%
Iron & steel 4.2%
Fuels 7.0%
Chemicals 8.6%
Transport equipment 10.2%
Machinery 17.7%

EXPORTS

Other
Transport equipment 2.5%
Fuels & energy 3.2%
Furniture 3.7%
Chemicals 9.9%
Food 19.4%
Machinery 23.9%

Source: EIU *Country Profile* (1989 figures).

BALANCE OF PAYMENTS

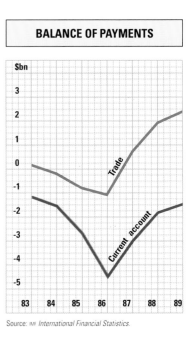

$bn

Trade

Current account

83 84 85 86 87 88 89

Source: IMF *International Financial Statistics*.

weapons on its territory, a position that Nato accepts but which has caused some internal political controversy.

Agricultural exports – cheese, beef, bacon – declining in importance since 1945, although Danish farmers still produce enough to feed three times the population. Fishing hit by falling prices, quota disputes and overcapacity. Most exports now manufactured goods, particularly in high-technology sectors. Agricultural machinery, cement, bricks and tiles are important.

Growth Electronics is fastest-growing industry, with 90% of production for export. Development of offshore hydrocarbon resources helping to reduce dependence on imported energy.

Problems Need to import most raw materials contributes to recurrent balance of payments problems and high external debt. Decline of fishing and shipbuilding industries has increased unemployment.

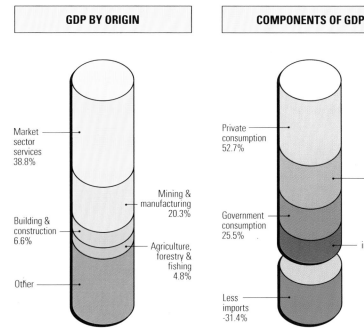

GDP BY ORIGIN

Market sector services 38.8%

Mining & manufacturing 20.3%

Building & construction 6.6%

Agriculture, forestry & fishing 4.8%

Other

COMPONENTS OF GDP

Private consumption 52.7%

Exports 34.8%

Government consumption 25.5%

Fixed investment 18.4%

Less imports -31.4%

Source: EIU *Country Report* (1989 figures).

THE FAROE ISLANDS

OFFICIAL NAME Faroe Islands.
CAPITAL CITY Tórshavn.
GEOGRAPHY An archipelago. *Area* 1,399 sq km (540 sq miles).
PEOPLE *Population* 48,000. *Density* 33 per sq km. *Ethnic groups* Scandinavian.
RELIGION Protestant 99% (Evangelical Lutheran 74%, Plymouth Brethren 20%, other 5%).
LANGUAGE Faroese and Danish.
EDUCATION Danish system. 1 university.
CLIMATE The Gulf Stream moderates the Arctic climate. Wet and cool winters, mild summers.
CURRENCY Faroese krone. Parity with Danish krone, which is also used.
PUBLIC HOLIDAYS As Denmark, plus Apr 25.
GOVERNMENT Semi-autonomous since 1948; sends 2 members to the Danish parliament.

Lying between Scotland and Iceland, the 18 inhabited Faroe Islands (there are 22 islands in all) have been administered by Denmark since 1380. They have their own government and parliament for internal affairs and decided not to join the EC with Denmark in 1973. About a third of the population lives on the main island, Streymoy. Fishing still accounts for 90% of exports and attempts are being made to diversify the economy which remains heavily dependent on Danish subsidies.

GREENLAND

OFFICIAL NAME Greenland.
CAPITAL CITY Nuuk-Godthåb.
GEOGRAPHY Mostly ice with some sandy or clay plains in the ice-free areas. *Area* 2,175,600 sq km (840,000 sq miles); ice-free area 341,700 sq km (131,930 sq miles).
PEOPLE *Population* 55,000. *Ethnic groups* Greenlander (includes Inuit) 82%, Danish 14%.
RELIGION Evangelical Lutheran 88%, other Protestant 10%.
LANGUAGE Danish and Greenlandic (Inuit).
EDUCATION Based on the Danish model, free, and compulsory to age 16.
CLIMATE Cold and bleak. Average monthly temperatures range from -8°C (18°F) to 10°C (50°F) in the south, to -22°C (-8°F) to 5°C (41°F) in the north.
CURRENCY Danish krone.
PUBLIC HOLIDAYS (*half day) Jan 1, 7, Maundy Thu, Good Fri, Easter Mon, 4th Fri after Good Fri, Ascension, Whit Mon, Jun 5*, 21, Dec 25–26.
GOVERNMENT 21-member legislature and 5-member executive; 2 members sent to the Danish parliament.

The world's largest island, Greenland came under Danish rule in 1380. A nationalist movement developed after the island was taken into the EC with Denmark in 1973 despite a majority vote by Greenlanders against joining. A 1979 referendum produced a large majority in favour of a degree of home rule and in 1985 Greenland withdrew from the EC. Seal-hunting, fishing and sheep-rearing are the main economic activities and the island still depends on substantial subsidies from Denmark, which is also its largest trading partner.

SCANDINAVIA

Aland (Ahvenanmae)

This group of 6,554 islands, 80 of them inhabited, lies between Sweden and Finland at the south end of the Gulf of Bothnia. The islands form an autonomous district of Finland (although Swedish is the main language) and send two representatives of their own to meetings of the Nordic Council.

Nordic Council

The five Nordic countries cooperate through the Nordic Council, an assembly that meets annually, and the Nordic Council of Ministers, whose membership consists of ministers responsible for the subjects under discussion. The Nordic Council's 87 members are elected annually by and from the parliaments of the various countries. The Faroes, Greenland and the Finnish Aland islands are each represented by two members of their own.

The Nordic Council countries form a common labour market, with reciprocal welfare benefits and a passport union.

Finland and the USSR

Until recently, the USSR frequently played a large part in Finnish politics. In the 1948 friendship treaty Finland agreed to resist any attack on the USSR through its territory, if necessary with Soviet assistance, and a barter trade agreement encouraged Finnish reliance on Soviet trade. However, since *glasnost*, the USSR has been cutting imports from Finland and failing to meet Finland's oil demands.

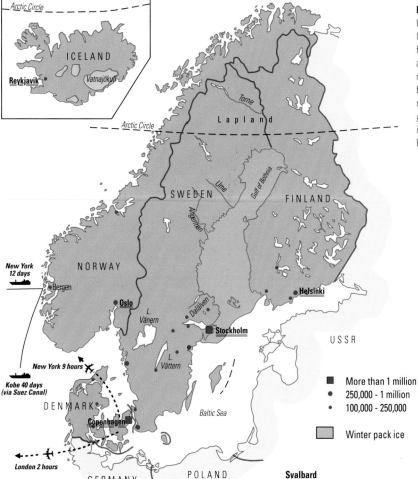

Lakes

Both Finland and Sweden are dotted with lakes, with 60,000 in Finland alone, making up 10% of the land area. Lake Vänern in Sweden is Western Europe's largest, with an area of 5,585 sq km (2,160 sq miles).

Seasonal ice

Ice blocks the Gulf of Bothnia for several months of the year. Farther north, the coast of Norway remains ice-free, warmed by the Gulf Stream.

- ■ More than 1 million
- ● 250,000 - 1 million
- · 100,000 - 250,000
- ▦ Winter pack ice

Svalbard

Svalbard, an archipelago in the Barents Sea, has been part of Norway since 1920, but nine other countries have mining rights there. Most of the inhabitants are Norwegian or Soviet coal miners. Spitsbergen, the largest island, was once an important whaling centre.

Efta

Finland, Iceland, Norway and Sweden belong to the European Free Trade Association, whose other members are Austria and Switzerland.

Efta was set up in 1960 with the aim of creating a single market including all countries in Western Europe. Free trade in manufactured goods was established among its members in 1966 and with European Community members in 1970. The UK and Denmark left to join the EC in 1972, Portugal in 1986.

The EC and Efta are to establish a European Economic Area by 1993, allowing Efta states trade benefits. However, the fears in Efta that the gaps between the EC and its neighbours will widen after 1992 have already prompted some states to apply for EC membership.

ICELAND

Iceland enjoys one of the world's highest standards of living, underpinned by a comprehensive social security system. Fishing generates 70% of export earnings and most jobs. The economy is therefore very vulnerable to falling fish prices and poor catches and the government has been forced into several devaluations of the currency in recent years.

The country is the most seismically active in the world. Its unique scenery of active volcanoes, *solfataras*, thermal springs and geysers provides the basis for a growing tourist industry. And its almost unlimited reserves of thermal and hydropower have stimulated plans to export electricity.

Political life is fragmented. Governments are usually coalitions and frequently torn by internal disputes. However, a rare agreement on wage and price restraint in February 1990, the "national accord", did result in inflation being brought under control.

Iceland is an active member of Efta and was dismayed by Sweden's decision in 1990 to seek EC membership, believing it undermined Efta's bargaining position with the Community over the proposed European Economic Area.

OFFICIAL NAME Republic of Iceland.
CAPITAL CITY Reykjavík.
GEOGRAPHY The interior is a glaciated tableland and most settlement is on the rocky coasts, whose fjords provide safe harbours for the fishing fleet. *Area* 103,000 sq km (39,800 sq miles).
PEOPLE *Population* 254,000. *Density* 2 per sq km. *Ethnic groups* Icelander 97%.
RELIGION Church of Iceland (Lutheran) 93%, other Lutheran 4%, RC 1%.
LANGUAGE Icelandic.
EDUCATION Free and compulsory for ages 7–16.
CURRENCY Icelandic króna.
PUBLIC HOLIDAYS Jan 1, Maundy Thu, Good Fri, Easter Mon, 1st day of summer, May 1, Ascension, Whit Mon, Jun 17, Aug 5, Dec 25–26.
GOVERNMENT Republic since 1944. The president is elected every 4 years as are the 63 members of the legislature, the Althingi, by PR; one-third forms an upper chamber.

SWEDEN

Sweden is the largest and most powerful Scandinavian state. It has the largest population, a wide industrial base, long experience of democracy and political stability; the Social Democrats have been in power for all but six years since 1932. As a neutral country it has also enjoyed a long period of peace.

Swedes have one of the highest standards of living in the world. A combination of taxation policy and a highly developed welfare state have all but eliminated extremes of wealth and poverty. Like other Nordic countries Sweden has prided itself on being an open society, in which political leaders are expected to be accessible. This helps explain why the assassination of Prime Minister Olof Palme in the spring of 1986 had such a deep impact.

Just two months after Mr Palme's death Swedish society was shocked again when radioactive clouds from the Chernobyl nuclear disaster in the Soviet Union passed across the country. Energy has been a major issue since the 1973–74 oil crisis bought home the country's vulnerability: Sweden has one of the highest per capita consumptions of imported oil in the world. With most hydropower potential already developed, the government turned to Sweden's rich uranium reserves and nuclear power as the quickest path to energy diversification; it now generates over 40% of electricity supplies. But public concern over environmental and safety factors led to a decision in 1980 to phase out nuclear power by 2010. However in 1991 the phase-out period was delayed as the government came under pressure from Swedish industry worried about the possible effects on competitiveness of more expensive energy.

Egalitarian social policies have not, in Sweden's case, militated against economic growth. For much of the 1980s the country enjoyed a boom, with rapidly rising production, low unemployment and industry working close to capacity. However, by the turn of the decade there were clear signs of over-heating and the January 1991 budget sought to cure the very un-Swedish problems of high inflation and decreasing production with a programme of austerity measures and public spending cuts. Politically, the most significant recent development has been parliament's support in 1990 for a proposal that Sweden join the EC. This was expected to lead to a formal application for membership. However, Sweden's enthusiasm for European economic integration is unlikely to extend to closer political union, if this involves compromising its traditional neutrality.

OFFICIAL NAME Kingdom of Sweden.
CAPITAL CITY Stockholm.
GEOGRAPHY 15% of Sweden lies inside the Arctic Circle; the Norrland, the northern region of mountains, forests and finger lakes, is almost uninhabited. The fertile central lowlands, where wide lakes and gravel ridges bear witness to glaciation, contain most of the population. The southern tip of the country has the stony uplands of Småland and the major agricultural region, Skåne. *Highest point* Kebnekaise 2,111 metres (6,930 feet). *Area* 449,964 sq km (173,730 sq miles).
PEOPLE *Population* 8.5m. *Density* 19 per sq km. *Ethnic groups* Swedish 95%, Finnish 2%.
RELIGION Church of Sweden (Evangelical Lutheran) 68%, RC 1%.
LANGUAGE Swedish. Also Finnish and Lapp.
EDUCATION Free and compulsory for ages 7–16. There are 34 universities and colleges.
CLIMATE Monthly average temperature ranges vary according to latitude: in south, from -3°C (27°F) to 18°C (64°F); in far north, from -14°C (7°F) to 14°C (57°F). Average rainfall is 400mm (16ins) in north, 550mm (22ins) in south.
CURRENCY Swedish krona.
PUBLIC HOLIDAYS Jan 1, 6, Good Fri, Easter Mon, May 1, Ascension, Whit Mon, Midsummer Day, All Saints, Dec 25–26.
GOVERNMENT Constitutional monarchy. The 349-member Riksdag is elected for 3 years; the Riksdag elects a prime minister, whose cabinet is the executive power.

EUROPE

IMPORTS AND EXPORTS

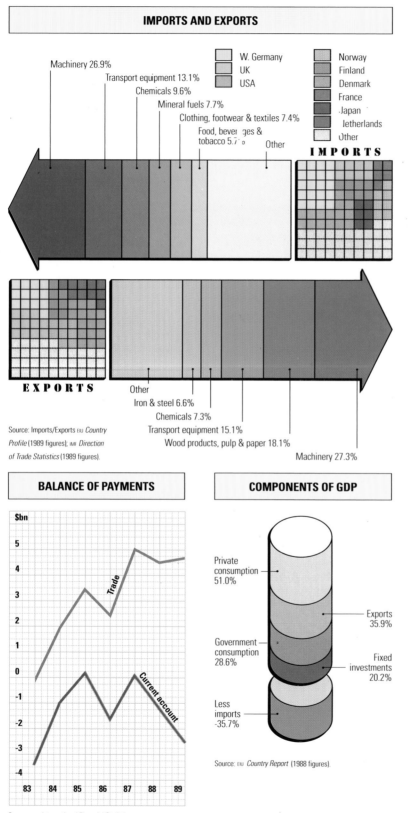

Machinery 26.9%

Transport equipment 13.1%

Chemicals 9.6%

Mineral fuels 7.7%

Clothing, footwear & textiles 7.4%

Food, beverages & tobacco 5.7%

Other

W. Germany
UK
USA

Norway
Finland
Denmark
France
Japan
Netherlands
Other

IMPORTS

EXPORTS

Other

Iron & steel 6.6%

Chemicals 7.3%

Transport equipment 15.1%

Wood products, pulp & paper 18.1%

Machinery 27.3%

Source: Imports/Exports EIU *Country
Profile* (1989 figures); IMF *Direction
of Trade Statistics* (1989 figures).

ECONOMIC PROFILE

Manufacturing the most important economic sector, particularly metallurgy, automotive engineering, timber and pulp and paper industries. One of the world's largest iron ore producers; copper, zinc, uranium also important. Decline in agriculture, but government striving to maintain 80% self-sufficiency in basic foods.

Growth Sophisticated high-technology goods – vehicles, electronics, telecommunications – finding wide export markets. Changes to financial regulations attracting foreign banks.

Problems Heavy dependence on imported oil. Shortage of popularly acceptable and cheap non-oil replacements for nuclear power, which is being phased out. Heavy subsidies have failed to save shipbuilding industry, once second largest in the world.

BALANCE OF PAYMENTS

$bn

Trade

Current account

83 84 85 86 87 88 89

Source: IMF *International Financial Statistics*.

COMPONENTS OF GDP

Private consumption 51.0%

Government consumption 28.6%

Less imports -35.7%

Exports 35.9%

Fixed investments 20.2%

Source: EIU *Country Report* (1988 figures).

GDP BY ORIGIN

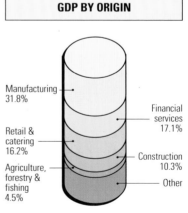

Manufacturing 31.8%

Retail & catering 16.2%

Agriculture, forestry & fishing 4.5%

Financial services 17.1%

Construction 10.3%

Other

NORWAY

Discovery of the Ekofisk oil field in the North Sea in 1970 enabled Norway, now Western Europe's second largest oil producer after the UK, to cut taxes while maintaining high public spending. As a result, Norwegians today enjoy a very high standard of living and an excellent national health and social security system. However, unemployment, at over 5%, is considered too high.

Norway's economic performance tends to reflect the price of oil, which accounts for 40% of export revenues. The 1986 price collapse plunged the country into economic crisis and led to the adoption of an austerity programme aimed at halting the boom in consumer spending and righting the trade balance. In contrast, the onset of the Gulf crisis in August 1990 and the subsequent rise in oil prices led to a doubling of the trade surplus in two months.

Deep divisions still exist over the question of Norway's membership of the EC. In 1972 the country voted narrowly to stay out. In October 1990 the issue led to the fall of the centre-right government. It was replaced by a minority Labour government which, although pro-membership, decided to shelve the problem until Efta and the EC secured an agreement over the proposed European Economic Area (EEA).

OFFICIAL NAME Kingdom of Norway.

CAPITAL CITY Oslo.

GEOGRAPHY As well as the mountainous western half of the Scandinavian peninsula, it includes the Svalbard Archipelago inside the Arctic Circle and several uninhabited northern islands. Repeated glaciation has created inland plateaus and hundreds of fjords on the coastline. There are 160,000 lakes; the interior is forested.
Highest point Galdhøpiggen 2,469 metres (7,526 feet).
Area Mainland 324,219 sq km (125,180 sq miles); islands 62,422 sq km (24,100 sq miles).

PEOPLE *Population* 4.2m. *Density* 13 per sq km (excluding islands). *Ethnic groups* Norwegian 98%.

RELIGION Church of Norway (Evangelical Lutheran) 88%, Pentecostalist 1%.

LANGUAGE Bokmål (Old Norwegian) and Landsmål or Nynorsk (New Norwegian). Also Lappish.

EDUCATION Free and compulsory for ages 7–16. 4 universities and 31 colleges.

CLIMATE West coast has marine climate with cool summers and mild, rarely freezing winters, moderated by the Gulf Stream; coastal rainfall can be as much as 2,000mm (80ins) a year: Inland summers are warmer, winters are colder, and there is less rain.

CURRENCY Norwegian krone .

PUBLIC HOLIDAYS Jan 1, Maundy Thu, Good Fri, Easter Mon, May 1, May 17, Ascension, Whit Mon, Dec 25–26.

GOVERNMENT Constitutional monarchy. The 165-member Storting is elected for 4 years by PR. The Storting divides into the Lagting and Odelsting. Executive power lies with a prime minister and state council

IMPORTS AND EXPORTS

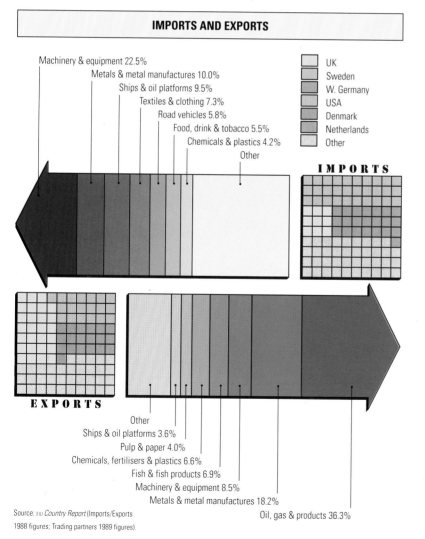

Machinery & equipment 22.5%
Metals & metal manufactures 10.0%
Ships & oil platforms 9.5%
Textiles & clothing 7.3%
Road vehicles 5.8%
Food, drink & tobacco 5.5%
Chemicals & plastics 4.2%
Other

UK
Sweden
W. Germany
USA
Denmark
Netherlands
Other

IMPORTS

EXPORTS

Other
Ships & oil platforms 3.6%
Pulp & paper 4.0%
Chemicals, fertilisers & plastics 6.6%
Fish & fish products 6.9%
Machinery & equipment 8.5%
Metals & metal manufactures 18.2%
Oil, gas & products 36.3%

Source: EIU *Country Report* (Imports/Exports 1988 figures; Trading partners 1989 figures).

COMPONENTS OF GDP

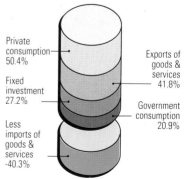

Private consumption 50.4%
Fixed investment 27.2%
Less imports of goods & services -40.3%
Exports of goods & services 41.8%
Government consumption 20.9%

Source: EIU *Country Report* (1989 figures).

ECONOMIC PROFILE

Older industries based on local raw materials: iron ore, timber, fish. Large oil and gas producer. Rugged terrain makes agriculture difficult; less than 3% of the land area is cultivated.

Growth Non-ferrous metals, engineering, chemical and fish exports are making economy less vulnerable to fluctuating oil prices.

Problems Oil production expected to decline steadily after 1995. Concentration on oil allowed other productive sectors to stagnate. Shipbuilding, once a major industry, in severe decline.

GDP BY ORIGIN

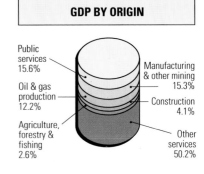

Public services 15.6%

Oil & gas production 12.2%

Agriculture, forestry & fishing 2.6%

Manufacturing & other mining 15.3%

Construction 4.1%

Other services 50.2%

Source: EIU *Country Report* (1989 figures).

FINLAND

Living in the shadow of the Soviet Union, the Finns have been keenly aware of their unique position. They are linked to Scandinavia by a long shared history but are separated from it by different ethnic and linguistic origins.

Fairly rapid industrialization has created a demographic imbalance, with small farms ceasing to be viable and people moving to the urban centres of the south. Yet a high level of agricultural self-sufficiency is regarded as vital, and Finland faces the problem of trying to protect domestic production while observing international agreements limiting government subsidies.

Increasing dependence on foreign trade has made Finland aware that even good housekeeping is no insulation against fluctuations in international markets. Financial and exchange controls have been loosened in recent years, bringing about a radical change in the financial market. Trade with the Soviet Union has been reduced since 1985 and replaced with exports to the West, but opinion on EC membership remains sharply divided.

In 1991 Finns, used to living standards which are among the highest in the world, were faced with falling private sector investment and rising unemployment. However, recession was not expected to lead to divisive tensions in Finnish society because the large number of political parties ensures the pursuit of consensus in decision-making, and because the trade unions were expected to act as much for the common good as in their members' interests.

OFFICIAL NAME Republic of Finland.

CAPITAL CITY Helsinki.

GEOGRAPHY Most is forested; 30% of the land is marshy and 10% is taken up by 55,000 mainly shallow lakes. Apart from mountains in the extreme north-west, the country is low-lying. One-third lies within the Arctic Circle. *Highest point* Haltia 1,324 metres (4,340 feet). *Area* 337,032 sq km (130,130 sq miles).

PEOPLE *Population* 5m. *Density* 15 per sq km. *Ethnic groups* Finnish 92%, Swedish 7%.

RELIGION Lutheran 90%, Greek Orthodox 1%.

LANGUAGE Finnish and Swedish. Also Lappish.

EDUCATION Comprehensive system, free and compulsory for ages 7–16. There are 22 universities and colleges of further education.

CLIMATE In the far north temperatures range from -30°C (-22°F) to 27°C (81°F); extremes are less marked further south. The Baltic freezes most years. Annual rainfall around 600mm (24ins).

CURRENCY Markka.

PUBLIC HOLIDAYS Jan 1, 12, Good Fri, Easter Mon, Apr 30, May 1, Ascension, Whit weekend, Jun 21, 22, Nov 2, Dec 6, 24–26.

GOVERNMENT Republic since 1919. The chief executive is the president, elected every 6 years by a college of 301 electors chosen by popular vote. The 200-member unicameral legislature, the Eduskunta, is elected by PR for a 4-year term, subject to dissolution by the president, who also appoints the prime minister and administrative council of state.

ECONOMIC PROFILE

Forests are the mainstay of Finland's prosperity, covering 65% of land area, with wood, paper and related industries providing about 40% of export earnings. Shipbuilding and manufacture of machinery for timber and paper industries are important. Highly mechanized cereal and dairy farming meets domestic requirements. Large copper reserves only major mineral resource.

Growth Forestry companies looking for expansion overseas. The emphasis domestically is on diversification. Grain surplus produced in recent years, leading to exports. Rapid growth in tourism.

Problems Industrial expansion constrained by shortage of skilled labour and need to import a major part of energy needs and many raw materials.

PORTUGAL

After a decade of political and social turmoil Portugal has settled down to face the challenges posed by EC entry in 1986 and the end of decades of isolationism.

In 1974 a coup brought 40 years of dictatorship to an end. In 1975 Portugal's African colonies were granted independence, large sections of the economy were nationalized and divisions within the armed forces became more evident. The 1976 elections made army chief Colonel António Eanes president, left the winning Socialists without a parliamentary majority and ushered in a decade of short-lived governments. The Socialists began Portugal's return to the European mainstream, applying for EC membership, but they were replaced by the Social Democrat-led centre-right in 1979. In 1983 the Socialists returned as the largest party and with the economy deteriorating rapidly formed a coalition with the Social Democrats. An IMF programme was implemented and EC entry finalized before the coalition collapsed in 1985.

A minority Social Democrat government was formed after the 1985 elections. It stole much of the Socialists' thunder, presiding over the 1985–87 economic boom and Portugal's EC entry. In 1986 Socialist leader Mário Soares became president; a year later the Social Democrats became the first party to win an absolute majority in parliament. Even so, the prime minister, Aníbal Cavaco Silva faced criticism for moving too slowly on privatization and social reforms. However, voters, who returned President Soares for a second term at the beginning of 1991, were in effect opting for the continuation of "cohabitation" between a left-of-centre president and right-of-centre government.

EC membership has given the economy a substantial jolt and Portugal is moving to complete integration by the mid-1990s. This is not easy for the poorest EC member, its backwardness a legacy of the years of dictatorship when private investment was discouraged and human resources neglected. Economic liberalization began in 1983 and has speeded up since 1986. EC grants, foreign investment and booming exports underpinned average annual growth of 4.7% between 1986–89. Growth subsequently slowed, but remained above the OECD average. There are still problems, however. Industry must shift away from low value-added goods and agricultural yields are a third of the EC norm with production still semi-subsistence in some areas. But Portugal's recent political stability has created a better environment for dealing with such problems.

OFFICIAL NAME Portuguese Republic.

CAPITAL CITY Lisbon.

GEOGRAPHY The River Tagus splits Portugal into 2 zones. To the north, 90% of the land is over 400 metres; most of the population lives in low, sheltered east-west valleys cut through plateaus and mountains. To the south, there are rolling lowlands. Much of the country is forested; soil is generally poor and droughts common. The coast is marked by capes and sandbars, with few good harbours. *Highest point* Estrela 1,993 metres (6,540 feet). *Area* 92,072 sq km (35,550 sq miles).

PEOPLE *Population* 10.5m. *Density* 112 per sq km. *Ethnic groups* Portuguese 99%.

RELIGION RC 95%, Protestant 1%.

LANGUAGE Portuguese.

EDUCATION Free and officially compulsory for 9 years, to be taken between ages 6 and 15; secondary education attendance well below EC average. 91 higher education institutions.

CLIMATE Mild and wet in winter, warm and dry in summer, with droughts in south. Rainfall highest in north, over 1,000mm (39ins) a year; around 700mm (27ins) in Lisbon. Temperatures average from 7°C (45F) in north in Jan to around 20°C (68°F) in south in Aug.

CURRENCY Escudo.

PUBLIC HOLIDAYS Jan 1, Shrove Tue, Good Fri, Apr 25, May 1, Corpus Christi, Jun 10, Jun 13 (Lisbon), Jun 24 (Oporto), Aug 15, Oct 5, Nov 1, Dec 1, 8, 25.

GOVERNMENT Republic. The head of state is the president, elected for a 5-year term. The 230-member unicameral legislative Assembléia da Republica is elected for a 4-year term. The president appoints the leader of the majority party as prime minister. Madeira and the Azores have been autonomous units within the republic since 1976.

ECONOMIC PROFILE

Traditional export-oriented businesses such as textiles and tourism are the mainstays. High level of imports, including 60% of food, most machinery and transport equipment and all oil. Remittances from migrant workers help bridge trade deficit.

Growth Paper companies, automotive and electrical component affiliates expanding fast. Services sector being modernized with much of the impetus coming from foreign banks and retailing concerns.

Problems Heavy industry, steel, chemicals, oil refining, uncompetitive in world markets, as are many traditional small companies. Agriculture is inefficient and backward.

IMPORTS AND EXPORTS

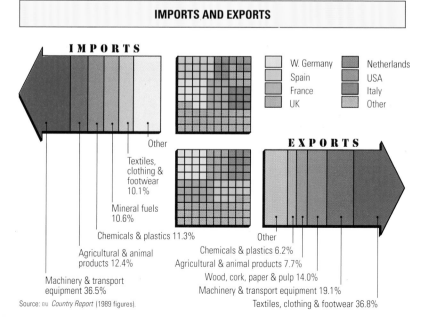

IMPORTS

W. Germany | Netherlands
Spain | USA
France | Italy
UK | Other

Other

Textiles, clothing & footwear 10.1%

Mineral fuels 10.6%

Chemicals & plastics 11.3%

Agricultural & animal products 12.4%

Machinery & transport equipment 36.5%

EXPORTS

Other

Chemicals & plastics 6.2%

Agricultural & animal products 7.7%

Wood, cork, paper & pulp 14.0%

Machinery & transport equipment 19.1%

Textiles, clothing & footwear 36.8%

Source: EIU *Country Report* (1989 figures).

THE IBERIAN PENINSULA

The Basque country

The Basques, who speak Europe's only surviving pre-Indo-European language, remained largely independent, living in parts of southern France and northern Spain, until the 19th century. The Basque separatist movement, Euscadi ta Askatasuna (Eta), has been active in Spain since the late 1960s; more than 600 people have died as a result of its actions.

Andorra

The principality of Andorra is a land locked enclave in the Pyrenees under the joint suzerainty of France and the Spanish bishop of Urgel. Agriculture and tourism are the main occupations, though low taxes have made it a centre of finance and duty-free trading.

Balearic Islands

Five large islands, including Mallorca, Menorca and Ibiza, and 11 islets form the Baleares autonomous region. The economy is based on agriculture, fishing and tourism.

Gibraltar

An awkward relic of empire, Gibraltar is a continuing irritant in relations between Spain and the UK. The Rock has been a British colony since 1713 and the 20,000 native Gibraltarians are determined that it will remain one. The British government has repeatedly reassured them that there will be no change in the colony's status without their consent, despite the reduction – accelerated in 1989 – in the British military presence and the closure of the naval dockyard, with serious consequences for the economy. The opening of the border with Spain in 1985 has brought significant benefits, however, giving the tourist industry a boost and helping to end labour shortages. Further potential lies in the development of an offshore financial centre and expansion of the port.

Tourism

Tourism has been Spain's major growth industry in the past two decades: by the mid-1980s it had become the most popular destination in the world, with arrivals exceeding 50m for the first time in 1987, bringing in around $13 billion in foreign exchange. However, a decline in visitors since the late 1980s has caused closures in facilities and investment losses. This is mainly due to changing trends and rising incomes in northern Europe, the origin of large amounts of tourism income. The fall is expected to continue, in spite of boosts from the Barcelona Olympics, the Seville Expo and the 500th anniversary celebrations of Columbus' voyage to the New World, all in 1992.

Portugal's tourist industry is on a much smaller scale, with around 16m visitors a year, more than half of them day-trippers from Spain. Income has been falling since 1988, although at a slower rate than in Spain, but with worse effects on the economy, which is more dependent on tourism.

The Azores and Madeira

Two groups of volcanic islands in the eastern Atlantic, the Azores and Madeira have been Portuguese colonies since their discovery in the 15th century. None of the islands had an indigenous population. Their colonists have relied on agriculture, fishing and, latterly, tourism. Since 1976 the two archipelagos have been autonomous regions within the Portuguese republic, with their own assemblies.

Canary Islands

An archipelago of seven large and numerous small islands off the Moroccan coast, the Canaries have been under Spanish rule since 1479. Agriculture and tourism are the main sources of income and employment. The islands belong to the EC, but do not participate in its common agricultural policy or customs union.

SPAIN

Spain has attracted much attention in recent years, and for good reason. For almost four decades the country was ruled by the dictator General Franco. His death in 1975 and the restoration of the monarchy in the person of King Juan Carlos inaugurated a period of rapid political change. A new constitution was adopted in 1978 and, notwithstanding the abortive 1981 coup, the country was generally regarded as a consolidated democracy by the time the Socialists under Felipe González came to power in 1982. In 1986, Spain joined the EC and confirmed its membership of Nato.

The success of Spain's transition to democracy is perhaps not surprising. In the 1960s and early 1970s the country experienced an "economic miracle", financed by foreign investment, tourism and migrant remittances. By 1975 Spain was well on its way to becoming an industrialized, urban society, with only 22% of the labour force in agriculture. Rapid growth brought a more even distribution of income and a significant rise in living standards for most Spaniards. Free education became available and the country's minimal welfare provisions were gradually improved. In other words, Spain had become in many respects not unlike its European neighbours.

The Union of the Democratic Centre (UCD), an amalgam of reformist groups, which governed from 1975–82 faced a number of problems. Spain is heavily dependent on imported oil and was badly hit by the 1974 oil crisis. But the UCD, preoccupied with consolidating Spain's fledgling democracy, was slow to tackle the resulting economic problems and by 1981 both inflation and unemployment had soared above 20%.

The relationship between the centre and regions was the other major issue. Centralizing forces have traditionally been strong, particularly during the Franco era, but regional consciousness has also remained powerful. The 1978 constitution paved the way for a process of political devolution which irritated the far right, which saw it as undermining Spanish national unity, without fully appeasing the demands for autonomy in Catalonia, the Basque country and Galicia. Today, Spain is effectively a federal state of 17 autonomous communi-

OFFICIAL NAME Kingdom of Spain.
CAPITAL CITY Madrid.
GEOGRAPHY The centre of Spain is a wide semi-arid plateau, the Meseta, bounded on the north and east by mountains and cut by a central range. The most extensive lowlands are in the north-east around the valley of the Ebro, on the east coast around Valencia and in the south around the valley of the Guadalquivir. *Highest point* (mainland) Mulhacén 3,478 metres (11,410 feet). *Area* 504,782 sq km (194,900 sq miles).
PEOPLE *Population* 39.4m. *Density* 78 per sq km. *Ethnic groups* Spanish 73%, Catalan 16%, Galician 8%, Basque 2%.
RELIGION RC 97%.
LANGUAGE Spanish (Castilian). Also Catalan, Galician, Basque, Andalusian.
EDUCATION Free and compulsory for ages 6–14. More than 30% of pupils are in private, mainly RC, schools subsidized by the state. There are 33 universities.
CLIMATE Temperate in the north, 9–18°C (48–64°F), with annual rainfall of over 1,000mm (39ins). More extreme in the centre, with hot, dry summers and cold winters; average temperatures 24°C (26°F) in July, 5°C (41°F) in Jan. Mediterranean in south.
CURRENCY Peseta.
PUBLIC HOLIDAYS (* not all areas) Jan 1, 6, Maundy Thu*, Good Fri, Easter Mon*, May 1, 15*, Corpus Christi, Jun 24, Jul 25, Aug 15, Oct 12*, Nov 1, Dec 6, 8*, 25–26*.
GOVERNMENT Parliamentary monarchy. The bicameral legislature, the Cortes, has a 350-member Congress of Deputies elected by PR for a 4-year term, and a Senate with 208 members. The chief executive, the president, is appointed by the monarch.

IMPORTS AND EXPORTS

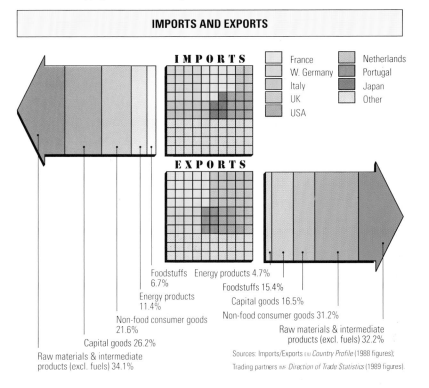

IMPORTS
France, W. Germany, Italy, UK, USA, Netherlands, Portugal, Japan, Other

EXPORTS

Foodstuffs 6.7%
Energy products 11.4%
Non-food consumer goods 21.6%
Capital goods 26.2%
Raw materials & intermediate products (excl. fuels) 34.1%

Energy products 4.7%
Foodstuffs 15.4%
Capital goods 16.5%
Non-food consumer goods 31.2%
Raw materials & intermediate products (excl. fuels) 32.2%

Sources: Imports/Exports EIU *Country Profile* (1988 figures); Trading partners IMF *Direction of Trade Statistics* (1989 figures).

BALANCE OF PAYMENTS

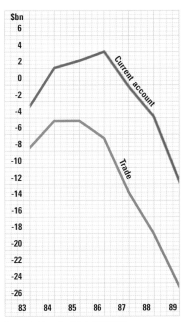

Current account
Trade

Source: IMF *International Financial Statistics*.

EUROPE

ties, each with its own executive, legislature and supreme court.

The Socialists, led by Felipe González, were the overwhelming victors of the 1982 elections. The next three years saw sweeping rationalization of the economy, in particular of older industries, high unemployment, and a gradual decline in inflation. This paved the way for renewed growth, fuelled by consumer demand and the fresh investments resulting from EC membership. Real GDP rose by 3.3% in 1986 and averaged 5.3% a year in 1987–89, well above that of Spain's European partners. By the turn of the decade GDP per head had reached $13,450, compared with the UK's $16,000. Growth slowed in 1990, with inflation rising to 7% and industrial output falling, and was expected to remain relatively low for the next two years.

However, there is still confidence in the economy's potential despite some clouds on the horizon. Tourism, which still represents 5% of GDP has been badly hit by recession. An overvalued peseta has encouraged very high interest rates which seriously damaged exports, and boosted inflation. However the government's room for manoeuvre was constrained by the ERM, which Spain joined in 1989.

The provision of a social structure and amenities in keeping with Spain's political and economic development has presented another challenge. In the immediate post-Franco period many instititions were modernized and divorce reintroduced. But reform lost its momentum after the early years of Socialist rule and the health and social services, and educational and legal systems are still chaotic in parts. Welfare benefits are well below the European norm, exacerbating the effects of unemployment, which is among the highest in the EC. The overwhelming support for the 1988 one-day general strike, the first for more than 50 years, owed much to discontent at the handling of social reforms and to popular feeling that the benefits of economic growth had become excessively concentrated in the hands of a minority.

The Socialists were re-elected in 1986 and 1989, helped by the lack of a credible opposition since the collapse of the UCD in 1982. However in 1989 the government's waning popularity resulted in the loss of its absolute parliamentary majority. It has since striven to present a more accommodating image, but a series of corruption scandals has done little to reduce popular cynicism. Even so a Socialist defeat in the 1993 elections seems improbable. The right-wing Popular Party (PP), led by the inexperienced José María Aznar, does not seem a viable alternative; although a PP alliance with the centrist Catalan and Basque nationalists could prove a challenge.

In the short-term 1992 is the key date in the Spanish calendar. It marks the completion of the transition period of Spain's EC membership. Spain will also host the Olympic Games in Barcelona and Expo '92 in Seville, as well as numerous celebrations to mark the 500th anniversary of the discovery of America.

ECONOMIC PROFILE

Services, except for tourism, less important than in most other EC countries. Composition of GDP stable; major changes within sectors. Industrial restructuring programme begun in early 1980s. Agricultural sector still substantial, increasingly specializing in high-value products for export. Spain is a major tourist destination and income helps balance persisting trade deficit.

Growth Surge of investment in industry since EC membership; expanding sectors include transport equipment and electrical machinery. Fruit and vegetable exports growing fast.

Problems Heavily dependent on imported oil. Steel, shipbuilding, chemicals and light engineering have contracted in the 1980s. Tourism hit by recession and down-market image of package sector.

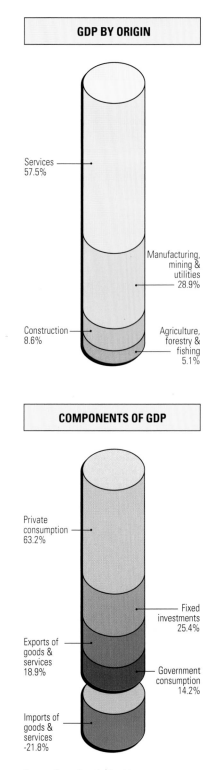

GDP BY ORIGIN

Services 57.5%

Manufacturing, mining & utilities 28.9%

Construction 8.6%

Agriculture, forestry & fishing 5.1%

COMPONENTS OF GDP

Private consumption 63.2%

Fixed investments 25.4%

Exports of goods & services 18.9%

Government consumption 14.2%

Imports of goods & services -21.8%

Source: EIU *Country Report* (GDP by origin 1988 figures; Components of GDP 1989 figures).

ITALY

The home of one of Europe's oldest civilizations, Italy is also one of its newest nations. It has been politically united only since 1870, and city or region is often still the primary unit of allegiance. Its people rank among the most prosperous in the world, yet there is an acute disparity between the wealthy industrial north and the poor, less developed Mezzogiorno.

There are other paradoxes. Italy is a major industrial power, ranking with the UK and France. Its business people, engineers and designers include some of the best in Europe, being adaptable, inventive and entrepreneurial. But they have to contend with a chronically inefficient bureaucracy and governments which lurch from crisis to crisis unable to cope with a growing national debt and the chaos of public finances.

Italy emerged from the second world war with a ruined economy and its political leaders disgraced by two decades of fascism and Mussolini's alliance with Hitler. The monarchy was abolished by popular referendum in 1946. A new constitution was drawn up two years later, a compromise between the competing forces of liberalism, socialism and Christian democracy. Subsequent elections brought a government dominated by the Christian Democrats to power; the Communists and Socialists were consigned to opposition.

The pattern of political power has changed little since. The Christian Democrats remain the largest party, dominating a succession of coalition governments until 1983. The Communists, the second largest party, have remained in opposition except for a brief period of compromise with the government in the late 1970s. The third major party, the Socialists, joined the governing coalition in the mid-1960s. Under their new leader Bettino Craxi they became more forceful in the 1980s, successfully challenging the Christian Democrats to lead two governments between July 1983 and March 1987.

Mr Craxi's first government lasted three years, making it the longest in postwar Italian history. The instability that led to some 50 different governments between 1945 and 1991 is inherent in Italy's electoral system and in the structure of its political parties. Not only has each government been formed from between three and five parties, but the major parties are themselves coalitions of competing factions. The Christian Democrats' return to government in 1987 was associated with a resurgence of factionalism between the left and centre of

OFFICIAL NAME Italian Republic.
CAPITAL CITY Rome.
GEOGRAPHY Much of Italy is upland, with the Alps in the north and the limestone Apennines making up the spine of the country and extending into Sicily. Earthquakes are common in southern and central regions, and there are active volcanoes in Sicily and on the Bay of Naples. The most important lowland area is the valley of the Po, containing the industrial centres of Turin and Milan. *Highest point* Mont Blanc 4,810 metres (15,780 feet). *Area* 301,225 sq km (116,300 sq miles).
PEOPLE *Population* 57.5m. *Density* 190 per sq km. *Ethnic groups* Italian 98%.
RELIGION RC 83%.
LANGUAGE Italian. Also French and German.
EDUCATION Free and compulsory for ages 6–14.
CLIMATE Temperate in the north, Mediterranean in the south and centre, with mild winters and long dry summers. Average temperatures around 25°C (77°F) in summer, 8°C (46°F) in winter, with local variations according to altitude.
CURRENCY Italian lira.
PUBLIC HOLIDAYS Jan 1, 6, Easter Mon, Apr 25, May 1, 12, Aug 15, Nov 1, 6, Dec 8, 25–26.
GOVERNMENT Republic since 1946. Italy has 20 regions, with varying degrees of autonomy. The head of state, the president of the republic, is elected for 7 years by a college of parliament and regional representatives. Parliament has 2 chambers, the 630-member Chamber of Deputies and the 315-member regional Senate, both elected by PR; the 2 chambers have equal powers. The chief executive is a council of ministers, whose leader is known as president of the council.

IMPORTS AND EXPORTS

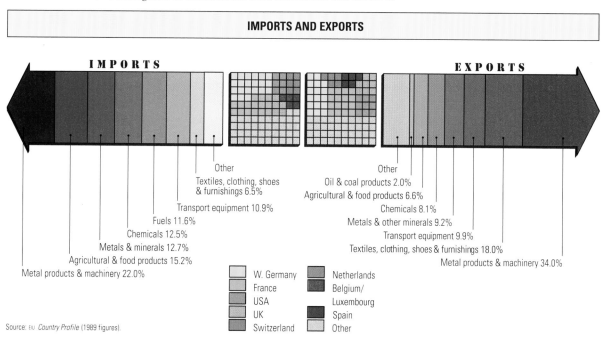

IMPORTS

EXPORTS

Other
Textiles, clothing, shoes & furnishings 6.5%
Transport equipment 10.9%
Fuels 11.6%
Chemicals 12.5%
Metals & minerals 12.7%
Agricultural & food products 15.2%
Metal products & machinery 22.0%

Other
Oil & coal products 2.0%
Agricultural & food products 6.6%
Chemicals 8.1%
Metals & other minerals 9.2%
Transport equipment 9.9%
Textiles, clothing, shoes & furnishings 18.0%
Metal products & machinery 34.0%

W. Germany
France
USA
UK
Switzerland
Netherlands
Belgium/Luxembourg
Spain
Other

Source: EIU *Country Profile* (1989 figures).

the party that threatened a new wave of short-lived governments in the 1990s. The late 1980s also brought divisions within the Communist party as it struggled to find a new political identity. The party's change of name in 1990 to the Democratic Party of the Left added to the anger of traditionalists and threatened a permanent factional split.

Such power struggles have encouraged corruption. Christian Democrat parliamentary dominance is complemented by a vast, complex network of patronage; other parties, particularly the Socialists, have followed suit. Together with instability, this is perhaps the major problem of Italian government, and one which is unlikely to be overcome in the absence of far-reaching institutional reform. The debate on reform was revived in 1990 but with little consensus on how to proceed.

Italy's economy has developed regardless of these and other handicaps, including a lack of natural resources and a dependence on imported raw materials and fuels second only to that of Japan among major industrial nations. Output doubled during the economic miracle of the 1950s and 1960s; by the 1970s income per head was approaching that of Italy's wealthier neighbours. Taking into account a massive black economy – estimated at 10–50% of GDP – the Italians were by 1987 claiming that they had overtaken the UK to become the world's fifth largest industrial power.

The economic transformation of Italy into an urbanized, industrial country has been paralleled by major social and demographic upheavals. The impact of growth has been unbalanced, however. The south remains poor and relatively undeveloped, with an inadequate infrastructure, although its problems have been alleviated by state investment. Its image remains tarnished by the power of organized crime: the Sicilian Mafia and the Neapolitan Camorra still undermine social and political order.

The south is more traditional than the north, but everywhere the transformation of social attitudes has been profound. Sexual mores have been revolutionized since the 1960s; despite the opposition of the Roman Catholic church, abortion and contraception are widely accepted and practised. However, the divorce rate remains low.

More generally, political and economic modernization has been incomplete and costly. An alienated labour force was one of the prices paid for the rapidity with which many Italian workers were transferred from agriculture to industry in the 1950s and 1960s. Urban terrorism, from both left and right, has been one of the consequences of Italy's blocked democracy, although it has subsided since reaching a peak in the 1970s. Another, and even more dangerous consequence has been a resurgence of regionalism and racial intolerance in the north, seen in the success of the anti-south Lombard League in the 1990 local elections.

ECONOMIC PROFILE

Economic growth led by manufacturing; export strengths lie mainly in medium- and low-tech products – industrial and office equipment, domestic appliances, vehicles, textiles, clothing, chemicals. Agriculture accounts for only 5% of GDP, producing mainly wheat, maize, rice, olives, wine and citrus fruit.

Growth White goods now account for third of European sales. Fiat vies with Audi/VW for leadership of European car market. Machine tools industry overtook USA in terms of total sales in 1988. Textiles and clothing moving successfully upmarket.

Problems Highly reliant on imported minerals and energy, a dependence likely to increase following rejection of nuclear power programme; also on food imports. Some traditional products – steel, textiles, clothing – suffering from Asian competition. Financial system remains fragmented; small, regionally based banks will have to merge to compete after 1992.

COMPONENTS OF GDP

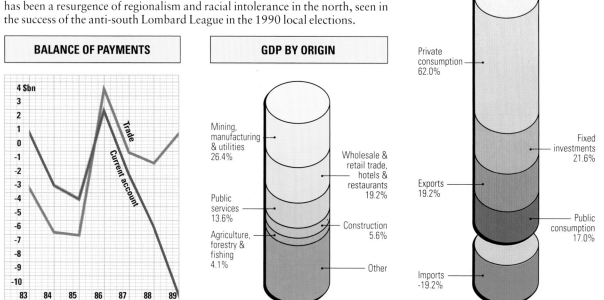

BALANCE OF PAYMENTS

4 $bn

Trade

Current account

83 84 85 86 87 88 89

Source: IMF *International Financial Statistics.*

GDP BY ORIGIN

Mining, manufacturing & utilities 26.4%

Public services 13.6%

Agriculture, forestry & fishing 4.1%

Wholesale & retail trade, hotels & restaurants 19.2%

Construction 5.6%

Other

Source: EIU *Country Profile* (1989 figures).

COMPONENTS OF GDP

Private consumption 62.0%

Fixed investments 21.6%

Exports 19.2%

Public consumption 17.0%

Imports -19.2%

The black economy

Italy has long been famous for its *economia sommersa* ; estimates of the black economy's contribution to GDP range from 10% to 50%. One study found that 54% of civil servants had second jobs, 33% sold goods within their ministries and 27% ran other businesses during working hours. The hidden economy boomed during the 1970s thanks to a combination of rigid labour laws and high taxes at a time when the official economy was in trouble. In 1987, a revision of government statistics to bring some informal economic activity into the official figures added 18% to estimates of national income at a stroke.

The regions

Italy's 20 regions have considerable autonomy, with powers over health, education and the police, although revenue comes from the central government. Each region has a legislative council, elected every five years. Five older regions have more autonomy than the rest: the two large islands, Sicily and Sardinia, French-speaking Valle D'Aosta, Trentino-Alto Adige, with its large German-speaking population, and Friuli-Venezia Giulia.

Differences between the regions reflect the country's north-south divide. The eight southern regions, the Mezzogiorno, cover 40% of the land area, contain 35% of the population but account for only about 25% of GDP. Even here there are wide disparities, with Calabria and Sardinia lagging far behind more developed regions such as Apulia. About a third of the workforce in parts of the south is still engaged in agriculture, compared with only 4% in Lombardy, the most densely populated region, which alone is responsible for one-third of the country's total GDP and 30% of exports. In 1989 the official rate of unemployment in the south was nearly three times that of the centre-north.

San Marino

Tourism accounts for 60% of revenue for this small, landlocked republic within Italy, and postage stamp sales for a further 10%. There is also some agriculture and light industry. The lack of customs restrictions makes San Marino an outlet for the illegal export of Italian currency and avoidance of value-added tax.

Vatican

An enclave in Rome, seat of the Holy See of the Roman Catholic church, and sustained entirely by investment income and voluntary contribution. At less than 1 sq km it is the smallest nation in the world, and the only one where Latin is the official language.

Energy

Italy is more dependent on imported energy than any other European country. Despite diversification during the oil shocks of the 1970s, oil still accounts for 58% of demand. Algeria remains a major supplier of natural gas, through the Transmed pipeline from Tunisia to Sicily, although consistently rising prices have prompted efforts to find alternative suppliers. Electricity is imported from France, Switzerland, Austria and Yugoslavia. Referenda in late 1987 ended Italy's nuclear power programme although increasing oil, gas and petrol consumption has prompted consideration of a further referendum on the nuclear issue.

■ More than 1 million
● 250,000 - 1 million
▢ The mezzogiorno

Italy is an enthusiastic supporter of European economic and political integration, working hard during its EC presidency in 1990 to hasten the process of monetary union. However, its record in enacting EC legislation is poor, and the later stages of monetary integration could prove problematic unless government spending and inflation are brought under control and the current account deficit is reduced. Unstable governments and a highly politicized bureaucracy will also hamper Italy's ability to compete in a more open Europe.

WORK FORCE

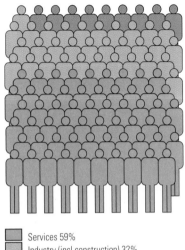

☐ Services 59%
☐ Industry (incl construction) 32%
☐ Agriculture, forestry & fishing 9%

Source: EIU *Country Profile* (1989 figures).

WAGES AND PRICES

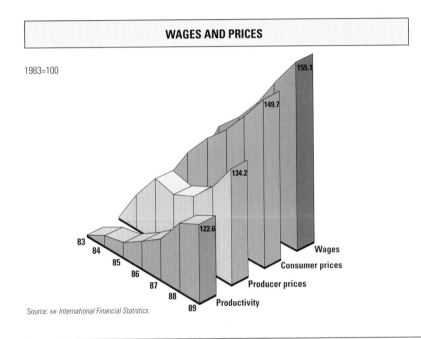

1983=100

155.1
149.7
134.2
122.6

Wages
Consumer prices
Producer prices
Productivity

83 84 85 86 87 88 89

Source: IMF *International Financial Statistics*.

MALTA

Seven years after independence, the Labour Party, led by Dom Mintoff, was the first to gain a majority vote in 1971. During Labour's 16 year rule, Malta withdrew from its close colonial relationship with the UK, and developed its non-aligned position, reflected in improved relations with the USSR, and with Libya, its major oil supplier. The departure of British forces in 1979 lost Malta a major source of income and enforced a hastened economic restructuring concentrating on export-oriented manufactures and tourism.

The Nationalist Party, led by Prime Minister Eddie Fenech Adami, won a narrow majority in the 1987 elections, and started to make good its election pledges; improvements in infrastructure boosted tourism receipts, and promotion as an offshore business centre is beginning to show results. By July 1990 Malta felt ready to apply for EC membership. However, it will be 1993, at the earliest, before it learns the fate of its application because of the EC moratorium on admitting new members until completion of the single market.

OFFICIAL NAME Republic of Malta.
CAPITAL CITY Valletta.
GEOGRAPHY The limestone archipelago lies 93km south of Sicily and 200km north of Libya. Only Malta, Gozo and Cornino are inhabited. Malta's rugged north and west coasts give way to deep harbours on the east. *Highest point* 249 metres (820 feet). *Area* 316 sq km (120 sq miles).
PEOPLE *Population* 349,000. *Density* 1,104 per sq km. *Ethnic groups* Maltese 96%, British 2%.
RELIGION RC 97%, Anglican 1%.
LANGUAGE Maltese and English. Also Italian.
EDUCATION Free and compulsory for ages 5–16. There is 1 university. Over 8% of spending is on education.
CLIMATE Mediterranean, with average annual temperature of 18°C (64°F), around 25°C (77°F) in summer. Annual rainfall 560mm (22ins), most in winter.
CURRENCY Maltese pound.
PUBLIC HOLIDAYS Jan 1, Feb 10, Mar 19, 31, Good Fri, May 1, Jun 7, 29, Aug 15, Sep 8, 21, Dec 8, 13, 25.
GOVERNMENT Independent since 1964, republic since 1974. The 69-member legislature, the House of Representatives, is elected every 5 years and elects a president who appoints the prime minister and the cabinet.

GREECE, TURKEY & CYPRUS

The Kurdish problem

Kurdish speakers make up some 15% of Turkey's total population and are in a majority in eight south-eastern provinces flanking Syria, Iran and Iraq. However, the Kurds are not officially recognized as a separate ethnic group, although the ban on the Kurdish language was lifted in early 1991.

The separatist Workers Party of Kurdistan (the PKK) supports the creation of a Kurdish national homeland within Turkey and wages guerrilla war against the Turkish authorities; around 2,000 deaths, mostly of Kurdish villagers, occured between 1984 and 1990. Turkey's problems with its own Kurdish minority was one of the reasons behind the government's initial reluctance to grant entry to hundreds of thousands of Iraqi Kurdish refugees in the aftermath of the 1991 Gulf war.

Tourism

Greece has been one of Europe's most popular destinations since the 1960s. The number of visitors expanded to around 7.5m a year in the late 1980s, although the amount spent by each continues to decline. However, terrorist problems and the Gulf crisis reduced Greece's attraction in the early 1990s, and the fall is forecast to continue.

As Greek tourist resorts have neared saturation point, the country has lost business to Turkey, which was one of the fastest-growing tourist destinations in the 1980s, with a peak of $2.6 billion in receipts in 1988. Again problems in the Gulf and a slackening of demand from Western Europe reduced income.

The Dardanelles and Bosporus

The straits separating European and Asiatic Turkey have long been of strategic significance. The Dardanelles (Turkish name Canakkale Bogazi) linking the Aegean Sea with the Sea of Marmara are 65km (40 miles) long and 1.6km (1 mile) wide at their narrowest point. The Bosporus (Istanbul Bogazi), from the Sea of Marmara to the Black Sea, is 32km (20 miles) long and narrows to only 640m (2,100 feet). The Bosporus is spanned at Istanbul by two suspension bridges.

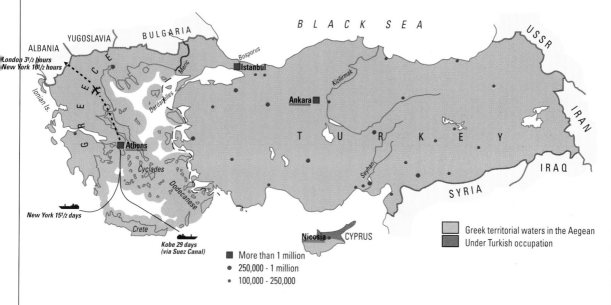

Greek territorial waters in the Aegean
Under Turkish occupation

More than 1 million
250,000 - 1 million
100,000 - 250,000

The Aegean

The territorial dispute between Greece and Turkey over the Aegean Sea centres on two issues: the continental shelf and airspace, both defined in international law as the same. Turkey does not claim Greek islands in the Aegean close to its coast, but does claim half the continental shelf, partly for security reasons, partly for its mineral resources. This runs counter to Greece's desire to extend its territorial waters to a 12-mile limit, which would bring the area it controls within a few kilometres of the Turkish coast in places and block Turkey's access to international waters.

Both countries depend heavily on military aid from the USA, which maintains bases in both countries in exchange for military assistance, provided in a 7:10 ratio to allow Greece, with a smaller standing army, to achieve a balance of power.

Divided island

Cyprus's 1960 constitution provided for a Greek president and Turkish vice-president, and a council of ministers containing seven Greeks and three Turks. Tension between the two communities came to a head in 1963, after President Makarios declared his intention of revising the constitution. The coup that overthrew Archbishop Makarios in 1974 was swiftly followed by the Turkish invasion and effective partition of the island. The Turkish north unilaterally declared independence in 1983 as the Turkish Republic of North Cyprus, so far recognized only by Turkey. Each community has its own president, ministers, judiciary and education system.

Cleaning up the Mediterranean

Seventeen of the 18 Mediterranean countries signed the Barcelona convention in 1976, setting aside national rivalries in a concerted effort to combat pollution. Further agreements followed on cleaning up discharges of sewage, industrial waste and agricultural pesticides; marine reserves have been designated to protect wildlife. Over 80 marine laboratories carry out long-term monitoring of pollution. The programme has made considerable progress: by the late 1980s, four out of five Mediterranean beaches were regarded as being safe for swimmers. But the migration every summer of 100m tourists to shores where 130m people already live will continue to put enormous pressure on local efforts to fight pollution.

GREECE

Greece is on the periphery of Western Europe in more than just a geographical sense. Ostracized during the dictatorship of the colonels from 1967 to 1974, it did not join the EC until 1981. The election victory later that year of the Panhellenic Socialist Movement (Pasok), led by Andreas Papandreou, not only gave Greece its first socialist government but also brought early promises of taking Greece out of Nato and of a referendum on EC membership.

The proposed fundamental changes to Greece's relationships with its neighbours and allies failed to materialize, but there were also signs of intermittent discord. The Pasok administration blew hot and cold on the question of US bases; the Reagan administration countered with accusations that Greece was soft on Middle East terrorism and not pulling its weight as a Nato member. Relations with Turkey, already blighted by the 1974 Turkish invasion of Cyprus, were further shaken by arguments over territorial waters and mineral exploration of the Aegean. However, by the late 1980s tensions had diminished as Greece's allies learned to distinguish between internal politicking and serious policy statements. The government also became more conciliatory, to the extent that Mr Papandreou initiated a dialogue with Turkey in 1988.

The Pasok government fell at elections in June 1989 amid reports of high-level embezzlement and abuse of power. Almost a year of ineffective coalition governments later the electorate voted in the conservative New Democracy Party, led by Constantine Mitsotakis. He became prime minister with a parliamentary majority of one seat in April 1990 and was immediately faced with the task of re-establishing firm government. The country's economic problems, already evident in the later years of socialist rule, had become critical during the year of inaction. Under strong pressure from the EC the New Democracy government introduced an austerity programme, cutting the social welfare programme and closing or privatizing state-owned industries. Attempts were also made to curb Greece's notorious "black economy".

The gap between Greece and its EC partners, in terms both of economic management and income per head, remains wide. Partisan politics and the cumbersome state bureaucracy remain the biggest obstacles to growth. But there is confidence that the tough economic policies are working, although elements of the bureaucracy remain resistant to change, a cause of much chagrin both to foreign investors and the Greek business community. The approach of the single European market has helped to galvanize Greek industry into unprecedented activity. There are hopes that closer European economic ties will act as a similar engine for change in the cumbersome bureaucratic machine.

OFFICIAL NAME Hellenic Republic.

CAPITAL CITY Athens.

GEOGRAPHY Greece is a country of mountainous peninsulas and rugged islands, themselves the tops of submerged ranges. River valleys, small basins in the mountains and coastal plains are the only lowland areas and contain most of the population. Agriculture is limited to less than 25% of the land. Much of the bedrock is porous limestone, and rivers tend to be short, with erratic flows. There are frequent earthquakes. *Highest point* Mount Olympus 2,917 metres (9,570 feet). *Area* 131,957 sq km (50,950 sq miles).

PEOPLE *Population* 9.9m. *Density* 76 per sq km. *Ethnic groups* Greek 95%, Macedonian 2%, Turkish 1%, Albanian 1%.

RELIGION Greek Orthodox 98%, Muslim 1%.

LANGUAGE Greek.

EDUCATION Free and officially compulsory for ages 6–15, though enrolment is below 75%. There are 14 universities.

CLIMATE Mediterranean, with hot, dry summers. Average temperatures in Athens 28°C (82°F) in July, 9°C (48°F) in Jan; cooler in north of country. West has highest rainfall.

CURRENCY Drachma.

PUBLIC HOLIDAYS Jan 1, Jan 6, Mon before Shrove Tue, Mar 25, Greek Orthodox Good Fri–Easter Mon, May 1, 7th Mon after Easter Mon, Aug 15, Oct 28, Dec 25–26.

GOVERNMENT Republic. A 300-member parliament is elected for a 4-year term. The president, ceremonial head of state, is elected by parliament for 5 years; he appoints the majority leader in parliament as prime minister and chief executive.

ECONOMIC PROFILE

Agriculture and manufacturing are mainstays. Large balance of payments deficit; foreign exchange earnings mainly from tourism, also shipping. Olive oil, citrus fruits, sugar and wine exported.

Growth Mining and quarrying, oil refining, clothing, some agricultural products such as yoghurt. Tourism continues to expand.

Problems Tobacco, footwear and leather, machinery and transport equipment industries are in decline. Increasing demand for imported manufactured goods.

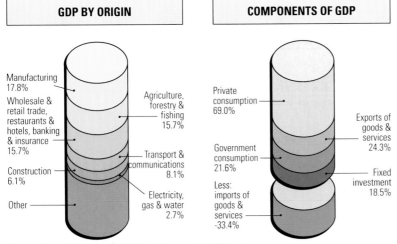

GDP BY ORIGIN	COMPONENTS OF GDP

Manufacturing 17.8%
Wholesale & retail trade, restaurants, hotels, banking & insurance 15.7%
Construction 6.1%
Other
Agriculture, forestry & fishing 15.7%
Transport & communications 8.1%
Electricity, gas & water 2.7%

Private consumption 69.0%
Government consumption 21.6%
Less: imports of goods & services -33.4%
Exports of goods & services 24.3%
Fixed investment 18.5%

Source: EIU *Country Profile* (GDP by origin 1989 figures; Components of GDP 1988 figures).

IMPORTS AND EXPORTS

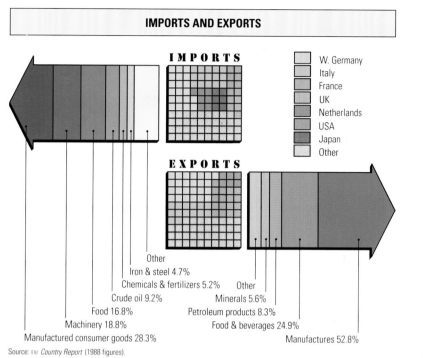

IMPORTS

W. Germany
Italy
France
UK
Netherlands
USA
Japan
Other

EXPORTS

Other
Iron & steel 4.7%
Chemicals & fertilizers 5.2%
Crude oil 9.2%
Food 16.8%
Machinery 18.8%
Manufactured consumer goods 28.3%

Other
Minerals 5.6%
Petroleum products 8.3%
Food & beverages 24.9%
Manufactures 52.8%

Source: EIU *Country Report* (1988 figures).

BALANCE OF PAYMENTS

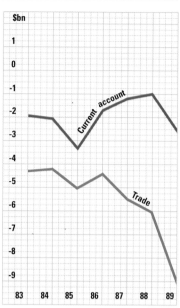

Current account

Trade

Source: IMF *International Financial Statistics*; EIU *Country Report*.

TURKEY

Since the second world war Turkey has alternated between periods of democracy and military rule. The most recent military intervention was initiated by General, later President, Kenan Evren, who seized power in 1980 and put an end to widespread terrorism and economic chaos.

With the old parties and their leaders banned, the 1983 elections reflected only a partial restoration of democracy. The victory of the centrist Motherland Party (Anap) under Turgut Ozal, heralded a new era of stability and economic vigour; Mr Ozal felt confident enough, following his re-election in 1987, to apply for EC membership in the same year.

The application was received in Brussels politely but with little enthusiasm. Despite impressive economic growth – averaging 7.3 % between 1981 and 1988 – income per head is still way below the EC average, and economic booms have been accompanied by steep inflation and a heavy debt burden. Turkey's human rights record and disputes with Greece, notably over Turkey's 1974 occupation of northern Cyprus, are additional obstacles to membership.

Mr Ozal became president in 1990, as the introduction of consumer credit for the first time fuelled a new inflationary boom. The onset of the Gulf crisis brought this swiftly to an end, and provided the government with an opportunity to bring domestic demand under control. Its actions were expected to be tempered, however, by the prospect of general elections, due before the end of 1992. In trying to restore the current account to surplus, equal emphasis was expected to be placed on boosting exports. With this in mind the government called for improved market openings for exports when offered compensation for Turkey's role in enforcing sanctions against Iraq during the Gulf war.

OFFICIAL NAME Republic of Turkey.

CAPITAL CITY Ankara.

GEOGRAPHY Thrace, the area north-west of the Bosphorus, is mostly lowland, but the bulk of the country, Anatolia, is made up of seismically active young mountain chains, highest in the east of the country. Less than 10% of Turkey, mostly around the coasts, is level or gently sloping. *Highest point* Mt Ararat 5,165 metres (16,950 feet). *Area* 780,576 sq km (301,380 sq miles).

PEOPLE *Population* 50.6m. *Density* 65 per sq km. *Ethnic groups* Turkish 87%, Kurdish 9%, Arab 2%.

RELIGION Sunni Muslim 99%, Christian 0.5%.

LANGUAGE Turkish. Also Kurdish and Arabic.

EDUCATION Officially compulsory for 5 years, to be taken between ages 6 and 14; free to university level. Around 20% of secondary pupils attend private schools. There are 28 universities.

CLIMATE Much of interior is semi-arid, with continental extremes of temperature. Winters cold, around 0°C (32°F) in Ankara in Jan, down to -40°C (-40°F) in eastern mountains; summers warm, around 23°C (71°F) in Ankara in July, hotter on Mediterranean coast.

CURRENCY Turkish lira.

PUBLIC HOLIDAYS (* some areas only) Jan 1, Seker Bayram, Apr 23, May 1, May 19, Kurban Bayram, Aug 30, Oct 28*–29.

GOVERNMENT Republic. The 1982 constitution provides for a 450-member national assembly, elected for a 5-year term by a form of PR. The executive's powers are limited by a constitutional court and a national security council, which is dominated by the military and headed by the president.

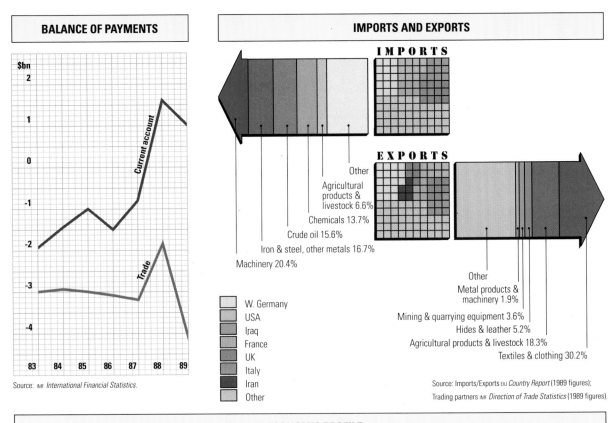

BALANCE OF PAYMENTS

$bn

Current account

Trade

83 84 85 86 87 88 89

Source: IMF *International Financial Statistics*.

IMPORTS AND EXPORTS

IMPORTS

EXPORTS

Other
Agricultural products & livestock 6.6%
Chemicals 13.7%
Crude oil 15.6%
Iron & steel, other metals 16.7%
Machinery 20.4%

Other
Metal products & machinery 1.9%
Mining & quarrying equipment 3.6%
Hides & leather 5.2%
Agricultural products & livestock 18.3%
Textiles & clothing 30.2%

W. Germany
USA
Iraq
France
UK
Italy
Iran
Other

Source: Imports/Exports EIU *Country Report* (1989 figures);
Trading partners IMF *Direction of Trade Statistics* (1989 figures).

ECONOMIC PROFILE

Agriculture overtaken by manufacturing, though still important: key crops are cotton, tobacco, wheat, hazelnuts, dried fruit, silk and olives. Remittances from migrant workers in western Europe, notably Germany, declining. Clothing and textiles important exports following industrialization.

Growth Machinery, iron and steel, chemicals. Tourism has been a growth area.

Problems Dependent on imports of oil and other fuels. High inflation rates and foreign debt burden threaten recent high growth rates. Fiscal difficulties arise from the failure to tax effectively agricultural incomes.

CYPRUS

This small but strategically placed Mediterranean island gained independence from the UK in 1960. Its partition dates from 1974 when Turkish troops invaded the north, responding both to a Greek right-wing coup that had overthrown President Makarios and to the beleaguered state of the Turkish-Cypriot minority. Repeated UN efforts to heal the island's divisions have come to nothing.

After 1974 the Greek south prospered as never before. Wealth was generated by specialized agriculture (potatoes, avocados, exotic fruits), substantial income from the British bases and invisibles, such as offshore banking, shipping and above all tourism. Manufacturing (clothing, shoes, plastics) is becoming less important as the customs union with the EC takes full effect. In contrast, the Turkish north has had only limited success in breaking out of its diplomatic isolation to market its agricultural produce and tourism potential.

OFFICIAL NAME Republic of Cyprus.
CAPITAL CITY Nicosia.
GEOGRAPHY A hot central plain is flanked by the Kyrenian mountains to the north and the Troödos massif to the south. *Area* 9,251 sq km (3,570 sq miles).
PEOPLE *Population* 687,000. *Ethnic groups* Greek 81%, Turkish 19%.
RELIGION Greek Orthodox 77%, Muslim 18%.
LANGUAGE Greek and Turkish. Also English.
EDUCATION Free, and compulsory for ages 5–11.
CLIMATE Mediterranean with above-average rainfall.
CURRENCY Cyprus pound.
PUBLIC HOLIDAYS (* Greek; + Turkish) Jan 1, 6*, 19*, Apr 1, 23+, Easter*, May 1, Ramazam Bayram+, May 19+, Jul 20+, Qurban Bayram+, Aug 30+, Oct 1, Birth of Prophet+, Oct 28*, 29+, Nov 15+, Dec 25–26*.
GOVERNMENT Democratic republic. The Turkish Republic of Northern Cyprus is not internationally recognized.

SWITZERLAND & AUSTRIA

Neutrality

Switzerland's long tradition of neutrality was recognized internationally when its borders were fixed by treaty in 1815. This has kept it at peace ever since but the policy of not entering into alliances is leaving it ever more isolated in an increasingly integrated Europe. There is mounting pressure to apply for EC membership, even though this will mean compromising not only neutrality but also a range of logistics particular to Switzerland and often critical to its economy.

Austria enshrined permanent neutrality in its constitution in 1955. Unlike Switzerland, it has used its neutral stance to act as a bridge between East and West and has taken a forthright stand on many world issues. The approach of 1992 prompted a number of Efta members to apply for EC membership, with Austria at the forefront.

The neutral status of Switzerland and Austria has made them popular sites for the headquarters of international organizations. Ten UN agencies, including the International Labour Organization, World Health Organization and the Office of the High Commissioner for Refugees, are based in Geneva, as are the International Red Cross, General Agreement on Tariffs and Trade and Efta. The Bank for International Settlements, the central banks' bank, has its headquarters in Basel. Vienna is home to Opec, the International Atomic Energy Agency and UN Industrial Development Organization, among others. Geneva has often been the site of sensitive political talks, including negotiations to end the Vietnam and Iran-Iraq wars.

Liechtenstein

The Principality of Liechtenstein lies on the foothills of the Alps and the floodplain of the Rhine between Austria and Switzerland, with which it has a postal and customs union. There is some industry, including machinery, precision instruments and dentistry equipment, and postal stamps make up 7.5% of government income. However, most revenue derives from its status as a company tax haven.

It is a constitutional democracy with a prince as head of state. Only two parties, the Progressive Citizens' Party and Fatherland Union, are represented in the 15-member Landtag or legislature. Referenda are called on all important issues. Diplomatic representation is via Switzerland.

■ More than 1 million
● 250,000 - 1 million
• 100,000 - 250,000

German speaking
French speaking
Italian speaking
Romansch speaking

The Alps

Europe's principal mountain range, the Alps stretch in parallel chains for over 1,000km (625 miles) from the French-Italian border to eastern Austria. The Alps are the source of many great European rivers, including the Rhine, Rhône and Po. Mont Blanc, at 4,807metres (15,770 feet), is the highest peak. There are railway tunnels at Col de Fréjus, Lotschberg, Simplon and St Gotthard; major passes are at Mont Cenis, Simplon, St Bernard, Gemmi, St Gotthard, Splugen, Stilfserjoch and Brenner. These attract long-distance road traffic between Italy and the rest of Western Europe. The environmental damage caused has led to moves, particularly in Switzerland, to impose restrictions on trucks in transit.

Languages

The historic isolation of different communities in Switzerland's mountainous terrain is reflected in its linguistic divisions. Six of the 26 cantons are French-speaking, there is one Italian-speaking canton on the Italian border, one with a significant community who speak Romansch; the rest of the country speaks German.

![Swiss flag] # SWITZERLAND

For more than 170 years, Switzerland has held itself aloof from the wars and diplomatic skirmishes that have washed around it. The Swiss are deeply proud of their neutrality and it has made the confederation a haven for political refugees and a headquarters for international organizations, such as the World Health Organization, the International Red Cross and the International Labour Organization.

Neutrality also left the Swiss free to make money in their own quiet, business-like way. The economy has become a model of steady prosperity, the richest in Europe in terms of income per head, and remarkably resilient in riding the ups and downs of world markets. Without natural resources, the Swiss have made the most of their human ones, using a skilled, highly paid workforce to develop a diversified industrial base, famous for quality products. The sophisticated and secretive banking system has enabled Switzerland to remain an international financial centre despite the deregulation of the 1980s.

The country's business success owes much to a profound work ethic and a record of industrial harmony: a no-strike agreement with the largest trade union has lasted since 1937. Politically, Switzerland is stable. Four parties – the Radicals, Christian Democrats, Social Democrats and Swiss People's Party – have run the country in harness along the same cautious lines since the late 1950s. There is the strong tradition of democracy in which local issues may be decided by a show of hands in the town square and national issues by referendum. However, such is the depth of conservatism that women did not get the vote in national elections until 1971.

On the face of it, the quality of life is good. Unemployment is almost non-existent, wages are high and Swiss towns display an affluence matched in few other countries. Swiss business continues to thrive, although it has been slow to exploit high-growth areas such as electronics and computers. But many young Swiss are disillusioned by their parents' bourgeois complacency and the lack of political change. The environment is an important issue and Green politics may be a force in future. The Swiss are under growing economic pressure to abandon their tradition of non-involvement – for example, there is a growing feeling that Switzerland should enter the EC. But the commitment to neutrality is unlikely to be surrendered while the country continues to thrive and prosper.

OFFICIAL NAME Swiss Confederation.

CAPITAL CITY Berne.

GEOGRAPHY Landlocked and mountainous, Switzerland is the source of many of Europe's great rivers. The west is bounded by the Jura, a wooded limestone range with upland meadows, while the Alps – split by the Rhône and Rhine valleys – cover the southern half of the country. Most of the population live on the central plateau, the Mittelland, which runs from Lake Geneva in the south-west to Lake Constance in the north-east. *Highest point* Dufourspitze 4,634 metres (15,200 feet). *Area* 41,288 sq km (15,941 sq miles).

PEOPLE *Population* 6.6m. *Density* 160 per sq km. *Ethnic groups* Swiss 86%, Italian 4%, French 2%, Spanish 2%, German 2%.

RELIGION RC 48%, Protestant 44%, Jewish 0.3%.

LANGUAGE German, French and Italian. Also Romansch.

EDUCATION Compulsory and free for ages 7–15. Education is administered at canton level and there are 26 different systems, with many private schools catering to overseas as well as Swiss students. 7 universities.

CLIMATE Wide variations: Atlantic in the west, Mediterranean in the south, continental in the east. Temperature varies with altitude. Annual rainfall over 1,000mm (39ins), except in dry pockets such as the Valais.

CURRENCY Swiss franc.

PUBLIC HOLIDAYS (* some cantons only) Jan 1–2, Good Fri, Easter Mon, Ascension, Whit Mon, May 1*, Aug 1*, Sep 5*, Dec 24*–26.

GOVERNMENT Federal Republic. Each of the 26 cantons and half cantons has its own system of courts, government and legislature. The Federal Assembly consists of a 46-member Council of State elected according to cantonal rules, generally by the majoritarian (first past the post) system, and a 200-member National Council elected mainly by PR, although in the smallest constituencies the majoritarian system is used. Laws can be submitted to a referendum at the request of 50,000 voters. The executive (federal council) is elected by the Federal Assembly for a period of 4 years; one of its number is elected annually as president of the council and serves as president of the confederation for representative purposes.

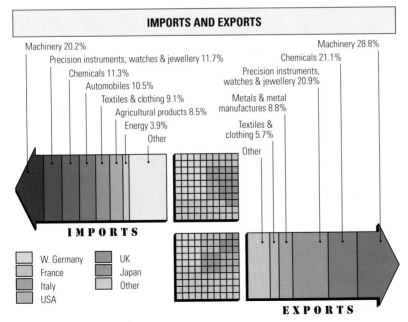

IMPORTS AND EXPORTS

Machinery 20.2%
Precision instruments, watches & jewellery 11.7%
Chemicals 11.3%
Automobiles 10.5%
Textiles & clothing 9.1%
Agricultural products 8.5%
Energy 3.9%
Other

Machinery 28.8%
Chemicals 21.1%
Precision instruments, watches & jewellery 20.9%
Metals & metal manufactures 8.8%
Textiles & clothing 5.7%
Other

IMPORTS

W. Germany
France
Italy
USA
UK
Japan
Other

EXPORTS

Source: EIU *Country Report* (1989 figures).

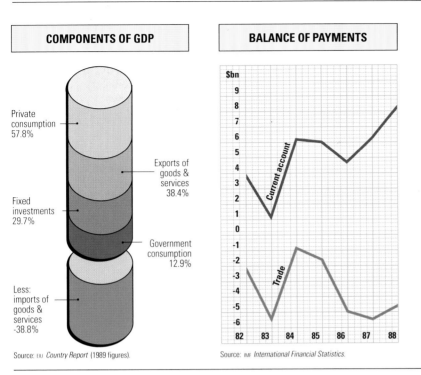

COMPONENTS OF GDP

Private consumption 57.8%

Exports of goods & services 38.4%

Fixed investments 29.7%

Government consumption 12.9%

Less: imports of goods & services -38.8%

Source: EIU *Country Report* (1989 figures).

BALANCE OF PAYMENTS

$bn

Current account

Trade

82 83 84 85 86 87 88

Source: IMF *International Financial Statistics.*

ECONOMIC PROFILE

Highly dependent on foreign trade: earns more than a third of GNP from exports; imports energy and more food per head than any other country. Economy mixed but traditionally strong in high-quality manufactured goods, especially precision instruments, machinery and chemicals, and in banking. Tourists also bring in foreign currency.

Growth Machinery and chemical industries benefiting from rationalization and shift towards specialized, high-technology products such as pharmaceuticals and medical equipment.

Problems Traditional exports such as textiles cut by acute labour shortages, high labour costs, currency fluctuations and changing world markets.

AUSTRIA

At the centre of the Austro-Hungarian empire until its dissolution in 1918, Austria was occupied by Nazi Germany in 1938; not until 1955, after ten years of occupation by allied forces, did it formally regain its independence.

Austria's post-war reconstruction was almost as remarkable as that of former West Germany, if on a smaller scale. Its success was due not least to the willingness of the partners in successive coalitions, the Socialist Party and Austrian People's Party, to play down ideological differences for the sake of social cohesion. About one-quarter of manufacturing industry was nationalized and, with generous government support, was a key factor in the consistent achievement of one of the highest growth rates in Europe.

But the success of state industry bred complacency; left largely to its own devices, it became cumbersome, inflexible and expensive to run. The growth rate by the mid-1980s was among Europe's lowest and Austria was burdened with a chronic budget deficit and huge public debt.

However, the late 1980s were something of a success for the Austrian economy. The state industry group OIAG was reorganized into seven holding companies under which 350 independent companies were grouped according to product lines and market segment. Priority was afforded to growth sectors such as chemicals and engineering, costs were slashed and assets disposed of. By 1989, the group had become profitable again; in February 1990 it was renamed Austrian Industries (AI). One effect of the OIAG rationalization has been to help reduce the budget deficit – from 4.7% of GNP in 1987 to 3.7% in 1989.

In July 1989 Austria formally applied for EC membership. Although the country is involved with Efta in negotiations with the community to establish a common economic area, full membership of the EC is now the priority. Austria has already adopted more directives and rules of the *acquis communitaire* than even some of the EC's members. However, its application to join is unlikely to be fully considered until after 1992. In the meantime the country has been trying to come to terms with the large influx of immigrants from Eastern Europe, which has caused social tension and a resurgence of nationalist sentiment.

OFFICIAL NAME Republic of Austria.

CAPITAL CITY Vienna.

GEOGRAPHY Most of the country is alpine or sub-alpine, with heavily wooded mountains and hills cut by the valleys of fast-flowing rivers. The plains around Vienna and the valley of the Danube in the north-east are the only lowland areas, and contain most of the population. *Highest point* Grossglockner 3,798 metres (12,460 feet). *Area* 83,855 sq km (32,370 sq miles).

PEOPLE *Population* 7.7m. *Density* 90 per sq km. *Ethnic groups* Austrian 96%, Yugoslavian 2%, Turkish 1%.

RELIGION RC 89%, other Christian 8%, Muslim 1%.

LANGUAGE German.

EDUCATION Free and compulsory for ages 6–15. There are 6 universities and 14 specialist university colleges.

CLIMATE Varies with altitude: in lowlands, average monthly temperatures -1–20°C (30–68°F); above 3,000 metres (9,800 feet) -11–2°C (12–36°F). Annual rainfall up to 1,000mm (39ins) in west, less in east.

CURRENCY Schilling.

PUBLIC HOLIDAYS Jan 1, 6, Easter Mon, May 1, Ascension, Whit Mon, Corpus Christi, Aug 15, Oct 26, Nov 1, Dec 8, 25–26.

GOVERNMENT Federal republic consisting of 9 provinces. The Federal Assembly consists of a 183-member National Council elected every 4 years by PR and a 63-member Federal Council elected by the provincial assemblies. The head of state, the president, is elected every 6 years by popular vote and is advised by a council of ministers, led by a chancellor.

195

EUROPE

ECONOMIC PROFILE

Manufacturing is the economy's mainstay. Agricultural production meets most food needs, with some surplus for export. Heavily dependent on imported energy supplies, although some oil and gas found in Lower Austria; hydroelectricity produces over a third of primary energy consumption. No nuclear power. Substantial foreign earnings from tourism.

Growth Chemicals, electronics and vehicles. Amendments to banking laws have helped financial sector improve profit margins.

Problems Budget deficit being brought under control; textiles and steel face declining markets and sometimes painful restructuring. Recent large influx of immigrants from eastern Europe has caused problems.

IMPORTS AND EXPORTS

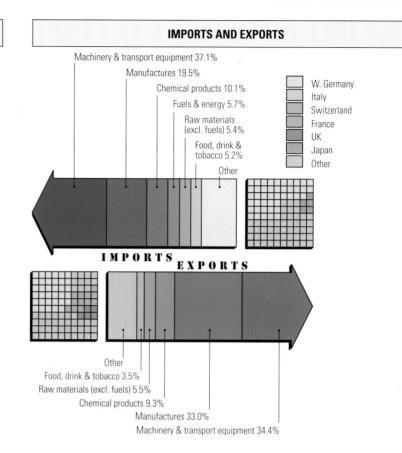

Machinery & transport equipment 37.1%
Manufactures 19.5%
Chemical products 10.1%
Fuels & energy 5.7%
Raw materials (excl. fuels) 5.4%
Food, drink & tobacco 5.2%
Other

W. Germany
Italy
Switzerland
France
UK
Japan
Other

IMPORTS EXPORTS

Other
Food, drink & tobacco 3.5%
Raw materials (excl. fuels) 5.5%
Chemical products 9.3%
Manufactures 33.0%
Machinery & transport equipment 34.4%

Source: EIU *Country Report* (1989 figures).

BALANCE OF PAYMENTS

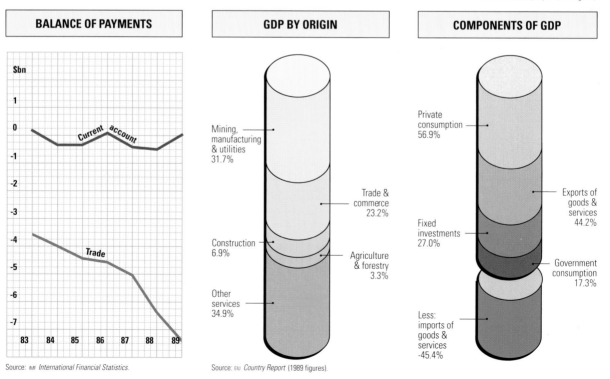

$bn

Current account

Trade

83 84 85 86 87 88 89

Source: IMF *International Financial Statistics*.

GDP BY ORIGIN

Mining, manufacturing & utilities 31.7%

Trade & commerce 23.2%

Construction 6.9%

Agriculture & forestry 3.3%

Other services 34.9%

Source: EIU *Country Report* (1989 figures).

COMPONENTS OF GDP

Private consumption 56.9%

Exports of goods & services 44.2%

Fixed investments 27.0%

Government consumption 17.3%

Less: imports of goods & services -45.4%

GERMANY

Formal unification of the two Germanys in October 1990 accomplished in one quick step the overriding mission of West German statesmanship during Europe's four post-war decades of ideological division. This dazzling but unexpected political triumph, made possible by the sudden end of the cold war, left the new Germany with an identity crisis and a whole host of problems.

When the allies divided Germany after the second world war large portions of eastern Germany were ceded to Poland; the remaining Soviet occupation zone became East Germany (DDR) with a population of 17m; and the three western zones became the Federal Republic of Germany (FDR) with a population of 60m and a land area roughly two and a half times the size of the DDR. With equal vigour both Germanys set about rebuilding their shattered economies but while the west benefited from Marshall Plan aid the east was made to pay huge war reparations to the USSR.

The post-war rivalry of the two German states quickly became a microcosm of the larger superpower conflict. This was because the German nation lived on as a legal fiction, and the democratically elected West German government laid claim to be its sole legitimate representative.

With its Hallstein doctrine, established in 1955, West Germany sought to isolate "the other Germany" by threatening to break off diplomacy with any country daring to recognize its Soviet-backed competitor. This was the decade of West Germany's *Wirtschaftswunder*, the economic miracle, when the economy grew by 8% a year. By 1955, West Germany's net national income had climbed an estimated 179% above the level extrapolated for the same region in 1936.

The first cracks were already showing in East Germany's rigid Stalinist system in the form of rising defections of frustrated professionals and skilled workers. By the end of 1953, East Germany had lost 320,000 of its most productive citizens to the west. By 1961, the net loss of population to West Germany had reached 3.5m and the communist government in East Berlin built the notorious Berlin Wall in a desperate bid to stabilize the economy.

For a while it worked. After a new West German government under Willy Brandt came to power in 1969, West Germany abandoned the Hallstein doctrine, signed coexistence treaties with the Warsaw Pact countries and signalled its acquiescence to the continued existence of East Germany. Both Germanys entered the United Nations as equals. Tiny East Germany produced the highest

OFFICIAL NAME Federal Republic of Germany.
CAPITAL CITY Berlin.

GEOGRAPHY The northern third of the country is a plain cut by rivers and canals; both the North Sea and Baltic coastlines are indented with estuaries leading to major ports. More rivers intersect the central uplands, an area of forested low ranges and plateaus. In the south, the land rises to an extension of the Jura Mountains, which merge into the Bavarian Alps and the coniferous Black Forest. Dominating the west is the highly polluted Rhine; the Ruhr valley, home of new high-tech as well as older heavy industries, is the most densely populated area. The Elbe and its fertile valley is the focus of population in the east. *Highest point* Zugspitze 2,963 metres (9,720 feet). *Area* 357,048 sq km (137,810 sq miles).

PEOPLE *Population* 78m. *Density* 217 per sq km. *Ethnic groups* German 94%, Turkish 2%, Yugoslavian 0.7%, Italian 0.6%.

RELIGION Protestant 54%, RC 37%, Muslim 2%.

LANGUAGE German.

EDUCATION Compulsory and free for 9 years between 6 and 18. Education is the responsibility of the Länder rather than the federal government. Well-developed higher education system.

CLIMATE Temperate and variable. Temperature -3–1°C (27–34°F) in Jan, 16–19°C (61–66°F) in July. Temperatures higher in southern valleys and lower on highlands with more rain. Spring and autumn often overcast. Rainfall around 600mm (25ins) in the north, 2,000mm (80ins) in the Alps.

CURRENCY Deutschmark.

PUBLIC HOLIDAYS (* some Länder only) Jan 1, 6*, Good Fri, Easter Mon, May 1, Ascension, Whit Mon, Corpus Christi*, Aug 15*, Oct 3, Nov 1*, Repentance Day, Dec 25–26.

GOVERNMENT Federal republic, consisting of 16 regions (Länder). The federal government deals only with defence, foreign affairs and finance. The legislature has 2 houses: the Bundesrat (upper house), a 45-member federal council appointed by the governments of the Länder, and the Bundestag (lower house), a 663-member federal assembly, 519 from the west, 144 from the east, largely elected in a mixed system of PR and single-member constituencies. The assembly elects the chief executive, the federal chancellor, who appoints the cabinet. The head of state is a president elected by a college of the assembly and regional legislatures.

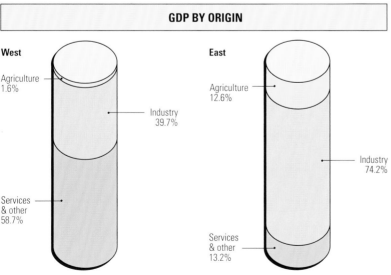

GDP BY ORIGIN

West
Agriculture 1.6%
Industry 39.7%
Services & other 58.7%

East
Agriculture 12.6%
Industry 74.2%
Services & other 13.2%

Source: EIU *Country Report;* EIU *Eastern European Risk Service* (West 1989 figures; East 1987 figures).

EUROPE

Foreign troops

Around 800,000 troops are stationed in Germany; half are Soviet troops in the east, and the rest, consisting of US, British, French, Belgian, Dutch and Canadian, in the west. The thaw in the cold war, however, prompted discussions on defence cuts in Europe and new arms limits were agreed in Paris in November 1990 at the Conference on Security and Co-operation in Europe, although mistrust on each side remains. Germany will lose all Soviet forces by 1994 and there will be major reductions in Nato troops during the early 1990s.

Guest workers

Official estimates show a foreign population of over 5m throughout Germany, mostly living in western Germany where the booming economy sucked in migrant workers, many of them from Turkey, in the 1960s and 1970s. High levels of immigration continued into the 1980s, resulting in part from the former West Germany's liberal asylum laws. However, with growing unemployment following reunification and an increasing number of easterners looking for work in the west, the government has been trying to persuade those carrying foreign passports to return to their native homes.

The Treuhandanstalt

Established in 1990, the Treuhandanstalt is the trust body to which ownership of some 8,000 state-owned former East German firms was transferred. It is charged with privatizing and restructuring where it can, liquidating where it must. By early 1991 about 1,200 firms had been sold, mainly to western German buyers. About one-third of the remainder were expected to have to close.

The environment

West Germany took a lead in the EC in adopting more environmentally conscious policies. On the other hand, like most Eastern European countries, East Germany's post-war priority was developing the heavy and extraction industries, with no regard for the ecological effects. Resources were wasted through outdated industrial production methods and inefficiency. The chemical industry, the worst culprit, is the origin of 60% of total eastern sulphur dioxide emissions and 53% of the dust. The River Elbe has near lethal levels of cadmium, mercury and other heavy metals. Estimates of the costs to repair industry range from DM38–47 billion annually over 10 years, not including the social and economic costs of the great number of plants and factories likely to be forced into closure for environmental reasons.

standard of living in Eastern Europe, became the most important Soviet trading partner and mobilized its youth with a sports programme that consistently harvested unparalleled crops of Olympic medals. Yet the regime was never able to reward the industriousness of its people with a lifestyle that came anywhere near that of those who lived in West Germany; a disparity made clear by East German access to West German television and radio broadcasting.

The orderliness of West German society, considered by many Europeans to be stifling and over-bureaucratic, was critical to its post-war economic success. It was reflected in a record of harmonious labour relations that was the envy of the West, and a degree of worker participation in management that would have threatened disaster elsewhere. Firms such as BMW, Bosch and Beyer AG acquired an international reputation for quality, and helped turn West Germany into the world's third largest economy and biggest exporter. West German economic success eroded class differences, encouraged a relaxed outlook and brought a quality of life matched by few in the world. Western Germans continue to pay themselves well, buy expensive cars and high-quality consumer goods, and take long holidays abroad. Western German cities, clean and increasingly well-provided with cultural and leisure facilities, have reflected this affluence.

Resolving the considerable disparities in wealth is the essential challenge facing those who will shape the new Germany. It will be a complex, expensive and lengthy process. Taxes have already risen to help pay the costs of unification. Huge investment is needed to rebuild eastern Germany's decrepit industrial base and infrastructure. One estimate puts the cost of updating eastern Germany's transport system alone – re-instating pre-war rail links and dealing with the 56% of motorways described by the Transport Ministry as being in "catastrophic condition"– at DM 100 billion. Business has reacted positively, realising the long-term economic potential of the unified country, but until the industrial regeneration is well under way the government will have to come to terms with the social and economic consequences of high unemployment and public discontent.

The ease and dangers of underestimating the difficulties ahead are already apparent. The first estimate of the cost of unification, made in mid-1990, suggested a bill of under DM 100 billion over five years, with annual expenditure diminishing rapidly from 1992 onwards. By 1991 DM100 billion had become the cost per year of dealing with the public sector alone. Monetary union has caused problems that the Kohl government did not foresee or chose to ignore. The cultural differences between the two peoples have proved more marked than anticipated, and the skills and technology gap will mean that unemployment in the western states will fall, while in the east there will be dramatic rises, with attendant increases in social tensions. Educating those from the east in the ways of the west will take time. Meanwhile, those in the west are worried that the political and economic stability and the high standard of living they have enjoyed may be under threat.

Unification and the great changes in Eastern Europe appear to have eliminated Germany's security concerns, however. The Warsaw Pact has crumbled and eastern Germany has committed its troops to Nato; the 300,000 Soviet

ECONOMIC PROFILE

Too crowded for large-scale agriculture and sparsely endowed with natural resources, Germany has concentrated on industrial production. Leading export-oriented manufacturing industries are automotive engineering, machinery and plant engineering, electronics and electrical engineering and chemicals. Innovation and consistently high investment in research and development ensuring western industry's international competiveness. Western German workforce conscientious, highly skilled and well paid.

Growth New domestic production capacity coming on stream throughout the early 1990s should squeeze out surge in imports which initially filled demand gap of newly-integrated eastern Germany, and ensure further economic expansion. Heavy government outlays to rebuild infrastructure of the eastern states will sustain solid growth for vital capital goods producers.

Problems Economic integration of eastern Germany gradually reversing the country's balance of payments picture, with western exports of investment capital evaporating. Rising deficit spending risks forcing the country to compete in international capital markets as a net borrower after playing leading lending role in 1980s. Risk of polarization of German society as impoverished east comes to terms with prosperous west.

troops remaining in eastern Germany are due to return home by 1994. But the constitution bars military adventures abroad and the country's unwillingness to take an active part in the 1991 Gulf war reinforced the impression that Germans want no part in another military adventure. A succession of politicians has also taken great pains to dispel any lingering fear among the country's neighbours of resurgent German nationalism, and to emphasize that Germany's future lies within the secure political framework of a united Europe.

Germany is already the economic anchor of the EC. Unification will occupy it for much of the next decade but it should result in Germany becoming an even more dominant economy. The process will also serve to highlight some of the practical difficulties of closer European economic and political union.

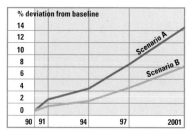

ECONOMIC SCENARIO

Source: IMF *German Unification*

The above graph shows two possible courses for the growth of Germany's real GDP. Scenario A assumes a high demand in eastern Germany leading to rapid growth in production. Scenario B is less optimistic, predicting high demand but less buoyant investment and thus slower growth, higher unemployment and greater east-west migration.

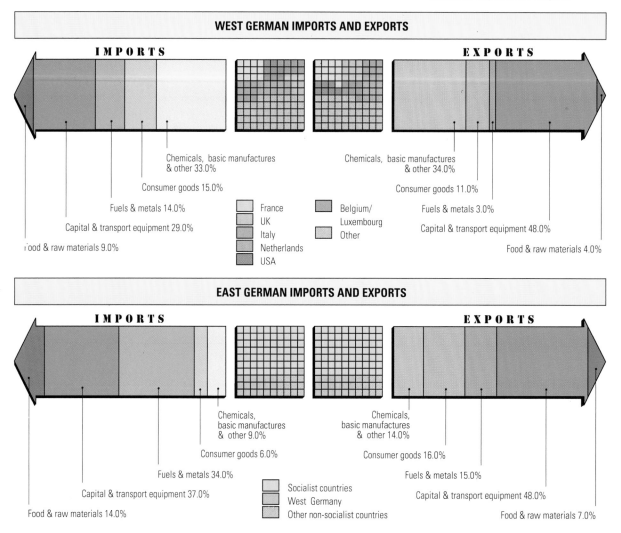

WEST GERMAN IMPORTS AND EXPORTS

IMPORTS

Chemicals, basic manufactures & other 33.0%

Consumer goods 15.0%

Fuels & metals 14.0%

Capital & transport equipment 29.0%

Food & raw materials 9.0%

EXPORTS

Chemicals, basic manufactures & other 34.0%

Consumer goods 11.0%

Fuels & metals 3.0%

Capital & transport equipment 48.0%

Food & raw materials 4.0%

France
UK
Italy
Netherlands
USA
Belgium/Luxembourg
Other

EAST GERMAN IMPORTS AND EXPORTS

IMPORTS

Chemicals, basic manufactures & other 9.0%

Consumer goods 6.0%

Fuels & metals 34.0%

Capital & transport equipment 37.0%

Food & raw materials 14.0%

EXPORTS

Chemicals, basic manufactures & other 14.0%

Consumer goods 16.0%

Fuels & metals 15.0%

Capital & transport equipment 48.0%

Food & raw materials 7.0%

Socialist countries
West Germany
Other non-socialist countries

Source: West Germany EIU Country Report (1989 figures); East Germany EIU Country Report; EIU *East European Risk Service* (1988 figures).

EMPLOYMENT BY SECTOR

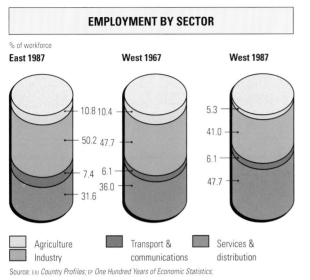

% of workforce

East 1987 **West 1967** **West 1987**

East 1987: 10.8, 50.2, 7.4, 31.6

West 1967: 10.4, 47.7, 6.1, 36.0

West 1987: 5.3, 41.0, 6.1, 47.7

- Agriculture
- Industry
- Transport & communications
- Services & distribution

Source: EIU *Country Profiles*; EP *One Hundred Years of Economic Statistics*;
ILO *Yearbook of Labour Statistics*.

INDUSTRIAL OUTPUT

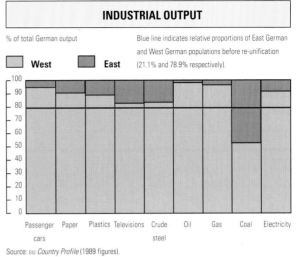

% of total German output

Blue line indicates relative proportions of East German and West German populations before re-unification (21.1% and 78.9% respectively).

- West
- East

Passenger cars, Paper, Plastics, Televisions, Crude steel, Oil, Gas, Coal, Electricity

Source: EIU *Country Profile* (1989 figures).

OWNERSHIP

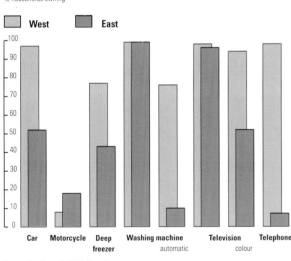

% households owning

- West
- East

Car, Motorcycle, Deep freezer, Washing machine automatic, Television colour, Telephone

Source: *The Economist* (1988 figures).

CONSUMER SPENDING PATTERNS

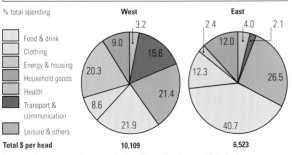

% total spending

West   **East**

West: 3.2, 9.0, 15.6, 20.3, 21.4, 8.6, 21.9

East: 2.4, 4.0, 2.1, 12.0, 12.3, 26.5, 40.7

- Food & drink
- Clothing
- Energy & housing
- Household goods
- Health
- Transport & communication
- Leisure & others

Total $ per head   10,109   6,523

Source: EIU *Consumer spending patterns in the EC*; Euromonitor *European Marketing Data and Statistics* (1988 figures).

SOCIAL PROFILE

Employment Unification has led to a reduction in unemployment in western Germany, but to a massive increase in the east. The Treuhandanstalt, the body handling the sale and restructuring of former DDR state industries, quickly became known as the "job-killer", as its closure of uneconomic concerns pushed unemployment to 500,000 in the first months after unification. Another 1.8m workers were placed on short-time contracts. The dramatic loss of jobs in the east was expected to peak at the end of 1991 at around 1.8m unemployed and 2m short-time workers.

Welfare By April 1991, 808,000 eastern German workers had joined the unemployment queue. Although most received more in welfare payments from unified Germany than from their pre-unification salaries, this still left them worse off than their west German counterparts. The government also subsidized short-term workers in the east, paying 65% of their wages; their companies the rest. However, the cushion of the short-term working scheme was due to be phased out within less than a year of unification. And with eligibility for full unemployment benefit lasting only a year, and plans also to phase out energy subsidies, the prospects were for a renewed rise in social tension if the eastern German economy did not begin to pick up.

Consumerism East Germans spent little on consumer durables prior to unification because there was little for them to buy. Unification brought choice, and eastern Germans plumped for western products, even though rejection of goods from eastern factories only exacerbated unemployment problems. Western German companies initially met demand by increasing production in their exisiting factories, but they are now starting to invest heavily in the east. Although most easterners are expected to have reached 1990/91 western German living standards by 1995, disparities between the economies of the two parts of Germany are expected to remain marked well into the next century.

EASTERN EUROPE

The states of Eastern Europe were carved after the first world war from the remains of the great empires (Prussian, Russian, Austro-Hungarian and Turkish) which dominated the map in 1913. After 1945 the Soviet Union created a cordon of satellite states in order to form a united front and a barrier against the perceived threat from the West. Twice it intervened to preserve the alliance; in Hungary in 1956 and Czechoslovakia in 1968.

However, following changing policies in the USSR, communists in both Hungary and Poland were forced into a dialogue with the opposition in late 1988 and agreed to recognize opposition parties and to hold free elections. In the course of 1989 "people power" led to the toppling of communist regimes in all other East European countries with the exception of Albania.

Capitals & regional capitals
- ■ More than 1 million
- ● 250,000 – 1 million
- • 100,000 – 250,000

Nationalism

The removal of the *Pax Sovietica*, together with declining standards of living, has served to accentuate long-dormant ethnic rivalries, raising questions about boundaries and the continued viability of some states. Ethnic and national questions were a feature of almost all state elections held after communist rule.

Comecon and the Warsaw Pact

The Council for Mutual Economic Assistance, formed in 1949 to share resources and to help development of the member states, had limited success. The Warsaw "treaty of friendship, cooperation and mutual assistance" was signed in 1955 providing a single military command in Moscow and obliging signatories to assist each other in the event of an attack.

The collapse of communist regimes in Eastern Europe has led to a distancing from the USSR, with calls for radical economic reforms and a reduction in domestic arms spending and the removal of Soviet troops. Nato's London declaration that it no longer viewed the Warsaw Pact states as adversaries increased pressure for the dissolution of the organization, and, with a growing desire to establish links with prosperous Western Europe and the EC, Comecon is seen as a relic of the cold war divisions of Europe, and the 1990s will see major changes in the defence and economic allegiances of countries in Eastern Europe.

Environment

The great emphasis the communists placed on the extractive and heavy industries and poor regard for pollution controls, has made for environmental disaster in many parts of Eastern Europe. Particularly notorious is the triangle between Dresden, Katowice and Mlada Boleslav where industrial regions of Poland, the former DDR and Czechoslovakia meet. The conversion of industry will be hugely costly and will take time.

Climate

Most of the region has a continental climate, with warm summers and cold winters. Summer temperatures can be as high as 28°C (82°F) in Bulgaria, winter ones as low as -60°C (-76°F) in Poland. Most rainfall is in the warm months.

POLAND

Under the leadership of the independent trade union Solidarity, Poland was the first of the Soviet Union's Eastern European satellites to challenge communist rule during the 1980s. However, it was the last to achieve a totally freely elected parliament; the mid-1989 elections, in which the communists were defeated, were only partially contested. A Solidarity-led coalition government subsequently began dismantling the apparatus of communist rule and negotiated with Moscow a timetable for the withdrawal of Soviet troops.

It also propounded a radical reform programme which was approved by the IMF. Aimed in the long-run at achieving a market economy, its more immediate target was to bring hyperinflation under control. The "big bang" of January 1990 made the zloty internally convertible and other measures included trade liberalization and tight monetary, fiscal and wage controls. Inflation initially fell dramatically from its 1989 peak of 1,000%. But so too did industrial production and living standards, while unemployment soared.

However, exports to the West have expanded and the private sector is growing, augmented by the first sell-off of state enterprises in November 1990. Yet, despite encouragement, foreign investors are hesitant because of economic and political uncertainties. Poland's foreign debt remains huge and unserviceable. Western governments recommended a 30% debt forgiveness in early 1991; the government said 80% was necessary for market-led growth.

Political uncertainties centre on whether the Poles are prepared to go on tolerating rising unemployment and falling living standards. A resurgence of inflation in late 1990 fuelled renewed militancy among farmers and trade unionists, and indicated that they might be losing patience with Lech Walesa who was elected national president in November 1990. The government faced fully contested parliamentary elections in 1991 against a background of growing internal divisions over economic policy.

OFFICIAL NAME Republic of Poland
CAPITAL CITY Warsaw.
GEOGRAPHY Most is lowland, part of the central European plain; to the south lie the Sudety Mountains and the Carpathians. The Baltic coast consists of swamps and dunes; inland, there is a belt of lakes. Most agriculture and industry is in the centre. *Highest point* Tatry 2,499 metres (8,200 feet). *Area* 312,677 sq km (120,730 sq miles).
PEOPLE *Population* 37.9m. *Density* 119 per sq km. *Ethnic groups* Polish 99%.
RELIGION RC 95%, Polish Orthodox 1%.
LANGUAGE Polish.
EDUCATION Free and compulsory for ages 7–14. There are 11 universities and 18 technical universities.
CLIMATE Temperate in the west; continental in the east. Summers short and hot, autumns mild, winters long, cold and snowy. Monthly average Warsaw temperature -6–24°C (21–75°F).
CURRENCY Zloty.
PUBLIC HOLIDAYS Jan 1, Easter Mon, May 1, 3, Corpus Christi, Aug 1, Nov 1, 11, Dec 25–26.
GOVERNMENT Democratic republic. The parliament consists of an upper chamber (Senate) of 100 seats and a lower chamber (Sejm) of 460 seats. The head of state is the president, elected by popular vote.

ECONOMIC PROFILE

Largest East European economy, a major source of raw materials and fuel, especially coal. Loss-making heavy industries such as shipbuilding and steel. Farming largely in private hands, but food supplies inadequate. Exports manufactured goods to the East; raw materials, food and light industrial products to the West.

Growth Potential for growth in small but vibrant private sector, freed from government controls. Joint ventures with Western partners being encouraged.

Problems Industry needs re-equipping and restructuring away from reliance on heavy metals and fuel. Shortages of energy – 80% supplied by coal – inevitable unless efficiency improves.

IMPORTS AND EXPORTS

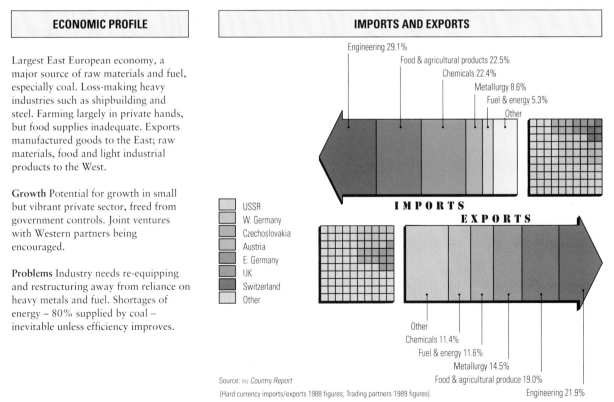

Engineering 29.1%
Food & agricultural products 22.5%
Chemicals 22.4%
Metallurgy 8.6%
Fuel & energy 5.3%
Other

IMPORTS

EXPORTS

USSR
W. Germany
Czechoslovakia
Austria
E. Germany
UK
Switzerland
Other

Other
Chemicals 11.4%
Fuel & energy 11.6%
Metallurgy 14.5%
Food & agricultural produce 19.0%
Engineering 21.9%

Source: EIU *Country Report*

(Hard currency imports/exports 1988 figures; Trading partners 1989 figures).

CZECHOSLOVAKIA

In November 1989 Czechoslovakia's "velvet revolution" banished the communists from government and signalled the end of one-party rule. Two decades earlier reform attempts from within the Communist Party, the "Prague Spring" of 1968, had been crushed by Soviet tanks. The subsequent return to conformity was managed by Gustáv Husák. Under his repressive stewardship growth faltered and the overdue modernization of the country was postponed.

Mikhail Gorbachev's gospel of *glasnost* and *perestroika* was received without enthusiasm by President Husák. In 1987 he was replaced by Milos Jakes who proved unable to satisfy growing political and economic aspirations. By October 1989 there were scenes of mass protest in Prague. Two months later Václav Havel, the playwright and dissident who had helped found the small but influential Charter 77 opposition group, had become president. The efforts to restore political pluralism culminated in June 1990 in the first free elections since 1946. They were a triumph for Civic Forum, the broad-based coalition of opposition groups which led the revolution. But euphoria and optimism soon gave way to more sober reflections and in early 1991 Civic Forum split over the key problem of how fast economic reform should be tackled. The other main issue for post-communist Czechoslovakia is resurgent Slovak nationalism.

Czechoslovakia has many of the problems of centrally-planned economies: a budget deficit equivalent to 70% of national income and overdependence on heavy industry and on ex-Comecon trading partners. More positively it has a manageable foreign debt and a skilled, adaptable workforce. Moves towards a market economy began after mid-1990. Laws to encourage foreign investment allowed for the privatization of small enterprises, the creation of joint-stock companies and the liberalization of foreign trade. The koruna was devalued and made internally convertible in January 1991. Some controls over prices were retained in an effort to slow inflation, but a sharp fall in living standards was seen as an inevitable cost of the transition to a market economy.

OFFICIAL NAME The Czech and Slovak Federated Republic.

CAPITAL CITY Prague.

GEOGRAPHY Around 65% is upland, 20% mountains and 10% lowland. The west is dominated by the Bohemian massif, a hilly, undulating basin surrounded by mountain ranges. The Carpathian Mountains are the major feature of the east. *Highest point* Gerlachovsky 2,663 metres (8,740 feet). *Area* 127,899 sq km (49,370 sq miles).

PEOPLE *Population* 15.6m. *Density* 122 per sq km. *Ethnic groups* Czech 64%, Slovak 31%, Magyar 4%.

RELIGION RC 70%, Czechoslovak church 15%.

LANGUAGE Czech and Slovak.

EDUCATION Free and compulsory for ages 6–16.

CLIMATE Mixed. Mean annual temperatures of -4°C (25°F) in the highlands, 10.5°C (51°F) in the lowlands. Rainfall is highest in summer.

CURRENCY Koruna.

PUBLIC HOLIDAYS Jan 1, Easter Mon, May 1, 9, Jul 5–6, Oct 28, Dec 25–26.

GOVERNMENT A democratic federal republic since 1990. The 300-member bicameral Federal Assembly is elected by PR for a 4-year term. It elects a president who is head of state and appoints the prime minister and cabinet. The 200-member Czech and 150-member Slovak national councils handle local affairs.

ECONOMIC PROFILE	IMPORTS AND EXPORTS

Extensive but increasingly obsolete industrial capacity including vehicles, glass, footwear, textiles and ceramics. Large coal deposits, plus copper and zinc. Agriculture is a long way short of self-sufficiency. Forests are large and productive.

Growth Gold deposits discovered mid-1980s. Reform programme under way to install a market system as soon as possible; involves price liberalization and privatization.

Problems Failure to modernize industry has undermined quality and export competitiveness. Labour and energy shortages and low agricultural productivity compound difficulties of transition to free-market economics. Popular resentment of social costs threatening political stability and could slow economic reform.

Source: EIU *Country Profile* (Imports/Exports 1988 figures; Trading partners 1989 figures).

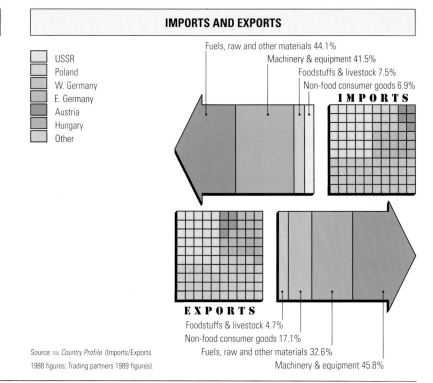

USSR
Poland
W. Germany
E. Germany
Austria
Hungary
Other

IMPORTS
Fuels, raw and other materials 44.1%
Machinery & equipment 41.5%
Foodstuffs & livestock 7.5%
Non-food consumer goods 6.9%

EXPORTS
Foodstuffs & livestock 4.7%
Non-food consumer goods 17.1%
Fuels, raw and other materials 32.6%
Machinery & equipment 45.8%

HUNGARY

In March and April 1990 Hungarians voted for their first freely elected government since the second world war. They opted for a centre-right coalition headed by the Hungarian Democratic Forum (HDF). The elections were the culmination of a process which began in 1988 when ageing President János Kádár and his old guard were ousted by reformers within the ruling communist Hungarian Socialist Workers' Party (HSWP).

President Kádár had come to power in the wake of Soviet suppression of the 1956 revolution. Despite this he had become a popular leader, allowing a modicum of political freedom and promoting economic reform. But by the mid-1980s the failure to tackle the economy's fundamental problems and years of heavy borrowing had provoked the crisis that led to his downfall. During the months that followed it became clear that the HSWP was split over not only reform but also the party's future role. Democratic pressures began to increase: parliament, hitherto a rubber-stamp body, began to assert its independence; new press freedoms encouraged debate and greater political expectations. A number of opposition groups began to challenge the HSWP's authority and in early 1989, no longer able to look to Moscow for support, the central committee agreed to accept a multi-party system. Parliament's move in October 1989 to end the party's "leading role" in society signalled the final collapse of its power.

Under Prime Minister József Antall the HDF-led coalition announced its intention to redirect the economy along free-market principles, reducing the state's share in the economy from 80% to 20%. A major drive towards privatization was initiated, price controls relaxed, and in mid-1990 Hungary established the region's first stock market. The government is looking to foreign investment to ease the transition from reliance on heavy industry to lighter, more high-tech enterprises. Budapest has been chosen as the location of the EC's first regional office, a sign that Hungary is a front-runner in the race among former Comecon members to join the Community.

OFFICIAL NAME The Hungarian Republic.
CAPITAL CITY Budapest.
GEOGRAPHY A lowland country, mostly 80–200 metres (250–650 feet) in altitude, surrounded by mountains. The great and little Hungarian plains are separated by the Hungarian highlands, but the dominant geographical feature is the Danube and its tributary the Tisza, which flood regularly in spring and summer. One-sixth of the country is forested. *Highest point* Kékes 1,015 metres (3,330 feet). *Area* 93,030 sq km (35,920 sq miles).
PEOPLE *Population* 10.6m. *Density* 114 per sq km. *Ethnic groups* Magyar (Hungarian) 93%.
RELIGION Christian 83% (RC 54%, Protestant 22%, other 7%), Jewish 1%.
LANGUAGE Magyar.
EDUCATION Free from the age of 3 and compulsory for ages 6–16. There are 9 universities and 9 technical universities.
CLIMATE Continental, with an annual rainfall of 500–750mm (20–30ins); average temperatures around 0°C (32°F) in winter, 20°C (68°F) in summer.
CURRENCY Forint.
PUBLIC HOLIDAYS Jan 1, Mar 15, Easter Mon, May 1, Aug 20, Oct 23, Dec 25–26.
GOVERNMENT A democratic republic since 1990. The 386-member unicameral national assembly is elected for 5 years; 176 members are elected from single-member constituencies, 152 from party lists in the regions, and the rest by PR. The president, elected by the national assembly, is head of state.

IMPORTS AND EXPORTS

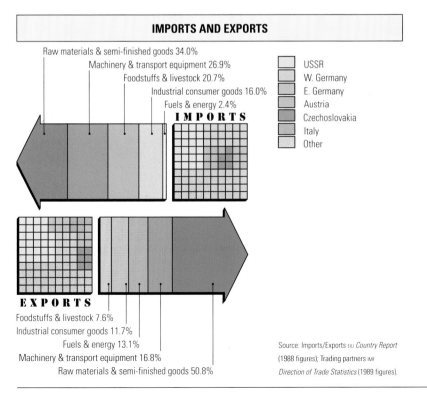

Raw materials & semi-finished goods 34.0%
Machinery & transport equipment 26.9%
Foodstuffs & livestock 20.7%
Industrial consumer goods 16.0%
Fuels & energy 2.4%
IMPORTS

USSR
W. Germany
E. Germany
Austria
Czechoslovakia
Italy
Other

EXPORTS
Foodstuffs & livestock 7.6%
Industrial consumer goods 11.7%
Fuels & energy 13.1%
Machinery & transport equipment 16.8%
Raw materials & semi-finished goods 50.8%

Source: Imports/Exports EIU *Country Report* (1988 figures); Trading partners IMF *Direction of Trade Statistics* (1989 figures).

ECONOMIC PROFILE

Heavy industry and agriculture are mainstays of the economy. Major producer and exporter of buses, bulk agricultural products – world's largest exporter of broiler chickens – and computer software. Limited mineral resources apart from bauxite and recently discovered copper.

Growth Western joint ventures growing fast, bringing in new technology and management styles. Tourism growing even more rapidly. Ambitious nuclear power programme.

Problems Much industry inefficient and unprofitable, saddled with outdated equipment and hopelessly uncompetitive with the west. Energy resources cannot meet demand because of inefficient use.

YUGOSLAVIA

Modern Yugoslavia emerged from the victory of Tito's partisans in 1945 and the ideological split with the USSR three years later. It developed unique forms of political and economic organization with power devolved to the regions and workers gaining at least theoretical control over their workplaces. Since 1948 Yugoslavia has sought the middle way in foreign policy, playing a central role in founding the non-aligned movement.

After Tito's death in 1980 a collective presidency took over. It formed part of the decentralization of the 1970s which aimed at preventing ethnic rivalry but in practice weakened the central authorities. By the end of 1989 the economy was in a parlous state with inflation above 2,000%. Under the prodding of the IMF, Prime Minister Ante Markovic pushed through free-market measures to reduce inflation and boost investment and trade. Within months inflation had been cut to almost zero, but began to take off again in mid-1990 as most of the republics ignored central directives and increased spending on subsidies. Bankruptcies and unemployment were also on the rise, but the chances of recovery depended on the federal authorities' ability to reassert financial discipline.

By the end of 1990 it had become clear that the forces of nationalism and political rivalry were in danger of overwhelming the fragile unity of Yugoslavia's loose federation of states. The first multi-party elections since 1945 were held during the year and the communists (renamed Socialists) were ousted in four of the six republics, retaining power only in Serbia and Montenegro. They were replaced mainly by nationalists, who in Slovenia and Croatia indicated a desire to loosen federal ties further. Even in Serbia, the largest republic, the Socialists under Slobodan Milosevic seemed more a nationalist than pan-Yugoslavian party.

The bitter memories of ethnic hostilities in the pre-Tito era surfaced in 1991. Fighting broke out between Serbs and Croats, and the country faces a very difficult period. A new, looser form of association seems the most likely outcome. Its success will depend on the skills of the country's political leaders, despite attempts at intervention by EC governments.

OFFICIAL NAME Socialist Federal Republic of Yugoslavia.

CAPITAL CITY Belgrade.

GEOGRAPHY Most people live in the Pannonian lowlands drained by the Danube in the north-east. Forested mountains run behind the other population centre of the Adriatic coast. *Highest point* Triglav 2,864 metres (9,400 feet). *Area* 225,804 sq km (98,770 sq miles).

PEOPLE *Population* 23.5m. *Density* 92 per sq km. *Ethnic groups* Serbian 36%, Croatian 20%, Muslim 9%, Slovene 8%, Albanian 8%, Macedonian 6%, Montenegrin 3%, Hungarian 2%, Gypsy 1%.

RELIGION Serbian Orthodox 35%, RC 26%, Muslim 9%.

LANGUAGE Serbo-Croatian. Also Slovene, Macedonian, Albanian and Hungarian.

EDUCATION Free and compulsory for ages 7–15. There are 19 universities.

CLIMATE Mediterranean on coast, continental inland. Temperatures are around 20°C (70°F) in summer, close to freezing in winter. Rainfall is steady.

CURRENCY Yugoslav dinar.

PUBLIC HOLIDAYS (* certain republics only): Jan 1–2, Apr 27*, May 1–2, Jul 4, 7*,13*, 22*, 27*, Aug 2*, Oct 11*, Nov 1*, 29–30.

GOVERNMENT Federal republic comprising six republics and two autonomous provinces. Each republic and province has a 3-chamber assembly.

ECONOMIC PROFILE

Manufacturing, notably assembly and processing, and mining are the economic mainstays. Textiles, transport, electrical equipment and chemicals are among main exports. Leading European producer of copper, bauxite, silver, bismuth, mercury. Agriculture, largely cereals and livestock, is labour-intensive, employing 25% of the workforce; world's ninth largest wine producer. Tourism helps offset trade deficit.

Growth Potential for export-led growth with liberalization of trade/foreign exchange regime. Exports of iron and steel products increasing as competing EC industries decline. Lower labour costs benefit shipbuilding. Joint ventures promoted.

Problems Stress on import substitution created industries that find it hard to compete on world markets. Oil and gas reserves cannot meet demand. Many raw materials and manufactured goods imported.

IMPORTS AND EXPORTS

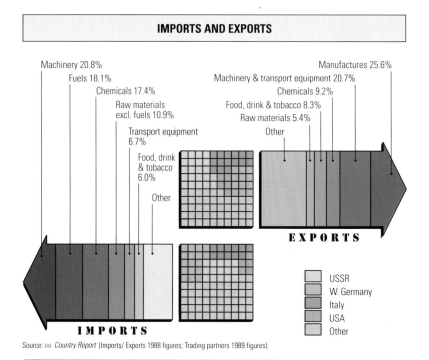

Machinery 20.8%
Fuels 18.1%
Chemicals 17.4%
Raw materials excl. fuels 10.9%
Transport equipment 6.7%
Food, drink & tobacco 6.0%
Other

Manufactures 25.6%
Machinery & transport equipment 20.7%
Chemicals 9.2%
Food, drink & tobacco 8.3%
Raw materials 5.4%
Other

EXPORTS

IMPORTS

USSR
W. Germany
Italy
USA
Other

Source: EIU *Country Report* (Imports/ Exports 1988 figures; Trading partners 1989 figures).

ALBANIA

Albania achieved independence in 1912 after centuries as part of the Ottoman empire. In 1944 the staunchly pro-communist Albanian Workers' Party (AWP) took control, led by Enver Hoxha until his death in 1985. For decades Albania took a fierce pride in its isolation, describing itself as the world's sole surviving bastion of Marxism-Leninism.

Efforts after 1944 to expand and diversify industrial and agricultural production met with some success. However, growth rates have fallen markedly and it has been impossible to generate sufficient food and consumer goods to keep pace with population growth of 2.1%, the highest in Europe.

Mr Hoxha's successor, Ramiz Alia, initially continued his predecessor's policies, but after the momentous shift away from communism in Eastern Europe in the late 1980s, it became clear that Albania would have to adapt. As a result the government began to admit failures, especially in the economic field. In 1990 it declared its intention to establish relations with the USA and Soviet Union and to participate in the Helsinki process.

Other grudging reforms included the legalization of religion, foreign investment and peasants' rights to sell their produce. Free elections were held in March 1991, and confirmed the communists in power. Two months later, however, a crippling general strike brought the government down. An interim coalition government was formed to rule until elections scheduled for 1992.

OFFICIAL NAME Socialist People's Republic of Albania.
CAPITAL CITY Tirana.
GEOGRAPHY The Balkan Mountains take up 70%; 40% is forest. Clay and sand lowlands along the coast and valleys are the most populous parts. *Area* 28,748 sq km (11,100 sq miles).
PEOPLE *Population* 3.1m. *Density* 111 per sq km. *Ethnic groups* Albanian 93%, Gypsy 2%, Greek 2%.
RELIGION Muslim 20%, Christian 5%.
LANGUAGE Albanian.
EDUCATION Free and compulsory for ages 7–15.
CLIMATE Mediterranean along the coast; more extreme inland. Average July temperature 25°C (77°F). Average annual rainfall 1,400mm (55ins).
CURRENCY Lek.
PUBLIC HOLIDAYS Jan 1, 11, May 1, Nov 7, 28–29.
GOVERNMENT Communist republic. The party controls elections to the 250-member people's assembly. There is a 15-member praesidium whose president is head of state, and a council of ministers whose chairman is head of government.

ROMANIA

Romania is still trying to adjust to life after the nightmare of the Ceausescu era. Now widely regarded as one of the communist world's most repressive leaders, Nicolae Ceausescu was for many years lauded in the West because of his independent stance towards Moscow.

Heavy industrial investment combined with worsening trade terms to cause severe debt problems by the end of the 1970s. During the 1980s President Ceausescu subordinated economic policy to repayment of foreign debt, slashing imports and directing the majority of domestic output to exports. By 1989 Romania was a net creditor nation, but ordinary Romanians were hungry and cold, with food and energy savagely rationed. At the same time President Ceausescu embarked on plans to bulldoze 7,000 villages and rehouse their inhabitants in agro-industrial complexes. This aroused international protest and suspicions that the aim was to disperse the 2m-strong Hungarian minority.

President Ceausescu was the last communist leader to fall during 1989 and his departure was the most violent. He and his wife were executed on Christmas Day. He was succeeded by a National Salvation Front (NSF) interim government. The NSF was far from being an opposition movement (many members were former Ceausescu associates) and its victory in the May 1990 multi-party elections aroused controversy. Suspicions deepened when President Ion Iliescu brought miners to Bucharest to help disperse anti-government demonstrations. Exasperation with the weakness of the parliamentary opposition subsequently led to the formation of the Civic Alliance, a focal point for the strikes and demonstrations which had become the main channel for opposition.

Economic policy under the new government has been gradualist. Collective farms were allowed to allocate land for private use, small industrial concerns were permitted, the currency was devalued and most consumer subsidies were removed. But shortages of basic foodstuffs and consumer goods continued and foreign investment was discouraged by political instability. The NSF's reluctance to embrace effective market reform, with its inevitable social costs, was a result of both the street protests and internal divisions between technocrat ministers and a conservative mainstream imbued with the habits of communist rule.

OFFICIAL NAME Republic of Romania.
CAPITAL CITY Bucharest.
GEOGRAPHY The Carpathians and Transylvanian Alps run across the centre; to their west and north lie the Transylvanian tablelands. The population is concentrated in the fertile plains of the south and east, especially the Danube valley. The delta on the Black Sea has fishing and tourist industries. *Highest point* Moldoveanul 2,543 metres (8,340 feet). *Area* 237,500 sq km (91,700 sq miles).
PEOPLE *Population* 23.2m. *Density* 98 per sq km. *Ethnic groups* Romanian 89%, Hungarian 8%, German 2%.
RELIGION Orthodox Christian 80% (Romanian 70%, Greek 10%), Muslim 1%.
LANGUAGE Romanian.
EDUCATION Free and compulsory for ages 6–16. There are 7 universities and 5 technical universities.
CLIMATE Variations according to altitude; the climate in the south-east lowlands is almost Mediterranean. Generally, summers hot and humid with a monthly average temperature of 23°C (73°F); winter average -3°C (27°F). Average annual rainfall 660mm (26ins).
CURRENCY Leu.
PUBLIC HOLIDAYS Jan 1–2, Easter Mon, Dec 1, 25–26.
GOVERNMENT Republic. A new constitution is due to be introduced by December 1992. Under interim provisions the directly elected president is head of state and nominates the prime minister. The bicameral legislature comprises a 119-seat Senate and a 387-seat Assembly of Deputies, both elected by modified PR.

BULGARIA

Bulgaria has traditionally been the USSR's closest ally in Eastern Europe. The friendship between the two nations dates back to 1878 when Tsarist Russia liberated Bulgaria from 500 years of Turkish domination. A rigidly Stalinist response to dissent after Todor Zhivkov took over in 1954 made Bulgaria one of the most secure and compliant Soviet satellites.

Although popular opposition to President Zhivkov had been growing, it was his own party colleagues who finally ousted him in November 1990. The new leaders promised greater freedoms, multi-party elections and economic restructuring and, despite pressure from nationalists, moved to end the forced assimilation of the Turkish minority. The Communist Party transformed itself into the Bulgarian Socialist Party (BSP) prior to multi-party elections in June 1990. A disunited and unconvincing opposition and a conservative peasantry gave it an electoral majority, but not the 75% needed to carry through major constitutional reforms.

By the end of 1990 the economy was in a disastrous state. Foreign debt, at $10 billion, was more than twice the previous estimate. Industry and agriculture were in rapid decline, and food shortages and hoarding were rife. Energy was another problem. Bulgaria lacks its own energy resources. After years of subsidized dependence on the USSR, it now had to pay for oil at world prices; shortages were becoming critical.

The government seemed to lack the appetite for sweeping economic reform, and opponents claimed that the BSP had made little effort to dismantle the power structures of the former regime. A general strike precipitated the resignation of Prime Minister Andrei Lukanov in November 1990. Dimitar Popov, his successor, freed prices and prepared a reform programme which included privatization. Prices rose sharply, with unemployment set to follow. Bulgarians were looking to the West for the help to tide them through a period of crisis.

OFFICIAL NAME Republic of Bulgaria.
CAPITAL CITY Sofia.

GEOGRAPHY The north of the country is taken up by the rolling, fertile Danube plain, rising to the Balkans. Farther south other mountain ranges, all running east-west, have deep gorges and sheltered upland basins, in one of which lies Sofia. The sandy beaches of the Black Sea coast support a thriving tourist industry. *Area* 110,912 sq km (42,820 sq miles).

PEOPLE *Population* 9m. *Density* 81 per sq km. *Ethnic groups* Bulgarian 87%, Turkish 8.5%, Macedonian 2.5%, Gypsy 2%.

RELIGION Eastern Orthodox 27%, Muslim 8%, Protestant 1%, RC 1%.

LANGUAGE Bulgarian, written in Cyrillic script. Also Turkish and Macedonian.

EDUCATION Free from the age of 3 and compulsory for ages 6–16.

CLIMATE A country of temperature extremes. In Sofia averages range from -5°C (23°F) in winter to 28°C (82°F) in summer. Annual rainfall varies from 450mm (18ins) in the north-east to 1,200mm (48ins) in the mountains. Hail and thunder storms common in spring and summer.

CURRENCY Lev.

PUBLIC HOLIDAYS Jan 1, Mar 3, Easter Mon, May 1, 24, Sep 9, Dec 25.

GOVERNMENT A new constitution under preparation in 1991. In the interim the government comprises a directly elected president who is head of state and nominates the prime minister. The unicameral national assembly has 200 members elected by PR and 200 by simple majority.

IMPORTS AND EXPORTS

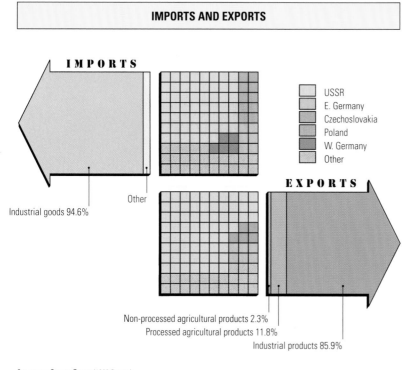

IMPORTS

Industrial goods 94.6%

Other

- USSR
- E. Germany
- Czechoslovakia
- Poland
- W. Germany
- Other

EXPORTS

Non-processed agricultural products 2.3%
Processed agricultural products 11.8%
Industrial products 85.9%

Source: EIU *Country Report* (1989 figures).

ECONOMIC PROFILE

Agriculture and basic manufacturing still the core of the economy. New high-tech industries starting to make a contribution. Sales of agricultural products to west – canned fruit and vegetables, cigarettes, wine – bring in hard currency. Other major exports include construction steels, aluminium ingots, machinery and equipment.

Growth Electronics is fastest-growing sector. Promotion of joint ventures and tourism. High priority given to nuclear programme and expansion of the biotechnology industry.

Problems Shortages of energy (supplying only one third of needs) and foreign exchange crippling industrial and agricultural output. Fork-lift truck production, the largest industry, in long-term decline, and others – chemicals, engineering – stagnant.

THE SOVIET UNION

Enormous endeavour and sacrifice succeeded in turning the Soviet Union from a backward agrarian society when the Bolsheviks took over in 1917 into a super-power by the 1970s. As it entered the 1990s it began to look as though much of the effort had been in vain. Traditional Soviet communism was in dramatic decline as the Soviet Union faced an economic and political crisis which threatened the very existence of the union.

Since 1917 the Soviet Union has been attempting to catch up with the West. Forced modernization was effected under Stalin but at the price of enormous waste of human and material resources; output per head is still, on some estimates, only one-fifth that of the USA. Two subsequent presidents attempted reform: Khrushchev a more efficient use of resources; and Brezhnev made modest efforts to streamline the communist system. Both failed, blocked by an entrenched bureaucracy and the system's inbuilt inertia. Only in defence and space did the USSR achieve international recognition, but this was against a background of a stagnating economy by the late 1970s.

The selection of KGB head Yuri Andropov to the party leadership in 1982 marked a more determined attempt by the Communist Party to deal with the need for reform. Mr Andropov's death fifteen months later, and his replacement by the traditionalist Konstantin Chernenko, delayed necessary changes. It was a protégé of Mr Andropov's, Mikhail Gorbachev, who succeeded Mr Chernenko in March 1985, and finally confronted the serious problems facing the USSR.

President Gorbachev was unaware of the depth of the crisis when he took over. He later admitted that his first two years in office and his economic policy of *uskorenie* (acceleration) were ineffective. Failure made him more radical, and *perestroika* (restructuring) and *glasnost* (openness) were aimed at influencing all aspects of Soviet economic and political life. Individual enterprises and workers were, in theory, to have a greater say in how production goals should be achieved, and elements of the market economy were introduced. An element of choice in elections at local level and a freer press were intended to make government officials more responsive to the people and give the average Soviet citizen a sense that participation could change the system.

Internationally the great shift engineered by Mikhail Gorbachev transformed the image of the Soviet Union abroad. New thinking in foreign policy, prompted in part by the crippling cost of the military to the civilian economy, led to the

GEOGRAPHY The Soviet Union qualifies as the largest country in the world, occupying one-sixth of the land surface. Most people live in the great western plain bounded in the south by the Caucasus and Carpathians and in the east by the Urals. Beyond the Urals are the low, featureless and relatively uninhabited Siberian plains. The mountain chains marking the length of the southern border extend into plateaus in central Siberia and rise again in the mountainous Kamchatka peninsula. Several areas, especially in the far east, are volcanically active. The north falls inside the Arctic Circle and forms a continuous, largely uninhabited belt of tundra. *Highest point* Communism Peak 7,495 metres (24,590 feet). *Area* 22,402,200 sq km (8,649,500 sq miles).

PEOPLE *Population* 289m. *Density* 13 per sq km. *Ethnic groups* Russian 52%, Ukrainian 16%, Uzbek 5%, Belorussian 4%, Kazakh 2%, Tatar 2%, Azerbaijan 2%, Armenian 2%, Georgian 1%, Moldavian 1%, Tadzhik 1%, Lithuanian 1%, Turkmen 1%.

RELIGION Russian Orthodox 22%, Muslim 11%, Protestant 2%, RC 1%, Jewish 1%.

LANGUAGE Russian (59%), Ukrainian (15%), Uzbek (4%). There are 112 recognized languages in all and 5 alphabets.

EDUCATION Free at all levels and compulsory for ages 7–17, with proposals to bring the starting age down to 6. There are 894 institutes of higher education.

CLIMATE An enormous climatic range, but predominantly a continental, extreme climate; temperatures range from -60°C (-94°F) in Siberia to 50°C (122°F) in the central deserts. Average temperatures in Moscow vary from -12°C (10.5°F) in Jan to 18°C (64.5°F) in July.

CURRENCY Rouble.

PUBLIC HOLIDAYS Jan 1, Mar 8, May 1–2, 9, Oct 7, Nov 7–8.

GOVERNMENT The Soviet Union was a federation of 15 separate republics, each with its own Supreme Soviet (parliament) and government. The Communist Party of the Soviet Union (CPSU) was the only legal party until 1988. The Congress of People's Deputies elected the 500-member USSR Supreme Soviet of the union, which since 1989 amended the constitution several times. The December 1990 constitution allowed for an executive president with extensive powers. But all these arrangements collapsed in August 1991, to be replaced by provisional bodies dominated by the republics.

BREAKING UP The abortive August 1991 coup set in train momentous changes in what had been the Union of Soviet Socialist Republics. Independence was swiftly granted to the three Baltic republics as the union moved towards a looser federation of sovereign states to be known – at least in the short term – as the Union of Sovereign States. At the time this book went to press it was impossible to be certain about almost anything in the Soviet Union. The Soviet economic statistics quoted or illustrated in the *Atlas* are, of course, for the former USSR. It will be some time before there are useful statistics for the individual republics.

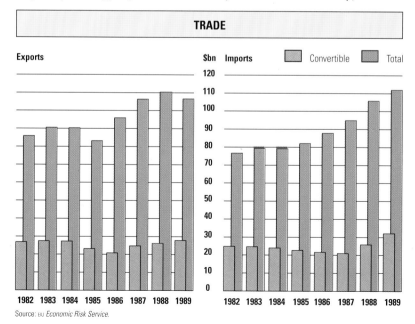

TRADE

Exports — Imports — $bn — Convertible — Total

1982 1983 1984 1985 1986 1987 1988 1989

Source: EIU *Economic Risk Service.*

EUROPE

scrapping of the ideological imperative in the conduct of inter-state relations and the adoption of the concept of security interdependence. Warmer relations with the USA, reflected in arms-control treaties, followed the withdrawal from Afghanistan, the retreat from Eastern Europe, the dissolution of the Warsaw Pact and the negotiation of a treaty to allow German unification.

Meanwhile, at home *glasnost* had dramatic effects, unleashing a separatist surge in the republics, and a wave of unprecedented criticism of government. But by 1990 it was clear that the parallel attempt to restructure the Soviet economy had failed. *Perestroika* was full of contradictions. The Soviet economy stagnated further, as attempts at reform were blocked by bureaucrats, realizing that moving closer to a market economy would deprive them of influence. Plant managers and workers reacted suspiciously to directives from the centre; increasingly, instructions were simply ignored. Shortages were exacerbated by farmers withholding their produce, and the increase in barter between individual republics and between factories; in

Urals

Traditional border between European and Asiatic Russia, this mineral-rich mountain range stretches from the Arctic to the Kazakh steppes. Highest point Mt Narodnaya, 1,894metres (6,210 feet).

BALTIC STATES

The three Baltic states, independent between the world wars, were occupied by Soviet forces and incorporated into the USSR in 1940; incorporation confirmed by plebiscites in 1944. Each declared independence in 1990, claiming that the plebiscite was a fraud and they were never legally part of the USSR. Independence was recognized August 1991.

Estonia is closely related linguistically and ethnically to Finland. Estonian SSR founded and included in USSR 1940. **Population 2m (Estonian 62%), area 45,100 sq km (17,400 sq miles).**

Latvia was successively under German, Polish and Swedish rule before coming under Russian domination in the 18th century. Latvian SSR founded and included in USSR 1940. **Population 3m (52% Latvian), area 64,600 sq km (24,942 sq miles).**

Lithuania formed a dual monarchy with Poland from the 16th to 18th centuries, stretching over much of modern Belorussia and western Ukraine. Lithuanian SSR founded and included in USSR 1940. In 1990 Lithuania was the first republic to declare independence from the USSR. **Population 4m (79% Lithuanian), area 65,200 sq km (25,200 sq miles).**

WESTERN REPUBLICS

Moldova (Moldavia) Moldavian SSR founded following Soviet army occupation of Bessarabian region of Romania. In 1990 language was recognized as Romanian, and republic renamed Moldova. Independence declared August 1991. **Population 4m (64% Moldavian), area 33,700 sq km (13,000 sq miles).**

Ukraine Second most populous Soviet republic. Slavic nation occupying territory of former Kievan Rus princedom. Ukrainian SSR founded 1917, included in USSR 1922. Holds own seat in UN. Independence declared August 1991. **Population 51m (72% Ukrainian), area 603,700 sq km (233,100 sq miles).**

Belorussia Smallest Slav nation, once part of Lithuania. Holds own seat at UN. Belorussia SSR founded 1919, included in USSR since 1922. Independence declared August 1991. **Population 10m (79% Belorussian), area 207,600 sq km (80,200 sq miles).**

Russian Federation

Russian Soviet Federal Socialist Republic Largest Soviet republic, stretching from Baltic to Arctic and Pacific. Includes Moscow, St Petersburg and most other large Soviet cities. RSFSR founded 1917, included in USSR 1922. **Population 144m (83% Russian), area 17,075,400 sq km (6,592,800 sq miles).**

CAUCASUS

Armenia The Armenians, an ancient Indo-European people, have lived in Transcaucasia since 6th century BC. Claim to have been first Christian kingdom. Persian part of Armenia conquered by Russians in 1828. Short-lived independent Armenian Republic overrun by Soviet army 1920 and Armenian SSR founded. Independence declared 1991. **Population 3m (93% Armenian), area 29,800 sq km (11,500 sq miles).**

Azerbaijan Original Iranian population turkicized by Seljuk Turks in 8th century. Persian khanate of Gulistan ceded to Russia 1813. Independent republic fell to Soviet forces and Azerbaijan SSR founded April 1920. **Population 7m (78% Azerbaijanian), area 86,600 sq km (33,400 sq miles).**

Georgia Ancient people speaking unique Caucasian language. Allied with Russia under Treaty of Georgievsk 1783. Independent Menshevik republic from 1918 until conquered by Soviet forces and Georgian SSR founded 1920. In 1990 Georgia declared independence. **Population 5m (69% Georgian), area 69,700 sq km (26,900 sq miles).**

Arctic circle

The longest sea coast – over 6,000km (3,700 miles) – is by the Arctic Ocean. The coast is sparsely settled and the sea to the north frozen over for nine months of the year, from October to June.

Population

70% of the population lives west of the Urals, less than 10% in Siberia and the far east. Russians still largest ethnic group, but the population growth rate in central Asian republics is close to 3%, compared with less than 1% in the Russian Federation.

Baikal

The world's deepest lake, at 1,620 metres (5,310 ft). 636 km (395 miles) long and an average 50km (30 miles) wide, it contains one-fifth of all fresh water in the world's lakes. Unique flora and fauna, but cellulose factories at southern end have caused severe pollution since 1960s.

■ More than 1 million

● 250,000 - 1 million

CENTRAL ASIA

Most of the region became part of Russia in the second half of the 19th century, by either conquest or alliance. Four of the five republics are Turkic speaking.

Uzbekistan Conquered by imperial Russia 1865–84. After 1917 revolution part of Soviet Turkestan. Uzbek SSR founded 1924. Considerable tensions between Tadzhiks and Uzbeks, and Kirgiz and Uzbeks have resulted in bloodletting. Declared independence August 1991. **Population 18m (69% Uzbek), area 447,400 sq km (172,700 sq miles).**

Turkmenistan Last Central Asian territory to be conquered by Russia, 1878–85. After October revolution part of Soviet Turkestan. Turkmen SSR founded 1924. Declared independence August 1991. **Population 3m (68% Turkmen), area 488,100 sq km (188,500 sq miles).**

Kirgizstan (Kirgizia) Turkic people closely related to Kazakhs. Accepted Russian protection in 1855; conquest completed 1876. After the revolution an autonomous oblast (province), then an autonomous republic within Russian Federation. Kirgiz SSR founded

1936. **Population 4m (52% Kurgiz), area 198,500 sq km (76,600 miles).**

Kazakhstan The second-largest Soviet republic in area. In 1731 the khan of the Little Horde (one of three Kazakh hordes) accepted Russian rule in return for military aid. Russians established control by 1850s. In 1920 became an autonomous republic within the Russian Federation. Kazakh SSR founded 1936. In 1991 Kazakhstan formed informal economic alliance with the Russian Federation, Belorussia and the Ukraine to introduce market economy from below. **Population 16m (36% Kazakh), area 2,717,300 sq km (1,049,200 sq miles).**

Tadzhikistan Conquered by Russians in 1860s–70s. Part of Soviet Uzbekistan until 1924. Tadzhik SSR founded 1929. Russians and Germans, around 10% of the population, now leaving due to ethnic tensions. Declared independence August 1991. **Population 5m (59% Tadzhik), area 143,100 sq km (55,300 sq miles).**

effect parallel *ad hoc* economies, beyond the Kremlin's control, were emerging. It became clear to Western observers that Soviet politicians and economists lacked a sophisticated understanding of how the existing Soviet economy worked, let alone how it might be turned to follow market disciplines. The ability to measure the performance of Soviet industry was not even in place, and previous performance figures – based, except in the military economy, on meeting production targets, irrespective of quality – were inflated and therefore useless. In 1991 an energy crisis loomed, as oil production declined.

President Gorbachev responded to the successive crises by taking more nominal power to the Soviet presidency at the expense of parliament and the party, successfully excluding the latter from the day-to-day running of economic life. In December 1990 he went further, becoming executive president, and totally subordinating the government and party to himself. The attempt to make the economy more responsive by decree was doomed to failure, however, as was that to solve the related question of the future shape of the union. The Baltic states, Armenia, Georgia and Moldova, disillusioned with his economic reforms, wanted to leave the union. The Ukraine and the massive Russian Federation, under the charismatic Boris Yeltsin, pressed for a loose federation, dominated by stronger republics, each with a directly-elected president. Yeltsin himself triumphed in Russia's presidential election in June 1990.

The failure of the August 1991 coup to replace Mikhail Gorbachev with a hard-line regime of the old school transformed the situation. The result was a weakened Gorbachev, a stronger Yeltsin, the end of Communist Party supremacy and the beginning of the break-up of the union. The Baltic republics were granted independence. The move to a looser federation of independent republics, or possibly to a complete dissolution of the union, had begun in earnest.

ECONOMIC PROFILE

Comprehensive natural-resource base makes self-sufficiency almost feasible. Oil and coal output is declining and costs of extraction increasing. Natural gas output may have peaked. Energy and raw materials make up most export income. Heavy industrial base in desperate need of modernization. Transport network is proving less and less capable of coping with demands made on it. Agriculture has considerable potential, but only if released from central control. Huge imports of grain from West will continue.

Growth No sector now growing fast, almost all in decline. Service sector expanding through private business.

Problems Economic growth low or negative, since late 1970s. Technological change in defence and space but sluggish elsewhere. Few manufactured goods competitive on world markets. Low oil prices and less oil to export will lead to a decline in hard-currency earnings, making the acquisition of Western technology increasingly difficult. Pollution appalling, especially by chemical and oil industries. The short-term outlook is grim.

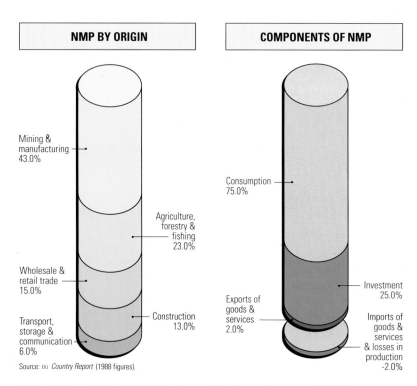

NMP BY ORIGIN

Mining & manufacturing 43.0%
Agriculture, forestry & fishing 23.0%
Wholesale & retail trade 15.0%
Construction 13.0%
Transport, storage & communication 6.0%

Source: EIU *Country Report* (1988 figures).

COMPONENTS OF NMP

Consumption 75.0%
Investment 25.0%
Exports of goods & services 2.0%
Imports of goods & services & losses in production -2.0%

Soviet statisticians publish fiscal data in the form of net material product. NMP has no exact parallel in Western financial figures, and is most useful for internal analysis as shown here. It is of less value for year-on-year comparisons, because NMP does not allow properly for inflation and it fails to reflect developments in the service sector.

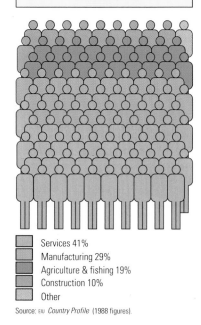

WORK FORCE

Services 41%
Manufacturing 29%
Agriculture & fishing 19%
Construction 10%
Other

Source: EIU *Country Profile* (1988 figures).

NATIONALITIES

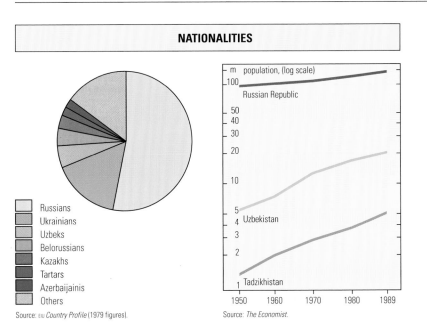

Russians
Ukrainians
Uzbeks
Belorussians
Kazakhs
Tartars
Azerbaijainis
Others

Source: EIU *Country Profile* (1979 figures).

Source: *The Economist*.

Demographic patterns

Although the Russian population is still just over half of the total population, extrapolation of present growth rate trends suggests that it will soon lose its majority position; the population is growing fastest in the Muslim Central Asian republics and the Caucasus. The composition of the army has provided a focus for Russian concerns about the changing ethnic balance; Muslims now make up 30–40% of soldiers and their loyalty is questioned.

NATIONAL INCOME

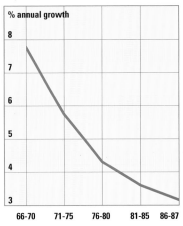

Soviet statistics, as estimated by the CIA, showed a steady decline in growth throughout the 1970s and 1980s. However, the decision to publish more open economic statistics has revealed an even bleaker picture than suspected, with GNP falling by 8% in early 1991.

IMPORTS AND EXPORTS

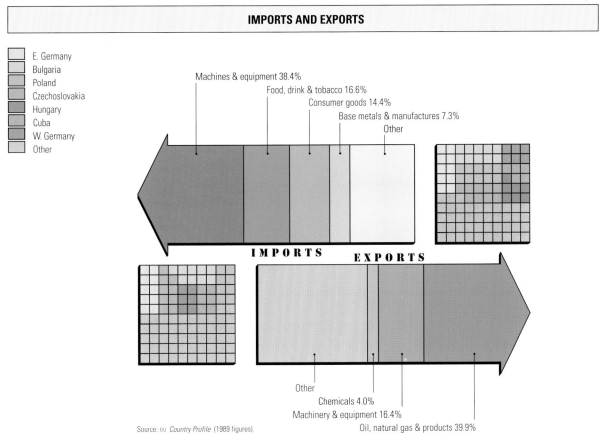

E. Germany
Bulgaria
Poland
Czechoslovakia
Hungary
Cuba
W. Germany
Other

Machines & equipment 38.4%
Food, drink & tobacco 16.6%
Consumer goods 14.4%
Base metals & manufactures 7.3%
Other

IMPORTS

EXPORTS

Other
Chemicals 4.0%
Machinery & equipment 16.4%
Oil, natural gas & products 39.9%

Source: EIU *Country Profile* (1989 figures).

213

INDIAN SUBCONTINENT

Afghan refugees

At least 5m refugees left Afghanistan after the Soviet invasion in 1979 and the subsequent guerrilla war; over 3m are in Pakistan, the rest in Iran. The refugee communities were a focus for resistance to the Soviet occupation and a channel for foreign military aid to the *mujahideen* within Afghanistan. Continued fighting after the Soviet withdrawal condemned the refugees to more years in exile.

Drugs

The troubled border between Pakistan and Afghanistan has been fertile ground for the drugs trade in the past decade. Pakistan became the world's biggest heroin producer and exporter in the early 1980s, after the Islamic revolution in Iran and tough action against producers in the Myanmar-Thailand-Laos Golden Triangle cut off other sources of supply. Under US pressure, the Pakistani government has made efforts to crack down on the trade, but it has been unable to do much about opium grown across the border in Afghanistan, which helped to finance the guerrilla war against Soviet occupation.

Language

India's official languages are Hindi and English, spoken by 30% of the population. The constitution also recognizes 16 regional languages of which the most widely spoken are Telugu, Bengali, Marathi, Tamil, Urdu and Gujarati.

Food and climate

Indian agriculture depends on the monsoon, which brings 80% of annual rainfall between June and September. India once suffered catastrophic famines when the monsoon failed but the "green revolution" has transformed food supplies over the past 20 years through use of irrigation, fertilizers and improved seed varieties. India is now self-sufficient in food grains, with surpluses to see it through the bad years, but the benefits of the green revolution have been uneven, favouring the medium-sized farmer and failing to ensure a supply of food for the rural, landless poor.

Islands

Three groups of islands form part of India. The Andaman and Nicobar Islands in the Bay of Bengal became an Indian state in 1950. The two groups contain over 300 islands. The Andaman Islands were a British penal colony until 1945; the mountainous Nicobar group to the south was occupied by Denmark for almost a century before being annexed by the British in 1869. The Lakshadweep or Laccadive Islands lie 300km (190 miles) off India's south-west coast. Ten of the 27 coral islands are inhabited.

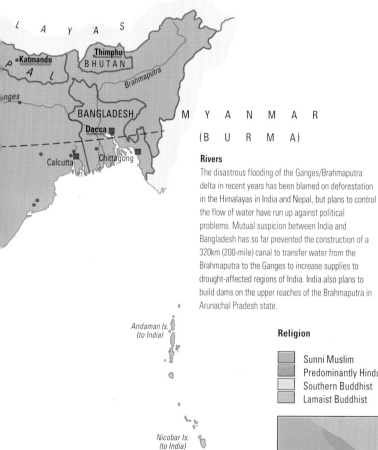

Kashmir

The northern state of Jammu and Kashmir, with a Hindu ruler and a Muslim majority population, sought separate status in 1947, but attached itself to India after an attack by Pakistan. Fighting ended in 1949 after a UN-negotiated ceasefire but war broke out again over the issue in 1965 and 1972; the border in Kashmir follows the ceasefire line. Relations repeatedly deteriorated in the 1980s after accusations that Pakistan was supporting the Sikh separatist movement in the Punjab, and in early 1990 after the uprising of Muslim secessionists in Kashmir. The situation remained fragile, although both sides appeared keen to avoid war.

The Himalayas

A series of parallel mountain ranges, rising towards the Tibetan plateau in the north, the Himalayas stretch from the Pamir Mountains in the Soviet Union to the borders of Assam and China in the east, about 2,400km (1,500 miles) away. The Himalayas contain the world's highest mountains, with eight peaks over 8,000 metres (26,250 feet) high.

CHINA

L A Y A S

Katmandu

Thimphu
BHUTAN

Brahmaputra

nges

BANGLADESH

MYANMAR

Dacca

(BURMA)

Calcutta

Chittagong

Rivers

The disastrous flooding of the Ganges/Brahmaputra delta in recent years has been blamed on deforestation in the Himalayas in India and Nepal, but plans to control the flow of water have run up against political problems. Mutual suspicion between India and Bangladesh has so far prevented the construction of a 320km (200-mile) canal to transfer water from the Brahmaputra to the Ganges to increase supplies to drought-affected regions of India. India also plans to build dams on the upper reaches of the Brahmaputra in Arunachal Pradesh state.

Andaman Is.
(to India)

Nicobar Is.
(to India)

Religion

Sunni Muslim
Predominantly Hindu
Southern Buddhist
Lamaist Buddhist

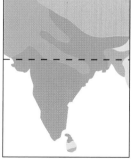

■ More than 1 million
● 250,000 - 1 million

AFGHANISTAN

Afghanistan has balanced uncomfortably between the Soviet Union and the Western powers. Britain invaded twice in the 19th century to maintain the country as a buffer against the Russian empire. British and Soviet recognition of Afghan independence in 1921 temporarily removed the country from the arena of great power conflict.

A left-wing coup in 1972 deposed the monarchy and established a republic. A further military coup in 1978 handed power to the Moscow-oriented People's Democratic Party of Afghanistan (PDPA). Clumsy implementation of radical policies and internal divisions produced political chaos and a succession of palace coups. In 1979 Soviet forces invaded, ostensibly responding to government appeals. The Soviet action aroused widespread hostility. Opposition groups – although divided by religious and political differences – fought an unrelenting resistance war, with military aid from the USA and the cooperation of Pakistan. The *mujahideen* (holy warriors) undermined government control over large areas and inflicted heavy losses on Soviet troops.

After lengthy negotiations between Pakistan, the two super-powers and Kabul, agreement was reached in 1988 to end external interference. The withdrawal of Soviet troops, a key element of the agreement, was completed in 1989. The expected collapse of the PDPA and victory of the mujahideen did not ensue, however. Instead, growing divisions within the opposition and the PDPA's failure to effect national reconciliation seemed to be pushing Afghanistan back into its traditional pattern of tribal fiefs lightly administered from Kabul.

The war severely disrupted the predominantly agricultural economy. Fruit and carpets are the main traditional exports. Natural gas became increasingly important in the 1980s; the Soviet decision to cap the wells in 1989 was another blow to the economy.

OFFICIAL NAME Republic of Afghanistan.
CAPITAL CITY Kabul.
GEOGRAPHY The south of the country is a desert plateau. Most people live in the north, in the fertile plains and foothills beneath the high mountains of the Hindu Kush. *Area* 647,500 sq km (250,000 sq miles).
PEOPLE *Population* 18.6m. *Density* 28 per sq km. *Ethnic groups* Pushtun or Pathan 50%, Tadzhik 25%, Uzbek 9%, Hazarah 3%.
RELIGION Muslim 99% (Sunni 87%, Shia 12%).
LANGUAGE Pushtu and Dari, a dialect of Persian. Also many minority languages.
EDUCATION Compulsory for ages 7–15.
CLIMATE Continental, with extreme temperatures, especially at altitude. At Kabul, average monthly temperature range is -3°C (27°F) to 25°C (77°F). Annual rainfall ranges from 75mm (3ins) to 1,300mm (50ins).
CURRENCY Afghani.
PUBLIC HOLIDAYS Mar 16, 21, 1st day of Ramadan, Apr 27, May 1, Id al-Fitr, Id al-Adha, Aug 18, Ashoura, Mouloud.
GOVERNMENT Republic since 1973. The People's Democratic Party of Afghanistan (renamed Watan, or Homeland, Party June 1990) was the only permitted party 1978–87, when the formation of other parties was allowed. Under the February 1989 state of emergency, a 20-member Supreme Council for the Defence of the Homeland, headed by the president and comprising mainly PDPA members, took over executive responsibilities from the council of ministers.

PAKISTAN

Created by the partition of British India into Muslim and Hindu areas, the state that came into being in August 1947 comprised two widely separated regions, West and East Pakistan. Conflict between the two led to a bitter civil war in 1971. After Indian intervention, East Pakistan seceded and became Bangladesh. Regional tensions persisted in West Pakistan. Violent conflicts between rival groups have been aggravated by an influx of arms resulting from the war in neighbouring Afghanistan.

In 1977, the army overthrew the first elected civilian government, led by Zulfikar Ali Bhutto. Chief of staff General Zia ul-Haq ruled for eight years under martial law. Mr Bhutto was convicted of murder and hanged. A controlled move towards civilian institutions culminated in 1985 in the lifting of martial law, but General Zia remained president and commander of the army.

His death in an air crash in 1988 accelerated the transition to civilian rule. Mr Bhutto's daughter Benazir was appointed prime minister after elections in November, but a strong showing by Zia's followers in the Punjab promised heightened regional tensions. As in the past, the survival of civilian leadership depended on the consent of the army. In August 1990, in what was widely seen as a withdrawal of army consent, the president dismissed Miss Bhutto. After elections in October, a prime minister more acceptable to the military establishment, Nawaz Sharif, a Zia protégé and chief minister of the Punjab, was installed.

The economy has grown rapidly but depends heavily on external resources. A chronic trade deficit is funded by remittances from workers abroad and by heavy foreign lending. A severe fiscal crisis has resulted from a combination of tax evasion and exemptions for the agricultural sector.

OFFICIAL NAME Islamic Republic of Pakistan.
CAPITAL CITY Islamabad.
GEOGRAPHY The Himalayas in the far north feed rivers that run through a scrubby plateau to Pakistan's heartland: the flat alluvial flood plain of the Indus. In the west the mountainous border with Afghanistan gives way to the Baluchistan plateau and deserts. *Highest point* Mt Godwin Austen (K2) 8,611 metres (28,250 feet). *Area* 769,095 sq km (307,370 sq miles).
PEOPLE *Population* 96.2m. *Density* 121 per sq km. *Ethnic groups* Punjabi 66%, Sindhi 13%, Pushtun 8%.
RELIGION Muslim 97%, Hindu 2%, Christian 1%.
LANGUAGE Urdu. Also English, Punjabi, Pushtu, Sindhi, Saraiki and others.
EDUCATION Free for ages 5–18 but non-compulsory.
CLIMATE Continental, with daily temperature ranges of 15°C (60°F); average 4°C (39°F) in Jan, over 40°C (105°F) in summer. Rainfall 750–900mm (30–35ins) in the mountains, but less than 500mm (20ins) elsewhere.
CURRENCY Pakistani rupee.
PUBLIC HOLIDAYS (*for Christians only) Mar 23, Good Fri*, Easter Mon*, Eid ul-Fitr (Apr), Eid ul-Azha (Jun), Aug 14, Sep 6, 11, Nov 9, Dec 25*–26*, Jama Tul Wida, 9th & 10th of Muharram, Eid I Milad Un abi.
GOVERNMENT Federal republic since 1947. The bicameral legislature consists of an 87-member Senate elected by the 4 provincial assemblies for 6 years, and a 237-member National Assembly elected for 5 years.

ECONOMIC PROFILE

Wheat is main food crop; cotton is grown for domestic market and for export. Industry is dominated by textiles and food processing. Remittances from overseas workers have shrunk in recent years, but still bring in more income than any single commodity export.

Growth Output of both food and cash crops has grown significantly, if erratically. Natural gas production has risen sharply, as has output of food processing and chemical industries.

Problems Production of cotton cloth in decline. External demand for cotton and rice exports fluctuates dramatically. Dependence on oil contributes to trade deficit. Heavy debt service burden.

IMPORTS AND EXPORTS

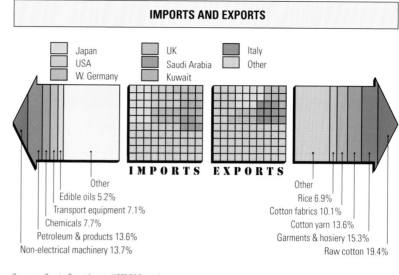

Japan
USA
W. Germany
UK
Saudi Arabia
Kuwait
Italy
Other

IMPORTS EXPORTS

Other
Edible oils 5.2%
Transport equipment 7.1%
Chemicals 7.7%
Petroleum & products 13.6%
Non-electrical machinery 13.7%

Other
Rice 6.9%
Cotton fabrics 10.1%
Cotton yarn 13.6%
Garments & hosiery 15.3%
Raw cotton 19.4%

Source: EIU *Country Report*: Imports (1987/88 figures); Exports (1988/89 figures); Trading Partners (1987/88 figures).

INDIA

Today, as at independence in August 1947, the vast majority of India's people work small plots of land and live in simple village communities. For them, poverty and insecurity are still the dominant facts of life. Yet India has also developed a complex urban society and a sizeable middle class. Social divisions are eased somewhat by nationalist political traditions and democratic institutions. Indians are more firmly attached to their own culture than many in the third world. Internationally, these attitudes translated in the early years of independence into a pioneering role in the non-aligned movement, although border tensions with China and Pakistan drew India towards the Soviet Union. At home, a tradition of concern for the poor is upheld by both individuals and government. There have been significant advances in extending literacy, education and health care, although huge inequalities remain.

Economic progress has been slow but sure. Growth has not been rapid but it has firm foundations. Heavy foreign debt has been avoided by financing investment largely from domestic savings; both industry and government have made determined efforts to promote technological self-sufficiency. The country can now maintain food reserves to meet demand even in shortage years. On the other hand, poor environmental management has caused serious problems with deforestation and loss of vital top soils.

India's democratic institutions have survived, but the Indian National Congress party, architect of independence, is a shadow of its former self. Congress was split by the radical economic policies of Indira Gandhi, who took office in 1966, two years after the death of her father, India's first prime minister Jawaharlal Nehru. Politics became bitterly factionalized and Mrs Gandhi's response was authoritarian, culminating in the declaration of a state of emergency in 1975. The Janata party ousted Mrs Gandhi in the 1977 elections, but she was returned to power two years later.

Divisions in the body politic have been paralleled by tensions among the diverse linguistic, religious and cultural groups. In the northern state of Punjab, economic prosperity generated a new political assertiveness among the Sikh people, building upon their well-established sense of cultural identity. Their grievances increasingly found expression in violence against the Punjab's Hindu minority. In 1984, Mrs Gandhi herself became a casualty, when her Sikh

OFFICIAL NAME Republic of India.
CAPITAL CITY New Delhi.
GEOGRAPHY To the south of the Himalayas a wide and densely populated alluvial plain contains the Ganges, Indus and Brahmaputra. Peninsular India consists of the Deccan plateau fringed by a coastal plain. *Highest point* Nanda Devi 7,817 metres (25,650 feet). *Area* 3,287,590 sq km (1,269,350 sq miles).
PEOPLE *Population* 800m. *Density* 243 per sq km. *Ethnic groups* Mainly Indo-Aryan and Dravidian. Also Mongoloid and Australoid.
RELIGION Hindu 83%, Muslim 11%, Christian 3%, Sikh 2%, Buddhist 1%, Jain 1%.
LANGUAGE Hindi and English. Also many minority languages.
EDUCATION Government aiming at free and compulsory education for ages 6–14.
CLIMATE Tropical, monsoon season Jun–Oct. Annual rainfall 750–1,500mm (30–60ins) in most areas. Average annual temperatures from around 13°C (55°F) in northern highlands to 25–30°C (77–86°F) on coast.
CURRENCY Indian rupee.
PUBLIC HOLIDAYS Vary from state to state. Pongal (Jan), Jan 26, Maha Shivaratri, Holi (Mar), Ram Navami, Buddha Purinama (May), Id ul-Fitr (June), Id uz-Zuha, Dussehra, Guru Nanak's birthday, 15 August, 2 October, Mahatma Gandhi's birthday, Divali, December 25–26.
GOVERNMENT Federal republic. Each of the 25 states has its own elected legislature and governor appointed by the federal president. The legislative parliament has a 245-member Council of States elected for 6 years by the state assemblies and a 543-member House of the People (Lok Sabha) elected for 5 years from single-member constituencies. The chief executive is the prime minister. Head of state is the president, elected by a college of parliament and the state assemblies.

ASIA

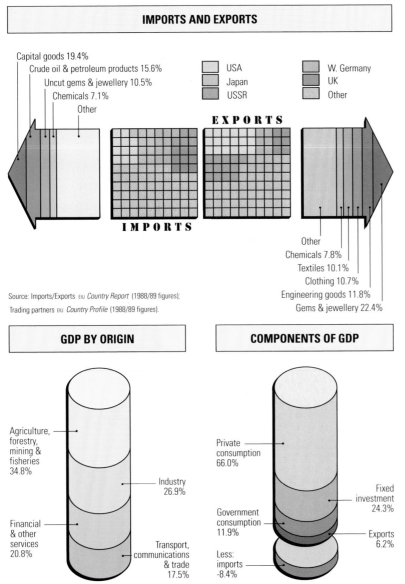

IMPORTS AND EXPORTS

Capital goods 19.4%
Crude oil & petroleum products 15.6%
Uncut gems & jewellery 10.5%
Chemicals 7.1%
Other

USA
Japan
USSR

W. Germany
UK
Other

EXPORTS

IMPORTS

Other
Chemicals 7.8%
Textiles 10.1%
Clothing 10.7%
Engineering goods 11.8%
Gems & jewellery 22.4%

Source: Imports/Exports *EIU Country Report* (1988/89 figures);
Trading partners *EIU Country Profile* (1988/89 figures).

GDP BY ORIGIN

Agriculture,
forestry,
mining &
fisheries
34.8%

Industry
26.9%

Financial
& other
services
20.8%

Transport,
communications
& trade
17.5%

COMPONENTS OF GDP

Private
consumption
66.0%

Fixed
investment
24.3%

Government
consumption
11.9%

Exports
6.2%

Less:
imports
-8.4%

Source: EIU *Country Report* (Origins of GDP 1988/89 figures; Components of GDP 1986/87 figures).

ECONOMIC PROFILE

Most people work on the land, but the industrial sector is large and diverse, its contribution to GDP almost as large as that of agriculture. "Green revolution" technologies have boosted crop yields, especially of wheat, but much agriculture still on a subsistence basis, dependent on annual monsoon. Exports account for only a small proportion of output; efforts being made to strengthen sectors such as clothing, engineering, chemicals.

Growth Development of new reserves boosted oil production in early 1980s. Wide range of consumer and capital goods industries expanding fast. Services, particularly tourism, contributing a growing share of GDP.

Problems Traditional exports such as tea and jute declining, as is cotton textile industry. Many more sophisticated capital goods still imported. Higher foreign borrowing likely to be needed to sustain current account deficit.

BALANCE OF PAYMENTS

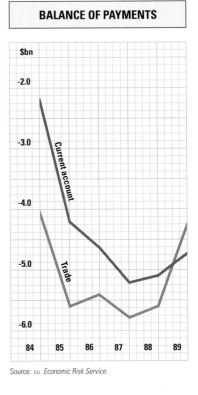

$bn

Current account

Trade

84 85 86 87 88 89

Source: EIU *Economic Risk Service*.

bodyguards took revenge for the storming of the Golden Temple, the Sikhs' holiest shrine and stronghold of militants. The terrible violence that followed her death did enormous damage to national unity. Rajiv Gandhi took his mother's place, but was voted out of office in November 1989, to be succeeded by two short lived non-Congress governments.

In the run-up to elections in May 1991 the fragility of Indian democracy was once more exposed when Rajiv Gandhi was assassinated at a political rally. The elections were postponed, but fears of rising tensions spreading into widespread violence proved unfounded. The political situation remained in flux, however, with three major political groupings contending for power: the Congress machine; the Janata Dal of V P Singh and its allies seeking to mobilize the dispossessed, lower caste and Muslim voters in particular; and most ominously, the Bharatija Janata Party (BJP), invoking a strident Hindu nationalism that would consign the various minorities to second-class status.

NEPAL

Until 1990 Nepal was one of the few states in which the monarch held real power. Then a wave of popular demonstrations swept away the partyless system of government, and reduced the king to a constitutional ruler. An interim government, dominated by a coalition of the long-banned Nepali Congress Party and the communist left, promised a new constitution and multi-party elections.

Nepal's subsistence economy is precariously dependent on the rains and liberal amounts of foreign aid. Periodic Indian border restrictions during the late 1980s underlined Nepal's reliance on its southern neighbour, and one of the interim government's first acts was to end a long-standing trade dispute.

OFFICIAL NAME Kingdom of Nepal.
CAPITAL CITY Kathmandu.
GEOGRAPHY Three-quarters of Nepal is ruggedly mountainous. The only lowland is the fertile Tarai plain along the southern border. The land rises through forested foothills to a system of mountain ranges divided by glacial basins where most of the population lives. The high Himalayas in the north are uninhabited. *Highest point* Mt Everest 8,848 metres (29,030 feet). *Area* 140,797 sq km (54,360 sq miles).
PEOPLE *Population* 17.6m. *Density* 119 per sq km. *Ethnic groups* Nepali 54%, Bihari 19%, Tamang 6%, Newari 4%, Tharu 4%.
RELIGION Hindu 90%, Buddhist 5%, Muslim 3%.
LANGUAGE Nepali. Also Bihari, Tamang and other languages.
EDUCATION Free and compulsory for ages 6–11; few girls are educated. There is one university.
CLIMATE Sub-tropical on the plain, temperate in the mountain valleys, alpine or arctic on the peaks. Annual rainfall 1,500–2,000mm (60–80ins) in the east, half that in the west. Kathmandu temperatures range between 2°C (35°F) and 30°C (86°F).
CURRENCY Nepalese rupee.
PUBLIC HOLIDAYS Jan 11, 29, Feb 18, Shivaratri, Mar 8, New Year, Buddha's Birthday, Apr 10, Indra Jatra, Dasain Durga-Puja festival, Oct 24, Tihar , Nov 7, Dec 17, 28.
GOVERNMENT Constitutional monarchy since April 1990. The king is head of state and appoints a council of ministers on recommendation of the prime minister.

BHUTAN

A landlocked kingdom in the eastern Himalayas, Bhutan is one of the world's poorest countries. King Jigme Singye Wangchuk is head of state and government, although external affairs are "guided" by India under a 1949 treaty.

The economy is predominantly agricultural, with maize and rice the staple foods. Fruit and cardamon are the main cash crops. Timber production is also important, and with cement, talcum powder, stamps and tourism earns foreign exchange – but not enough to avert dependence on grants from India and elsewhere.

OFFICIAL NAME Kingdom of Bhutan.
CAPITAL CITY Thimphu.
GEOGRAPHY Most of the people live in flat, fertile valleys, that run north-south through the centre of the country. Farther north, by the ill-defined border with Tibet, the peaks are over 7,000 metres (23,000 feet). *Highest point* Kula Kangri 7,554 metres (24,780 feet). *Area* 46,500 sq km (17,954 sq miles).
PEOPLE *Population* 1.3m. *Density* 28 per sq km. *Ethnic groups* Bhutia 61%, Gurung 15%, Assamese 13%.
RELIGION Buddhist 70%, Hindu 25%, Muslim 5%.
LANGUAGE Dzongkha (Tibetan/Burmese).
EDUCATION Non-compulsory; free where available. Teaching is in English, with a British-style syllabus.
CLIMATE Temperate, varying with altitude. Dry in the extreme north, hot and humid on the Duars plain. Average monthly temperatures in the valleys range from 5°C (41°F) in Jan to 17°C (63°F) in July.
CURRENCY Ngultrum. Indian rupee also used.
PUBLIC HOLIDAYS Nov 11, Dec 17. Buddhist lunar holidays also observed.
GOVERNMENT Modified constitutional monarchy.The king is head of government and, supported by his personal advisers, shares power with the council of ministers, the national assembly and the Buddhist head abbot.

CHAGOS ARCHIPELAGO

The British Indian Ocean Territory now consists only of the Chagos Archipelago. It is held by the UK, despite Mauritian claims, and is home to the US military base on Diego Garcia. The original inhabitants were evacuated before the construction of the base; it has a temporary British and US population.

OFFICIAL NAME British Indian Ocean Territory.
GEOGRAPHY The isolated series of small coral atolls lies some 1,800km (1,100 miles) east of the Seychelles. *Area* 60 sq km (20 sq miles).
PEOPLE *Population* 2,900.
LANGUAGE English.
CURRENCY US dollar and UK pound.
GOVERNMENT UK territory.

MALDIVES

Consistent with its isolation in the Indian Ocean, the Maldives remains economically dependent on the sea, with fish products accounting for 45% of export earnings. Small quantities of coconuts, grains and yams are produced, but virtually all food has to be imported – as do most essential consumer and capital goods.

Tourism, a growth industry in the 1980s, might be threatened if there is renewed evidence of political instability such as the 1988 coup attempt which was suppressed with Indian help.

OFFICIAL NAME Republic of Maldives.
CAPITAL CITY Malé.
GEOGRAPHY The archipelago consists of more than 1,200 coral islands, none of them large and only 202 inhabited. They are grouped into 19 atolls for administrative purposes. *Area* 298 sq km (120 sq miles).
PEOPLE *Population* 206,000. *Density* 691 per sq km. *Ethnic groups* Mainly Sinhalese.
RELIGION Sunni Muslim.
LANGUAGE Dhivehi. Also English, Arabic and Hindi.
EDUCATION Non-compulsory. There are three systems: traditional Koranic schools, Divehi primary schools, and English primary and secondary schools.
CLIMATE Tropical and humid, with annual average temperature around 27°C (81°F). Rainfall varies between 2,500mm (100ins) and 4,000mm (160ins).
CURRENCY Rufiyaa.
PUBLIC HOLIDAYS Jan 7, Id al-Fitr, Id al-Adha, Jul 26, Muharram, Mouloud, Nov 11, Dec 10.
GOVERNMENT Republic, independent since 1965. The president, elected every 5 years, is head of state and chief executive. Legislative power is held by the 48-member Citizens' Council. Each atoll is partly self-governing. There are no political parties.

SRI LANKA

Communal violence has blighted the prospects of Sri Lanka, which has come some way in diversifying an economy traditionally based on rice growing and tea exports through the development of light industry and tourism.

The conflict between the Sinhalese majority of the south (74% of the population) and the northern Tamil people (18%) is the most serious problem facing the country. Heavy-handed government treatment of demands for local autonomy caused young Tamils to turn to violence. After anti-Tamil riots in 1983 the conflict escalated into civil war. Under pressure from India, the government met many Tamil demands in 1987 and allowed an Indian peacekeeping force into the country. The Indians failed to crush the main separatist group, the Tamil Tigers. In the south the Janatha Vimukti Peramuna (JVP) – which combines fierce Sinhalese nationalism with crude Marxism – launched a violent campaign against concessions to the Tamils and the Indian presence.

President Junius Jayawardene retired at the beginning of 1989, after dominating Sri Lankan politics for more than a decade. His conservative United National Party (UNP) won a decisive electoral victory in 1977 over the Sri Lanka Freedom Party of Mrs Sirimavo Bandaranaike and her populist programme. The UNP introduced a new constitution based on a presidential system of government and in 1982 used a national referendum to postpone a general election for a further six years.

Despite violence and intimidation, the election of Mr Jayawardene's successor took place on schedule, resulting in a narrow victory for Ranasinghe Premadasa, the former prime minister. He initiated a no-holds-barred offensive which broke the JVP and ordered the Indian forces home. The withdrawal was completed in March 1990. Subsequent negotiations with the Tigers quickly broke down. The violence and economic disruption that plagued the country in the 1980s looked set to continue well into the 1990s.

OFFICIAL NAME Democratic Socialist Republic of Sri Lanka.
CAPITAL CITY Colombo.
GEOGRAPHY From the south-central highlands the land falls by steppes to a rolling coastal plain, narrow in the south and west and broad in the north. Rivers are generally short, and rainfall heaviest in the south. The uplands and wet zone are most densely populated. *Highest point* Pidurutalagala 2,524 metres (8,280 feet). *Area* 65,610 sq km (25,330 sq miles).
PEOPLE *Population* 16.6m. *Density* 257 per sq km. *Ethnic groups* Sinhalese 74%, Tamil 18%, Moor 7%.
RELIGION Buddhist 70%, Hindu 15%, Christian 8%, Muslim 7%.
LANGUAGE Sinhala. Also Tamil and English.
EDUCATION Free and compulsory for ages 5–15.
CLIMATE Tropical monsoon; monthly temperatures 25–29°C (77–84°F). Main rainy season, May–Oct; secondary season, Dec–Mar.
CURRENCY Rupee.
PUBLIC HOLIDAYS Jan 14–15, Feb 4, Good Fri, Wesak Full Moon Poya Day, May 22, Hadji, Dec 25, Ramzan. (also numerous Full Moon Poya Days – Buddhist holidays).
GOVERNMENT Republic since 1948. The chief executive and head of state is a president who is not accountable to parliament; he appoints the prime minister and the cabinet. Parliament is elected by PR; there are no by-elections.

BANGLADESH

Bangladesh, the former eastern region of Pakistan, has had an unsettled history since its birth in 1971 out of a bitter civil war which was resolved by Indian intervention. Four military coups followed and two heads of state, including Sheikh Mujibur Rahman, the country's founding father, died violently in office.

President Hossain Mohammad Ershad, who came to power in a military coup in 1982, resigned as army chief to take up the civilian presidency in 1986. He faced opposition from political parties founded by the two murdered presidents: Sheikh Mujib's Awami League and the Bangladesh National Party (BNP) of General Zia-ur Rahman, who was killed in 1988. Their regular mass protests added to political instability but did not threaten the regime as long as the opposition remained disunited and the army backed Ershad. In late 1990 these conditions ceased to hold and Ershad was toppled from power. The BNP won a plurality of seats in the first free parliamentary elections since independence and General Zia's widow, Begum Khaleda Zia, became prime minister.

Such conflicts have often been overshadowed by the elements. Storms and flooding during the monsoon season continue to take a terrible toll of life and property. Discussion of flood control schemes with India, begun in the mid-1970s, has been hampered by an atmosphere of mutual suspicion.

Bangladesh is one of the poorest and most densely populated countries in the world. It is heavily dependent on foreign aid, with an agricultural economy based on rice growing in the Ganges delta. International demand for jute, the principal export crop, has long been in decline, but substantial reserves of coal, oil and natural gas await development.

OFFICIAL NAME People's Republic of Bangladesh.
CAPITAL CITY Dhaka.
GEOGRAPHY Most of the country is the flat, low-lying and extremely fertile flood plains and deltas of the Ganges and Brahmaputra. The south-east is hilly and thickly forested. *Area* 143,998 sq km (55,600 sq miles).
PEOPLE *Population* 104.5m. *Density* 726 per sq km. *Ethnic groups* Mainly Bengali.
RELIGION Muslim 85%, Hindu 7%, Buddhist 0.6%, Christian 0.3%.
LANGUAGE Bangla.
EDUCATION Non-compulsory. Only primary education (5–10) is free. There are 6 universities.
CLIMATE Tropical monsoon; monthly temperatures 21–28°C (70–82°F). Rainy season Jun–Sep. Cyclonic storms occur in the Bay of Bengal.
CURRENCY Taka.
PUBLIC HOLIDAYS Jan 1, Mar 26, Shahid Day, Easter, Jemedahbida, Id al-Fitr, May 1, Buddha Purinama, Id al-Adha, Durga Puja, Mouloud, Nov 7, Dec 16, 25–26.
GOVERNMENT Republic since 1971. The elected president is head of state and chief executive; the 330-member parliament includes 30 non-elected women.

CHINA

China is home to more than one-fifth of the human race, and is the world's most populous nation. It is also one of the poorest, and the outcome of its desperate search for the fast lane to economic growth will have global repercussions. The Chinese have immense pride staked on their success. Their civilization was ahead of Europe for most of recorded history. Traditionally, they see themselves as the "Middle Kingdom" of refinement and technology, surrounded by ignorant barbarians.

A decline set in roughly 200 years ago, steep enough to rank China now among the poverty-stricken nations of the world. GNP is only about $300 per head; that of the USA is 50 times bigger. It will be a long and arduous haul before China can achieve the modernity and prosperity the West now takes for granted.

Increasingly effete emperors ruled China until well into the 20th century, by which time national weakness and breakdown had allowed Western and Japanese imperialism to nibble away at the country's edges – Britain in Hong Kong, Japan in Taiwan, the tsars in Siberia. Sun Yat-sen led the republican forces to victory in 1912 but could not unify them. Precious resources were destroyed in civil war between the right-wing Kuomintang (or Nationalist) party and the communists, and in resisting Japan's invasion in the 1930s. By the time peace returned with the communist victory in 1949, at least 10m lives had been lost and the stock of infrastructure and productive assets was gravely depleted.

Since 1949 the country has been ruled by the Long March generation of communist leaders who rose to prominence during the struggles of the previous decades. The political changes that have occurred reflect both policy disagreements and intense personal loyalties and rivalries. The party leadership began by alienating the country's entrepreneurial talent. Then in 1958, impatient with slow economic growth, they launched Mao Zedong's "Great Leap Forward", an ill-prepared campaign to accelerate development. The resulting chaos was compounded by exceptional weather setbacks, leading to famine. Similar failure attended the Cultural Revolution of the late 1960s, which aimed to re-establish socialist ideals. Its actual result was a costly suspension of all education for a decade and the loss of the regime's credibility.

Only after Mao's death in 1976 were more pragmatic, less interventionist

OFFICIAL NAME People's Republic of China.

CAPITAL CITY Beijing.

GEOGRAPHY The plateau of Tibet in the south-west, where many great Asian rivers have their sources, is the highest in the world at over 4,000 metres (13,120 feet). Around it to the north and east is a wide arc of basins and plateaus from the desert of Takla Makan in the north-west to the rocky south-eastern shore. To the east rolling hills and plains are drained and shaped by the Huang He, Chang Jiang and Xi Jiang rivers. Cultivation (and population) is concentrated in the northern half of the area, where flatter terrain makes up for lower rainfall. Extensive coastal plains end in flat, sandy beaches north of Shanghai and a rugged shore marked by bays and islands to the south. *Highest point* Mt Everest 8,848 metres (29,030 feet). *Area* 9,561,000 sq km (3,692,000 sq miles).

PEOPLE *Population* 1,096m. *Density* 114 per sq km. *Ethnic groups* Han 93%, Zhuang 1.3%.

RELIGION Confucian 20%, Buddhist 6%, Taoist 2%, Muslim 2%.

LANGUAGE 93% of the population speaks one of 5 main Sino-Tibetan dialects: Mandarin; Cantonese, Fukienese, Hakka and Wu. Putonghua (based on Mandarin and formulated in 1949 to simplify language difficulties) is now the state language.

EDUCATION Non-compulsory and fee-paying at all levels.

CLIMATE Sub-tropical in the south-east, but continental in the interior. 4,000mm (1,579ins) of rain can fall in the south-east, less than 250mm (10ins) in large areas of the arid north-west. Winter temperatures range from -28°C (-18.5°F) in the extreme north, dominated by the Siberian air mass, to 20°C (68°F) in the sheltered south. The summer range is much smaller. Typhoons hit the southern coast every summer.

CURRENCY Renminbi/yuan.

PUBLIC HOLIDAYS Jan 1, Spring Festival, May 1, Aug 1, October 1–2, Chinese New Year.

GOVERNMENT Communist republic since 1949. There are 22 provinces, 5 autonomous regions and 3 municipalities. Political power is held by the Chinese Communist Party, whose congress elects a central committee and politburo every five years; the latter sets policy and controls administrative, legal and executive appointments. The legislature is the unicameral National People's Congress (NPC), whose 2,970 deputies are elected indirectly for 5 years by regional bodies and the People's Liberation Army. The NPC elects a standing committee, an executive state council of premier and ministers, and a president who is head of state.

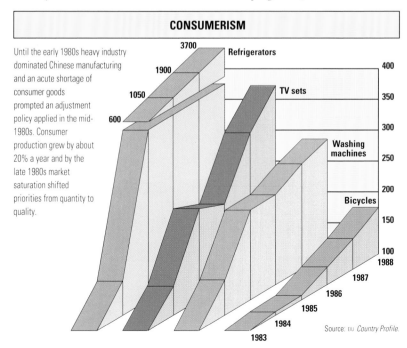

CONSUMERISM

Until the early 1980s heavy industry dominated Chinese manufacturing and an acute shortage of consumer goods prompted an adjustment policy applied in the mid-1980s. Consumer production grew by about 20% a year and by the late 1980s market saturation shifted priorities from quantity to quality.

Refrigerators
TV sets
Washing machines
Bicycles

3700
1900
1050
600

400
350
300
250
200
150
100

1988
1987
1986
1985
1984
1983

Source: EIU *Country Profile.*

policies adopted, under the leadership of Deng Xiaoping. In the countryside these have largely been successful. The urban population is quicker to produce a political backlash if its own interests are under threat. The many demonstrations and strikes which rocked China's cities in 1988–89, culminating in the June 1989 massacre in Beijing's Tiananmen Square, were strictly an urban phenomenon.

The economic reforms since 1980 have seen farming, although still conducted on collectively-owned land, carried out by families largely free from bureaucratic fetters. Heavy industry remains state-owned, but with management increasingly independent of central controls. Light industry, with the service trades, has become the preserve of small collectives, cooperatives and a new army of private entrepreneurs and self-employed. Yet many politically powerful party members cling to the old socialist dreams, hoping to be more prudent than Mao Zedong, but aiming for the same goal.

Freeing the peasants from the dead hand of the people's commune released sufficient energy (and greed) to hoist the major grain harvests – rice, wheat and maize – by 40% in the decade after 1976. But the other side of the coin has been neglect of irrigation works, coupled with industry's inability to produce enough fertilizer. The government has also fought shy of sharply raising staple food crop prices for farmers, fearing the spectre of inflation. Whether the official target of 500m tonnes (550m US tons) of cereals a year by 1999 can be achieved is therefore uncertain. Other agricultural sectors, especially cash crops and vegetables, are in a healthy state. Farmers as a whole have never been better off. Only a return to the polarization of incomes, as the state either ceases to protect the weak or curbs the resourceful cultivator, could spoil the picture.

Loosening the reins for market-led production was paralleled by more social and political freedom as well, to the delight of the, albeit small, professional middle class. But it also led to higher crime figures and unprecedented levels of official corruption and bribery. Top government officials voiced their concern about falling standards of public morality, and corruption, nepotism and censorship were the principal targets of the students who led the Tiananmen Square uprising.

Until 1989 Deng Xiaoping managed to hold together an uneasy alliance of conservatives and reformers, tilting the balance towards the latter in the hope

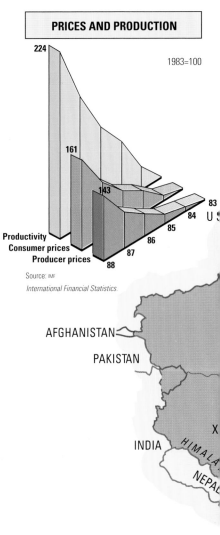

PRICES AND PRODUCTION

1983=100

224
161
143
83
84
85
86
87
88

Productivity
Consumer prices
Producer prices

Source: IMF
International Financial Statistics.

AFGHANISTAN
PAKISTAN
INDIA
HIMALA
NEPAL

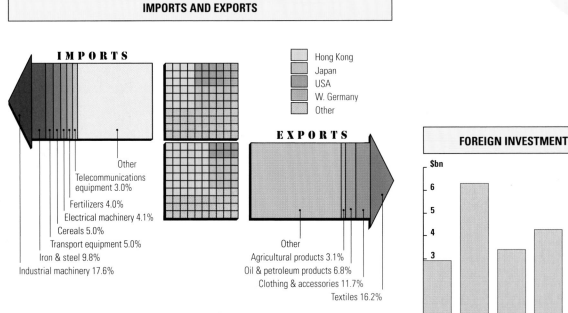

IMPORTS AND EXPORTS

IMPORTS

Hong Kong
Japan
USA
W. Germany
Other

Other
Telecommunications equipment 3.0%
Fertilizers 4.0%
Electrical machinery 4.1%
Cereals 5.0%
Transport equipment 5.0%
Iron & steel 9.8%
Industrial machinery 17.6%

EXPORTS

Other
Agricultural products 3.1%
Oil & petroleum products 6.8%
Clothing & accessories 11.7%
Textiles 16.2%

FOREIGN INVESTMENT

$bn
6
5
4
3

1984 1985 1986 1987 1988

Source: EIU *Country Profile.*

Source: Imports/Exports EIU *Country Profile* (1989 figures);
Trading partners IMF *Direction of Trade Statistics* (1989 figures).

Population distribution

Population is heavily concentrated in the fertile plains and river basins of the south-east; by comparison, the arid north-west is virtually uninhabited. 90% of the population inhabits 15% of the land and nearly half of Chinese are urbanized. Population densities range from over 600 people per square kilometre in Jiangsu province, north of Shanghai, to only two in Xizang autonomous region (Tibet). Over 60 Chinese cities have populations exceeding 1m. The number is much higher if suburbs are included.

Languages

Putonghua (Mandarin) has been adopted as the national language. Although the written language is the same throughout China, five main dialects are spoken: Mandarin (including Peking) in the north; Cantonese (or Yue); Fukienese (or Min); Hakka and Wu. The Pinyin system of transliteration for Mandarin was officially adopted in 1958.

■ More than 1 million

Major cities

Population in millions, including suburbs (1985).

Shanghai	12.2
Beijing	9.6
Tianjin	8.1
Shenjang	7.5
Wuhan	6.4
Guangzhou	5.9

Border disputes

Talks on delineating the 8,000km/5,000-mile border with the USSR have progressed since 1986, when Soviet leader Mikhail Gorbachev accepted China's definition of the Amur river boundary in the north.

China and India went to war in 1962 over their disputed border in the Himalayas. The issue has not been settled, although India has recently shown willingness to yield its claim to land China took in 1962 if China gives up its claim to part of the Indian state of Arunchal Pradesh.

Tension has been high on the border with Vietnam since 1979, fuelled by Vietnam's treatment of its Chinese population and its invasion of Cambodia. The two have also clashed over their claims to the Spratly and Paracel Islands in the South China Sea.

Time zones

All of China is eight hours ahead of GMT.

Special Economic Zones

The four Special Economic Zones (SEZs) were set up in 1979, aiming to attract foreign investment through tax and other incentives to produce foods for export. Growth rates have been disappointing, particularly in the largest zone, Shenzhen, bordering Hong Kong's New Territories. Two of the other zones, Shantou and Zhuhai are, like Shenzhen, in Guangdong province; the fourth, Xiamen, is in neighbouring Fujian.

Tibet

Tibet was occupied by the People's Liberation Army of China in 1950, although border areas had been the subject of dispute for many years. The Dalai Lama, spiritual leader of the Tibetans, had already fled to India and established a government in exile when the Chinese proclaimed the Autonomous Region of Tibet in 1965.

In 1961 the International Commission of Jurists produced a report accusing China of committing genocide in Tibet. Subsequent human rights abuses have been largely ignored by Western governments, and concessions from the Dalai Lama (awarded the Nobel Peace Prize in 1989) have failed to alter China's stance.

Tibet is a valuable source of minerals, including uranium, and timber.

that they would continue the process of change after his death. This strategy collapsed when, confronted by the Tiananmen demonstrators, he threw in with the hardliners. After the army brutally suppressed the uprising and re-established the authority of the party leadership an altogether less liberal regime emerged. Still under Deng Xiaoping, the new leadership remains committed to basic economic reforms but has rejected political liberalization. And with Deng Xiaoping's reformist protégées discredited, there is an intense succession crisis under way behind the public facade of unity.

For Chinese, unlike most other peoples, religion is not the source of ethics. There is no universal ethic in Buddhism or the other religions that China practises; Confucianism limits its demands to relations within the family. The extended family is so strong and tight, in spite of communist intrusions, that its web of obligation overrides those to party or state. (That is one reason why the government has had difficulty enforcing its strict family planning policy to contain damaging population growth.) The practical response to adversity tends to be superstition. The Chinese are unusually addicted to charms, rituals, lucky numbers, astrology and geomancy.

Isolated for millennia from other civilizations, China was again cut off under Mao Zedong. Deng Xiaoping opened the door to the West, facilitating trade, investment, travel, training and other forms of foreign intercourse. But the events of mid-1989 were a violent reminder of the continuing power of those within the party who fear contamination by Western ideas of social and political freedom.

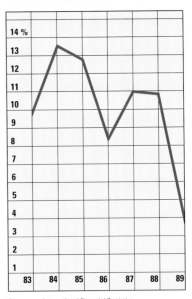

GNP GROWTH

Source: IMF *International Financial Statistics*;
EIU *Country Report*.

ECONOMIC PROFILE

Primarily an agricultural economy; rice, wheat and pigs the main products. Industry mostly developed in few centres around Beijing, Shanghai, Wuhan and Guangzhou; primitive and highly labour-intensive elsewhere. Textiles and consumer electrical goods are important exports, along with rice, processed meat and vegetables, oil and coal. Superabundance of manpower, exported for construction projects overseas.

Growth Farming was biggest beneficiary of economic reforms in 1980s, but all-round growth trend strong. Chemical (especially fertilizer), vehicle, power and construction industries likely to be growth leaders in 1990s.

Problems Urgent need to encourage enterprise in society used to bureaucracy. Serious energy shortage hampers industry. Transport infrastructure poorly developed. Economic reforms in 1980s made cash crops more profitable than cereals, leading to major cereal imports.

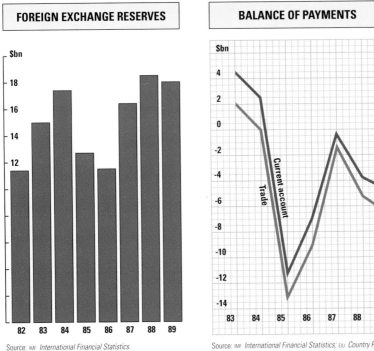

FOREIGN EXCHANGE RESERVES

Source: IMF *International Financial Statistics*.

BALANCE OF PAYMENTS

Source: IMF *International Financial Statistics*; EIU *Country Profile*.

China has in recent years run a trade surplus; the current account plunged into deficit in 1985, when imports surged after a poor grain harvest and relaxation of curbs on imports of consumer goods. Efforts to boost exports, including devaluation, and strong inflows from tourism helped reduce the deficit in subsequent years. The deficits ate into foreign exchange reserves, which had reached an all-time high in 1984, but these resumed a rising trend after an export boom in 1987. Income from China's substantial foreign investments and from the export of labour are significant foreign exchange earners.

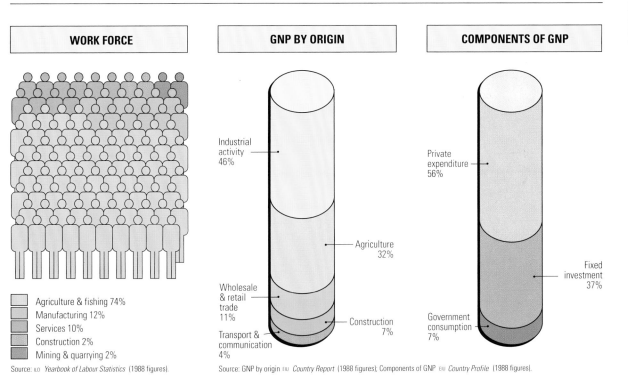

WORK FORCE

- Agriculture & fishing 74%
- Manufacturing 12%
- Services 10%
- Construction 2%
- Mining & quarrying 2%

Source: ILO *Yearbook of Labour Statistics* (1988 figures).

GNP BY ORIGIN

- Industrial activity 46%
- Agriculture 32%
- Wholesale & retail trade 11%
- Construction 7%
- Transport & communication 4%

COMPONENTS OF GNP

- Private expenditure 56%
- Fixed investment 37%
- Government consumption 7%

Source: GNP by origin EIU *Country Report* (1988 figures); Components of GNP EIU *Country Profile* (1988 figures).

POPULATION GROWTH

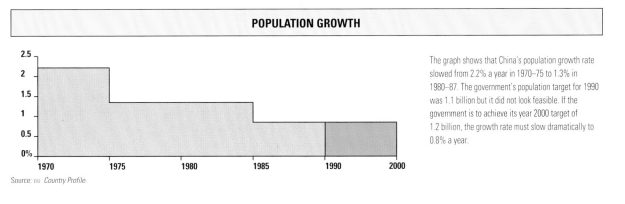

The graph shows that China's population growth rate slowed from 2.2% a year in 1970–75 to 1.3% in 1980–87. The government's population target for 1990 was 1.1 billion but it did not look feasible. If the government is to achieve its year 2000 target of 1.2 billion, the growth rate must slow dramatically to 0.8% a year.

Source: EIU *Country Profile*.

MONGOLIA

Wedged in the high central Asian plateau between the USSR and China, Mongolia is too weak to be neutral. It was heavily dependent on Soviet military and political support until a 1987 agreement by Moscow to reduce its presence. In March 1990 the communist old guard stepped down after months of popular demonstrations, paving the way for multi-party elections. The ruling Mongolian People's Revolutionary Party won the poll, somewhat soothing Chinese anxieties about reform. China claimed sovereignty over Mongolia until 1950, and there are more people of Mongolian origin in China than in Mongolia itself.

The economy is traditionally based on animal husbandry; there are 22m sheep, goats, cattle and horses. Steady industrial development based on indigenous coal and oil has taken place in recent decades. Wool, hides, fluorspar and copper are exported. Oil, vehicles, fertilizer, sugar and consumer goods are the chief imports.

OFFICIAL NAME Mongolian People's Republic.
CAPITAL CITY Ulan Bator.
GEOGRAPHY Largely high, rolling steppes with mountains to the north and the Gobi Desert in the south. *Area* 1,565,000 sq km (604,250 sq miles).
PEOPLE *Population* 2.1m. *Density* 1 per sq km. *Ethnic groups* Khalkha 84%, Kazakh 5%, Durbet 3%.
RELIGION Shamanist 31%, Buddhist 2%, Muslim 1%.
LANGUAGE Khalka Mongolian. Also Kazakh.
EDUCATION Compulsory for ages 6–16.
CLIMATE Continental, with very cold, dry winters and warm summers; low rainfall.
CURRENCY Tugrik or Tögrög.
PUBLIC HOLIDAYS Jan 1, Mongolian New Year, Mar 8, May 1, Jul 11, Nov 7, Dec 31.
GOVERNMENT Communist-dominated republic since 1924.

EAST ASIA

The four "Little Dragons"

Asia's four "Little Dragons" – Hong Kong, Singapore, South Korea and Taiwan – have achieved impressive export-led growth and rapid development of manufacturing and services. Excepting Hong Kong, their approach has been characterized by a high level of state intervention in their economies, high spending on education and training and pragmatic, authoritarian government.

Investment by Japan, which took advantage of lower labour costs in the four newly industrializing countries to set up plants for the assembly of electronic and other goods, helped to set these countries on the road to rapid economic growth. They now need to emulate Japan's shift from labour-intensive manufacturing to more capital-intensive sectors, such as electronics, as labour costs start to rise. With small domestic markets they must export to survive, and growth will be hindered by the falling market prompted by world recession. They must also meet the growing demands of their people for more democracy and a fairer share of the benefits of prosperity.

The Mekong

The longest river in South-East Asia, the Mekong has its source in China's Qinghai province. It forms the border between Laos and both Myanmar and Thailand. In Cambodia to the south, a huge freshwater lake, Tonle Sap, acts as a natural flood reservoir for the Mekong. During the rainy season the Tonle Sap river linking the Mekong to the lake reverses its flow and floods an area three times its normal size. In Vietnam the Mekong separates into four main branches and enters the South China Sea through a delta.

Climate

South-East Asia has a tropical climate strongly influenced by monsoon winds. Thailand, Malaysia, the Philippines, Vietnam, Cambodia and Laos have heavy rainfall during the May–October south-west monsoon; Indonesia's rainy season runs from December to March. Temperatures vary little from month to month, averaging 22–32°C (72–90°F), and humidity is high throughout the year.

Korea has an extreme continental climate, with cold winters and hot summers. Winter winds bring cold dry air from Siberia; in summer, warm moist winds blow from the Pacific. June to September are the wettest months. North Korea has severe winter weather, with temperatures as low as -13°C (9°F).

The Golden Triangle

The area where Thailand, Laos and Myanmar meet on the banks of the Mekong river has long been notorious as a source of opium and heroin. Parts of eastern Myanmar are controlled by war-lords who use drug smuggling to finance their struggle against the government.

Macao

An enclave on the Chinese coast that was once Portuguese, Macao is now Chinese under Portuguese administration and is due to be ceded fully to China in 1999. The Portuguese governor acts on domestic affairs in consultation with the legislative assembly, 6 of whose 17 members are directly elected. Foreign affairs are the preserve of the Portuguese president. Macao's industry centres on textile manufacture, although tourism and gambling are gaining greater importance.

Asean

Founded in 1967, the Association of South East Asian Nations (Asean) has proved one of the more successful regional organizations in the developing world. Asean has given its members a collective say in world affairs, through a regular dialogue with the USA, the EC and Japan. It has been particularly prominent in seeking a settlement in Cambodia although here the aims of Indonesia, which seeks to contain Chinese influence, have conflicted with those of its Asean partners, whose priority is curbing Vietnam. Economic cooperation has been less fruitful as most Asean members produce a similar range of commodities and thus compete on world markets. Intra-Asean trade is only about 30% of the total, but is expected to grow. Founder members were Malaysia, Thailand, Singapore and the Philippines. Brunei joined in 1984. Papua New Guinea is an observer.

Los Angeles 22 days

*New York
21 hours*

Japanese investment

Japan, the leading trading partner and source of foreign investment for many East Asian countries, increased investment in the four "Little Dragons" by 15–25% a year throughout the 1980s. Now, as their labour costs rise and their currencies appreciate against the dollar, Japan is turning to other countries in the region offering lower costs: Indonesia, Malaysia, the Philippines and Thailand. However, the road to rapid economic growth will not be as smooth for these countries, all dependent on raw material exports vulnerable to fluctuating world commodity prices. Meanwhile, Japan's investment flow is beginning to slow.

The Spratlys and Paracels

The Spratlys, or Nanshan Islands, in the South China Sea probably rank as the most disputed scraps of land in the world. No less than five nations have a claim to some or all of the islands, which lie on major international trade routes in an area regarded as promising for oil exploration. Vietnam, the Philippines, Malaysia and Taiwan all maintain garrisons on various islets; in early 1988, the arrival of Chinese marines near Vietnamese-held islands led to a brief naval battle followed by angry diplomatic exchanges. Earlier, the Chinese ousted Vietnam from the Paracels, another island group further north.

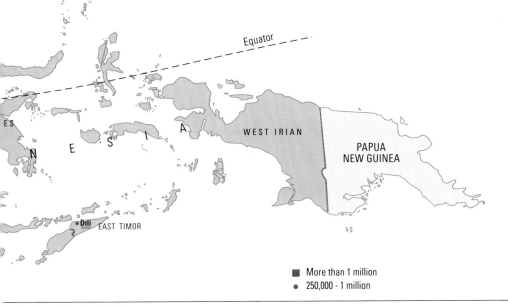

■ More than 1 million
● 250,000 - 1 million

SOUTH KOREA

The Koreans, an ethnically cohesive, linguistically united people, enjoyed over a thousand years as a unified, independent kingdom until the Japanese annexation of 1910. After Japan's defeat in 1945 Korea was divided into Soviet and American zones of occupation and then in 1948 into two hostile republics. The north's invasion of the south in 1950 led to three years of war, in which the UN supported the south and China the north. The two sides were left glaring at each other across a ceasefire line not far from the 38th parallel, which marked the original US and Soviet zones.

South Korea gave priority to education and made owner-occupation by smallholders the basis of land tenure. In 1962 a military government, seeking an engine for growth in a country with few natural resources, initiated a strategy of export-oriented industrialization. It depended on South Korea's one major asset: cheap but well-educated labour. The next quarter century was one barely interrupted boom, with GNP growth averaging 8.8% a year. Positive agricultural policies maintained self-sufficiency in food grains, with some of the world's highest rice yields.

South Korea at the start of the 1990s was in a state of transition. In domestic politics, it was moving slowly from military dictatorship to a more democratic system. In international relations erstwhile communist countries had moved towards recognition of South Korea, and even North Korea had relaxed its hostility sufficiently to agree to "talks about talks". In economic terms, the question is not if South Korea will leave developing country status behind and join the OECD, but when.

Before it does, the government will have to complete the liberalization of the economy, allowing market forces the main role in determining resource allocation. This will help transform the country's export position, making it less

OFFICIAL NAME Republic of Korea.

CAPITAL CITY Seoul.

GEOGRAPHY Basically mountainous, the population is concentrated in the arable river valleys and along the coastal plain. The plain is wider on the west coast, where there are many rias and offshore islands, than on the east, where the Taebaek range often falls sheer into the sea. *Highest point* Halla San 1,950 metres (6,400 feet). *Area* 99,222 sq km (38,310 sq miles).

PEOPLE *Population* 41.9m. *Density* 423 per sq km. *Ethnic groups* Korean.

RELIGION Buddhist 37%, Christian 30%, Confucian 17%, Chundo Kyo 4%.

LANGUAGE Korean.

EDUCATION Free and compulsory for ages 6–12. 90% of those eligible are enrolled in higher education; there are more than 100 university-level institutions. Education accounts for 20% of total government expenditure.

CLIMATE Continental, with an average temperature range from -5°C (23°F) in winter to 27°C (81°F) in summer, more extreme in the interior. Annual rainfall is 1,000–1,400mm (40–55ins).

CURRENCY South Korean won.

PUBLIC HOLIDAYS Jan 1–3, Chinese New Year, Mar 1, Apr 5, May 5, Buddha's birthday, Jun 6, Jul 17, Aug 15, Choo-Suk, Oct 1, 3, 9, Dec 25.

GOVERNMENT Republic since 1948. The 1987 constitution gives executive power to a president directly elected for a single term of 5 years; the legislative National Assembly is elected for 4 years. Serving military officers are banned from membership of the state council, which consists of the president, prime minister and their appointees.

ECONOMIC PROFILE

Export-led growth dominated by labour-intensive manufactures, especially textiles, clothing and footwear. Agriculture protected from market forces to maintain self-sufficiency in food.

Growth Motor vehicles, aerospace, computers, advanced materials, nuclear power, financial services are all growth areas. Government R&D spending to double in real terms in less than five years.

Problems Oil and most industrial raw materials imported. The problems of success: rising labour costs, inflationary pressures.

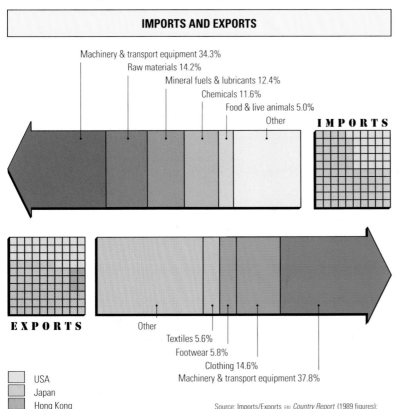

IMPORTS AND EXPORTS

Machinery & transport equipment 34.3%
Raw materials 14.2%
Mineral fuels & lubricants 12.4%
Chemicals 11.6%
Food & live animals 5.0%
Other

IMPORTS

EXPORTS

Other
Textiles 5.6%
Footwear 5.8%
Clothing 14.6%
Machinery & transport equipment 37.8%

USA
Japan
Hong Kong
Other

Source: Imports/Exports EIU *Country Report* (1989 figures);
Trading partners IMF *Direction of Trade Statistics* (1989 figures).

reliant on manufactures sold on the basis of cheap labour, more on high-quality, high-technology goods sold under the brand names of major South Korean corporations. Already, with some difficulty, it is coping with a swing from current account deficit to surplus. The world's fourth largest debtor in the early 1980s, South Korea should become an international creditor by 1992.

South Korea's new role as a developed economy is likely to be evident in its relations with China, whose cheap labour it will seek to employ in joint ventures. It could also affect links with the USSR, whose Siberian raw materials it may help to develop. The country's determination to reach the economic first rank makes a successful transition to democracy essential, since it depends on persuading people with marketable technological skills that South Korea is a country worth staying in, or returning to. The shift to democracy in turn makes the technological priority inevitable: now that it is no longer politically possible to suppress workers' demands for a larger share of the new prosperity, South Korea's days as a cheap labour market are numbered. The move into current account surplus has not been without its problems – posing a choice between unwanted currency appreciation and an inflationary growth of foreign exchange reserves – because of the restrictions on South Koreans investing abroad. Economic liberalization is being forced on South Korea by the success of a quasi-command economy.

The dynamism of South Korea is beyond doubt and with some political skill the country should fulfil the expectations of the 1990s. An overwhelmingly urban community, with a falling and ageing rural population, it will be a much more open economy. It will export goods such as cars and consumer electronics and become a major importer of raw materials. Ordinary South Koreans are likely to demand a much greater allocation of resources to the social sectors; its highly-educated workforce will be able to generate the financial surpluses to satisfy their demands, although growth is unlikely to continue at current spectacular rates.

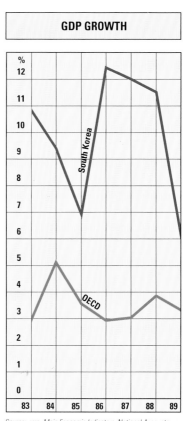

GDP GROWTH

Source: OECD *Main Economic Indicators, National Accounts;* EIU *Economic Risk Service.*

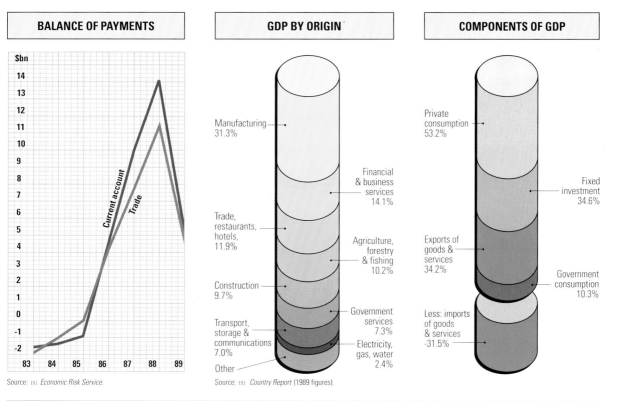

BALANCE OF PAYMENTS

Source: EIU *Economic Risk Service.*

GDP BY ORIGIN

Source: EIU *Country Report* (1989 figures).

COMPONENTS OF GDP

 ## NORTH KOREA

The communist regime of North Korea, imposed by the USSR in 1945 and supported by China during the Korean war, has since managed to play one against the other. It is characterized by one of the world's most extreme personality cults, surrounding its leader, Kim Il Sung, and his designated heir Kim Jung Il. Policies have combined the economic centralism and party dominance of 1950s communism with a stubborn desire for national independence.

Agriculture is collectivized and has been fairly successful. The emphasis of development has been on heavy industry, not least to support a formidable war machine that is estimated to absorb about 25% of GNP. After early impressive growth, industry has become increasingly old-fashioned and produces little saleable abroad. Exports, primarily to other communist countries, were worth $65 per head in 1986, compared with $816 in South Korea. Imports on credit from the non-communist world have been largely ruled out by North Korea's default on debt repayments after a failed bid in the early 1970s to modernize with the help of Western capital goods.

There have been few signs of the reforms being undertaken by most of North Korea's erstwhile political allies. How long this can continue is questionable. A prerequisite for the maintenance of the regime has been the effective isolation of North Koreans from the outside world. But the government is being forced to re-examine this self-imposed quarantine by South Korea's burgeoning relations with the USSR and China. Very tentative feelers have been put out to the USA, and there have been new moves on talks with South Korea.

OFFICIAL NAME Democratic People's Republic of Korea.
CAPITAL CITY Pyongyang.
GEOGRAPHY Mountains run down the eastern side of the country. More than half the population is urbanized; major settlements are on the wide western and narrow eastern coastal plains. *Area* 120,538 sq km (46,540 sq miles).
PEOPLE *Population* 21.9m. *Density* 181 per sq km. *Ethnic groups* Predominantly Korean.
RELIGION Shamanist 16%, Chundo Kyo 14%, Buddhist 2%, Christian 1%.
LANGUAGE Korean.
EDUCATION Free and compulsory for ages 5–16. 46 universities.
CLIMATE Continental, with monthly average temperatures ranging from -3°C (27°F) to 24°C (75°F). Annual rainfall is 1,000mm (40ins), most in Jun–Sep.
CURRENCY North Korean won.
PUBLIC HOLIDAYS Jan 1, Feb 16, Mar 8, Apr 15, May 1, Aug 15, Sep 9, Oct 10, Dec 27.
GOVERNMENT Communist republic since 1948. The Korean Workers' Party (KWP) has been in power since 1949. The president is elected by the Supreme People's Assembly, whose 655 members are elected unopposed.

 ## HONG KONG

After 150 years as a British colony, Hong Kong will become a "special administrative region" of China in mid-1997. Under the 1984 agreement governing the transition, China has pledged that the territory will enjoy full economic autonomy and be free to pursue capitalism for at least 50 years. The "one country, two systems" principle reflects Hong Kong's importance to China as a source of commercial, technical and marketing skills, as well as almost a third of its export earnings.

Hong Kong's small hinterland means that the territory relies on China for

OFFICIAL NAME Territory of Hong Kong.
CAPITAL CITY Victoria.
GEOGRAPHY The mainland and islands of Hong Kong are a partly drowned old mountain range. Between Hong Kong island and the Kowloon peninsula is one of the great deep-water harbours of the world. The terrain is steep and hilly; land is at such a premium that much has been reclaimed from the sea. Inland, north of the Kowloon ridge, are the New Territories, the focus of agriculture and rapidly expanding dormitory towns. *Highest point* Tai Mo Shan 957 metres (3,140 feet). *Area* 2,916 sq km (1,130 sq miles).
PEOPLE *Population* 5.7m. *Density* 5,364 per sq km. *Ethnic groups* Chinese 97%, British 0.5%.
RELIGION Buddhist 18%, Christian 18%, Taoist 14%, Confucian.
LANGUAGE Chinese, mainly Cantonese, and English.
EDUCATION Education is free and almost universal for ages 6–14. There are 2 universities.
CLIMATE Sub-tropical, with an annual average temperature of 21°C (70°F) and a rainfall of 2,160mm (85ins), more than half of which falls in Jun–Aug. Winters are dry and sunny, summers humid.
CURRENCY Hong Kong dollar.
PUBLIC HOLIDAYS Jan 1, Chinese New Year, Easter, Apr 5, Queen's Official Birthday, Tuen Ng, last Sat and Mon in Aug, Aug 29, Mid-Autumn festival, Chung Yeung festival, Dec. 25–27.
GOVERNMENT UK dependent territory. It is administered by a British-appointed governor with a nominated executive council and a legislative council of 57 members.

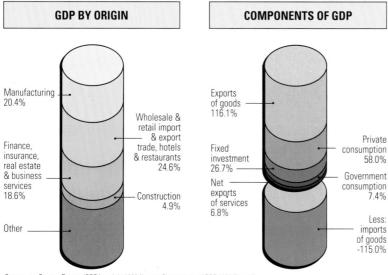

GDP BY ORIGIN

Manufacturing 20.4%
Finance, insurance, real estate & business services 18.6%
Other
Wholesale & retail import & export trade, hotels & restaurants 24.6%
Construction 4.9%

COMPONENTS OF GDP

Exports of goods 116.1%
Fixed investment 26.7%
Net exports of services 6.8%
Private consumption 58.0%
Government consumption 7.4%
Less: imports of goods -115.0%

Source: EIU *Country Report* (GDP by origin 1988 figures; Components of GDP 1989 figures).

IMPORTS AND EXPORTS

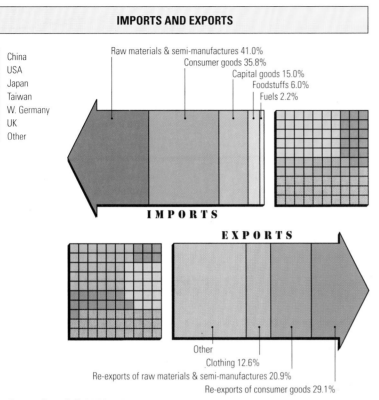

China
USA
Japan
Taiwan
W. Germany
UK
Other

Raw materials & semi-manufactures 41.0%
Consumer goods 35.8%
Capital goods 15.0%
Foodstuffs 6.0%
Fuels 2.2%

IMPORTS

EXPORTS

Other
Clothing 12.6%
Re-exports of raw materials & semi-manufactures 20.9%
Re-exports of consumer goods 29.1%

Source: EIU *Country Profile* (1989 figures).

ECONOMIC PROFILE

No resources save deep-water port and people, so trade is mainstay and ingenuity in adding value is crucial. Manufacturing – garments, electronics, toys, plastics – developed only in post-war years and is beset by high costs. Services, especially banking and tourism, now strong.

Growth Upswing in activities oriented towards China: trade, particularly booming entrepôt trade between China and other countries; industrial subcontracting to Chinese labour; provision of services and technology. Construction, printing and publishing also thriving.

Problems Uncertainty about future leading to drain of skills and investment. Many raw materials and most food and water are imported, largely from China. Land is short and has to be reclaimed from the sea. Several industries past competitive peak; shipping fleet mothballed because of world contraction. Offshore currency markets favour Singapore.

most of its food and water as well as many raw materials. And much of Hong Kong's recent prosperity is based on the efforts of refugees who, following the creation in 1949 of the People's Republic of China, exchanged communism for the *laissez-faire* policies of a British colonial government that viewed the territory primarily as a free port. Hong Kong has become the world's biggest container port, largest garment exporter and tenth biggest trader. GDP per head is the highest in Asia after Japan and Brunei.

Trading, especially as an entrepôt, was the mainstay of the economy until the mid-1950s, when it began to be replaced by manufacturing – firstly of textiles, then of electronics. Since the mid-1980s most new manufacturing investment has been in the neighbouring Chinese province of Guangdong, where labour costs are lower; Hong Kong's continuing industrial growth has been based on re-exports of Chinese origin. Financial services have emerged as the new engine of growth. Hong Kong is now one of the world's largest financial centres.

Government intervention in the economy is minimal and restricted mainly to the provision of support services. Housing and transport are particular areas of achievement. Half the population lives in public housing, while the mass-transit railway is one of the most advanced in the world.

The Chinese, who form 97% of the population, have begun taking over many old British firms. Australian, American and, particularly, Japanese corporations also began investing during the 1980s. After the June 1989 Tiananmen Square massacre in Beijing, the pace of investment noticeably slowed. Emigration, especially of professionals, speeded up. The British government's controversial 1990 decision to give 50,000 "key" personnel and their dependents the "emergency exit" of a full British passport was aimed at stemming the loss. China also attempted to provide verbal reassurance, but confidence that it would honour its pledges after 1997 has been severely jolted. Hong Kong is traditionally a place where quick returns are expected, so a litmus test of Tiananmen's longer-term effects will be investment levels after 1993.

BALANCE OF PAYMENTS

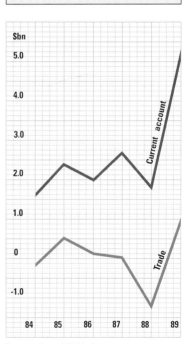

Source: EIU *Economic Risk Service*.

TAIWAN

Taiwan has been one of the economic miracles of the post-war years. An island about the size of the Netherlands, overcrowded and with no significant natural resources, it has achieved astonishing rates of economic growth. Most extraordinary of all, this prosperity has been created under the rule of a government founded on a political fantasy. The ruling nationalist party, the Kuomintang (KMT), claims to be the legitimate ruler of all of China, from the Spratly Islands in the South China Sea to Tibet.

The roots of this bizarre and forlorn claim lie in the Chinese civil war. In the late 1940s, as defeat loomed at the hands of the communists, the KMT under General Chiang Kai-shek, fled the mainland. During the two years that culminated in the foundation of the communist People's Republic of China in 1949 more than 1.5m soldiers, officials, camp followers and others descended on the former Japanese colony, then known as Formosa. The new regime, styling itself the Republic of China, was greeted with much resentment by the island's 8m native Taiwanese, and imposed with considerable brutality.

The dream of a return to the mainland has gradually faded and from unpromising beginnings the KMT has built an economic success. A far-sighted land reform in the 1950s created the agricultural basis for rapid industrialization. From the 1960s labour-intensive manufacturing became the cornerstone of the economy, fuelling an export boom that helped sustain impressive growth rates. From 1953 to 1989, Taiwan's annual average GDP growth was 8.8%. The authoritarian KMT has progressively reformed itself, and in 1987 lifted the 40-year-old state of martial law.

By the late 1980s the economy was dominated by foreign trade and manufacturing. Exports account for 50% of current GDP; nearly all exports are manufactures. Taiwan's success was built behind protective tariff barriers, and with an undervalued currency. Growing dependence on the US market, however, exposed Taiwan to pressure to reform its trading practices. In 1987 it responded with wide-ranging tariff cuts and plans for economic restructuring and liberalization. The aim is to move Taiwan upmarket, into consumer electronics and the bottom end of the information technology industry.

OFFICIAL NAME Republic of China.

CAPITAL CITY Taipei.

GEOGRAPHY An eroded central mountain range running roughly north-south plunges steeply into the sea on the east coast but gives way gradually on the west to populous terraced tablelands and alluvial plains. The west coast is lined with lagoons and sand dunes. *Highest point* Hsin-kao Shan 3,997 metres (13,110 feet). *Area* 36,000 sq km (13,900 sq miles).

PEOPLE *Population* 19.9m. *Density* 552 per sq km. *Ethnic groups* Han Chinese 98%, Indonesian 2%.

RELIGION Buddhist 43%, Taoist 21%, Christian 7%.

LANGUAGE Mandarin Chinese. Also local dialects.

EDUCATION Free and compulsory for ages 6–15. There are 16 universities.

CLIMATE Sub-tropical, moderated by the Kuroshio current, giving long warm summers averaging 25–30°C (77–86°F) and mild winters with a mean of 15°C (59°F). Average rainfall is 2,500mm (100ins), around double that in the eastern highlands; typhoon season is Jul–Sep.

CURRENCY New Taiwan dollar.

PUBLIC HOLIDAYS Jan 1, Chinese New Year, Mar 29, Apr 5, Dragon Boat festival, mid-autumn Moon festival, Sep 28, Oct 10, 25, 31, Nov 1–2, Dec 25.

GOVERNMENT Republic. The head of state and chief executive is a president, elected for a 6-year term by the National Assembly, which is dominated by life-term members, as is the main legislative body.

IMPORTS AND EXPORTS

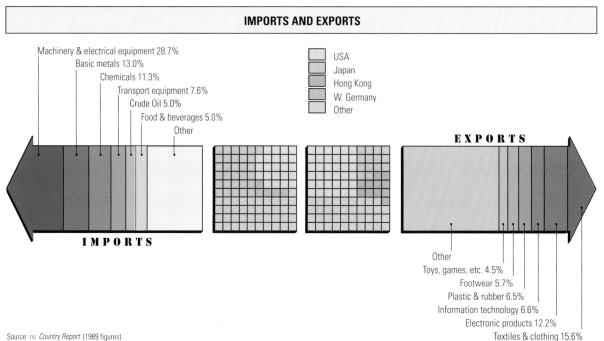

Machinery & electrical equipment 28.7%
Basic metals 13.0%
Chemicals 11.3%
Transport equipment 7.6%
Crude Oil 5.0%
Food & beverages 5.0%
Other

USA
Japan
Hong Kong
W. Germany
Other

IMPORTS

EXPORTS

Other
Toys, games, etc. 4.5%
Footwear 5.7%
Plastic & rubber 6.5%
Information technology 6.6%
Electronic products 12.2%
Textiles & clothing 15.6%

Source: EIU *Country Report* (1989 figures).

With huge reserves of foreign exchange, negligible foreign debt and a versatile and educated workforce, Taiwan is well equipped to make this transition. Living standards have risen fast enough to sustain a soaring import bill. New freedom to remit foreign currency has led to an accumulation of foreign assets. The main threats to its prosperity are beyond Taiwan's control: recession or protectionism in the United States, and – although less acute now – mainland intervention. For all its economic progress, Taiwan remains a diplomatic pariah, recognized by only a handful of countries. China has shifted from threats to the blandishments of a "one country, two systems" approach to encourage Taiwan back into the pan-Chinese fold. But Taiwan's rulers and, as far as can be judged, its people remain adamant in favouring international political isolation to reunification.

ECONOMIC PROFILE

Transformed in 40 years from producer of rice and sugar to an economy reliant on manufacturing. Labour-intensive food processing, textiles, garments, toy and plastic products industries giving way to more automated industries.

Growth Electronics and computers overtaking food processing industries as

leading contributors to GDP, although textiles holding their own and increasing value added.

Problems Creaking financial system; state-owned banks being gradually privatized. Environment ravaged by rapid industrialization; pollution control becoming a major political issue and extra cost to investors.

GDP GROWTH

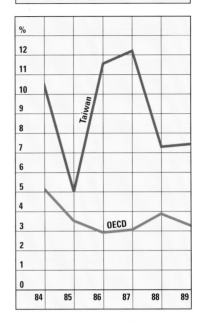

Source: OECD *Main Economic Indicators, National Accounts;* EIU *Country Report.*

GDP BY ORIGIN

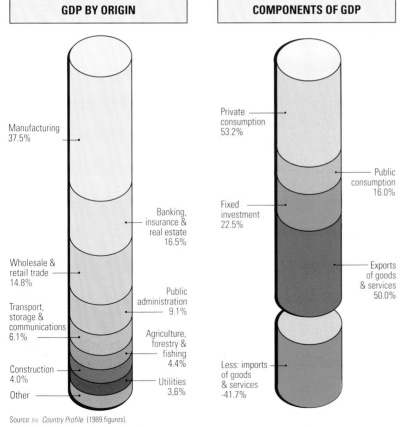

Manufacturing 37.5%

Banking, insurance & real estate 16.5%

Wholesale & retail trade 14.8%

Public administration 9.1%

Transport, storage & communications 6.1%

Agriculture, forestry & fishing 4.4%

Construction 4.0%

Utilities 3,6%

Other

Source: EIU *Country Profile* (1989 figures).

COMPONENTS OF GDP

Private consumption 53.2%

Public consumption 16.0%

Fixed investment 22.5%

Exports of goods & services 50.0%

Less: imports of goods & services -41.7%

BALANCE OF PAYMENTS

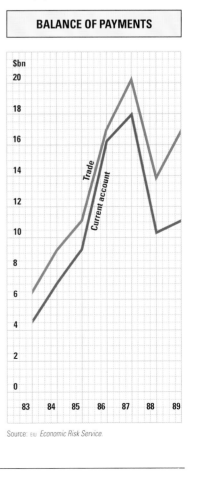

Source: EIU *Economic Risk Service.*

JAPAN

Japan was the first country outside Europe and the USA to adopt modern capitalism. It has been so successful that its average income level is now higher than that of the USA. This is despite a social structure quite different from that of Western countries, and based on Confucian family values. Japan also cut itself off for 200 years, until the mid-19th century, helped by the 150km of sea that separates it from the Asian mainland.

The physical nature of the land makes Japan distinctive in other ways. It is subject to earthquakes and so mountainous that only one-sixth of the area can be farmed or lived on, making the population density twice that of Europe and providing the rationale for Japan's concern for social harmony. Another consequence of land shortage is that the average farm is very small, necessitating cooperative rather than individual or household cultivation. This has resulted in a surprisingly uncompetitive agricultural sector. Over a quarter of food has to be imported.

Conscious westernization began in the 1870s. When Japan joined the victors of the first world war, having already separately vanquished China and Tsarist Russia and annexed Taiwan and Korea as spoils, it expected recognition as an equal. Instead, it was snubbed at the Versailles peace conference and at the subsequent negotiations to balance the Pacific navies. Militarists took over in the 1930s, establishing a fascist regime at home and attacking China and South-East Asia. The bombing of Pearl Harbor in 1941 triggered total US involvement in the second world war and, ultimately, the atom bombs on Hiroshima and Nagasaki.

After the war, the Japanese threw themselves into the work of pursuing their economic hopes, helped by US occupation reforms: land redistribution, the break-up of monopolies, multi-party parliamentary democracy (under a figurehead emperor) and the rule of law. The almost complete lack of natural resources meant a high dependence on foreign trade. Japan became of necessity the most successful exporting nation as well as, eventually, the world's biggest foreign investor with the largest foreign exchange reserves.

Political stability underpinned these achievements; the conservative Liberal Democratic Party (LDP) has ruled since 1948. Socialist, Communist and Buddhist Clean Government opposition parties have shown few signs of being able to win power, although in 1989 it seemed briefly that LDP dominance might be threatened when scandal forced the resignation of two prime ministers in just

OFFICIAL NAME Nihon.

CAPITAL CITY Tokyo.

GEOGRAPHY The archipelago has four main islands – Honshu, Shikoku, Kyushu and Hokkaido – and about 4,000 small ones. It lies on a fault line and there are more than 1,000 earth tremors annually, and occasional major quakes. Two-thirds of the land area is mountainous and thickly forested; only 15% of the country, mostly the coastal plains, is cultivable, and is intensively exploited for largely arable agriculture. Industrial and urban development is concentrated in a strip along Honshu's south coast. *Highest point* Mt Fuji 3,776 metres (12,390 feet). *Area* 372,313 sq km (143,750 sq miles).

PEOPLE *Population* 122.8m. Over 75% urbanized. *Density* 325 per sq km; 1,500 per sq km if uninhabitable areas are excluded. *Ethnic groups* Japanese 99%.

RELIGION Shinto 87%, Buddhist 73% (most Japanese profess both).

LANGUAGE Japanese.

EDUCATION Compulsory for ages 6–15, with plans to increase the leaving age to 18. A third of school-leavers go to one of more than 400 universities.

CLIMATE Pacific coast has hot, humid summers and cold, dry winters. Sea of Japan coast has heavy winter snowfalls. Hokkaido has very cold winters, down to -10°C (14°F), and short, warm summers. Southern Kyushu is sub-tropical.

CURRENCY Yen.

PUBLIC HOLIDAYS Jan 1, 15, Feb 11, Mar 21, Apr 29, May 3, 5, Sep 15, 23, Oct 10, Nov 3, 23, Dec 23.

GOVERNMENT Constitutional monarchy. The emperor is head of state. Executive power is vested in a cabinet and prime minister. The 512-member House of Representatives is elected for 4 years, and its decisions are largely rubber-stamped by the 252-member House of Councillors.

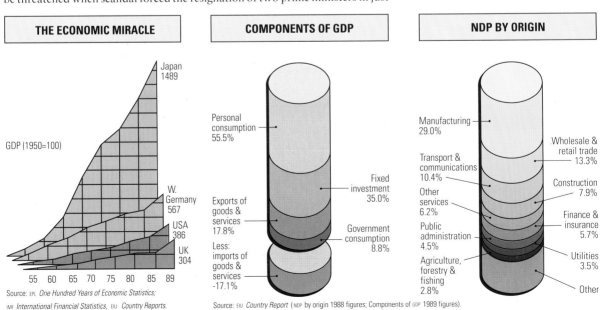

THE ECONOMIC MIRACLE

GDP (1950=100)

Japan 1489
W. Germany 567
USA 386
UK 304

55 60 65 70 75 80 85 89

Source: EPL *One Hundred Years of Economic Statistics*; IMF *International Financial Statistics*, EIU *Country Reports*.

COMPONENTS OF GDP

Personal consumption 55.5%
Exports of goods & services 17.8%
Less: imports of goods & services -17.1%
Fixed investment 35.0%
Government consumption 8.8%

NDP BY ORIGIN

Manufacturing 29.0%
Transport & communications 10.4%
Other services 6.2%
Public administration 4.5%
Agriculture, forestry & fishing 2.8%
Wholesale & retail trade 13.3%
Construction 7.9%
Finance & insurance 5.7%
Utilities 3.5%
Other

Source: EIU *Country Report* (NDP by origin 1988 figures; Components of GDP 1989 figures).

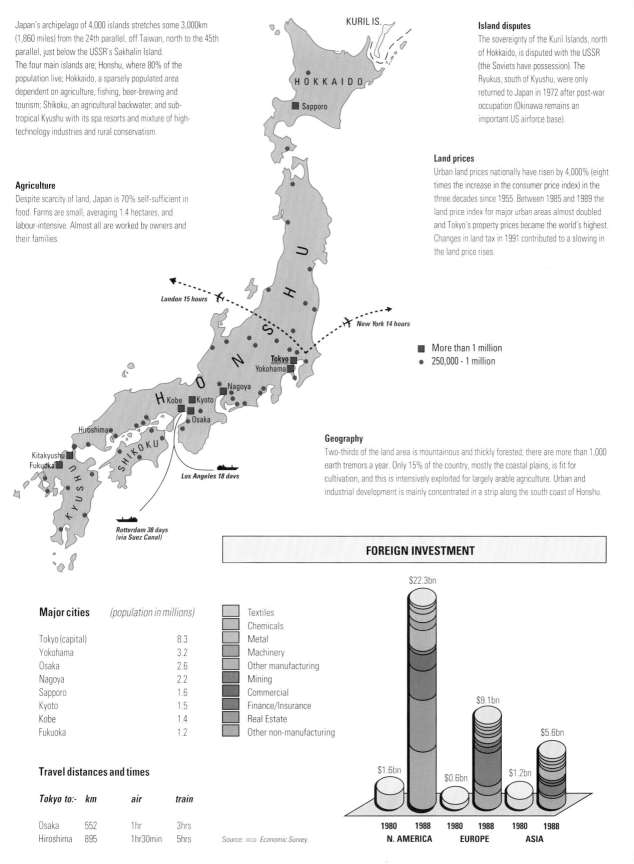

Japan's archipelago of 4,000 islands stretches some 3,000km (1,860 miles) from the 24th parallel, off Taiwan, north to the 45th parallel, just below the USSR's Sakhalin Island. The four main islands are; Honshu, where 80% of the population live; Hokkaido, a sparsely populated area dependent on agriculture, fishing, beer-brewing and tourism; Shikoku, an agricultural backwater; and sub-tropical Kyushu with its spa resorts and mixture of high-technology industries and rural conservatism.

Agriculture

Despite scarcity of land, Japan is 70% self-sufficient in food. Farms are small, averaging 1.4 hectares, and labour-intensive. Almost all are worked by owners and their families.

KURIL IS.

HOKKAIDO

■ Sapporo

H O N S H U

London 15 hours

New York 14 hours

Tokyo ■
Yokohama

Nagoya

Kobe ■ Kyoto
Osaka

Hiroshima

Kitakyushu ■
Fukuoka

SHIKOKU

Los Angeles 18 days

KYUSHU

Rotterdam 38 days
(via Suez Canal)

■ More than 1 million
● 250,000 - 1 million

Island disputes

The sovereignty of the Kuril Islands, north of Hokkaido, is disputed with the USSR (the Soviets have possession). The Ryukus, south of Kyushu, were only returned to Japan in 1972 after post-war occupation (Okinawa remains an important US airforce base).

Land prices

Urban land prices nationally have risen by 4,000% (eight times the increase in the consumer price index) in the three decades since 1955. Between 1985 and 1989 the land price index for major urban areas almost doubled and Tokyo's property prices became the world's highest. Changes in land tax in 1991 contributed to a slowing in the land price rises.

Geography

Two-thirds of the land area is mountainous and thickly forested; there are more than 1,000 earth tremors a year. Only 15% of the country, mostly the coastal plains, is fit for cultivation, and this is intensively exploited for largely arable agriculture. Urban and industrial development is mainly concentrated in a strip along the south coast of Honshu.

FOREIGN INVESTMENT

Major cities	(population in millions)
Tokyo (capital)	8.3
Yokohama	3.2
Osaka	2.6
Nagoya	2.2
Sapporo	1.6
Kyoto	1.5
Kobe	1.4
Fukuoka	1.2

Textiles
Chemicals
Metal
Machinery
Other manufacturing
Mining
Commercial
Finance/Insurance
Real Estate
Other non-manufacturing

$22.3bn

$9.1bn

$5.6bn

$1.6bn

$0.6bn

$1.2bn

Travel distances and times

Tokyo to:-	km	air	train
Osaka	552	1hr	3hrs
Hiroshima	895	1hr30min	5hrs

Source: OECD Economic Survey.

1980	1988	1980	1988	1980	1988
N. AMERICA		EUROPE		ASIA	

five months, and temporarily boosted support for the Socialists. External stability is provided by the USA-Japan Security Treaty, under which the Americans guarantee Japan's defence in the light of the (American-drafted) post-war constitution, which renounces war and the use of force in foreign relations. Until the 1980s spending on the Self-Defence Forces, as they are called, was kept below 1% of national income (though this was still enough to make Japan one of the world's biggest spenders on defence). Even after this self-restraint was officially breached by Prime Minister Yasuhiro Nakasone in 1986, Japan's military profile remained far lower than that of other countries. Whether pacifism is entrenched in public life, or whether a new wave of militarism is on the horizon, is a matter of debate.

Japan's diffidence in security terms is matched by psychological unreadiness for a full international role. Few Japanese speak foreign languages well enough, or are ready to risk a career outside the familiar domestic mainstream, to staff world organizations like the UN. There is also a bedrock of racial prejudice, especially against blacks. Relations with neighbouring countries, notably the Koreas, China and South-East Asia, where there is some mutual awareness, are often sour. Reliance on imported materials nevertheless leads Japan to a low-key diplomacy that makes few enemies.

WORK FORCE

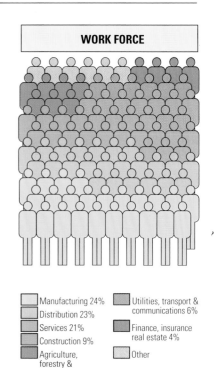

	Manufacturing 24%		Utilities, transport & communications 6%
	Distribution 23%		Finance, insurance real estate 4%
	Services 21%		
	Construction 9%		Other
	Agriculture, forestry & fishing 7%		

Source: EIU *Country Profile* (1988 figures).

ECONOMIC PROFILE

The world's most successful industrial nation, with steel, ships, motor vehicles and machinery as main products. Most manufactures exported. Until late 1980s few services sold abroad, but now annual exports exceed $50 billion. Invests $140 billion of long-term capital abroad annually, the most in the world. Agriculture only 3% of GDP, producing mainly rice. Fishing fleet is world's largest.

Growth Information technology is fastest growing industry, along with deregulated telecommunications and financial markets. Banking and securities now moving to foreign centres as well. Atomic energy has doubled capacity in five years to make

Japan the fourth largest nuclear generating power. Construction booming.

Problems Old industries like textiles, shipbuilding, steel and semi-conductors losing out to third world producers, especially South Korea and Taiwan. Even Japanese passenger vehicles increasingly made by subsidiaries abroad. Shipping hit by world contraction. Lack of mineral and energy sources: world's largest oil importer. Timber inadequate as local forests inaccessible for exploitation.

IMPORTS AND EXPORTS

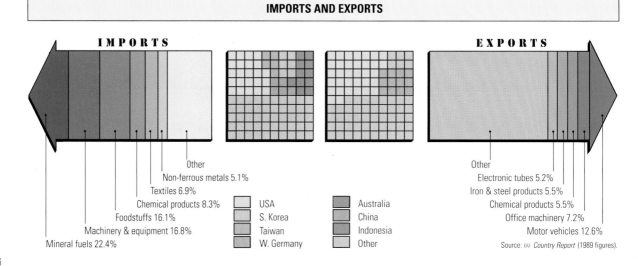

IMPORTS

Other
Non-ferrous metals 5.1%
Textiles 6.9%
Chemical products 8.3%
Foodstuffs 16.1%
Machinery & equipment 16.8%
Mineral fuels 22.4%

	USA		Australia
	S. Korea		China
	Taiwan		Indonesia
	W. Germany		Other

EXPORTS

Other
Electronic tubes 5.2%
Iron & steel products 5.5%
Chemical products 5.5%
Office machinery 7.2%
Motor vehicles 12.6%

Source: EIU *Country Report* (1989 figures).

WAGES AND PRICES

1983=100

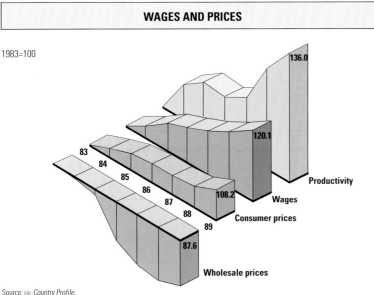

- 136.0 Productivity
- 120.1 Wages
- 108.2 Consumer prices
- 87.6 Wholesale prices

83 84 85 86 87 88 89

Source: EIU *Country Profile.*

GETTING OLDER

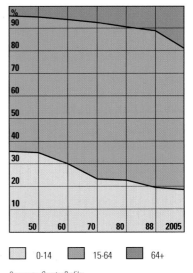

0-14   15-64   64+

Source: EIU *Country Profile;*
EPL *One Hundred Years of Economic Statistics.*

Longevity is yet another indicator of Japan's high standard of living but spells high welfare bills for the future.

Japan is subject to more international misunderstanding than any other important country. The language is highly ambiguous: attempting to avoid the impolite "no", a Japanese can mislead a foreigner into thinking he means "yes". Law is seen as a means of reconciling two parties, rather than of administering justice. Repression of the individual in the interests of the group – family, company, nation – is carried further than in most societies. The group ethic is thus the key to Japanese society, and one that not many foreigners comprehend. Lone pioneers like Akio Morita of Sony and Soichiro Honda are generally admired, but others in the literary and artistic fields, like Yukio Mishima, the *harakiri* novelist, are not. Decision by consensus, or by apparent consensus, is preferred to autocratic leadership. Life-long employment is on the wane, given technological advances and rapid changes in corporate structure, but is still expected by both sides of industry.

The world first became aware of Japan's "economic miracle" in 1964, when Tokyo hosted the Olympic Games. Since then Japanese industry has raced ahead, achieving leadership in electronic and automobile exports and alarming customers by the size of its trade surplus. The revaluation of the yen, which had been artificially held down, helped to check the imbalance, but complaints continue that the Japanese domestic market remains largely closed to Western and third world exports, despite tariff reductions and other liberalization measures in the 1980s. Deregulation of Tokyo's financial market began after 1985. An important consequence of the dearer yen was a flood of Japanese investment and tourism overseas, together with more aid to developing countries.

New problems confront Japan. As the population ages the welfare burden on industry and on the next generation of taxpaying employees is increasing. The work ethic is relaxing, with smaller families, financial affluence, the "leisure boom" and westernization. The education system, however outstanding, tends to discourage the creativity that the economy will need.

Import dependency, especially in oil, remains a worry. Industrial and commercial success itself brings its own frustrations, with higher costs and reduced international competitiveness, although Japanese corporations have so far proved skilful in absorbing the former. The national will that has driven Japan so far will be needed even more in future.

BALANCE OF PAYMENTS

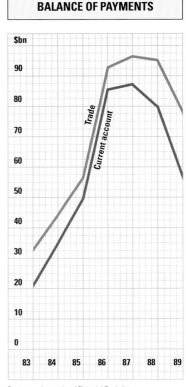

$bn

Trade

Current account

83 84 85 86 87 88 89

Source: IMF *International Financial Statistics.*

MYANMAR (BURMA)

In the 1950s Burma exported rice, teak and gems and was self-sufficient in oil. In 1987 the UN declared it a "least developed country". Rice was scarce and oil had to be imported. Burma's prosperity was a casualty of the mixture of Buddhism, isolationism and state control practised after the army took power in 1962.

The British colony became independent in 1948. The new government was immediately under attack from a host of guerrilla movements, and the memory of this period has haunted Burmese politics ever since. In 1962 the army, led by General Ne Win, overthrew the government. The military, which first ruled directly and then through the Burma Socialist Programme Party (BSPP), formed in 1974, has since been dominant. Under BSPP rule the formal economy, dominated by state monopolies, grew unresponsive.

A botched attempt at economic reform in 1987 sent prices soaring and set off an explosion of political protest. Mass demonstrations forced General Ne Win's resignation as party chairman in July 1988 and subsequently the reimposition of direct military rule. The military promised genuine reform and elections, but viciously suppressed the demonstrations. After pressure from Burma's main aid donors, elections were held in May 1990. The opposition won 392 of the 485 seats contested. But there seemed little likelihood of an early return to civilian rule. The military refused to cede power and the opposition, powerless to dislodge it, was forced to renounce the results and agree to a new transition agenda.

OFFICIAL NAME Union of Myanmar.
CAPITAL CITY Yangon (Rangoon).
GEOGRAPHY Most Burmese live in the valley and delta of the Irrawaddy, which is hemmed in on three sides by mountain ranges and steep plateaus. *Area* 676,552 sq km (261,220 sq miles).
PEOPLE *Population* 39.3m. *Density* 58 per sq km. *Ethnic groups* Burman 68%, Shan 7%, Karen 7%.
RELIGION Buddhist 87%, Christian 6%.
LANGUAGE Burmese. Also tribal languages.
EDUCATION Free where available, but non-compulsory.
CURRENCY Kyat.
PUBLIC HOLIDAYS Jan 4, Feb 12, Mar 2, 27, Maha Thingyan, Apr 17, May 1, Id al-Adha, July 19, Divali, Tazaungdaing Festival, National Day, Dec 3, 25, full moons in Mar, May, Aug and Oct.
GOVERNMENT Military-dominated republic. All executive power is held by the State Law and Order Restoration Council (Slorc). Political parties have been permitted since 1989.

THAILAND

Thailand alone in South-East Asia avoided colonization, a success which owes something to its famous national pragmatism. Since the 19th century its kings have been modernizers. In 1932 the monarchy gracefully accepted an end to absolutism when the military demanded it. A succession of military strongmen held sway for most of the next four decades, accommodating in turn the British, French, Japanese and Americans. An unprecedented popular explosion in 1973 introduced Thailand to democracy. But the military intervened in 1977, launching a coup – the 13th since 1932 – against a government it thought too right-wing.

"Semi-democracy" has since prevailed. The pillars of the system remain the monarchy, the military, the bureaucracy and the political parties; but the balance has changed. Reverence for the king has been the only constant, ensuring that his rare political interventions are decisive. The military has been less obtrusive, but still reserves the right to intervene. It claims credit for having blunted Vietnamese expansionism by luring home-grown communists out of the jungle, although schisms among the rebels were at least as important.

A former army commander, Prem Tinsulanond, enjoyed a record uninterrupted term as prime minister from 1980 to 1988. His successor Chartchai Choonhavan, a long-retired soldier with stronger business than military connections, became the first elected prime minister for 12 years. In February 1991, however, the military high-command, fearful that its prerogatives were being threatened, launched a successful coup. By harping on the undoubted venality of the civilian politicians and installing a cabinet of non-partisan technocrats the military won popular support for its move. The king's support was the final seal of approval.

Well into the 1960s Thailand's wealth rested on growing rice and exporting the surplus. The Vietnam war encouraged diversification into export crops, the development of infrastructure and the beginnings of a manufacturing base. By the mid-1980s political stability had helped Thailand become a favourite South-East Asian location for foreign manufacturers. Manufacturing has contributed more to GDP than agriculture since 1984. Textiles overtook rice as the leading

OFFICIAL NAME Kingdom of Thailand.
CAPITAL CITY Bangkok.
GEOGRAPHY The northern mountains, outriders of the Himalayas, extend along the western borders into the Malay peninsula. The east of the country is taken up by the Khorat plateau, 200 metres (650 feet) high, whose rolling terrain gives way to swampland along the Mekong river. In the heart of the country is a great fertile plain drained by the Chao Phraya river, whose wide delta contains the capital. *Highest point* Doi Inthanon 2,595 metres (8,510 feet). *Area* 513,115 sq km (198,115 sq miles).
PEOPLE *Population* 55.4m. *Density* 108 per sq km. *Ethnic groups* Thai 54%, Lao 28%, Chinese 11%, Malay 4%, Khmer 3%.
RELIGION Buddhist 95%, Muslim 4%.
LANGUAGE Thai.
EDUCATION Compulsory for ages 7–14.
CURRENCY Baht.
PUBLIC HOLIDAYS Jan 1, Magha Puja, Apr 6,13, Visakha Puja, May 5, Royal Ploughing Ceremony, Asalha Puja, Khao Phansa, Aug 12, Oct 23, Dec 5, 10, 31.
GOVERNMENT Constitutional monarchy. The king is head of state and appoints a prime minister on the advice of a bicameral National Assembly. The 268 members of the non-party Senate are appointed by the king for 6 years, while the 357 members of the House of Representatives are elected for a 4-year term.

GDP BY ORIGIN

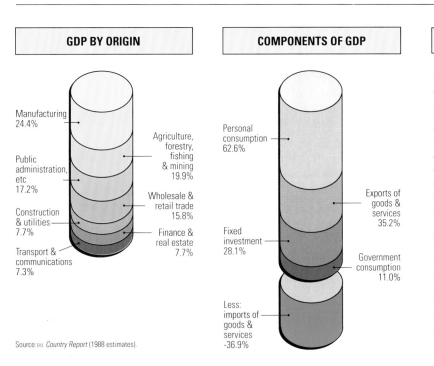

Manufacturing
24.4%

Public
administration,
etc
17.2%

Construction
& utilities
7.7%

Transport &
communications
7.3%

Agriculture,
forestry,
fishing
& mining
19.9%

Wholesale &
retail trade
15.8%

Finance &
real estate
7.7%

Source: EIU *Country Report* (1988 estimates).

COMPONENTS OF GDP

Personal
consumption
62.6%

Fixed
investment
28.1%

Less:
imports of
goods &
services
-36.9%

Exports of
goods &
services
35.2%

Government
consumption
11.0%

ECONOMIC PROFILE

Rice, mainstay of domestic economy and chief export, still covers half planted area, alongside newer crops like maize, sugar, tapioca. Other valuable commodity exports: rubber, tin, teak. Manufacturing is largely confined to food processing, with some consumer goods produced for domestic market. Export and heavy industries – cement, petrochemicals – are now developing.

Growth Foreign investment fuelling boom in labour-intensive export industries – textiles, electronics, shoes, toys – but tourism now leading foreign exchange earner. Automobile sector increasing level of local content and moving into regional exports. Large natural gas discoveries offer chance to end dependence on imported oil.

Problems Inadequate infrastructure a constraint on growth. Education system not coping with expanding demand for skilled labour. Rice no longer a reliable earner in glutted world market; new exports face quota problems. Forests destroyed by uncontrolled logging.

export in 1985.

For all their recent successes, the Thais are handicapped in their attempt to emulate South Korea in a dash for growth. Economic activity remains focused on the kingdom's traditional hub, Bangkok, and the central plain. With a population of 8m, Bangkok Metropolis is 40 times larger than any other Thai city. Its clogged port and overloaded telephone and road systems are symptomatic of an infrastructure pushed beyond its limits by rapid growth. New investment and the dispersion of economic activity have become urgent priorities that will test the capacity, and ultimately the stability, of Thailand's political system.

IMPORTS AND EXPORTS

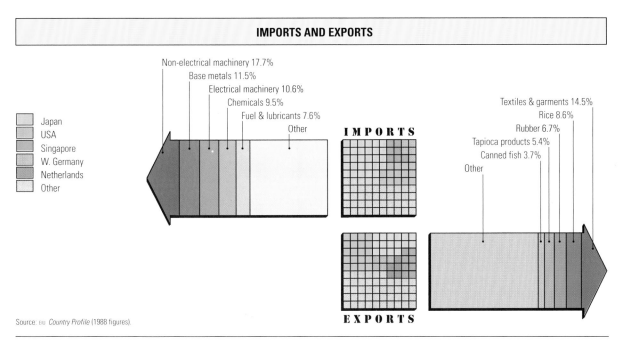

Non-electrical machinery 17.7%

Base metals 11.5%

Electrical machinery 10.6%

Chemicals 9.5%

Fuel & lubricants 7.6%

Other

IMPORTS

Japan
USA
Singapore
W. Germany
Netherlands
Other

Textiles & garments 14.5%

Rice 8.6%

Rubber 6.7%

Tapioca products 5.4%

Canned fish 3.7%

Other

EXPORTS

Source: EIU *Country Profile* (1988 figures).

ASIA

LAOS

Mountainous, landlocked, sparsely populated, Laos is one of geography's victims. For centuries it suffered from the competing ambitions of Thailand and Vietnam. The French colonized it for strategic reasons. After they left in 1953, Laos endured two decades of civil war, aggravated by the wider regional conflict. The communist Pathet Lao movement brought stability when it took power in 1975, but also isolation and further stagnation. Now GDP per head is among the world's lowest; 85% of the population are subsistence farmers.

After 1975 Vietnam kept a large military contingent in Laos and packed ministries with advisers. Late in 1986, the Laotian politburo announced a version of *perestroika*. The chief consequence has been commercial openings to Thailand and China, reducing dependence on Vietnam. Moves to lessen state control have seen over 80% of public enterprises made autonomous of the central planning system. Recent plans to encourage alternative crops to opium (in 1989 Laos was ranked third largest producer) have improved relations with the USA.

OFFICIAL NAME Lao People's Democratic Republic.
CAPITAL CITY Vientiane.
GEOGRAPHY The population is concentrated on the east bank of the Mekong and the Bolovens plateau in the south. *Area* 236,800 sq km (91,400 sq miles).
PEOPLE *Population* 3.9m. *Density* 16 per sq km. *Ethnic groups* Lao 99%.
RELIGION Buddhist 58%, Animist.
LANGUAGE Lao. Also local languages.
EDUCATION Free; state sector only.
CURRENCY New Kip.
PUBLIC HOLIDAYS Apr 13–15, May 1, Dec 2.
GOVERNMENT Communist republic since 1975. The president is head of state, exercising executive power through a council of ministers. The legislative, 79-member Supreme People's Assembly, is elected for a 5-year term. The Lao People's Revolutionary Party is the only legal party.

VIETNAM

When Vietnam's northern and southern halves were reunited in 1976 the country became the world's third most populous communist nation. A decade later it was still burdened by war, against Cambodia rather than France or the USA, and remained frustrated in its centuries-old struggle for effective independence.

The 1978 invasion of Cambodia made Vietnam a Soviet dependent, crippling the diplomatic opening to the West implicit in Vietnam's 1976 application to join the IMF. Doctrinaire policies compounded economic isolation, inhibiting recovery from the war.

Reform was the watchword after the 1986 party congress, but an en-trenched bureaucracy ensured that economic change, though real, was halting. The generous 1988 foreign investment code aroused some interest, but an economic breakthrough depends on the successful conclusion of a settlement in Cambodia and the USA lifting its trade embargo.

OFFICIAL NAME Socialist Republic of Vietnam.
CAPITAL CITY Hanoi.
GEOGRAPHY Most is mountainous rain forest, apart from river deltas in the north and south and a coastal plain. *Area* 329,566 sq km (127,246 sq miles).
PEOPLE *Population* 64.4m. *Density* 195 per sq km. *Ethnic groups* Vietnamese 88%, Chinese 2%, Thai 2%.
RELIGION Buddhist 55%, Christian 8%.
LANGUAGE Vietnamese. Also French and English.
EDUCATION Free for ages 6–16.
CURRENCY New dong.
PUBLIC HOLIDAYS Jan 1, Feb 3, Apr 7, 30, May 1, Sep 2–3, Tet.
GOVERNMENT Communist republic since 1976. The Communist Party of Vietnam is the only permitted party. A 496-member National Assembly, elected every 5 years, is the highest state authority. It elects an executive council of ministers and a council of state and must approve all domestic and foreign policy.

CAMBODIA

Once the "gentle kingdom" – isolated, but blessed with rich soils and the largest freshwater lake in South-East Asia – Cambodia (Kampuchea) has recently gained an altogether different reputation, thanks to the genocidal policies of the Khmer Rouge. After their overthrow in 1979 by Vietnam, civil war ensued between the People's Republic of Kampuchea, installed and sustained by Vietnam, and the tripartite Coalition Government of Democratic Kampuchea, of which the Khmer Rouge was the strongest component. The coalition had international recognition and support from China, the USA and Asean. Its most acceptable face was Prince Norodom Sihanouk.

By the late 1980s the economy was barely subsisting on rice. Child mortality was higher only in Afghanistan. Increasingly denied aid and credits, even by the Eastern bloc, trade dwindled to a trickle. Fears of a Khmer Rouge takeover, in the wake of Vietnam's 1988–89 troop withdrawal, generated sufficient superpower pressure to bring the Cambodian parties to agreement in September 1990 on a UN interim administration in the country.

OFFICIAL NAME State of Cambodia.
CAPITAL CITY Phnom Penh.
GEOGRAPHY Around 90% of Cambodians live on the low alluvial plain around the Mekong and Tonle Sap Lake. East of the Mekong the land climbs gradually to forested mountains and plateaus. *Area* 181,035 sq km (69,898 sq miles).
PEOPLE *Population* 7.7m. *Density* 42 per sq km. *Ethnic groups* Khmer 93%, Vietnamese 4%, Chinese 3%.
RELIGION Buddhist 88%, Muslim 2%, Christian 1%.
LANGUAGE Khmer.
CURRENCY Riel.
PUBLIC HOLIDAYS Jan 7, New Year, Apr 17, May 1, Sep 22.
GOVERNMENT Under 1981 constitution legislative power is vested in a 123-member National Assembly, elected for a 5-year term. The assembly elects an executive council of state, whose chairman is head of state, and an administrative council of ministers.

MALAYSIA

By the late 1980s Malaysia's ambition to become a newly industrializing country before the turn of the century looked within reach. Already an upper middle-income country (in World Bank parlance), with GNP per head approaching US$2,000, Malaysia is modestly populated and endowed with abundant natural resources. The world's largest producer of rubber and palm oil, and the second largest of tin, it has also begun to exploit its plentiful oil and timber reserves. Successful diversification into resource processing and export industries after 1960 made manufacturing a key economic sector. A foray into heavy industrialization followed, with Japan and the East Asian "Little Dragons" consciously adopted as models.

Complicated politics clouds this considerable economic good fortune. Malaysia owes its intricate patchwork of races and religions largely to the British, who in the 19th century imported Chinese and Indians to work the tin mines and rubber estates of the Malay peninsula. The Muslim Malays remained in the majority but were economically marginalized. In 1963 the 11 peninsular states of Malaya joined with the predominantly tribal Borneo states of Sarawak and Sabah, 530km (330 miles) across the South China Sea, and the overwhelmingly Chinese island of Singapore to form the federation of Malaysia. It was a potentially explosive ethnic configuration.

Three times since independence in 1957 the delicate social fabric has looked in danger of unravelling. After independence the three-party Alliance, representing the three main ethnic groups, continued to hold power, dominated by the United Malays National Organisation (UMNO). The principle of Malay hegemony was vigorously challenged by Lee Kuan Yew in 1965; Singapore was asked to leave the federation. Four years later, in the heated aftermath of a general election, serious race riots in Kuala Lumpur shocked the communities into a new consensus. This involved a broadened governing coalition, the National Front, agreement to avoid sensitive debate and the New Economic Policy (NEP), which aimed to increase the share of corporate holdings in Malay hands to 30% by 1990.

The third challenge to the system was posed when the hard-driving Dr

OFFICIAL NAME Federation of Malaysia.

CAPITAL CITY Kuala Lumpur.

GEOGRAPHY Malaysia consists of a mountainous peninsula and the northern part of the island of Borneo. Almost three-quarters of the land area is tropical rain forest or swamp forest. The majority of the peninsular population is concentrated on the wider western coastal plain, where short, swift rivers flood seasonally. Villages on stilts and colonial cities built on rubber and tin fortunes are typical settlements on the peninsula. The territories in Borneo of Sarawak and Sabah are rugged and forested, and are predominantly rural, with the few cities mostly populated by Chinese. *Highest point* Mt Kinabalu 4,101 metres (13,450 feet). *Area* 329,749 sq km (127,320 sq miles), of which the peninsula is 131,587 sq km (50,810 sq miles).

PEOPLE *Population* 16.9m. *Density* 51 per sq km. *Ethnic groups* Malay and other indigenous 60%, Chinese 31%, Indian, Pakistani and Bangladeshi 8%.

RELIGION Muslim 53%, Buddhist 17%, Chinese folk religions 12%, Hindu 7%, Christian 6%.

LANGUAGE Malay. Also Chinese, English, Tamil, Iban Dusun, Bajan and other local dialects.

EDUCATION Free for ages 6–19. Education takes up 18% of government spending. There are 7 universities.

CURRENCY Ringgit.

PUBLIC HOLIDAYS Chinese New Year, Hari Rya Puasa, May 1, 9, 15th day of 4th Moon, Birthday of HM the Yang di-Pertuan Agong, 1st Wednesday in Jun, Hari Raya Haji, Muharram, Aug 31, Mouloud, Deepavali, Dec 25.

GOVERNMENT Federation of 13 states and 1 federal territory (Kuala Lumpur). Nine of the states have hereditary monarchs and these elect one of their number head of state for 5 years. The legislature has 2 houses: the 177 members of the Dewan Rakyat are elected for 5 years; the Dewan Negara has 58 members, 26 elected by the state assemblies and the remainder royal appointees. Executive power is held by the prime minister and cabinet, responsible to the legislature.

IMPORTS AND EXPORTS

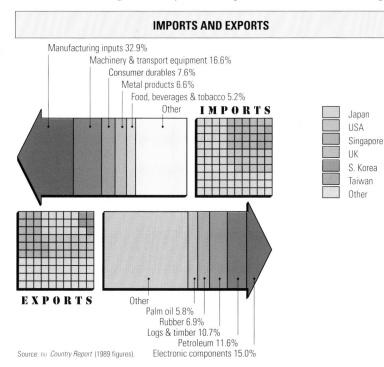

Manufacturing inputs 32.9%
Machinery & transport equipment 16.6%
Consumer durables 7.6%
Metal products 6.6%
Food, beverages & tobacco 5.2%
Other
IMPORTS

Japan
USA
Singapore
UK
S. Korea
Taiwan
Other

EXPORTS
Other
Palm oil 5.8%
Rubber 6.9%
Logs & timber 10.7%
Petroleum 11.6%
Electronic components 15.0%

Source: EIU *Country Report* (1989 figures).

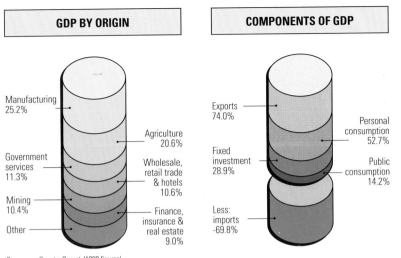

GDP BY ORIGIN

Manufacturing 25.2%

Government services 11.3%

Mining 10.4%

Other

Agriculture 20.6%

Wholesale, retail trade & hotels 10.6%

Finance, insurance & real estate 9.0%

Source: EIU *Country Report* (1989 figures).

COMPONENTS OF GDP

Exports 74.0%

Fixed investment 28.9%

Less: imports -69.8%

Personal consumption 52.7%

Public consumption 14.2%

ECONOMIC PROFILE

Rubber and tin traditional mainstays, with rice providing subsistence base. Later supplemented by crude oil, timber and palm oil, and manufactured exports – local resource-based, electronics, textiles. Drive to create heavy industries – the "national car", steel, cement – giving way to emphasis on secondary sector products.

Growth Still scope for expansion in wood and latex-based industries. Coal and petrochemicals in early stages of major development programmes; tin emerging from 1985 crash. Several major construction projects – highways, gas pipeline and refinery – to run into 1990s.

Problems Palm oil and cocoa production nearing their limits. Healthy trade surplus eroded by services deficit caused by inadequate domestic shipping, port and insurance facilities. Rice losing out to export crops and imports rising.

Mahathir Mohamad became prime minister in 1981, the first Malay commoner to hold the office. Amid mounting resentment of the NEP in all communities and growing doubts about the government's industrialization plans, the economy slowed in 1985. The National Front lost much of the Chinese vote in the 1986 general election. The following year Dr Mahathir narrowly survived a challenge to his leadership of UMNO from the aristocratic former finance minister Tengku Razaleigh Hamzah, who then split away to form a new, multi-ethnic opposition coalition, Semangat '46.

The split seemed to presage the breakdown of the old system. But Dr Mahathir retained the upper hand over his rival, despite growing criticism of his autocratic style. Using his control of the state apparatus he held the loyalty of two key elements of the Malay community: the bureaucracy and the farmers. An easing of economic pressures also helped, with export demand, investment and growth recovering and the government taking a more pragmatic approach to achieving the NEP's targets.

BRUNEI

Oil and gas, which account for some 70% of GDP and 99% of exports, have restored Brunei's fortunes. The once mighty Malay sultanate had fallen on hard times when Royal Dutch/Shell found oil at Seria in 1929. Its lowest point was in the 19th century, when the British made it a protectorate, squeezed into the present two small enclaves.

Independence came in 1984 and power has remained firmly in the hands of the sultan's family, although a few technocrats have been brought in lower down the political ladder. Deployment of the sultanate's wealth abroad has sometimes looked feckless, but opportunities for spending on domestic economic diversification are limited. Earnings from overseas investments now comfortably exceed oil and gas revenues.

Limited political activity has been permitted since independence, but parties have failed to flourish. Government employees, about two-thirds of the labour force, are banned from political activity. The ordinary Bruneian – enjoying the benefits of a womb-to-tomb welfare state and undemanding public-sector employment – has proved indifferent to politics.

OFFICIAL NAME Sultanate of Brunei.

CAPITAL CITY Bandar Seri Begawan.

GEOGRAPHY Settlements are confined to the river valleys and a narrow coastal plain, where mangrove swamps separate fertile areas of peat and alluvium. *Area* 5,765 sq km (2,230 sq miles).

PEOPLE *Population* 233,800. *Density* 41 per sq km. *Ethnic groups* Malay 65%, Chinese 20%.

RELIGION Muslim 65%, also Buddhist and Christian.

LANGUAGE Malay. Also Chinese and English.

EDUCATION Free and along Islamic lines.

CURRENCY Brunei dollar.

PUBLIC HOLIDAYS Jan 1, Chinese New Year, Feb 23, Leilat al-Meiraj, 1st day of Ramadan, Revelation of Quran, Id al-Fitr, May 31, Jul 15, Hari Raya Haji, Muharram, Mouloud, Dec 25.

GOVERNMENT Absolute monarchy. The sultan governs by decree through appointed councils.

SINGAPORE

Already too mature to be tagged a newly industrializing country, Singapore has grown at an almost steady 7% a year since splitting from the Malaysian federation in 1965, to become the richest of the Asian "Little Dragons".

After separation from Malaysia, the island city state was an unlikely front-runner in South-East Asia. Lee Kuan Yew and his colleagues in the People's Action Party (PAP) found themselves masters of a port city without an agricultural hinterland or natural resources. Its small population was mostly Chinese in a region of Malays. The implications of this inheritance were both economic and political.

Singapore's economic success has depended on agile management to maintain an edge over potential rivals. An entrepôt and British military base when it became internally self-governing in 1959, Singapore was recognizably the child of its founder, Sir Stamford Raffles. He saw what could be made of a muddy Malay fishing village standing astride the sea route from India to China. The British made the island a trading post and base for their foray into South-East Asia.

British withdrawal east of Suez and the aspirations of Singapore's neighbours forced a break with the past. In the 1960s and 1970s the strategy was growth through labour-intensive and export-oriented industrialization. This succeeded beyond expectations, helped by a boom in domestic construction and the

OFFICIAL NAME Republic of Singapore.
CAPITAL CITY Singapore.
GEOGRAPHY An infertile island at the southern tip of the Malay peninsula, from which it is separated by the narrow Johore strait, Singapore has one of the largest ports in the world. The rugged granitic centre of the island gives way to sandy hills on the east and a series of scarps on the west. Much of the northern sector is mangrove swamp. *Highest point* Bukit Timah 177 metres (580 feet). *Area* 625.6 sq km (241.5 sq miles)
PEOPLE *Population* 2.7m. *Density* 4,293 per sq km. *Ethnic groups* Chinese 77%, Malay 15%, Indian and Sri Lankan 6%.
RELIGION Taoist 29%, Buddhist 27%, Muslim 16%, Christian 10%, Hindu 4%.
LANGUAGE Malay, Chinese, English and Tamil.
EDUCATION Free, but non-compulsory. English is the main language of instruction. There are 6 universities.
CURRENCY Singapore dollar.
PUBLIC HOLIDAYS Jan 1, Chinese New Year, Good Fri, May 1, Hari Raya Puasa, Vesak Day, Hari Raya Haji, Aug 9, Deepavali, Dec 25 .
GOVERNMENT Republic since 1965. Parliament elects a president as head of state every 4 years. The 81 members of parliament are elected from single and multi-member constituencies for 5 years; the People's Action Party has won almost every seat since 1972. Executive power lies with a cabinet headed by a prime minister.

ECONOMIC PROFILE

Entrepôt, financial services centre and commodities exchange for the region. Industrialization based on labour-intensive export processing, shipbuilding and repair, and oil refining. Maintaining competitive edge by moving into high-tech manufacturing and support for R&D. Well-developed infrastructure and government attuned to the needs of multinationals for flexible trade and investment policies.

Growth Export-led growth sustained by strong demand for electronic products

and computer peripherals. Bidding to take over Hong Kong's role as secondary financial centre for East Asia.

Problems Dependence on trade makes Singapore vulnerable to protectionist pressures, particularly in the USA. Labour shortages forcing some businesses to move elsewhere.

IMPORTS AND EXPORTS

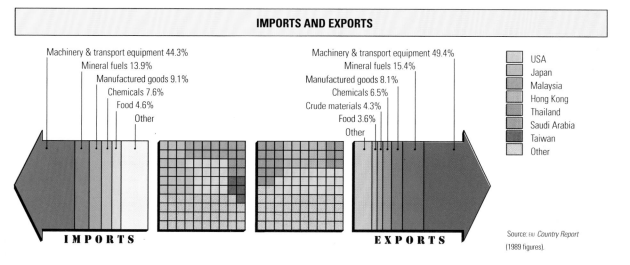

Machinery & transport equipment 44.3%
Mineral fuels 13.9%
Manufactured goods 9.1%
Chemicals 7.6%
Food 4.6%
Other

IMPORTS

Machinery & transport equipment 49.4%
Mineral fuels 15.4%
Manufactured goods 8.1%
Chemicals 6.5%
Crude materials 4.3%
Food 3.6%
Other

EXPORTS

USA
Japan
Malaysia
Hong Kong
Thailand
Saudi Arabia
Taiwan
Other

Source: EIU *Country Report* (1989 figures).

regional oil industry. In the late 1970s mainstays like oil refining began to look shaky and competition loomed from exporters elsewhere in the region. The government launched a second industrial revolution, to move the economy towards skill- and capital-intensive industries with high added value.

All went well until 1985, when GDP for once fell. After another bout of self-examination the course was adjusted. The goal was now to establish a new-style entrepôt, relying on Singapore's efficiency, infrastructure and skills to become a regional hub, a transport and communications centre where multinationals would set up regional headquarters and base their high-tech and R&D operations. The economy took off once more.

Survival has also been the dominant theme in politics. In the beleaguered 1960s every PAP cadre seemed to believe that he was under siege in a hostile region. Mr Lee's authoritarian instinct, sharpened in his battles with the left, was that politics was a luxury for Singapore. Social policy has often amounted to social engineering, whether in the famously strict litter laws or in efforts to encourage selective breeding. Some of the consequences are now being felt, as high local wages cut into export competitiveness and government opposition to immigration denies Singapore an easy answer to labour shortages.

Mr Lee finally stepped down as prime minister in November 1990, but – thorough as always – he has nurtured a "second generation" leadership team to succeed his own. Under prime minister Goh Chok Tong it inherits a Singapore of wealthy owner-occupiers that seems assured of a niche in the safer post-Vietnam world of Asean partnership and superpower detente and one that may benefit considerably as a result of the uncertainties over Hong Kong's future. Although Mr Goh's style of government was expected to be less stern than that of his formidable predecessor, he was not expected to deviate far from Lee Kuan Yew's bracing agenda.

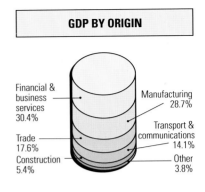

GDP BY ORIGIN

Financial & business services 30.4%
Manufacturing 28.7%
Transport & communications 14.1%
Trade 17.6%
Construction 5.4%
Other 3.8%

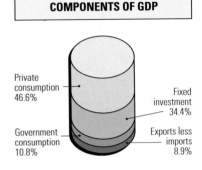

COMPONENTS OF GDP

Private consumption 46.6%
Fixed investment 34.4%
Government consumption 10.8%
Exports less imports 8.9%

Source: EIU *Country Report* (1989 figures).

INDONESIA

Indonesia's independent history changed course in October 1965, when troops led by General Suharto put down a supposedly communist-inspired coup. The coup attempt became the pretext for the bloody suppression of what was then the largest communist party outside China and the USSR. General Suharto supplanted President Sukarno, leader of the bitter independence struggle against the Dutch from 1945 to 1949.

Mr Sukarno's last years in power had been marked by political turmoil and economic collapse. Since independence, Indonesia had seemed perpetually on the brink of disintegration, with separatist movements throughout the archipelago fighting under regionalist or Islamic banners.

President Suharto and the military took depoliticization and development as their watchwords. US-trained technocrats stabilized the economy and ushered in a period of rapid growth, greatly aided by rising oil prices. In the 1970s oil came to account for 70% of export earnings and over half of tax receipts. Not only did income per head improve but also social indicators like life expectancy, living standards and literacy. Some major successes such as rice self-sufficiency and family planning have been achieved, largely as a result of government *diktat*.

General Suharto also abandoned his predecessor's anti-Western rhetoric and his bid for international prominence as leader of the world's fifth most populous country and largest Islamic state. A pragmatic, low-key approach was adopted in international affairs, leading to improved relations with the West and with Indonesia's neighbours, partners in Asean after 1967.

Weakening oil prices in the 1980s eroded the economy's most secure revenue base and helped cause a massive rise in foreign debt. A series of deregulatory packages since 1986 has stimulated other exports, especially manufactured products. Oil and gas now account for less than 50% of earnings. Corruption

OFFICIAL NAME Republic of Indonesia.

CAPITAL CITY Jakarta.

GEOGRAPHY There are nearly 14,000 islands in Indonesia, 930 of them inhabited. Most are rugged, sometimes volcanic, and covered with rain forest. The larger islands – Sumatra, Java, Southern Borneo, Sulawesi and Irian Jaya – contain the majority of the population. Most live in river valleys, alluvial coastal plains or on terraced mountain sides. *Highest point* Puncak Jaya 5,030 metres (16,500 feet). *Area* 1,904,569 sq km (735,360 sq miles).

PEOPLE *Population* 163m. *Density* 86 per sq km. *Ethnic groups* Javanese 40%, Sundanese 15%, Indonesian 12%, Madurese 5%.

RELIGION Muslim 88%, Christian 7%, Hindu 2%.

LANGUAGE Bahasa, Indonesian and others.

EDUCATION Free and compulsory for ages 7–13. 73 universities (48 state, 25 private).

CURRENCY Rupiah.

PUBLIC HOLIDAYS Jan 1, Leilat al-Meiraj, Good Fri, Ascension, Id al-Fitr, Id al-Adha, Muharram, Aug 17, Mouloud, Dec 25.

GOVERNMENT Military-dominated republic. The president, who is both chief executive and head of state, is elected for 5-year terms. The People's Consultative Assembly includes a legislative House of Representatives, with 400 elected and 100 appointed members.

and nepotism still distort policy-making, but the trend is away from state intervention and towards greater participation by private investors.

Java, with 7% of the land area but 60% of the population, is Indonesia's political core. But most of the oil, minerals, timber and plantation crops that provide the country's wealth come from the "outer islands". Secessionism is now largely confined to the eastern fringe of the archipelago in Irian Jaya and East Timor, both unwillingly incorporated well after independence.

Formal politics has become a sedate affair. They are dominated by Golkar, the military-backed coalition of functional groups which regularly wins elections against the two permitted political parties. The real power struggles are conducted out of public view within the military, which invokes the doctrine of "dual function" to justify its involvement in civilian affairs.

General Suharto may seek a sixth term in 1993, when he will be 72. He has no obvious successor and there are suspicions that he feels he must hold on to power to protect his family's extensive interests. But there are also signs that the military might prefer to see him retire. It has indicated it would be happy to field its own candidate should he decide not to run. The military establishment reacted badly to the elevation to the vice-presidency in 1988 of Lieutenant General Sudharmono – who seems to favour a diminishing military role in politics – and saw to it that he was replaced as chairman of Golkar by a retired general more to their liking. The military sees itself as the sole guarantor of stability in Indonesia; whenever it feels that the people need to be reminded of this, it has only to conjure up the communist bogey.

ECONOMIC PROFILE

Agrarian rice-based economy exporting agricultural commodities – edible oils, coffee, tea, rubber, tobacco – minerals, oil and natural gas. Import-substitution industries – textiles, cement, steel, vehicles – developed under heavy protection, being tested by trade liberalization; drive to reduce dependence on oil exports.

Growth Export-oriented manufacturing set to grow strongly, with ambitious plans to develop the aircraft industry and electronics; expansion also in minerals processing, furniture and handicrafts. Plans to revive shelved petrochemical projects. Inter-island shipping and ports being modernized and deregulated. Tourism is booming.

Problems Oil production set to decline unless new discoveries made. Financial sector hampered by over-regulation. Capital goods still a major import item. Costs of servicing debt continue to rise.

IMPORTS AND EXPORTS

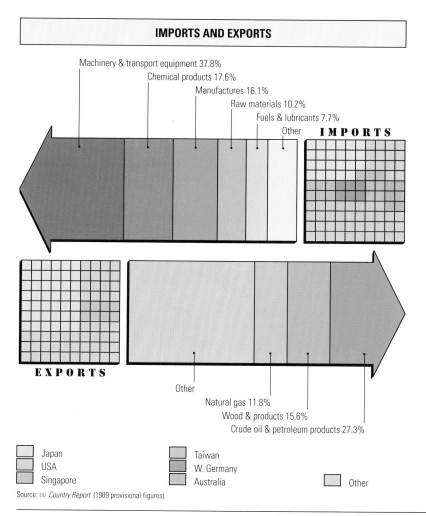

Machinery & transport equipment 37.8%
Chemical products 17.6%
Manufactures 16.1%
Raw materials 10.2%
Fuels & lubricants 7.7%
Other

IMPORTS

EXPORTS

Other
Natural gas 11.8%
Wood & products 15.6%
Crude oil & petroleum products 27.3%

Japan
USA
Singapore
Taiwan
W. Germany
Australia
Other

Source: EIU *Country Report* (1989 provisional figures).

GDP BY ORIGIN

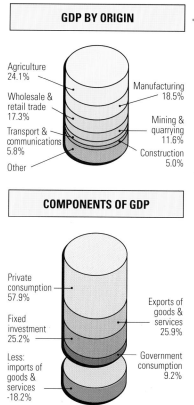

Agriculture 24.1%
Wholesale & retail trade 17.3%
Transport & communications 5.8%
Other
Manufacturing 18.5%
Mining & quarrying 11.6%
Construction 5.0%

COMPONENTS OF GDP

Private consumption 57.9%
Fixed investment 25.2%
Less: imports of goods & services -18.2%
Exports of goods & services 25.9%
Government consumption 9.2%

Source: EIU *Country Report* (1988 provisional figures).

EAST TIMOR

For 400 years, East Timor was a neglected backwater of the Portuguese empire, known largely for its superior coffee. Portugal promised self-determination in 1975, but Indonesia's nervous generals, seeing the Fretilin independence movement as an attempt to establish a communist beachhead in the East Indies, invaded and annexed the territory. Tens of thousands of Timorese died in the invasion and subsequent conflict.

The UN has not recognized the takeover and the government has yet to yield to international pressure to lift restrictions on access to the territory, despite promises to do so. East Timor remains effectively closed to the outside world.

OFFICIAL NAME East Timor.
CAPITAL CITY Dili.
GEOGRAPHY The territory comprises the eastern half of a rugged volcanic island in the chain that runs from Sumatra. *Highest point* 2,920 metres (9,580 feet). *Area* 14,874 sq km (5,740 sq miles).
PEOPLE *Population* 631,000. *Density* 42 per sq km. *Ethnic groups* Indonesian/Malay, Melanesian.
RELIGION Christian 39%, Animist.
LANGUAGE Tetum and other local languages. Also Indonesian and Portuguese.
CURRENCY Indonesian rupiah.

THE PHILIPPINES

Three hundred years of Spanish rule, followed by nearly 50 years under the Americans have left their cultural marks on the Philippines. Catholicism and constitutionalism both run deep. It was the first Asian country to win independence from Western colonialism, in 1946. Economic and security relations with the USA remain strong, if sometimes acrimonious.

After independence graft and corruption came to play an increasingly important role in politics, reaching their apogee under Ferdinand Marcos. Mr Marcos won the 1965 elections, and was the first Philippine president to be re-elected. He then extended his rule by declaring martial law in 1972. The pretext was the insurgencies of the communist New People's Army (NPA) and the southern Muslim Moro National Liberation Front. The armed forces, in a position of real power for the first time, proved incapable of restoring peace. From being a localized irritant, the NPA had become a nationwide force by the early 1980s.

During his two decades in power Mr Marcos substantially increased links with the USA. His administration has been credited with massive infrastructure programmes, but they were achieved at the expense of increasing foreign debts.

OFFICIAL NAME Republic of the Philippines.
CAPITAL CITY Manila.
GEOGRAPHY Most of the islands in the archipelago are mountainous, with most ranges running from north to south. Some of the islands are coral and some volcanic – there are 10 active volcanoes – and many have narrow coastal plains. Most of the population lives in intermontane plains on the larger islands, or on the coastal strips. Around 40% of the land is forested. *Highest point* Mount Apo 2,954 metres (9,690 feet). *Area* 300,000 sq km (116,000 sq miles).
PEOPLE *Population* 60m. *Density* 200 per sq km. *Ethnic groups* Cebuano 24%, Tagalog 24%, Ilocano 11%, Hiligaynon 10%, Bicolano 7%, Samar-Leyte 5%, Pampanga 3%.
RELIGION Christian 93% (RC 85%, other 8%), Muslim 4%.
LANGUAGE Filipino, Tagalog and English. Also Spanish and local languages.
EDUCATION Free and compulsory for ages 7–12. Secondary education (13–17) also free in some areas. 55 universities.
CURRENCY Philippine peso.
PUBLIC HOLIDAYS Jan 1, Feb 25, Maundy Thu, Good Fri, May 1, 6, Jun 12, last Sun in Aug, Sep 11, 21, Nov 1, 30, Dec 25, 30–31.
GOVERNMENT Republic since 1946. The 1987 constitution provides for a bicameral legislature with a president, elected for a single 6-year term, as head of state and chief executive. The 24-member Senate is elected for a 5-year term. The House of Representatives serves a 3-year term; it has 200 elected members and up to 50 others appointed by the president to represent various minority groups.

ECONOMIC PROFILE

Agriculture the main employer, producing rice and maize for domestic consumption and coconuts and sugar for export. Manufacturing originally based on local agricultural and mineral resources. Import-substitution industries – notably assembly of consumer goods – developed in 1950s and 1960s, bringing industry's contribution to GDP level with that of agriculture. Ambitious programme to build heavy industrial base launched in 1981 became casualty of economic austerity; most projects abandoned. New emphasis on agri-business and small-scale labour-intensive industries.

Growth Mining, tourism and financial sector recovering from setbacks of Marcos years. Main motors of manufacturing growth are garments, semiconductors and other export industries. Food and timber processing receiving official encouragement. Buoyant domestic and export demand stimulating investment.

Problems Sugar suffered from low world prices, coconuts from neglect, both from "cronyism". Forests seriously depleted. Continued dependence on commodity exports does little to create jobs. Half of labour force unemployed or underemployed; high level of emigration. Debt service burden has forced rescheduling, making banks reluctant to lend new money. Privatization of government corporations proceeding very slowly.

IMPORTS AND EXPORTS

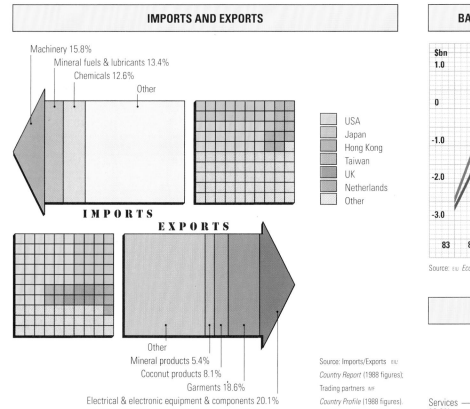

Machinery 15.8%
Mineral fuels & lubricants 13.4%
Chemicals 12.6%
Other

IMPORTS

EXPORTS

USA
Japan
Hong Kong
Taiwan
UK
Netherlands
Other

Other
Mineral products 5.4%
Coconut products 8.1%
Garments 18.6%
Electrical & electronic equipment & components 20.1%

Source: Imports/Exports EIU *Country Report* (1988 figures); Trading partners IMF *Country Profile* (1988 figures).

BALANCE OF PAYMENTS

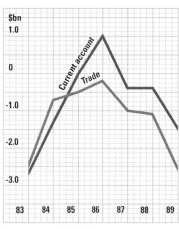

$bn
Current account
Trade
1.0
0
-1.0
-2.0
-3.0
83 84 85 86 87 88 89

Source: EIU *Economic Risk Service*.

GDP BY ORIGIN

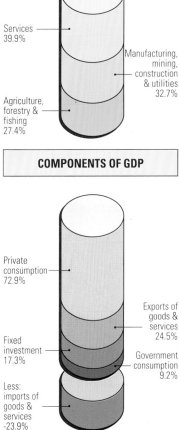

Services 39.9%
Manufacturing, mining, construction & utilities 32.7%
Agriculture, forestry & fishing 27.4%

COMPONENTS OF GDP

Private consumption 72.9%
Exports of goods & services 24.5%
Fixed investment 17.3%
Government consumption 9.2%
Less: imports of goods & services -23.9%

Source: EIU *Country Report* (1988 figures).

Worsening economic problems were compounded by the system of "cronyism", which gave trading monopolies to Mr Marcos's chief supporters.

The assassination in August 1983 of Mr Marcos's chief political rival, Benigno Aquino, minutes after his return from exile, marked the beginning of the end for Mr Marcos. The assassination triggered mass demonstrations. Foreign creditors suspended the short-term loans that underpinned the economy, investment dried up and capital fled. By 1985 GDP per head was back to 1975 levels, and foreign debt had become insupportable.

Blatantly rigged elections in February 1986 triggered a new wave of popular protest. This "people power", backed by the church, and by key sections of the military brought to power Mr Aquino's widow, Corazon ("Cory").

Mrs Aquino then sought to unite the country. A new constitution was approved, limiting presidential powers, and Philippine-style democracy began functioning again. The new administration quickly wound up the cronies' trading monopolies and rescheduled foreign bank debts. Uniting the disparate anti-Marcos elements in the cabinet was more difficult. There were five coup attempts in the president's first 18 months. By shedding the liberals in her cabinet, Mrs Aquino tried to win over the malcontents.

But in December 1989 the military rebels tried again, and might have succeeded if the USA had not indicated its willingness to give military support to the president. Mrs Aquino's standing was further weakened by her ineffectual response to the economy's mounting problems, the resurgence of the NPA after a brief ceasefire in 1987, and the government's indecision in the negotiations over the future of US bases. Pressures on her to resign before the 1992 elections began to grow, but the absence of an obvious heir could leave the succession to one of her political opponents.

SOUTH PACIFIC

Micronesia

Micronesia, the northernmost group of Pacific islands, stretches in an arc from the Northern Mariana Islands, south-east of Japan, to Tuvalu, north of Fiji.

The economies of Micronesia are among the tiniest in the world. Most islands are coral atolls with poor-quality soils; subsistence farming is the main occupation, although copra is a source of export earnings and fishing and tourism are being developed. A select few, notably Nauru, have rich phosphate reserves.

Spain, Germany, Japan, the UK and USA have all controlled parts of the region at various times. The Northern Mariana, Caroline and Marshall Islands came under US administration by UN mandate in 1947 as the Trust Territory of the Pacific Islands. Most gained effective independence when the trusteeship came to a formal end in 1986, although the USA remains responsible for defence and security and provides economic aid. Guam, largest of the Marianas, elected to remain part of the USA and is an important military base. The status of Palau, an island in the Caroline group but not part of the Federated States of Micronesia formed by the rest, remains unsettled because of a dispute over the USA's rights to store nuclear materials on the island.

Anzus

The Anzus security treaty was signed in 1951 to coordinate the collective defence efforts in the Pacific of the USA, Australia and New Zealand. New Zealand's decision in 1985 to ban ships carrying nuclear weapons from its ports led the USA to suspend joint military exercises under the Anzus pact. This has put the pact's future in doubt, as Australia is also reviewing its defence arrangements.

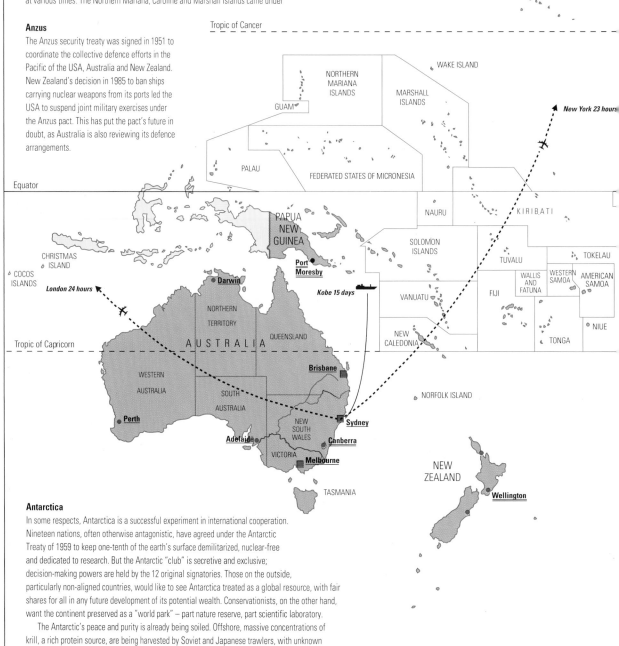

Antarctica

In some respects, Antarctica is a successful experiment in international cooperation. Nineteen nations, often otherwise antagonistic, have agreed under the Antarctic Treaty of 1959 to keep one-tenth of the earth's surface demilitarized, nuclear-free and dedicated to research. But the Antarctic "club" is secretive and exclusive; decision-making powers are held by the 12 original signatories. Those on the outside, particularly non-aligned countries, would like to see Antarctica treated as a global resource, with fair shares for all in any future development of its potential wealth. Conservationists, on the other hand, want the continent preserved as a "world park" – part nature reserve, part scientific laboratory.

The Antarctic's peace and purity is already being soiled. Offshore, massive concentrations of krill, a rich protein source, are being harvested by Soviet and Japanese trawlers, with unknown effects on future stocks.

The South Pacific Forum

This is the main organization grouping the independent and self-governing states of the region. Established in 1971, it has focused attention on issues such as nuclear testing, fishing rights and the independence of New Caledonia. Economic and trade concerns are handled by the South Pacific Bureau for Economic Cooperation (Spec), set up in 1973. This has negotiated duty-free access to Australian and New Zealand markets for the smaller islands.

Nuclear tests and nuclear-free zones

France's programme of nuclear tests in the Pacific has united most nations of the region in opposition. The Treaty of Rarotonga, establishing a South Pacific nuclear-free zone, was signed in 1985 by Australia, New Zealand, Papua New Guinea and most of the smaller Pacific island nations. The treaty, which prohibits the possession, testing and use of nuclear weapons, came into force in December 1986. Of the five major nuclear powers, the USSR and China have signed the treaty; France, the UK and the USA have refused to adhere to it.

Exclusive economic zones

Attempts to regulate access to the potential wealth of the oceans led to the adoption in 1982 of the UN Convention on the Law of the Sea. This puts 40% of the world's oceans under the control of coastal states, giving them rights over economic activity and responsibility for environmental protection within a 200-nautical mile exclusive economic zone. Deep seabed areas are designated the "common heritage of mankind", to be controlled by an International Seabed Authority. About 160 nations have signed the convention, but it will come into effect only when 60 have ratified it. However, leading industrial nations, including the UK and the USA, have refused to sign, arguing that it gives insufficient representation to countries with technology for deep sea mining.

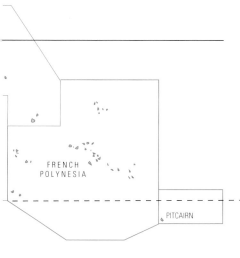

FRENCH POLYNESIA

PITCAIRN

■ More than 1 million
● 250,000 - 1 million

Polynesia

The nuclear age has dispelled the notion of the Polynesian islands as an unspoiled earthly paradise. France governs 120 of the islands, scattered across the South Pacific, and has tested its nuclear weapons at Mururoa Atoll in the Tuamotu archipelago since 1966, despite the mounting protests of Pacific nations and environmentalist groups. The presence of large numbers of French troops is a boost to the economy of the islands, particularly Tahiti. So too is tourism, but high costs and the destruction of the environment caused by the tourists themselves is starting to keep visitors away. Coconuts are the major cash crop and copra the largest export, but the total value of exports covers only about a quarter of the cost of imports each year.

The Samoan Islands, north-east of Fiji, are split between Western Samoa, independent since 1962, and US-administered American Samoa. Tuna-canning plants are a major source of employment in American Samoa but the islands' economies depend on aid, remittances and, to a limited extent, tourism.

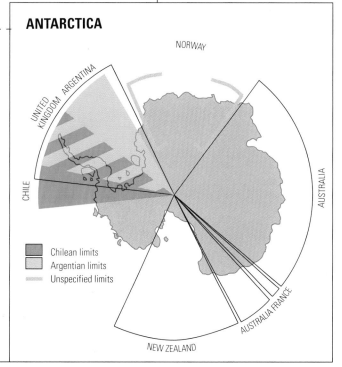

ANTARCTICA

NORWAY

UNITED KINGDOM ARGENTINA

CHILE

AUSTRALIA

AUSTRALIA FRANCE

NEW ZEALAND

■ Chilean limits
■ Argentian limits
▬ Unspecified limits

 # AUSTRALIA

Long seen as an alien European outpost at the extremity of Western civilization, Australia is increasingly coming to terms with its location. The old Anglo-Australian identity is being replaced by one based on new multicultural relationships and an awareness of being part of Asia and the Pacific, which is reflected in the re-direction of the economy. Strategic thinking, too, stresses self-reliance and good regional diplomacy, although the military alliance with the USA, which took Australian troops to Vietnam in the early 1970s, remains axiomatic.

The heritage of education and social reform that gained Australia a reputation as a "working man's paradise" at the turn of the century still has meaning in a highly democratic but also highly competitive society. Most Australians are descended not from convicts but from free immigrants bent on bettering their lot. Ethnically the population is now 75% British or Irish in origin; the rest is mainly the product of post-war immigration. This brought in Italians, Greeks and other Europeans and, more recently, Asians, whose arrival marked the dismantling of the infamous "white Australia" policy that banned non-white entry for 100 years. Ironically, the group that has most clearly been excluded from the emerging multicultural consensus is that of the Aboriginal Australians, who form 1% of the population and whose special relationship with the land has yet to be properly recognized.

Australian politics is almost exclusively masculine. The federal government co-exists (uneasily at times) with state governments who guard their independence jealously. The tension between central and state governments is exacerbated by the three-year electoral cycle. With a transferable vote system that prevents overwhelming majorities and because of the independence of the states the Australian system has maintained political stability and excitement simultaneously.

Despite its vastness, Australia is one of the world's most highly urbanized nations. Well over 80% of its people live in cities, almost all in the well-watered, fertile belt stretching along the south-east coast from Brisbane to Adelaide and in a pocket around Perth in the west. Their easy-going ethos masks a concern for family security that is reflected in very high levels of home ownership and of personal savings.

Traditionally, Australia depended on its agricultural and pastoral products. It has been the world's leading wool producer since the 19th century; it is also the largest beef exporter and a major wheat grower. Minerals, important since the gold rushes of the 1850s, have boomed in recent years to become the leading export sector and turning Australia into one of the world's largest producers. It is the biggest exporter of iron ore and aluminium, the second biggest of coal,

OFFICIAL NAME Commonwealth of Australia.
CAPITAL CITY Canberra.
GEOGRAPHY Australia is by far the flattest and driest of the continents. Its vast, barren and largely uninhabited interior, the outback, is a low, rolling plateau dotted with dry salt lakes. In the south it gives straight onto the sea, but elsewhere it is bordered by coastal mountain ranges. In the south-east the wooded Great Dividing Range separates the outback from a hilly and fertile coastal region that contains most of the population. The northern coasts and the Queensland peninsula are covered with tropical rain forest and the southern island of Tasmania is cool and mountainous. *Highest point* Mt Kosciusko 2,228 metres (7,310 feet). *Area* 7,686,848 sq km (2,967,910 sq miles).
PEOPLE *Population* 16.5m. *Density* 2 per sq km. *Ethnic groups* Australian 78% (Aborigine 1%), British and Irish 8%, Asian 4% Italian 2%, New Zealander 2%, Greek 1%, Yugoslavian 1%.
RELIGION Anglican Church of Australia 26%, RC 26%, Uniting Church 5%, Presbyterian 4%, Methodist 3%, Greek Orthodox 3%, Muslim 1%.
LANGUAGE English. Also Aboriginal languages.
EDUCATION Free to university level and compulsory for ages 6–15. There are 25 universities. Education is a joint responsibility of state and federal governments.
CLIMATE Tropical and sub-tropical, with wet summers in the north; temperate with wet winters in east and south. Inland is mostly hot desert, with clear skies and extremes of temperature.
CURRENCY Australian dollar.
PUBLIC HOLIDAYS Jan 1, Jan 26, Good Fri, Easter Mon, Apr 25, Jun 12, Dec 25–26. Also state holidays.
GOVERNMENT Parliamentary monarchy The head of state is the British monarch, represented by a governor-general. The 6 states and 2 territories are largely autonomous. The bicameral federal parliament comprise, a Senate with 12 members from each state and 2 from each territory, and a House of Representatives with 148 members elected for a 3-year term.

IMPORTS AND EXPORTS

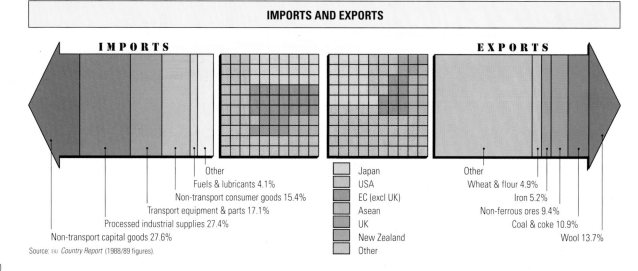

IMPORTS

Other
Fuels & lubricants 4.1%
Non-transport consumer goods 15.4%
Transport equipment & parts 17.1%
Processed industrial supplies 27.4%
Non-transport capital goods 27.6%

Japan
USA
EC (excl UK)
Asean
UK
New Zealand
Other

EXPORTS

Other
Wheat & flour 4.9%
Iron 5.2%
Non-ferrous ores 9.4%
Coal & coke 10.9%
Wool 13.7%

Source: EIU *Country Report* (1988/89 figures).

nickel and zinc, and an important supplier of lead, gold, tin, tungsten and uranium. Australia is 70% self-sufficient in oil and plans have been mooted to develop offshore oilfields in conjunction with Indonesia. It is also a continent of natural beauty, and tourism is thriving.

Even so, the country faces a number of economic problems and challenges. Extended droughts periodically devastate agricultural output. But oversupply is also a recurring threat and as a commodity exporter Australia is vulnerable to fluctuations in its international markets. The 1990 collapse of the world wool market, for instance, left the industry in crisis and created a wool mountain costing A$1 billion a year to store, equivalent to one-quarter of the budget surplus. If the economy is to reduce this vulnerability it must start adding value to key exports by beginning some part-processing, especially of minerals.

Australia's manufacturing sector is dangerously weak for a supposedly developed and balanced economy. Manufacturing remains the largest single contributor to GDP, but its share has declined steadily, in part as a result of formidable competition from Australia's Asian neighbours. Restructuring has yet to yield any significant export successes and Australia's high transport costs are a formidable obstacle to reducing dependence on domestic markets. Australia's skills base also requires urgent attention if the country is to expand its role as a supplier of technological and scientific advice to the region.

But the biggest challenge of all for this isolated country with a small domestic market is to develop and diversify its trade links. The last two decades have seen a major reorientation of the country's trading patterns. The UK, once the country's principal trading partner, has become far less significant since it joined the EC. Two-thirds of Australia's trade is now with the Pacific rim, with Japan as the country's principal trading partner and the USA second in importance. Links with the Middle East, Europe and Latin America must also be nurtured, although the prospect of the single European market and formation of new trading blocs in the Americas is causing growing concern to a country hit hard by recession in the early 1990s and dependent on free trade for its prosperity.

ECONOMIC PROFILE

A major world producer of raw materials. Minerals now main export earner, though agricultural products – wool, beef, wheat, fruits, sugar – still account for 40% of exports. Relatively small manufacturing sector, developed behind protective barriers, beginning to restructure in search of new markets.

Growth Mineral production expanding, as is tourism. Competing effectively and expanding overseas in selected areas: food and drink, media and entertainment, transport, electronic communications. Increasingly important investor and trader in Pacific region.

Problems Manufacturing's contribution to GDP has fallen from 30% to 16% since 1950s. High current account deficits from heavy borrowing – foreign debt equals 30% of GDP. A growing wool mountain, equal to about a year's production.

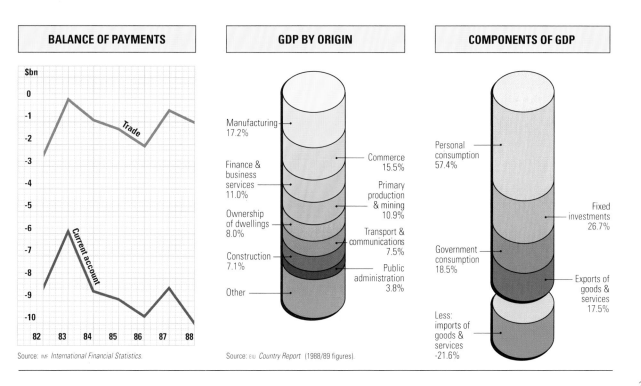

BALANCE OF PAYMENTS

Source: IMF *International Financial Statistics.*

GDP BY ORIGIN

Manufacturing 17.2%
Finance & business services 11.0%
Ownership of dwellings 8.0%
Construction 7.1%
Other
Commerce 15.5%
Primary production & mining 10.9%
Transport & communications 7.5%
Public administration 3.8%

Source: EIU *Country Report* (1988/89 figures).

COMPONENTS OF GDP

Personal consumption 57.4%
Government consumption 18.5%
Less: imports of goods & services -21.6%
Fixed investments 26.7%
Exports of goods & services 17.5%

NEW ZEALAND

At one time New Zealand seemed to have everything: an advanced social democracy with high living standards, European and Maori cultures in harmonious co-existence, and a land of unpolluted beauty and fertility. The idyll evaporated in the 1970s when the UK joined the EC. Britain had been the market for 70% of New Zealand's exports and supplied most of its manufactured goods; after EC membership UK purchases fell to less than 10% of exports. New markets in the Middle East and east Asia have not filled the gap. Manufactures still have to be imported at high cost and there is a serious balance of payments problem. The country has also had to rethink defence policy. Objections to the visits of US nuclear warships led to New Zealand's ejection from the Anzus alliance and defence policy now emphasizes cooperation with other South Pacific nations.

All these changes have forced a formerly secure nation to reconsider its position. New Zealand has had to dismantle much of its state-directed economy, float the currency, encourage new industries and import-substitution, and seek success through even greater efficiency. Farm subsidies were slashed, halving farm incomes; state concerns were privatized. New markets were sought and an agreement signed with Australia to phase in free trade. Fish, timber, wood-pulp and iron export industries have been set up and natural gas discoveries have eased fuel shortages.

The free-market medicine has yet to work, however. Growth levels remain low despite some success in reducing inflation and improving the current account. The country's farmers are among the most efficient in the world, but they face restricted access to vital EC and American markets. The weakening currency has made exports more competitive but increased sales have not compensated for the loss of value.

The social consequences of the country's economic problems include rising unemployment and violent crime. The traditional exodus to Australia has also increased and race relations have deteriorated. Efforts to find a solution were not helped by growing divisions within the Labour government in the late 1980s. The election in 1990 of the National Party under prime minister Jim Bolger ended the political uncertainty. But the announcement of a new welfare system and other reforms could not obscure the continuing bleak outlook for the economy.

OFFICIAL NAME New Zealand.

CAPITAL CITY Wellington.

GEOGRAPHY Two-thirds of New Zealand is covered with evergreen forest. There are two major and several smaller islands. South Island is mountainous and scenic, with glaciers, lakes and fast-flowing rivers; most settlement is on the alluvial east coast plains. North Island is less rugged but volcanically active, with many hot springs and geysers; the volcanic central plateau, rolling down into Hawke Bay, is the centre of the dairy industry. Auckland, on its isthmus, has harbours in both the Tasman sea and the Pacific; the area to the north has poor soils and sub-tropical vegetation. *Highest point* Mt Cook 3,764 metres (12,350 feet). *Area* 268,676 sq km (103,740 sq miles).

PEOPLE *Population* 3.3m. *Density* 13 per sq km. *Ethnic groups* New Zealander 84% (Maori 9%), British 6%, Australian 1.5%, Samoan 1%, Dutch 1%.

RELIGION Church of England 26%, Presbyterian 16%, RC 14%, Methodist 5%, Baptist 2%.

LANGUAGE English. Also Maori.

EDUCATION Free and compulsory for ages 6–15. There are 7 universities.

CLIMATE Temperate and generally sunny. Average annual temperature 9°C (48°F) in south, 15°C (59°F) in north, with no seasonal extremes. Annual rainfall 600–1,500mm (24–60ins), more in mountains, evenly spread through the year.

CURRENCY New Zealand dollar.

PUBLIC HOLIDAYS Jan 1–2, 21, Feb 6, Good Fri, Easter Mon, Apr 1, 25, June 3, Oct 28, Dec 25–26.

GOVERNMENT Parliamentary monarchy. The head of state is the British monarch, represented by a governor-general. The legislative House of Representatives has 97 members elected every 3 years; 4 seats are reserved for Maoris. Head of government is the prime minister who appoints the cabinet.

ECONOMIC PROFILE

Overwhelmingly dependent on agricultural exports such as wool, frozen lamb, butter. Few mineral resources, but self-sufficient in coal; hydro-power and natural gas supplies help reduce oil imports. Most manufactured goods imported.

Growth Exports of timber, wood pulp, coal, iron, aluminium, frozen fish and specialized foods, such as kiwi fruit and venison; tourism.

Problems Vulnerable to fluctuating prices and markets for agricultural exports. Policies to diversify and liberalize slow to take effect.

IMPORTS AND EXPORTS

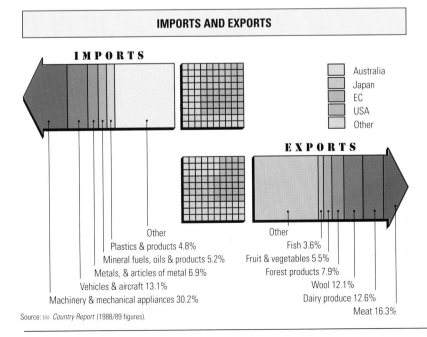

IMPORTS

Australia
Japan
EC
USA
Other

Other
Plastics & products 4.8%
Mineral fuels, oils & products 5.2%
Metals, & articles of metal 6.9%
Vehicles & aircraft 13.1%
Machinery & mechanical appliances 30.2%

EXPORTS

Other
Fish 3.6%
Fruit & vegetables 5.5%
Forest products 7.9%
Wool 12.1%
Dairy produce 12.6%
Meat 16.3%

Source: EIU *Country Report* (1988/89 figures).

CHRISTMAS ISLAND

GEOGRAPHY *Area* 135 sq km (52 sq miles).
PEOPLE *Population* 2,000. *Ethnic groups* Chinese 55%,
Malay 24%, European 12%.
LANGUAGE English.
CURRENCY Australian dollar.
GOVERNMENT Australian external territory.

Christmas Island, in the Indian Ocean,
is administered by Australia. Phosphate
mining has been the main economic
activity; tourism is expected to replace it
as the phosphate reserves run out.

COCOS ISLANDS

GEOGRAPHY *Area* 14 sq km (5.4 sq miles).
PEOPLE *Population* 616. *Ethnic groups* Malay 63%,
Australian 34%, European 3%.
LANGUAGE English.
CURRENCY Australian dollar.
GOVERNMENT Australian external territory.

Only two of the 27 Cocos Islands are
inhabited. Coconuts are the sole cash
crop, postage stamps the only other
source of revenue. In 1984 the 600
inhabitants voted for integration with
Australia.

NORFOLK ISLAND

GEOGRAPHY *Area* 35 sq km (14 sq miles).
PEOPLE *Population* 2,400. *Density* 67 per sq km. *Ethnic
groups* European, Polynesian and European/Polynesian.
LANGUAGE English and Norfolk (Old English/Tahitian).
CURRENCY Australian dollar.
GOVERNMENT Australian external territory.

Norfolk Island was a penal colony in
the late 18th and early 19th centuries;
in 1856 it was settled by immigrants
from overcrowded Pitcairn Island. The
island has been an Australian external
territory since 1913 but has its own
legislative assembly.

MELANESIA

PAPUA NEW GUINEA

OFFICIAL NAME Papua New Guinea.
CAPITAL CITY Port Moresby.
GEOGRAPHY The territory includes several smaller
islands as well as the eastern half of the island of New
Guinea, which has a mountainous interior covered by
tropical rain forest. There are few towns; 85% of the
population is rural. *Area* 461,691 sq km (178,260 sq
miles).
PEOPLE *Population* 3.6m. *Density* 7 per sq km. *Ethnic
groups* Papuan 83%, Melanesian 15%.
RELIGION Protestant 58%, RC 33%, Anglican 5%,
Animist.
LANGUAGE English. Also Pidgin English, Hiri Motu
(Melanesian Pidgin) and 700 other languages and
dialects.
EDUCATION Free but non-compulsory for ages 7–13.
There are 2 universities.
CLIMATE Tropical, with temperatures of 23–32°C
(73–90°F) year-round. Annual rainfall of at least
2,000mm (80ins), rising to 7,000mm (276ins) in
highlands; driest May–Aug.
CURRENCY Kina.
PUBLIC HOLIDAYS Jan 1, Good Fri, Easter Mon, June
16, Jul 23, Sep 16, Dec 25–26.
GOVERNMENT Parliamentary monarchy. The head of
state is the British monarch, represented by a governor-
general who acts on the advice of the executive council.
The council is responsible to a 109-member parliament.

Independent from Australia since 1975,
Papua New Guinea has been a
relatively stable democracy within the
Commonwealth, with a fifth of its
budget provided by Australia. Coffee,
copra and cocoa are still important, but
exports are now dominated by
minerals, especially copper. Large new
copper deposits have been found and
gold production from the Ok Tedi and
other mines is increasing. Oil
production was due to start in 1992.
  Economic policy has emphasized
equitable growth, reduction of
dependence on Australia and job
creation. These aims were undermined
by events on Bougainville island where
demands for a greater share in the
earnings of the giant Panguna mine
escalated into a secessionist struggle.
The mine was mothballed in 1989 with
serious economic consequences. Moves
towards a peaceful settlement led to
hopes in 1991 that it might be re-opened.

SOLOMON ISLANDS

GEOGRAPHY *Area* 28,446 sq km (10,983 sq miles).
PEOPLE *Population* 310,000. *Density* 11 per sq km.
Ethnic groups Melanesian 93%, Polynesian 4%,
Micronesian 1.4%.
LANGUAGE English. Also Pidgin and many local
languages and dialects.
CURRENCY Dollar.
GOVERNMENT Parliamentary monarchy. The head of
state is the British monarch, represented by a governor-
general who acts on the advice of the prime minister
and cabinet. The legislative body is the 38-member
parliament.

The development of the Solomon
Islands is hampered by the
mountainous, densely forested terrain
of the six main islands. Settlements are
scattered and transport difficult.
Subsistence farming provides a living
for 90% of the population. Tuna fish is
the main export earner, followed by
timber, copra and palm oil, but prices
for all these products have been poor in
recent years. Faced with persistent
trade and budget deficits, the
government has been forced to seek
finance from the multilateral agencies.
Political activity is turbulent, highly
democratic and focused more on
personalities than policies. Perhaps the
islands' biggest challenge is a
population growth rate of 3.5% a year.

VANUATU

GEOGRAPHY *Area* 14,800 sq km (5,700 sq miles).
PEOPLE *Population* 143,000. *Ethnic groups* Melanesian
94%, European 2%.
LANGUAGE Pidgin, English and French. Also many
local languages and dialects.
CURRENCY Vatu.
GOVERNMENT Republic since 1980. The head of state
is the president, elected by an electoral college.
Executive power lies with a prime minister, elected by
and from the 46-member parliament, and a council of
ministers.

A unique colonial history as a
condominium – popularly known as
the "pandemonium" – governed jointly

by France and the UK has left the former New Hebrides with an independent attitude. The first Pacific state to join the non-aligned movement, Vanuatu also opened diplomatic relations with Cuba and China, and with the Soviet Union, which in 1986 signed a fishing agreement giving it access to Vanuatu's ports. Evidence the following year of a Libyan presence prompted Australian criticism, which was roundly rejected by the outspoken Father Walter Lini, Anglican priest and prime minister since independence in 1980. Since then, however, Vanuatu has developed friendlier relations with its former colonial rulers.

Independence was accompanied by a rebellion on the francophone island of Espiritu Santo. In recent years Father Lini's authority has been challenged by a split in the ruling anglophone party, which in 1988 precipitated a constitutional crisis and coup attempt.

Most Vanuatuns live by subsistence farming; copra is the main export earner.

NEW CALEDONIA

GEOGRAPHY *Area* 19,058 sq km (7,358 sq miles).
PEOPLE *Population* 164,000. *Ethnic groups* Melanesian 43%, European (mainly French) 37%, Wallisian 8%, Polynesian 4%.
LANGUAGE French. Also many local languages and dialects.
CURRENCY Pacific franc.
GOVERNMENT French overseas territory. There are 4 regional areas with limited self-government. 2 deputies are sent to the French national assembly.

New Caledonia is bitterly divided over the issue of independence from France. The indigenous Melanesian people, the Kanaks, mostly support it but now represent less than half the population; French settlers, many of whom came to the island from Algeria, are resolutely opposed. The sometimes violent conflict between the two has been defused by a plan for increased local self-government leading to independence in 1998; but the low turnout in the referendum that approved it leaves its future in some doubt.

The economy depends on a single

commodity, nickel, which accounts for nearly 90% of export earnings and of which New Caledonia was the world's largest producer during the 1960s. It is still the third largest source, and has about 40% of world reserves. Copra and coffee are also exported, but France continues to provide about one-third of the government budget.

FIJI

GEOGRAPHY *Area* 18,274 sq km (7,056 sq miles).
PEOPLE *Population* 717,000. *Ethnic groups* Indian 50%, Fijian 45%, European 2%, Rotuman 1%.
RELIGION Christian 50%, Hindu 41%, Muslim 8%.
LANGUAGE English, Fijian and Hindustani.
CURRENCY Fiji dollar.
GOVERNMENT Republic since 1987. The head of state is the president. Quasi-civilian government based on presidential decree is in place until a new constitution is approved.

Fiji today is still living with the legacy of colonialism. In the late 19th century, the British brought in Indian workers for the sugar plantations; in time, the Indians came to outnumber the Fijian population but were discriminated against in political representation and land ownership rights. A new electoral system adopted at independence in 1970 aimed to ensure a racial balance in the legislature, but politics continued to be dominated by racial issues.

A crisis was provoked by the April 1987 election, which brought to power the first government with a majority of ministers of Indian origin. Two military coups followed, a republic was declared, the constitution revoked and Fiji's membership of the Commonwealth suspended. A constitution was drawn up designed to give the Melanesian population a permanent majority in parliament. The Indians responded by voting with their feet, many taking their valuable skills elsewhere.

Political instability had a disastrous effect on tourism, a major source of foreign exchange, but the sector has recovered well. Sugar remains the main cash crop; attempts to encourage small-scale industrial development are still in their infancy.

GUAM

GEOGRAPHY *Area* 541 sq km (209 sq miles).
PEOPLE *Population* 129,000. *Ethnic groups* Chamorro 45%, Caucasian 25%, Filipino 21%, Korean 3%, Micronesian 3%.
LANGUAGE English and Chamorro.
CURRENCY US dollar.
GOVERNMENT Self-governing US territory.

NORTHERN MARIANAS

GEOGRAPHY *Area* 471 sq km (182 sq miles).
PEOPLE *Population* 31,600. *Density* 69 per sq km.
LANGUAGE English. Also local languages and dialects.
CURRENCY US dollar.
GOVERNMENT US commonwealth territory.

FEDERATED STATES OF MICRONESIA

GEOGRAPHY *Area* 825 sq km (318 sq miles).
PEOPLE *Population* 91,300. *Density* 130 per sq km.
LANGUAGE English. Also local languages and dialects.
CURRENCY US dollar.
GOVERNMENT Self-governing state in free association with USA. Formerly part of US Trust Territory of the Pacific Islands.

MARSHALL ISLANDS

GEOGRAPHY *Area* 180 sq km (69 sq miles).
PEOPLE *Population* 35,000.
LANGUAGE English. Also local languages and dialects.
CURRENCY US dollar.
GOVERNMENT Self-governing republic in free association with USA. Formerly part of US Trust Territory of the Pacific Islands.

PALAU

GEOGRAPHY *Area* 460 sq km (178 sq miles).
PEOPLE *Population* 14,000. *Density* 28 per sq km.
LANGUAGE English. Also local languages and dialects.
CURRENCY US dollar.
GOVERNMENT Self-governing republic since 1981.

NAURU

GEOGRAPHY *Area* 21.3 sq km (8 sq miles).
PEOPLE *Population* 8,042. *Density* 378 per sq km.
LANGUAGE Nauruan and English.
CURRENCY Australian dollar.
GOVERNMENT Republic since 1968.

KIRIBATI

GEOGRAPHY *Area* 728 sq km (281 sq miles).
PEOPLE *Population* 68,200. *Density* 79 per sq km.
LANGUAGE English and I-Kiribati (Micronesian dialect).
CURRENCY Kirabati-Australian dollar.
GOVERNMENT Independent republic since 1979.

POLYNESIA

TONGA

GEOGRAPHY *Area* 748 sq km (289 sq miles).
PEOPLE *Population* 94,500. *Density* 126 per sq km.
LANGUAGE Tongan (Polynesian) and English.
CURRENCY Pa'anga or Tongan dollar.
GOVERNMENT Monarchy. The king is head of state and head of government. He appoints, and presides over, a privy council which acts as the cabinet. There is a unicameral legislative assembly which comprises the king and 28 members. There are no political parties.

TUVALU

GEOGRAPHY *Area* 158 sq km (61 sq miles).
PEOPLE *Population* 8,230.
LANGUAGE Tuvaluan (Samoan) and English.
CURRENCY Tuvaluan dollar/Australian dollar.
GOVERNMENT Parliamentary monarchy.

WALLIS & FUTUNA

GEOGRAPHY *Area* 274 sq km (106 sq miles).
PEOPLE *Population* 12,400. *Density* 45 per sq km.
LANGUAGE French. Also Wallisian and Futunian.
CURRENCY Pacific franc.
GOVERNMENT French overseas territory.

WESTERN SAMOA

GEOGRAPHY *Area* 2,842 sq km (1,097 sq miles).
PEOPLE *Population* 159,000.
LANGUAGE Samoan and English.
CURRENCY Tala or Western Samoan dollar.
GOVERNMENT Parliamentary monarchy.

AMERICAN SAMOA

GEOGRAPHY *Area* 199 sq km (77 sq miles).
PEOPLE *Population* 32,300.
LANGUAGE Samoan and English.
CURRENCY US dollar.
GOVERNMENT Self-governing US territory.

NIUE

GEOGRAPHY *Area* 259 sq km (100 sq miles).
PEOPLE *Population* 2,530.
LANGUAGE Niue (a Polynesian language) and English.
CURRENCY New Zealand dollar.

GOVERNMENT Self-governing territory in free association with New Zealand.

TOKELAU

GEOGRAPHY *Area* 12.2 sq km (4.7 miles).
PEOPLE *Population* 1,690.
LANGUAGE Tokelauan and English.
CURRENCY New Zealand dollar.
GOVERNMENT New Zealand overseas territory.

COOK ISLANDS

GEOGRAPHY *Area* 241 sq km (93 sq miles).
PEOPLE *Population* 19,000.
LANGUAGE English and Polynesian languages.
CURRENCY Cook Islands dollar.
GOVERNMENT Internally self-governing state in free association with New Zealand.

FRENCH POLYNESIA

GEOGRAPHY *Area* 4,000 sq km (1,500 sq miles).
PEOPLE *Population* 189,000. *Density* 45 per sq km. *Ethnic groups* Polynesian 68%, mixed 15%, European 12%, Chinese 5%.
LANGUAGE French. Also Polynesian languages including Tahitian.
CURRENCY Pacific franc.
GOVERNMENT French overseas territory. Two deputies are sent to the French national assembly.

PITCAIRN ISLANDS

GEOGRAPHY *Area* 5 sq km (2 sq miles).
PEOPLE *Population* 49. *Ethnic groups* European, Polynesian and European/Polynesian.
LANGUAGE English and English/Tahitian.
CURRENCY New Zealand dollar.
GOVERNMENT British dependent territory.

THE MIDDLE EAST

Lebanon

Many Middle East conflicts have been fought out in the suburbs of Beirut: Lebanese Christian against Lebanese Muslim, Israeli against Palestinian, Shia against Sunni. After the end of the Iran-Iraq war in 1988, Iraq supplied anti-Syrian Christian militias with weapons. In October 1990 the Syrians finally crushed General Michel Aoun's rebellion against the government of Christian Maronite President Elias Hrawi.

Lebanese militias

Amal Shia organization set up by Musa Sadr in early 1970s. Support mainly from poor Shias in the south and Beqaa valley. Nabih Berri became leader after Sadr disappeared during a visit to Libya in 1978.

Hizbollah Umbrella organization of radical Shias with links with Iran. Led by Shaikh Muhammad Hussein Fadlallah and Shaikh Ibrahim al-Amin.

Tawhid Radical Sunni movement led by Shaikh Said Shaban and based in Tripoli. Rumoured to have links with Iran.

Kataib Founded in 1930s by Pierre Gemayel. Traditionally represented the dominant Maronite groups. Military wing has been absorbed into the Lebanese Forces.

Lebanese Forces Military wing, led by Samir Geagea, of the Lebanese Front, a coalition of Maronite leaders dominated by the Kataib. The strongest single militia grouping.

Fatah The biggest single Palestinian movement, founded in 1957 and headed by Yasser Arafat. Under the umbrella of the Palestine Liberation Organization (PLO).

Fatah Revolutionary Council Not a member of the PLO; involved in protracted feud with the Fatah group.

The Kurds

There are 17m Kurds in the region dispersed in Iran, Iraq, Syria, Turkey and the USSR, and radical Kurdish movements have long sought an independent homeland. Iraq mounted chemical weapons attacks against its Kurdish population at the end of the Iran-Iraq war. Iraq's defeat in the Gulf war led to Kurdish rebellions in northern Iraq in early 1991, which disintegrated in the face of superior Iraqi military strength, forcing hundreds of thousands of Iraqi Kurds into Turkey and Iran and necessitating a massive international relief effort.

1947 UN approves partition plan for Palestine
1948 Foundation of state of Israel; Arab-Israeli war
1949 Ceasefire leaves Israel with a third more territory than agreed in UN partition plan
1952 King Farouk of Egypt overthrown by army officers, led by Gamal Abdel Nasser
1953 Coup in Iran removes Prime Minister Muhammad Mossadeq, who had supported nationalization of oil industry. Death of King Abdel Aziz Ibn Saud, founder of Saudi Arabia
1956 Egypt nationalizes Suez canal; British, French and Israelis attack
1958 Iraqi monarchy overthrown
1962 Military coup in Yemen; Egypt and Saudi Arabia support opposing sides in ensuing civil war
1963 Shah of Iran assumes control of government
1967 Six-Day war; Israel occupies West Bank, Golan Heights, Sinai and Gaza Strip. South Yemen becomes independent

1970 Sultan of Oman overthrown by his son, Qaboos. Death of Nasser; succeeded by Anwar Sadat. Civil war in Jordan; Palestinian guerrillas expelled. Military coup in Syria
1971 Bahrain, Qatar and the Trucial States become independent
1973 October war: Egypt recaptures part of Sinai; Opec restricts oil supply in response to Western support for Israel
1975 King Faisal of Saudi Arabia assassinated by a nephew. Lebanese civil war begins
1977 Anwar Sadat visits Jerusalem
1979 Iranian revolution; flight of shah; seizure of US embassy in Tehran. Camp David peace agreement signed by Egypt and Israel; Egypt expelled from Arab League. Muslim extremists occupy Grand Mosque at Mecca

1980 Iran-Iraq war begins
1981 Sadat assassinated; succeeded by Hosni Mubarak
1982 Israel invades Lebanon; massacre at Sabra and Chatila refugee camps
1985 Israel withdraws from Lebanon
1987 Most Arab states restore diplomatic relations with Egypt
1988 Palestinian *intifada* (uprising) in occupied territories; Palestine National Council sets up government in exile and recognizes Israel's right to exist. Ceasefire in Iran-Iraq war; peace talks begin
1990 Unification of North and South Yemen in May; Iraq invades and annexes Kuwait in August
1991 UN-sanctioned and US-led allied forces expel Iraq from Kuwait; UN Security Council resolutions accepted by Saddam Hussein.

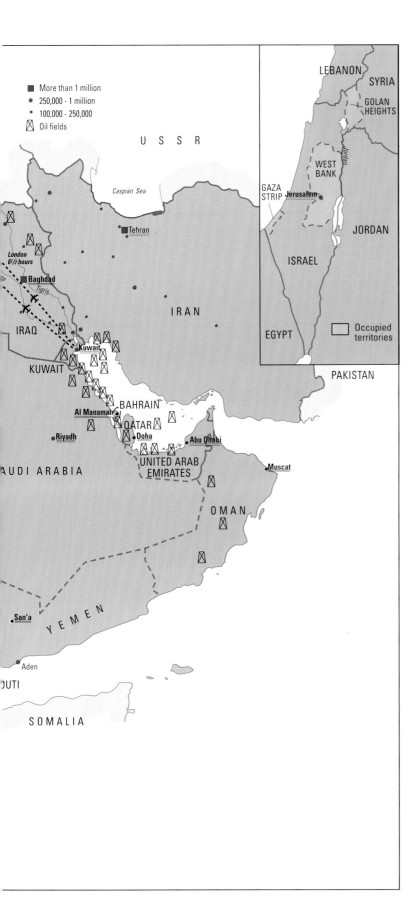

THE MIDDLE EAST

- ■ More than 1 million
- ● 250,000 - 1 million
- • 100,000 - 250,000
- ⋈ Oil fields

U S S R

Caspian Sea

■Tehran

London 6½ hours

■Baghdad
Tigris

IRAN

IRAQ

Kuwait

KUWAIT

BAHRAIN

Al Manamah

QATAR

Doha

•Riyadh

Abu Dhabi

AUDI ARABIA

UNITED ARAB
EMIRATES

•Muscat

OMAN

YEMEN

•San'a

•Aden

JUTI

SOMALIA

LEBANON
SYRIA
GOLAN
HEIGHTS

WEST
BANK

Jordan

GAZA
STRIP

Jerusalem

JORDAN

ISRAEL

EGYPT

☐ Occupied
territories

PAKISTAN

THE MIDDLE EAST

SYRIA

Syria's recent role in the Lebanon and in the 1990–91 Gulf crisis has done much to restore in Western eyes the credibility lost through its alleged involvement in terrorism. Its implication in the 1986 attempt to blow up an Israeli airliner in London led to the UK severing diplomatic ties and the United States and EC imposing sanctions. However the condemnation lessened as Syria emerged as a regional arbiter, firstly in Beirut securing the release of hostages and then as mediator between Iran and the other Gulf states.

Syria's political rehabilitation accelerated after the 1988 ceasefire between Iran and Iraq and its involvement with the allied forces after Iraq's invasion of Kuwait in 1990. As a result Syria was expected to play a key role in determining the new regional political structure.

Syria's primary aim in Lebanon has been to increase its influence in the region by fostering unity under its own aegis. The Shia Amal militia has been its main ally, but Syria has also capitalized on splits within the Christian Maronite camp.

In power since 1970, Hafez Assad has won recognition as an astute politician who has retained power by playing rivals against each other. Many senior government positions are held by members of his minority Alawi sect and opposition is ruthlessly suppressed.

With falling living standards and a non-military foreign debt of over $5 billion, Syria is heavily dependent on Arab aid. Recent oil discoveries have provided greater economic independence and Syria's stance during the 1991 Gulf war has been rewarded with substantial financial aid.

ECONOMIC PROFILE

Traditionally an agricultural economy, but mineral and manufactured exports gaining importance. Main exports: oil and oil products, textiles and foods. Cotton is the main cash crop. Most machinery and spares imported.

Growth Recent finds of high-grade crude have cut import needs. Emphasis on developing chemicals, cement, textiles, leather, paper and electrical goods. Entered 1990s with a healthy trade surplus.

Problems Economy long dependent on large-scale Arab aid. Balance of payments highly vulnerable to international oil market developments and fluctuations in cotton prices. Significant loss in workers' remittances, as well as rise in unemployment, as some 100,000 migrant workers returned from Kuwait in wake of 1990–91 Gulf crisis. Debt service a heavy burden.

OFFICIAL NAME Syrian Arab Republic.

CAPITAL CITY Damascus.

GEOGRAPHY The short, sandy Mediterranean coastline gives way to a littoral mountain range whose continuation forms the border with Lebanon and merges with the southern Golan Heights. The west is by far the most populous region, the rest of the country being a rocky desert plain cut in two by the Euphrates river, whose course supports a second area of population. *Highest point* Mt Hermon 2,814 metres (9,230 feet). *Area* 185,180 sq km (71,500 sq miles).

PEOPLE *Population* 12m. *Density* 65 per sq km. *Ethnic groups* Arab 89%, Kurdish 6%.

RELIGION Muslim 90% (Sunni 72%, Alawi 11%, Druze 3%, other 4%), Christian 9%.

LANGUAGE Arabic. Also Kurdish, Armenian and local dialects.

EDUCATION Compulsory for ages 6–12. There are 4 universities.

CLIMATE Sub-tropical on the coast, with a dry season May–Oct; continental in the interior, with temperatures ranging from below freezing to close to 50°C (120°F). Annual rainfall around 1,000mm (40ins) in the west, less than 100mm (4ins) in the east.

CURRENCY Syrian pound.

PUBLIC HOLIDAYS Jan 1, Leilat al-Meiraj, Mar 8, Greek Orthodox Easter, Id al-Fitr, Id al-Adha, Jul 23, Hijra New Year, Sep 1, Mouloud, Oct 6, Nov 16, Dec 25.

GOVERNMENT Socialist republic. Head of state is a president, directly elected for a 7-year term, who appoints the vice-president, prime minister and council of ministers. The 195-member People's Assembly is directly elected for a 4-year term. The ruling body is National Progressive Front of five socialist parties, headed by the Baath Arab Socialist Party.

IMPORTS AND EXPORTS

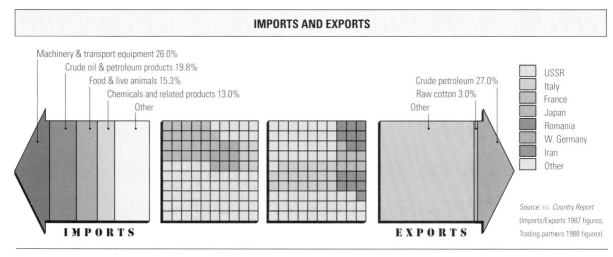

Machinery & transport equipment 26.0%
Crude oil & petroleum products 19.8%
Food & live animals 15.3%
Chemicals and related products 13.0%
Other

Crude petroleum 27.0%
Raw cotton 3.0%
Other

USSR
Italy
France
Japan
Romania
W. Germany
Iran
Other

IMPORTS

EXPORTS

Source: EIU *Country Report*
(Imports/Exports 1987 figures;
Trading partners 1988 figures).

IRAQ

The August 1988 ceasefire with Iran brought welcome, if temporary, relief to Iraq after eight years of war. The declared reason for President Saddam Hussein's disastrous assault on Iran was disputed territory along the Shatt al-Arab waterway, Iraq's outlet to the sea. But he was also supported by Western opposition to the spread of pro-Iranian Islamic fundamentalism.

A British mandate from 1918 until independence in 1932, Iraq remained under British influence until the 1958 revolution swept away the Hashemite monarchy. Three coups in the next decade manifested the struggle between communists and pan-Arab Baathists. The Baathist triumph in 1968 led to the rise of the dictator Saddam Hussein.

The 1975 Algiers Agreement ended Iran's support for Iraq's Kurdish separatists, freed Iraq from dependence on the Soviet Union and allowed it to draw closer to the West. Its huge oil wealth financed an ambitious economic development programme which was halted by the start of the war with Iran in 1980. Financial support from conservative Arab states, combined with Soviet and Western willingness to provide weapons, enabled Saddam Hussein to build up the world's fourth largest army.

In August 1990, after accusing Kuwait of sabotaging the Iraqi economy by exceeding its Opec oil quota, Iraq invaded and then annexed the country. The UN imposed mandatory sanctions and a US-led multinational military force was set up to counter any further Iraqi aggression. After Iraq ignored a final UN deadline to withdraw from Kuwait, war ensued in January 1991. By early March Saddam Hussein had capitulated. Much of Iraq's infrastructure had been destroyed and untold numbers of Iraqis died in the conflict.

The war brought to the fore fundamental regional unrest from the Kurds in the north and Shia rebels in the south. Iraq now faces years of reconstruction and hardship; the speed of recovery depends on the establishment of a regime acceptable to Iraq's neighbours and the West.

OFFICIAL NAME Republic of Iraq.
CAPITAL CITY Baghdad.
GEOGRAPHY The cultivated valley of the Tigris and Euphrates is bounded by mountains to the north-east and desert to the west. *Highest point* Rawanduz 3,658 metres (12,000 feet). *Area* 434,924 sq km (167,930 sq miles).
PEOPLE *Population* 18m. *Density* 41 per sq km. *Ethnic groups* Arab 77%, Kurdish 19%, Turkish 2%.
RELIGION Muslim 96%, Christian 3%.
LANGUAGE Arabic. Also Kurdish and Turkish.
EDUCATION Free and compulsory for ages 6–12.
CLIMATE Continental. May–Oct is very hot, averaging 35°C (95°F), and dry, while there are widespread frosts in winter. Generally, rainfall is less than 500mm (20ins).
CURRENCY Iraqi dinar.
PUBLIC HOLIDAYS Jan 1, 6, Feb 8, Leilat al-Meiraj, May 1, Id al-Fitr, Jul 14, Id al-Adha, Muharram, Ashoura, Mouloud.
GOVERNMENT One-party republic since 1958. The chief executive is the president, elected by the 9-man revolutionary command council, which shares legislative power with a 250-member National Assembly elected for 4 years.

ECONOMIC PROFILE

Dominance of oil – 98% of exports – reinforced by centralized control of economy. Agriculture employs one-third of population but contributes less than 10% of GNP; net food importer. Drive to industrialize in late 1970s emphasized use of oil and gas as feedstock. State-owned heavy industry produces steel, textiles, cement, bitumen and pharmaceuticals.

Growth Oil sales rose sharply after Iran-Iraq ceasefire. Oil refining, petrochemicals, cement and phosphates were also set to expand. Combined effects of UN sanctions and war-damage has thrown the country into a critical situation. Recovery in GDP dependent on resumption of normal trading relations and the restoration of essential services and infrastructure.

Problems Iraqi economy damaged by war with Iran and devastated by 1991 Gulf war. Foreign debt of more than $100 billion. Financial support for recovery likely to be heavily conditional.

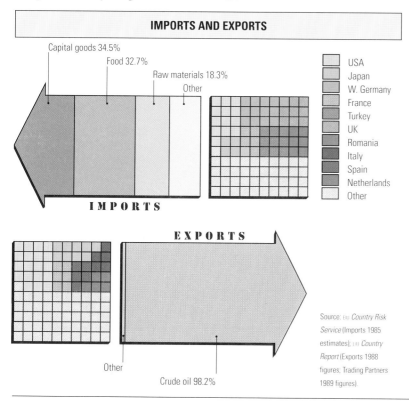

IMPORTS AND EXPORTS

Capital goods 34.5%
Food 32.7%
Raw materials 18.3%
Other

USA
Japan
W. Germany
France
Turkey
UK
Romania
Italy
Spain
Netherlands
Other

IMPORTS

EXPORTS

Other
Crude oil 98.2%

Source: EIU *Country Risk Service* (Imports 1985 estimates); EIU *Country Report* (Exports 1988 figures; Trading Partners 1989 figures).

IRAN

Iran's Islamic revolution in 1979 created a new threat to the conservative Arab states of the Gulf region; it was seen as a beacon for Islamic fundamentalists in other Arab states to challenge the corruption of their own governments. Iran's Islamic message found listeners throughout the region; and accordingly every regime has been forced, to some extent, to listen to the growing voice of fundamentalism. Saudi Arabia, although itself founded on fundamentalist principles, was one of the first to feel the strength of revolutionary fervour when militants took control of the Great Mosque in Mecca in 1979, a violent episode echoed when Saudi police killed more than 400 Iranian pilgrims during the Mecca riots in 1987. Moreover, civil unrest in Egypt and other north Africa states, while touched off by economic grievances, often carried the flavour of militant Islam.

The hostility of the conservative Gulf states was, in these circumstances, understandable; the hostility of their Western allies was, however, more carelessly caused by the siege of the US embassy in Tehran, Iran's support for terrorism and the taking of hostages, and the endless tirade against the West for its imperialism and materialism. As a result, Iran had few supporters in its war with Iraq.

The ceasefire in 1988 brought about a reversal of roles. War-weary Iran, seeking aid to reconstruct its battered economy, began to court the West which now felt free to condemn Iraq's ruthless treatment of its rebellious Kurdish and Shia communities.

OFFICIAL NAME Islamic Republic of Iran.
CAPITAL CITY Tehran.
GEOGRAPHY The centre of Iran is a high arid basin dotted with oases and with a vast, dry salt lake, the Kavir, at its heart. The basin is surrounded by a ring of mountains whose fertile foothills are extensively farmed. A marshy coastal plain lies along the south coast of the Caspian sea and a desert strip along the Persian Gulf. Most settlement is in the north and west; the south and east are principally inhabited by nomads. *Highest point* Qolleh-ye Damavand 5,604 metres (18,390 feet). *Area* 1,648,000 sq km (636,000 sq miles).
PEOPLE *Population* 48m. *Density* 30 per sq km. *Ethnic groups* Persian 45%, Azerbaijan 16%, Kurdish 8%.
RELIGION Shia Muslim 93%, Sunni Muslim 5%.
LANGUAGE Farsi (Persian). Also Azerbaijani, Turkish, Kurdish, Baluchi, Arabic and others.
EDUCATION Free for ages 6–11. Ccmpulsory 6–14 where available. Mixed-sex schools being phased out.
CLIMATE Continental and dry, especially in summer. Average monthly temperatures range from 2°C (36°F) in Jan to 30°C (86°F) in July, with recorded extremes of -18°C (0°F) and 55°C (131°F).
CURRENCY Rial.
PUBLIC HOLIDAYS Feb 11, Mar 20–24, Leilat al-Meiraj, Apr 1–2, Id al–Fitr, Jun 4, 5, Id al–Adha, Ashoura, Mouloud.
GOVERNMENT Islamic republic. Since the overthrow of the shah in 1979, Iran has had an Islamic constitution. The president, who is chief executive, and the 270-member legislature, the Consultative Assembly, are elected every 4 years. All laws must be approved for their constitutional and Islamic correctness by the 12-member Council of Guardians.

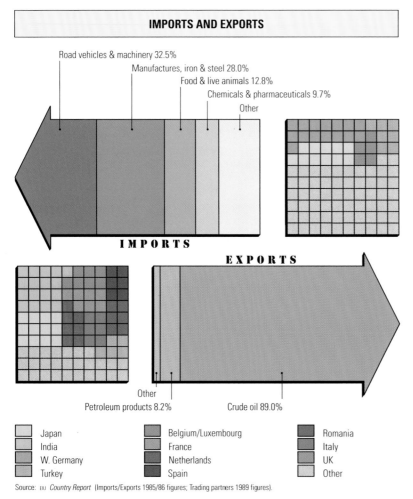

IMPORTS AND EXPORTS

Road vehicles & machinery 32.5%
Manufactures, iron & steel 28.0%
Food & live animals 12.8%
Chemicals & pharmaceuticals 9.7%
Other

IMPORTS

EXPORTS

Other
Petroleum products 8.2%
Crude oil 89.0%

Japan	Belgium/Luxembourg	Romania
India	France	Italy
W. Germany	Netherlands	UK
Turkey	Spain	Other

Source: EIU *Country Report* (Imports/Exports 1985/86 figures; Trading partners 1989 figures).

When the war with Iraq ended, Iran's oil production was running at barely half the level under the shah and being sold for less than half the price. The disadvantages of dependence on oil have been hotly debated, but restoring revenue from this source seemed the only feasible way of mobilizing finance for reconstruction. The war promoted the arms industry but little else; shortages of inputs forced the closure of many ambitious schemes. Lack of foreign exchange made countertrade deals the preferred vehicle for new business with overseas contractors. Efforts were made to diversify exports by including large-scale sales of carpets or pistachio nuts in barter trade. Attempts to reverse the serious neglect of agriculture under the shah's rule have yet to stem the drift away from rural areas that started in the 1960s, adding to social pressures in the cities. Around 55% of the population are urban residents, of whom more than 6m live in the fastest growing city, Tehran, where there is a serious housing shortage.

Iran's ability to finance its war with Iraq without borrowing on the international market and its scrupulous repayment of interest on pre-revolutionary loans earned it valuable credibility during the post-war reconstruction phase. Peace also meant that economic and political discontent could no longer be sublimated in the cause of a holy war against Iraq. Many Iranians were tired of clerical rule and of the increasingly desperate poverty that the state of war had imposed.

Iran's increasingly robust political system has proved a safeguard against instability; parliament is open by regional standards, although more controlled than it was in the early 1980s. Ayatollah Khomeini died in mid-1989 and was succeeded by Ali Khamenei. His informal coalition with the powerful parliamentary speaker and commander-in-chief of the armed forces, Hashemi Rafsanjani (who was subsequently elected president), appeared to confirm a shift in power away from the radicals and towards the pragmatic moderates seeking better relations with the West in the interests of economic reconstruction.

The country's return to international respectability was expected to be helped by its stance during the 1990–91 Gulf crisis. Despite pressure from domestic fundamentalists, the government remained determinedly neutral, offering to act as a peace-broker. Subsequent events tended to confirm Iran's desire for better relations with the EC and United States.

ECONOMIC PROFILE

Oil and gas production backbone of economy; agriculture recovering from neglect during free-spending years of shah's regime. Traditional exports – caviar, carpets, pistachio nuts, fresh and dried fruit – a tiny proportion of total. Resumption of industrial development depends on foreign partners' willingness to conclude barter or buyback deals.

Growth Reconstruction offers plenty of scope if finance can be raised. Oil sector will initially get priority for funds, followed by armed forces, housing and power. Plans to complete petrochemical schemes and increase natural gas exports.

Problems Recovery from war damage and 1990 earthquake will take years, although assistance from Western and Arab countries more likely since Iran's neutral position in Gulf crisis improved relations. Shortages of foods and consumer goods; power supplies unreliable. Weak currency raises import costs. Erratic government attitude to private sector discourages investment.

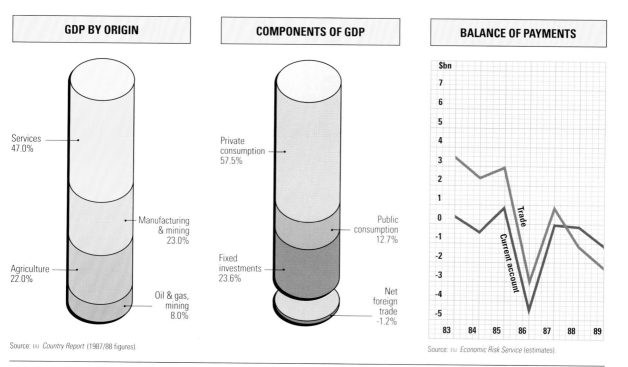

GDP BY ORIGIN

Services 47.0%
Manufacturing & mining 23.0%
Agriculture 22.0%
Oil & gas, mining 8.0%

Source: EIU *Country Report* (1987/88 figures).

COMPONENTS OF GDP

Private consumption 57.5%
Public consumption 12.7%
Fixed investments 23.6%
Net foreign trade -1.2%

BALANCE OF PAYMENTS

$bn

Trade
Current account

83 84 85 86 87 88 89

Source: EIU *Economic Risk Service* (estimates).

LEBANON

The elegance that once characterized Beirut as the hub of the Middle East is long gone, destroyed by the indiscriminate violence that has scarred Lebanon since 1975. The conflict which exploded that year had at its heart Muslim resentment towards the historical pre-eminence of the Christians, a group supported by a complex power-sharing arrangement that had not been revised since 1943. Attempts by Syria to impose a package offering Muslims equal representation in parliament failed to satisfy Muslim groups resentful of Christian power. The Syrian invasion in 1976 prevented an outright victory for the Muslim leftists and the PLO, and appeared to have ended the civil war.

In reality this was merely the start of the downward spiral. Two Israeli invasions followed; the first, in 1978, allowed Israel to hand control of the southern border area to its Christian allies. The second, in 1982, was aimed at the destruction of the PLO, but attracted notoriety when the Christian Lebanese Forces massacred the inhabitants of Palestinian refugee camps. When the Israelis withdrew, Syria resumed its efforts to secure national reconciliation, intervening in strength in 1987. Failed attempts at reform by President Amin Gemayel left Lebanon without any overall government and maverick Christian leader, General Michel Aoun, took advantage.

His two-year rebellion was crushed in October 1990 by Syrian forces and their allies. The national government of Elias Hrawi, a pro-Syrian Maronite Christian, set about consolidating its power with the support of most Lebanese. However, there is little prospect of a rapid end to Lebanon's internal strife.

ECONOMIC PROFILE

Banking and commerce traditionally largest contributors to GDP but badly affected by civil war. Exports of fruit and vegetables much reduced. Industrial base well developed and diversified by regional standards – oil refining, cement, textiles, light industries.

Problems Beirut has lost its role as services and recreational centre of the Middle East. Much of industry and agriculture destroyed or seriously disrupted. Most commerce through unofficial channels, controlled by one or other of warring factions.

OFFICIAL NAME Republic of Lebanon.
CAPITAL CITY Beirut.
GEOGRAPHY Most settlement is along the sedimentary coastal plain and the lower slopes of the Lebanon Mountains. Lying between them and a range on the Syrian border lies the Beqaa valley, another population centre. *Area* 10,400 sq km (4,000 sq miles).
PEOPLE *Population* 2.8m. *Density* 271 per sq km. *Ethnic groups* Lebanese Arab 83%, Palestinian Arab 10%, Armenian 5%, Kurdish 1%.
RELIGION Muslim 65% (Shia 33%, Sunni 25%, Druze 7%), Christian 35% (Maronite 25%, other 10%).
LANGUAGE Arabic.
EDUCATION Free but non-compulsory state schools; secondary and higher education dominated by private schools.
CLIMATE Summers are hot (32°C/90°F) and dry; average winter temperatures 16°C (61°F) on the coast, 10°C (50°F) inland. Annual rainfall is around 750mm (30ins) on the coast, double that on the heights.
CURRENCY Lebanese pound.
PUBLIC HOLIDAYS Jan 1, Feb 9, Mar 22, Leilat al-Meiraj, Good Fri–Easter Mon (both the Orthodox and Western Easters are celebrated), Ascension, Id al-Fitr, Id al-Adha, Muharram, Aug 15, Ashoura, Mouloud, Nov 1, 22, Dec 25, 31.
GOVERNMENT Republic since 1941. Normal political life is only now being revived after long period of suspension. Formerly, a 99-member legislative national assembly, its seats allocated on religious lines, was elected by PR; and the chief executive was a president elected by the assembly from among the Maronites.

JORDAN

Jordan's identity is inextricably linked with the creation of Israel in 1948. During the first Arab-Israeli war that followed, Jordan absorbed the Palestinian West Bank as well as large numbers of refugees; today at least 60% of Jordan's population is Palestinian. The West Bank, lost to the Israelis in 1967, remains the heartland of any possible Palestinian state. King Hussain's sudden announcement in August 1988 that Jordan was severing its links with the West Bank was a recognition that the PLO and not Jordan was the legitimate representative of the Palestinian people. While Jordan's perceived support for Iraq during the 1990–91 Gulf crisis increased the Hashemite kingdom's popularity at home, it seriously damaged Jordan's political and economic standing in the region and with the West.

Natural resources are restricted to phosphates, which account for 30% of exports, potash and oil shale; agriculture is largely confined to the Jordan valley. Jordan, facing a balance of payments crisis, depends on remittances from migrants working in the Gulf, service industries and technology transfer; all this was damaged by the international embargo against Iraq which has devastated the Jordanian economy.

OFFICIAL NAME The Hashemite Kingdom of Jordan.
CAPITAL CITY Amman.
GEOGRAPHY Four-fifths of Jordan is a rocky desert. Most people live on the north-western plateaus, on either side of the Rift Valley. *Area* 97,740 sq km (37,740 sq miles) including West Bank.
PEOPLE *Population* 4m (including West Bank). *Ethnic groups* Arab 98%, Circassian 1%.
RELIGION Muslim (mainly Sunni) 93%, Christian 5%.
LANGUAGE Arabic.
EDUCATION Free and compulsory for ages 5–11.
CLIMATE Summers dry and hot, winters cold. Annual rainfall 400mm (16ins) in uplands.
CURRENCY Jordanian dinar.
PUBLIC HOLIDAYS Jan 1, Leilat al-Meiraj, Id al-Fitr, May 25, Id al-Adha, Aug 11, Mouloud, Raa's Alsaneh Alhijreyeh.
GOVERNMENT Constitutional monarchy. The king is chief executive, aided by a Council of Ministers. The legislative assembly consists of the Senate of 40 members and the Chamber of Deputies of 80 members.

ISRAEL

The war that followed the creation of Israel in 1948 left the new state with one-third more territory than it had been awarded by the UN partition plan. The flight of Palestinian Arabs was offset by a doubling of the Jewish population in three years through immigration. The 1967 war left Israel in control of more Arab territory, to which it still clings. Today, 60% of Israel's 3.5m Jews were born in Israel; some 2.2m Arabs live under Israeli rule, 1.4m of them in the Occupied Territories.

Absorbing the new Jewish immigrants presented massive social and economic challenges in the new state's early years. These were, however, successfully met and the economy grew by a real annual average of 10% between 1950 and 1973. But the legacies of those stressful years, in the form of a centralized and monopolistic economic structure and the enforced integration of people from diverse backgrounds, were eventually revealed after the 1973 Arab-Israeli war abruptly ended the era of rapid growth.

The past two decades have seen a transformation in the make-up of Israeli society, with the founding generation, whose roots were mostly socialist and eastern European, giving way gradually and reluctantly to Israeli-born leaders and managers, many of whose parents came from Muslim countries. The Likud and Labour parties governed in a series of uneasy coalitions throughout the 1980s, at times joined by some of the plethora of mini-parties created by a proportional representation system that guarantees seats in parliament to any party that gets more than 1% of the popular vote. The price of their support has included the promotion of religious orthodoxy. This has meant an increase in nationalism, but the popular culture and high level of technological achievement underline the strong Western orientation of society.

The problem of Arab enmity has partially receded since the peace treaty with Egypt in 1979, but the Palestinian-Israeli conflict, exacerbated by the continued occupation of the West Bank, Gaza Strip and East Jerusalem, has returned to centre stage. The *intifada* (uprising) that began in late 1987 has been a powerful catalyst for Palestinian nationalism and has heightened the split between the Israelis who wish to hold on to the occupied territories and those prepared to yield them in return for a credible peace. Israel's military prowess, built up to resist an external threat, has proved ill equipped to deal with what is essentially an internal political problem. The sight of the Israeli army in confrontation with Palestinian youths throwing stones and petrol bombs severely tarnished the country's image and eroded its international support just at a period when the Palestine Liberation Organization (PLO) was gaining new international

OFFICIAL NAME State of Israel.

CAPITAL CITY Jerusalem.

GEOGRAPHY Most Israelis live on the coastal plain or the hills and mountains of the north and centre. To the east, the Jordan runs in a rift valley between the Sea of Galilee and the heavily saline Dead Sea, the lowest place on earth at 396 metres (1,300 feet) below sea level. The southern wedge of the country is taken up by the Negev Desert. *Highest point* Har Meron 1,208 metres (3,960 feet). *Area* 20,700 sq km (8,000 sq miles).

PEOPLE *Population* 4.4m. *Density* 202 per sq km. *Ethnic groups* Jewish 83%, Arab 14%.

RELIGION Jewish 83%, Muslim 13%, Christian 2%, Druze 2%.

LANGUAGE Hebrew and Arabic. Also Yiddish.

EDUCATION Free to university level and compulsory for ages 5–15. There are 6 universities.

CLIMATE Mainly sub-tropical, with deserts in the south. Average temperature is around 20°C (68°F) on the coast, 32°C (90°F) in the southern desert. Annual rainfall, almost all falling Oct–Apr. is often as low as 25mm (1in) in the south, but rising to 2,000mm (80ins) around the Sea of Galilee.

CURRENCY Shekel.

PUBLIC HOLIDAYS Mar 30, Apr 5, 18, May 19, Sept 9, 10, 18, 23, 30. Muslim and Christian holidays observed by respective minorities.

GOVERNMENT Republic. The head of state is a president, elected for 5 years by the Knesset, a 120-member legislature elected by PR for a 4-year term. The executive consists of a cabinet, usually representative of the majority coalition, and a prime minister who is usually from the dominant coalition party.

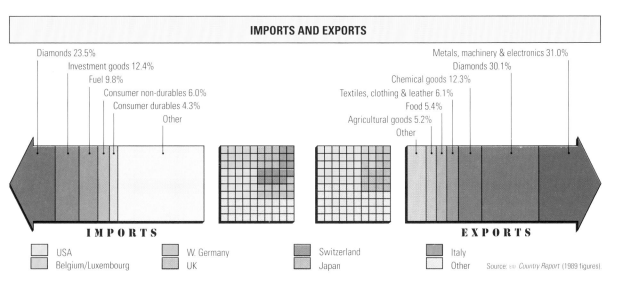

IMPORTS AND EXPORTS

Diamonds 23.5%
Investment goods 12.4%
Fuel 9.8%
Consumer non-durables 6.0%
Consumer durables 4.3%
Other

Metals, machinery & electronics 31.0%
Diamonds 30.1%
Chemical goods 12.3%
Textiles, clothing & leather 6.1%
Food 5.4%
Agricultural goods 5.2%
Other

IMPORTS

EXPORTS

☐ USA
☐ Belgium/Luxembourg
☐ W. Germany
☐ UK
☐ Switzerland
☐ Japan
☐ Italy
☐ Other   Source: EIU *Country Report* (1989 figures).

respectability through its decision to recognize Israel's right to exist and renounce the armed struggle in preparation for a peace conference. However the limited resumption of terrorism and the PLO's support for Iraq during the 1990–91 Gulf crisis has made it harder for the US administation to force Israel into a meaningful dialogue with the PLO.

The need to find a solution to the Palestinian issue is coupled with the need to prepare for the open international economy of the 1990s. Israel will not be able to align itself with its major trading partners – the EC and United States – until it has extricated itself both from its entanglement in the occupied territories and its overregulated and government-dominated economic structure. Failure here will lead to growing political isolation, economic stagnation and a steady loss of human and financial capital. Success will enable Israel to generate or free the resources needed to tackle its social problems and return to stable growth.

ECONOMIC PROFILE

Intensive high-yield agriculture, much of it on a cooperative basis, has provided self-sufficiency and export capacity. Diversified industrial base, with former export leaders – electronics, metallurgy, weapons – giving way in recent years to textiles, clothing, food products. Major diamond-cutting centre. Successful austerity measures have brought inflation to more manageable levels.

Growth Citrus fruit and vegetable exports to European markets. High-tech science-based industries – chemicals, biotechnology, aerospace and agricultural technology – offer growth and export prospects, but also face strong international competition. "Non-interventionist" role during 1990–91 Gulf crisis permitted Israel to ask USA for $10 billion in aid.

Problems Military spending a heavy drain on resources. Almost all energy imported. Tourism hit by Palestinian uprising.

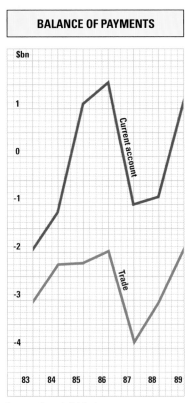

BALANCE OF PAYMENTS

Source: EIU *Economic Risk Service.*

EGYPT

Egypt, the foundation of Arab socialism and solidarity in the 1960s, is today essentially capitalist and pro-Western. Despite this change of character it has regained much of its traditional authority in the region since late 1987 when most Arab states restored diplomatic ties, severed after Egypt's peace treaty with Israel in 1979.

The death of President Nasser in 1970 ended an experiment that had involved the nationalization of industries, land reform and the takeover of foreign assets, including – most crucially for Egypt's image in the third world – the nationalization of the Suez canal in 1956. Nasser's influence waned after Egypt's disastrous defeat by Israel in 1967. His successor, Anwar Sadat, expelled Soviet advisers and began dismantling the top-heavy bureaucracy.

In 1974, President Sadat moved away from centralized economic management and instituted the open-door policy, aimed at encouraging foreign and domestic private investment. A period of prosperity ensued, although largely dependent on four non-industrial sources of revenue: remittances from Egyptians working abroad, oil, tourism and Suez canal tolls. The policy is criticized today for having stimulated service industries at the expense of vital agricultural and industrial development.

Although Sadat's treaty with Israel relieved the country of its military burden and enhanced its credibility with institutions such as the IMF, it lost Egypt the prestige in the Arab world earned by its performance in the 1973 war with Israel. Domestic anger at the peace treaty drew strength from the Iranian revolution and the reaction to mounting corruption, providing the context for Sadat's assassination in 1981 by Islamic militants.

The new president, Hosni Mubarak, lacked the charisma of his predecessors

OFFICIAL NAME Arab Republic of Egypt.

CAPITAL CITY Cairo.

GEOGRAPHY Egypt is almost entirely desert; a narrow, extremely fertile strip along the floodplain of the Nile and its delta is the only cultivable land. Most of the country is flat. *Highest point* Mt Katherîna 2,642 metres (8,670 feet). *Area* 1,001,449 sq km (386,660 sq miles).

PEOPLE *Population* 51.8m. *Density* 52 per sq km. *Ethnic groups* Arab 99.7%.

RELIGION Muslim 94%, Christian 6%.

LANGUAGE Arabic.

EDUCATION Compulsory for ages 6–12 and free at all levels.

CLIMATE Dry, with hot summers 30°C (86°F) and mild winters 16°C (61°F). Even on the Mediterranean coast rainfall is less than 200mm (8ins).

CURRENCY Egyptian pound.

PUBLIC HOLIDAYS Sham El Nessim, Sinai Liberation Day, 1st Bairam, Workers' Day, Evacuation Day, 2nd eve of 2nd Bairam, 2nd Bairam, Revolution Day, Prophet Mohammed's birthday, Army Forces Day, Suez City and National Liberation Day , Victory Day.

GOVERNMENT Republic since 1953. The 458-member legislative People's Assembly is elected for 5 years by PR. The chief executive is the president, nominated by a two-thirds majority of the assembly and elected by referendum for a 6-year term.

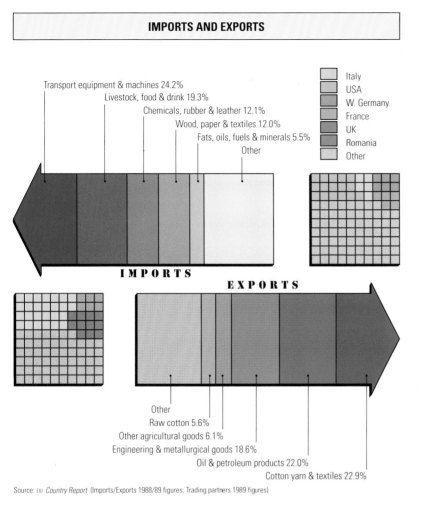

IMPORTS AND EXPORTS

Transport equipment & machines 24.2%
Livestock, food & drink 19.3%
Chemicals, rubber & leather 12.1%
Wood, paper & textiles 12.0%
Fats, oils, fuels & minerals 5.5%
Other

Italy
USA
W. Germany
France
UK
Romania
Other

IMPORTS

EXPORTS

Other
Raw cotton 5.6%
Other agricultural goods 6.1%
Engineering & metallurgical goods 18.6%
Oil & petroleum products 22.0%
Cotton yarn & textiles 22.9%

Source: EIU *Country Report* (Imports/Exports 1988/89 figures; Trading partners 1989 figures).

ECONOMIC PROFILE

Agriculture, leading employer, concentrated in Nile flood plain and delta. Food prices kept low to benefit urban consumers. Cotton is main cash crop, aided by heavy subsidies. Industry, largely import-substitution, developed in public sector, being slowly privatized and restructured.

Growth Reconciliation with Arab world raising hopes of new investment. Arms industry profited from Iran-Iraq war and has found new export markets. Plans to expand vehicle assembly, iron and steel, and to start production of power station equipment.

Problems Agriculture periodically threatened by low Nile waters, as well as soil salinity and growing pressure on land. Fears of unrest resulting from cautious IMF-imposed economic reforms. Workers' remittances and tourism severely hit by 1990–91 Gulf crisis.

BALANCE OF PAYMENTS

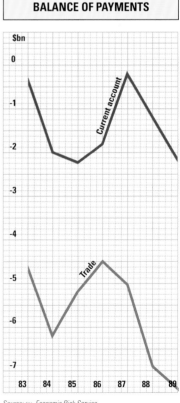

Source: EIU *Economic Risk Service*.

but has unhesitatingly fulfilled his pledge to steer the nation towards democracy. A genuine opposition to the ruling National Democratic Party emerged after the first comparatively fair elections in 1984. The press has been liberalized, providing a lively forum for the expression of most political opinions.

A coalition led by the Muslim Brotherhood became the main parliamentary opposition in the 1987 elections. President Mubarak seemed to have welcomed this, in the hope that the body politic would neutralize the fundamentalists by co-opting them. But the militants remain as violent as ever, and Egypt's middle classes fear an experiment in Islamic government.

Egypt's new regional respectability has given it the confidence to edge away from its strong ties with the USA and be more critical of Israel. These moves betoken a revival of radicalism founded upon support for the Palestinian uprising, discontent with a very high inflation rate and a feeling that the poor are being made to pay for economic measures prescribed by the IMF.

The economy has been boosted by IMF and other loans, a rescheduling of much of its estimated $50 billion foreign debt, increased US aid and favourable trade relations with the Soviet Union. The tourist industry, however, was severely hit by the 1990–91 Gulf crisis. Egypt has to import 60% of the food it needs, at a cost of $4 billion a year for a population that continues to grow by over 2% a year. Egypt's support of the allies during the 1990–91 Gulf crisis resulted in the writing-off of US military debt worth $7 billion and pledges of an unprecedented amount of foreign aid.

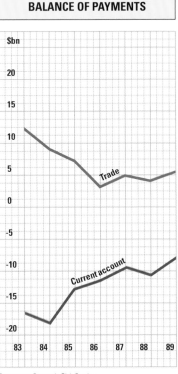

SAUDI ARABIA

Saudi Arabia, with one-quarter of the world's oil reserves, has experienced both the benefits and the costs of an oil-dependent economy. It built a modern infrastructure with the extra revenues from the quadrupling of oil prices in 1973, but was thrown into recession when a glut in the market undermined prices in the mid-1980s.

The slump in oil revenues dislocated plans to adjust the industry. Schemes to replace foreign workers with Saudis and to encourage the private sector to take over the running of industrial projects, particularly in setting up downstream industrial plants at the new industrial cities of Jubail and Yanbu, became irrelevant.

Rapid development has put growing pressure on a society largely founded on traditional values. The kingdom is governed by the Al-Saud family; King Fahd and his full brothers form the ruling clique and no opposition is tolerated. The conservative views of the Islamic clergy are heeded, particularly since the Iranian revolution of 1979. The occupation of the Great Mosque in Mecca that year by Muslim zealots tested the regime. It responded by curtailing overt personal extravagance and discussing proposals for a quasi-democratic *majlis al-shura* (consultative council). The kingdom's obligation to act as host each year to millions of pilgrims to Mecca exposes it to disruptive influences from abroad; in 1987 Saudi police killed 400 Iranian pilgrims demonstrating against the royal family and its alliance with the USA.

Iraq's invasion of Kuwait in August 1990 and the subsequent war posed the most serious threat to stability in the kingdom's history. Despite Iraq's total defeat, Saudi Arabia faces continued difficulties: Arab radicals might be antagonised if the maintenance of a foreign military force is required to protect the kingdom.

The kingdom's oil reserves give it considerable political muscle. It used oil as a weapon after the 1973 Arab-Israeli war to garner support for the Arab cause, but it remains torn between support for the Palestinians and its military dependence on the USA. One of the kingdom's main problems has been how to adopt Western technology and economic methods while preserving the strict form of Islam that is its foundation. Contamination by foreign values through, *inter alia*, an extensive education programme, threatens a culture that forbids alcohol, cinema and dancing and imposes strict Islamic penalties for crimes such as murder, theft and adultery.

OFFICIAL NAME Kingdom of Saudi Arabia.
CAPITAL CITY Riyadh.
GEOGRAPHY Basically a sloping plateau, rising sheer – except for a narrow coastal plain in the south – from the Red Sea and sloping gently eastward through sandy deserts to salt flats and marshes on the east coast. There are no permanent rivers. The south-eastern quarter of the country is almost totally empty and half the Saudi population are nomadic herdsmen. Mecca and Medina, Islam's holiest cities, are on the high ground to the west. *Highest point* 3,133 metres (10,280 feet). *Area* 2,150,000 sq km (830,000 sq miles).
PEOPLE *Population* 14m. *Density* 6 per sq km. *Ethnic groups* Arab.
RELIGION Muslim 99% (Sunni 85%, other 14%).
LANGUAGE Arabic.
EDUCATION Free but non-compulsory.
CLIMATE Summers very hot, with temperatures generally above 38°C (100°F); average winter temperatures 14–23°C (57–73°F). Although the coast is oppressively humid, rainfall is very low; southern desert can remain dry for years.
CURRENCY Riyal.
PUBLIC HOLIDAYS Apr 15–18, Jun 22–25, Sep 23.
GOVERNMENT Absolute monarchy. The king appoints a council of ministers; the prime minister is invariably a member of the royal family.

BALANCE OF PAYMENTS

$bn

Source: EIU *Economic Risk Service.*

ECONOMIC PROFILE

Economy previously based on subsistence agriculture and nomadic herding transformed by discovery of oil. Oil production fuelled rapid development of infrastructure and oil-related heavy industry – refining, petrochemicals, fertilizers, steel. Irrigated agriculture, developed at high cost, has brought self-sufficiency in wheat and eggs.

Growth Banks and industry recovering from mid-1980s slump. Light industry promoted on industrial estates. Continued heavy spending on defence programme. Mineral resources, including gold, silver, copper, coal and bauxite, await development.

Problems Much economic activity still reliant on government spending and hence on oil revenues. Private industry inhibited by small Gulf market. New heavy industries entering overcrowded markets. Enormous financial commitment to US-led allied operations in the 1991 Gulf war, coupled with expected budget deficits suggest that the kingdom will become an international borrower.

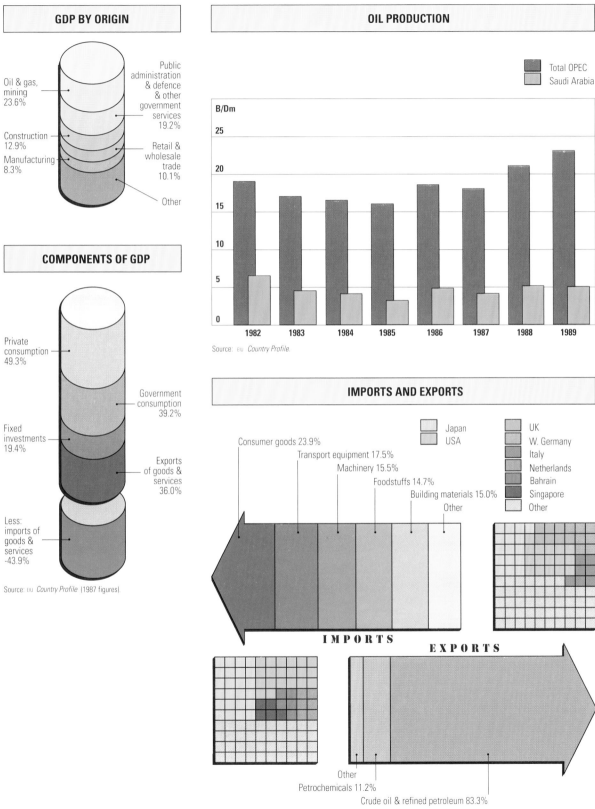

GDP BY ORIGIN

Oil & gas, mining 23.6%

Public administration & defence & other government services 19.2%

Construction 12.9%

Manufacturing 8.3%

Retail & wholesale trade 10.1%

Other

COMPONENTS OF GDP

Private consumption 49.3%

Government consumption 39.2%

Fixed investments 19.4%

Exports of goods & services 36.0%

Less: imports of goods & services -43.9%

Source: EIU *Country Profile* (1987 figures).

OIL PRODUCTION

Total OPEC
Saudi Arabia

B/Dm

25
20
15
10
5
0

1982   1983   1984   1985   1986   1987   1988   1989

Source: EIU *Country Profile.*

IMPORTS AND EXPORTS

Japan
USA

UK
W. Germany
Italy
Netherlands
Bahrain
Singapore
Other

Consumer goods 23.9%
Transport equipment 17.5%
Machinery 15.5%
Foodstuffs 14.7%
Building materials 15.0%
Other

IMPORTS

EXPORTS

Other
Petrochemicals 11.2%
Crude oil & refined petroleum 83.3%

Source: EIU *Country Report* (1988 figures).

THE MIDDLE EAST

 KUWAIT

Until the Iraqi invasion of August 1990 it appeared that the discovery of oil in 1938 had given Kuwait the financial security to resist the expansionist aims of its three great neighbours, Saudi Arabia, Iraq and Iran. Its oil reserves were the third largest in the non-communist world, with a lifespan of around 250 years. Oil wealth enabled the Al-Sabah family, which has ruled Kuwait since 1752, to consolidate its political power. By developing and running an efficient and very generous welfare state system it won the loyalty of most of both the 550,000 indigenous Kuwaitis and the 1.5m other residents.

Kuwait was the first and most successful Gulf state to invest its oil wealth in both downstream industries and non-oil sectors. Its overseas refineries and petrol stations guaranteed a market for Kuwaiti crude oil, while its overseas investments – $8 billion a year – now earn more than its oil industry.

During the Iran-Iraq war Kuwait, along with other Gulf states, felt obliged to support Iraq against the spread of Iranian radicalism with massive financial aid. However, an ungrateful Iraq renewed its claims to Kuwaiti territory and accused it of economic sabotage. Iraq eventually invaded Kuwait in August 1990 and formally annexed it. A US-led multilateral force was formed and the UN adopted mandatory economic sanctions against Iraq. In January 1991 a short but devastating war began. Iraq was heavily defeated and was ejected from Kuwait, but not before it had plundered almost everything which was transportable, torched Kuwait's oil fields and destroyed installations. In the aftermath of the war, popular revenge for the Iraqi invasion was largely directed at Kuwait's long-term Palestinian population, which was subjected to harassment and repression. Physical reconstruction of the country, expected to cost at least $100 billion, was due to be paralleled by political reform, with the Al-Sabah family promising a more democratic form of government.

OFFICIAL NAME State of Kuwait.
CAPITAL CITY Kuwait.
GEOGRAPHY Most is flat, rocky desert, with a few low hills and little surface water. The land around the Bay of Kuwait is irrigated and cultivated and supports most of the highly urbanized population. *Highest point* 299 metres (980 feet). *Area* 17,818 sq km (6,880 sq miles).
PEOPLE *Population* 2m. *Ethnic groups* Arab 84% (Kuwaiti 42%, other 42%), Asian 15%.
RELIGION Muslim 92%, Christian 6%.
LANGUAGE Arabic.
EDUCATION Free to university level but non-compulsory. There is 1 university.
CLIMATE Hot; daytime temperatures of 50C (120°F) are common. Annual rainfall 25–200mm (1–8ins); Apr–Sep always dry.
CURRENCY Kuwaiti dinar.
PUBLIC HOLIDAYS Jan 1, Feb 25, Leilat al-Meiraj, Id al-Fitr, Id al-Adha, Muharram, Mouloud.
GOVERNMENT Monarchy. The emir is head of state and chief executive. The 1962 constitution provides for a national assembly of 50 members elected by literate adult male civilians. This was dissolved in 1986, when the emir announced he would rule by decree. After the 1991 Gulf war the emir promised a more democratic form of government would be introduced.

 BAHRAIN

Historically a pearling, fishing and trading centre, Bahrain led the region in developing oil, discovered in 1932. When production waned in the 1970s, the island diversified into communications and banking just as Lebanon, the region's traditional services centre, tumbled into civil war.

Bahrain's cosmopolitan history and industrial sector made for a social awareness shading towards political radicalism that persisted after independence in 1971. The National Assembly was dissolved in 1975. The Iranian revolution, four years later, sparked off demonstrations among the Shia majority calling for an Islamic republic. The early 1980s were further punctuated by Shia agitation, with Iran responding to Bahrain's support for Iraq by repeating historic claims to the island; the ceasefire in the Iran-Iraq war in 1988 came as welcome relief.

The oil sector still provides 20% of GDP and 60% of government revenues although reserves are running low; heavy use of the refinery by Saudi Arabia bolstered revenue in the early 1980s. An aluminium smelter, iron pelletizing plant and dry dock form the beginnings of an industrial base, and joint ventures with investors from the OECD have been encouraged. The banking sector, which includes both onshore and offshore activity, went through a troubled patch both in the mid-1980s recession and particularly following Iraq's invasion of Kuwait in 1990. The sector accounts for 14% of GDP and the flight of capital and loss of business confidence has had a severe impact.

OFFICIAL NAME State of Bahrain.
CAPITAL CITY Al Manamah.
GEOGRAPHY Bahrain island, most of the land area, has a centre of rocky, barren hills and sand and salt marshes to the south and west. The north and north-west is irrigated and contains most of the population. *Highest point* Jabal ad-Dukhan 135 metres (440 feet). *Area* 622 sq km (240 sq miles).
PEOPLE *Population* 420,000. *Density* 670 per sq km. *Ethnic groups* Bahraini 70%.
RELIGION Muslim 85% (Shia 50%, Sunni 35%), Christian 7%.
LANGUAGE Arabic and English.
EDUCATION Free but non-compulsory. Private and religious schools co-exist with the state system.
CLIMATE Hot and humid, though annual rainfall is less than 100mm (4ins). Average temperatures range from less than 20°C (68°F) in Dec–Mar to more than 29°C (84°F) in May–Oct.
CURRENCY Bahrain dinar.
PUBLIC HOLIDAYS Jan 1, Leilat al-Meiraj, 1st day of Ramadan, Id al-Fitr, Id al-Adha, Muharram, Ashoura, Mouloud, Dec 16.
GOVERNMENT Monarchy. Final independence from the UK was gained in 1971. The emir now rules by decree through an appointed council of state.

UNITED ARAB EMIRATES

British interest in the Trucial States in the 19th century centred on its concern to protect the sea route to India. The seven states that eventually formed the United Arab Emirates (UAE) – Abu Dhabi, Dubai, Sharjah, Ajman, Umm al-Qawain, Ras al-Khaimah and Fujairah – might have been nine, but Bahrain and Qatar decided not to join the federation on its birth in 1971, opting for independence in their own right.

Shaikh Zayed, ruler of Abu Dhabi, the largest and wealthiest emirate, became president of the federation, with the late Shaikh Rashid, ruler of entrepreneurial Dubai, as prime minister. The dominance of Abu Dhabi, the largest oil producer, was enhanced in 1973 when oil prices quadrupled. Dubai, however, capitalized on its long trading relationship with Iran during the Iran-Iraq war, as well as keeping its dry dock in business repairing war-damaged vessels. Despite rapid infrastructural development, the changes brought by the emirates' new wealth have not done away with the old ways of life. Strongly entrenched traditions remain, as does the shaikhs' council, which has held the federation together in troubled times. The UAE's support for the US-led alliance in the 1990–91 Gulf crisis came in the form of substantial financial assistance and deployment of some men to the Arab alliance.

Lack of coordination between the emirates has limited attempts to move away from total dependence on oil revenues, leaving the federation with too many banks, too many ports and airports and much duplication of industrial capacity.

OFFICIAL NAME United Arab Emirates.

CAPITAL CITY Abu Dhabi Town.

GEOGRAPHY The area consists of a strip of desert sand and salt flats along the rocky southern coast of the Gulf. *Highest point* Jabal Hafit 1,189 metres (3,900 feet). *Area* 83,600 sq km (32,300 sq miles).

PEOPLE *Population* 1.6m. *Density* 21 per sq km. *Ethnic groups* (residents and citizens) Indian, Iranian and Pakistani 50%, Arab 42%, European 8%.

RELIGION Muslim (mainly Sunni) 89%, Christian 6%.

LANGUAGE Arabic.

EDUCATION Compulsory for ages 6–12.

CLIMATE Hot and dry, with mild winters. Annual rainfall 75–100mm (3–4ins). Average temperatures 18°C (64°F) in Jan, 33°C (91°F) in July; summer temperatures up to 46°C (115°F).

CURRENCY Dirham.

PUBLIC HOLIDAYS Jan 1, Leilat al-Meiraj, start of Ramadan, Id al-Fitr, Id al-Adha, Aug 2, 6, Oct 11, Dec 2, 25.

GOVERNMENT Federation of emirates. Each of the seven shaikhs is an absolute monarch in his own territory, and the seven form the federal supreme council of rulers, who elect a federal president and vice-president from among their number. There are no political parties.

IMPORTS AND EXPORTS

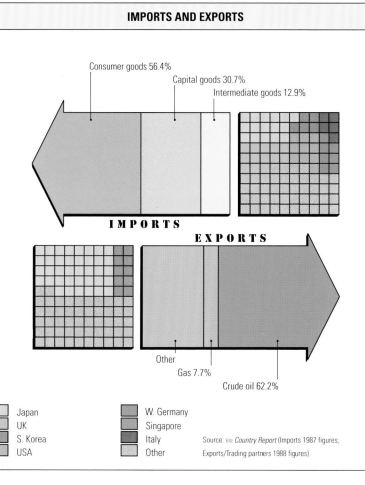

Consumer goods 56.4%
Capital goods 30.7%
Intermediate goods 12.9%

IMPORTS

EXPORTS

Other
Gas 7.7%
Crude oil 62.2%

Japan
UK
S. Korea
USA

W. Germany
Singapore
Italy
Other

Source: EIU *Country Report* (Imports 1987 figures; Exports/Trading partners 1988 figures).

GDP BY ORIGIN

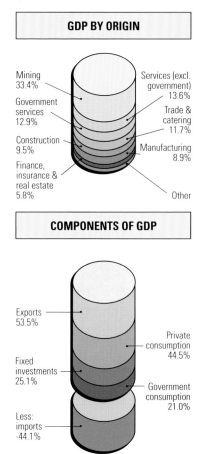

Mining 33.4%
Services (excl. government) 13.6%
Government services 12.9%
Trade & catering 11.7%
Construction 9.5%
Manufacturing 8.9%
Finance, insurance & real estate 5.8%
Other

COMPONENTS OF GDP

Exports 53.5%
Private consumption 44.5%
Fixed investments 25.1%
Government consumption 21.0%
Less: imports -44.1%

Source: EIU *Country Report* (1988 figures).

QATAR

Qatar was the first Arab Gulf state to start an industrial programme to diversify away from oil. Its cement, steel and fertilizer plants are relatively efficient but cannot compete in glutted world markets. Doha, the capital, and the place where most people live, competes unsuccessfully with Bahrain as a business and leisure centre.

Qatar became independent from the UK in 1971, soon after the creation of the United Arab Emirates. The country has been ruled by Shaikh Khalifa since 1972 after his cousin was deposed in February that year. Its foreign policy is expressed mainly in concert with the Gulf Co-operation Council (GCC), although it is in dispute with another GCC member, Bahrain, over a series of islands. In 1986, the Qatar army raided the disputed Fasht ad-Dibal coral reef, seizing foreign workers who were building a Bahraini coastguard station. There have been indications of increased spending on defence, but the dispute is now being settled by arbitration.

Dependence on hydrocarbons remains strong, accounting for 80% of government revenues and 80% of exports. The government, known for cautious management, responded to the unpredictable oil market after 1986 by refusing to produce an annual budget, allocating funds month by month as earnings permitted.

Completion of most essential infrastructure has led to an exodus of migrant workers depressing domestic demand. New activity is accompanying development of the vast North Field gas reserves, set to continue well into the next century, promising a secure income as oil declines. The non-oil sectors, however, have performed poorly. The initial loss of confidence because of the 1990–91 Gulf crisis should not unduly hamper construction projects and Qatar did not suffer capital flight to the same degree as other GCC states.

OFFICIAL NAME State of Qatar.

CAPITAL CITY Doha.

GEOGRAPHY A barren, sandy, almost entirely featureless and waterless peninsula in the Persian Gulf, most settlement is on the eastern side, the location of the capital and oil reserves. *Highest point* Dukhan Heights 98m (320 feet). *Area* 11,000 sq km (4,200 sq miles).

PEOPLE *Population* 341,000. *Density* 32 per sq km. *Ethnic groups* Arab.

RELIGION Muslim 92%, Christian 6%, Hindu 1%.

LANGUAGE Arabic. Also English.

EDUCATION Free but non-compulsory, at all levels. There is 1 university.

CLIMATE Hot and dry, with annual rainfall less than 100mm (4ins). Summer temperatures over 30°C (86°F); winters relatively mild, around 18°C (64°F).

CURRENCY Riyal.

PUBLIC HOLIDAYS Feb 22, Sep 3, Id al-Fitr, Id al-Adha.

GOVERNMENT Absolute monarchy. The emir is head of state and chief executive, and appoints an administrative council of ministers and an advisory council. There is no legislature.

OMAN

Oman had three primary schools and 10km of tarred roads in 1970 when Sultan Said was ousted, with British help, by his son Qaboos. Sultan Said, too old to adapt to the changes brought by the start of oil production in 1967, had imposed a nightly curfew in the capital, Muscat, and banned such symbols of decadence as spectacles and radios.

Sultan Qaboos, trained in the British army, set out to develop Oman rapidly and to end the civil war in the southern province of Dhofar. By 1976 the war was over and the return of highly-educated exiles from the West accelerated development, which generally eschewed prestige projects in favour of spending on infrastructure, education and health. Oil reserves proved larger than expected and astute management reduced the impact of falling prices. Oil revenues still account for 90% of government income. In addition, limited amounts of copper are exported from mines; light industry is expanding; and a stock market has been set up. Rugged scenery offers potential for the nascent tourist industry.

Sultan Qaboos ended Oman's isolation and developed an independent foreign policy. Previously tense relations with neighbouring South Yemen gradually improved during the 1980s. Oman has also opened diplomatic relations with the USSR and, like the UAE, has maintained close ties with Iran. Defence and internal security eat up over 40% of the annual budget, and Oman has close military links with the UK and USA, which stem from its strategic position at the mouth of the Gulf.

Oman, because of its distance from the conflict, avoided the crash in business confidence that hit other Gulf states during the 1990–91 crisis. It also benefited from windfall profits in the hydrocarbon sector.

OFFICIAL NAME Sultanate of Oman.

CAPITAL CITY Muscat.

GEOGRAPHY Most of Oman is a flat desert with scattered oases. The Hajar Mountains shield a narrow, settled coastal plain on the Gulf of Oman. There are also settlements on the landward, less steep, side of the mountains. *Highest point* Jabal ash-Sham 3,018 metres (9,900 feet). *Area* 212,457 sq km (82,030 sq miles).

PEOPLE *Population* 1.3m. *Ethnic groups* Arab 87%, Baluchi 4%.

RELIGION Ibadi Muslim 74%, Sunni Muslim 25%.

EDUCATION Non-compulsory. There is 1 university, but priority is given to provision of adult literacy centres.

LANGUAGE Arabic.

CLIMATE Hot and dry, with high humidity on coasts. Average temperatures around 35°C (95°F) in summer, around 22°C (72°F) in winter. Annual rainfall 75–100mm (3–4ins).

CURRENCY Rial Omani.

PUBLIC HOLIDAYS Leilat al-Meiraj, 1st day of Ramadan, Id al-Fitr, Id al-Adha, Muharram, Ashoura, Mouloud, Nov 18–19.

GOVERNMENT Absolute monarchy. The sultan appoints an administrative cabinet and an advisory consultative assembly. There are no political parties.

YEMEN

On 22 May 1990 the Yemen Arab Republic (YAR) and the People's Democratic Republic of Yemen (PDRY), more commonly known as North and South Yemen, officially merged to form the most populous state of the Arabian peninsula. The northern city of Sana'a became the unified capital and its leader, Ali Abdullah Saleh, became the head of state. The two parts of the country had their own history before unity.

In the north traditional spiritual leaders, the Zaydi imams, had held onto power despite repeated uprisings until nationalist officers proclaimed the YAR in 1962. Civil war followed, with Saudi Arabia backing the imams, and Egypt the republicans. After Egypt withdrew its support, a compromise coalition government was formed in 1970 but violence and upheaval continued. President Saleh came to power in 1978 resulting in relative political stability, although the government's *de facto* control was limited to the major urban areas.

The PDRY was created as a result of military and administrative expansion from Aden, the Indian Ocean port seized by Britain in 1839. From the 1950s onwards British colonial policy came under increasing pressure from a nationalist movement. Its militancy began in the 1960s, when the UK's attempt to create a south Arabian federation ran up against rivalry between Adeni merchants and the tribal rulers of the interior. In 1966 the British initiated a two-year transition to independence but the threat of civil war in November 1976 forced a premature handover of power to the National Liberation Front. Post-independence politics were both bloody and militantly Marxist.

Moves towards greater cooperation in the late 1980s witnessed the joint oil exploration project in a disputed border area. The combination of new political thinking in Aden, encouraged by Soviet reforms, and the YAR's greater economic independence from Saudi Arabia as a result of the start of oil exports, also acted as catalysts for unity.

Yemen faces serious economic problems. The chronic ills of the two former Yemen states, which propelled them into unification, have been further exacerbated by the political consequences of the 1990–91 Gulf crisis. The government's pro-Iraqi position resulted in Saudi Arabia expelling at least 1m Yemeni workers. The resulting loss of earnings – the country's major source of foreign exchange – will plunge the country into a deeper recession. And the returning workers will exacerbate unemployment problems at a time when much-needed Gulf aid is likely to be cut back.

OFFICIAL NAME Republic of Yemen.

CAPITAL CITY Sana'a.

GEOGRAPHY Most inhabitants live in the west which benefits from higher rainfall, especially on the Yemeni highlands which are cultivated by terracing. The interior is a barren plateau, with a few settlements on the south flowing wadis. The northern edge of the plateau roughly marks the border with Saudi Arabia. *Highest point* Jabal an Nabi Shu'ayb 3,760 metres (12,340 feet). *Area* 536,869 sq km (217,740 sq miles).

PEOPLE *Population* 12.5m. *Density* 23 per sq km. *Ethnic groups* Arab 97%, Somali 1%, Indian & Pakistani 1%.

RELIGION Muslim 100% (Zaydi Shia 47%, Sunni 53%).

EDUCATION Primary education available for ages 7–13, but non-compulsory.

LANGUAGE Arabic.

CLIMATE The western coast is hot and humid, maximum 43–45°C (109–113°F), with little rainfall. The highland interior is cooler and receives monsoon rainfall, average 500–1,000 mm (20–40ins).

CURRENCY Yemeni rial, Yemeni dinar.

PUBLIC HOLIDAYS Leilat al-Meiraj, 1st day of Ramadan, Id al-Fitr, 22 May, Id al-Adha, Muharram, Ashoura, 6 Sept, Mouloud, 14 Oct.

GOVERNMENT Multi-party democracy since 1990. Five member Presidential Council, with 5-year terms, assisted by a 45-member Advisory Council; 25 from the north and 20 from the south.

GDP BY ORIGIN

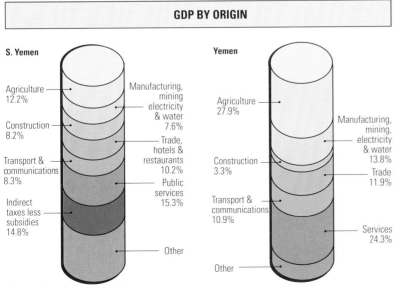

S. Yemen

Agriculture 12.2%
Construction 8.2%
Transport & communications 8.3%
Indirect taxes less subsidies 14.8%
Manufacturing, mining electricity & water 7.6%
Trade, hotels & restaurants 10.2%
Public services 15.3%
Other

Yemen

Agriculture 27.9%
Construction 3.3%
Transport & communications 10.9%
Manufacturing, mining, electricity & water 13.8%
Trade 11.9%
Services 24.3%
Other

Source: EIU *Country Reports* (1987 figures).

GDP GROWTH

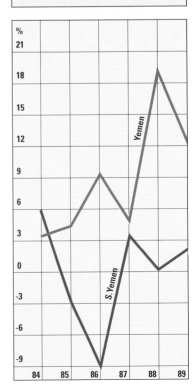

Source: EIU *Country Profile and Report.*

NORTH AFRICA

Western Sahara

After Spain abandoned the colony in 1976, Western Sahara came increasingly under the control of Morocco which lays claim to the territory in disregard of the indigenous independence movement, Polisario. The Polisario government-in-exile, the Sahrawi Arab Democratic Republic, is widely recognized and the war for Western Sahara has strained Morocco's relations with its neighbours and many African states. Both sides accepted a UN peace plan in 1988 and have had formal diplomatic contacts. Yet, progress has been slow and Polisario has stepped up its military activity since 1989 in an effort to jolt the kingdom towards compromise. The UN is attempting to organize a referendum in the territory on the question of self-determination, although Morocco is attempting to set strict conditions on who is eligible to vote.

Ceuta and Melilla

Two enclaves on the Moroccan coast, Ceuta and Melilla, were retained by Spain when Morocco became independent in 1956. The population of the two cities is mainly Spanish in origin, although the Arab population has grown rapidly in recent years. Morocco formally claims the two enclaves but relations with Spain remain relatively cordial.

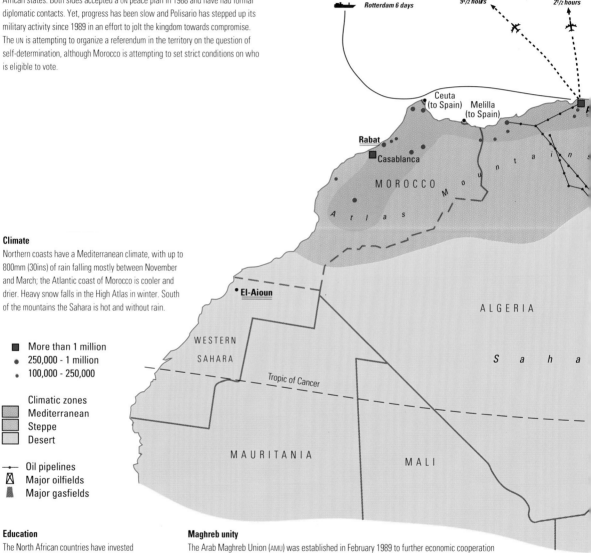

Climate

Northern coasts have a Mediterranean climate, with up to 800mm (30ins) of rain falling mostly between November and March; the Atlantic coast of Morocco is cooler and drier. Heavy snow falls in the High Atlas in winter. South of the mountains the Sahara is hot and without rain.

- ■ More than 1 million
- ● 250,000 - 1 million
- · 100,000 - 250,000

Climatic zones
- Mediterranean
- Steppe
- Desert

- ⊷ Oil pipelines
- ⊠ Major oilfields
- ▲ Major gasfields

Education

The North African countries have invested heavily in education, which is generally compulsory from 7 to 15, although female education remains a lower priority than male. Algeria has come close to its aim of providing nine years' schooling; education accounts for a quarter of the government budget. There is also strong emphasis on promoting technical skills through higher education. Libya, enrolled more than 10% of the population in higher education by the mid-1980s.

Maghreb unity

The Arab Maghreb Union (AMU) was established in February 1989 to further economic cooperation between its five members: Algeria, Libya, Mauritania, Morocco and Tunisia. Its major achievement has been a commitment signed in July 1990 to form a full customs union by 1995 as concern mounts about the impact of the EC single market. Equally, the AMU gives its members a channel through which to negotiate with the EC on issues such as aid, Arab migrant workers and security.

However, regional tensions between its members have threatened the AMU from its inception and it is unlikely that it will ever progress to the political union envisaged by the Libyan leader Moammar Qaddafi. In particular, the five states took very different stances over the 1990–91 Gulf crisis, reflecting their differences on pan-Arab solidarity. The populations of the Maghreb became increasingly radicalized by the war against Iraq and the entire region has experienced increasing unrest. Such a climate is unlikely to encourage further moves towards Maghreb cooperation.

Oil and gas

North Africa's most important economic link with western Europe is as a supplier of oil and gas. Although its oil reserves are likely to be exhausted in little over 30 years, Algeria's gas reserves rank seventh in size in the world and it is the EC's third largest supplier with plans for expansion. Libya's crude oil is of high quality and in 1990 reserves were estimated at 45–50 billion barrels, including potential offshore reserves gained as a result of Libya's victory in maritime border disputes with Tunisia and Malta.

Pipe dreams

The enormous oil revenues earned by Algeria and Libya have enabled them to undertake bold construction projects. The success of the Trans-Mediterranean pipeline, which has linked Algeria's gas fields with Italy since 1983, has prompted plans for a second pipeline to carry gas to Spain and possibly beyond into western Europe. In Libya, the Great Man-Made River pipeline is only a third completed and there are grave doubts as to the environmental impact and even the agricultural necessity of the project.

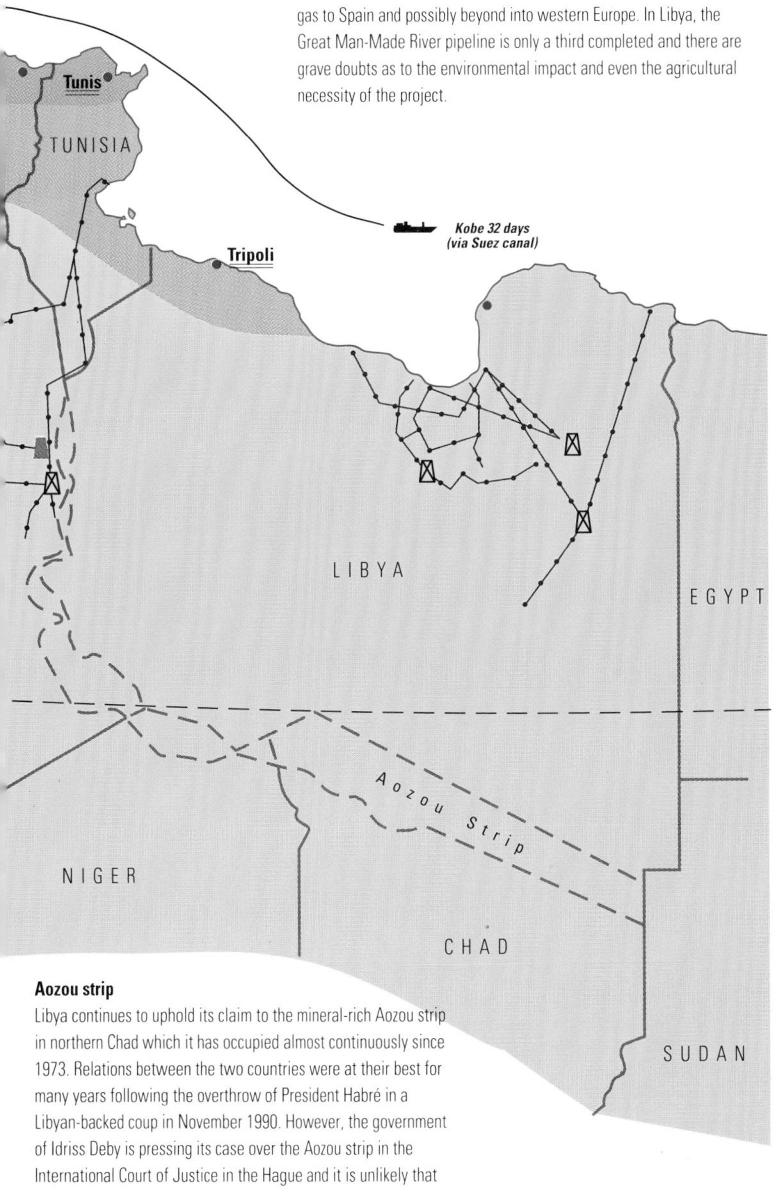

Tunis

TUNISIA

Tripoli

*Kobe 32 days
(via Suez canal)*

L I B Y A

E G Y P T

A o z o u   S t r i p

N I G E R

C H A D

S U D A N

Aozou strip

Libya continues to uphold its claim to the mineral-rich Aozou strip in northern Chad which it has occupied almost continuously since 1973. Relations between the two countries were at their best for many years following the overthrow of President Habré in a Libyan-backed coup in November 1990. However, the government of Idriss Deby is pressing its case over the Aozou strip in the International Court of Justice in the Hague and it is unlikely that any agreement will be reached soon.

AFRICA

MOROCCO

King Hassan II has survived several attempts on his life and power since he came to the throne in 1961. Ostensibly a constitutional monarch, he nevertheless retains an autocratic hold on government. The 1980s saw the emergence of a limited degree of independent political expression, but any signs of Islamic fundamentalism have been forcefully suppressed.

King Hassan has established Morocco as a leading conservative force in Afro-Arab politics, making his mark as a mediator in Middle East politics. However, his tenacity over the Western Sahara issue has lost him friends in Africa and inflated the defence budget, helping push external debt to $22 billion by 1989.

The import bill will not fall until agricultural productivity improves and greater food self-sufficiency is achieved. The lengthy depression of world phosphate prices has been partly mitigated by adding value to production, but mineral resources generally are unremarkable. Tourism offers more potential, since Morocco is already a popular destination. The sector is attracting foreign investment and the government hopes to extend this to other economic areas through recent liberalization measures.

OFFICIAL NAME Kingdom of Morocco.
CAPITAL CITY Rabat.
GEOGRAPHY Bordered on the north by the Mediterranean Sea, on the west by the Atlantic Ocean, the south by the Sahara Desert and the east by the Atlas Mountains, Morocco is almost a continental "island". The mountains also constitute a precious watershed, with rivers flowing down into the dry, sandy plains and plateaus which cover two-thirds of the territory. The mountains separate the fertile west and north from the near-Saharan south and east. *Highest point* Toubkal 4,165 metres (13,670 feet). *Area* 710,850 sq km (274,460 sq miles).
PEOPLE *Population* 23.4m. *Density* 33 per sq km. *Ethnic groups* Arab/Berber 99%.
RELIGION Muslim 99%, Christian 1%.
LANGUAGE Arabic. Also French, Berber and Spanish.
CURRENCY Dirham.
PUBLIC HOLIDAYS Jan 1, Mar 3, 1st day of Ramadan, May 1, Id al-Fitr, Id al-Adha, Muharram, Ashoura, Aug 14, Mouloud, Nov 6, 18.
GOVERNMENT Constitutional monarchy. The king rules with a chamber of representatives of 306 members, two-thirds elected by universal suffrage and the remainder by an electoral college of employer, worker and professional groups. Ministers are appointed by the king. There are around 10 officially recognized political parties.

IMPORTS AND EXPORTS

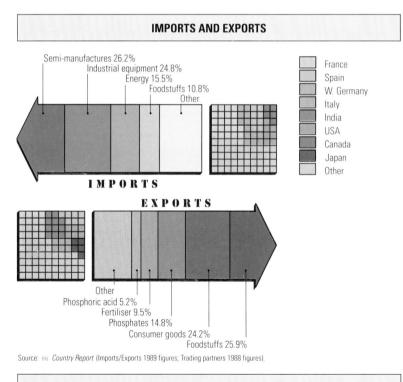

Semi-manufactures 26.2%
Industrial equipment 24.8%
Energy 15.5%
Foodstuffs 10.8%
Other

France
Spain
W. Germany
Italy
India
USA
Canada
Japan
Other

IMPORTS

EXPORTS

Other
Phosphoric acid 5.2%
Fertiliser 9.5%
Phosphates 14.8%
Consumer goods 24.2%
Foodstuffs 25.9%

Source: EIU *Country Report* (Imports/Exports 1989 figures; Trading partners 1988 figures).

ECONOMIC PROFILE

Agriculture still employs nearly half the working population, producing wheat, barley and beans for home market; citrus fruits, olive oil, wine, figs and dates for export. Phosphates are biggest export earner.

Growth Tourism. Strong and expanding fishing and textile industries.

Problems Heavy external debt burden; stagnant world phosphate market. Hopes of extracting oil from shale depend on sustained high oil prices.

BALANCE OF PAYMENTS

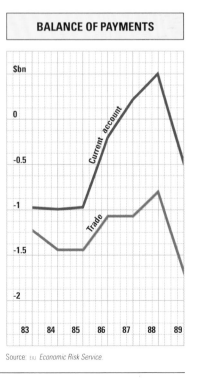

$bn

0

-0.5

-1

-1.5

-2

Current account

Trade

83 84 85 86 87 88 89

Source: EIU *Economic Risk Service*.

TUNISIA

The peaceful overthrow in November 1987 of President Habib Bourguiba by his prime minister, Zine el-Abidine Ben Ali, ended fears of a bitter succession struggle. Mr Bourguiba led Tunisia to independence from France in 1956 and tried to create a westernized, largely secular state in his own image. In his last years he presided over a confused and divided government, as the Islamic opposition gathered support among Tunisians struggling to make ends meet.

Mr Ben Ali consolidated support by emphasizing national reconciliation. He announced amnesties for thousands of prisoners and invited the opposition to take part in drawing up policy aims and in a revived electoral process.

While maintaining Tunisia's commitment to Western alliances and liberal economic policies, Mr Ben Ali stressed its Arab-Islamic identity, undercutting the fundamentalists' appeal. Relations with Libya improved sharply, to the benefit of plans for Maghreb unity.

The mid-1980s slump in oil prices exacerbated a growing economic crisis and in 1986 the government called for IMF assistance in implementing an economic liberalization programme. The policies required were not far removed from those already in place and Tunisia, as a result, has had fewer difficulties adjusting than some other countries. Recent droughts have created some unwelcome problems, but the country has remained one of the IMF's star pupils.

OFFICIAL NAME Republic of Tunisia.
CAPITAL CITY Tunis.
GEOGRAPHY The northern half of Tunisia is the eastern end of the Atlas range. Forests cover the mountains. The fertile valleys and small areas of flat land along the generally rocky northern coast support most of the population. The centre of the country is a depression dotted with salt lakes, the south a largely uninhabited semi-desert upland. *Area* 163,610 sq km (63,170 sq miles).
PEOPLE *Population* 7.8m. *Density* 48 per sq km. *Ethnic groups* Arab 98%, Berber 1.5%, French 0.2%.
RELIGION Muslim 99.5%, Christian 0.3%.
LANGUAGE Arabic. Also French and Berber.
CURRENCY Tunisian dinar.
PUBLIC HOLIDAYS Jan 1, Mar 20–21, Apr 9, May 1, Id al-Seghir, May 1, Id al-Kebir, Jul 25, Aug 13, Oct 15.
GOVERNMENT Republic since 1956. The head of state and chief executive is a president, elected for a 5-year term, as are the 141 members of the legislative National Assembly. A multi-party state since 1981.

ECONOMIC PROFILE

Based on Mediterranean produce – olive oil, citrus fruit and textiles. Oil accounted for half of export earnings in early 1980s but has declined in importance as fields have been worked out. Tourism now crucial.

Growth Dependent on further expansion of services sector. A number of international banks have set up operations in Tunis. Joint ventures supplying the EC market are being encouraged.

Problems Agriculture has been hit by drought. Economy vulnerable to fluctuating oil and phosphate prices and the volatile tourism market.

IMPORTS AND EXPORTS

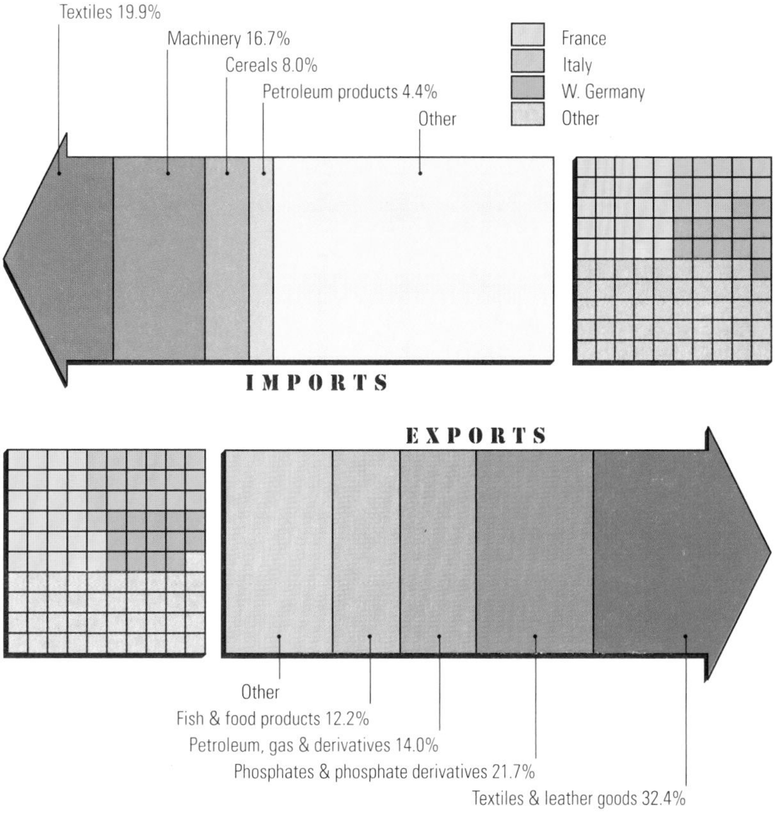

Textiles 19.9%
Machinery 16.7%
Cereals 8.0%
Petroleum products 4.4%
Other

France
Italy
W. Germany
Other

IMPORTS

EXPORTS

Other
Fish & food products 12.2%
Petroleum, gas & derivatives 14.0%
Phosphates & phosphate derivatives 21.7%
Textiles & leather goods 32.4%

Source: EIU *Country Report* (1988 figures).

275

ALGERIA

The October 1988 riots left hundreds dead and shattered Algeria's hard-won image of political stability. The Front de Libération Nationale (FLN) retained power but with its legitimacy, stemming from its role in the bitter 1954–62 independence war against France, undermined. President Chadli Benjedid responded with unprecedented political reforms (allowing the formation of opposition parties) which complemented the overhaul of the socialist economy begun in the early 1980s.

The fundamentalist Front Islamique du Salut's (FIS) victory in the June 1990 local elections was a shock which first raised the prospect of Algeria going the way of Iran, and becoming an Islamic fundamentalist state. The FIS raised the stakes again in the run-up to the 1991 general election, with demands for a change in the voting laws, presidential elections, and for the immediate establishment of an Islamic State. Following fundamentalist riots in Algiers, President Chadli dismissed the government, postponed elections and imposed a state of emergency.

Continuing reform of the bureaucracy and state industry as part of the economic liberalization process is vital if growth rates are to be raised. Against opposition from party hardliners and trade unionists, state companies have been given considerable autonomy, and private agriculture and foreign investment have been encouraged. Oil reserves are dwindling, but hydrocarbons remain crucial with 75% of export earnings still coming from sales of gas, condensates and refined products.

In many respects the FLN government has been better respected abroad than at home. Charged with being a terrorist haven in the 1960s, Algeria became a leading international mediator in the 1980s. Moves towards regional unity, long an important policy in Algiers, bore fruit in 1989 in the form of the Arab Maghreb Union with its goal of a "Maghreb EC" by 1995.

OFFICIAL NAME People's Democratic Republic of Algeria.

CAPITAL CITY Algiers.

GEOGRAPHY Much of Africa's second largest country is a dry sandstone plateau, largely uninhabited, that merges into the Sahara Desert. The Atlas Mountains separate the plateau from the Mediterranean, with a coastal plain where the major cities, Algiers and Oran, are situated. *Highest point* Mt Tahat 2,918 metres (9,570 feet) *Area* 2,381,741 sq km (919,600 sq miles).

PEOPLE *Population* 22.5m. *Density* 9 per sq km. *Ethnic groups* Arab 83.5%, Berber 16%.

RELIGION Muslim 99%, Christian 0.5%.

LANGUAGE Arabic. Also Berber and French.

CURRENCY Algerian dinar.

PUBLIC HOLIDAYS Jan 1, Id al-Fitr, May 1, Jun 19, Id al-Adha, Jul 5, Ashoura, Mouloud, Nov 1.

GOVERNMENT Republic since 1962. The unicameral National People's Assembly has 295 members elected for 5 years by universal suffrage. The president, also elected every 5 years, is head of state and appoints a prime minister who initiates legislation. A multi-party state since 1989.

ECONOMIC PROFILE

Economic development continues to rely on exports of oil, natural gas and associated products. Agriculture, mainstay of the colonial economy, fell into deep decline after independence and large-scale food imports are necessary.

Growth Agricultural production gradually increasing, with some products – fruit, wine – available for export. Steel and some other manufactured goods now being exported. New economic policies could open the way for development of tourism and service industries.

Problems Insufficient diversification to avoid dependence on shrinking hydrocarbon reserves to pay for food imports and to service debts. Restructuring of industry handicapped by shortages of hard currency, bureaucracy, poor training and overmanning.

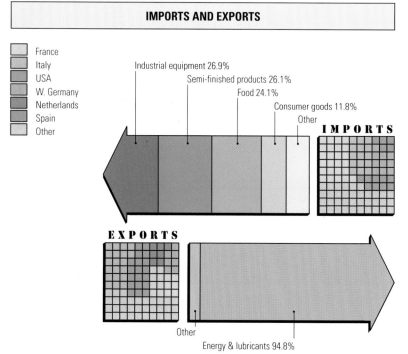

IMPORTS AND EXPORTS

France
Italy
USA
W. Germany
Netherlands
Spain
Other

Industrial equipment 26.9%
Semi-finished products 26.1%
Food 24.1%
Consumer goods 11.8%
Other

IMPORTS

EXPORTS

Other
Energy & lubricants 94.8%

Source: EIU *Country Profile* (Imports/Exports 1988 figures; Trading partners 1989 figures).

LIBYA

It is not just the revolutionary rhetoric of Colonel Moammar Qaddafi that has set Libya apart. In 1951 the former Italian colony became independent, the first African colony to do so. King Idris took over one of the world's poorest states; scrap metal from the second world war battlefields was its main export. But since oil exports began in 1961 Libya has been transformed into a country with a GDP comparable to that of Egypt.

Colonel Qaddafi's 1969 coup was a product of rising third world radicalism and resentment over the lack of popular benefits from the oil wealth. He has been best known for his abolition of conventional government institutions, support for radical movements and confrontation with the USA and its allies.

Until the 1980s occasional stirrings of revolt were kept in check by repression and the distribution of still considerable resources among a population of less than 4m. Opposition to the regime has not died; Islamic fundamentalism and the pro-democracy tide sweeping the rest of the continent are the most recent challenges to its authority. But the popular sweeteners are fewer. Falling oil revenues during the 1980s forced drastic measures after 1988 to rescue the economy, including some liberalization and private enterprise activities.

OFFICIAL NAME The Great Socialist People's Libyan Arab Jamahiriya.
CAPITAL CITY Tripoli.
GEOGRAPHY Mostly desert, with fertile uplands in the extreme east and west. Inland the country is largely uninhabited; the majority of the population is concentrated in the cities along the Mediterranean coast. *Area* 1,759,540 sq km (679,360 sq miles).
PEOPLE *Population* 3.6m. *Density* 2 per sq km. *Ethnic groups* Arab/Berber 100%.
RELIGION Muslim 97%.
LANGUAGE Arabic.
CURRENCY Libyan dinar.
PUBLIC HOLIDAYS Leilat al-Meiraj, Mar 28, Id al-Fitr, Jun 11, Id al-Adha, Muharram, Ashoura, Sep 1, Mouloud, Oct 7.
GOVERNMENT Independent since 1951. Republic since 1969. The Arab Socialist Union is the only permitted party. The head of state is the revolutionary leader, elected by the 1,112 members of the General People's Congress.

GDP BY ORIGIN

Services 33.1%
Oil & natural gas 29.6%
Construction 12.3%
Other

Source: EIU *Country Report* (1987 estimates).

ECONOMIC PROFILE

Oil reserves are enough to last for 60 years, but revenues running at less than half their 1980 peak until 1990-91 Gulf crisis. Agriculture is confined to coastal areas and oases.

Growth The project to pipe groundwater from beneath the Sahara to coastal areas would transform agriculture if completed. Huge investments in petrochemicals, steel and aluminium industries.

Problems Falling oil prices hit development of industry and infrastructure. Much food is imported.

COMPONENTS OF GDP

Private consumption 35.0%
Fixed investments 25.0%
Government consumption 32.0%
Exports 48.0%
Less: imports -40.0%

IMPORTS AND EXPORTS

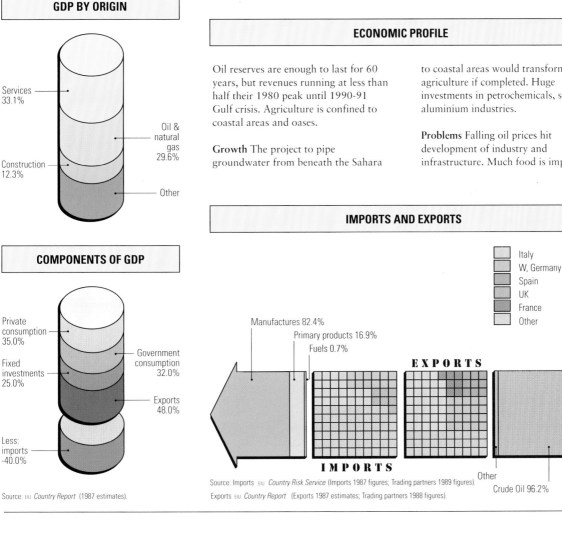

Italy
W, Germany
Spain
UK
France
Other

Manufactures 82.4%
Primary products 16.9%
Fuels 0.7%

EXPORTS

IMPORTS

Other
Crude Oil 96.2%

Source: Imports EIU *Country Risk Service* (Imports 1987 figures; Trading partners 1989 figures).
Exports EIU *Country Report* (Exports 1987 estimates; Trading partners 1988 figures).

WEST AFRICA

Ecowas and CEAO

West Africa has two overlapping economic communities. The Communauté Economique de l'Afrique de l'Ouest (CEAO), set up in 1974, is exclusively francophone. CEAO's main objective is to liberalize trade among members; its recent history has been marred by allegations of financial irregularities.

All CEAO's members also belong to the Economic Community of West African States (Ecowas), established a year later, which has a total of 16 members. Ecowas aims to establish first a customs union and then a full common market. Progress has been slow, hindered by the fact that the region's economies are competitive rather than complementary, and the multiplicity of different currencies used.

Concern to avoid domination of the organization by Nigeria, the region's economic giant, led to the establishment of the Ecowas Fund for Cooperation, Compensation & Development to help redress the balance by ensuring that members did not suffer losses from Ecowas operations and funding development projects in the poorer states. A regional bank, Ecobank, is also being set up. CEAO consists of Benin, Burkina Faso, Côte d'Ivoire, Mali, Mauritania, Niger and Senegal; Togo has observer status. Ecowas consists of CEAO members plus Cape Verde, Gambia, Ghana, Guinea, Guinea-Bissau, Liberia and Nigeria.

Senegambia

The confederation between Senegal and its much smaller neighbour, Gambia, had its origins in the July 1981 coup attempt against Gambia's president Sir Dawda Jawara. Senegalese troops were invited to help put down the coup. Their intervention precipitated discussions on forming the confederation, which were finalized by the end of the year.

Plans for a monetary and customs union and integration of the educational and legal systems foundered with the dissolution of the confederation in September 1989. A new friendship and cooperation treaty was signed in January 1991 but full political union seems unlikely.

The Franc Zone

Unlike most African countries, franc zone members – mainly former French colonies – have the advantage of a freely convertible currency. The CFA franc, used by most African franc zone members, is linked to the French franc at a fixed rate and is backed by the French treasury. West African members of the franc zone – Benin, Burkina Faso, Côte d'Ivoire, Mali, Niger, Senegal and Togo – form the Union Monétaire Ouest-Africaine and share a common central bank, Banque Centrale des Etats de l'Afrique de l'Ouest. All are also members of Banque Ouest-Africaine de Développement. Six central African countries and the Comoros, in the Indian Ocean, are also franc zone members.

- More than 1 million
- 250,000 - 1 million
- 100,000 - 250,000
- Major oilfields
- Areas at risk of desertification

Desertification

Twenty-five years of declining rainfall and growing population pressures in the semi-arid Sahelian belt have contributed to the gradual southward advance of the Sahara. The world's attention was first drawn to the problem by the Sahelian famine of 1973, when 100,000 people died. That crisis was caused by drought, but the roots of the problem lay in the previous two decades of better-than-average rainfall, when cash crop cultivation and settlement expanded on to marginal land. Over-grazing, over-cultivation, deforestation and poor irrigation are the main causes of desertification; the process is reversible, if the land is given time to rest and reclaimed through tree-planting and terracing, but such techniques have yet to be applied on a large scale.

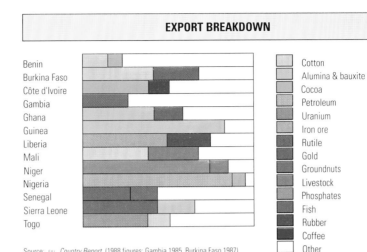

EXPORT BREAKDOWN

Benin
Burkina Faso
Côte d'Ivoire
Gambia
Ghana
Guinea
Liberia
Mali
Niger
Nigeria
Senegal
Sierra Leone
Togo

Cotton
Alumina & bauxite
Cocoa
Petroleum
Uranium
Iron ore
Rutile
Gold
Groundnuts
Livestock
Phosphates
Fish
Rubber
Coffee
Other

Source: EIU *Country Report* (1988 figures; Gambia 1985, Burkina Faso 1987).

Dependency

West African countries are particularly vulnerable to commodity price falls. Most are dependent on the export of one or two products.

Climate

Coastal and southern areas have two rainy seasons, in May–June and October; further north these merge into one, from July to September. Average annual rainfall ranges from 600–2,000mm (25–80ins); temperatures range from 18–32°C (65–90°F). The dry season is subject to the hot dusty harmattan wind blowing from the north-east.

Ethnic and linguistic groups

Colonial frontiers, preserved after independence, took little account of the geographical distribution of African peoples. One of the greatest difficulties faced by African governments has been in building national consciousness and unity from a diversity of ethnic and tribal groups; old loyalties and rivalries live on. Nigeria, for example, has more than 250 ethnic groups; Côte d'Ivoire more than 60. The languages spoken are just as numerous, although most West African languages belong to the Niger-Congo family, spoken by more than 150m people across the west and centre of the continent. The main West African languages include Wolof and Mandinke in the far west and the Kwa languages of the Ashante people of Ghana and the Yoruba and Igbo of southern Nigeria.

Education

The economic difficulties suffered by many West African countries during the 1980s have threatened their achievements in raising educational standards since independence. The rate of growth of enrolment in education fell during the 1980s, as governments were forced to cut back on education spending and the cost to families rose. In most West African countries, the majority of children receive some primary education: 77% of the age group in Côte d'Ivoire, for example, 92% in Nigeria. Far fewer go on to secondary schools: less than 30% in both these cases.

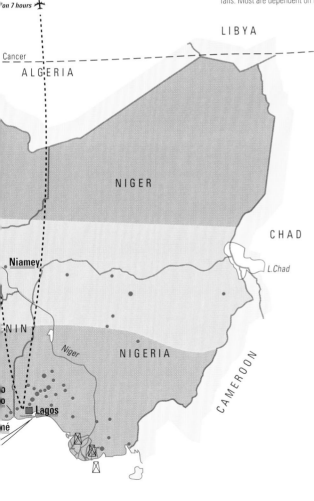

MAURITANIA

One of the last countries to abolish slavery, in 1980, Mauritania was led by Mokhtar Ould Daddah from independence in 1960 until the military took over in 1978. Maaouya Ould Sid'Ahmed Taya became Mauritania's fourth military leader in 1984. A promised return to civilian rule has been delayed by ethnic unrest, particularly the 1989 conflict with Senegal which saw retaliatory deportations of Senegalese Mauritanians and Mauritanian Moors living in Senegal.

The traditional economy is based on nomadic livestock rearing, although this has declined since the 1960s with the development of mining and fishing. Less than 1% of the country receives enough rain for arable farming and land competition has added to racial tensions. Several dam projects undertaken in the 1980s should open up large areas to irrigated cultivation. Exploitation of Mauritania's vast iron ore reserves began in 1963 but suffered during the 1970s from recession in the world steel industry. Output began to recover in the 1980s as markets improved and new deposits were brought into production. However, fishing is now the main foreign exchange earner.

OFFICIAL NAME Islamic Repubic of Mauritania.
CAPITAL CITY Nouakchott.
GEOGRAPHY Around 40% is Sahara Desert, 30% semi-desert. There is a narrow band of fertile land along the Senegal river. *Area* 1,030,700 sq km (397,950 sq miles).
PEOPLE *Population* 1.9m. *Density* 2 per sq km.
RELIGION Muslim 99%, Christian 0.5%.
LANGUAGE Arabic and French.
CURRENCY Ouguiya.
PUBLIC HOLIDAYS Jan 1, Leilat al-Meiraj, May 1, Id al-Fitr, May 25, Id al-Adha, Tabaski, Mouloud, Nov 28.
GOVERNMENT Military-dominated republic. The Comité Militaire de Salut National (CMSN) has ruled by decree since 1978. Head of state is the president of the CMSN. All political parties are banned.

MALI

In the 14th century Timbuktu was the religious and cultural centre of a vast empire stretching as far as the Atlantic. Today the World Bank ranks the landlocked remnant of that empire as one of the poorest countries in the world.

After independence in 1960 Modibo Keita's government sought to create its own style of socialism. But economic performance was poor and in 1968 President Keita was ousted in a military coup led by Moussa Traoré. Mali returned to one-party civilian rule in 1979. However, 12 years later President Traoré's refusal to heed growing demands for the establishment of a multi-party democracy led to riots in the capital, Bamako, and precipitated his downfall in a military coup in March 1991. The new ruling military promised elections before the end of 1992.

The early independence years saw a great expansion of the state's role in the economy, but since 1981 the government has pursued a programme of liberalization. Cotton is the country's leading export.

OFFICIAL NAME Republic of Mali.
CAPITAL CITY Bamako.
GEOGRAPHY Large and landlocked, with two crucial arteries, the Senegal and Niger rivers which provide vital irrigation, means of access, and a source of fish. *Area* 1,240,190 sq km (478,770 sq miles).
PEOPLE *Population* 8.2m. *Density* 7 per sq km.
RELIGION Muslim 90%, Christian 1%, Animist.
LANGUAGE French. Also local languages.
CURRENCY CFA franc.
PUBLIC HOLIDAYS Jan 1, 20, May 1, Korité, May 25, Tabaski, Sep 22, Mouloud, Baptism of the Prophet, Nov 19, Dec 25.
GOVERNMENT Republic since 1960. The president is the head of state and government and is elected every 5 years. There is an 82-member national assembly serving a 3-year term.

NIGER

Niger is predominantly a rural economy with 90% of the population still dependent on agriculture. Livestock was the main export until the early 1970s when exploitation of the country's uranium reserves started. Rising uranium revenues and good rains brought Niger unaccustomed prosperity from 1975 to 1979, but this was quickly succeeded by economic crisis as uranium demand collapsed and periodic drought returned. Better days returned after 1986 as the pace of uranium sales quickened, the rains returned and a series of IMF-backed reform programmes encouraged a sharp rise in aid levels.

After independence in 1960 Niger was led by President Diori Hamani until he was overthrown in 1974 by the autocratic Lieutenant-Colonel Seyni Kountché. Colonel Ali Saibou succeeded after President Kountché's death in 1987 and his personal popularity helped him survive the political turbulence generated by cutbacks in civil service employment and rising ethnic unrest. In late 1990 he conceded a return to multi-party rule, pending the results of a constitutional review commission whose main challenge was to balance the competing demands of Niger's Hausa majority with those of the Zarma political élite.

OFFICIAL NAME Republic of Niger.
CAPITAL CITY Niamey.
GEOGRAPHY The largest state in West Africa, Niger is landlocked and two-thirds is desert. Minimal rainfall along the Nigerian border permits limited cultivation while the Niger river provides some pasture land. *Area* 1,267,000 sq km (489,000 sq miles).
PEOPLE *Population* 7.2m. *Density* 6 per sq km.
RELIGION Muslim 88%, Christian 0.5%, Animist.
LANGUAGE French. Also local languages.
CURRENCY CFA franc.
PUBLIC HOLIDAYS Jan 1, May 1, Id al-Fitr , Id al-Adha, Aug 3, Id al-Kebir, Mouloud, Dec 18, 25.
GOVERNMENT Military-dominated republic. Head of state is a president nominated by the Mouvement National pour la Société de Développement (MNSD), the sole legal party, and confirmed by universal suffrage to serve a maximum of two 7-year terms. The 93-member National Assembly serves a 7-year term.

THE GAMBIA

A ribbon enclave within Senegal, The Gambia has survived as a multi-party democracy since independence from Britain in 1965 despite periods of instability. Senegalese support to quell the 1981 coup attempt led to the formation of the Senegambia Confederation. But The Gambia's reluctance to proceed with integration into its larger neighbour led to the break up of the Confederation eight years later.

About 50% of arable land is given over to groundnuts, the major export. Rice is the staple food but production has fallen behind demand. Tourism has been the star of the economy; arrivals rose from just 300 in 1966 to 150,000 in 1990.

OFFICIAL NAME Republic of The Gambia.
CAPITAL CITY Banjul.
GEOGRAPHY On average only about 25km wide, bordering the Gambia river. Much is mangrove swamp and marsh. *Area* 11,295 sq km (4,360 sq miles).
PEOPLE *Population* 699,000. *Density* 62 per sq km.
RELIGION Muslim 85%, Christian 3%, Animist.
LANGUAGE English. Also local languages.
CURRENCY Dalasi.
PUBLIC HOLIDAYS Jan 1, Feb 18, Good Fri, Id al-Fitr, Id al-Adha, Aug 15, Mouloud, Dec 25.
GOVERNMENT Republic since 1970. Executive power is vested in the president, elected for a 5-year term.

SENEGAL

The jewel in the crown of France's African colonies, Senegal inherited the region's leading port and its best road network at independence in 1960.

Political life was dominated by Léopold Senghor from well before independence until 1980 when he handed power to his prime minister, Abdou Diouf. Senegal is also one of Africa's few long-established multi-party democracies, although only the Parti Démocratique Sénégalais (PDS) offers any real challenge to the ruling Parti Socialiste (PS).

Relative political stability has been in stark contrast to the vicissitudes of the economy. From being one of the region's leaders, Senegal today is impoverished, suffering from chronic balance of payments deficits and a heavy burden of foreign debt. This has been due to factors including a steady decline in rainfall over the last 30 years, deteriorating terms of trade for its key exports, groundnuts and phosphates, inappropriate policies and government inefficiency. Since the early 1980s a number of IMF-backed restructuring programmes have been undertaken, but their success has been constrained by continuing adverse weather and price conditions. However, tourism is on the increase, particularly in the south, and fishing is another growth area, although the territorial waters are plundered by foreign fleets.

OFFICIAL NAME Republic of Senegal.
CAPITAL CITY Dakar.
GEOGRAPHY Dakar is on the volcanic Cape Verde peninsula, the country's focus. To the north-east is a savannah basin falling to the River Senegal. To the south is the enclave of The Gambia. *Area* 196,192 sq km (75,750 sq miles).
PEOPLE *Population* 6.8m. *Density* 36 per sq km.
RELIGION Muslim 91%, Christian 6%, Animist.
LANGUAGE French. Also local languages.
CURRENCY CFA franc.
PUBLIC HOLIDAYS Jan 1, Feb 1, Good Fri, Easter Mon, Apr 4, May 1, Ascension, Korité, Whit Mon, Tabaski, Assumption, Mouloud, Nov 1, Dec 25.
GOVERNMENT Republic since 1960. The government is responsible to the president and is controlled by the National Assembly. Legislative and presidential elections are held every 5 years.

IMPORTS AND EXPORTS

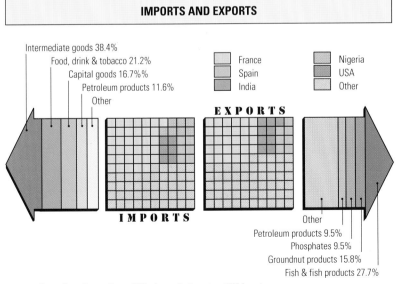

Intermediate goods 38.4%
Food, drink & tobacco 21.2%
Capital goods 16.7%%
Petroleum products 11.6%
Other

France
Spain
India

Nigeria
USA
Other

EXPORTS

IMPORTS

Other
Petroleum products 9.5%
Phosphates 9.5%
Groundnut products 15.8%
Fish & fish products 27.7%

Source: EIU *Country Report* (Imports/Exports 1988 estimates; Trading partners 1988 figures).

BALANCE OF PAYMENTS

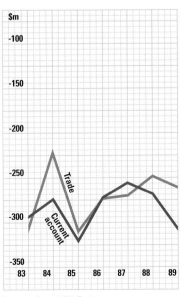

$m

Trade

Current account

Source: EIU *Economic Risk Service.*

CAPE VERDE

This former Portuguese colony has been a leader of moves towards greater democracy in Africa. Political liberalization began in 1988 and culminated in January 1991 in the surprise electoral defeat of the Partido Africano da Independência de Cabo Verde (PAICV), which had been in power since independence in 1975 and was respected for its probity in government. A month later President Aristide Pereira suffered a similar shock losing the presidential elections by a large margin to the moderate Antonio Mascarenhas Monteiro, leader of the victorious Movimento para Democracia.

Two-thirds of Cape Verdeans live abroad. Their remittances are vital to an economy with few natural resources, minimal exports other than fish, and subject to endemic drought. Policy has perforce been pragmatic, focusing on economic liberalization and the establishment of a free-trade area.

OFFICIAL NAME Republic of Cape Verde.
CAPITAL CITY Praia.
GEOGRAPHY An arid archipelago of 10 islands and 5 islets. *Area* 4,033 sq km (1,560 sq miles).
PEOPLE *Population* 370,000. *Density* 91 per sq km.
RELIGION RC 98%, Protestant 2%.
LANGUAGE Portuguese. Also Creole Portuguese.
EDUCATION Compulsory for ages 7–14.
CURRENCY Cape Verde escudo.
PUBLIC HOLIDAYS Jan 1, 20, Mar 8, May 1, June 20, Aug 3, 27, Sept 24, Nov 14, Dec 25.
GOVERNMENT Republic since 1975. A September 1990 amendment to the 1981 constitution abolished the country's one-party status. The 83-member National Assembly serves a 5-year term. Head of state is a president elected by universal suffrage every 5 years.

GUINEA-BISSAU

At independence in 1974 Luiz Cabral's socialist government inherited an economy devastated by 11 years of independence war with Portugal. Efforts to rebuild the key agricultural sector, which generates 50% of GDP, were hindered by inappropriate policies and an emphasis on prestige projects. President Cabral was overthrown in 1980 by his prime minister, João Bernardo Vieira, who initiated an IMF-supported stabilization programme aimed at liberalizing the economy and encouraging investment and higher agricultural production.

It has had some success. Output of rice, the staple food, has expanded rapidly and cashew nuts have overtaken goundnuts as the main export. New cash crops are being developed and a start has been made on exploiting the country's rich fishing grounds. However, boundary disputes have delayed the development of offshore oil discoveries, and large phosphate and bauxite reserves have yet to be exploited.

The government has fallen in step with moves towards greater democracy in Africa. In August 1990 President Vieira announced a programme to achieve a multi-party system by 1993.

OFFICIAL NAME Republic of Guinea-Bissau.
CAPITAL CITY Bissau.
GEOGRAPHY The country consists of many coastal islands and the Bissagos archipelago, as well as the mainland with its deeply indented coast. The land behind the coastal plain is fairly flat, and crossed by meandering rivers edged with mangrove swamps. *Area* 36,125 sq km (13,950 sq miles).
PEOPLE *Population* 940,000. *Density* 26 per sq km.
RELIGION Muslim 30%, Christian 4%, Animist.
LANGUAGE Portuguese. Also Guinean Creole.
CURRENCY Peso.
PUBLIC HOLIDAYS Jan 1, 20 , Mar 8, May 1, Jun 20, Aug 3, 27, Tabaski, Nov 14, Dec 25.
GOVERNMENT Republic since 1974. The president is head of state and chief executive. He heads a 15-member council of state.

GUINEA

Twenty-five years of autocratic rule under Ahmed Sekou Touré followed independence in 1958. His policies of state control led to economic stagnation and turned the country into a food importer.

The military government that took over after his death in 1984 has been beset by internal divisions, but under President Lansana Conté it has worked hard to restore growth. An IMF-backed recovery programme has emphasized liberalization, privatization and foreign investment.

Although agriculture remains the base of the economy, mining provides most export and government revenues. Bauxite contributes about 70% of export earnings; Guinea has a third of the world's known high-grade reserves. Diamond exports are also important and gold production is increasing. The country's huge iron ore reserves are yet to be exploited.

A complex timetable to restore multi-party democracy by the mid-1990s was unveiled in 1989.

OFFICIAL NAME Republic of Guinea.
CAPITAL CITY Conakry.
GEOGRAPHY A 280km (174-mile) coastline gives way to four very different regions: the west, with its marshes and winding rivers; the middle region, with the mountainous Fouta Djallon massif and the source of the Niger; the forests of the south-east; and the savannah of the Haute Guinée region. *Area* 245,857 sq km (944,926 sq miles).
PEOPLE *Population* 6.9m. *Density* 28 per sq km.
RELIGION Muslim 69%, Christian 1%, Animist.
LANGUAGE French. Also local languages.
CURRENCY Guinean franc.
PUBLIC HOLIDAYS Jan 1, Easter Mon, May 1, Id al-Fitr, Aug 27, Sep 28, Oct 2, Mouloud, Nov 1, 22, Dec 25.
GOVERNMENT Republic since 1958. The constitution and national assembly were suspended in 1984. Rule is by decree of the Comité Militaire de Redressement National (CMRN). The president of the CMRN is head of state.

SIERRA LEONE

Siaka Stevens, who retired in 1985 after 17 years as president, handed a troubled economy to his hand-picked successor, Joseph Momoh. Agriculture had been in decline for decades, inflation, public spending and the debt burden were rising and smuggling, corruption and the informal sector were flourishing.

President Momoh has made little headway in efforts to tackle these problems, falling out with the IMF and World Bank over structural adjustment measures. Discussions to restore links with the two bodies began in 1990 but it will be years before the country realizes the full benefit of its varied natural resources. Rutile, or titanium ore, diamonds, bauxite, coffee and cocoa are the main exports. The country also has iron and gold reserves and fisheries and tourism potential.

Popular discontent has forced President Momoh to acknowledge the need for greater democracy. A constitutional review began in late 1990 preparatory to the possible introduction of a multi-party system.

OFFICIAL NAME Republic of Sierra Leone.
CAPITAL CITY Freetown.
GEOGRAPHY From the Loma Mountains in the northeast the land falls in three distinct zones to the highly indented, rugged coastline which gives the country its name. *Area* 71,740 sq km (27,700 sq miles).
PEOPLE *Population* 4m. *Density* 55 per sq km.
RELIGION Muslim 40%, Christian 9%, Animist.
LANGUAGE English. Also local languages.
CURRENCY Leone.
PUBLIC HOLIDAYS Jan 1, Good Fri, Easter Mon, Apr 27, Id al-Fitr, Id al-Adha, Mouloud, Dec 25–26.
GOVERNMENT Republic since 1971. Independent since 1961. Executive power is vested in the president, elected for a 7-year term of office, and in a cabinet appointed by him. The only recognized political party is the ruling All People's Congress (APC).

CÔTE d'IVOIRE

Rapid economic growth, averaging 6.7% a year, underpinned Côte d'Ivoire's reputation in the 1970s as an exemplar to Africa of the benefits of liberalism and foreign investment. However, the 1980s brought severe recession which has shown little sign of abating with the new decade, despite IMF-supported austerity programmes. The country's problems have several causes, notably the protracted depression of prices for its main export, cocoa, of which it is the world's largest producer; and the rising costs of servicing the debt incurred to finance ambitious development projects.

Austerity measures have been supported by repeated reschedulings of the $14.5 billion external debt. There have also been moves to privatize parastatals and to diversify the key agricultural sector. A range of cash crops is produced, but cocoa and the second export, coffee, account for 60% of both cultivated land and foreign exchange earnings.

Félix Houphouët-Boigny has been the dominant political figure for more than 40 years, and president since independence in 1960. In 1990 he bowed to mounting pressure for democracy; the first multi-party elections were held in November. They produced a landslide victory for his ruling Parti Démocratique de la Côte d'Ivoire (PDCI) and in the preceding presidential poll, the octogenarian Mr Houphouët-Boigny, himself, was re-elected for a seventh term.

OFFICIAL NAME Côte d'Ivoire.
CAPITAL CITY Abidjan.
GEOGRAPHY The land drops from mountain ranges in the north through savannah to the dense tropical forests of the south. The coastline running west from Fresco is marked by high cliffs and rocky inlets; the rest has sandy beaches and lagoons but no natural ports because of barrier reefs; Abidjan port was set up only in 1950. *Area* 322,463 sq km (124,504 sq miles).
PEOPLE *Population* 12.1m. *Density* 37 per sq km.
RELIGION Christian 32%, Muslim 24%, Animist.
LANGUAGE French. Also local languages.
CURRENCY CFA franc.
PUBLIC HOLIDAYS Jan 1, Good Fri, Easter Mon, May 1, Ascension, Id al-Fitr, Whit Mon, Id al-Adha, Assumption, Nov 1, 11, Dec 7, 25, Ramadan, Tabaski.
GOVERNMENT Republic since 1960. The head of state and chief executive is the president, elected for a 5-year term, who appoints a council of ministers. The 175 members of the National Assembly, are also elected every 5 years. Multi-party democracy since May 1990.

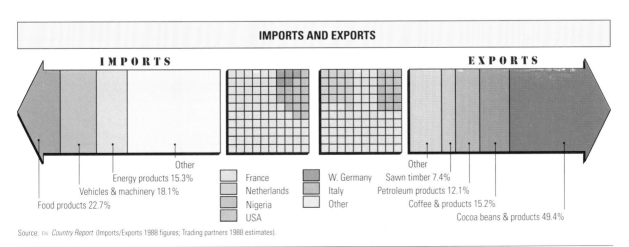

IMPORTS AND EXPORTS

IMPORTS

Other
Energy products 15.3%
Vehicles & machinery 18.1%
Food products 22.7%

France
Netherlands
Nigeria
USA

W. Germany
Italy
Other

EXPORTS

Other
Sawn timber 7.4%
Petroleum products 12.1%
Coffee & products 15.2%
Cocoa beans & products 49.4%

Source: EIU *Country Report* (Imports/Exports 1988 figures; Trading partners 1988 estimates).

GHANA

Ghana was the first of Britain's West African colonies to become independent, in 1957. Its first president, Kwame Nkrumah, influenced the rest of the continent with his theories of pan-African socialism. But at home nationalization and a costly industrialization programme wreaked havoc on the economy. The cocoa industry, key to the country's prosperity, went into steep decline.

Fifteen years of ineffective, predominantly military governments followed the overthrow of President Nkrumah in 1966. In 1981, with the country on the verge of economic collapse, the charismatic Jerry Rawlings took power. He proved an unexpected but effective ally of the IMF, his popularity enabling him to impose tough austerity measures. Recently there have been encouraging signs of recovery, with a return of real growth rates, a revival of cocoa and timber production and new investment in gold mining. However, the social costs have been high and despite attempts to soften the impact of austerity, life for ordinary Ghanaians is still very hard.

Some tentative moves towards a restoration of elected government were made in 1989 with the holding of district-level elections. However, the pressure for change was expected to grow following the formation in 1990 of opposition groups demanding greater democracy. The government itself seemed to be split between single- and multi-party advocates.

OFFICIAL NAME Republic of Ghana.
CAPITAL CITY Accra.
GEOGRAPHY The Volta basin occupies a vast area in the east, with an artificial lake of 8,500 sq km (3,300 sq miles). It is bordered on the north and south by plateaus up to 600 metres (1,970 feet) above sea level. Much of the central Ashanti region is covered in forest which is now much reduced from its original huge acreage. The Akwapim-Togo mountain range runs from the eastern edge of the Volta basin to the sea near Accra. The coastline is generally low with little natural shelter. *Area* 238,537 sq km (92,100 sq miles).
PEOPLE *Population* 14.4m. *Density* 60 per sq km.
RELIGION Christian 62%, Muslim 16%, Animist.
LANGUAGE English. Also local languages.
CURRENCY Cedi.
PUBLIC HOLIDAYS Jan 1, Mar 6, Good Fri, Easter Mon, Jun 4, Jul 5, Dec 25–26, 31.
GOVERNMENT Independent republic since 1957. The constitution was suspended in 1981. Government is by decree of the 9-member Provisional National Defence Council. Political parties are banned.

IMPORTS AND EXPORTS

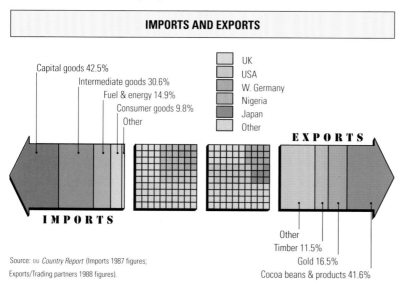

Capital goods 42.5%
Intermediate goods 30.6%
Fuel & energy 14.9%
Consumer goods 9.8%
Other

UK
USA
W. Germany
Nigeria
Japan
Other

EXPORTS

IMPORTS

Other
Timber 11.5%
Gold 16.5%
Cocoa beans & products 41.6%

Source: EIU *Country Report* (Imports 1987 figures; Exports/Trading partners 1988 figures).

BALANCE OF PAYMENTS

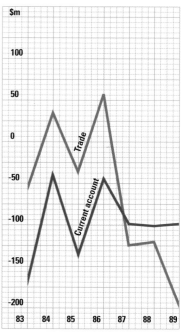

$m

Trade

Current account

Source: EIU *Economic Risk Service*.

ECONOMIC PROFILE

Once world's leading cocoa producer, now in fifth place. Diamonds, gold, timber, bauxite and manganese also exported. State-owned industries were developed in the 1960s but stagnated until recently. They are now being sold to the private sector.

Growth Cocoa and timber exports recovering fast. New gold rush has begun – exports could bring in $1 billion a year in 1990s. Growing foreign investment interest in fishing, tourism and agro-industry.

Problems Depressed prices of cocoa and other export commodities. Falling production of diamonds. Loss of export revenue through smuggling to neighbouring countries. High unemployment and inflation testing government commitment to austerity policies.

LIBERIA

Founded by freed slaves from the USA, Liberia has been an independent republic since 1847. American influence has remained strong. The economy is predominantly agricultural. Rubber is the main cash crop, although iron ore has overtaken it as the leading export commodity.

The slaves' descendants governed Liberia until 1980 when Samuel Doe's bloody coup began his rule of harsh repression. Under US pressure he held elections in 1985, but they were crudely managed to confirm him in power. In 1989 a former associate, Charles Taylor, invaded from Côte d'Ivoire. His forces held most of the country by mid-1990, but fierce fighting continued with troops loyal to President Doe and to another rival, Prince Yormie Johnson. A West African peacekeeping force intervened but a ceasefire was not achieved until November, two months after President Doe was murdered by Prince Johnson's forces. The peacekeeping force sought to establish an interim government, but it was not recognised by Taylor and the power struggle continued. It threatened to escalate into a regional conflict when elements of Taylor's force began incursions into Sierra Leone, fighting alongside opponents of President Momoh's regime.

OFFICIAL NAME Republic of Liberia.
CAPITAL CITY Monrovia.
GEOGRAPHY Hills and generally low mountain ranges rise behind a costal plain. Surf, cliffs and lagoons make access from the Atlantic Ocean difficult. *Area* 111,369 sq km (43,000 sq miles).
PEOPLE *Population* 2.5m. *Density* 21 per sq km.
RELIGION Muslim 15%, Christian 10%, Animist.
LANGUAGE English. Also local languages.
CURRENCY Liberian dollar and US dollar.
PUBLIC HOLIDAYS Jan 1, Feb 11, Mar 12, 15, Good Fri, Apr 11–12, May 14, Jul 26, Aug 24, Nov 6, 12, 29, Dec 25.
GOVERNMENT Republic since 1847. Bicameral parliament rendered ineffective by civil war. An interim government was appointed in August 1990 by a conference of Economic Community of West Africa (Ecowas) heads of state. The National Democratic Party of Liberia (NDPL), led by Charles Taylor, also claimed to be the legitimate government. Neither was recognized internationally.

BURKINA FASO

The former Upper Volta, renamed in 1984, has had a turbulent history. The coup which brought Captain Blaise Compaoré to power in 1987 was the fifth since independence in 1960. President Compaoré moderated the radical, nationalist policies of his predecessor, Thomas Sankara, and in 1990 announced plans to establish multi-party democracy by the end of 1991.

The country is one of the world's poorest and heavily dependent on external aid. Almost 90% of the population relies on subsistence agriculture and many augment their income as migrant labourers. The modern sector is state-dominated. The country's landlocked position, poor infrastructure and recent radical policies have discouraged foreign investment, except in mining. Cotton and livestock are the main exports, but gold is increasingly important. Zinc production is planned to start in 1994 and there are large manganese reserves.

OFFICIAL NAME Burkina Faso.
CAPITAL CITY Ouagadougou.
GEOGRAPHY Landlocked. The country sits astride two ecological zones: sahelian in the north and wooded savannah in the south. Rivers mainly drain south to the Volta or the Niger. *Area* 274,122 sq km (105,840 sq miles).
PEOPLE *Population* 8.7m. *Density* 30 per sq km.
RELIGION Muslim 43%, Christian 12%, Animist.
LANGUAGE French. Also local languages.
CURRENCY CFA franc.
PUBLIC HOLIDAYS Jan 1, 3, Easter Mon, May 1, Ascension, Id al-Fitr, Whit Mon, Id al-Adha, Aug 4, Assumption, Mouloud, Nov 1, Dec 25.
GOVERNMENT Republic since 1960. Legislative power rests with the Front Populaire (FP). A return is planned to multi-party democracy.

TOGO

For more than two decades after taking power in 1967 President Gnassingbé Eyadéma was the absolute and virtually unchallenged ruler of this former French colony. By April 1991, however, his political survival had begun to look increasingly uncertain. A wave of strikes had already forced him to make promises of reform when mass protests broke out in Lomé. The army's brutal response – 26 people were beaten to death – only added new impetus to the demands for democracy and it became a matter of "when" not "if" political change would occur.

Agriculture is the mainstay of the economy, accounting for almost 40% of GDP. Cocoa, cotton and coffee are important exports, but phosphates are the key foreign exchange earner, providing 50% of the total. Ambitious industrialization plans in the 1970s contributed mainly to a sharp increase in foreign debt, which combined with the collapse of phosphate prices in 1975 to precipitate a financial crisis. This still restrains the economy, although IMF-backed stabilization measures have restored modest growth.

OFFICIAL NAME Togolese Republic.
CAPITAL CITY Lomé.
GEOGRAPHY The indented coastline is only 56km (35 miles) wide. Inland lies a tableland giving way to wooded mountains and then an infertile dry plateau. *Area* 56,785 sq km (21,930 sq miles).
PEOPLE *Population* 3.3m. *Density* 58 per sq km.
RELIGION Christian 37%, Muslim 30%, Animist.
LANGUAGE French. Also local languages.
CURRENCY CFA franc.
PUBLIC HOLIDAYS Jan 1, 13, 24, Easter Mon, Apr 24, May 1, Ascension, Whit Mon, May 26, Assumption, Nov 1, Dec 25.
GOVERNMENT Republic since 1960. The head of state is the executive president, elected for a 7-year term. The 77-member National Assembly is elected every 5 years. The only legal party is the Rassemblement du Peuple Togolais (RPT).

BENIN

Benin is primarily an agricultural economy, with commerce, mainly with Nigeria and much of it illicit, the other principal economic activity. Offshore oil production began in 1982, but output has been disappointing, declining steadily since the 1985 peak. Palm oil has been overtaken by cotton as the leading export; both, like oil, were badly affected by falling prices in the 1980s.

Financial mismanagement by the military government of Mathieu Kérékou made Benin's economic problems worse. Popular discontent came to a head in December 1989 when nationwide strikes by public-sector employees over wage arrears paralysed the economy. After 17 years in power President Kérékou was forced to renounce Marxism, concede IMF-backed economic reforms and promise a return to multi-party democracy. The military government was dissolved in March 1990, handing power to an interim administration. Elections were held a year later and brought defeat for President Kérékou and his party at the hands of the coalition Union pour le Triomphe du Renouveau Démocratique led by Nicephore Soglo, who had acted as interim prime minister.

OFFICIAL NAME Republic of Benin.
CAPITAL CITY Cotonou.
GEOGRAPHY Fairly flat, fertile land, rising to mountains in the north-west, lies behind a 100km (62-mile) coastline and an area of lagoons. *Area* 112,622 sq km (43,484 sq miles).
PEOPLE *Population* 4.5m. *Density* 40 per sq km.
RELIGION Christian 20%, Muslim 15%, Animist.
LANGUAGE French. Also local languages.
CURRENCY CFA franc.
PUBLIC HOLIDAYS Jan 1, Easter Mon, May 1, 4, 15, Aug 1, 15, Ramadan, Id al-Fitr, Sept 4, Oct 26, Nov 1, 30, Dec 25, 31.
GOVERNMENT Independent republic since 1960. Executive power rests with the president and his appointed cabinet. The president serves a maximum of two terms. Multi-party activity resumed March 1990.

NIGERIA

Democratic government has proved elusive in this unruly nation of more than 100m people. Civilians have ruled for a total of only nine years since independence in 1960. The most recent civilian government, that of President Shehu Shagari, lasted four years before the military took power again in 1983. The idealistic and rigid General Muhammadu Buhari was in turn replaced in a bloodless coup two years later by the more pragmatic General Ibrahim Babangida.

Oil production started in the late 1950s and since 1973 has been the mainstay of the economy, accounting for about 95% of export earnings and almost 80% of federal revenues. Oil riches have proved a mixed blessing, however. Construction boomed in the 1970s and early 1980s, with foreign contractors lining up to build the oil refineries, steel works and vehicle assembly lines that were to ensure Nigeria's economic future. Meanwhile, the public developed a taste for imported foods and consumer goods and agriculture was neglected. Cocoa exports halved; cotton and groundnut exports all but ceased.

By the mid-1980s Nigeria was saddled with foreign debts of $26 billion. President Babangida's task of restoring economic discipline was made harder by the collapse of oil prices in 1986, which halved export earnings to $6.1 billion in

OFFICIAL NAME Federal Republic of Nigeria.
CAPITAL CITY Lagos (Abuja after 1992).
GEOGRAPHY The coastline, much of it bordered by mangrove swamp, is intersected by numerous creeks; the south-east coast, dominated by the Niger river delta, is the location of the offshore oil reserves. Inland lies an area of tropical rain forest and bush. Savannah and woodland cover much of the central upland area; the Jos plateau is the watershed of hundreds of streams and small rivers flowing as far as Lake Chad and the Niger and Benue rivers. The far north, bordering the Sahara, is mainly savannah. Spectacular highlands line the eastern border with Cameroon. *Highest point* Vogel peak 2,040 metres (6,690 feet). *Area* 923,768 sq km (356,670 sq miles).
PEOPLE *Population* 113m. *Density* 122 per sq km.
RELIGION Christian 50%, Muslim 45%, Animist.
LANGUAGE English. Also local languages.
CURRENCY Naira.
PUBLIC HOLIDAYS Jan 1, Good Fri, Easter Mon, May 1, Id al-Fitr, Id al-Kebir, Id al-Adha, Oct 1, Mouloud, Dec 25–26.
GOVERNMENT Federal republic, independent since 1960. Civilian constitution suspended December 1983. Federal legislation is by decree of the Armed Forces Ruling Council (AFRC) which appoints the administrative council of ministers as well as the 21 state governors. Chairman of the AFRC is the national president. Proceeding with timetable for a return to civilian rule and general and presidential elections by October 1992. Only two parties have been permitted by the AFRC to register to contest the elections.

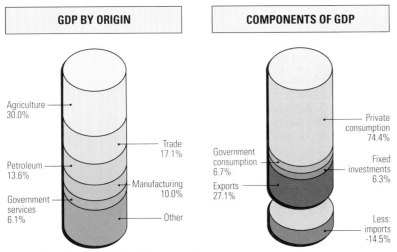

GDP BY ORIGIN

Agriculture 30.0%
Trade 17.1%
Petroleum 13.6%
Manufacturing 10.0%
Government services 6.1%
Other

COMPONENTS OF GDP

Private consumption 74.4%
Government consumption 6.7%
Fixed investments 6.3%
Exports 27.1%
Less: imports -14.5%

Source: EIU *Country Report* (GDP by origin 1988 figures; Components of GDP 1987/88 figures).

IMPORTS AND EXPORTS

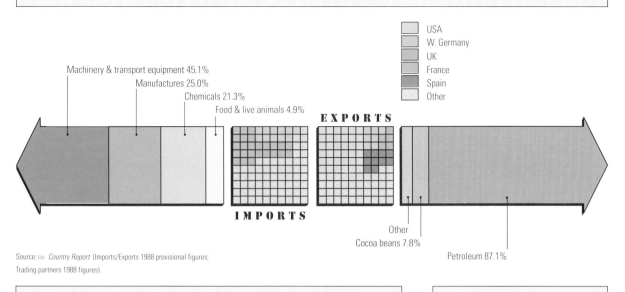

USA
W. Germany
UK
France
Spain
Other

Machinery & transport equipment 45.1%
Manufactures 25.0%
Chemicals 21.3%
Food & live animals 4.9%

EXPORTS

IMPORTS

Other
Cocoa beans 7.8%
Petroleum 87.1%

Source: EIU *Country Report* (Imports/Exports 1988 provisional figures;
Trading partners 1988 figures).

ECONOMIC PROFILE

An agricultural economy, exporting cocoa, groundnuts and cotton, transformed by oil exports. Oil financed the development of new industries – refining, petrochemicals, steel, cement, vehicles, agricultural processing – but work on many projects has been halted by payments problems.

Growth Agricultural and other non-oil exports starting to revive. Government pressing ahead with petrochemicals and LNG schemes.

Problems Industry starved of spares and inputs. Tortuous debt rescheduling negotiations have delayed new lending and investment.

BALANCE OF PAYMENTS

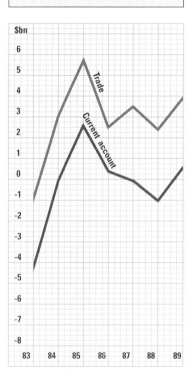

Source: EIU *Economic Risk Service.*

just 12 months. Drastic policy changes were introduced. The trade system was liberalized, agricultural marketing was put into private hands, a foreign exchange auction system was introduced, and an extensive programme of privatization was announced. Because of popular hostility to the IMF, elaborate arrangements were made with the fund to obtain approval for the measures without appearing to succumb to an official austerity programme. This enabled some of Nigeria's debt to be rescheduled despite rocky relations with creditors.

The new policies soon started to show results, notably the revival of food and export crop production. Industry has reduced its dependence on imports but capacity utilization is still barely 40%. The costs of reform have been borne largely by ordinary Nigerians who have faced high unemployment and a general decline in living standards. The rise in oil prices after August 1990 was expected to provide some relief, giving the government leeway to boost public spending.

From the start President Babangida insisted that his rule was temporary. In August 1987 a complex timetable was issued aimed at bringing a return to civilian rule by October 1992. The president seemed determined not only to see it through, but also to try to set up a structure free from the weaknesses of the old civilian governments. Only two political parties were to be allowed to contest the elections, and most former politicians were barred from standing as candidates. However, as 1992 approached there were signs (not least the April 1990 coup attempt) that the country remained split by the old factional, ethnic and religious rivalries and that political stability could prove as elusive as ever.

CENTRAL AFRICA

The Franc Zone and CEEAC

Cameroon, Central African Republic, Chad, Congo, Gabon and Equatorial Guinea are members of the Franc Zone. All share a central bank, and belong to an economic and monetary union, the Union Douanière et Economique de l'Afrique Centrale (UDEAC).

In 1983, a new organization was set up, the Communauté Economique des Etats de l'Afrique Centrale (CEEAC), with the aim of creating a common market including all central African countries. CEEAC's members are the six UDEAC states plus Zaire, Rwanda, Burundi and São Tomé and Príncipe.

Ethnic and linguistic groups

Zaireans speak more than 250 different languages, but four predominate: Lingala, Kikongo, Tshiluba and Swahili. There are about a dozen major ethnic groups. Cameroon is similarly diverse: Bantu-speaking peoples dominate in the south, Sudanic and Afroasiatic languages are spoken in the north. The country's colonial history also left it with two official languages: French and English. The largest ethnic group in Gabon and mainland Equatorial Guinea is the Fang.

The Congo (Zaire)

After the Nile, the longest river in Africa at 4,670km (2,910 miles), the Congo or Zaire drains a basin second only in size to that of the Amazon. Rising in south-east Zaire, the river crosses the Equator twice before entering the Atlantic. It flows through Zaire for much of its length and forms part of that country's border with Congo; the two capitals, Kinshasa and Brazzaville, face each other on opposite banks.

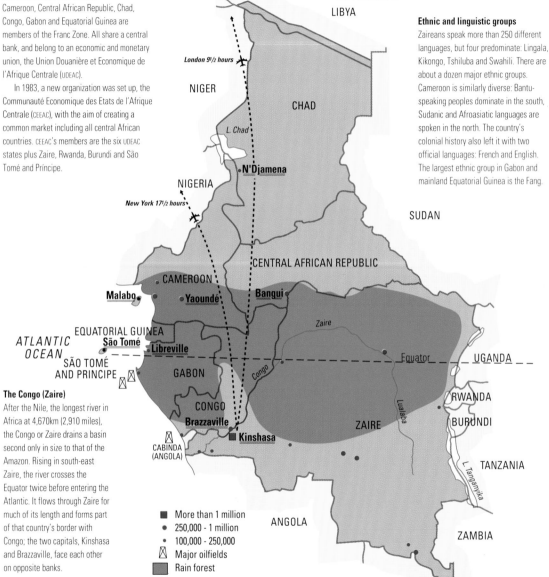

- ■ More than 1 million
- ● 250,000 - 1 million
- • 100,000 - 250,000
- ⊠ Major oilfields
- ▨ Rain forest

Climate

Most of the region has an equatorial climate, with rain all year and temperatures averaging 28–31°C (82–88°F). Parts of Zaire and Cameroon have a more moderate climate; northern Cameroon is semi-arid. A small area on Mount Cameroon is one of the three wettest places in the world, receiving more than 10,000mm (394ins) a year.

Education

Congo and Gabon provide compulsory education from the ages of 6 to 16. Both highly urbanized countries, they have been more successful in expanding educational opportunities than vast and diverse Zaire, which transferred responsibility for education to the state from the Roman Catholic church in 1972. In the recent climate of economic austerity there have been hints that this decision might be reversed.

CHAD

Since independence in 1960, Chad has been dominated by almost continuous civil war. The internecine strife was exacerbated by the growing involvement of Libya, which in 1973 annexed the mineral-rich Aozou strip in the north. Hopes for peace were raised in 1987 when President Hissène Habré decisively defeated the Libyan-supported opposition. However, President Habré proved unwilling to renounce partisan politics and slow to embrace democratic change. In December 1990 he was overthrown after three weeks of fighting by Idriss Deby, a top military commander during the 1980s desert war. President Deby promised to replace one-party politics with multi-party democracy and moved to establish non-partisan credentials, forming a broad-based government.

The World Bank ranks Chad as the world's third poorest country. The overwhelmingly agricultural economy has been devastated by war and drought. Donors are supporting efforts to increase production of cotton, the main export, and there are plans to exploit oil reserves in the Lake Chad basin.

OFFICIAL NAME Republic of Chad.
CAPITAL CITY Ndjamena.
GEOGRAPHY Landlocked; semi-desert in the north giving way to savannah in the centre. Most people live in the south-west around the Lake Chad basin. *Area* 1,284,000 sq km (496,000 sq miles).
PEOPLE *Population* 5.5m. *Density* 4 per sq km.
RELIGION Muslim 44%, Christian 33%, Animist 23%.
LANGUAGE French. Also Arabic and local languages.
CURRENCY CFA franc.
PUBLIC HOLIDAYS Jan 1, Easter Mon, Id al-Fitr, May 1, 25, Whit Mon, Id al-Adha, June 7, Aug 11, Maloud, Nov 1, 28.
GOVERNMENT Republic since 1960. The 1989 constitution was suspended in December 1990. A 33-member council of state, chaired by the president, was established as the ruling body. A return to multi-party democracy has been promised, but no timetable set.

CAMEROON

Cameroon's striking diversity extends from its varied climate and ethnic groupings (over 200 in all) to its mixed German, French and British colonial heritage and its broad range of economic resources and activities.

Agriculture is the cornerstone of an economy which averaged growth of around 7.5% a year from 1970 to 1986 when the fall in oil prices precipitated recession. Cotton is grown in the north, cocoa and coffee in the west and centre. In the south-west the Cameroon Development Corporation, the country's largest employer, produces rubber, palm oil, tea and bananas. Oil production began in 1977, passing its peak in the mid-1980s. Known reserves are expected to run out in the 1990s. Industrial development has favoured small-scale enterprises; the few major projects undertaken have generally been unsuccessful.

Cameroon is officially bilingual but the francophone domination of government and the public sector rankles with the anglophone minority. After more than two decades of autocratic rule President Ahmadou Ahidjo handed the reins to his prime minister, Paul Biya, in 1982. President Biya's looser grip on government allowed ethnic tensions to surface and corruption to spread. The government's failure in 1990 to respond to demands for greater democracy with more than vague promises of multi-party politics, in contrast to neighbouring Gabon and Zaire, increased the prospects of instability.

OFFICIAL NAME Republic of Cameroon.
CAPITAL CITY Yaoundé.
GEOGRAPHY The flat northern provinces are sub-Sahelian and frequently suffer from drought. The uplands in the west around Mt Cameroon, with its volcanic soils, support a wide range of crops. The south is generally flat and covered in dense forest. *Highest point* Mt Cameroon 4,070 metres (13,350 feet). *Area* 475,442 sq km (183,570 sq miles).
PEOPLE *Population* 11.5m. *Density* 23 per sq km.
RELIGION Christian 50%, Animist 25%, Muslim 20%.
LANGUAGE French and English. Also local languages.
CURRENCY CFA franc.
PUBLIC HOLIDAYS Jan 1, Feb 11, Good Fri, Easter Mon, May 1, 20, Ascension, Djoulde Soumae, Sheep festival, Dec 10, 25.
GOVERNMENT Republic since 1960. The president, elected every 5 years, is head of state and chief executive. Legislative power is vested in the 180-member National Assembly, also elected every 5 years. The Cameroon People's Democratic Movement (CPDM) is the only official political party.

IMPORTS AND EXPORTS

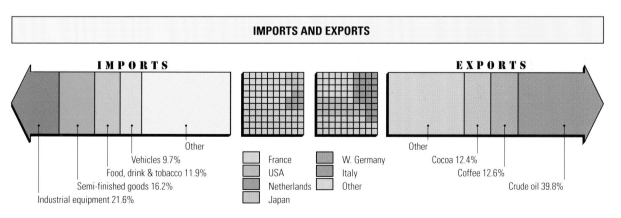

IMPORTS

Other
Vehicles 9.7%
Food, drink & tobacco 11.9%
Semi-finished goods 16.2%
Industrial equipment 21.6%

France
USA
Netherlands
Japan
W. Germany
Italy
Other

EXPORTS

Other
Cocoa 12.4%
Coffee 12.6%
Crude oil 39.8%

Source: EIU *Country Report* (1987/88 figures).

SÃO TOMÉ AND PRÍNCIPE

São Tomé and Príncipe became independent in 1975, ending over 500 years of repressive colonization by Portugal. President Manuel Pinto da Costa's left-wing government inherited a cocoa-dependent economy which went into rapid decline in the face of wholesale nationalization of the plantations and the collapse of world cocoa prices. In 1985 the government announced a policy U-turn, embarking on a liberalization programme. The cocoa sector is being revived and attempts are being made to diversify into tourism and new exports.

Economic liberalization was accompanied by political democratization. This culminated in the January 1991 parliamentary elections which saw the ruling Movimento de Libertação de São Tomé e Príncipe (MLSTP) defeated by the Partido da Convergência Democrática (PCD). President Pinto da Costa's announcement that he would not be contesting the March presidential elections left the way clear for Miguel Travoada to win the poll.

OFFICIAL NAME Democratic Republic of São Tomé and Príncipe.
CAPITAL CITY São Tomé.
GEOGRAPHY Both islands are volcanic. *Area* 964 sq km (370 sq miles).
PEOPLE *Population* 117,400. *Density* 122 per sq km.
RELIGION Christian 97% (RC 92%).
LANGUAGE Portuguese. Also local languages.
CURRENCY Dobra.
PUBLIC HOLIDAYS Jan 1, Good Fri, Easter Mon, May 1, Ascension, Whit Mon, Assumption, Oct 5, All Saints, Dec 1, 25.
GOVERNMENT Republic since 1975. The 1990 constitution ushered in multi-party democracy. The head of state is a president, elected for a maximum of two 5-year terms.

GABON

Gabon's oil wealth has underpinned impressive economic growth; real GDP rose by an average 4.4% a year between 1960 and 1982. The low oil prices of the late 1980s ushered in a new climate of austerity, but the country still has black Africa's highest GDP per head. Other resources include manganese, uranium, iron ore and the products of the rain forest which blankets the country.

President Omar Bongo has been in power since 1967. Like many of his long-ruling African contemporaries he has been forced to concede popular demands for an end to one-party government. However, his Parti Démocratique Gabonais (PDG) easily retained a parliamentary majority in the October 1990 multi-party elections, the first in 20 years.

OFFICIAL NAME Republic of Gabon.
CAPITAL CITY Libreville.
GEOGRAPHY An 800km (500-mile) coastline is marked by deep estuaries in the north, giving way to sandy lagoons in the south. There are three separate small mountain chains in the north, south-east and south, but the overwhelming landscape features are the thick forest, which covers 85% of land area, and an extensive network of rivers and swamps. *Area* 267,667 sq km (193,350 sq miles).
PEOPLE *Population* 1.2m. *Density* 4 per sq km.
RELIGION Christian 95% (RC 64%), Animist 1%, Muslim 1%.
LANGUAGE French. Also local languages.
CURRENCY CFA franc.
PUBLIC HOLIDAYS Jan 1, Mar 12, Easter Mon, Id al-Fitr, Whit Mon, May 1, Whit Mon, Id al-Adha, Aug 17, Mouloud, Nov 1, Dec 25.
GOVERNMENT Republic since 1960. Executive power is vested in the president, who is elected for a 7-year term and may be re-elected. The 120-member National Assembly is elected every 5 years. Since the abolition in 1990 of the political monopoly of the Parti Démocratique Gabonais (PDG), the largest parliamentary party forms the government under a prime minister.

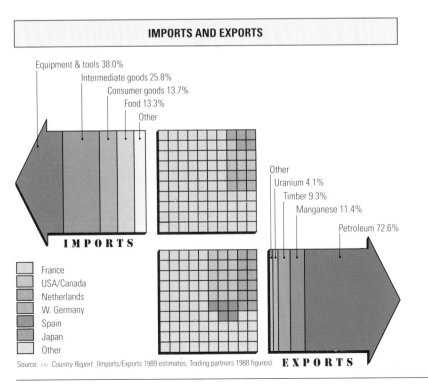

IMPORTS AND EXPORTS

Equipment & tools 38.0%
Intermediate goods 25.8%
Consumer goods 13.7%
Food 13.3%
Other

IMPORTS

Other
Uranium 4.1%
Timber 9.3%
Manganese 11.4%
Petroleum 72.6%

France
USA/Canada
Netherlands
W. Germany
Spain
Japan
Other

Source: EIU *Country Report* (Imports/Exports 1989 estimates; Trading partners 1988 figures).

EXPORTS

CENTRAL AFRICAN REPUBLIC

The Central African Republic (CAR) achieved brief notoriety in the mid-1970s under the self-styled emperor Jean-Bedel Bokassa. His excesses eventually prompted France, which has always retained close links with its former colony, to intervene to remove him in 1979. A short period of civilian rule was ended by the 1981 military coup which brought General André Kolingba to power. He established a one-party state under the Rassemblement Démocratique Centrafricain (RDC) and has pursued policies emphasizing economic and political stability. Pressure for greater democracy increased in 1990 as elsewhere in the continent. President Kolingba initially resisted the demands for pluralism, but he was expected eventually to have to yield on political reform.

The economy is predominantly agricultural, with coffee, cotton, timber and tobacco the main exports after diamonds. Other resources include gold (mined in small quantities) and uranium, which has yet to be exploited.

OFFICIAL NAME Central African Republic.
CAPITAL CITY Bangui.
GEOGRAPHY Landlocked. Predominantly plateau, covered by savannah in the south. The north is part of the Sahara desert. *Area* 622,984 sq km (240,540 sq miles).
PEOPLE *Population* 2.8m. *Density* 4 per sq km.
RELIGION Christian 84%, Animist 12%, Muslim 3%.
LANGUAGE French. Also Sango.
CURRENCY CFA franc.
PUBLIC HOLIDAYS Jan 1, Mar 29, Easter Mon, May 1, Ascension, Whit Mon, Jun 30, Aug 13, Assumption, Nov 1, Dec 1, 25.
GOVERNMENT Independent republic since 1960. Head of state and chief executive is the president, elected for a 6-year term. The 52-seat legislative National Assembly is elected every 5 years. The Rassemblement Démocratique Centrafricain (RDC) is the sole legal party.

EQUATORIAL GUINEA

This former Spanish colony once boasted the highest income per head in Africa thanks to the world's best cocoa, grown on the island of Fernando Póo (now Bioko). But independence in 1968 was followed by 11 years of bloody dictatorship under Macías Nguema which left the economy in ruins.

In 1979 the dictator was overthrown by his nephew, Teodoro Nguema. There has since been a very gradual improvement in the economy. Discipline has been brought to policy-making and the cocoa plantations have been rehabilitated. Entry into the franc zone in 1985 brought the advantage of a convertible currency and new commercial ties with France.

Political progress, however, has been minimal. The president has payed lipservice to democratic reform but power has remained in the hands of his Esangui clan, corruption is rampant and there are persistent reports of human rights abuses.

OFFICIAL NAME Republic of Equatorial Guinea.
CAPITAL CITY Malabo.
GEOGRAPHY The capital is on Bioko, a volcanic island off the Cameroon coast. The other principal area is a mainland territory, Río Muni, consisting of a narrow coastal plain and upland plateau. *Area* 28,051 sq km (10,830 sq miles).
PEOPLE *Population* 430,000.
RELIGION RC 89%, Animist 5%, Muslim 0.5%.
LANGUAGE Spanish. Also local languages.
CURRENCY CFA franc.
PUBLIC HOLIDAYS Jan 1, Mar 5, Good Fri, Easter Mon, May 1, 25, Dec 10, 25.
GOVERNMENT Republic since 1968. Head of state and chief executive is the president, elected for a 7-year term. The 41-member National Assembly serves a 5-year term. The sole official political party is the Partido Democrático de Guinea Ecuatorial (PDGE).

CONGO

The Parti Congolais du Travail (PCT) came to power in 1969. Over the next 20 years, although Marxist-Leninist in ideology, the government showed increasing economic pragmatism. Western capital was used to develop the offshore oil fields in the 1970s. After the oil price crash of 1986 cut revenues and exacerbated the problems of a large debt service burden, the government sought IMF support for its structural adjustment plans. The process gained momentum in 1989 when President Sassou-Nguesso won party support for a variety of liberalization measures, including privatization of some parastatals.

Along with economic liberalization there were moves towards political reform, particularly after December 1989. Marxism-Leninism was dropped in favour of more general socialist goals and a commitment to move to a multiparty system. The achievement of pluralism was not likely to ease the path of economic reform. Congo's powerful trade unions are strongly in favour of political reform, but were expected to line up with PCT traditionalists in opposing moves towards privatization and job cuts.

OFFICIAL NAME People's Republic of Congo.
CAPITAL CITY Brazzaville.
GEOGRAPHY Dense rain forest intersected by numerous river gorges lies behind the narrow coastal plain. The Niari valley in the east has fertile soils. *Area* 342,000 sq km (132,000 sq miles).
PEOPLE *Population* 1.94m. *Density* 5 per sq km.
RELIGION Christian 75%, Animist 20%, Muslim 3%.
LANGUAGE French. Also local languages.
CURRENCY CFA franc.
PUBLIC HOLIDAYS Jan 1, Good Fri, Easter Mon, May 1, Aug 15, Dec 25.
GOVERNMENT Independent republic since 1960. The sole legal party, the Parti Congolais du Travail (PCT) elects a central committee chairman who is head of state and chief executive. The 153-member National Assembly serves a 5-year term. A return to multi-party democracy has been promised.

ZAIRE

Zaire is Africa's third largest country with enormous variations in climate and terrain and abundant natural resources. Its size, however, has been a major barrier to realizing this potential; Kinshasa, the capital, is as far from the second city, Lubumbashi, as Paris is from Moscow. The lack of basic infrastructure, particularly transport, is still the most immediate constraint on growth.

Poor communications helped President Mobutu Sese Seko keep an iron grip on the country for 25 years after seizing power in 1965. So too did an astute use of divide-and-rule tactics against his many opponents. His economic policies were more erratic. Alternating bouts of nationalization and privatization, combined with rampant corruption and declining commodity prices during the 1980s to undermine the country's innate strengths. Living standards plummeted; in 1987 Zaire was classified by the World Bank as one of the world's poorest countries. In early 1990 a wave of strikes and student unrest, reflecting the democratic tide sweeping the continent, forced President Mobutu to announce a programme to make Zaire a multi-party democracy. There were doubts about his true intentions, but his room for manoeuvre was limited when Zaire's key donors indicated that aid would be linked to democratization and improvements in his government's human rights record. Donor support is crucial to efforts to restore economic growth.

Zaire's strengths include exceptionally rich mineral resources, which generate over 60% of export revenues. Copper is the most important followed by cobalt, of which Zaire is the world's largest producer. Exports also include diamonds, coffee and oil. During the 1970s plans to turn the country into a regional industrial centre generated a number of giant development projects such as the Maluku steel works and the Inga hydroelectric scheme. Few were completed and their main contribution has been to Zaire's foreign debt. In the 1980s the government changed tack, leaving industrial growth to the private sector and relaxing controls on foreign investment.

OFFICIAL NAME Republic of Zaire.
CAPITAL CITY Kinshasa.
GEOGRAPHY The country is focused around the Congo (Zaire) river. Its mouth provides Zaire with a short Atlantic coastline. Upriver the natural vegetation is tropical rain forest. To the south the land rises to the savannah of Shaba province. The vast forest areas are sparsely populated, but Kinshasa, with 3m inhabitants, is one of Africa's largest cities. *Highest point* Ruwenzori 5,000 metres (16,400 feet). *Area* 2,344,885 sq km (905,370 sq miles).
PEOPLE *Population* 34.5m. *Density* 15 per sq km.
RELIGION Christian 90% (RC 48%), Animist 5%, Muslim 1%.
LANGUAGE French. Also local languages.
CURRENCY Zaire.
PUBLIC HOLIDAYS Jan 1, 4, May 1, 20, Jun 24, 30, Aug 1, Oct 14, 27, Nov 17, 24, Dec 25.
GOVERNMENT Republic since 1960. The head of state and chief executive is the president, elected every 7 years. The president appoints the executive council whose members are known as state commissioners. The unicameral Legislative Council is elected every 5 years. The Mouvement Populaire de la Révolution (MPR) is the only officially recognized political party, but a programme for transition to a multi-party system by 1992 was announced in 1990.

IMPORTS AND EXPORTS

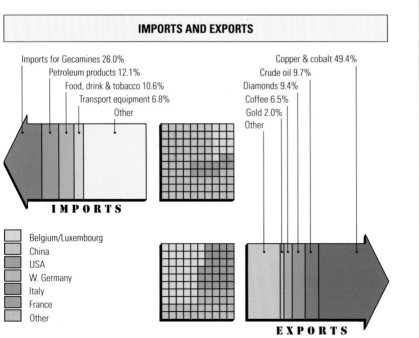

Imports for Gecamines 26.0%
Petroleum products 12.1%
Food, drink & tobacco 10.6%
Transport equipment 6.8%
Other

IMPORTS

Copper & cobalt 49.4%
Crude oil 9.7%
Diamonds 9.4%
Coffee 6.5%
Gold 2.0%
Other

Belgium/Luxembourg
China
USA
W. Germany
Italy
France
Other

EXPORTS

Source: EIU *Country Report* (Imports 1987 figures; Exports/Trading partners 1988 figures).

BALANCE OF PAYMENTS

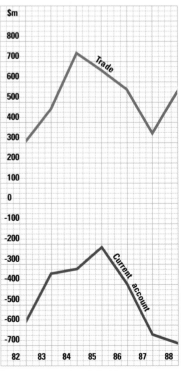

Source: IMF *International Financial Statistics*.

EAST AFRICA

Climate

Eastern coastal areas have a tropical climate, with two rainy seasons and temperatures averaging 22–32°C (72–90°F); annual rainfall averages 1,200mm (47ins). The Kenyan and Ethiopian highlands are cooler. Lake Victoria, Africa's largest lake, has a strong influence on the climate of the countries on its shores – Uganda, Rwanda, Burundi and parts of Tanzania – bringing heavy rainfall to adjoining areas. Northern Sudan has a desert climate with rainfall of only 160mm (6ins) a year.

Sudanese refugees

Sudan has suffered two civil wars since independence in 1956. The first lasted 17 years; the second began in 1983. Both had their origins in the African south's fear of domination by the Arab north; an attempt to impose Islamic law is the issue at the root of the current conflict. It was estimated that around 750,000 people had died and up to 9m more were at risk from war and drought-induced famine by mid-1991. At least 500,000 had sought refuge in neighbouring Ethiopia.

Ethnic and linguistic groups

The ethnic groups of East Africa are as diverse as anywhere on the continent. Ethiopia, an empire established by conquest in the 19th century, has 76 nationalities and 286 languages. The Oromo is the largest ethnic group followed by Amhara and Tigrinya speakers. About 40% of Sudan's people are of Arab origin, but there are 19 major ethnic groups. Conflict between the Arab north and African south has dominated Sudan's independent history. A similar divide in Uganda, between the Bantu peoples of the south and the Nilotic groups in the north, has also been a source of ethnic tension. Swahili, originally the language of the East African coast, has become the *lingua franca* of much of the region, spoken as a first or second language by many of the people of Kenya and Tanzania and even parts of eastern Zaire.

Education

Kenya and Tanzania have led the way in expanding education since independence. Primary education in Kenya is free and, although it is non-compulsory, enrolment is virtually universal. Secondary education has also expanded fast, to account for about 20% of the age group. Only a tiny proportion go on to higher education, however. Tanzania, too, with free and compulsory education from 7 to 14 has achieved enrolment and literacy rates above the African average. Elsewhere, the results are less impressive, although great strides have been made. Often, too, earlier achievements are threatened by growing economic difficulties and the problems of bringing education to scattered communities in rural areas.

Ethiopian refugees

Ethiopia annexed Eritrea, a former Italian colony on the Red Sea, in 1962. For almost thirty years Eritrean separatist groups fought for independence. The Tigray separatist movement has also been a force to be reckoned with since the late 1970s. Both groups had established control over their regions prior to the overthrow of President Mengistu by a coalition of rebel forces in 1991, and were the main channels of relief supplies to famine-hit areas. The rebellion and famine led to a huge exodus of refugees, an estimated 1m crossing the border into neighbouring Sudan, and 140,000 to Djibouti.

Somali refugees

Ethiopia and Somalia went to war over the disputed Ogaden region in 1977–78; hundreds of thousands of refugees fled to Somalia after the Ethiopian victory. Twelve years later the war to overthrow the Siyad Barre regime caused Somali refugees to flood into Ethiopia and other neighbouring states.

More than 1 million

250,000 - 1 million

100,000 - 250,000

SUDAN

Africa's largest country, Sudan has twice been devastated by civil war between the southern, African minority and the northern, Arabized-Muslim majority. Both conflicts stem from the south's rejection of perceived efforts at political, economic and religious domination by the north. The first war, settled in 1972, lasted 17 years and cost 500,000 lives. The second began in 1983 and has already caused more deaths, largely from war-induced famine in the south.

The return of democratic government in 1986, after 16 years of military rule, raised hopes of peace. But prime minister Sadiq al-Mahdi's fragile coalition administration was incapable of decisive government. It was overthrown in June 1989 by the pro-Islamic fundamentalist Revolutionary Command Council (RCC) headed by General Omar Hassan al-Bashir. The RCC's subsequent efforts to establish an Islamic republic scotched all chances of an end to the war and led to unprecedented repression in the north. Political parties were banned and political opponents imprisoned, tortured and executed.

The economy went into decline in the late 1970s as earnings from the key export, cotton, began to fall and debt servicing costs to climb. The collapse has been accelerated by war, devastating drought and the failure of successive governments to implement coherent economic reforms. The country's $12 billion debt has also continued to strangle recovery and to create problems with the IMF and other creditors.

OFFICIAL NAME Republic of Sudan.
CAPITAL CITY Khartoum.
GEOGRAPHY Most of Sudan is a featureless plain through which the Nile and its tributaries flow, with highland to the east and west. In the east are the Red Sea Hills; in the far west the barren Darfur massif. Much of the Nile valley is cultivable. In the south is the Sudd, one of the world's largest swamplands. *Area* 2,505,800 sq km (967,500 sq miles).
PEOPLE *Population* 21.6m. *Density* 9 per sq km.
RELIGION Muslim 73%, Christian 9%, Animist.
LANGUAGE Arabic. Also English and local languages.
CURRENCY Sudanese pound.
PUBLIC HOLIDAYS Jan 1, Mar 3, Apr 6, Sham an-Nassim, Id al-Fitr, May 1, Jul 1, Id al-Adha, Muharram, Mouloud, Dec 25.
GOVERNMENT Republic since 1956. After the June 1989 coup the 151-seat national assembly was replaced by a military, 15-member Revolutionary Command Council for National Salvation and a joint military-civilian cabinet.

IMPORTS AND EXPORTS

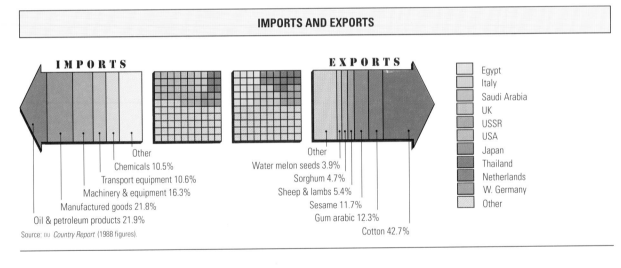

IMPORTS

Other
Chemicals 10.5%
Transport equipment 10.6%
Machinery & equipment 16.3%
Manufactured goods 21.8%
Oil & petroleum products 21.9%

EXPORTS

Other
Water melon seeds 3.9%
Sorghum 4.7%
Sheep & lambs 5.4%
Sesame 11.7%
Gum arabic 12.3%
Cotton 42.7%

Egypt
Italy
Saudi Arabia
UK
USSR
USA
Japan
Thailand
Netherlands
W. Germany
Other

Source: EIU *Country Report* (1988 figures).

DJIBOUTI

A semi-desert enclave squeezed between Ethiopia and Somalia, Djibouti has survived through support from France and clever diplomacy by Hassan Gouled Aptidon, president since independence in 1977.

The economy is based on services, centred on the port, the French garrison and the railway to Addis Ababa, which account for about two-thirds of GDP. With minimal natural resources and most land too poor for cultivation, Djibouti's prospects depend on its ability to become a regional service centre. The country has been remarkably stable, with President Hassan Gouled balancing the Issa (Somali) majority and the Afar minority in his one-party government. But now over 70, he is due to retire in 1993 and there have been signs of unrest among the Afars, as well as growing pressure from opposition groups for greater democracy.

OFFICIAL NAME Republic of Djibouti.
CAPITAL CITY Djibouti.
GEOGRAPHY Mountainous, with a low plateau in the south. *Area* 22,000 sq km (8,500 sq miles).
PEOPLE *Population* 483,000. *Density* 30 per sq km.
RELIGION Muslim 94%, Christian 6%.
LANGUAGE French. Also Arabic.
CURRENCY Djibouti franc.
PUBLIC HOLIDAYS Jan 1, Id al-Fitr, May 1, Jun 27, Id al-Adha, Muharram, Mouloud, Dec 25.
GOVERNMENT Republic since 1977. Rassemblement Populaire pour le Progrès (RPP) the only permitted party since 1981. The executive president is elected for a maximum of two, 6-year terms.

ETHIOPIA

In 1974 Ethiopia exchanged one despot, Emperor Haile Selassie, for another, President Mengistu Haile Mariam. The ideology changed from feudal to neo-communist, but failed to solve the problems of drought, under-development and Eritrean, Tigrean and Oromo rejection of Amhara rule.

Ethiopia is one of the world's poorest countries. Overgrazing, deforestation and failed agricultural policies have left it vulnerable to famine; the war against the rebel groups has not helped. Over 1m people died in 1984–85, and drought devastated the country again in 1990 and 1991. The government, with the support of its socialist allies waning, began losing heavily to the Eritreans and Tigreans in 1990. In May 1991 rebel forces took Addis Ababa, and President Mengistu fled to Zimbabwe. US-sponsored peace talks secured promises of elections in 1992, but otherwise failed to reconcile Ethiopian divisions.

OFFICIAL NAME People's Democratic Republic of Ethiopia.
CAPITAL CITY Addis Ababa.
GEOGRAPHY Much of the country is mountainous. *Area* 1,221,900 sq km (471,800 sq miles).
PEOPLE *Population* 47.8m. *Density* 38 per sq km.
RELIGION Christian (Coptic) 49%, Muslim 31%.
LANGUAGE Amharic. Also English, Italian and local languages.
CURRENCY Birr.
PUBLIC HOLIDAYS (* Coptic Holidays) Jan 7*, 19*, Mar 2, Apr 6, Id al-Fitr, May 1, Id al-Adha, Sep 12, 27*, Mouloud.
GOVERNMENT Military-dominated socialist republic. All candidates for the 835-seat National Assembly must be members of the Ethiopian Democratic Unity Party.

SOMALIA

Somalia has been ravaged by drought, floods and war. It has few natural resources: bananas dominate exports. After President Siyad Barre seized power in 1969, imposing a military-dominated dictatorship, economic policy became increasingly centralist. Policy differences led to a break with the IMF in 1987 and a sharp fall in aid. Economic reform measures were introduced in 1989, but donor concern over human rights abuses prevented a recovery of aid levels.

Soviet advisers were expelled in 1977 when Moscow refused to support Somalia in its war with Ethiopia over the disputed Ogaden. The USA then became a major donor, but distanced itself from the regime as repression increased during the 1980s. Opposition was strongest among the northern Issaqs. Sporadic fighting became civil war in 1988 and spread to the centre and south. In early 1991, with most of the country under opposition control, Siyad Barre's rule was over. But, with no widely accepted successor, his escape into exile in Kenya was not expected to bring a quick end to the turmoil.

OFFICIAL NAME Somali Democratic Republic.
CAPITAL CITY Mogadishu.
GEOGRAPHY A dry, scrubby plateau rises behind the wide Indian Ocean coastal plain. The narrow Gulf of Aden coastal plain gives way to montane forest. *Area* 637,700 sq km (246,200 sq miles).
PEOPLE *Population* 6.8m. *Density* 10 per sq km.
RELIGION Sunni Muslim 99.8%.
LANGUAGE Somali. Also Arabic, English and Italian.
CURRENCY Somali shilling.
PUBLIC HOLIDAYS Jan 1, Id al-Fitr, May 1, Jun 26, Jul 1, Id al-Adha, Ashoura, Mouloud, Oct 21–22.
GOVERNMENT Military-dominated socialist republic. Independent since 1960. The leader of the sole legal party, the Somali Revolutionary Socialist Party, is president and chief executive.

UGANDA

Described by Winston Churchill as the "pearl of Africa", Uganda was almost torn apart by internecine strife after independence in 1962. Seven changes of government, four of them violent, and two civil wars left one of the continent's most promising economies in ruins and a worrying legacy of factionalism and corruption. Since President Yoweri Museveni took power in 1986 there has been relative peace. His daunting task has been to maintain stability, restore economic growth and return the country to democracy.

Export production is still low and industry is only gradually being rebuilt, but economic progress has been encouraging. Growth has averaged 7% a year since 1987; inflation dropped from over 200% in 1986 to under 30% in 1990. After a slow start aid donors have proved generous, although the debt burden remains a big problem. More serious still is Aids, which is threatening to decimate the population and undermine much of the economic recovery. Rebel activity continues in the north and east, but President Museveni has made great strides towards restoring political stability since 1988. Agreements have been made with opposition groups and government representation widened. The government favours a one-party system, but the pluralist voice remains powerful. General elections have been postponed until 1995, but pressure may bring them forward.

OFFICIAL NAME Republic of Uganda.
CAPITAL CITY Entebbe.
GEOGRAPHY A landlocked lakeland country, the south and east comprise Lake Victoria and its basin. The Victoria Nile flows from it, through the country's heartland. Ice-capped mountains straddle the equator in the west. The north of the country is a high, scrubby plateau. *Area* 236,036 sq km (91,130 sq miles).
PEOPLE *Population* 12.6m. *Density* 52 per sq km.
RELIGION Christian 75%, Muslim 15%, Animist.
LANGUAGE English. Also local languages.
CURRENCY New shilling.
PUBLIC HOLIDAYS Jan 1, Mar 25, Good Fri, Easter Mon, Id al-Fitr, May 1, Id al-Adha, Oct 9, Dec 25,
GOVERNMENT Republic since 1962. The head of state and chief executive is the president. The legislative National Resistance Council comprises 210 elected members and 68 presidential nominees; all serve a 6-year term. There are registered political parties, but political activity has been suspended by the government.

KENYA

Kenya's much-vaunted political stability is looking increasingly fragile. Internal tensions, linked to extreme economic inequalities and traditional ethnic rivalries, were highlighted by the 1982 coup attempt. President Daniel arap Moi's response was to imprison dissidents and curb basic liberties. When opposition resurfaced in 1989 in the form of demands for a multi-party democracy, his reaction was even stronger. However, this time the opposition had wider support and the repression led to riots in July 1990, as well as warnings from donors that aid flows were at risk. President Moi's immediate reaction was defiant, but with the multi-party lobbyists unlikely to fade away he faced the choice of making significant concessions or of courting political and economic crisis.

Kenya's pro-Western stance and its market-oriented economy have attracted generous foreign aid. It underpins the country's current account deficit and since 1985 has helped keep economic growth ahead of one of the world's highest population growth rates (4% a year), despite the collapse in coffee prices.

OFFICIAL NAME Republic of Kenya.
CAPITAL CITY Nairobi.
GEOGRAPHY The African Rift Valley sweeps through the eastern half of the country, filled in the arid north by Lake Turkana. High volcanic mountains around the valley give way to a low, sloping plateau, most of it scrubland. The high ground supports agriculture; the drier valley floor and plains are home to herds of game, much of it in extensive reserves. *Area* 582,645 sq km (224,950 sq miles).
PEOPLE *Population* 21.1m. *Density* 37 per sq km.
RELIGION Christian 70%, Muslim 6%, Animist.
LANGUAGE Swahili and English. Also local languages.
CURRENCY Kenya shilling.
PUBLIC HOLIDAYS Jan 1, Good Fri, Easter Mon, May 1, Id al-Fitr, Jun 1, Id al-Adha, Oct 20, Dec 12, 25–26.
GOVERNMENT Republic since 1964. Independent since 1963. The head of state and chief executive is a president, elected for a 5-year term. Since 1982, the Kenyan African National Union has been the only permitted party. The legislature is a 188-member National Assembly.

ECONOMIC PROFILE

Coffee and tea are major cash crops; also pyrethrum and sisal. Robust light industrial sector, particularly in food and beverage processing and engineering. Tourism, oil refining and entrepôt trade for landlocked neighbours important foreign-exchange earners. The most developed financial sector in East Africa.

Growth Tourism recently overtook coffee as leading foreign-exchange earner. Horticultural exports, airfreighted to Europe, growing fast. Industry being encouraged to go for export growth.

Problems Shortage of fertile land and rapidly growing population. Heavily dependent on imported oil, although hydroelectric and geothermal power sources are being developed.

IMPORTS AND EXPORTS

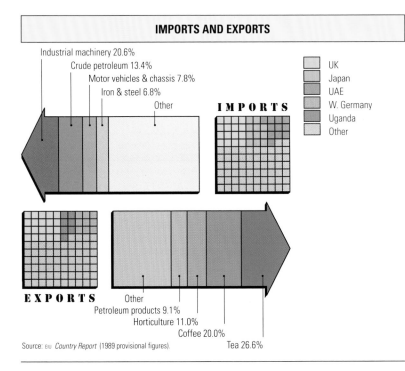

Industrial machinery 20.6%
Crude petroleum 13.4%
Motor vehicles & chassis 7.8%
Iron & steel 6.8%
Other

IMPORTS

UK
Japan
UAE
W. Germany
Uganda
Other

EXPORTS
Other
Petroleum products 9.1%
Horticulture 11.0%
Coffee 20.0%
Tea 26.6%

Source: EIU *Country Report* (1989 provisional figures).

BALANCE OF PAYMENTS

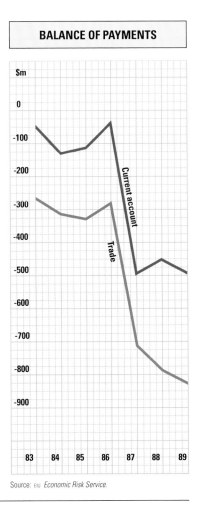

$m

Current account

Trade

83 84 85 86 87 88 89

Source: EIU *Economic Risk Service*.

RWANDA

Rwanda is one of the world's poorest countries, its limited natural resources coming under pressure from a rapidly growing population. President Juvenal Habyarimana, who seized power in 1973, has won the backing of aid donors for plans to sustain and diversify the mainly agricultural economy. Rwanda has largely avoided the ethnic violence between the minority Tutsi and majority Hutu which has bedevilled Burundi, but there has been growing anger among Rwandan refugees who cannot return home because the government says the country is over-populated. In October 1990 an armed invasion from Uganda, involving about 8,000 Rwandan refugees, posed a real threat to the government before a ceasefire was agreed. President Habyarimana decided to speed up the process of domestic political reform begun earlier in 1990, with a view to having a multi-party system in place by the end of 1991.

OFFICIAL NAME Republic of Rwanda.
CAPITAL CITY Kigali.
GEOGRAPHY A landlocked upland plateau. *Area* 26,338 sq km (10,170 sq miles).
PEOPLE *Population* 5.7m. *Density* 218 per sq km.
RELIGION Christian 82%, Muslim 1%.
LANGUAGE Kinyarwanda and French.
CURRENCY Rwanda franc.
PUBLIC HOLIDAYS Jan 1, 28, Easter Mon, May 1, Ascension, Whit Mon, Jul 1, 5, Aug 15, Sep 25, Oct 26, Nov 1, Dec 25.
GOVERNMENT Republic since 1962. The head of state and chief executive is the president, directly elected for a 5-year term, who appoints his own council of ministers.

BURUNDI

Burundi's history since independence in 1962 has been dominated by periodic violence rooted in the political and economic dominance of the Tutsi minority over the Hutu majority. The 1988 outbreak of ethnic rivalry caused the death of up to 20,000 people. In an effort to bring lasting peace President Pierre Buyoya, who replaced Jean-Baptiste Bagaza after the 1987 coup, has promised a new constitution which is to be submitted to a national referendum. Aid donors have supported his plans, but President Buyoya is vulnerable to those within the Tutsi élite opposed to change, especially greater Hutu participation in politics.

Burundi is poor. Coffee accounts for 80% of export earnings. Small amounts of tea and cotton are also exported, but most agricultural land is given over to subsistence crops.

OFFICIAL NAME Republic of Burundi.
CAPITAL CITY Bujumbura.
GEOGRAPHY A landlocked upland plateau. *Area* 27,834 sq km (10,750 sq miles).
PEOPLE *Population* 5.1m. *Density* 185 per sq km.
RELIGION RC 78%, Protestant 5%, Animist.
LANGUAGE Kirundi. Also French and Swahili.
CURRENCY Burundi franc.
PUBLIC HOLIDAYS Jan 1, Easter Mon, May 1, Ascension, Jul 1, Assumption, Sep 18, Nov 1, Dec 25.
GOVERNMENT Independent republic since 1962. The military government, in power since since 1987, is being replaced by a reformed single party, the Union pour le Progrès National (Uprona).

TANZANIA

For over 20 years after independence in 1961 Tanzania was moulded by the self-help socialism of its first president, Julius Nyerere. Under his direction Tanzania achieved comparatively high welfare and educational standards, and basic human liberties were respected. But President Nyerere failed to increase agricultural productivity and the state sector performed badly. Initiative was stifled by an increasingly inefficient and corrupt party bureaucracy. The oil price hikes of the 1970s, world recession and the consequent drop in prices of Tanzania's principal exports all contributed to the country's economic decline in the 1980s.

Mr Nyerere stepped down as president in 1985 but retained the party leadership until August 1990. His successor, Ali Hassan Mwinyi, and a handful of technocrats have battled against the old guard to restore incentives and the disciplines of a market economy. Recovery has been slow and hampered, among other things, by an inadequate transport system. However, tourism could be a growth sector and basic goods are back in the shops. The pace of economic liberalization was expected to speed up after President Mwinyi became party leader in 1990. But having finally consolidated his power-base, he may face a new political challenge from growing calls for moves towards multi-party democracy.

A mainly agricultural economy, Tanzania's exports are dominated by coffee, cotton, sisal, cashew nuts, tea and, from Zanzibar, cloves. Output from both the agricultural and state-dominated industrial sectors has improved since 1986 as a result of the economic reforms and an increase in foreign aid which has improved the availability of foreign exchange for essential imports.

OFFICIAL NAME United Republic of Tanzania.
CAPITAL CITY Dar es Salaam.
GEOGRAPHY Tanzania is mostly a rolling plateau, bounded in the north and west by lakes Tanganyika, Malawi and Victoria. Africa's highest peak, Mount Kilimanjaro, lies on the border with Kenya. A narrow coastal strip and the offshore islands of Zanzibar and Pemba are flat and edged with coral and mangrove swamps. *Area* 945,087 sq km (364,900 sq miles).
PEOPLE *Population* 23.9m. *Density* 25 per sq km.
RELIGION Christian 43%, Muslim 30%, Animist.
LANGUAGE Swahili. Also English and local languages.
CURRENCY Tanzanian shilling.
PUBLIC HOLIDAYS Jan 12, Feb 5, Good Fri, Easter Mon, Id al-Fitr, Apr 26, May 1, Id al-Haji, July 7, Dec 9, 25.
GOVERNMENT Republic since 1962. Independent since 1961. The executive president is nominated by the only recognized party, Chama cha Mapinduzi, and elected by universal suffrage for a 5-year term. The legislative National Assembly is elected for 5 years and comprises up to 156 members from the mainland and Zanzibar. Zanzibar has its own assembly for internal matters.

AFRICA

IMPORTS AND EXPORTS

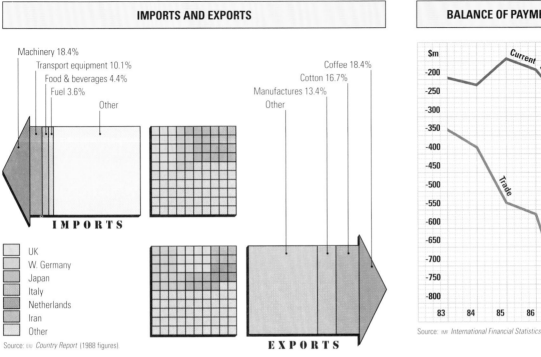

Machinery 18.4%
Transport equipment 10.1%
Food & beverages 4.4%
Fuel 3.6%
Other

Coffee 18.4%
Cotton 16.7%
Manufactures 13.4%
Other

IMPORTS

UK
W. Germany
Japan
Italy
Netherlands
Iran
Other

EXPORTS

Source: EIU *Country Report* (1988 figures).

BALANCE OF PAYMENTS

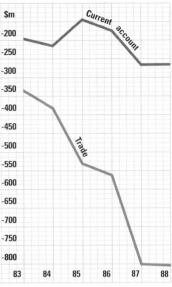

Current account

Trade

Source: IMF *International Financial Statistics*.

MADAGASCAR

OFFICIAL NAME Democratic Republic of Madagascar.
CAPITAL CITY Antananarivo.
GEOGRAPHY One of the world's largest islands, its spine is a rain-forested, mountainous plateau, tumbling into the ocean on the east and sloping more gently to a scrubby coastal plain in the west. The south is desert. *Area* 587,041 sq km (226,650 sq miles).
PEOPLE *Population* 9.9m. *Density* 17 per sq km.
RELIGION Christian 43%, Muslim, Animist.
LANGUAGE Malagasy. Also French.
CURRENCY Madagascar franc.
PUBLIC HOLIDAYS Jan 1, Mar 29, Good Fri, Easter Mon, May 1, Ascension, Whitsun, Jun 26, Nov 1, Dec 25, 30.
GOVERNMENT Republic since 1960. The head of state and chief executive is a president, heading a supreme revolutionary council. A legislative National People's Assembly is elected for 5 years.

Madagascar is more a small continent than an island, its people and their language of Indonesian rather than African origin. Over 150,000 plant and animal species are unique to Madagascar, but they are threatened by widespread deforestation and soil erosion. Pioneering "debt-for-nature" swap schemes have recently increased funding for vital nature conservation work, while provid-

ing opportunities to write off debt.

The government that took over at independence in 1960 stayed close to France, but a resurgence of Malagasy nationalism in 1972 led to the departure of French troops and advisers. A period of turmoil followed, ended by the emergence in 1975 of Didier Ratsiraka as the strong man of a "humanist-Marxist" regime. President Ratsiraka brought relative stability. All political parties, including his own Arema party, belonged to the National Front for the Defence of the Revolution and contested elections under its umbrella. In the late 1980s worsening poverty, food shortages and unpopular economic reforms focused opposition to the government. Pluralist politics formally returned in March 1990 when the National Front coalition was ended, but only after President Ratsiraka had won another seven-year mandate in the 1989 elections.

Madagascar has maintained strong ties with the EC (its major trade partner). The economy has moved from the nationalizations and central control of the early Ratsiraka years, to the late 1980s liberalization of marketing, investment and the exchange rate, which has made Madagascar a test case for free-market reforms. But, despite the policy shifts, the economy has remained

in the doldrums. In the search for new investment and growth President Ratsiraka in 1990 broke ranks with the OAU and restored economic ties with South Africa.

COMOROS

OFFICIAL NAME Federal Islamic Republic of the Comoros.
CAPITAL CITY Moroni.
GEOGRAPHY A volcanic archipelago, its three main islands, Njadidja, Mwali and Nzwami, have forested centres and swampy coasts enclosing heavily cultivated fertile strips. *Area* 1,852 sq km (720 sq miles).
PEOPLE *Population* 484,000. *Density* 261 per sq km.
RELIGION Muslim 99.7%, Christian.
LANGUAGE Arabic. Also French and Comorian.
CURRENCY Comorian franc.
PUBLIC HOLIDAYS Leilat al-Meiraj, 1st day of Ramadan, Id al-Fitr, Jul 6, Id al-Adha, Muharram, Ashoura, Mouloud, Nov 27.
GOVERNMENT Republic since 1975. An executive president is elected every 6 years, while the legislative federal assembly serves a 5-year term.

Comoros has had two successful coups since it broke free from France in 1975. The first, shortly after independence, deposed President Ahmad Abdallah; the second, in 1978, staged by European mercenaries, returned him to power.

Financed by South Africa, the mercenaries stayed on. They kept President Abdallah in office until 1989 when he was killed in an argument with mercenary leader, Bob Denard. His successor, Said Djohar, was confirmed in office after general elections in March 1990 and pledged to return the country to democracy.

Most of the population are subsistence farmers, but more than half of the islands' food is imported. The main exports face shrinking world markets. Tourism has been the main growth area, with heavy South African investment. President Djohar has promised to pursue the economic liberalization programme begun by his predecessor.

MAURITIUS

OFFICIAL NAME Mauritius.
CAPITAL CITY Port Louis.
GEOGRAPHY A volcanic island surrounded by coral reefs, its mountainous, forested centre gives way to vast plantations of sugar-cane in the valleys and around the coast. *Area* 2,040 sq km (790 sq miles).
PEOPLE *Population* 1.04m. *Density* 508 per sq km.
RELIGION Hindu 53%, RC 28%, Muslim 16%.
LANGUAGE English. Also French and Creole.
CURRENCY Mauritian rupee.
PUBLIC HOLIDAYS Jan 1, 2 New Year, Thaipoosam Cavadec, Feb 12, Maha Shivaraatree, Chinese Spirit Festival, Mar 12, Independence Day, Ougadi, Id al-Fitr, May 1, Ganesh Chaturthi, All Saints, Divali, Dec 25.
GOVERNMENT Independent Commonwealth state. The head of state is the British monarch, represented by a governor-general. A legislative assembly of up to 71 members (plus 8 "best losers") is elected for a 5-year term.

Until recently Mauritius was one of Africa's success stories. The growth of clothing manufacture in the Export Processing Zone (EPZ) and of tourism encouraged high growth rates in the 1970s and 1980s and moderated the economy's vulnerability to fluctuations in the price of sugar, the main export crop. Since the late 1980s, however, growth has slowed markedly as the EPZ has come up against problems of rising wages, labour shortages and protectionism in its main markets. The government

is now encouraging further diversification but it is expected to be some years before former high growth rates are restored.

MAYOTTE

OFFICIAL NAME Territory of Mayotte.
CAPITAL CITY Dzaoudzi.
GEOGRAPHY The coral-fringed volcanic island has heathland in the centre and agriculture in the lowlands. *Area* 375 sq km (145 sq miles).
PEOPLE *Population* 73,000. *Density* 179 per sq km.
RELIGION Muslim 97%, Christian 3%.
LANGUAGE French. Also local languages.
CURRENCY French franc.
GOVERNMENT French overseas *collectivité territoriale*. The French government is represented by a prefect; Mayotte sends a deputy to the French national assembly.

Mayotte voted to remain part of France when the other three Comoros islands declared independence in 1975. Comoros has continued to press its claims to the island, backed by the UN, but Mayotte's politicians limit their ambitions to attaining the status of a department of France.

Vanilla and the essential oil ylang-ylang are the main exports. The island depends on French aid; it has also received investment from South Africa.

SEYCHELLES

OFFICIAL NAME Republic of Seychelles.
CAPITAL CITY Victoria.
GEOGRAPHY A scattered archipelago of over 100 granitic and coralline islands, four of which – Mahé, Praslin, Silhouette and La Digue – support almost all the population. *Area* 453 sq km (175 sq miles).
PEOPLE *Population* 66,000. *Density* 146 per sq km.
RELIGION Christian 98% (RC 90%), Hindu 1%.
LANGUAGE English. Also French and Creole.
CURRENCY Seychelles rupee.
PUBLIC HOLIDAYS Jan 1–2, May 1, Independence Day, Good Fri, Easter Sat, Easter Mon, Jun 5, 9, Corpus Christi, Assumption, Nov 1, Immaculate Conception, Dec 25.
GOVERNMENT Republic since 1976. The only

recognized party is the Seychelles People's Progressive Front. A president is elected unopposed for a 5-year term as head of state and chief executive.

President Albert René's government has made efforts to diversify away from dependence on upmarket tourism by expanding fishing, agriculture and light industry. But the tourist industry still accounts for more than 50% of foreign earnings.

Tourism is particularly vulnerable to political upsets. President René himself came to power in a coup in 1977, a year after independence from the UK. His exiled enemies continue to plot his downfall, although he has indicated his intention of stepping down in 1994.

RÉUNION

OFFICIAL NAME Department of Réunion.
CAPITAL CITY Saint-Denis.
GEOGRAPHY The volcanic island has a mountainous, forested centre surrounded by an intensively cultivated coastal plain full of sugar plantations. *Area* 2,510 sq km (970 sq miles).
PEOPLE *Population* 579,000.
RELIGION RC 96%, Muslim 2%.
LANGUAGE French.
CURRENCY French franc.
GOVERNMENT Overseas department of France. It is administered through a government commissioner aided by councils elected to deal with purely local matters. 5 deputies are sent to the French national assembly.

Occupied by France as a penal colony in the mid-17th century, Réunion today is the main French military base in the Indian Ocean. The people of Réunion have consistently opposed complete independence.

The economy has long been based on sugar; its processing and the production of rum are the only significant industries.

SOUTHERN AFRICA

SADCC

One of the most successful of African development organizations, the Southern African Development Co-ordination Conference (SADCC) was founded in 1979 by nine southern African states: Angola, Botswana, Mozambique, Tanzania, Zambia, Zimbabwe, Lesotho, Malawi and Swaziland. Namibia became the 10th member in 1990. Their explicit aim is to reduce their economic dependence on South Africa. SADCC initially concentrated on freeing its members from the need to use lengthy and costly transport routes to South African ports by raising finance to rehabilitate rail and road links from landlocked states like Zimbabwe and Malawi to the Mozambican ports of Beira, Maputo and Nacala, and Dar es Salaam in Tanzania. These schemes have been a considerable success; around 30% of Zimbabwe's freight, for example, now passes through Beira, although Mozambican rebel activity remains a problem. The peace in Angola has raised hopes of putting the Benguela railway, once an important export route for the Zambian and Zairean copperbelts, back in action.

SADCC does not confine itself to transport projects; the emphasis is on coordination of efforts in a wide variety of areas: agriculture, mining, energy, industry and tourism.

The PTA

The 17-member Preferential Trade Area for Eastern and Southern Africa aims to liberalize trade, encourage economic cooperation and create a regional common market. Trade within the region has been stimulated by adoption of a common list of goods from member states to be given preferential treatment, although insistence on majority local ownership has raised objections from countries like Kenya and Zimbabwe, where foreign firms often hold large stakes in local companies. Establishment of a PTA clearing house and use of a common unit of account has reduced the need to use scarce convertible currency in trade between member states. PTA member states are: Angola, Burundi, Comoros, Djibouti, Ethiopia, Kenya, Lesotho, Malawi, Mauritius, Mozambique, Rwanda, Somalia, Swaziland, Tanzania, Uganda, Zambia and Zimbabwe.

Refugees

Southern Africa has one of the largest concentrations of refugees and displaced people in the world. Over 2m people have been forced to leave their homes within their own countries; 1m more have fled to neighbouring countries. The vast majority are fleeing not from drought or natural disaster but from man-made catastrophes.

Most come from Mozambique, where a rebel movement, the Mozambique National Resistance, has caused widespread destruction for over a decade. About 800,000 Mozambicans have fled to Malawi, where they now represent about 10% of the population, placing a huge burden on the country's slender resources. Hundreds of thousands more are in Zimbabwe, Tanzania, Zambia and Swaziland. Close to half Mozambique's population are at risk, deprived of the means to feed themselves.

The civil war in Angola caused massive displacement of people and most countries of the region provided a home for some of the thousands of South Africans who fled their country's apartheid policies.

Climate

Mozambique and Angola have a tropical climate on the coast. Inland, Zimbabwe and Zambia receive most of their rain between November and March. Much of Namibia and Botswana and parts of South Africa have a desert climate. Temperatures average 20–30°C (68–86°F) and annual rainfall ranges from 24mm (1in) on the Namibian coast to 2,000mm (78ins) in Zimbabwe's eastern highlands. In the extreme south there are dry summers and wet, mild winters on the Mediterranean pattern.

■ More than 1 million
● 250,000 - 1 million
• 100,000 - 250,000

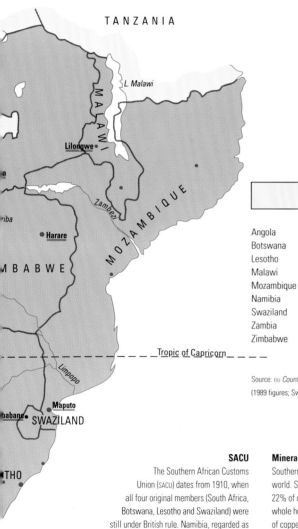

Ethnic and linguistic groups

Most of the peoples of southern Africa speak Bantu languages. The Bushmen or San of the Kalahari desert of Botswana and Namibia are linguistically and ethnically distinct: survivors of a Khoisan linguistic group that dominated the southern half of the continent 5,000 years ago. Among the largest ethnic groups are the Shona, who make up the majority of the population of Zimbabwe, and the Ovimbundu of Angola.

Education

Most countries in the region aim to provide education for all between the ages of 6 and 14, often free of charge. Zimbabwe, for example, has greatly increased spending on education since independence; in recent years education spending has been equivalent to over 12% of GDP and the primary school enrolment rate has reached 90%, from 50% in the late 1970s. In many countries, however, economic pressures mean that achievements in these fields fall far short of aspirations. In Angola and Mozambique, especially, years of civil war have severely disrupted educational efforts; the Mozambique rebel movement has made schools and health centres a particular target. Provision of secondary education in most countries lags behind that for younger children.

"Homelands"

Variously known as "national states", "homelands" or "Bantustans", these states were created as part of the white South African policy of "separate development". Four of the states — Bophuthatswana, Ciskei, Transkei and Venda — are nominally independent, with their own governments and citizenship and separate legal and tax systems. In practice, small and fragmented as they are, they lack any real autonomy and are dependent on South African aid. They have not received international recognition.

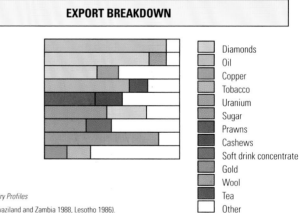

EXPORT BREAKDOWN

Angola
Botswana
Lesotho
Malawi
Mozambique
Namibia
Swaziland
Zambia
Zimbabwe

Diamonds
Oil
Copper
Tobacco
Uranium
Sugar
Prawns
Cashews
Soft drink concentrate
Gold
Wool
Tea
Other

Source: EIU *Country Profiles*

(1989 figures; Swaziland and Zambia 1988, Lesotho 1986).

SACU

The Southern African Customs Union (SACU) dates from 1910, when all four original members (South Africa, Botswana, Lesotho and Swaziland) were still under British rule. Namibia, regarded as an unofficial member while under South African administration, joined after independence in 1990. South Africa sets and collects customs duties for all the SACU members and distributes a share to the other four. The union is an important source of income for the smaller states, but it also provides South Africa with a captive market for its goods behind significant protective barriers.

Minerals

Southern Africa arguably contains the most wealthy and varied concentrations of minerals in the world. South Africa alone has about 49% of the world's known gold reserves, 86% of its platinum, 22% of diamonds, 4% of antimony, 83% of chrome, 48% of manganese, 64% of vanadium, plus a whole host of minor strategic minerals, like titanium, nickel and fluorspar. Zambia has huge reserves of copper and cobalt; Zimbabwe has a little of almost all of South Africa's range of minerals. Botswana, like South Africa and Zimbabwe, has huge coal reserves, as well as some of the world's richest diamond deposits. Namibia has huge reserves of diamonds, uranium, copper, lead, zinc and other metals.

ANGOLA

Angola should be one of Africa's richest countries. It has large reserves of oil and diamonds and plenty of fertile land. But very little of this potential has been realized, outside the enclave of the oil sector. This is mainly due to the 1975–1991 civil war between the government, backed by the USSR and Cuba, and the União Nacional para a Independência Total de Angola (Unita) guerrillas, backed by South Africa and the USA.

The settler exodus at independence in 1975 and subsequent austere Marxist policies did little to help the deteriorating economy. Industry collapsed and production of non-oil exports, notably coffee and diamonds, declined steeply. By mid-1988 over 1.5m people had been displaced because of the war.

In December 1988 South Africa and Cuba agreed to withdraw their forces from Angola. Subsequent peace talks between the government and Unita were beset by mutual mistrust, but war-weariness and the changing priorities of their main supporters have pushed them towards a peace settlement. Talks sponsored by the Portuguese government led to a cease-fire in May 1991, under the supervision of an American, Soviet and Portuguese-backed commission. Multi-party elections were scheduled for 1992.

OFFICIAL NAME People's Republic of Angola.
CAPITAL CITY Luanda.
GEOGRAPHY High plateau apart from a coastal plain that merges in the north with the Congo delta. The vegetation ranges from forest in the north through savannah to near-desert on the southern coast. *Area* 1,246,700 sq km (481,354 sq miles).
PEOPLE *Population* 9.7m. *Density* 7 per sq km.
RELIGION Christian 90% (RC 70%, Protestant 20%), Animist.
LANGUAGE Portuguese. Also local languages.
CURRENCY Kwanza.
PUBLIC HOLIDAYS Jan 1, Feb 4, Mar 27, Apr 14, May 1, Aug 1, Sep 17, Nov 11, Dec 1, 10, 25.
GOVERNMENT Independent republic since 1975. The National People's Assembly has 223 members who serve a 5-year term. Head of state is the executive president.

ZAMBIA

After more than two decades of relative stability Zambia faces an uncertain future. In 1990 President Kenneth Kaunda was forced by mass rioting to acknowledge popular rejection of one-party government and to concede multi-party elections within a year. The outcome of the poll hinged on the opposition's ability to remain united. The victor faced the unenviable task of dealing with Zambia's profound problems.

These stem from its dependence on copper for almost 90% of export earnings. The decline in copper prices since 1975 has trapped Zambia in a vicious circle of rising debt and falling output and living standards. To add to the country's plight, copper reserves are nearing exhaustion.

Policy changes since 1983 boosted the agricultural sector, but their impact was limited by the failure of successive austerity programmes. Government reluctance to liberalize the economy was accompanied by the international community's failure to provide effective relief for Zambia's massive debt.

OFFICIAL NAME Republic of Zambia.
CAPITAL CITY Lusaka.
GEOGRAPHY Landlocked; mainly upland plateau country with elevations declining westwards. Most people live in the central Copperbelt area and along the line of rail south to Livingstone. *Area* 752,614 sq km (290,586 sq miles).
PEOPLE *Population* 7.8m. *Density* 10 per sq km.
RELIGION Christian 72%, Animist.
LANGUAGE English. Also local languages.
CURRENCY Zambian kwacha.
PUBLIC HOLIDAYS Jan 1, Mar 11 , Easter Mon, May 1, 24 , Jul 5, 8, Aug 5, Oct 24, Dec 25.
GOVERNMENT Republic since 1964. The executive president appoints a prime minister and cabinet. The United National Independence Party (UNIP) was the sole legal party from 1972 to December 1990 when the constitution was amended to allow multi-party politics.

IMPORTS AND EXPORTS

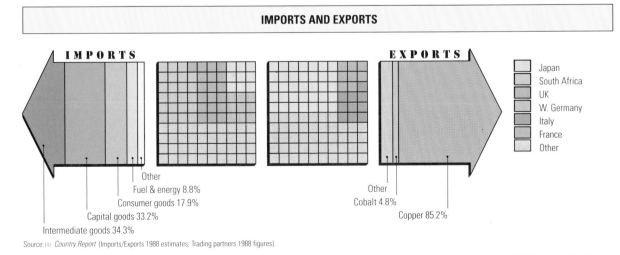

IMPORTS

EXPORTS

Japan
South Africa
UK
W. Germany
Italy
France
Other

Other
Fuel & energy 8.8%
Consumer goods 17.9%
Capital goods 33.2%
Intermediate goods 34.3%

Other
Cobalt 4.8%
Copper 85.2%

Source: EIU *Country Report* (Imports/Exports 1988 estimates; Trading partners 1988 figures).

MALAWI

President Hastings Banda, in power since before independence in 1964, has pursued idiosyncratic policies. He has been sympathetic to South Africa and, until recently, hostile to most of his left-leaning neighbours. His autocratic rule brooks no opposition; potential successors have quickly fallen out of favour.

Economic policies have been conservative, emphasizing private-sector agriculture. At first, austere housekeeping and high agricultural productivity fuelled impressive growth in a country with few natural assets apart from fertile soils. The early 1980s brought recession as structural weaknesses emerged, prices of the main exports fell and trade routes through neighbouring Mozambique were disrupted.

Recent economic reforms emphasizing new exports and the upgrading of peasant agriculture have helped restore growth. After pressure from aid donors, programmes have been started to improve health and education levels, which are below African averages.

OFFICIAL NAME Republic of Malawi.

CAPITAL CITY Lilongwe.

GEOGRAPHY Landlocked, Malawi lies at the southern end of the Rift Valley along the eastern shore of Lake Malawi. *Area* 118,484 sq km (45,750 sq miles).

PEOPLE *Population* 8.6m. *Density* 72 per sq mile.

RELIGION Christian 57%, Muslim 16%, Animist.

LANGUAGE English. Also local languages, especially Chichewa.

CURRENCY Malawi kwacha.

PUBLIC HOLIDAYS Jan 1, Mar 3, Good Fri, Easter Mon, May 14, Jul 6, Oct 17, Dec 21, 25–26.

GOVERNMENT Republic since 1964. Head of state and government is the president. Dr Hastings Banda was made president for life in 1971. The National Assembly comprises 112 elected members and an unlimited number of presidential nominees. The Malawi Congress Party (MCP) is the only legal party.

MOZAMBIQUE

Portuguese settlers fleeing at independence in 1975 left behind a bankrupt economy bereft of skilled workers. The Frelimo government, under the charismatic Samora Machel, set out to provide education and healthcare for all; but the erratic application of socialist policies did nothing to arrest the economy's decline. The civil war against the Mozambique National Resistance (MNR) set the seal on the country's collapse.

The MNR rebels, until recently receiving South African support, systematically destroyed the country's infrastructure and terrorized the rural population. Over 1m people became refugees; almost half the remaining population became dependent on aid as food production collapsed. Output of the few exports declined steeply; by the mid-1980s earnings were less than half the pre-independence level.

After 1984 Frelimo began to move away from socialist policies and to open Mozambique to the West. The political and economic realignment continued under Joaquím Chissano, who became president after Samora Machel's death in an air crash in 1986. Mr Chissano has also overseen moves to democratize the constitution and to negotiate a settlement with the MNR.

OFFICIAL NAME Republic of Mozambique.

CAPITAL CITY Maputo.

GEOGRAPHY Most of the country is lowland, cut by many rivers. South of the Zambezi the coastal plain is a wide, rolling grassland supporting subsistence agriculture; farther north the plain narrows, rising to a savannah plateau on the eastern banks of Lake Malawi. *Area* 799,380 sq km (308,561 sq miles).

PEOPLE *Population* 15.4m. *Density* 19 per sq km.

RELIGION Christian 16%, Muslim 16%, Animist.

LANGUAGE Portuguese. Also local languages.

CURRENCY Metical.

PUBLIC HOLIDAYS Jan 1, Feb 3, Apr 7, May 1, Jun 25, Sep 7, 25, Dec 25.

GOVERNMENT Republic since 1975. The Frente de Libertação de Moçambique (Frelimo) was the only permitted party until December 1990 when the constitution was amended to allow a multi-party system. The president is head of state, chief executive and chairman of the permanent commission of a 250-member legislative National Assembly.

BOTSWANA

One of the world's poorest countries at independence in 1966, with cattle its only export, Botswana has been transformed by its huge diamond resources. Expanding diamond output during the 1980s fuelled one of the world's fastest economic growth rates, despite a protracted drought that reduced the cattle herd by one-third.

With reserves of almost $3 billion and low external debt, the main problem is to diversify the economy and provide jobs for a growing population.

Although Botswana is one of Africa's few long-standing multi-party democracies, the same party has been in power since independence – the Botswana Democratic Party (BDP). The decision in 1990 by the smaller opposition parties to unite could pose the BDP with its first real electoral challenge, especially in the urban areas.

OFFICIAL NAME Republic of Botswana.

CAPITAL CITY Gaborone.

GEOGRAPHY Basically a dry red sandstone plateau, it has salt lakes and swamps in the north and desert – part of the Kalahari – in the south and west. *Area* 557,570 sq km (215,279 sq miles).

PEOPLE *Population* 1.2m. *Density* 2 per sq km.

RELIGION Christian 50%, Animist.

LANGUAGE English and Setswana.

CURRENCY Pula.

PUBLIC HOLIDAYS Jan 1–2, Good Fri–Easter Mon, Ascension, July 15–16, Sep 30, Oct 1, Dec 25–26.

GOVERNMENT Republic since 1966. Executive power is exercised by a directly elected president who is an ex-officio member of a 38-seat National Assembly, which is elected for a 5-year term.

ZIMBABWE

After a decade of civil war Zimbabwe achieved independence in 1980 under the leadership of Robert Mugabe. His reconciliation policy encouraged many whites to stay, but failed to win over dissidents from the Matabele minority. Sporadic guerrilla activity only ended after the December 1987 agreement merging President Mugabe's party with that of his main rival, Joshua Nkomo. The merger created a *de facto* one-party state. Popular opposition, linked to corruption scandals, has forced Mr Mugabe to suspend plans to formalize Zimbabwe's one-party status.

The economy, forced by the international sanctions of 1967–79, is one of Africa's most diversified and sophisticated. Despite a commitment to socialism, government policy has been pragmatic; the private sector still dominates many areas. Modernization of mining and industry has been hampered by foreign exchange shortages caused by the country's exemplary debt repayment record. Innovative agricultural policies have produced massive grain surpluses.

The government's main task is to generate the high growth needed to create jobs for a rapidly increasing labour force. To this end a liberalization process focusing on export generation was begun in 1989.

OFFICIAL NAME Republic of Zimbabwe.
CAPITAL CITY Harare.
GEOGRAPHY A landlocked upland of varying relief regions, ranging from the mountainous eastern highlands to the lowveld of the Zambezi basin in the north and Limpopo basin in the south. *Area* 390,580 sq km (150,800 sq miles).
PEOPLE *Population* 8.8m. *Density* 23 per sq km.
RELIGION Christian 70%, also Muslim, Hindu and Animist.
LANGUAGE English, Shona and Ndebele.
CURRENCY Zimbabwe dollar.
PUBLIC HOLIDAYS Jan 1, Good Fri, Easter Mon, Apr 18, May 1, 25, Aug 11, 12, Dec 25–26.
GOVERNMENT Republic since 1980. Bicameral parliament replaced in 1990 by a 150-member unicameral House of Assembly, comprising 120 elected constituency representatives, 8 provincial governors, 10 customary chiefs and 12 presidential nominees. Head of state and chief executive is the president elected by universal suffrage for a 5-year term.

IMPORTS AND EXPORTS

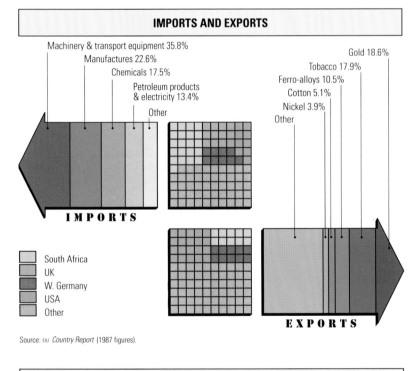

Machinery & transport equipment 35.8%
Manufactures 22.6%
Chemicals 17.5%
Petroleum products & electricity 13.4%
Other

Gold 18.6%
Tobacco 17.9%
Ferro-alloys 10.5%
Cotton 5.1%
Nickel 3.9%
Other

IMPORTS

South Africa
UK
W. Germany
USA
Other

EXPORTS

Source: EIU *Country Report* (1987 figures).

BALANCE OF PAYMENTS

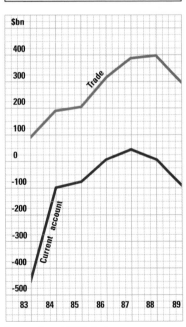

Source: EIU *Economic Risk Service*.

ECONOMIC PROFILE

Diversified agriculture producing tobacco, sugar, cotton, tea, coffee, beef and grains for export; almost self-sufficient in food crops. Rich mineral resources include gold, nickel, copper, tin and coal. Manufacturing and service sectors amongst the most sophisticated in Africa.

Growth Sanctions were a forcing house for industry. Metal products and processing most important sub-sectors; others include vehicles, textiles and pharmaceuticals .

Problems Constraints on investment of foreign exchange shortages. Rising unemployment.

NAMIBIA

Namibia became independent in March 1990, bringing to an end 70 years of South African rule, the last 20 of which were in defiance of the UN. The South West Africa People's Organization (Swapo), which began the war for independence in 1966, convincingly won the 1989 independence elections on a platform of unity, reconciliation and gradual economic and social change.

Under the leadership of President Sam Nujoma, Swapo seemed determined to fulfil its election pledges once in power. Spending on health and education was increased, but economic policies emphasized the continuation of a mixed economy. This pragmatism ensured no immediate mass exodus of the whites who still control most of trade and industry.

Namibia is well endowed with resources, including diamonds, uranium and rich offshore fishing grounds. The mining industry contributes 90% of export earnings and 40% of GDP, and is largely controlled by multinational companies which enjoyed unusually generous tax incentives under South African rule. The government was expected to revise these to ensure a fairer division of revenue.

OFFICIAL NAME Republic of Namibia.
CAPITAL CITY Windhoek.
GEOGRAPHY Desert predominates: the Namib along the coast and the Kalahari in the east and south. Most settlement is on a central plateau and along the course of the Kunene and the Okavango rivers, which with the Orange are the only permanent watercourses. *Area* 824,168 sq km (318,213 sq miles).
PEOPLE *Population* 1.3m. *Density* 2 per sq km.
RELIGION Christian 96% (Lutheran 50%, RC 20%).
LANGUAGE English. Also local languages, German and Afrikaans.
CURRENCY South African rand.
PUBLIC HOLIDAYS Jan 1, Good Fri–Easter Mon, May 1, Ascension, Oct 1, Dec 10, 25–26.
GOVERNMENT Became an independent republic on March 21, 1990. Head of state is an executive president directly elected for a maximum of two 5-year terms. The legislative national assembly comprises 72 elected members and up to 6 non-voting presidential nominees.

SWAZILAND

Tradition still rules in this fertile, landlocked state sandwiched between South Africa and Mozambique. King Mswati III came to the throne prematurely in 1986, aged only 18. His coronation was intended to end the palace power struggles of the interregnum that followed the death in 1982 of his father, King Sobhuza II, who had reigned for over 60 years and overseen the country's independence in 1968. The young king, who seems to share the autocratic tendencies of his father, faces a difficult task in reconciling traditional social structures with the demands of an increasingly urban population.

Sugar, citrus and wood pulp underpin the modern export-oriented economy and the country has reserves of asbestos, coal and diamonds. Dependence on South Africa as a source of imports, capital and jobs is heavy. Growth since 1985 has been helped by the success of efforts to attract new private investment; most has been from South Africa-based firms.

OFFICIAL NAME Kingdom of Swaziland.
CAPITAL CITY Mbabane.
GEOGRAPHY Most of the country is savannah, with altitudes ranging from the highveld in the west to the lowlands of the east where irrigated, export agriculture is concentrated. *Area* 17,107 sq km (6,605 sq miles).
PEOPLE *Population* 726,000. *Density* 42 per sq km.
RELIGION Christian 77%, Animist.
LANGUAGE English and siSwati (Swazi).
CURRENCY Lilangeni.
PUBLIC HOLIDAYS Jan 1, Good Fri–Easter Mon, Apr 19, 25, Ascension, Jul 22, Umhlanga Reed Dance, Sep 6, Oct 24, Incwala Day, Dec 25–26.
GOVERNMENT Modified absolute monarchy. The king rules through a nominated prime minister and council of ministers. The bicameral parliament comprises a 50-member House of Assembly, and a 20-member Senate. Political parties are banned.

LESOTHO

Lesotho became formally independent in 1966. However, as one of the world's poorest countries with little cultivable land, it has in practice remained a client economy of South Africa. Most imports come from South Africa, which also employs about half the male labour force in its mines. Economic ties will become even closer during the 1990s with the completion of phase one of the $4 billion Highlands water scheme. Its rivers are one of Lesotho's few natural resources and the scheme aims at increasing jobs and revenue by selling water to South Africa.

Political power has been in the hands of a military government since 1986. It has pledged a return to civilian rule by 1992. Doubts were thrown over this timetable in 1990 when the military first forced King Moshoeshoe II into exile and then deposed him, replacing him with his son, Letsie III. King Moshoeshoe had been a critic of the military and sceptical of its democratic intentions.

OFFICIAL NAME Kingdom of Lesotho.
CAPITAL CITY Maseru.
GEOGRAPHY An enclave within South African territory, Lesotho is a high volcanic plateau, more than half of it above 2,000m, the source of the Orange and Tugela rivers. Most of the country is savannah, with forests in the deep-cut river valleys. *Area* 30,344 sq km (11,716 sq miles).
PEOPLE *Population* 1.7m. *Density* 56 per sq km.
RELIGION Christian 82% (RC 39%), Animist.
LANGUAGE English and Sesotho.
CURRENCY Loti.
PUBLIC HOLIDAYS Jan 1, 20, Mar 12, 21, Good Fri, Easter Mon, May 2, Ascension, Family Day, National Sports Day, Oct 4, Dec 25–26.
GOVERNMENT A hereditary monarchy. Executive and legislative powers are vested in the king, advised by a 5-member military council and a council of ministers.

SOUTH AFRICA

The arrival of the Boers, Dutch colonists, in 1652 marked the start of white settlement in South Africa. During the next two centuries their descendants established independent republics to escape the second wave of colonists, the British who were attracted by the rich mineral, especially gold, deposits which are the foundation of South Africa's wealth. Defeat in the Anglo-Boer war (1899–1902) stimulated a nationalism defined by opposition to British influence and the determination to entrench white supremacy over the black majority.

The Afrikaner National Party (NP) came to power in 1948. A republic was declared in 1961 and South Africa left the British Commonwealth. Apartheid policies were systematically implemented to deny blacks access to economic and political power. But black nationalist groups, of which the African National Congress (ANC) has always been the most powerful, persisted in opposing white domination. After it was banned in 1960 the ANC established external bases to maintain a campaign of international diplomacy and a largely symbolic armed struggle.

From the 1950s to 1970s South Africa proved a valuable Western ally in the cold war, notwithstanding limited sanctions imposed by the USA, Western Europe (excluding the UK) and the Commonwealth. Political isolation, however, did not deter the NP from its efforts to make the black majority "disappear" by creating "Bantustans", or tribal "homelands". Four were eventually granted "independence", but have never been internationally recognized. Sanctions also forced the country to become more self-sufficient. New energy sources were developed, including oil and gas from coal, and manufacturing grew into the largest economic sector. These factors helped fuel strong economic growth in the 1960s and early 1970s.

The failure of the homelands policy combined with violent disturbances, such as the 1976 Soweto uprising, to encourage the beginnings of a split between the *verligte* (enlightened) and *verkrampte* (hardline) wings of the NP. The economy was also important. Growth slowed after the mid-1970s and the economy moved into recession during the 1980s. In part this was due to slower growth in South Africa's main markets, but equally important was the impact of sanctions.

Under P. W. Botha, who became prime minister in 1978, the pass laws were repealed, some petty apartheid restrictions ended and African trade unions legalized. After much opposition a new constitution was introduced in 1984 providing for a tricameral parliament involving whites, coloureds and Indians

OFFICIAL NAME Republic of South Africa.
CAPITAL CITY Cape Town (legislative), Pretoria (administrative).
GEOGRAPHY Most of South Africa is a wide, rolling tableland, dropping down to a generally narrow coastal plain in a series of dramatic escarpments. Semi-desert in the west gives way to a high central basin covered in savannah and bisected by the Orange River, and to lush grasslands and forest in Natal in the east. A range of mountains lies along the southern coast. *Area* 1,222,161 sq km (471,880 sq miles).
PEOPLE *Population* 30.2m. *Density* 27 per sq km. *Ethnic groups* Bantu 68%, European 18%, coloured 11%, Asian 3%.
RELIGION Christian 59%, African churches 17%, Hindu 2%, Muslim 1%, Jewish 1%.
LANGUAGE Afrikaans. Also English, Zulu, Xhosa and other African languages.
EDUCATION There have been separate systems for whites, blacks, Indians and coloureds, but schools are gradually being desegregated. Education is compulsory for ages 7–15 for whites, 7–11 for blacks and varies from state to state for others. The races mix at university level; the 10 white and 9 black universities were desegregated in 1985.
CURRENCY Rand.
PUBLIC HOLIDAYS Jan 1, Apr 6, 13, 16, May 7, 24, 31, Oct 10, Dec 16, 25–26.
GOVERNMENT Republic. Direct adult suffrage is limited to white, coloured (mixed race) and Asian voters; the black majority are disenfranchised. There are 3 separate assemblies, each passing legislation relating to its own racial group. The white House of Assembly has 178 members, the coloured House of Representatives 85, and the Asian House of Delegates 45. There is no black chamber. Legislation from all chambers has to be passed by the state president who is also head of state and chief executive. The president is elected for the duration of parliament (usually 5 years) by a college of 88 delegates from the 3 chambers of parliament.

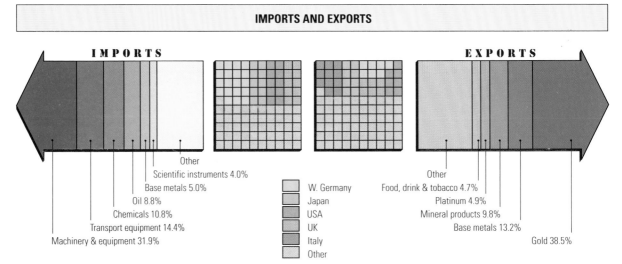

IMPORTS AND EXPORTS

IMPORTS

Other
Scientific instruments 4.0%
Base metals 5.0%
Oil 8.8%
Chemicals 10.8%
Transport equipment 14.4%
Machinery & equipment 31.9%

EXPORTS

Other
Food, drink & tobacco 4.7%
Platinum 4.9%
Mineral products 9.8%
Base metals 13.2%
Gold 38.5%

W. Germany
Japan
USA
UK
Italy
Other

Source: EIU *Country Report* (Imports/Exports 1988 figures; Trading partners 1989 figures).

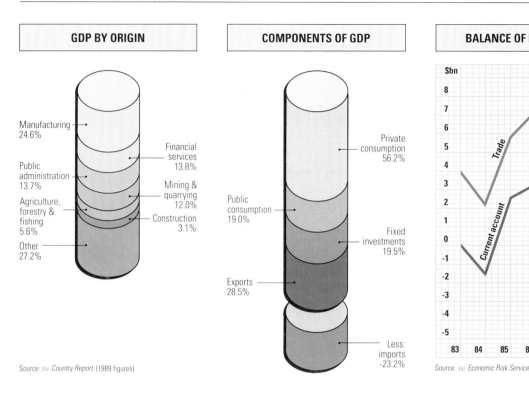

GDP BY ORIGIN

Manufacturing 24.6%

Financial services 13.8%

Public administration 13.7%

Mining & quarrying 12.0%

Agriculture, forestry & fishing 5.6%

Construction 3.1%

Other 27.2%

Source: EIU *Country Report* (1989 figures).

COMPONENTS OF GDP

Private consumption 56.2%

Public consumption 19.0%

Fixed investments 19.5%

Exports 28.5%

Less: imports -23.2%

BALANCE OF PAYMENTS

$bn

Trade

Current account

83 84 85 86 87 88 89

Source: EIU *Economic Risk Service*.

and an executive president instead of prime minister. But the exclusion of Africans combined with the impact of economic recession to revive militant black opposition. The imposition of a state of emergency in 1985 and new sanctions exacerbated the economy's problems and led to a heavy flight of capital. The government, however, remained secure despite losing votes to the right-wing Conservative Party (CP) in the 1987 and 1989 general elections.

The political stalemate was broken after President Botha resigned in February 1989 and handed over to F. W. de Klerk. Convinced of the need for real political reform President de Klerk unbanned the ANC and allied organizations in February 1990 and released Nelson Mandela, the veteran ANC leader, in jail since 1963. The government also committed itself to negotiating a new constitution and to scrapping all remaining apartheid legislation, including the Group Areas and Population Registration Acts, the two pillars of apartheid.

During 1990, President de Klerk and Mr Mandela discussed the removal of obstacles to a constitutional convention, but progress was slow. Further problems were created when traditional rivalries between members of Chief Manga Sotho Buthelezi's conservative Inkatha movement and ANC supporters erupted into unprecedented violence, leaving thousands dead. In January 1991 Mr Mandela and Chief Buthelezi signed a peace accord, but their fragile hold over their youthful supporters became clear as the violence continued.

Evidence of progress, however, was sufficient to persuade the EC to lift its voluntary ban on investment. International sanctions were expected to erode further after the repeal of the main apartheid laws, promised by de Klerk before the end of 1991. Such a move would be welcome news for the economy. Despite moves towards greater liberalization there were few signs of an end to recession at the start of the new decade. Renewed large-scale foreign investment is vital for sustained growth . But there is little prospect of this until a stable new political order is established. In 1991 President de Klerk and Mr Mandela appeared to be moving close to achieving the conditions for a multi-party conference on the constitution for the "new South Africa".

ECONOMIC PROFILE

Wealth founded on gold and diamonds; also an exporter of agricultural products, particularly fruit and vegetables, and a wide range of strategic minerals unavailable elsewhere. Manufacturing developed to substitute for imports, dominated by iron and steel, engineering, vehicles and chemicals. Coal is major energy source. When international sanctions are lifted, the tourist industry could make an increasing contribution.

Growth Arms exports are thriving. Recent small-scale discoveries of oil and natural gas. The country could provide a focus for regional economic growth once regional conflicts are resolved.

Problems Fluctuations of gold price lead to wild swings in export earnings. Sanctions cutting off export markets and political instability hitting business confidence. Disinvestment has made the country a net capital exporter. Unemployment among blacks a major economic, social and political problem; annual GDP growth of 5% is needed just to stop the jobless total rising.

GLOSSARY

ACP (African, Caribbean and Pacific) The 66 ACP members, almost all ex-colonies of EC members, receive a large proportion of the Community's overseas aid budget and under the Lomé Convention are allowed free entry to the Western European market for 99% of their exports.

Aladi Asociación Latinoamericana de Integración, the 11-member Latin American trade integration organization, based in Montevideo (*see* pages 101, 144).

AMU (Arab Maghreb Union) The agreement set up in 1989 between Algeria, Libya, Mauritania, Morocco and Tunisia, working towards a common market and united diplomatic stance (*see* page 272).

Andean Pact The 5-member group of South American states, based in Lima, which aims to establish a free-trade area (*see* page 101).

Arab League The organization set up in 1945 to strengthen cooperation among independent Arab states; based in Tunis (*see* page 256).

Arctic climate No warm season; warmest month below 10°C (50°F).

Asean Association of South East Asian Nations, founded in 1967, based in Jakarta (*see* pages 101, 227).

Balance of payments The record of a country's transactions with the rest of the world during a given period. The current account of the balance of payments consists of:
• "visible" trade: merchandise (*see* trade balance)
• "invisible" trade: receipts and payments for services such as banking, tourism, shipping and insurance, plus dividend and interest payments
• private transfers, such as remittances from workers abroad
• official transfers, such as payments to international organizations.
The capital account consists of:
• short- and long-term transactions relating to a country's external assets and liabilities.
Adding the current account balance and the net investment balance gives the "basic" balance of payments. As the overall balance of payments must be in equilibrium, any surplus or deficit in the basic balance is accounted for by changes in foreign exchange reserves, borrowing from or lending to international institutions and public-sector foreign-currency borrowing. All countries also record errors and omissions (or a balancing item) which in some cases can be very large (*see* page 86).

Benelux Benelux Economic Union (Belgium, Luxembourg and the Netherlands).

Bleu Belgium and Luxembourg Economic Union.

Capital goods Assets which are capable of generating income and which have themselves been produced; machines, plant and buildings.

Caricom The 13-member Caribbean Community and Common Market, based in Georgetown, Guyana (*see* pages 101, 137).

Cash crop A crop grown for sale, generally for export rather than for domestic consumption.

CFA (Communauté Financière Africaine/ African Financial Community) Its members, most of the francophone African nations, share a common currency, the CFA franc, which is maintained at a fixed rate of FFr1 = 50 CFA francs by the French treasury (*see* Franc Zone, pages 101, 278).

CFP (Communauté Française du Pacifique/ French Pacific Community) Analogous to the CFA.

CIF (Cost, insurance, freight) Trade statistics usually record imports on a CIF basis, thus including the cost of shipping goods to the country. To determine the visible trade balance for balance of payments purposes the figures must be adjusted to a free-on-board (FOB) basis; the difference between CIF and FOB figures is included in the balance of payments as invisibles.

CMEA See Comecon.

Comecon The Council for Mutual Economic Assistance (*see* page 100).

Commonwealth The association of independent states comprising the UK and most of its former dependencies (*see* page 100).

Competitiveness The index of a country's labour costs relative to those of its trading partners.

Components of GDP Domestic production by type of expenditure.

Constant prices Used to adjust nominal values to constant or real values by removing the effects of inflation.

Continental climate Hot summers, cold winters: typical of the interior of a continent. Coldest month below 0°C (32°F); warmest month above 10°C (50°F).

Convertible currency A currency that can be freely exchanged for another or for gold.

Countertrade The generic term for trade involving the exchange of goods for goods rather than for money. The various forms of countertrade include barter, a straight exchange of goods for goods; counter-purchase, where a country selling goods to another promises to spend its receipts from the sale on purchases from that other country within a given period; and buy-back, where a company builds a factory in another country and agrees to be paid in output from the factory.

DAC Development Assistance Committee, the OECD committee responsible for promoting aid to developing countries (*see* page 104).

Debt rescheduling An agreement between a country and its creditors to spread out debt repayments over a longer period than originally scheduled. Interest rates should continue to flow, although repayment of capital is delayed; the lender is often payed an extra fee for agreeing to the rescheduling. Rescheduling of official debt is negotiated through the Paris Club, that of commercial bank debt through the London Club.

Debt-service ratio A country's interest and capital repayments on foreign debt as a percentage of export earnings in a given period. Used to gauge a country's ability to continue servicing the debt: the higher the debt-service ratio, the more burdensome the payments.

Dependency A foreign territory governed by another country.

EBRD European Bank for Reconstruction and Development set up to aid East European recovery.

EC European Community (*see* pages 100, 158).

Ecowas Economic Community of West African States (*see* pages 101, 278).

ECSC European Coal and Steel Community (*see* page 158).

ECU European Currency Unit, made up of defined percentages of each EC member's national currency.

EEA European Economic Area, aiming to ease trade barriers between the EC and other European countries; due to come into effect from 1993.

Efta European Free Trade Association (*see* pages 100, 176).

EMS European Monetary System, created in 1979 to aid the management of exchange rates between currencies of the European Community.

Entrepôt An international trading centre for import and re-export of goods, usually a port.

ERM Exchange Rate Mechanism. Each EC member's currency has an agreed "central rate". The ERM parity grid is a network of exchange rate boundaries which cannot be overstepped.

Euratom European Atomic Energy Community (*see* page 158).

Factor cost The cost of producing an item, including materials and labour, as distinct from its market price.

FAO Food and Agriculture Organization (*see* UN).

Fiscal policy The budgetary stance of central government: the manipulation of taxation and expenditure to control demand for goods and services and the level of economic activity.

FOB (Free on board) Exports are normally valued FOB in trade statistics to exclude the transport costs paid by the importing country (*see* CIF).

Franc Zone The currency zone including former French colonies in Africa and French dependencies in the Pacific which use the CFA (*see* CFA) and CFP (*see* CFP) francs (*see* pages 101, 278, 288).

French overseas departments An integral part of the French Republic with an administrative structure similar to that of the *départements* within France.

French overseas territory A subdivision of the French Republic, with elected representation to the French parliament.

Gatt General Agreement on Tariffs and Trade, instituted in 1947 to liberalize trade and prevent discrimination. More than 100 countries are signatories. The Uruguay talks were re-opened in 1991 after disagreements concerning agricultural subsidies in late 1990 threatened Gatt's future. (*See* page 86.)

GCC Gulf Co-operation Council, the 6-member economic and security organization of Arab Gulf states (*see* page 100).

GDP (gross domestic product) The best measure of a country's level of economic activity, GDP is the total value of a country's annual output of goods and services, discounted for depreciation. It is normally valued at market prices; GDP can, however, be valued at factor cost, by subtracting indirect taxes and adding subsidies. To eliminate the effects of inflation, GDP growth is usually expressed in constant prices.

GDP by origin Domestic production broken down into type of activity. The categories vary but the usual ones are mining, agriculture, manufacturing and government and private services.

Gécamines The giant Zaire mining company owned by the state (see page 292).

Glasnost *See* page 209.

GMP (Gross Material Product) Equal to NMP plus capital consumption.

GMT (Greenwich Mean Time) Time based on the meridian at Greenwich in the UK. International standard.

GNP (gross national product) Equal to GDP plus residents' income from investments abroad minus income accruing to non-residents from investments in the country.

IBRD (International Bank for Reconstruction and Development, generally known as the World Bank) Set up to aid reconstruction in post-war Europe, the IBRD is now mostly concerned with lending to developing countries to finance development projects that cannot obtain finance on commercial capital markets. It is the largest single source of development aid and its lending in recent years has increasingly focused on economic policy reforms, as well as individual development projects, bringing it closer to the role of the IMF (*see* IMF). The IBRD itself borrows and lends on commercial terms, lending largely to higher-income developing countries. Its soft-loan agency, the International Development Association, is financed by contributions from rich countries. It lends to the poorest countries on very concessional terms. The International Finance Corporation aims to promote the private sector in developing countries; it lends and takes equity stakes and encourages participation in companies by other development banks and commercial companies (*see* page 91).

IDA International Development Association (*see* IBRD).

ILO International Labour Organization.

IMF (International Monetary Fund) The policeman of the international financial system, the IMF provides short-term balance of payments support to its members. Its assistance is conditional on a country carrying out an agreed programme of economic reforms; other lenders generally make the presence of an IMF programme a condition for aid or debt rescheduling.

Members pay subscriptions, or quotas, to the IMF and can borrow up to a certain multiple of their quota (for membership *see* page 91). In 1970, the IMF introduced the Special Drawing Right as a reserve currency (*see* SDR).

Inflation/deflation Inflation is the rate at which prices increase. An economy is said to have inflationary tendencies if there is pressure on prices to rise, and deflationary if they are falling. Explanations of the causes of inflation vary, but they usually relate to excess demand, high costs or money supply increases.

kwh kilowatts per hour.

Liquidity Either the speed with which financial assets can be turned into cash, or the volume of turnover in a financial market.

London Club An informal grouping of commercial banks responsible for negotiating rescheduling of debt with creditor countries.

m million.

Mediterranean climate Hot summers, warm winters, affected by trade winds in summer, westerlies in winter. It occurs on the west side of large land masses between latitudes 30-60°.

Monetary policy Government control of the quantity of money in the economy. Connected to interest and exchange rate policies. The economic doctrine of monetarism maintains a direct link between excessive money growth and rising inflation and holds that the money supply can have no more than a temporary effect on real output (*see* Supply-side policies).

Nato (North Atlantic Treaty Organization) The alliance for the defence of the West against the Soviet Union. Formed in 1949, it includes the USA and Canada and most Western European nations. France withdrew in 1966 from the military command of the alliance and East Germany joined when it became unified with West Germany in 1990 (*see* page 101).

NDP (net domestic product) Differing from gross domestic product in that it discounts for depreciation.

NMP (net material product) A measure of economic performance often used by communist countries. Gross material product differs from gross domestic product by excluding the value of services; NMP also discounts for depreciation.

Oapec Organization of Arab Petroleum Exporting Countries, set up in 1968 and based in Kuwait (*see* page 100).

OAU Organization of African Unity, set up in 1963 to promote unity and solidarity among African states; based in Addis Ababa (*see* page 100).

Observer status The right to observation at an organization's meetings but not of direct participation.

OECD Organization for Economic Co-operation and Development, the "rich countries' club", established in 1961 to promote economic growth in its 24 member countries and the expansion of world trade; based in Paris (*see* page 100).

OIAG (Österreichische Industrieholding Aktiengesellshaft), the Austrian holding company for nationalized industries established in 1970.

Opec (Organization of Petroleum Exporting Countries), set up in 1960 and based in Vienna (*see* pages 100, 256).

Organization of River Plate Basin Countries Based in Brasília, it coordinates multinational development projects in the zone (*see* page 101).

Pamscad The IBRD's Programme of Action to Mitigate the Social Costs of Adjustment (*see* Structural adjustment).

Paris Club An informal grouping of Western government officials responsible for negotiation with countries in difficulties with debt repayments. The club is run by the French treasury (*see* Debt rescheduling).

Perestroika *See* page 209.

PR Proportional representation, an electoral system designed to allocate seats roughly in proportion to the votes. Several different systems exist. Germany's 5% vote threshold eliminates the smallest parties. Ireland's single transferable vote (STV) system allows voters to rank their preferences but gives only a rough approximation to proportionality.

Price-earnings ratio The current market price of a company's shares expressed as a multiple of total earnings per share over the previous accounting year. It provides an indication of whether a company's share price is too high or too low compared with those of its competitors.

Privatization The sale of state assets, particularly state-owned industries, to the private sector.

Producer price inflation The rate of growth of the index of producer prices, the price of goods "at the factory gate".

Productivity The ratios of proportionate changes in inputs of resources to changes in the outputs of goods and services. Labour productivity is measured by an index of man-hours divided into an index of output.

PTA Preferential Trade Area for Eastern and Southern Africa (*see* pages 101, 300).

Real terms Figures expressed in real terms have been adjusted to allow for inflation.

SADCC Southern African Development Co-ordination Conference (*see* pages 101, 300).

SDR (Special Drawing Right) The reserve currency introduced by the IMF in 1970, intended to replace gold and national currencies in settling international transactions. The IMF uses SDRS for book-keeping purposes and issues them to member countries. Their value is based on a basket of the five most widely traded currencies: the US dollar, Deutschmark, pound sterling, Japanese yen and French franc. SDRS are increasingly being used for lending by commercial banks and for accounting purposes by some multinational companies.

Soft loan Money lent on concessionary terms, generally at lower interest rates or with longer maturities than could be obtained in the commercial lending market.

Structural adjustment Shorthand for the package of economic reforms being implemented by many developing countries, particularly in Africa, at the urging of organizations such as the IMF and IBRD and Western donor governments. Policies adopted include trade and investment liberalization, currency devaluation, privatization of state-owned companies, removal of consumer price subsidies, increased agricultural producer prices to stimulate food and export production and tighter fiscal policy. The political cost of adjustment programmes has proved too high for some governments despite help from the Pamscad programme (*see* Pamscad).

Sub-tropical climate Warmest month above 22°C (72°F); coolest month between 0°C (32°F) and 18°C (65°F).

Supply-side policies Measures to promote the efficiency of production by improving the responsiveness of labour, goods and capital markets. Founded on a belief that the stimulation of demand can have no long-term effect on the real economy, only on prices.

TCE tonne of coal equivalent.

Temperate climate Mild winters, warm summers, rainfall throughout the year. Coolest month above 0°C (32°F) but below 18°C (65°F); warmest month above 10°C (50°F) but below 22°C (72°F).

Terms of trade The ratio between import and export prices, measuring the purchasing power of a country's exports in terms of the imports in needs. Terms of trade is expressed as an index to show changes over a period of time. When the index rises, terms of trade improve.

Territory A state under the control of another.

Trade balance The record of a country's exports and imports of merchandise. Sometimes referred to as the visible balance and sometimes used more loosely as a synonym for the current account balance (*see* Balance of payments).

Tropical climate Very hot and generally humid. No winter: coolest month above 18°C.

UN United Nations, set up in 1945, after the collapse of the League of Nations, to encourage world peace and security. It incorporates a number of specialized agencies; *see* Unctad, Unesco, WHO, Gatt, FAO and IMF.

Unctad United Nations Conference on Trade and Development.

Unesco United Nations Educational, Scientific and Cultural Organization.

Value added The value of output minus the cost of raw materials and other inputs. Used to quantify the contribution of an industry to GDP.

Warsaw Pact The security agreement which existed between Eastern European states and the Soviet Union (*see* pages 101, 202).

WHO World Health Organization (*see* UN).

World Bank *See* IBRD.

Every care has been taken in the compilation of this book, which went to press in May 1991, but no responsibility can be accepted for the accuracy of the data presented.

Figures may not add up to totals and percentage breakdowns to 100% because of rounding. Statistical definitions and quality will vary from country to country, thus affecting comparability. On maps, where a city falls outside population categories included in the key, a black town-stamp is used.

Recognition of a state by the UN is taken to be authoritative. Thus East Timor is given a separate entry although it has been occupied for several years, whereas the South African "homelands" are not. Germany and Yemen are now shown as united countries, although their statistics, based on previous years, reflect the situation prior to unification.

Capital city The place named is generally the administrative centre which can differ from the legislative or judicial centre.

Climate The *Glossary* gives a definition of climate types. Temperatures, unless otherwise indicated, refer to the monthly average.

Education Official schooling requirements are given.

Geography The area is rounded to the nearest square kilometre and nearest ten square miles. It includes water recognized as part of the territory.

Government Suffrage should be assumed to be universal unless otherwise specified.

Imports and exports The ultimate source or destination can differ from the country indicated; sources of imports are usually the last country of shipment, which may not be the country of production.

Language Official and widespread languages are given first, then minority and unofficial languages.

Official name The English translation of the official name is given since, in all but a few cases, this is the name used in international forums such as the UN.

Population Country populations are based on the most recent census and exclude expatriates. Non-nationals are included in some censuses and not in others. Census ethnic categories are used and style may vary; comparisons between countries may not always be valid. In general Mestizo refers to mixed

European/American Indian, and Mulatto refers to mixed European/African. Percentages in each ethnic group are to the nearest 1%. Population density is averaged over the whole area.

Public holidays Public holidays are given in sequence according to the Gregorian calendar. If the holiday is not on a fixed date it is named. Muslim holidays are determined by a lunar calendar and so change position in relation to the Gregorian calendar, occurring 10 or 11 days earlier each year.

Religion Religious breakdowns in censuses vary in degree of detail and the titles of categories. Animism is a general term for nontheistic and tribal religions; since it is often coexistent with other religious beliefs, the proportion of animists in a population is not quantified. Atheists are omitted.

Editorial Sources

The Banker
British Geological Survey:
  World Mineral Statistics
British Petroleum:
  Statistical Review of World Energy
Carbon Dioxide Information Analysis
  Centre
Central Intelligence Agency
Chambers World Gazetteer
Commerzbank
Deutsche Bank
The Economist
The Economist Books:
  Vital World Statistics
  Pocket World in Figures
The Economist Intelligence Unit (EIU):
  Consumer Spending Patterns in the EC
  Country Risk Service
  Country Profiles
  Country Reports
  East European Risk Service
The Economist Publications
  Limited(EPL):
    *One Hundred Years of Economic
    Statistics*
Euromonitor:
  *European Marketing Data
  and Statistics*
Europa Year Book
European Community:
  *The Community Budget: The Facts
  and Figures*
Executive Office of the President:
  *Budget of the United States
  Government*

Food and Agriculture Organization:
  Production Yearbook
Freedom House:
  Survey of Freedom
International Institute for Strategic
  Studies:
    The Military Balance
International Labour Organization:
  Yearbook of Labour Statistics
International Monetary Fund:
  German Unification
  Direction of Trade Statistics
  International Financial Statistics
International Finance Corporation:
  Emerging Stock Markets Factbook
Larrouse:
  Atlas Geostrategique
Lloyd's Shipping Register
Nasa Goddard Institute for
  Space Studies
Nuexco Annual Review
Organization of Economic Cooperation
  and Development:
    Development Cooperation
    Economic Outlook
    Economic Survey
    Main Economic Indicators
    National Accounts
Smithsonian Institute:
  *Tropical Rainforests:
  A Disappearing Treasure*
Statistical Abstract of the United States
United Nations:
  Demographic Yearbook
  Energy Statistics Yearbook
  Human Development Report
  Industrial Statistics Yearbook
  *International Trade Statistics
  Yearbook*
  Map of Desertification
  Monthly Bulletin of Statistics
  National Accounts Statistics
  Statistical Yearbook
  World Population Prospects
Unesco:
  UN Statistical Yearbook
World Bank:
  World Debt Tables
  World Tables
World Bureau of Metal Statistics
World Health Organization:
  World Health Statistics Annual
World Meteorological Organization:
  *Long-Range Transport of Sulphur in
  the Atmosphere and Acid Rain*
World Resources Institute:
  World Resources Report

GENERAL INDEX

MAP INDEX

A

Harrat Nawāşif **69** G 4
Harricana **17** M 5
Harrington Harbour **17** Q 5
Harris **32** B 3
Harrisburg **19** L 3
Harrismith **76** D 5
Harrison **19** H 4
Harrison Bay **14** G 1
Harrisonburg **19** L 4
Harrisville **19** K 3
Harrogate **32** C 4
Harry S. Truman Reservoir **19** H 4
Harsprånget **34** GH 2
Harstad **34** G 2
Harsvik **34** E 3
Hartford **19** M 3
Hartlepool **32** C 4
Hartola **34** J 3
Harts Range **62** E 3
Hartwell Lake **19** K 5
Harūt **69** J 5
Harvey (N.D., U.S.A.) **18** G 2
Harvey (Western Australia) **62** B 5
Harwich **32** D 4
Haryana **54** C 2
Hasalbag **51** K 3
Hasan Langī **50** F 5
Hasançelebi **39** E 3
Hasār **50** F 3
Hassan **54** C 5
Hasse **33** E 4
Hassela **34** G 3
Hässleholm **35** F 4
Hastings (MN, U.S.A.) **19** H 3
Hastings (NE, U.S.A.) **18** G 3
Hastings (New Zealand) **65** R 8
Hastings (U.K.) **32** D 4
Hasvik **34** H 1
Hat Hin **55** H 3
Hat Yai **55** H 6
Hatanbulag **52** E 2
Haţeg **38** B 1
Hathras **54** C 2
Hatisar **55** F 2
Hatta **54** C 3
Hattah **63** G 5
Hattfjelldal **34** F 2
Hattiesburg **19** J 5
Haud **75** GH 3
Hauge **35** E 4
Haugesund **35** DE 4
Haugsdorf **37** G 2
Haukeligrend **35** E 4
Haukipudas **34** HJ 2
Haukivesi **34** J 3
Haukivuori **34** J 3
Hauraki Gulf **65** R 8
Haut-Zaïre **74** CD 4
Havana **19** K 7
Havana **21** F 3
Haverhill (MA, U.S.A.) **19** M 3
Havern **34** G 3
Havířov **33** G 5
Havlíčkův Brod **33** G 5
Havøysund **34** H 1
Havran **38** C 3
Havre **18** E 2
Havre-Saint-Pierre **17** P 5
Havsa **38** C 2
Havza **39** E 2
Hawaii **61** E 1
Hawaiian Islands **61** E 1
Hawera **65** Q 8
Hawi **61** E 1
Hawick **32** C 3
Hawke Bay **65** R 8
Hawke Harbour **17** Q 5
Hawker **63** F 5
Hawkers Gate **63** G 4
Hawkwood **63** J 4
Hawng Luk **55** G 3
Hawr al Ḩabbānīyah **69** G 2
Hawr al Ḩammār **69** H 2
Hawr as Sa'dīyah **69** H 2
Hawrā' **69** H 5
Hawthorne **18** C 4
Hay **15** O 4
Hay (N.S.W., Austr.) **63** G 5
Hay River (N.W.T., Can.) **15** O 3
Hayes **15** T 4
Hayjān **69** G 5
Hayl **69** K 4
Haymana **39** D 3
Hayraboly **38** C 2
Hayrān **69** G 5
Hays **18** G 4
Hayward **18** B 4
Hazar Gölü **39** E 3
Hazarajat **51** H 4
Hazard **19** K 4

Hazaribagh **54** E 3
Hazebrouck **36** D 1
Hazelton **15** M 4
Hazlehurst **19** K 5
Hazleton **19** L 3
Hazlett, Lake **62** D 3
Hazro **39** F 3
He Xian **52** F 6
Head of Bight **62** E 5
Heales-ville **63** H 6
Hearne **19** G 5
Hearst **16** L 6
Hebei **53** G 3
Hebel **63** H 4
Hebian **52** F 3
Hebrides, Inner **32** B 3
Hebrides, Outer **32** B 3
Hebron (Newfoundl., Can.) **17** P 4
Heby **35** G 4
Hecate Strait **14** L 5
Hechi **52** E 6
Hechuan **52** E 4
Hede **34** F 3
Hedemora **35** G 3
Hedmark **34** F 3
Heerenveen **32** E 4
Hefa **68** E 2
Hefei **53** G 4
Hegang **49** NO 6
Heide (F.R.G.) **33** E 4
Heidelberg **33** E 5
Heidenheim **33** F 5
Heilbronn **33** E 5
Heiligenblut **37** F 2
Heiligenstadt **33** F 4
Heilong Jiang **49** O 6
Heilongjiang **53** JK 1
Heimaey **34** A 3
Heimahe **52** C 3
Heimdal **34** EF 3
Heinola **34** J 3
Hemkut **55** FG 2
Heishan **53** H 2
Heishui **52** D 4
Hejian **53** G 3
Hejiang **52** E 5
Hejing **51** M 2
Heka **52** C 3
Hekimhan **39** E 3
Helan **52** E 3
Helena (AR, U.S.A.) **19** H 5
Helena (MT, U.S.A.) **18** D 2
Helensville **65** Q 8
Helgeland **34** F 2
Helgoländer Bucht **33** E 4
Hella **34** A 3
Hellas **38** B 3
Helmsdale **32** C 3
Helmstedt **33** F 4
Helong **53** J 2
Helsingborg **35** F 4
Helsingfors **35** J 3
Helsingör **35** F 4
Helsinki **35** J 3
Helwan → Ḩulwān **68** E 3
Hemnesberget **34** F 2
Hemse **35** G 4
Henan **52** D 4
Henan **52** F 4
Henares **36** C 3
Henbury **62** E 3
Hendek **38** D 2
Henderson **18** C 4
Henderson (N.C., U.S.A.) **19** L 4
Henderson (TX, U.S.A.) **19** H 5
Hendersonville (N.C., U.S.A.) **19** K 4
Hendersonville (TN, U.S.A.) **19** J 4
Hendrik Verwoerd Dam **76** D 6
Heng Xian **52** E 6
Henganon **64** E 3
Hengduan Shan **52** C 5
Hengshan **52** E 3
Hengshan **52** F 5
Hengshui **52** G 3
Hengyang **52** F 5
Henik Lakes **15** S 3
Hennan **34** G 3
Henryetta **19** G 4
Henzada **55** G 4
Hepu **52** E 6
Hequ **52** F 3
Heraklia **68** F 1
Herat **51** G 4
Hérault **36** D 3
Herbert **15** Q 5
Hercegnovi **38** A 2
Hercegovina **37** G 3
Heredia **20** F 5
Hereford (TX, U.S.A.) **18** F 5

Hereford (U.K.) **32** C 4
Herford **33** E 4
Hermanas **20** B 2
Hermidale **63** H 5
Hermiston **18** C 2
Hermosillo **18** D 6
Hernandarias **28** EF 4
Hernani **36** C 3
Herning **35** E 4
Heroica Alvarado **20** C 4
Heroica Tlapacoyan **20** C 4
Herrera **28** D 4
Herrera de Pisuerga **36** C 3
Herrljunga **35** F 4
Hervey Bay **63** J 3-4
Heshun **52** F 3
Hess **14** L 3
Hessen **33** E 4
Hexigten Qi **53** G 2
Heyuan **52** F 6
Heywood (Victoria, Austr.) **63** G 6
Heze **52** G 3
Hezheng **52** D 3
Hialeah **19** K 6
Hibbing **19** H 2
Hidalgo **20** C 3
Hidalgo del Parral **18** E 6
Hidrolândia **27** G 4
Higginsville **62** C 5
High Level **15** O 4
High Point **19** L 4
High Prairie **15** O 4
High River **15** P 5
Highrock Lake (Man., Can.) **15** RS 4
Highrock Lake (Sask., Can.) **15** Q 4
Higuerote **24** E 1
Higüey **21** J 4
Hiitola **34** J 3
Hiiumaa **35** H 4
Hijar **36** C 3
Ḩila **57** G 5
Hildesheim **33** EF 4
Hill Bank **20** E 4
Hill Grove **63** H 2
Hill Island Lake **15** Q 3
Hillcrest Center **18** C 4
Hilleröd **35** F 4
Hillsboro (IL, U.S.A.) **19** HJ 4
Hillsboro (TX, U.S.A.) **19** G 5
Hillston **63** H 5
Hillswick **32** C 2
Ḩilo **61** E 1
Hilvan **39** E 3
Hilversum **32** DE 4
Ḩimā **69** G 5
Himara **38** A 2
Himatnagar **54** B 3
Himi **53** L 3
Himmetdede **39** E 3
Ḩimş **68** F 2
Hin Heup **55** H 4
Hindarun **54** C 2
Hindmarsh, Lake **63** G 6
Hindu Kush **51** HJ 3
Hindubagh **51** H 4
Hindupur **54** C 5
Hindustan **42** FG 4
Hinganghat **54** C 3
Hingoli **54** C 4
Ḩinīs **39** F 3
Hinnøya **34** G 2
Hinobaan **57** F 2
Hinton **15** O 5
Hirado **53** J 4
Hirakud Reservoir **54** D 3
Hirara **53** J 6
Hirfanlı Barajı **39** D 3
Hiriyur **54** C 5
Hirosaki **53** LM 2
Hiroshima **53** K 4
Hirson **36** D 2
Hirtshals **35** E 4
Hirvensalmi **34** J 3
Ḩismā **68** F 3
Ḩişn al 'Abr **69** H 5
Hispaniola **21** H 4
Hissar **54** C 2
Ḩīt **69** G 2
Hita **53** K 4
Hitachi **53** M 3
Hite **18** D 4
Hitra **34** E 3
Hjälmaren **35** G 4
Hjerkinn **34** E 3
Hjo **35** F 4
Hjørring **35** E 4
Ho Chi Minh **55** J 5
Hoa Binh **55** HJ 3
Hoai Nhon **55** J 5

Hoare Bay **17** P 2
Hobart (OK, U.S.A.) **18** G 4
Hobart (Tasmania, Austr.) **64** L 9
Hobbs **18** F 5
Hobo **24** C 3
Hoboksar **51** M 1
Hobro **35** EF 4
Hodal **54** C 2
Hodeida **69** G 6
Hodgson Downs **62** E 2
Hodh **70** D 5
Hódmezővásárhely **38** B 1
Hodna, Chott el **71** F 1
Hodonin **33** G 5
Hof **33** F 4
Höfdakaupstadur **34** AB 2
Höfn **34** B 3
Hofors **35** G 3
Hofsá **34** B 2
Höfu **53** K 4
Höganäs **35** F 4
Hoggar **71** F 4
Hoggar → Ahaggar **71** G 4
Hoh Sai Hu **52** B 3
Hoh Xil Hu **52** B 3
Hohhot **52** F 2
Hoi An **55** J 4
Hoi Xuan **55** J 3
Hokitika **65** Q 9
Hokkaidō **53** M 2
Hokksund **35** E 4
Hokmābād **50** F 3
Hol **35** E 3
Holanda **26** C 3
Holbæk **35** F 4
Holbrook **18** D 5
Holdenville **19** G 4
Holdrege **18** G 3
Hole Narcipur **54** C 5
Holguín **21** G 3
Holitna **14** F 3
Höljes **35** F 3
Hollabrunn **37** G 2
Holland **19** J 3
Holly Springs **19** HJ 5
Hollywood (FL, U.S.A.) **19** L 6
Holman Island **15** O 1
Hólmavík **34** A 2
Holmestrand **35** EF 4
Holmsjön **34** FG 3
Holmsund **34** H 3
Holstebro **35** E 4
Holsteinburg **17** R 2
Holy Cross **14** E 3
Holyhead **32** C 4
Holyoke (CO, U.S.A.) **18** F 3
Holyoke (MA, U.S.A.) **19** M 3
Homalin **55** G 3
Hombre Muerto, Salar de **28** C 4
Home Bay **17** O 2
Home Hill **63** H 2
Homer **14** G 4
Homestead (FL, U.S.A.) **19** K 6
Homestead (Queensland, Austr.) **63** H 3
Homewood **19** J 5
Hommelstö **34** F 2
Homnabad **54** C 4
Homoljske Planina **38** B 2
Homosassa **19** K 6
Homs **68** F 2
Hon Chong **55** H 5
Hon Gai **55** J 3
Honavar **54** B 5
Honda **24** C 3
Honduras **20** E 5
Hönefoss **35** F 3
Honey Lake **18** B 3
Hong Kong **52** FG 6
Honghe **52** D 6
Hongliuhe **52** B 2
Hongliuyuan **52** BC 3
Hongor **52** F 1
Hongqizhen **52** E 7
Hongsa **55** H 4
Honguedo, Détroit d' **17** P 6
Hongyuan **52** D 4
Hongze **53** G 4
Hongze Hu **53** G 4
Honiara **65** G 3
Honkajoki **34** H 3
Honnali **54** C 5
Honningsvåg **34** J 1
Honolulu **61** E 1
Honrubia **36** C 4
Honshū **53** KL 3
Hood River **18** B 2
Hoogeveen **32** E 4
Hooghly **54** E 3
Hooker Creek **62** E 2
Hoonah **14** K 4

K

L

O

S

Samch'ŏnp'o 53 J 4
Same (Indonesia) 57 G 5
Sámi 38 B 3
Samirah 69 G 3
Samka 55 G 3
Samo Alto 28 B 5
Samoa Islands 60 D 3
Sambor 37 G 2
Samokov 38 B 2
Sámos 38 C 3
Samothráki 38 C 2
Samothráki 38 C 2
Sampaga 57 E 4
Sampit 56 D 4
Sampit, Teluk 56 D 4
Sampun 65 F 3
Samrong 55 H 5
Samsang 54 D 1
Samsun 39 E 2
Samthar 54 C 2
Samtredia 39 F 2
Samus' 47 QR 4
Samut Prakan 55 H 5
Samut Songkhram 55 H 5
San' ä' 69 G 5
San Agustín de Valle Fértil 28 C 5
San Andrés 21 F 5
San Andrés del Rabanedo 36 B 3
San Andrés Tuxtla 20 D 4
San Angelo 18 F 5
San Antonia de Cortés 20 E 4-5
San Antonio 18 G 6
San Antonio 24 E 3
San Antonio (Chile) 28 B 5
San Antonio (Portugal) 70 A 1
San Antonio (Uruguay) 28 E 5
San Antonio Abad 36 D 4
San Antonio Bay 19 G 6
San Antonio de Caparo 24 D 2
San Antonio de los Cobres 26 C 5
San Antonio del Tachira 24 D 2
San Antonio Oeste 29 D 7
San Bernadetto del Tronto 37 F 3
San Bernardino 18 C 5
San Bernardo (Chile) 28 BC 5
San Bernardo (Mexico) 18 D 6
San Blas 18 E 6
San Blas 20 A 3
San Blas 20 B 2
San Borja 26 C 3
San Buenaventura 20 B 2
San Carlos (Argentina) 28 C 4
San Carlos (Argentina) 28 C 5
San Carlos (Chile) 29 B 6
San Carlos (Mexico) 20 C 3
San Carlos (Nicaragua) 20 F 5
San Carlos (Philippines) 57 F 1
San Carlos (Uruguay) 28 EF 5
San Carlos de Bariloche 29 B 7
San Carlos de Río Negro 24 E 3
San Carlos del Zulia 24 D 2
San Casme 28 E 4
San Cataldo 37 F 4
San Clemente 18 C 5
San Cristóbal (Argentina) 28 D 5
San Cristóbal (Dominican Rep.) 21 HJ 4
San Cristóbal (Galápagos Is., Ecuador) 24 B 6
San Cristóbal (Solomon Is.) 65 H 4
San Cristóbal (Venezuela) 24 D 2
San Cristóbal de las Casas 20 D 4
San Custodio 24 E 3
San Diego 18 C 5
San Dona di Piave 37 F 2
San Estanislao 26 E 5
San Esteban de Gormaz 36 C 3
San Felipe (Chile) 28 B 5
San Felipe (Colombia) 24 E 3
San Felipe (Mexico) 18 D 5
San Felipe (Mexico) 20 B 3
San Felipe (Venezuela) 24 E 1
San Feliu 36 D 3
San Felíu de Guixols 36 D 3
San Fernando (Chile) 29 B 5
San Fernando (Mexico) 20 C 3
San Fernando (Philippines) 57 J 1
San Fernando (Spain) 36 B 4
San Fernando (Trinidad and Tobago) 25 F 1
San Fernando de Apure 24 E 2
San Fernando de Atabapo 24 E 3
San Francisco (U.S.A.) 18 B 4
San Francisco (Argentina) 28 D 5
San Francisco de Arriba 20 B 2
San Francisco de Macoris 21 HJ 4
San Francisco del Chañar 28 D 4
San Francisco del Monte de Oro 28 C 5
San Francisco del Oro 18 E 6
San Francisco del Rincón 20 B 3
San Francisco Javier 36 D 4
San Gil 24 D 2
San Giovanni in Fiore 37 G 4

San Gregorio (Chile) 29 B 9
San Gregorio (Uruguay) 28 E 5
San Hilario 18 D 7
San Ignacio 26 D 4
San Ignacio (Argentina) 29 E 6
San Ignacio (Belize) 20 E 4
San Ignacio (Bolivia) 26 C 3
San Ignacio (Mexico) 18 D 6
San Ignacio (Paraguay) 28 E 4
San Isidro (Argentina) 28 DE 5
San Isidro (Costa Rica) 20 F 6
San Isidro (Peru) 24 C 5
San Jacinto 24 C 2
San Javier (Argentina) 28 D 5
San Javier (Bolivia) 26 D 4
San Javier (Chile) 29 B 6
San Javier (Spain) 36 C 4
San Javier (Uruguay) 28 E 5
San Joaquín 26 D 3
San Joaquin River 18 BC 4
San Jorge, Bahia de 18 D 5
San Jorge, Golfo 29 C 8
San Jorge, Golfo de 36 D 3
San Jose (CA, U.S.A.) 18 B 4
San José (Costa Rica) 20 F 6
San José (Guatemala) 20 D 5
San Jose (Philippines) 57 F 1
San Jose (Philippines) 57 J 1
San José de Amacuro 25 F 2
San Jose de Buenavista 57 F 1
San José de Chiquitos 26 D 4
San José de Feliciano 28 E 5
San José de Gracia 18 E 6
San José de Guanipa 25 F 2
San José de Jáchal 28 C 5
San José de Mayo 28 E 5
San José de Ocuné 24 DE 3
San José del Cabo 18 E 7
San José del Guaviare 24 D 3
San Juan (Argentina) 28 C 5
San Juan (Dominican Rep.) 21 H 4
San Juan (Peru) 26 A 4
San Juan (Puerto Rico) 21 J 4
San Juan (Venezuela) 24 E 2
San Juan Bautista (Paraguay) 28 E 4
San Juan Bautista (Spain) 36 D 4
San Juan Bautista Tuxtepec 20 C 4
San Juan de Guadalupe 20 B 3
San Juan de los Cayos 24 E 1
San Juan del Norte 20 F 5
San Juan del Rio 20 BC 3
San Juana (Venezuela) 24 E 2
San Julián 29 C 8
San Justo 28 D 5
San Lorenzo (Argentina) 28 D 5
San Lorenzo (Ecuador) 24 C 3
San Lucas (Bolivia) 26 C 5
San Lucas (Mexico) 18 D 7
San Luis (Argentina) 28 C 5
San Luis (Mexico) 18 D 6
San Luís (Venezuela) 24 E 1
San Luis de la Paz 20 BC 3
San Luis Gonzaga, Bahia 18 D 6
San Luis, Lago de 26 D 3
San Luis Obispo 18 B 4
San Luis Potosi 20 B 3
San Luis Rio Colorado 18 D 5
San Marcos (Colombia) 24 C 2
San Marcos (Mexico) 20 B 3
San Marcos (Mexico) 20 C 4
San Marcos (TX, U.S.A.) 18 G 5-6
San Marino 37 F 3
San Martín (Colombia) 24 D 3
San Martín (Spain) 36 C 3
San Martín de los Andes 29 B 7
San Martín, Lago 29 B 8
San Mateo 18 B 4
San Matías 20 C 4
San Matías, Golfo 29 D 7
San Miguel (El Salvador) 20 E 5
San Miguel (Peru) 26 B 3
San Miguel de Allende 20 BC 3
San Miguel de Horcasitas 18 D 6
San Miguel de Huachi 26 C 4
San Miguel de Tucumán 28 C 4
San Miguel del Padrón 21 F 3
San Miguel Sole de Vega 20 C 4
San Nicolás 28 D 5
San Nicolás (Mexico) 20 B 2
San Nicolás (Peru) 26 A 4
San Onofre 24 C 2
San Pablo (Argentina) 29 C 9
San Pablo (Bolivia) 26 C 5
San Pablo (Philippines) 57 F 1
San Pedro (Argentina) 26 D 5
San Pedro (Argentina) 28 DE 5
San Pedro (Dominican Rep.) 21 J 4
San Pédro (Ivory Coast) 72 C 5
San Pedro (Mexico) 20 B 2
San Pedro (Paraguay) 28 E 5

San Pedro de Arimena 24 D 3
San Pedro de Atacama 26 C 5
San Pedro de las Bôcas 25 F 2
San Pedro de Lloc 24 BC 5
San Pedro Pochutla 20 C 4
San Pedro Sula 20 E 4
San Quintin 18 C 5
San Quintin, Bahia de 18 C 5
San Rafael (Argentina) 28 C 5
San Rafael (Bolivia) 26 D 4
San Rafael (Chile) 29 B 6
San Rafael (Mexico) 20 B 2
San Ramón 26 AB 3
San Ramón de la Nueva Orán 26 D 5
San Remo 37 E 3
San Roque 36 B 4
San Salvador (El Salvador) 20 E 5
San Salvador de Jujuy 26 C 5
San Sebastian (Argentina) 29 C 9
San Sebastián (Spain) 36 C 3
San Severo 37 G 3
San Silvestre 24 D 2
San Telmo 18 C 5
San Vicente (Mexico) 18 C 5
San Vicente (Philippines) 57 J 1
San Vicente de Cañete 26 A 3
San Vicente de la Barquerq 36 C 3
San Vicente del Raspeig 36 CD 4
Sanagir 54 C 2
Sanain 39 F 2
Sanana 57 G 4
Sanandaj 50 D 3
Sananduva 28 F 4
Sanâw 69 J 5
SanCarlos 24 BC 2
Sancarlos 24 E 2
Sánchez 21 J 4
Sanchor 54 B 3
Sancti Spiritus 21 G 3
Sand 35 E 4
Sand Point 14 EF 4
Sandai 56 D 4
Sandakan 56 E 2
Sandanski 38 B 2
Sandarne 34 E 3
Sandefjord 35 EF 4
Sanderson 18 F 5
Sandia 26 C 3
Sandikli 38 D 3
Sandila 54 D 2
Sandnes 35 E 4
Sandnessjöen 34 F 2
Sandomierz 33 H 4
Sandoway 55 F 4
Sandspit 14 L 5
Sandstone (MN, U.S.A.) 19 H 2
Sandstone (Western Australia) 62 B 4
Sandur 32 A 1
Sandusky 19 K 3
Sandvig 35 FG 4
Sandvika 35 F 4
Sandviken 35 G 3
Sandwich Bay (Newfoundl., Can.) 17 Q 5
Sandwip 55 F 3
Sandy Desert, Great 62 C 3
Sandy Lake 15 J 5
Sandy Lake 16 J 5
Sandy Point 55 F 5
Sandykachi 51 G 3
Sangamner 54 B 4
Sangareddipet 54 C 4
Sangayán, Isla 26 A 3
Sanger 18 C 4
Sanggau 56 D 3
Sangha 73 GH 5
Sangiyn Dalay Nuur 48 GH 6
Sangju 53 J 3
Sangkhla Buri 55 G 5
Sangkulirang, Teluk 57 E 3
Sangli 54 B 4
Sangre Grande 25 F 1
Sangri 52 B 5
Sangrur 54 C 1
Sangüesa 36 C 3
Sangzhi 52 F 5
Sanikiluaq 17 M 4
Sanjawi 51 H 4
Sanjiang 52 E 5
Sanjö 53 L 3
Sankt Martin 37 G 2
Sankt Michel 34 J 3
Sankt Pölten 37 G 2
Sankt Veit an der Glan 37 F 2
Sanlúcar de Barrameda 36 B 4
Sanmen 53 H 5
Sanmenxia 52 F 4
Sanming 53 G 5
Sannär 68 E 6
Sannikova 78
Sannikova, Proliv 49 PQ 1

Sanok 33 H 5
Sant' Agata di Militello 37 F 4
Sant' Antioco 37 E 4
Santa Ana 18 D 5
Santa Ana (Bolivia) 26 C 3
Santa Ana (CA, U.S.A.) 18 C 5
Santa Ana (Ecuador) 24 BC 4
Santa Ana (El Salvador) 20 DE 5
Santa Barbara (CA, U.S.A.) 18 B 5
Santa Barbara (Mexico) 18 E 6
Santa Barbara Channel 18 B 5
Santa Bárbara do Sul 28 F 4
Santa Catalina (Argentina) 26 C 5
Santa Catalina (Chile) 28 C 4
Santa Catarina (Brazil) 28 F 4
Santa Clara (CA, U.S.A.) 18 B 4
Santa Clara (Colombia) 24 E 4
Santa Clara (Cuba) 21 F 3
Santa Clara (Mexico) 18 E 6
Santa Clotilde 24 D 4
Santa Comba 36 B 3
Santa Cruz (Amazonas, Brazil) 24 D 5
Santa Cruz (Argentina) 29 C 9
Santa Cruz (Bolivia) 26 D 4
Santa Cruz (CA, U.S.A.) 18 B 4
Santa Cruz (Chile) 29 B 5
Santa Cruz (Costa Rica) 20 E 5
Santa Cruz (Espírito Santo, Brazil) 27 HJ 5
Santa Cruz (Pará, Brazil) 25 H 4
Santa Cruz (Peru) 24 C 5
Santa Cruz (Philippines) 57 F 1
Santa Cruz (Philippines) 57 H 1
Santa Cruz de la Palma 70 B 3
Santa Cruz de la Zarza 36 C 4
Santa Cruz de Mudela 36 C 4
Santa Cruz de Tenerife 70 B 3
Santa Cruz del Sur 21 G 3
Santa Cruz do Rio Pardo 27 G 5
Santa Cruz do Sul 28 F 4
Santa Cruz, Isla (Galápagos Is., Ecuador) 24 B 6
Santa Cruz Islands (Solomon Is.) 65 J 4
Santa Elena 24 B 4
Santa Elena de Uairén 25 F 3
Santa Fé (Argentina) 28 D 5
Santa Fé (Goiás, Brazil) 27 F 4
Santa Fe (N.M., U.S.A.) 18 E 4
Santa Filomena 27 G 2
Santa Helena 25 JK 4
Santa Inês 25 J 4
Santa Ines, Bahía 18 D 6
Santa Inés, Isla 29 B 9
Santa Isabel 25 G 5
Santa Isabel 26 D 3
Santa Isabel (Argentina) 29 C 6
Santa Isabel (Solomon Is.) 65 G 3
Santa Isabel do Araguaia 25 J 5
Santa Juana 24 E 2
Santa Júlia 25 G 5
Santa Lucía (Uruguay) 28 E 5
Santa Maria (Amazonas, Brazil) 25 F 4
Santa María (Amazonas, Brazil) 25 G 4
Santa María (Argentina) 28 C 4
Santa Maria (CA, U.S.A.) 18 B 4
Santa María (Rio Grande do Sul, Brazil) 28 F 4
Santa Maria, Bahia de 18 E 6
Santa María de Ipire 24 E 2
Santa María del Oro 20 A 2
Santa Maria del Río 20 B 3
Santa Maria dos Marmelos 25 F 5
Santa Marta 24 D 1
Santa Marta, Ría de 36 B 3
Santa Olalla del Cala 36 B 4
Santa Rita (Colombia) 24 D 3
Santa Rita (N.M., U.S.A.) 18 E 5
Santa Rita (Venezuela) 24 E 2
Santa Rita do Araguaia 27 F 4
Santa Rosa (Argentina) 28 C 5
Santa Rosa (Argentina) 29 CD 6
Santa Rosa (Argentina) 29 CD 6
Santa Rosa (Bolivia) 26 C 3
Santa Rosa (CA, U.S.A.) 18 B 4
Santa Rosa (Colombia) 24 E 3
Santa Rosa (N.M., U.S.A.) 18 F 5
Santa Rosa (Peru) 24 C 5
Santa Rosa (Rio Grande do Sul, Brazil) 28 F 4
Santa Rosa de Cabal 24 C 3
Santa Rosa de Copán 20 E 4-5
Santa Rosa de la Roca 26 D 4
Santa Rosalia 18 D 6
Santa Sylvina 28 D 4
Santa Teresa (Espírito Santo, Brazil) 27 H 5
Santa Teresa (Goiás, Brazil) 27 G 3
Santa Teresinha 27 F 3
Santa Vitória do Palmar 28 F 5
Santafé (Spain) 36 C 4
Santai 52 E 4
Santan 56 E 4
Santana 27 H 3
Santana do Livramento 28 EF 5
Santander (Colombia) 24 C 3

U

V

W

Y